Praise for the Seventh Edition of *Security Analysis*

With wit and discipline, Seth Klarman and his team of contributors show their timeless wisdom in this update of the investment classic *Security Analysis*. The book is right for this moment and will be right for a long time to come. Readers can profit greatly by reading and acting.

> —**Lawrence H. Summers**, former treasury secretary and president emeritus, Harvard University

The financial system and markets are extremely complex and constantly changing. While we must never stop learning and being prepared for unpredictable events, we also must remember that there are certain bedrock principles that don't change—and these are the great and enduring lessons of Graham and Dodd. By turns instructive and insightful, Seth Klarman's depth of experience in a rapidly changing financial ecosystem vividly brings these new lessons to life in this seventh edition of *Security Analysis*.

> —**Jamie Dimon**, chairman and CEO, JPMorgan Chase & Co.

Any investor at any level would benefit immensely from reading this seventh edition of Graham and Dodd's timeless *Security Analysis*. While value investing has stood the test of time, it's not a static process. Indeed, the best practitioners are constantly evolving with the changing political, societal, and economic landscape while maintaining the discipline espoused by Graham and Dodd almost 90 years ago.

> —**Stan Druckenmiller**, CEO, Duquesne Family Office

Graham and Dodd's *Security Analysis* is both a classic and a technical guidepost for leaders at the intersection of business and investing. The individual contributors to the seventh edition are the "All Stars" of investing, including Warren Buffett and Seth Klarman. They share their unique and thoughtful insights, which will undoubtedly help light the way for the next generation who follow in their footsteps.

> —**Kenneth I. Chenault**, chairman and managing director, General Catalyst; former chairman and CEO, American Express

The many insightful commentaries make the seventh edition of *Security Analysis* the best yet. It remains essential reading for all serious value investors.

> —**Bruce Greenwald**, professor emeritus of asset management and finance, Columbia Business School

If *Security Analysis* is the bible for value investors, the seventh edition is the New Testament. Seth Klarman and company are faithful prophets, divining how Graham and Dodd may have approached market events they could have never anticipated—from a globe flooded with free money and zero interest rates to the creation of cryptocurrencies and meme stocks. Whether you're steeped in the tenets of value investing or just a curious neophyte, this book is required reading. It's an affirmation of faith designed to hearten true believers and convert wayward speculators into righteous investors.

> —**Becky Quick**, anchor, CNBC

The seventh edition of Graham and Dodd's eternal text—*Security Analysis*—is an instructive and impressive build on enduring principles that have influenced generations of investors, including me. The new content captures evolving market conditions, shifting standards, and recent developments in investment management, while also reinforcing that staying-power and patience remain the surest way to succeed at value investing.

> —**Laurence D. Fink**, chairman and chief executive officer, BlackRock, Inc.

The influx of financial data, constant evolution of the economy, and advances in behavioral finance are changing the art of investing. Having taught a course on *Security Analysis* at Columbia Business School for three decades, I appreciate this edition's blend of continuing wisdom and contemporary commentary. It's essential reading for the serious investor.

—**Michael Mauboussin**, head of Consilient Research, Counterpoint Global—Morgan Stanley Investment Management

SECURITY ANALYSIS

Security Analysis Prior Editions

Graham and Dodd: *Security Analysis*, First Edition (1934)

Graham and Dodd: *Security Analysis*, Second Edition (1940)

Graham and Dodd: *Security Analysis*, Third Edition (1951)

Graham, Dodd, Cottle, and Tatham: *Security Analysis*, Fourth Edition (1962)

Graham, Dodd, Cottle, Murray, Block, and Leibowitz: *Security Analysis*, Fifth Edition (1988)

Graham, Dodd, Klarman, Grant, and Greenwald: *Security Analysis*, Sixth Edition (2009)

SECURITY ANALYSIS

PRINCIPLES AND TECHNIQUE

SEVENTH EDITION

BENJAMIN GRAHAM
AND DAVID L. DODD

EDITED BY SETH A. KLARMAN

New York   Chicago   San Francisco   Lisbon   London   Madrid
Mexico City   Milan   New Delhi   San Juan   Seoul
Singapore   Sydney   Toronto

1 2 3 4 5 6 7 8 9   LCR   28 27 26 25 24 23

ISBN   978-1-264-93240-5
MHID   1-264-93240-5

e-ISBN   978-1-264-93275-7
e-MHID   1-264-93275-8

Library of Congress Cataloging-in-Publication Data

Names: Graham, Benjamin, 1894–1976 author. | Dodd, David L. (David Le Fevre), 1895–1988 author. | Klarman, Seth A., 1957– author.
Title: Security analysis : principles and techniques / Seth Klarman, Benjamin Graham & David L. Dodd.
Description: Seventh edition. | New York, NY : McGraw Hill, [2023] | Includes bibliographical references and index.
Identifiers: LCCN 2023002396 (print) | LCCN 2023002397 (ebook) | ISBN 9781264932405 (hardback) | ISBN 9781264932757 (ebook)
Subjects: LCSH: Securities—United States. | Investment analysis. | Speculation.
Classification: LCC HG4521 .G67 2023 (print) | LCC HG4521 (ebook) | DDC 332.60973—dc23/eng/20230512
LC record available at https://lccn.loc.gov/2023002396
LC ebook record available at https://lccn.loc.gov/2023002397

McGraw Hill books are available at special quantity discounts to use as premiums and sales promotions or for use in corporate training programs. To contact a representative, please visit the Contact Us pages at www.mhprofessional.com.

McGraw Hill is committed to making our products accessible to all learners. To learn more about the available support and accommodations we offer, please contact us at accessibility@mheducation.com. We also participate in the Access Text Network (www.accesstext.org), and ATN members may submit requests through ATN.

BENJAMIN GRAHAM AND DAVID DODD forever changed the theory and practice of investing with the 1934 publication of *Security Analysis*. The nation, and indeed the rest of the world, was in the grips of the Great Depression, a period that brought unprecedented upheaval to the financial world. In 1940, the authors responded with a comprehensive revision. The second edition of *Security Analysis* is considered by many investors to be the definitive word from the most influential investment philosophers of our time.

Around the world, *Security Analysis* is still regarded as the fundamental text for the analysis of stocks and bonds. It is also considered to be the bible of value investing. As we approach 90 years of *Security Analysis*, McGraw Hill is proud to publish this seventh edition.

This new edition retains many chapters from the classic 1940 edition, and also features lively and practical essays written by a stellar team of today's leading value investors and financial writers. The result is a contemporary bible of value investing.

Additional chapters from the 1940 second edition are available for download at www.mhprofessional.com/ SecurityAnalysis7.

Many shall be restored that now are fallen,
and many shall fall that now are in honor.

—HORACE, "ARS POETICA"

Contents

PART I
Survey and Approach

PART II
Fixed-Value Investments

PART III
Senior Securities with Speculative Features

PART IV
Theory of Common-Stock Investment.
The Dividend Factor

PART V
Analysis of the Income Account. The Earnings
Factor in Common-stock Valuation

PART VI
Balance-Sheet Analysis. Implications of Asset Values

PART VII
Additional Aspects of Security Analysis.
Discrepancies Between Price and Value

PART VIII
Contemporary Concepts in Value Investing

Foreword

by Warren E. Buffett

There are four books in my overflowing library that I particularly treasure, each of them written more than 50 years ago. All, though, would still be of enormous value to me if I were to read them today for the first time; their wisdom endures though their pages fade.

Two of those books are first editions of *The Wealth of Nations* (1776), by Adam Smith, and *The Intelligent Investor* (1949), by Benjamin Graham. A third is an original copy of the book you hold in your hands, Graham and Dodd's *Security Analysis*. I studied from *Security Analysis* while I was at Columbia University in 1950 and 1951, when I had the extraordinary good luck to have Ben Graham and Dave Dodd as teachers. Together, the book and the men changed my life.

On the utilitarian side, what I learned then became the bedrock upon which all of my investment and business decisions have been built. Prior to meeting Ben and Dave, I had long been fascinated by the stock market. Before I bought my first stock at age 11—it took me until then to accumulate the $115 required for the purchase—I had read every book in the Omaha Public Library having to do with the stock market. I found many of them fascinating and all interesting. But none were really useful.

My intellectual odyssey ended, however, when I met Ben and Dave, first through their writings and then in person. They laid out a road map for investing that I have now been following for 57 years. There's been no reason to look for another.

Beyond the ideas Ben and Dave gave me, they showered me with friendship, encouragement, and trust. They cared not a whit for reciprocation—toward a young student, they simply wanted to extend a one-way street of helpfulness. In the end, that's probably what I admire most about the two men. It was ordained at birth that they would be brilliant; they elected to be generous and kind.

Misanthropes would have been puzzled by their behavior. Ben and Dave instructed literally thousands of potential competitors, young fellows like me who would buy bargain stocks or engage in arbitrage transactions, directly competing with the Graham-Newman Corporation, which was Ben's investment company. Moreover, Ben and Dave would use current investing examples in the classroom and in their writings, in effect doing our work for us. The way they behaved made as deep an impression on me—and many of my classmates—as did their ideas. We were being taught not only how to invest wisely; we were also being taught how to live wisely.

The copy of *Security Analysis* that I keep in my library and that I used at Columbia is the 1940 edition. I've read it, I'm sure, at least four times, and obviously it is special.

But let's get to the fourth book I mentioned, which is even more precious. In 2000, Barbara Dodd Anderson, Dave's only child, gave me her father's copy of the 1934 edition of *Security Analysis*, inscribed with hundreds of marginal notes. These were inked in by Dave as he prepared for publication of the 1940 revised edition. No gift has meant more to me.

The Timeless Wisdom of Graham and Dodd

by Seth A. Klarman

The world of investments is one of unlimited choices, significant opportunity, and great rewards, as well as shifting landscapes, untold nuances, and serious perils. Against that backdrop, investors must weigh multiple and sometimes competing objectives: generating income, growing principal over time, protecting against loss and the ravages of inflation, and maintaining a degree of liquidity to provide future flexibility and meet unexpected needs. Finding the right balance is essential.

To do so, investors need a guidebook that offers them not a plan to succeed in a particular moment but rather a set of principles to steer them through any and all environments. In 1934, in the depths of the Great Depression, Benjamin Graham and his colleague, David Dodd, produced such a volume, *Security Analysis*, detailing how to sort through thousands of different common stocks, preferred issues, and bonds and identify those worthy of investment. Over the ensuing 90 years, during which it has remained consistently in print, *Security Analysis* has been crowned the bible of value investing. The stringing together of their very names—"Graham and Dodd"—has become synonymous with this sensible and timeless approach.

The sixth edition of *Security Analysis* was published in the middle of the worst financial crisis since Graham and Dodd's time. The edition in your hands builds on the sixth and reflects on new events in the markets and the current economic backdrop and business landscape, as well as developments in the field of investment management and security analysis. As with the sixth edition, we have assembled leading practitioners and market observers to update and provide commentary on the content of the book's acclaimed second edition. In our attempt to distill what has changed over the years, we have striven to separate reality and enduring wisdom from what is ephemeral, protean, and illusory. Although markets have evolved enormously in the past nine decades and the book's historic examples show their age, you will see in the pages that follow that many of the value investing principles at the heart of *Security Analysis* are just as applicable today as ever.

The heft and detail of *Security Analysis* immediately suggest that it is not an easy read. Today's aspiring investors and early-career practitioners may wonder whether it's worth the effort. The other contributors and I strongly believe that it would indeed be time well-spent.

ENDURING PRINCIPLES

Change is the one constant in the investment world, and for any investment book to pass the test of time, it must hold universal. A successful investment philosophy, such as value investing, must address the challenges in navigating change, remaining flexible in approach and tactics while grounded in basic, unwavering principles. The alternative—a strategy that blows with the wind—almost ensures being perpetually whipsawed by volatile markets and burdened by frenetic trading.

Many of the details in the original *Security Analysis* belong to another era. The earliest editions implicitly describe a smokestack economy in which steam-driven locomotives race across the landscape to deliver a cornucopia of manufactured goods. Today, the U.S. and global economies are increasingly characterized by tens of millions of men and women at keyboards and screens, gathering, tracking, and analyzing data for the information economy, while countless others are energetically engaged in the burgeoning service economy.

Many of the companies mentioned in the early editions have been merged, restructured, or liquidated out of existence, and some of the tools and methods Graham and Dodd used are outmoded or losing relevance. Book value, for example, is far less relevant for investors today than a century ago. Graham and Dodd recommended that investors purchase stocks trading for less than two-thirds of net working capital, defined as working capital less all other liabilities. Many stocks fit this criterion during the Depression years; far fewer do today.

Yet while many of Graham's examples and tools have been eclipsed by the passage of time, the general principles of Graham and Dodd still hold true because the investor behaviors that drive markets are fixed in human nature, and market inefficiencies can always be found. Generations of investors have adopted the teachings of this book and successfully implemented them across highly varied market environments, geographies, asset classes, and securities types. This would delight the authors, who hoped to set forth principles that would "stand the test of the ever-enigmatic future." (First Edition Preface)

Graham and Dodd witnessed and wrote about how they navigated through the financial markets of the 1930s, an era of protracted economic depression and extreme risk aversion. The decade that began in the late 1920s encompassed the best and then the worst of times in the markets—the euphoric run-up to the 1929 peak, the October 1929 crash, and the relentless grinding down of the Depression years. Though distant from today, exploring such a period remains valuable. After all, each new day has the potential to throw a curveball: a war, a pandemic, a macroeconomic shock, a real estate crash, a financial crisis, the unexpected failure of a prominent company, a sovereign default, a broad-based technological upheaval, or dramatic political or regulatory change. People tend to assume that tomorrow will look very much like today, and most of the time, it does. But every once in a while, conditions change abruptly and conventional wisdom is turned on its head. In those times, many investors don't know what to do and may become paralyzed; they need a guiding philosophy, and Graham and Dodd offer an excellent one. "We have striven throughout," they write, "to guard the student against overemphasis upon the superficial and the temporary," which is "at once the delusion and the nemesis of the world of finance." (First Edition Preface) It is during periods of tumult and upheaval that a value-investing philosophy is especially beneficial.

FLUCTUATING SHARE PRICES ARE A MAJOR DRIVER OF OPPORTUNITY

Graham and Dodd remind us that stocks represent fractional ownership interests in a business and bonds are senior claims on that business. The most important element of an investor's return from an equity investment is the cash flows generated by the underlying business itself. When McDonald's sells billions of hamburgers, the owner of 1% of the company's shares sells tens of millions. The value of every business is thus inexorably related to its current and future financial performance.

In valuing businesses, markets will often be inefficient, causing securities prices to under- or overshoot. Emotional overreactions can, for a time, overpower fundamentals. When prices overshoot, euphoria is eventually overtaken by reality, causing them to retrench. When they undershoot, investors can take advantage of such mispricings to pick up a fractional interest in a business at bargain levels. Over the long run, as current uncertainties and temporary business difficulties are resolved, share prices tend to gravitate toward the value of the underlying businesses—and bargain-hunting value investors enjoy a profit.

Share prices, in themselves, hold no particular informational value. Day-to-day, they are set by the forces of supply and demand and driven more by the whims, beliefs, and exigencies of other buyers and sellers than by a measured, rational assessment of business performance and prospects. Unexpected developments, heightened uncertainty, and moment-by-moment capital flows exacerbate short-term market volatility, and prices sometimes depart from a company's underlying value. Small changes in assumptions or sentiment can cause wild price swings, as can be observed from the prices of the shares of scores of fast-growing but still unprofitable technology and biotech companies in recent years.

These fluctuations give rise to one of the greatest challenges of investing. While an analysis of a company and its value can be spot on, the stock market can fail to reward that insight and can even appear to refute it. Indeed, an investor may not be rewarded for quite some time, and perhaps experience sizable paper losses. Investors, therefore, can *be* right yet *appear* wrong, to themselves and to anyone who looks.

While at first blush this may seem to be a problem, it is actually an opportunity. Graham and Dodd's philosophy maintains that the financial markets themselves are the ultimate creator of opportunity. On any given day, some securities may be priced more or less correctly, others not. But in the long run, fundamentals are what drive business value. Graham is credited with explaining: "In the short run, the market is a voting machine, but in the long run it is a weighing machine." By acknowledging and taking advantage of this dichotomy, investors can profit from bargains as they patiently wait for the underlying fundamental value of a business to be reflected in its share price.

Those who are able to develop reliable investment convictions about the securities in which they plan to invest and can tolerate significant market fluctuations and potential drawdowns will benefit when the undervaluation they perceive becomes even more egregious, as long as they have the fortitude to hang on and ideally add to their holdings. (Somewhat counterintuitively, extreme undervaluation can serve as its own catalyst, attracting not only bargain hunters in the public markets but also opportunistic buyers of the whole business.) Just as market fluctuations can appear to refute accurate analysis, prices may temporarily seem to validate incorrect conclusions. Investors who gain confidence from rising market prices, for example, may make the mistake of gaining additional conviction in their investments at the very moment when they are, in fact, becoming less and less attractive.

Learning to love markdowns is critical for long-term investment success. Key is the ability to retain the perspective that markdowns represent the opportunity to buy an additional stake in a business at an even better price, and that a markdown is a loss only if you sell. From this vantage point, what seems on the surface like bad news is actually a positive development. Obviously, in the face of a downdraft, it is incumbent on investors to regularly check their analysis and reaffirm their conclusions, especially in the face of sudden and surprising price declines, to assess whether the price action may reflect important information—either of new developments or information that your own analysis may have missed or misunderstood.

Investors who lack confidence and staying power, or who are under onerous short-term performance pressures, are prone to bailing out when the prices of what they own move lower. Investors must be resolute in the face of withering criticism from clients and superiors and their own self-doubt during protracted periods of underperformance. (That's why for those managing other people's money, having patient, long-term-oriented clients is crucial.) At the other end of the spectrum, investors who are overly confident are prone to confirmation bias, meaning that they exult over the elements that confirm their thesis while filtering out or looking past anything that may tend to disprove it.

Investors must do the work to develop conviction regarding an investment thesis, checking and rechecking their analysis before they act. At the same time, they must remain open to updated information and new perspectives, and thus to changing their minds as warranted and without bias. They must walk a tightrope of developing strong convictions but holding them lightly.

It is also important to recognize that while the outcomes of investments are determined by the fundamentals of the underlying businesses in which you invest, the returns are inextricably linked to the purchase price. The less you pay relative to underlying value, the higher your investment returns will be; discipline matters in both buying and selling. In the words of Graham and Dodd, "the price [of a security] is frequently an essential element, so that a stock . . . may have investment merit at one price level but not at another." (First Edition Preface) The old adage sums it up: Price may be what you pay, but value is what you get.

AT THE CORE OF VALUE INVESTING: BUYING A DOLLAR AT A DISCOUNT

Value investing, whether in Graham and Dodd's day or ours, is the practice of purchasing securities or assets for less than they are worth— buying the proverbial dollar for 50 cents. Value investors can profit two ways: both from the cash flows generated by the underlying business and from a capital gain when the market better recognizes the underlying value and reprices the security. They also benefit from an important margin of safety conferred by the bargain purchase. A margin of safety provides room for error, imprecision, bad luck, or the vicissitudes of the economy and stock market. It offers a degree of downside protection. While some might mistakenly consider value investing a mechanical tool for identifying statistical bargains (i.e., stocks whose price-to-book or price-to-earnings ratio falls below a certain level), it is, in actuality, a comprehensive investment philosophy based on performing in-depth fundamental analysis, pursuing long-term investment results, resisting crowd psychology, and limiting risk.

Identifying and buying bargains is the sweet spot of value investors. But how much of a bargain to require in order to buy or continue to hold is a matter of art and not science, a judgment call. Price targets for buying and selling must be set and then regularly adjusted to reflect all currently available information.

Value investors should plan to completely exit a security by the time it reaches its full value; owning overvalued securities and hoping they appreciate further is a game for speculators. Indeed, value investors should typically begin selling at a 10% to 20% discount to their assessment of a security's underlying value—the exact discount based on the liquidity of the security, the possible presence of a catalyst for value realization, the quality of management, the degree of leverage employed by the business, and their own confidence regarding the assumptions underlying their analysis. Exiting an investment "too early" and "leaving money on the table" may be frustrating, but it is far less painful than attempting to get out after it's too late. Round-tripping an investment—watching it go up, failing to sell it, and watching it go back down—can be psychologically unsettling and economically costly. Disciplined selling, on the other hand, can open opportunities to exit your position and then possibly reinvest back into a company you already know well at an improved price.

One might think of value investing as the marriage of a contrarian streak and a calculator, the mixing of deep, fundamental analysis with a propensity for going against the grain. Having a differentiated viewpoint is essential. In the stock market, good news isn't helpful if it's already baked into investor expectations.

DRIVERS OF FINANCIAL MARKET INEFFICIENCY

What drives financial market inefficiency? Investors, being human, sometimes buy or sell for emotionally charged reasons, such as exuberance or panic. They periodically alter their decision-making, not in response to investment fundamentals, but to recent performance that significantly expanded or shrank their own net worth. They might not want to miss out on a trend their peers have been profiting from. They can be lulled into complacency and even risk-seeking behavior by the momentum of the market. They might find it hard to maintain a contrarian view that has, so far, been costly. They might also overreact to surprises, particularly a quarterly earnings shortfall or an unexpected credit-rating downgrade. They may be overwhelmed by the analytical challenges involved with rapid corporate change, complexity, or heightened uncertainty. Investors always need to fight the tendencies to warm to investments whose price has been rising and bail on those whose price has been falling.

Security prices deviate from fundamental value for myriad other reasons as well. One is that investors may well have very different visions of reality; some are inveterate optimists while others are pessimists. Some become cheerleaders for their holdings, falling in love with their hypotheses. Investors' time horizons also differ, as do their expectations for the future. A university endowment or philanthropic foundation may be able to take a truly long-term perspective, but a couple nearing retirement age and expecting to soon begin living on their nest egg cannot. Individual risk tolerances also vary, both for interim price fluctuations but also, more important, for the prospect of a permanent loss of capital. Income needs from a portfolio differ as well, and some investors may be forced to exit a stock that omits its dividend or a bond that defaults, regardless of price.

In addition to all of these reasons for market inefficiency, people will always be subject to their own behavioral biases, as Daniel

Kahneman brilliantly describes in *Thinking, Fast and Slow* (2013). People tend to anchor to the price they paid for an investment and then stubbornly hold onto the investment when it runs into trouble, irrationally waiting for it to return to the price they paid for it to get out without a loss when selling might have been the right thing to do. And after a financial loss, people often become more risk-averse, causing them to possibly miss out on the next fat pitch. People tend to overestimate the future likelihood of events that they recently experienced, and under-rate the possibility of events that haven't lately occurred. The cumulative effect of investors committing many small irrational acts can result in significant mispricings. A major challenge for investors is to be aware of, fight, and overcome their own biases, relying instead on objective realities and truths; this way, they can profit from mispricings rather than contribute to them.

Another reason to expect ongoing securities mispricings is that many investors must adhere to institutional constraints that limit their behavior. Such constraints are usually well-intentioned, but they nevertheless detract from market efficiency because they limit the pool of potential buyers and sellers for some securities. Many investment funds, for example, are required by their charters to operate within narrow silos that restrict ownership of investments to those that have an investment-grade credit rating, pay a cash dividend, or are listed on an exchange. Others are restricted to a single industry. But in investing, price is king. Almost any security is a "buy" at one price, a "hold" at another, and a "sell" at yet another. Anything that prevents investors from buying or selling the most compelling opportunities available is a constraint that can lead to inferior performance.

So how does a value investor take advantage of, rather than succumb to, all these sources of inefficient and noneconomic behavior? At my firm, The Baupost Group, we actively and deliberately seek to create a culture that minimizes the risk of irrational or biased behavior.

We work in teams to regularly incorporate fresh information and new perspectives into our analysis and calmly debate our decisions. We also work to ensure that we are not limited by institutional constraints. We search for opportunity by surveying, analyzing, and tracking the securities and assets we believe are most likely to be inefficiently priced. Those are often found in the gaps between traditional investment silos and include newly distressed or downgraded debt instruments; companies undergoing rapid corporate change such as mergers, major asset sales, and spin-offs; and situations involving great uncertainty, such as those subject to major litigation. We regularly pull at the threads of one interesting situation to find others; we look for patterns based on past investment successes. We rummage through the list of "new lows," knowing that out-of-favor securities can be an attractive source of bargains. We search expansively for potential opportunity and then dig deeply to verify that each situation is truly undervalued. Even after we buy, we keep digging.

THE ART OF BUSINESS VALUATION

While value investing is about buying into businesses at discounts to their fair value, doing so is by no means a paint-by-numbers exercise. It is not simply the practice of buying securities trading at the lowest multiples of recent earnings, cash flows, or book value. After all, sometimes a stock sports a low valuation multiple for good reason: troubling trends, competitive challenges, a broken business model, hidden liabilities, protracted and potentially crippling litigation, or incompetent or corrupt management. Investors must consider every potential investment with skepticism and humility, relentlessly hunting for additional information while realizing that they will never know everything about a company.

So how exactly do we ascertain value in order to recognize if a bargain is available? There are a number of useful methodologies, among them the calculation of the present value of estimated future cash flows; applying sensible multiples of relevant income-statement, balance-sheet, and cash flow metrics; assessing the private-market value of a company (i.e., the value a knowledgeable third party would reasonably pay for the business); and establishing the breakup value (i.e., the amount to be realized if the various segments of a business were sold separately to the highest bidders). Value cannot usually be captured in a single-point estimate, and an investor would be wise to consider all these methodologies to determine a plausible range of value.

Each of these methodologies has its strengths and weaknesses. Private-market value can fluctuate with the moods of the market and swings of the economy, and sometimes there are few if any private bids available for a given asset. Such transactions are also typically dependent on the availability and cost of financing. Applying multiples, on the other hand, has the benefit of relying on observable financial metrics. This approach may be more objective on the surface, but insisting on very low purchase multiples may inadvertently filter for lower quality or deteriorating businesses or fail to capture the value inherent in rapidly growing subsidies. While Graham considered corporate earnings, dividend payments, and book value to be the most important metrics in analyzing a stock, for example, most value investors today look past those factors to focus on the generation of free cash flow (i.e., the cash produced annually from the operations of a business after all capital expenditures are made and changes in working capital are considered). Investors turned to this approach because earnings reported under GAAP can differ materially from the cash actually generated by a business. For example, depreciation and amortization are noncash charges that alter the reported bottom line and mask actual cash generation. Contrariwise, some business activities gobble up cash but aren't expensed, such as accumulations of potentially obsolete inventories or uncollectable receivables.

Taking a multiple of appropriately calculated current cash flows, however, might not capture the crucial element of a business's value. Ultimately, it is the future cash flows of a business that matter. If assessing the drivers of a company's current cash flow is an imperfect art, evaluating the likely path of future cash flows is even more daunting, especially as past may not be prologue.

Given the difficulty of such forecasting, Graham and Dodd believed this was an endeavor best avoided. In the preface to the first edition of *Security Analysis*, the authors said, "Some matters of vital significance, *e.g.*, the determination of the future prospects of an enterprise, have received little space, because little of definite value can be said on the subject." (First Edition Preface) But in today's investing world, something can and in fact must be said about future cash flow. Clearly, a company that generates $1 per share of cash flow today that is reasonably expected to grow to $2 per share of cash flow five years from now is worth considerably more than one with no growth. The quality and source of these cash flows are also relevant. It matters whether the growth is organic or is expected to come from acquisitions, is steady or cyclical, and whether large capital investments are necessary to achieve it. A further complication is that companies can increase their cash flows in many different ways. They can sell the same volume of goods but at a higher unit price, or sell more goods albeit at the same, or an even lower, price. They might change their product offerings, to sell more of the higher profit-margin items, or they may develop an entirely new product line. Cash flow growth from cutting costs has very different ramifications for a company than the growth that occurs from expanding one's customer base; when expenses are trimmed, muscle may be lost as well as fat. Such decisions, inevitably, also impact customer satisfaction and competitor response. Obviously, some forms of growth are worth more than others. Investors need to dig into the details to understand the true growth characteristics of a business and value them properly. Ultimately, despite Graham and Dodd's understandable reservations about the difficulties of projecting the future, in the context of today's rapid and powerful disruption of existing businesses, and the steady formation of promising new ones, it is simply not possible to disregard the trajectory of growth or decline when determining the valuation of a business.

Investors using the discounted cash flow method must also choose an appropriate discount rate to apply to a company's cash flows. Valuations can be very sensitive to this subjective variable, especially for high-growth businesses, much of whose expected cash flow generation lies far in the future. To set the proper discount rate, investors must assess the quality, consistency, and riskiness of the company's cash flows. The best businesses usually have such attributes as strong barriers to entry, limited capital requirements, organic growth, repeat customers, significant pricing power, high margins, low risk of technological obsolescence, competitive moats, and thus strong, sustained, and increasing free cash flow. In many cases, the growth of such businesses is interwoven with those of other enterprises so that they become larger and more profitable as other companies execute their plans. The highest-quality businesses deserve to have their cash flows discounted at a lower rate than other businesses, conferring a higher valuation multiple. How much higher, however, is a subject of never-ending calibration and debate.

In all of these valuation analyses, investors must also attempt to assess the skills, capabilities, priorities, and core values of a company's top management. Talented managers clearly enhance the cash flows and improve the capital-allocation decisions of the businesses they lead, but managerial ability can't easily be quantified. As Graham and Dodd noted, "Objective tests of managerial ability are few and far from scientific." (Sixth Edition Introduction) But unmistakably, a management's acumen, integrity, and motivation make a huge difference in shareholder returns. The past actions of any management team, whether in their current or previous roles, are perhaps the most reliable guide to future behavior. Alignment of their incentives with the interests of shareholders is also crucial.

In addition to running the business well, managers have many other ways to positively impact investor returns. These include timely share repurchases, prudent use of leverage, and astute acquisitions. Managers who are unwilling to make shareholder-friendly decisions risk their companies turning into "value traps." They may be undervalued but ultimately poor investments, because the assets are likely to remain underutilized and cash flows may be squandered. Such underperforming companies should not necessarily be shunned, however, because those firms often attract activist investors seeking to join the board, change management, improve decision-making, and unlock value. Investors must also decide whether to take the risk of investing—at any price— with management teams who seemingly put their own interests ahead of those of shareholders. While the shares of such companies may sell at a steep discount, the discount may be warranted because the value that belongs to the equity holders today may instead be spirited away or squandered tomorrow. In other words, the actual future cash flow generation cannot be included in a discounted cash flow analysis because those cash flows will never find their way to the investor.

Ultimately, valuation is as much an art as it is a science, and judgment is constantly required. An investor's analytical, left-brain skills must be married to her softer, right-brain skills so she can add nuance and alternative perspectives to her rigorous analysis. In the end, the most successful value investors bear in mind this inherent imprecision as they combine detailed business research and valuation work with endless discipline and patience, deep curiosity, intellectual honesty, and optimally, the judgment that comes with years of analytical and investment experience.

NAVIGATING THE AGE OF BIG DATA
AND TECHNOLOGICAL DISRUPTION

In the search for investment opportunity, the financial analysis of businesses and securities has become increasingly sophisticated over the years. Even Benjamin Graham's pencil, one of the sharpest of his era, might not be sharp enough today. Now anyone on Wall Street can build a detailed financial model of any business, since vast amounts of data can be summoned, at little or no cost, at the touch of a finger. But since that information is readily available to everyone now, it confers no obvious edge. The advantage comes when an investor has an analytical edge or insight that allows her to draw better conclusions.

Benjamin Graham and David Dodd acknowledged that they could not anticipate the multitude of changes that would sweep through the investment world over the ensuing years. Technological advances in particular often have a compounding effect that almost ensures more rapid change; new technologies stand on the shoulders of a long chain of previous breakthroughs. Today, accelerating technological change and the disruption it can wreak are regular features of the investment landscape. The robust venture capital industry nearly guarantees that there will be prolific formation of new businesses and intense competition in many or most industries. Furthermore, the steady pace of corporate mergers and acquisitions is bound to materially alter and even transform large numbers of businesses over very short periods.

Investors need an investment approach with principles that are constant and practices that are flexible, so they can navigate through change, assessing challenges facing incumbent firms as well as the newly fertile soil that can nourish the rapid growth of extraordinary new ones. What makes a business successful in one era may apply less in another, not because the approach isn't a sound one, but because the environment has radically shifted, tastes have changed, or the competition has caught up—or even leapt ahead.

Graham's world was analog; today's is almost completely digital. Companies today sell products and utilize technologies that Graham and Dodd could never have envisioned. Many enjoy first-mover advantages, rapid and unprecedented scalability, massive competitive moats, low or zero marginal cost of production, and network effects that make the business more profitable and more formidable the larger it grows. *Security Analysis* offers, of course, no examples of how to value a software developer, internet search engine, or smartphone manufacturer, but its analytical tools will be useful in evaluating almost any company, assess the value of its marketable securities, and determine the presence of a margin of safety. Questions of predictability, persistence, growth, business strategy, liquidity, and risk cut across businesses, markets, nations, and time.

Over the past quarter century, the internet has enabled the formation of an enormous number of businesses that simply were not imaginable before, some of the best in the world. One such example is Google (now Alphabet), which collects and analyzes vast and growing quantities of data that give the company an insurmountable advantage in providing increasingly targeted advertising. This capability has enabled the company to completely disrupt the traditional advertising business, building a deeper and deeper moat.

Thanks to the internet and the burgeoning growth of venture capital, an entrepreneur can now envision a business or even an industry that has never existed before, and he or she can raise venture funding, grow the fledgling enterprise exponentially at little or no cost, and if executed successfully, create a new market leader. This revolution arrived so rapidly that value investors found themselves in an unfamiliar position: many apparent bargains, evaluated on the basis of a continuation of historic cash flows, were turning out not to be bargains at all. Many such companies were not sound businesses facing a temporary down cycle as in Graham's day. Rather, they had become endangered by technological disruption from innovations that simultaneously destroyed their incumbent businesses while birthing phenomenal new ones that ate their lunch.

Technology, a word not found in the index of the first four editions of *Security Analysis*, has obviously become a predominant force in understanding and conducting business analysis. In short, companies develop and market technology, figure out how to use it to improve their operations, or live in fear of it overtaking them. It's now a fact of life, the 800-pound gorilla in almost every room. Technology unleashes a torrent of change, which means that the cash flows of a business today might tell you little about its future prospects; but it's the future cash flows, as previously discussed, that are the true determinant of value.

While Graham was interested in companies that produced consistent earnings, analysis in his day was less sophisticated regarding why some companies' earnings might be more resilient than others. Investors today examine businesses but also business models to identify the best ones. The bottom-line impact of changes in revenues, profit margins, product mix, and other variables is carefully studied by managements and financial analysts alike. Investors know that businesses do not exist in a vacuum; competitors, suppliers, and customers can greatly influence corporate profitability. They also understand that the rapid pace of innovation means that business circumstances can change quickly. Analysts evaluating fast-growing companies must consider not only the current volume of business, but also the potential demand for that product or service and its total addressable market (TAM) in order to assess for how long a company's growth might persist and when it might taper. Similarly, analysts think about the "right to win" of a business, the market share it might reasonably compete for, based on its cost structure and product advantages. While assessing future prospects of businesses in newly created industries is always difficult, investors would fall short if they failed to analyze and place a value on likely future growth or consider when and whether that growth might lead to enhanced profitability and cash flow.

In earlier eras, one's best guess of tomorrow's business performance was an extension of today's. But now, because of new technologies spurring astonishing growth in many industries and technological disruptions mortally wounding many incumbent businesses, tomorrow is much less likely to look like today than it was in Graham's time; for some businesses, it will look significantly better, and for many others, much worse. This is an inversion of a core tenet of Graham and Dodd, that one's best guess of tomorrow begins with what you see today or with what you saw recently. Value investors have had to become better business analysts than ever before.

Value investors cannot ignore the future. They must assign value to rapid and sustainable growth in cash flows, but with caution. Given all the challenges and nuances to ascertaining future cash flows, there is risk in paying for cash flows that are not demonstrated in current financial performance but rather lie far off in an imagined future. Graham and Dodd observed that "analysis is concerned primarily with values which are supported by the facts and not those which depend largely upon expectations." (Sixth Edition Introduction) Strongly preferring the actual to the potential, they regarded the "future as a hazard which his [the analyst's] conclusions must encounter rather than as the source of his vindication." (Sixth Edition Introduction) Investors should be especially vigilant to not focus on growth exclusively, as that would increase the risk of overpaying. Again, Graham and Dodd were spot on in warning that "carried to its logical extreme, . . . [there is no price] too high for a good stock, and that such an issue was equally 'safe' . . . after it had advanced to 200 as it had been at 25." (Chap. 1) This precise mistake was made when stock prices surged skyward during the Nifty Fifty era of the early 1970s, the dot-com bubble of 1999–2000, and the low-interest-rate, post-economic stimulus stock market of 2021.

Today, business growth may have become more predictable for some companies. Many firms have built what appear to be better mousetraps, high-quality businesses with distinct capabilities that are speedily increasing their market shares. These businesses seem destined to grow well into the future, and investors who won't pay something for that growth may miss out on owning some of the best businesses in the world. Assessing the moats and scalability of such companies has become just as important in ascertaining value today as the reported book value of a company was in Graham and Dodd's time.

My firm's approach to analyzing the value of those businesses we believe are likely to consistently grow involves rigorous fundamental analysis and making conservative projections of future results over the next two to three years, then comparing the multiple of those cash flows to today's share price. If the multiple of near-future earnings is reasonable (i.e., significantly less than today's market multiple and no higher than low double-digits), then the downside is probably limited even if the rate of growth ultimately slows. Broadly speaking, we aim to earn for all our investments an internal rate of return, modeled under conservative assumptions, in at least the mid-teens, a level high enough to result in a margin of safety for our capital. Investments with lower prospective returns are not sufficiently mispriced to attract our interest.

MAINTAINING A LONG-TERM HORIZON: THE DIFFERENCE BETWEEN INVESTMENT AND SPECULATION

Far too many people buy stocks wanting to make money quickly. But reliable investment returns cannot be earned this way; value investing works only when allowed the fullness of time. In the short run, any security can trade at any price. If your goal is to make a quick buck, value investing will hold no interest. Speculators generally regard stocks as blips constantly in motion on an electronic screen, like the ball in a spinning roulette wheel, capable of generating gains for those who guess right. Those minute-by-minute fluctuations may generate excitement, but ultimately they are "random walks," unpredictable short-term meanderings. Since speculators foolishly decouple share prices from underlying business realities, they are often drawn to whatever has been going up in price, regardless of the foolishness of the valuation. They regularly mistake luck for skill, pointing to an upward price blip as proof that their gambling is paying off. Speculative approaches—which pay little or no attention to downside risk—are especially popular in rising markets. In heady times, few are sufficiently disciplined to maintain strict standards of valuation and risk aversion, especially at a time when many of those who have abandoned such standards are outpacing the pack and becoming rich.

In recent years, some have attempted to expand the definition of an investment to include any asset that has recently appreciated in price—or might soon: art, rare stamps and coins, wine collections, NFTs (nonfungible tokens), and hundreds of alternative (crypto) currencies. Because these items generate no present or future cash flows and have values that depend entirely on buyer whim, they should be regarded as speculations, not investments.

Ubiquitous 24/7/365 media coverage of the stock market has reinforced investors' overemphasis on the short term. The cheerleading television pundits exult at rallies and record highs and commiserate over market reversals; viewers get the impression that up is the only rational market direction, and that selling or sitting on the sidelines is not just a poor choice, it's may be even unpatriotic. These shows promote a herdlike mentality, blurring the lines between investing and speculation. Financial cable channels also create the false perception that one can reasonably formulate an opinion on everything pertinent to the financial markets. We live in a sound-bite culture that peddles the idea that investing is not painstaking or rigorous, but easy. There will never be a Graham and Dodd channel on cable business TV; human nature ensures it. That channel would be the broadcasting equivalent of watching paint dry.

Then there is the influence of social media. In recent years, speculators gathering on Reddit and other such platforms have gained notoriety for their involvement in "meme stocks," typically frail and even near-bankrupt companies that are often being sold short by hedge funds. This herd regards the stocks as speculative vehicles and treats them like a casino game. While occasionally their bull raids squeeze a short seller overexposed to a single name, the combination of poor fundamentals and overvaluation is toxic—and can be expected to sink most meme stocks over time. When you overpay and ignore fundamental value, you've almost certainly locked in future losses; you simply don't realize it yet.

VALUE INVESTING IS A RISK-AVERSE APPROACH

The proper goal of a long-term investor is not to make as much money as possible as quickly as possible. It's to earn good, sustainable returns and hang onto them. It's also to increase one's purchasing power over time, after taking inflation into account. Equities are able to support this objective in a way that most fixed-income investments cannot.

Unlike speculators and their preoccupation with quick gain, value investors strive to limit or avoid loss and thereby mitigate risk. When buying at a bargain price, one's downside is, by definition, truncated. Should the price fall from that level (assuming the value hasn't changed), the downside is further diminished—and the upside greater still. Contrary to academic theory, when a bargain becomes an even better bargain, you have both less risk and higher prospective return. What's key is having long-term capital that makes it possible to hold this perspective and benefit from it.

A risk-averse investor is one for whom the perceived benefit of any gain is less than the perceived cost of an equivalent loss.[1] Imagine how you would respond to the proposition of a coin flip that would either double your net worth or extinguish it. Most would respectfully decline to play. Such risk aversion is deeply ingrained in human nature. Yet many unwittingly set aside their risk aversion when the sirens of stock market speculation call.

The best way to guard against loss is to conduct deep and rigorous fundamental research. When a small slice of a business is offered through the stock market at a bargain price, it is helpful to evaluate it as if the whole business were being offered for sale there. This analytical anchor helps value investors remain focused on the pursuit of long-term results, rather than the profitability of their daily trading ledger.

DEFINING AND MANAGING RISK

Many academics and professional investors define risk in terms of the Greek letter beta, which they use as a measure of past share price volatility: meaning that a stock with a relative volatility that has been greater than the overall market's is seen as riskier than one whose volatility has been lower. From this perspective, the greater the risk, the greater the return. But value investors, who are inclined to think about risk differently—as the probability and amount of potential loss—find such reasoning absurd. A volatile stock can become particularly undervalued, in fact, and at a reduced price it may become a very low-risk investment.

---

[1] Losing money, as Graham noted, can be psychologically unsettling. Anxiety from the financial damage caused by recently experienced loss or the fear of further loss can significantly impede one's ability to take advantage of the next opportunity that comes along. If an undervalued stock falls by half while the fundamentals—after checking and rechecking—are confirmed to be unchanged, one should relish the opportunity to buy significantly more "on sale." But if one's net worth has tumbled along with the share price, it may be psychologically difficult to add to the position.

In the gravity-defying market environment that followed the 2008–2009 financial crisis, the most speculative investments regularly performed the best, and many institutional investors came to act as if return achieved is always commensurate with risk incurred. Specifically, they have made the decision to deliberately bear more risk to earn incremental return. But from a value-investing perspective, returns come from avoiding risk. When you take on additional risk, you always get the risk, but you may or may not achieve the return. Remember the carnage that comes when market bubbles burst. Stocks that investors eagerly bought at elevated prices based on overly optimistic assumptions find trouble attracting bids at much lower prices, even though at such levels the prospective returns could now outweigh the risks.

Risk must also be considered over a period of time. Any security, as mentioned, can trade at any price at a particular moment, but its value is ultimately tethered to the value of the underlying business. Short-term volatility can drive markdowns in the value of one's portfolio (a negative if you're forced to sell, and a positive if you can buy more). Longer term, the only risks that really matter are being overly optimistic on corporate cash flows or choosing an inadequate discount rate.

The risks of investing in securities are closely related to those of the underlying businesses. Some businesses are more secure in their market positions than others. A low-cost competitor with high-profit margins may have a considerable advantage, for example, and a high cost incumbent a dangerous disadvantage. Some companies are domiciled in unpredictable or unreliable locales, and investing in them may be overly risky. Some companies carry excessive leverage, while others have fortress-like balance sheets that can withstand just about any adversity. Every investor needs to establish her own willingness to incur such risks and determine how much expected return she will require to be paid for bearing them.

One of the most difficult questions for value investors is position sizing and its impact on portfolio diversification and risk. How much can you comfortably own of even the most attractive opportunities? I believe value investors should pack their portfolios with their best ideas; if you can tell the good from the bad, you should be able to distinguish the great from the good. However, one reasonable constraint on bulking up on individual holdings and creating a concentrated portfolio is the accompanying loss of liquidity. It's easier to sell stock representing 1% of a company than 5% or 10%. Investors should have a particularly strong conviction before amassing a highly concentrated position, as it will be much harder to exit.

Another risk consideration for value investors, as with all investors, is whether to utilize leverage. While some hedge funds and even endowments use leverage to enhance their returns, I side with those who prefer not to incur the added risks of margin debt. While leverage enhances the returns of successful investments, it magnifies the losses of unsuccessful ones. More important, nonrecourse (i.e., margin) debt raises risk to unacceptable levels because it jeopardizes one's staying power. Value investors should know that even if they are right in the long run, in the short run a security can trade at any price and holders need to have sufficiently strong footing to weather the worst of the storm. Otherwise, they may have to liquidate their position at a point of maximum loss, well before their insights can be rewarded. One risk-related consideration should be paramount above all others: the ability to sleep well at night, confident that your financial position is secure whatever the future may bring.

THE ACADEMIC VIEW

Although value investing has been a successful discipline for generations, one group largely ignores or dismisses it: academics. There's an old joke about the economist who came across a $20 bill on the sidewalk but didn't bother to pick it up, because if it were real someone else would have already grabbed it. Value investors are always on the hunt for that proverbial $20 bill—skeptical about its existence, but ready to pounce when it's found.

With elegant theories that purport to explain the real world, academics sometimes oversimplify and in so doing misunderstand it, because they rely on questionable assumptions regarding the existence of continuous markets, the presence of rational actors, the availability of perfect information, and zero transaction costs. One such theory, the Efficient Market Hypothesis, holds that security prices are always efficient, reflecting all available information about that security, an idea deeply at odds with Graham and Dodd's notion that there is great value in fundamental security analysis. Another academic concept, the Capital Asset Pricing Model, relates risk to return, but it always conflates market-correlated volatility, or beta, with risk. Modern Portfolio Theory applauds the benefits of diversification in constructing an optimal portfolio. But by insisting that once a portfolio is fully diversified higher expected return comes only with greater risk, MPT effectively repudiates value investing as a viable investment philosophy despite its long-term record of risk-adjusted investment outperformance.

Thanks to these theories becoming academic dogma, generations of students have been taught that security analysis is worthless and that they must prioritize portfolio diversification, allocating capital away from their best ideas (because in efficient markets there can be no good ideas) and spreading it into mediocre or poor ones. The very market inefficiencies that introductory finance textbooks brush away provide the opportunity for value investors to earn outsized returns over time.

THE IMPORTANCE OF PROCESS AND TEMPERAMENT

A necessary part of investing is being intellectually honest. Sometimes, you make money because your investment thesis was correct. Other times, you simply get lucky. Just because you made money doesn't mean you made a good investment, and just because you lost money doesn't mean you made a poor investment. In order to be successful over the long run, investors must distinguish skill from luck, and learn from successes and failures alike.

A sound investment process requires a disciplined approach to analysis and a healthy and informed debate over the merits of every investment. Emotion must be avoided. It's important for investment firms to build an environment where people with diverse perspectives and backgrounds can honestly and respectfully share their views. Decision-making must be examined over time, and postmortems must be conducted in order to improve future decision-making. The best investors focus on process rather than outcomes, because they know that good process eventually leads to better outcomes, while good outcomes are not necessarily reflective of good process and could reflect mere luck, not skill.

Investors need a plan that can succeed over a full market cycle, one they can stick to with conviction during the inevitable periods of underperformance. If you could predict the future meanderings of the market, you'd want to be fully invested at the bottom and get out at the top. But because we can't predict the path of share prices, the only way to proceed is to invest with the idea of holding your investments through thick and thin. This means buying investments with good upside potential and limited downside risk. But as Graham and Dodd argued so forcefully, we must remember that conditions will change. It makes little sense, for example, to pivot to a more defensive strategy after the market and economy have cratered, or to adopt a more aggressive strategy after the market has surged. In each case, that horse may well have already left the barn.

Living through the Great Depression, Benjamin Graham thought deeply about how to invest in the context of unpredictable and dramatic change. Mired in a downturn that seemed like it might go on forever, Graham nonetheless saw that it was temporary even if he couldn't know how long it would last, what would turn things around, or what might lie ahead. In the 1930s, Graham experienced a period of dramatic economic volatility and deep uncertainty, where the most impactful changes were driven by the vicissitudes of the business cycle. Companies had the capacity to produce goods, but customers had no money. The economy was not actively managed by central bankers the way it is today, and it was thus subject to higher volatility. There was no Fed "put" to support the stock market through periods of economic tumult.

Nevertheless, in an extremely challenging market, Graham and Dodd remained faithful to their principles. They knew that the economy and markets would sometimes go through painful cycles, and they also knew these periods must be endured because neither their beginning nor end could be reliably predicted. They expressed confidence, in the darkest days, that the economy and stock market would eventually rebound. As they noted: "While we were writing, we had to combat a widespread conviction that financial debacle was to be the permanent order." Even if you're fully expecting mean reversion for the economy as a whole, it's hard to maintain that view in the face of painful loss or persistent underperformance.

Over time, just as investors must deal with down cycles in which business results deteriorate and undervalued stocks become more deeply undervalued, they must also endure and remain disciplined during protracted up cycles in which bargains are scarce and investment capital seems limitless. Between 2010 and 2021, the financial markets performed exceedingly well by historic standards, rewarding the bulls while making downside protection seem a fool's errand, or at least an unnecessary waste. Fear of missing out (FOMO) replaced the fear of loss. The sole focus of most investors became earning a high return *on* capital, rather than ensuring the return *of* capital.

Capital-market manias regularly occur on a grand scale: Japanese stocks in the late 1980s, internet and technology stocks in 1999–2000, subprime mortgage lending in 2006, and high-growth though not yet profitable stocks, fixed income investments, and cryptocurrencies in 2020 and 2021. It's hard to bet against bubbles when you're in one; even experienced investors can wither under the market's relentless message that they are wrong. The pressure to succumb is enormous; many investment managers fear they'll lose business if they stand too far apart from the crowd or underperform for very long. FOMO can be a powerful force, but value investors must maintain a contrary stance as others around them lose their heads.

These days, value investors must also consider the propensity of the Federal Reserve to intervene in financial markets at the first sign of trouble. Amid severe turbulence, the Fed now typically lowers interest rates to prop up securities prices and restore investor confidence. When the economy slips into a downturn, the Fed quickly moves to buy bonds or cut rates. At such moments, Fed officials are trying to maintain orderly capital markets, but some money managers view Fed intervention as a virtual license to speculate. Aggressive Fed tactics to prop up markets, originally referred to as the "Greenspan Put" (and now the "Powell Put"), create a growing moral hazard that encourages speculation while prolonging and even exacerbating overvaluation. While Ben Graham recommended focusing on the bottom-up fundamentals of specific investments and largely ignoring macro factors, the Fed has become the 800-pound gorilla, something that cannot be ignored and a presence that tends to get its own way. In 2022, the Fed has begun to reverse these policies to combat elevated inflation, with uncertain longer-term impact.

My best advice for readers is to continue to invest bottom-up, while avoiding being completely wrong-footed by keeping one eye on the prevailing macro backdrop. To ignore the Fed's presence would be to put oneself fully at the mercy of policymaker overreach or misstep. Most important, value investors must fight the tendency to be lulled into a false sense of security by subdued volatility or elevated valuations that may swiftly reverse, and they must never rely on the Fed to rescue them from the overvalued investments they may make.

VALUE INVESTING IN 2022: CHALLENGES AND OPPORTUNITIES

Deep-pocketed, bargain-seeking competitors are the enemy of superior investment performance. Today's vast pools of capital ensure that few investments are completely orphaned or overlooked. Battalions of analysts, many of whom grew up reading prior editions of this very book, are peering into the nooks and crannies of every financial market. While there are many forces that can propel the prices of securities away from fundamental value, buy-side competition is consistently pushing in the other direction. Even a few competitors bidding for an investment can ruin a good thing; it takes only one aggressive buyer to fully correct a mispricing.

Yet the good news for value investors is that even with a large value-investing community, there are far more market participants who invest without a long-term value orientation. Most managers concentrate almost single-mindedly on the growth rate of a company's earnings or the momentum of its share price. Meanwhile, vast amounts of capital have been flowing into index funds to save money on fees and transaction costs. Index managers automatically buy the stocks in an index, doing no fundamental analysis to validate the purchases. Of course, with more and more investment capital being indexed, future mispricings may increasingly linger and the incremental returns achievable through fundamental analysis could start to rise.

In the parlance of Wall Street strategists, "value" underperformed "growth" for over a decade after the 2008–2009 financial crisis by nearly unprecedented margins. I set "value" and "growth" in quotation marks because these labels can be very misleading. Any stock, growing or not, can be under- or overvalued. Academics and Wall Streeters often use these labels as shorthand to identify the half of the market with the lowest multiples as "value" and the higher-multiple half as "growth," but that categorization is arbitrary. At times, well over half of the stocks in the market can be undervalued, and at other times bargains can be quite scarce.

This means that one reason for the periodic poor performance of "value" stocks comes from misunderstanding over a mere label. Those who define value investing as the purchase of the statistically lowest-multiple stocks (as measured by price to earnings, price to cash flow, price to book value, etc.) are making a serious error. As discussed, the rapid and well-funded innovation we observe every day has accelerated the demise of many "old economy" businesses. The stock market is hardly unaware of this. The obvious losers in this "creative destruction" fall in price to a low multiple of yesterday's results. But in a great many cases, this does not make them bargains. Many declining businesses are eroding faster than ever now. They are not value investments and should generally be avoided, except when the market has significantly overreacted and the situation can be assessed to be not as dire as commonly perceived.

The poor relative performance of "value" strategies in recent years has driven many investors to use other strategies, most prominently a "growth" approach. For many, there has been no price too high to pay for a rapidly growing and promising business. Thirteen years after the

Great Financial Crisis, more than a decade of meager interest rates had driven investors, even conservative ones, into larger and larger equity allocations. TINA ("There Is No Alternative") thinking drove them out of low-yielding bonds and into stocks and, for many endowments and pension funds, into illiquid and often risky alternative investments such as private equity and venture capital. This led to sizable excesses in the valuation of rapidly growing but still unprofitable businesses, many of which were not expected to produce their first profits or positive cash flows for years. Many slower-growing companies, in contrast, significantly lagged the market indices, trading at levels where they had become quite undervalued compared, for example, to what a private buyer might pay for them.

The shares of these more staid companies have often failed to attract large numbers of buyers in this market environment, because the disappointing performance of "value" strategies drove capital flows instead into "growth." The thinking was circular: put more money into what has worked, regardless of price, and avoid what hasn't worked, also regardless of price. This drives up the price of what has worked while reducing the price of what hasn't. This may seem like value hell, but it is actually driving prices in the direction of value heaven—meaning, exactly the sort of environment that Graham wrote about, a market in which undervalued companies were as unloved as overvalued companies were adored, one in which bargains became plentiful.

Value investors can build edge by taking a view that is longer-term than their competitors'. Because of the short-term, relative performance orientation of most investors and the constant performance comparisons they are subjected to, they can find it hard to look past a valley to imagine the next peak. Not many want to buy a stock if the next few quarters look disappointing, since stocks that fail to beat Wall Street's quarterly estimates are regularly thrashed. Even when short-term negatives have been more than fully baked into share prices, many hold back, waiting for obvious evidence of turnaround or recovery. In effect, they'd rather pay a higher price when the road ahead seems clear, even though by the time everyone can see what they see, the moment of greatest opportunity will have passed.

The pressures placed on professional investment managers cause them to act based on nonfundamental considerations. For example, many professional investors engage in certain career-management techniques, such as "window dressing" their portfolios at the end of calendar quarters by selling off losers (even if they are undervalued) while buying more of the winners (even if overvalued). This is because it's hard to keep defending a money-losing investment to disgruntled clients; being second-guessed is a common professional hazard. Of course, for truly long-term-oriented value investors, it's a wonderful thing that many potential competitors are thrown off course by constraints or behaviors that render them unable or unwilling to hold the very best investments.

Opportunity is often found where you least expect it, where you have never found it before, and where you have never even looked. During the Great Financial Crisis of 2008, one area of opportunity for my firm and for other value investors ended up being in residential mortgage-backed securities (RMBS) that fell under a dark cloud when the housing market collapsed. These securities, backed by slicing and dicing the cash flows from large pools of residential mortgages, were a Wall Street innovation that, like many, had not been stress-tested. Ratings downgrades caused the entire securitization market to shudder, and holders regurgitated enormous volumes of these suddenly disgraced issues. These now "toxic assets" plunged when it became apparent that investors would not recover par value. Prices began to discount a further plunge in housing prices, one which would have massively overshot fundamentals. Huge volumes of deeply discounted RMBS were available, offering a very attractive upside with quite limited downside. This example highlights that the bigger the mess, the better the value opportunity that may emerge.

Today's value investors also regularly find opportunity in the stocks and bonds of companies stigmatized on Wall Street because of their involvement in protracted litigation, accounting irregularities, financial distress, or scandals. These securities sometimes trade at bargain levels, where they become attractive to those who can remain stalwart in the face of bad news. For example, the debt of Steinhoff, a South African company with a large portfolio of European and South African retail businesses, came under tremendous selling pressure after a large accounting fraud was uncovered in December 2017, driving the bonds to a steep discount. But those intrepid enough to sleuth through the limited information available were able to bracket the extent of the fraud and find comfort that the pricing far more than discounted the fraud's extent. In general, for a value investor, companies that disappoint or surprise with lower-than-expected results, sudden management changes, accounting problems, or ratings downgrades are more likely to be sources of opportunity than the consistently strong performers are.

If there are no immediately compelling opportunities at hand, value investors should choose to wait rather than overpay, holding some cash in reserve. Compromising one's standards can lead to disaster. At various times in his career, including in his 2021 Berkshire Hathaway shareholder letter, Warren Buffett has stated that he has more cash to invest than he has good investments. As all value investors must do from time to time, Buffett exercises patience. While waiting, value investors should keep digging to identify new mispricings, uncover incremental kernels of information, and develop fresh insights. New opportunities will inevitably emerge. Importantly, value investors don't need the entire market to be bargain-priced, just 20 or 25 unrelated investments—a number sufficient for diversification of risk.

THE BURGEONING GROWTH OF INSTITUTIONAL INVESTING AND ALTERNATIVE INVESTMENT VEHICLES

One of the most important changes in the investment landscape over the past nine decades has been the ascendance of institutional investing. In the 1930s, individual investors dominated the stock market. In the 1950s, Keith Funston, then the president of the New York Stock Exchange, exhorted the public to "own your share of American business." But even as this message was being broadcast, pension funds and other institutions were amassing vast amounts of capital. Together with endowments and foundations, insurance companies, and sovereign wealth funds, as well as mutual funds and other commingled funds for individuals, these institutions came to dominate both the trading and ownership of publicly traded securities.

The advent of these large, professionally managed pools of capital have not brought a longer-term orientation to the financial markets. Institutional managers find it hard to have such an outlook when their committees and external consultants keep making increasingly short-term performance comparisons. Constant performance assessment inevitably leads to relative performance comparisons. As with animals in the wild, in investment management wandering from the herd is risky, subjecting managers to possible relative underperformance and client termination. While the only way to outperform the herd is to be different, only a few investors can weather the inevitable periods of relative underperformance.

A second major development in the world of institutional investing has been the rise of so-called alternative investments—a catch-all category that includes venture capital, leveraged buyouts, private equity, and private credit, as well as hedge funds. As the twenty-first century unfolded, they became all the rage among endowments, foundations, and pension and sovereign funds.

Thinking that traditional equity and debt markets are too expensive to provide adequate returns and increasingly too efficiently priced to possibly produce alpha (market outperformance), institutional investors have been allocating a growing portion of their assets under management to alternatives. In his 2000 book *Pioneering Portfolio Management*, the groundbreaking head of Yale's Investment Office, the late David Swensen, makes a strong case for these investments. He points to the historically inefficient pricing of many asset classes,[2] the record-high risk-adjusted returns of many alternative managers, the high dispersion between the best such managers and the rest of the pack, and the limited performance correlation between alternatives and other asset classes. He highlights the importance of choosing the right alternative managers by noting the large dispersion of returns between top-quartile and third-quartile performers. Many endowment managers have emulated Swensen by committing to these asset classes.

One of the most popular alternative asset classes today is private equity, a topic Graham and Dodd did not specifically address.[3] Though investing in private businesses may seem quite different from buying fractional interests in publicly traded companies, many of the analytical considerations regarding how each are valued are the same. The precise factors that can cause a stock to become mispriced obviously don't apply in private investments that don't trade on a market, but private investments can become mispriced for similar reasons. Under urgent

---

[2] Many investors make the mistake of thinking about returns to asset classes as if they are permanent. But returns are of course not inherent to any asset class; they result from the fundamentals of the underlying businesses *and* the price paid by investors. Capital pouring into an asset class can, reflexively, impair the ability of those investing in that asset class to continue to generate the anticipated returns.

[3] They did consider the relative merits of corporate control enjoyed by a private business owner versus the value of marketability enjoyed by a listed stock. (Chap. 28)

circumstances, a private company may be sold at a bargain price or accept a capital injection on favorable terms to the investor. They may suffer from a dysfunctional ownership group or poor management. While their holdings are illiquid, private equity investors gain a lever of corporate control to help drive business success and favorable investment outcomes. Control enables an investor not only to benefit from a disciplined approach, a bargain purchase, and timely buy and sell decisions, but also to enact more far-reaching measures, such as returning excess capital to the equity owners, changing a business plan, accelerating capital expenditures, making accretive acquisitions, exiting business units, and even selling the entire company.

Similarly, Graham and Dodd never addressed how to analyze direct investments in real estate (buildings of various use as well as land), a vast asset class that has become more popular with institutions. But there are bargains to be had in real estate, too, and they happen for all the same reasons—e.g., the seller has an urgent need for cash, an inability to perform proper analysis, differences in investor outlooks and time horizons, or investor disfavor or neglect. In a difficult real estate climate, tighter lending standards can constrain would-be buyers and cause even healthy properties to sell at distressed prices. Every building and every parcel of land can be seen as a candidate for investment; each holds the possibility of being mispriced. And as with private equity ownership, the owner of a building or land parcel has a nearly endless array of options: build or not, determine rents, refurbish or repurpose the building, finance or refinance, or exit. Graham and Dodd's principles—such as the stability of cash flows, sufficiency of return, analysis of downside risk, debt coverage ratios, and contingency analysis of what can go wrong— allow investors to identify real estate investments with a margin of safety in any market environment.

Graham and Dodd would have had trouble embracing one type of alternative investment—venture capital—because they would be unlikely to find a margin of safety in it.[4] While there is often the prospect of enormous upside in such an investment, there is also a very high risk of failure. Nor is it clear how to evaluate fledgling enterprises to see if the potential return justifies the risk. Naturally, investors with considerable risk tolerance and sophistication will want to participate in the businesses of tomorrow (and to buy in before they come public at what are generally particularly lofty valuations), by allocating a limited portion of capital to this sector while expecting a very bumpy ride. But investors should take note that the venture capital returns of 2020–2021 are virtually unprecedented and have benefitted greatly from exuberant public market valuations. Further, capital inflows have caused deal pricing at every stage of venture investing to be bid up considerably, increasing the probability that future returns will be lower.

These accelerating flows of capital into early-stage companies increases the likelihood that these nascent businesses may face intensified competition in the future. It's unclear whether the businesses enabled by ongoing technological advances can withstand the competitive forces unleashed by the burgeoning volumes of venture capital looking to back their current and future competitors.

Hedge funds, another alternative-asset class, and one with more than $3 trillions of capital under management, are pools of capital that invest in a wide array of instruments and markets and do so in varied ways. They are considered a category mainly because they have a common fee structure that typically pays the manager 1% to 2% of assets under management annually and roughly 20% (and sometimes

---

[4] Nor would they find one in highly leveraged buyouts, where businesses are purchased at high prices using mostly debt financing and a thin layer of equity capital. The only value investing rationale for venture capital or leveraged buyouts might be if they were regarded as mispriced call options.

more) of any returns generated. These funds had their start in the 1920s; Graham himself ran one of the first.

What would Graham and Dodd think about today's hedge funds? I believe they would consider them a mixed bag. Some pursue risk-averse strategies, carefully identifying mispricings and hedging risk. Others pursue short-term profits, employ enormous leverage, or make macroeconomic bets. Still others follow relative performance strategies, where they use fundamental investment analysis to buy what they regard as the best companies and sell short the worst companies. When done right, they may earn profits on both sides of the ledger. Illiquidity, lack of transparency, gargantuan size, embedded leverage, and some funds' hefty fees would no doubt raise red flags for Graham and Dodd, but they would probably approve of the hedge funds that practice value-oriented investment selection.

While Graham and Dodd emphasized limiting risk on a per investment basis, they also believed that diversification and hedging could protect the downside of an entire portfolio. (Chap. 1) Most hedge funds hold some securities that when considered in isolation may involve an uncomfortable degree of risk, but they attempt to offset the risks for the portfolio as a whole by employing hedging strategies such as the short sale of similar but higher multiple securities or market indices.

VALUE-INVESTING PRINCIPLES ARE RELEVANT BEYOND THE FINANCIAL MARKETS

Graham and Dodd's commonsense principles apply beyond the financial markets—such as in the search for baseball talent, as eloquently captured in Michael Lewis's 2003 book, *Moneyball*. The market for baseball players, like the market for stocks and bonds, is inefficient (and for many of the same reasons). In both investing and baseball, there is no single way to ascertain value, no one metric that tells the whole story, and there is voluminous information without a broad consensus on how to assess it. Decision-makers in both arenas misinterpret available data, misdirect their analyses, and reach inaccurate conclusions. In baseball, as in securities, executives often face pressures that cause them to overpay for talent because they fear standing apart from the crowd, doing something unpopular (such as failing to re-sign a superstar), and being criticized. They often have an excessively short-term orientation, driven by rabid fans, critical media, and impatient owners. They may make decisions for emotional, not rational, reasons. They become exuberant; they panic; they fear missing out; they may think they see patterns that aren't really there or don't apply. They fail to understand what is mean-reverting and what isn't. Baseball's value investors, like financial-market value investors, have achieved significant outperformance over time.

Moneyball did not delineate a static approach that would consistently outperform over time. Market inefficiencies in any endeavor attract competition and are often quickly corrected. In response to the dramatic success of early *Moneyball* adherents, baseball general managers have built sizable teams of data analysts. A key skill set in managing a baseball team, as with investing, is the ability to sort through proliferating masses of data to assign proper weights to disparate factors. There is, in baseball and investing, an endless process of identifying and building edge, and then having those edges whittled down by competition, changes in the market, and sometimes changes in the rules, until they are gone. Consequently, new sources of edge must constantly be identified and developed.

Baseball general managers have advanced the thinking and science of properly valuing baseball players beyond those represented in *Moneyball* to measure anything and everything that can be measured. New technologies allow teams to assess a catcher's pitch-framing skill as well as the spin rate of pitches and the response time of fielders after the ball has been hit. Just as with investing in the financial markets, the core principles will always apply, but the best applications of those principles will ebb and flow. The fact that Graham and Dodd's principles can help navigate the market for athletic talent attests to the universality and timelessness of their approach.

FINAL THOUGHTS

The essential characteristics of a value investor—patience and discipline—are rare. As Warren Buffett noted (in his famous article "The Superinvestors of Graham-and-Doddsville"), "[I]t is extraordinary to me that the idea of buying dollar bills for 40 cents takes immediately with people or it doesn't take at all. It's like an inoculation. If it doesn't grab a person right away, I find you can talk to him for years and show him records, and it doesn't make any difference."[5]

My own experience has been exactly the one that Buffett describes. My 1978 summer job and subsequent full-time employment at Mutual Shares, a no-load value-based mutual fund, set the course for my professional career. The planned liquidation of Telecor and spin-off of its Electro Rent subsidiary in 1980 forever imprinted in my mind the merit of fundamental investment analysis. A buyer of Telecor stock was effectively creating an investment in the shares of Electro Rent, a fast-growing equipment rental company, at the giveaway valuation of approximately one times cash flow. You always remember your first value investment.

If *Security Analysis* resonates with you—if you can resist speculating and sit on your hands at times—perhaps you have a disposition toward value investing. If not, at least this book will help you understand where you fit into the investing landscape and gain an appreciation for the value-investing community.

---

[5] "The Superinvestors of Graham-and-Doddsville," 1984; https://www8.gsb.columbia.edu/sites/valueinvesting/files/files/Buffett1984.pdf.

In a rising market, everyone makes money and a value philosophy may be unnecessary. But because there is no sure way to predict what the market will do, one needs to follow a value philosophy at all times. Value investors must remain hungry and agile, developing new areas of edge to replace those that are arbitraged away as more investors pile in. They must remain humble, intellectually honest, and deeply curious. They must be responsible stewards of capital, taking into account the influence of their companies on their customers, their communities, and the planet. And they must constantly hone their investment process and develop new insights into human behavior, including their own, while learning from mistakes and successes alike. Finally, they must fight the belief that the way things are today is the way they'll always be; history promises us otherwise. By controlling risk and limiting loss through extensive fundamental analysis, strict discipline, and endless patience, however, value investors can expect good results with limited downside.

The real secret to investing is that there is no secret to investing. Every important aspect of value investing has been made available to the public many times over, beginning in 1934 with the first edition of *Security Analysis*. That so many people fail to follow this timeless approach enables those who adopt it to be successful. I know of no long-time investor who regrets adhering to a value philosophy, and few will ever abandon this time-tested approach for another. Human nature guarantees that the hope for and pursuit of rapid and effortless gain will be with us forever. So as long as others succumb to the siren song of getting rich fast, value investing will remain, as it has been for some 90 years, a sound, low-risk, and successful approach. Truly, the concept of buying securities for less than they're worth never grows old. You may not get rich quickly, but you will keep what you have, and if the future of value investing resembles its past, you are likely to get rich slowly. As strategies go, this is the most that any reasonable investor can hope for.

PREFACE TO THE SECOND EDITION

The lapse of six years since first publication of this work supplies the excuse, if not the necessity, for the present comprehensive revision. Things happen too fast in the economic world to permit authors to rest comfortably for long. The impact of a major war adds special point to our problem. To the extent that we deal with investment policy we can at best merely hint at the war's significance for the future. As for security analysis proper, the new uncertainties may complicate its subject matter, but they should not alter its foundations or its methods.

We have revised our text with a number of objectives in view. There are weaknesses to be corrected and some new judgments to be substituted. Recent developments in the financial sphere are to be taken into account, particularly the effects of regulation by the Securities and Exchange Commission. The persistence of low interest rates justifies a fresh approach to that subject; on the other hand the reaffirmance of Wall Street's primary reliance on *trend* impels us to a wider, though not essentially different, critique of this modern philosophy of investment.

Although too great insistence on up-to-date examples may prove something of a boomerang, as the years pass swiftly, we have used such new illustrations as would occur to authors writing in 1939–1940. But we have felt also that many of the old examples, which challenged the future when first suggested, may now possess some utility as verifiers of the proposed techniques. Thus we have borrowed one of our own ideas and have ventured to view the sequel to all our germane 1934 examples as a "laboratory test" of practical security analysis. Reference to each such case, in the text or in notes, may enable the reader to apply certain tests of his own to the pretensions of the securities analyst.

The increased size of the book results partly from a larger number of examples, partly from the addition of clarifying material at many points, and perhaps mainly from an expanded treatment of railroad analysis and the addition of much new statistical material bearing on the exhibits of all the industrial companies listed on the New York Stock Exchange. The general arrangement of the work has been retained, although a few who use it as a text have suggested otherwise. We trust, however, that the order of the chapters can be revised in the reading, without too much difficulty, to convenience those who prefer to start, say, with the theory and practice of common-stock analysis.

Benjamin Graham and David L. Dodd

New York, New York

May, 1940

PREFACE TO THE FIRST EDITION

This book is intended for all those who have a serious interest in security values. It is not addressed to the complete novice, however, for it presupposes some acquaintance with the terminology and the simpler concepts of finance. The scope of the work is wider than its title may suggest. It deals not only with methods of analyzing individual issues, but also with the establishment of general principles of selection and protection of security holdings. Hence much emphasis has been laid upon distinguishing the investment from the speculative approach, upon setting up sound and workable tests of safety, and upon an understanding of the rights and true interests of investors in senior securities and owners of common stocks.

In dividing our space between various topics the primary but not the exclusive criterion has been that of relative importance. Some matters of vital significance, *e.g.*, the determination of the future prospects of an enterprise, have received little space, because little of definite value can be said on the subject. Others are glossed over because they are so well understood. Conversely we have stressed the technique of discovering *bargain issues* beyond its relative importance in the entire field of investment, because in this activity the talents peculiar to the securities analyst find perhaps their most fruitful expression. In similar fashion we have accorded quite detailed treatment to the characteristics of privileged senior issues (convertibles, etc.), because the attention given to these instruments in standard textbooks is now quite inadequate in view of their extensive development in recent years.

Our governing aim, however, has been to make this a critical rather than a descriptive work. We are concerned chiefly with concepts, methods, standards, principles, and, above all, with logical reasoning. We have stressed theory not for itself alone but for its value in practice. We have tried to avoid prescribing standards which are too stringent to follow, or technical methods which are more trouble than they are worth.

The chief problem of this work has been one of perspective—to blend the divergent experiences of the recent and the remoter past into a synthesis which will stand the test of the ever enigmatic future. While we were writing, we had to combat a widespread conviction that financial debacle was to be the permanent order; as we publish, we already see resurgent the age-old frailty of the investor—that his money burns a hole in his pocket. But it is the conservative investor who will need most of all to be reminded constantly of the lessons of 1931–1933 and of previous collapses. For what we shall call *fixed-value investments* can be soundly chosen only if they are approached—in the Spinozan phrase—"from the viewpoint of calamity." In dealing with other types of security commitments, we have striven throughout to guard the student against overemphasis upon the superficial and the temporary. Twenty years of varied experience in Wall Street have taught the senior author that this overemphasis is at once the delusion and the nemesis of the world of finance.

Our sincere thanks are due to the many friends who have encouraged and aided us in the preparation of this work.

Benjamin Graham and David L. Dodd
New York, New York
May, 1934

Benjamin Graham and *Security Analysis*: The Historical Backdrop

by James Grant

"It will simplify the Führer's whole work immensely if he need not first ask somebody if he may do this or that," the Associated Press quoted a Berlin informant on August 1, 1934, as saying of Adolf Hitler's ascension to the presidency of Germany. Set against such epochal events, a 727-page textbook on the fine points of value investing—the first edition of *Security Analysis*, by Benjamin Graham and David L. Dodd—must have seemed an unlikely candidate for bestsellerdom, then or later.

In his posthumously published autobiography, *The Memoirs of the Dean of Wall Street*, Benjamin Graham (1894–1976) thanked his lucky stars that he had entered the investment business in 1914, when stocks, the coming thing, were still a speculative afterthought.[1] The timing seemed not so propitious in 1934. From its 1929 peak to its 1932 trough, the Dow Jones Industrial Average had lost 87% of its value. At cyclical low ebb in 1933, the national unemployment rate had topped 25%. That the Great Depression had ended in 1933 was the considered judgment of the timekeepers of the National Bureau of Economic Research. Millions of Americans, however—not least, the

---

[1] Graham, *The Memoirs of the Dean of Wall Street*, edited by Seymour Chatman (New York: McGraw-Hill, 1996), p. 142.

relatively few who tried to squeeze a living out of a profitless Wall Street—had reason to doubt it.

The bear market and credit liquidation of the early 1930s gave the institutions of American finance a top-to-bottom scourging, and the tag ends that remained came in for rough handling in the first Roosevelt administration. Graham had learned his trade in the era of lightly regulated markets. He began work on *Security Analysis* as the Herbert Hoover administration was giving the country its first taste of thoroughgoing federal intervention during a peacetime economy. Graham was correcting page proofs as the Roosevelt administration was implementing its first radical forays into macroeconomic management. By 1934, there were laws to institute federal regulation of the securities markets, federal insurance of bank deposits, and federal price controls (not to put a cap on prices, as in later, inflationary times, but to put a floor under them). To try to prop up prices, the administration devalued the dollar. It is a testament to the quality of Graham's thought, not to mention the resiliency of America's financial markets, that *Security Analysis* gained and held its audience even as the economy was being turned upside down and inside out.

Five full months elapsed following publication of the first edition before Louis Rich got around to reviewing it in the *New York Times*. Who knows? Maybe the conscientious critic read every page. In any case, Rich gave the book a rave, albeit a slightly rueful one. "On the assumption," the critic wrote on December 2, 1934, "that despite the debacle of recent history there are still people left whose money burns a hole in their pockets, it is hoped that they will read this book. It is a full-bodied, mature, meticulous and wholly meritorious outgrowth of scholarly probing and practical sagacity. Although cast in the form and spirit of a textbook, the presentation is endowed with all the qualities likely to engage the liveliest interest of the layman."[2]

---

[2] Louis Rich, "Sagacity and Securities," *New York Times*, December 2, 1934, p. BR13.

How few laymen seemed to care about investing was brought home to Wall Street more forcefully with every passing year of the unprosperous post-Crash era. Just when it seemed that trading volume could get no smaller, or New York Stock Exchange seat prices no lower, or equity valuations more absurdly cheap, a new, dispiriting record was set. It required every effort of the editors of the Big Board's house organ, the *Exchange* magazine, to keep up a brave face. "*Must There Be* an End to Progress?" was the inquiring headline over an essay by the Swedish economist Gustav Cassel, published around the time of the release of Graham and Dodd's second edition in 1940 (the professor thought not).[3] "Why Do Securities Brokers Stay in Business?" the editors posed and helpfully answered, "Despite wearying lethargy over long periods, confidence abounds that when the public recognizes fully the value of protective measures which lately have been ranged about market procedure, investment interest in securities will increase." It did not amuse the Exchange that a New York City magistrate, sarcastically addressing a collection of defendants hauled into his court by the police for shooting craps on the sidewalk, had derided the financial profession. "The first thing you know," the judge had upbraided the suspects, "you'll wind up as stock brokers in Wall Street with yachts and country homes on Long Island."[4]

In ways now difficult to imagine, Murphy's Law was the order of the day; what could go wrong, did. "Depression" was more than a long-lingering state of economic affairs. It had become a worldview. The academic exponents of "secular stagnation," notably Alvin Hansen and Joseph Schumpeter, each a Harvard economics professor, predicted a long decline in American population growth. This deceleration, Hansen contended in his 1939 essay, "together with the failure of any really important innovations of a magnitude to absorb

---

[3] Gustav Cassel, "Must There Be an End to Progress?" *Exchange,* January 1940.

[4] *Exchange,* "Why Do Securities Brokers Stay in Business?" September 1940.

large capital outlays, weighs very heavily as an explanation for the failure of the recent recovery to reach full employment."[5]

Neither Hansen nor his readers had any way of knowing that a baby boom was around the corner. Nothing could have seemed more unlikely to a world preoccupied with a new war in Europe and the evident decline and fall of capitalism. Certainly, Hansen's ideas must have struck a chord with the chronically underemployed brokers and traders in lower Manhattan. As a business, the New York Stock Exchange was running at a steady loss. From 1933, the year in which it began to report its financial results, through 1940, the Big Board recorded a profit in only one year, 1935 (and a nominal one, at that). When an assistant professor of economics at Brown University, Chelcie C. Bosland, brought forth a book in 1937 entitled *The Common Stock Theory of Investment*, he remarked as if he were repeating a commonplace that the American economy had peaked two decades earlier at about the time of what was not yet called World War I. The professor added, quoting unnamed authorities, that American population growth could be expected to stop in its tracks by 1975.[6] Small wonder that Graham was to write that the acid test of a bond issuer was its capacity to meet its obligations not in a time of middling prosperity but in a depression (a test some 20% of today's largest 3,000 publicly traded companies would not come close to passing; indeed, according to Bloomberg, they failed to cover interest expense from operating cash flow even in the non-depression year of 2022).[7] Altogether, an investor in those days was well advised to keep up his guard. "The combination of a record high level for bonds,"

---

[5] James Grant, *The Trouble with Prosperity* (New York: Random House, 1996), p. 84.

[6] Chelcie C. Bosland, *The Common Stock Theory of Investment* (New York: Ronald Press, 1937), p. 74.

[7] Bloomberg News, "Zombie Firms Face Slow Death in the US as Easy-Credit Era Ends," May 31, 2022.

writes Graham in the 1940 edition, "with a history of two catastrophic price collapses in the preceding 20 years and a major war in progress is not one to justify airy confidence in the future." (Chap. 6)

Wall Street, not such a big place even during the 1920s boom, got considerably smaller in the subsequent bust. Ben Graham, in conjunction with his partner Jerry Newman, made a very small cog of this low-horsepower machine. The two conducted a specialty investment business at 52 Wall Street. Their strong suits were arbitrage, reorganizations, bankruptcies, and other complex situations. A schematic drawing of the financial district published by *Fortune* in 1937 made no reference to the Graham-Newman offices. Then again, the partnerships and corporate headquarters that did rate a spot on the Wall Street map were themselves—by the standards of twenty-first-century finance—remarkably compact. One floor at 40 Wall Street was enough to contain the entire office of Merrill Lynch & Co. And a single floor at 2 Wall Street was all the space required to house Morgan Stanley, the hands-down leader in 1936 corporate securities underwriting, with originations of all of $195 million. Compensation was in keeping with the slow pace of business, especially at the bottom of the corporate ladder.[8] After a 20% rise in the new federal minimum wage, effective October 1939, brokerage employees were entitled to earn at least 30 cents an hour.[9]

In March 1940, the *Exchange* documented the collapse of public participation in the stock market in all the detail its readers could want. In the first three decades of the twentieth century, the annual volume of trading had almost invariably exceeded the quantity of listed shares outstanding, sometimes by a wide margin. And in only one year between 1900 and 1930 had annual volume amounted to less than 50% of listed shares—the exception being 1914, the year in which

---

[8] *Fortune*, "Wall Street, Itself," June 1937.

[9] *New York Times*, October 3, 1939, p. 38.

the exchange was closed for four and a half months to allow for the shock of the outbreak of World War I to sink in. Then came the 1930s, and the annual turnover as a percentage of listed shares struggled to reach as high as 50%. In 1939, despite a short-lived surge of trading at the outbreak of World War II in Europe, the turnover ratio had fallen to a shockingly low 18.4%. "Perhaps," sighed the author of the study, "it is a fair statement that if the farming industry showed a similar record, government subsidies would have been voted long ago. Unfortunately for Wall Street, it seems to have too little sponsorship in officialdom."[10]

If a reader took hope from the idea that things were so bad that they could hardly get worse, he or she was in for yet another disappointment. The second edition of *Security Analysis* had been published only months earlier when, on August 19, 1940, the stock exchange volume totaled just 129,650 shares. It was one of the sleepiest sessions since the 49,000-share mark set on August 5, 1916. For the entire 1940 calendar year, volume totaled 207,599,749 shares— in 2022, a quiet hour's worth of volume and only 18.5% of the turnover of 1929, that year of seemingly irrecoverable prosperity. The cost of a membership, or seat, on the stock exchange sank along with turnover and with the major price indexes. At the nadir in 1942, a seat fetched just $17,000. It was the lowest price since 1897 and 97% below the record high price of $625,000, set—naturally—in 1929.

"'The Cleaners,'" quipped Fred Schwed, Jr., in his funny and wise book *Where Are the Customers' Yachts?* (which, like Graham's second edition, appeared in 1940), "was not one of those exclusive clubs; by 1932, everybody who had ever tried speculation had been admitted to membership."[11] And if an investor did, somehow, manage to avoid the

---

[10] *Exchange*, March 1940.

[11] Fred Schwed, Jr., *Where Are the Customers' Yachts?* (New York: Simon and Schuster, 1940), p. 28.

cleaners during the formally designated Great Depression, he or she was by no means home free. In August 1937, the market began a violent sell-off that would carry the averages down by 50% by March 1938. The nonfinancial portion of the economy fared little better than the financial side. In just nine months, industrial production fell by 34.5%, a sharper contraction even than that in the depression of 1920 to 1921, a slump that, for Graham's generation, had seemed to set the standard for the most economic damage in the shortest elapsed time.[12] The Roosevelt administration insisted that the slump of 1937 to 1938 was no depression but rather a "recession." The national unemployment rate in 1938 averaged 18.8%.

In April 1937, four months before the bottom fell out of the stock market for the second time in 10 years, Robert Lovett, a partner at the investment firm of Brown Brothers Harriman & Co., served warning to the American public in the pages of the mass-circulation *Saturday Evening Post*. Lovett, a member of the innermost circle of the Wall Street establishment, set out to demonstrate that there is no such thing as financial security—none, at least, to be had in stocks and bonds. The gist of Lovett's argument was that, in capitalism, capital is consumed and that businesses are just as fragile and mortal as the people who own them. He invited his millions of readers to examine the record, as he had done:

> If an investor had purchased 100 shares of the 20 most popular dividend-paying stocks on December 31, 1901, and held them through 1936, adding, in the meantime, all the melons in the form of stock dividends, and all the plums in the form of stock split-ups, and had exercised all the valuable rights to subscribe to additional stock, the aggregate market value of his total holdings on December 31,

---

[12] Benjamin M. Anderson, *Economics and the Public Welfare* (New York: Van Nostrand, 1949), p. 431.

1936, would have shown a shrinkage of 39% as compared with the cost of his original investment. In plain English, the average investor paid $294,911.90 for things worth $180,072.06 on December 31, 1936. That's a big disappearance of dollar value in any language.

In the innocent days before the crash, people had blithely spoken of "permanent investments." "For our part," wrote this partner of the eminent Wall Street private bank, "we are convinced that the only permanent investment is one which has become a total and irretrievable loss."[13]

Lovett turned out to be a prophet. At the nadir of the 1937–1938 bear market, one in five NYSE-listed industrial companies was valued in the market for less than its net current assets. Subtract from cash and quick assets all liabilities and the remainder was greater than the company's market value—that is, business value was negative. The Great Atlantic & Pacific Tea Company (A&P), the Walmart of its day, was one of these corporate zombies. At the 1938 lows, the market value of the common and preferred shares of A&P, at $126 million, was less than the net value of its cash, inventories, and receivables, conservatively valued at $134 million. In the words of Graham and Dodd, the still-profitable company was selling for "scrap." (Chap. 50)

A DIFFERENT ERA

Little about today's Wall Street would seem familiar to Benjamin Graham, from the old neighborhood itself (now largely residential) to the immensity of the dollars invested (the Depository Trust & Clearing Company processed securities trades in the sum of $2.37 quadrillion in 2021)[14] to the prevalence of index, or passive, investing (as of March 31, 2022, index mutual funds claimed $8.53 trillion in

---

[13] Robert A. Lovett, "Gilt-Edged Insecurity," *Saturday Evening Post,* April 3, 1937.

[14] DTCC 2021 annual report, p. 56.

assets, compared to $8.34 trillion in actively managed ones)[15] to the advent of commission-free trading (major brokerage houses dropped their rates to zero late in 2019) and the popularity of grading investment securities by the degree of compliance of their corporate issuers with the agenda of the "environmental, social and governance" reform movement.

Federal securities regulation was a new thing in the 1930s. What had preceded the Securities and Exchange Commission was, at its best, a regime of tribal sanction. Some things were simply beyond the pale, for instance, the solicitation of retail orders for initial public offerings (the risks and rewards of which were reserved for professionals). Both during and immediately after World War I, no self-respecting NYSE member firm would facilitate a client's switch from Liberty bonds into potentially more lucrative, if less patriotic, alternatives. There was no law against soliciting such a swap. Rather, according to Graham, it just wasn't done.[16]

A great many things weren't done in the Wall Street of the 1930s. Newly empowered regulators were resistant to financial innovation, transaction costs were high, and technology was (at least by today's digital standards) primitive. After the vicious bear market of 1937–1938, not a few investors decided they'd had enough. What was the point of it all? "In June 1939," approvingly writes Graham in a footnote in the second edition concerning financial innovation, "the S.E.C. set a salutary precedent by refusing to authorize the issuance of 'Capital Income Debentures' in the reorganization of the Griess-Pfleger Tanning Company, on the ground that the devising of new types of hybrid issues had gone far enough." (Chap. 5, Note 4)

---

[15] Morningstar Direct quoted in Allan Sloan, "The Democratization of Investing," Yahoo Finance, May 22, 2022.

[16] *The Memoirs of the Dean of Wall Street*, p. 169.

Safety is the essence of fixed-income investing, according to Graham, who develops the thought in words that continue to be quoted, if not strictly adhered to, today. Thus:

> Our primary conception of the bond as a commitment with limited return leads us to another important viewpoint toward bond investment. Since the chief emphasis must be placed on the avoidance of loss, bond selection is primarily a negative art. It is a process of exclusion and rejection, rather than of search and acceptance. (Chap. 6)

One can only speculate how Graham would have adapted this premise to the current era of ultra-low interest rates and to the existence, as recently as year-end 2021, of nearly $18 trillion dollars' worth of fixed-income securities worldwide quoted at nominal yields of less than zero. Far from a process of exclusion and rejection, bond investment, for the yield-famished savers of today, has become a desperate stampede for basis points—a process of inclusion and necessarily uncritical acceptance.

Nonetheless, in the 1940 edition, Graham records his support of the system of "legal lists," compendia of fixed-income securities authorized by state banking regulators for purchase by the savings banks under their charge. "Since the selection of high-grade bonds has been shown to be in good part a process of exclusion," he explains, "it lends itself reasonably well to the application of definite rules and standards designed to disqualify unsuitable issues." (Chap. 8)

The 1930s ushered in a revolution in financial disclosure. The new federal securities acts directed investor-owned companies to brief their stockholders once a quarter as well as at year-end. But the new standards were not immediately applicable to all public companies, and more than a few continued doing business the old-fashioned way, with their cards to their vests. One of these informational holdouts was none other than Dun & Bradstreet (D&B), the financial information company. Graham seemed to relish the irony of D&B not revealing "its own earnings to its own stockholders." (Chap. 3, Note 4) On the whole, by twenty-first-century standards, information in Graham's time was as slow moving as it was sparse. There were no conference calls, no automated spreadsheets, and no nonstop news from distant markets—indeed, not much truck with the world outside the 48 states. *Security Analysis* barely acknowledges the existence of foreign markets.

Such an institutional setting was hardly conducive to the development of "efficient markets," as today's economists style them—markets in which information is disseminated rapidly, human beings process it flawlessly, and prices incorporate it instantaneously. Graham, I think, would have scoffed at such an idea. Equally, he would have smiled at the discovery—so late in the evolution of the human species—that there was a place in economics for a subdiscipline called "behavioral finance." *Security Analysis* invites the reader to wonder what facet of investing is not behavioral. The stock market, Graham saw eight decades or so before the arrival of the 2021 "meme" stocks, is a source of entertainment value as well as investment value:

> Even when the underlying motive of purchase is mere speculative greed, human nature desires to conceal this unlovely impulse behind a screen of apparent logic and good sense. To adapt the aphorism of Voltaire, it may be said that if there were no such thing as common-stock analysis, it would be necessary to counterfeit it. (Chap. 27)

Anomalies of undervaluation and overvaluation—of underdoing it and overdoing it—fill these pages. It bemused Graham, but did not shock him, that so many businesses could be valued in the stock market for less than their net current assets, even during the late 1920s boom, or that, in the dislocations to the bond market immediately following World War I, investors could become disoriented enough to

assign a higher price and a lower yield to the Union Pacific First
Mortgage 4s than they did to the U.S. Treasury's own Fourth Liberty
4¼s. Graham writes of the "inveterate tendency of the stock market to
exaggerate." (Chap. 50) He would not have exaggerated much if he had
written, instead, "all markets."

Though he did not dwell long on the cycles in finance, Graham
was certainly aware of them. He could see that ideas, no less than
prices and categories of investment assets, had their seasons. The
discussion in *Security Analysis* of the flameout of the mortgage
guarantee business in the early 1930s anticipates the cyclically
recurrent race to the bottom in today's equity and credit markets.
Graham writes of his time and also of ours:

> The rise of the newer and more aggressive real estate bond
> organizations had a most unfortunate effect upon the policies of the
> older concerns. By force of competition they were led to relax their
> standards of making loans. New mortgages were granted on an
> increasingly liberal basis, and when old mortgages matured, they
> were frequently renewed in a larger sum. Furthermore, the face
> amount of the mortgages guaranteed rose to so high a multiple of the
> capital of the guarantor companies that it should have been obvious
> that the guaranty would afford only the flimsiest of protection in the
> event of a general decline in values. (Chap. 17)

Security analysis itself, too, is a cyclical phenomenon, as Graham
observed. In season, it holds a strong, intuitive appeal for the kind of
businessperson who thinks about stocks the way he or she thinks about
his or her own family business. What would such a fount of common
sense care about earnings momentum or Wall Street's pseudo-scientific
guesses about the economic future? Such an investor, appraising a
common stock, would much rather know what the company behind it
is worth. That is, he or she would want to study its balance sheet. Well,

Graham relates here, that kind of analysis went out of style when stocks started levitating without reference to anything except hope and prophecy. So by about 1927, fortune-telling and chart-reading had displaced the value discipline by which he and his partner were earning a very good living. It is characteristic of Graham that his critique of the "new era" method of investing is measured and not derisory. The old, conservative approach—his own—had been rather backward looking, Graham admits. It had laid more emphasis on the past than on the future, on stable earning power rather than tomorrow's earnings prospects. But new technologies, new methods, and new forms of corporate organization had introduced new risks as well as opportunities into the post–World War I economy. This fact—"the increasing instability of the typical business"—had blown a small hole in the older analytical approach that emphasized stable earnings power over forecast earnings growth. Beyond that mitigating consideration, however, Graham does not go. The new era approach, "which turned upon the earnings trend as the sole criterion of value, . . . was certain to end in an appalling debacle." (Chap. 28) Which, of course, it did, and—in the CNBC-driven markets of the twenty-first century—continues to do at intervals today.

A MAN OF MANY TALENTS

Graham, born Benjamin Grossbaum in London on May 9, 1894, sailed to New York with his family before he was two. Young Benjamin was a prodigy in mathematics, classical languages, modern languages, expository writing (as readers of this volume will see for themselves), and anything else that the then-superb New York City public schools had to offer. He had a tenacious memory and a love of reading—a certain ticket to academic success, then and now. His father's death at the age of 35 left him, his two brothers, and their mother in the social and financial lurch. Benjamin learned early to work and to do without.

No need here for a biographical profile of the principal author of *Security Analysis*: Graham's own memoir delightfully covers that ground. Suffice it to say that the high school brainiac entered Columbia College as an Alumni Scholar in September 1911 at the age of 17. So much material had he already absorbed that he began with a semester's head start, "the highest possible advanced standing."[17] He graduated number 2 in the class of 1914 and followed up his Phi Beta Kappa performance by writing a paper suggesting improvements in the teaching of calculus that *The American Mathematical Monthly* saw fit to publish.[18]

From these academic heights, Graham descended to the ground floor of Wall Street, beginning his career as a runner and board-boy at the New York Stock Exchange member firm of Newburger, Henderson & Loeb. Within a year, the trainee was playing the liquidation of the Guggenheim Exploration Company by astutely going long the shares of Guggenheim and short the stocks of the companies in which Guggenheim had made a minority investment, as his no-doubt bemused elders looked on: "The profit was realized exactly as calculated; and everyone was happy, not least myself."[19]

His masterwork, *Security Analysis*, did not come out of the blue. Long before he began teaching the advanced securities analysis course at Columbia University, in 1928 (with the assistance of David Dodd, his future *Security Analysis* collaborator), Graham had supplemented his income by contributing articles to the *Magazine of Wall Street*. His productions are unmistakably those of a self-assured and superbly educated Wall Street moneymaker. There was no need to quote expert opinion. He and the documents he interpreted were all the authority he needed. His favorite topics were the ones that he subsequently

[17] *The Memoirs of the Dean of Wall Street*, p. 106.

[18] Benjamin Graham, "Some Calculus Suggestions by a Student," *American Mathematical Monthly*, June 1917, vol. 24, no. 6, pp. 265–71.

developed in the book you hold in your hands. He was partial to the special situations in which Graham-Newman was to become so successful. Thus, when a high-flying and highly complex American International Corp. fell from the sky in 1920, Graham was able to show that the stock was cheap in relation to the evident value of its portfolio of miscellaneous (and not especially well disclosed) investment assets.[20] The shocking insolvency of Goodyear Tire and Rubber attracted his attention in 1921. "The downfall of Goodyear is a remarkable incident even in the present plenitude of business disasters," he writes, in a characteristic Graham sentence. (How many financial journalists, then or later, had "plenitude" on the tips of their tongues?) He shrewdly judged that Goodyear would be a survivor.[21] In the summer of 1924, he hit on a theme that would echo through *Security Analysis*: the evident non sequitur of stocks valued in the market at less than the liquidating value of the companies that issued them. "Eight Stock Bargains off the Beaten Track," says the headline over the Benjamin Graham byline: "Stocks That Are Covered Chiefly by Cash or the Equivalent—No Bonds or Preferred Stock Ahead of These Issues—an Unusually Interesting Group of Securities." In one case, that of Tonopah Mining, liquid assets of $4.31 per share towered over a market price of just $1.38 a share.[22]

For Graham, an era of sweet reasonableness in investment thinking seemed to end around the time he entered Wall Street. Before, say, 1914, the typical investor was a businessman who analyzed a stock or a bond much as he might a claim on a private business. He

---

[19] Ibid., p. 145.

[20] Benjamin Graham, "The 'Collapse' of American International," *Magazine of Wall Street*, December 11, 1920, pp. 175–176, 217.

[21] Benjamin Graham, "The Goodyear Reorganization," *Magazine of Wall Street*, March 19, 1921, pp. 683–685.

[22] Benjamin Graham, "Eight Stock Bargains off the Beaten Track," *Magazine of Wall Street*, July 19, 1924, pp. 450–453.

would naturally try to determine what the security-issuing company owned, free and clear of any encumbrances. If the prospective investment was a bond—and it usually was—the businessman-investor would seek assurances that the borrowing company had the financial strength to weather a depression.

"It's not undue modesty," Graham writes in his memoir, "to say that I had become something of a smart cookie in my particular field." His specialty was the carefully analyzed out-of-the-way investment: castaway stocks or bonds, liquidations, bankruptcies, arbitrage. Since at least the early 1920s, Graham had preached the sermon of the "margin of safety." As the future is a closed book, he urged in his writings, an investor, as a matter of self-defense against the unknown, should contrive to pay less than "intrinsic" value. Intrinsic value, as defined in *Security Analysis*, is "that value which is justified by the facts, e.g., the assets, earnings, dividends, definite prospects, as distinct, let us say, from market quotations established by artificial manipulation or distorted by psychological excesses." (Chap. 1)

He himself had gone from the ridiculous to the sublime (and sometimes back again) in the conduct of his own investment career. His quick and easy grasp of mathematics made him a natural arbitrageur. He would sell one stock and simultaneously buy another. Or he would buy or sell shares of stock against the convertible bonds of the identical issuing company. So doing, he would lock in a profit that, if not certain, was as close to guaranteed as the vicissitudes of finance allowed. In one instance, in the early 1920s, he exploited an inefficiency in the relationship between DuPont and the then red-hot General Motors. DuPont held a sizable stake in GM. And it was for that interest alone which the market valued the big chemical company. By implication, the rest of the business was worth nothing. To exploit this anomaly, Graham bought shares in DuPont and sold short the hedge-appropriate number of shares in GM. And when the market came to its senses, and the price gap between DuPont and GM widened in the expected direction, Graham took his profit.[23]

However, Graham, like many another value investor after him, sometimes veered from the austere precepts of safe-and-cheap investing. A Graham only slightly younger than the master who sold GM and bought DuPont allowed himself to be hoodwinked by the crooked promoter of a company that seems to not actually have existed—at least, not in anything like the state of glowing prosperity described by the manager of the pool to which Graham entrusted his money. An electric sign in Columbus Circle, on the Upper West Side of Manhattan, did bear the name of the object of Graham's misplaced confidence, Savold Tire. But as the author of *Security Analysis* confessed in his memoir, that could have been the only tangible marker of the company's existence. "Also, as far as I knew," Graham added, "nobody complained to the district attorney's office about the promoter's bare-faced theft of the public's money." Certainly, by his own telling, Graham didn't.[24]

By 1929, when he was 35, Graham was well on his way to fame and fortune. His wife and he kept a squadron of servants, including—for the first and only time in his life—a manservant for himself. With Jerry Newman, Graham had compiled an investment record so enviable that the great Bernard M. Baruch sought him out. Would Graham wind up his business to manage Baruch's money? "I replied," Graham writes, "that I was highly flattered—flabbergasted, in fact—by his proposal, but I could not end so abruptly the close and highly satisfactory relations I had with my friends and clients."[25] Those relations soon became much less satisfactory.

---

[23] Graham, *Memoirs*, p. 188.

[24] Ibid., pp. 181–184.

[25] Ibid., p. 253.

Graham relates that though he was worried at the top of the market, he failed to act on his bearish hunch. The Graham-Newman partnership went into the 1929 break with $2.5 million of capital. They controlled about $2.5 million in hedged positions—stocks owned long offset by stocks sold short and held, besides, about $4.5 million in outright long positions. It was bad enough that they were leveraged, as Graham later came to realize. Compounding that tactical error was a deeply rooted conviction that the stocks they owned were cheap enough to withstand any imaginable blow.

They came through the crash creditably: down by only 20% was, for the final quarter of 1929, almost heroic. But they gave up 50% in 1930, 16% in 1931, and 3% in 1932 (another relatively excellent showing), for a cumulative loss of 70%.[26] "I blamed myself not so much for my failure to protect myself against the disaster I had been predicting," Graham writes, "as for having slipped into an extravagant way of life which I hadn't the temperament or capacity to enjoy. I quickly convinced myself that the true key to material happiness lay in a modest standard of living which could be achieved with little difficulty under almost all economic conditions"—the margin-of-safety idea applied to personal finance.[27]

It can't be said that the academic world immediately clasped *Security Analysis* to its breast as the definitive elucidation of value investing, or of anything else. The aforementioned survey of the field in which Graham and Dodd made their signal contribution, *The Common Stock Theory of Investment*, by Chelcie C. Bosland, published three years after the appearance of the first edition of *Security Analysis*, cited 53 different sources and 43 different authors. Not one of them was named Graham or Dodd.

---

[26] Ibid., p. 259.

[27] Ibid., p. 263.

Edgar Lawrence Smith, however, did receive Bosland's full and respectful attention. Smith's *Common Stocks as Long Term Investments*, published in 1924, had challenged the long-held view that bonds were innately superior to equities. For one thing, Smith argued, the dollar (even the gold-convertible 1924 edition) was inflation-prone, which meant that creditors were inherently disadvantaged. Not so the owners of common stock. If the companies in which they invested earned a profit, and if a portion of that profit were retained in the business (thereby contributing to future earnings), the principal value of an investor's portfolio would tend "to increase in accordance with the operation of compound interest."[28]

Smith's timing was impeccable. Not a year after he published, the great Coolidge bull market erupted. *Common Stocks as Long Term Investments*, only 129 pages long, provided a handy rationale for chasing the market higher. That stocks do, in fact, tend to excel in the long run has entered the canon of American investment thought as a revealed truth (though it looked anything but obvious in the 1930s). For his part, Graham entered a strong dissent to Smith's thesis, or more exactly, its uncritical bullish application. It was one thing to pay 10 times earnings for an equity investment, he notes, quite another to pay 20 to 40 times earnings. Besides, the Smith analysis skirted the important question of what asset values lay behind the stock certificates that people so feverishly and uncritically traded back and forth. Finally, embedded in Smith's argument was the assumption that common stocks could be counted on to deliver in the future what they had done in the past. Graham was not a believer. (Chap. 27)

If Graham was a hard critic, however, he was also a generous one. In 1939 he was given John Burr Williams's *The Theory of Investment Value* to review for the *Journal of Political Economy* (no small honor for a Wall

---

[28] Grant, *The Trouble with Prosperity*, p. 43.

Street author-practitioner). Williams's thesis was as important as it was concise. The investment value of a common stock is the present value of all future dividends, the author proposed. Armed with that critical knowledge, Williams ventured to hope, investors might restrain themselves from bidding stocks back up to the moon again. Graham, in whose capacious brain dwelled the talents both of the quant and of the behavioral financier, voiced his doubts about that forecast. In order to apply Williams's method, he pointed out, one needed to make some very large assumptions about the future course of interest rates, the growth of profit, and the terminal value of the shares when growth stops. "One wonders," Graham mused, "whether there may not be too great a discrepancy between the necessarily hit-or-miss character of these assumptions and the highly refined mathematical treatment to which they are subjected." Graham closed his essay on a characteristically friendly note, commending Williams for the refreshing level-headedness of his approach and adding: "This conservatism is not really implicit in the author's formulas; but if the investor can be persuaded by higher algebra to take a sane attitude toward common-stock prices, the reviewer will cast a loud vote for higher algebra."[29]

Graham's technical accomplishments in securities analysis, by themselves, could hardly have carried *Security Analysis* through its many editions. After all, observes Roger F. Murray, who succeeded Graham as professor of the securities analysis course at Columbia Business School, "The Graham and Dodd approach . . . gains and loses adherents with the passing phases of the securities markets."[30] Not all readers of the Reddit message boards during the Covid-era speculative

[29] Benjamin Graham, "Review of John Burr Williams's *The Theory of Investment Value* (Cambridge, MA: Harvard University Press, 1938)," *Journal of Political Economy*, vol. 47, no. 2 (April 1939), pp. 276–278.

[30] Roger F. Murray, "Graham and Dodd: A Durable Discipline," *Financial Analysts Journal*, Sept.-Oct. 1984, vol. 40, no. 5, pp. 18–19, 22–23.

free-for-all found it necessary to familiarize themselves with the
concept of a margin of safety.

Rather, it's the intelligence, humanity, and good humor of *Security
Analysis* that to me explain the book's long life and the adoring loyalty
of Graham's readers. Was there ever a Wall Street moneymaker better
steeped than Graham in classical languages and literature *and* in the
financial history of his own time? I would bet "no" with all the
confidence of a value investor laying down money to buy a bargain.

Yet this great investment thinker and doer was, to a degree, a
prisoner of his own times. He could see that some of the experiences
through which he lived were unique, that the Great Depression was, in
fact, a great anomaly. If anyone understood the folly of projecting
current experience into the unpredictable future, it was Graham. Yet
this investment philosopher king, having spent 727 pages (not
including the gold mine of an appendix) describing how a careful and
risk-averse investor could prosper in every kind of macroeconomic
condition, arrives at a remarkable conclusion.

How should he invest? Graham asks, and he answers, at first
diffidently: Who is he to prescribe for the experienced financiers at the
head of America's philanthropic and educational institutions? But
then he takes the astonishing plunge. "An institution," Graham writes,
"that can manage to get along on the low income provided by high-
grade fixed-value issues should, in our opinion, confine its holdings to
this field. We doubt if the better performance of common-stock
indexes over past periods will, in itself, warrant the heavy
responsibilities and the recurring uncertainties that are inseparable
from a common-stock investment program." (Chap. 52)

Could the greatest value investor have meant that? Did the man
who stuck it out through ruinous losses in the Depression years and
went on to thrive in the prosperous postwar era really mean that
common stocks were not worth the bother? In 1940, with a new world

war fanning the Roosevelt administration's fiscal and monetary policies, high-grade corporate bonds yielded just 2.75%, while blue-chip equities delivered 5.1%. Did Graham mean to say that bonds were a safer proposition than stocks? Well, he did say it. If Homer could nod, so could Graham—and so can the rest of us, whoever we are. Let that, too, be a lesson.

Near the close of his memoirs, Graham allows himself to speculate on his legacy: "If my name has any chance of being remembered by future generations—assuming that there will be future generations—it will be as inventor of the Commodity Reserve Currency Plan."[31] Graham's plan, intermittently discussed but never implemented, was to iron out the business cycle by directing the U.S. Treasury to stabilize the price level by standing ready to buy and sell a portfolio of 30 basic raw materials at predetermined fixed prices. In effect, the gold standard would become one-thirtieth of a gold standard, with a potpourri of nongold materials furnishing the balance of the monetary collateral.

The truth is that Graham—amateur playwright, lifetime classicist, a founding spirit of the Chartered Financial Analyst movement—wrote his true legacy in the pages of this durable volume. Certainly, that would be Mr. Market's view. The $20,000 median value of a rare first edition copy represents a nearly 10% per annum rate of return from the original, 1934 cover price of $5.[32] And if that achievement falls a little short of the 10.8% compound annual return of the Standard & Poor's 500 over the same interval, with dividends reinvested, a Graham devotee will understand why. The nontaxable dividends that *Security Analysis* has paid its four generations of readers are more precious than the kind that a stockholder gets in the mail.

---

[31] *The Memoirs of the Dean of Wall Street*, p. 293.

[32] AbeBooks, "Security Analysis by Benjamin Graham, First Edition," June 27, 2022.

Problems of Investment Policy

Although, strictly speaking, security analysis may be carried on without reference to any definite program or standards of investment, such a specialization of functions would be quite unrealistic. Critical examination of balance sheets and income accounts, comparisons of related or similar issues, studies of the terms and protective covenants behind bonds and preferred stocks—these typical activities of the securities analyst are invariably carried on with some practical idea of purchase or sale in mind, and they must be viewed against a broader background of investment principles, or perhaps of speculative precepts. In this work we shall not strive for a precise demarcation between investment theory and analytical technique but at times shall combine the two elements in the close relationship that they possess in the world of finance.

It seems best, therefore, to preface our exposition with a concise review of the problems of policy that confront the security buyer. Such a discussion must be colored, in part at least, by the conditions prevailing when this chapter was written. But it is hoped that enough allowance will be made for the possibility of change to give our conclusions more than passing interest and value. Indeed, we consider this element of change as a central fact in the financial universe. For a better understanding of this point we are presenting some data, in conspectus form, designed to illustrate the reversals and upheavals in values and standards that have developed in the past quarter century.

The three reference periods 1911–1913, 1923–1925, and 1936–1938 were selected to represent the nearest approximations to "normal," or relative stability, that could be found at intervals during the past quarter century. Between the first and second triennium we had the

Financial and Economic Data for Three Reference Periods

Period	1911–1913			1923–1925			1936–1938		
	High	Low	Average	High	Low	Average	High	Low	Average
Business index*	118.8	94.6	107.9	174.9	136.0	157.9	164.9	106.0	137.0
Bond yields*	4.22%	4.02%	4.09%	4.82%	4.55%	4.68%	3.99%	3.36%	3.65%
Index of industrial stock prices*	121.6	92.2	107.6	198.6	128.6	153.4	293.4	124.8	211.1
Dow-Jones Industrial Average (per unit):									
Price range	94	72	82	159	86	112	194	97	149
Earnings	$8.69	$7.81	$8.12	$13.54	$10.52	$11.81	$11.41	$6.02	$9.14
Dividends	5.69	4.50	5.13	7.09	5.51	6.13	8.15	4.84	6.66
Price-earnings ratio†	11.6x	8.9x	10.1x	13.5x	7.3x	9.5x	21.2x	10.6x	16.3x
Dividend yield†	5.5%	7.1%	6.3%	3.9%	7.1%	5.5%	3.4%	6.9%	4.5%
U. S. Steel:‡									
Price range	82	50	65	139	86	111	178	53	96
Earnings per share	$11.00	$5.70	$7.53	$16.40	$11.80	$13.70	$11.22	(d)$5.30	$3.33
Dividends per share	5.00	5.00	5.00	7.00	5.25	6.42	1.40	Nil	0.42
Price-earnings ratio†	10.9x	6.6x	8.6x	10.1x	6.3x	8.1x	53.4x	15.9x	28.8x
Dividend yield†	6.1%	10.0%	7.7%	4.6%	7.5%	5.8%	0.2%	0.8%	0.4%
General Electric:§									
Price range	196	142	172	524	262	368	1,580	664	1,070
Earnings per share	$16.72	$12.43	$14.27	$32.10	$27.75	$30.35	$53.50	$23.40	$38.00
Dividends per share‖	10.40	8.00	8.80	19.80	19.80	19.80	53.50	21.85	38.90
Price-earnings ratio†	13.7x	10.0x	12.1x	17.2x	8.6x	13.8x	41.5x	17.5x	28.2x
Dividend yield†	4.5%	6.2%	5.1%	3.8%	7.6%	5.4%	2.5%	5.9%	3.6%

24

American Can:¶									
Price range	47	9	25	297	74	150	828	414	612
Earnings per share	$8.86	$0.07	$4.71	$32.75	$19.64	$24.30	$36.48	$26.10	$32.46
Dividends per share	Nil	Nil	Nil	7.00	5.00	6.00	30.00	24.00	26.00
Price-earnings ratio†	10.0x	1.9x	5.3x	12.2x	3.0x	6.2x	25.5x	12.7	18.8x
Dividend yield†	Nil	Nil	Nil	2.0%	8.1%	4.0%	3.1%	6.3%	4.2%
Pennsylvania R.R.:									
Price range	65	53	60	55	41	46	50	14	30
Earnings per share	$4.64	$4.14	$4.33	$6.23	$3.82	$5.07	$2.94	$0.84	$1.95
Dividends per share	3.00	3.00	3.00	3.00	3.00	3.00	2.00	0.50	1.25
Price-earnings ratio†	15.0x	12.2x	13.8x	10.9x	8.1x	9.2x	25.6x	7.2x	15.5x
Dividend yield†	4.6%	5.7%	5.0%	5.5%	7.3%	6.5%	2.5%	8.9%	4.1%
American Tel. & Tel.:									
Price range	153	110	137	145	119	130	190	111	155
Earnings per share	$9.58	$8.64	$9.26	$11.79	$11.31	$11.48	$9.62	$8.16	$9.05
Dividends per share	8.00	8.00	8.00	9.00	9.00	9.00	9.00	9.00	9.00
Price-earnings ratio†	16.5x	11.9x	14.8x	12.6x	10.4x	11.3x	21.0x	12.3x	17.1x
Dividend yield†	5.2%	7.3%	5.8%	6.2%	7.6%	6.9%	4.7%	8.1%	5.8%

* Axe-Houghton indexes of business activity and of industrial stock prices, both unadjusted for trend; yields on 10 high-grade railroad bonds—all by courtesy of E. W. Axe & Co., Inc.

† High, low, and average prices are compared with *average* earnings and dividends in each period.

‡ 1936-1938 figures adjusted to reflect 40% stock dividend.

§ Figures adjusted to reflect various stock dividends and split-ups between 1913 and 1930, equivalent ultimately to about 25 shares in 1936 for 1 share in 1912.

‖ Exclusive of one share of Electric Bond and Share Securities Corporation distributed as a dividend in 1925.

¶ 1936-1938 figures adjusted to reflect six-for-one exchange of shares in 1926.

war collapse and hectic prosperity, followed by the postwar hesitation, inflation, and deep depression. Between 1925 and 1936 we had the "new-era boom," the great collapse and depression, and a somewhat irregular recovery towards normal. But if we examine the three-year periods themselves, we cannot fail to be struck by the increasing tendency toward instability even in relatively normal times. This is shown vividly in the progressive widening of the graphs in Chart *A*, that follows, which trace the fluctuations in general business and industrial stock prices during the years in question.

It would be foolhardy to deduce from these developments that we must expect still greater instability in the future. But it would be equally imprudent to minimize the significance of what has happened and to return overreadily to the comfortable conviction of 1925 that we were moving steadily towards both greater stability and greater prosperity. The times would seem to call for caution in embracing any theory as to the future and for flexible and open-minded investment policies. With these caveats to guide us, let us proceed to consider briefly certain types of investment problems.

A. INVESTMENT IN HIGH-GRADE BONDS AND PREFERRED STOCKS

Bond investment presents many more perplexing problems today than seemed to be true in 1913. The chief question then was how to get the highest yield commensurate with safety; and if the investor was satisfied with the lower yielding standard issues (nearly all consisting of railroad mortgage bonds), he could supposedly "buy them with his eyes shut and put them away and forget them." Now the investor must wrestle with a threefold problem: safety of interest and principal, the future of bond yields and prices, and the future value of the dollar. To describe the dilemma is easy; to resolve it satisfactorily seems next to impossible.

1. Safety of Interest and Principal. Two serious depressions in the past twenty years, and the collapse of an enormous volume of railroad issues once thought safe beyond question, suggest that the future may have further rude shocks for the complacent bond investor. The old idea of "permanent investments," exempt from change and free from care, is no doubt permanently gone. Our studies lead us to conclude, however, that by sufficiently stringent standards of selection and reasonably frequent scrutiny thereafter the investor should be able to escape most of the serious losses that have distracted him in the past, so that his collection of interest and principal should work out at a satisfactory percentage even in times of depression. Careful selection must include a due regard to future prospects, but we do not consider that the investor need be clairvoyant or that he must confine himself to companies that hold forth exceptional promise of expanding profits. These remarks relate to (really) high-grade preferred stocks as well as to bonds.

2. Future of Interest Rates and Bond Prices. The unprecedentedly low yields offered by both short- and long-term bond issues may well cause concern to the investor for other reasons than a natural dissatisfaction with the small return that his money brings him. If these low rates should prove temporary and are followed by a rise to previous levels, long-term bond prices could lose some 25%, or more, of their market value. Such a price decline would be equivalent to the loss of perhaps ten years' interest. In 1934 we felt that this possibility must be taken seriously into account, because the low interest rates then current might well have been a phenomenon of subnormal business, subject to a radical advance with returning trade activity. But the persistence of these low rates for many years, and in the face of the considerable business expansion of 1936–1937, would argue strongly for the acceptance of this condition as a well-established result of a plethora of capital or of governmental fiscal policy or of both.

A new uncertainty has been injected into this question by the outbreak of a European war in 1939. The first World War brought about a sharp increase in interest rates and a corresponding severe fall in high-grade bond prices. There are sufficient similarities and differences, both, between the 1914 and the 1939 situations to make prediction too risky for comfort. Obviously the danger of a substantial fall in bond prices (from the level of early 1940) is still a real one; yet a policy of noninvestment awaiting such a contingency is open to many practical

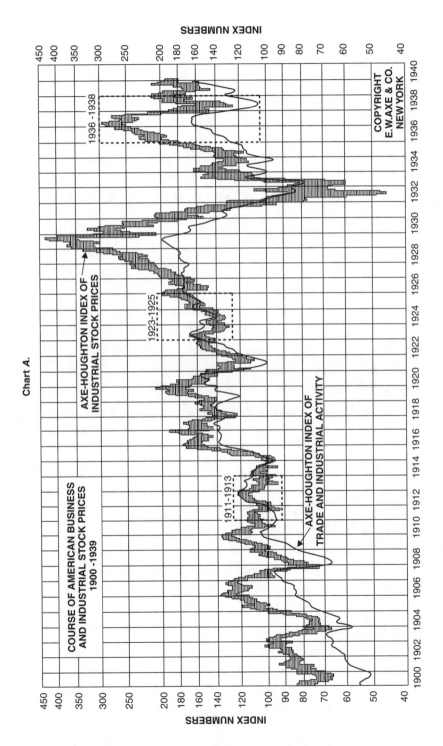

Chart A.

INDEX NUMBERS

COURSE OF AMERICAN BUSINESS
AND INDUSTRIAL STOCK PRICES
1900 -1939

AXE-HOUGHTON INDEX OF
INDUSTRIAL STOCK PRICES

AXE-HOUGHTON INDEX OF
TRADE AND INDUSTRIAL ACTIVITY

1936 -1938

1923-1925

1911-1913

COPYRIGHT
E.W.AXE & CO.
NEW YORK

INDEX NUMBERS

Chart *B.*

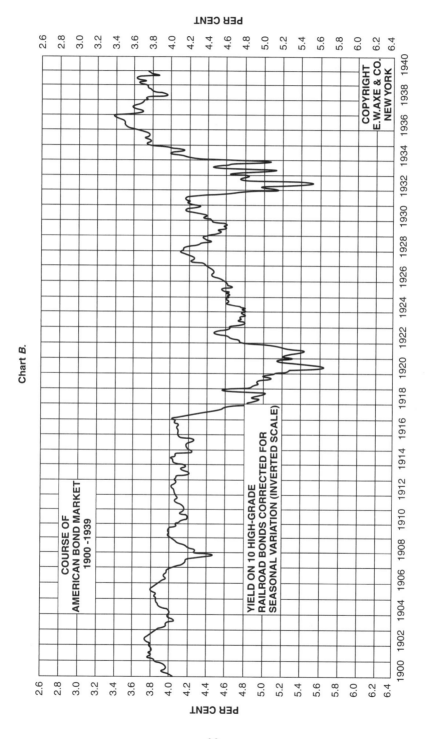

COURSE OF
AMERICAN BOND MARKET
1900 -1939

YIELD ON 10 HIGH-GRADE
RAILROAD BONDS CORRECTED FOR
SEASONAL VARIATION (INVERTED SCALE)

PER CENT

PER CENT

objections. Perhaps a partiality to maturities no longer than, say, fifteen years from purchase date may be the most logical reaction to this uncertain situation.

For the small investor, United States Savings Bonds present a perfect solution of this problem (as well as the one preceding), since the right of redemption at the *option of the holder* guarantees them against a lower price. As we shall point out in a more detailed discussion, the advent of these baby bonds has truly revolutionized the position of most security buyers.

3. The Value of the Dollar. If the investor were certain that the purchasing power of the dollar is going to decline substantially, he undoubtedly should prefer common stocks or commodities to bonds. To the extent that inflation, in the sense commonly employed, remains a possibility, the investment policy of the typical bond buyer is made more perplexing. The arguments for and against ultimate inflation are both unusually weighty, and we must decline to choose between them. The course of the price level since 1933 would seem to belie inflation fears, but the past is not necessarily conclusive as to the future. Prudence may suggest some compromise in investment policy, to include a component of common stocks or tangible assets, designed to afford some protection against a serious fall in the dollar's value. Such a hybrid policy would involve difficult problems of its own; and in the last analysis each investor must decide for himself which of the alternative risks he would prefer to run.

B. SPECULATIVE BONDS AND PREFERRED STOCKS

The problems related to this large class of securities are not inherent in the class itself, but are rather derived from those of investment bonds and of common stocks, between which they lie. The broad principles underlying the purchase of speculative senior issues remain, in our opinion, the same as they always were: (1) A risk of principal loss may not be offset by a higher yield alone but must be accompanied by a commensurate chance of principal profit; (2) it is generally sounder to approach these issues as if they were common stocks, but recognizing their limited claims, than it is to consider them as an inferior type of senior security.

C. THE PROBLEM OF COMMON-STOCK INVESTMENT

Common-stock speculation, as the term has always been generally understood, is not so difficult to understand as it is to practice successfully. The speculator admittedly risks his money upon his guess or judgment as to the general market or the action of a particular stock or possibly on some future development in the company's affairs. No doubt the speculator's problems have changed somewhat with the years, but we incline to the view that the qualities and training necessary for success, as well as the mathematical odds against him, are not vitally different now from what they were before. But stock speculation, as such, does not come within the scope of this volume.

Current Practice. We are concerned, however, with common-stock *investment*, which we shall define provisionally as purchases based upon analysis of value and controlled by definite standards of safety of principal. If we look to current practice to discern what these standards are, we find little beyond the rather indefinite concept that "a good stock is a good investment." "Good" stocks are those of either (1) leading companies with satisfactory records, a combination relied on to produce favorable results in the future; or (2) any well-financed enterprise believed to have especially attractive prospects of increased future earnings. (As of early 1940, we may cite Coca-Cola as an example of (1), Abbott Laboratories as an example of (2), and General Electric as an example of both.)

But although the stock market has very definite and apparently logical ideas as to the *quality* of the common stocks that it buys for investment, its *quantitative* standards—governing the relation of price to determinable value—are so indefinite as to be almost nonexistent. Balance-sheet values are considered to be entirely out of the picture. Average earnings have little significance when there is a marked trend. The so-called "price-earnings ratio" is applied variously, sometimes to the past, sometimes to the present, and sometimes to the near future. But the ratio itself can scarcely be called a standard, since it is controlled by investment practice instead of controlling it. In other words the "right" price-earnings ratio for any stock is what the market says it is.

We can find no evidence that at any time from 1926 to date common-stock investors as a class have sold their holdings because the price-earnings ratios were too high.

How the present practice of common-stock investors, including the investment trusts almost without exception, can properly be termed *investment*, in view of this virtual absence of controlling standards, is more than we can fathom. It would be far more logical and helpful to call it "speculation in stocks of strong companies." Certainly the results in the stock market of such "investment" have been indistinguishable from those of old-time speculation, except perhaps for the margin element. A striking confirmation of this statement, as applied to the years after the 1929 crash, is found by comparing the price range of General Electric since 1930 with that of common stocks generally. The following figures show that General Electric common, which is perhaps the premier and undoubtedly the longest entrenched investment issue in the industrial field today, has fluctuated more widely in market price than have the rank and file of common stocks.

Price Ranges of General Electric Common, Dow-Jones Industrials, and Standard Statistics' Industrial Stock Index, 1930–1939

Year	General Electric		Dow-Jones Industrials		Standard Statistics Industrials[1]	
	High	Low	High	Low	High	Low
1930	95 3/8	41 1/2	294.1	157.5	174.1	98.2
1931	54 3/4	22 7/8	194.4	73.8	119.1	48.5
1932	26 1/8	8 1/2	88.8	41.2	63.5	30.7
1933	30 1/4	10 1/2	108.7	50.2	92.2	36.5
1934	25 1/4	16 7/8	110.7	85.5	93.3	69.3
1935	40 7/8	20 1/2	148.4	96.7	113.2	72.8
1936	55	34 1/2	184.9	143.1	148.5	109.1
1937	64 7/8	34	194.4	113.6	158.7	84.2
1938	48	27 1/4	158.4	99.0	119.3	73.5
1939	44 5/8	31	155.9	121.4	118.3	86.7

[1] Weekly indexes of prices (1926 = 100) of 350 industrial issues in 1939 and 347 issues in earlier years.

It was little short of nonsense for the stock market to say in 1937 that General Electric Company was worth $1,870,000,000 and almost precisely a year later that it was worth only $784,000,000. Certainly nothing had happened within twelve months' time to destroy more than half the value of this powerful enterprise, nor did investors even pretend to claim that the falling off in earnings from 1937 to 1938 had any permanent significance for the future of the company. General Electric sold at 64$7/8$ because the public was in an optimistic frame of mind and at 27$1/4$ because the same people were pessimistic. To speak of these prices as representing "investment values" or the "appraisal of investors" is to do violence either to the English language or to common sense, or both.

Four Problems. Assuming that a common-stock buyer were to seek definite investment standards by which to guide his operations, he might well direct his attention to four questions: (1) the general future of corporation profits, (2) the differential in quality between one type of company and another, (3) the influence of interest rates on the dividends or earnings return that he should demand, and finally (4) the extent to which his purchases and sales should be governed by the factor of timing as distinct from price.

The General Future of Corporate Profits. If we study these questions in the light of past experience, our most pronounced reaction is likely to be a wholesome scepticism as to the soundness of the stock market's judgment on all broad matters relating to the future. The data in our first table show quite clearly that the market underestimated the attractiveness of industrial common stocks as a whole in the years prior to 1926. Their prices generally represented a rather cautious appraisal of past and current earnings, with no signs of any premium being paid for the possibilities of growth inherent in the leading enterprises of a rapidly expanding commonwealth. In 1913 railroad and traction issues made up the bulk of investment bonds and stocks. By 1925 a large part of the investment in street railways had been endangered by the development of the automobile, but even then there was no disposition to apprehend a similar threat to the steam railroads.

The widespread recognition of the factor of future growth in common stocks first asserted itself as a stock-market influence at a time when in fact the most dynamic factors in our national expansion (territorial development and rapid accretions of population) were no longer operative, and our economy was about to face grave problems of instability arising from these very checks to the factor of growth. The overvaluations of the new-era years extended to nearly every issue that had even a short period of increasing earnings to recommend it, but especial favor was accorded the public-utility and chain-store groups. Even as late as 1931 the high prices paid for these issues showed no realization of their inherent limitations, just as five years later the market still failed to appreciate the critical changes taking place in the position of railroad bonds as well as stocks.

Quality Differentials. The stock market of 1940 has its well-defined characteristics, founded chiefly on the experience of the recent past and on the rather obvious prospects of the future. The tendency to favor the larger and stronger companies is perhaps more pronounced than ever. This is supported by the record since 1929, which indicates, we believe, both better resistance to depression and a more complete recovery of earning power in the case of the leading than of the secondary companies. There is also the usual predilection for certain industrial groups, including companies of smaller size therein. Most prominent are the chemical and aviation shares—the former because of their really remarkable record of growth through research, the latter because of the great influx of armament orders.

But these preferences of the current stock market, although easily understood, may raise some questions in the minds of the sceptical. First to be considered is the extraordinary disparity between the prices of prominent and less popular issues. If average earnings of 1934–1939 are taken as a criterion, the "good stocks" would appear to be selling about two to three times as high as other issues. In terms of asset values the divergence is far greater, since obviously the popular issues have earned a much larger return on their invested capital. The ignoring of asset values has reached a stage where even current assets receive very little attention, so that even a moderately successful enterprise is likely to be selling at considerably less than its liquidating value if it happens to be rich in working capital.

The relationship between "good stocks" and other stocks must be considered in the light of what is to be expected of American business generally. Any prediction on the latter point would be highly imprudent; but it is in order to point out that the record of the last fifteen years does not in itself supply the basis for an expectation of a long-term upward movement in volume and profits. In so far as we judge the future by the past we must recognize a rather complete transformation in the *apparent* outlook of 1940 against that in 1924. In the earlier year a secular rise in production and a steady advance in the figure taken as "normal" were accepted as a matter of course. But so far as we can see now, the 1923–1925 average of industrial production, formerly taken as 100 on the Federal Reserve Board's index,[1] must still be considered as high a normal as we have any right to prognosticate. Needless to say, the investor will not deny the *possibility* of a renewed secular rise, but the important point for him is that he cannot count upon it.

If this is the working hypothesis of the present stock market, it follows that stock buyers are expecting in general a further growth in the earnings of large companies *at the expense* of smaller ones and of favorably situated industries at the expense of all others. Such an expectation appears to be the theoretical basis for the high price of the one group and the low prices found elsewhere. That stocks with good past trends and favorable prospects are worth more than others goes without saying. But is it not possible that Wall Street has carried its partiality too far—in this as in so many other cases? May not the typical large and prosperous company be subject to a twofold limitation: first, that its very size precludes spectacular further growth; second, that its high rate of earnings on invested capital makes it vulnerable to attack if not by competition then perhaps by regulation?

Perhaps, also, the smaller companies and the less popular industries as a class may be definitely undervalued, both absolutely and in

---

[1] In 1940 the Board revised this index. New components were added, and the average of 1935–1939 was adopted as the base.

relation to the favored issues. Surely this can be true in theory, since at *some* price level the good stocks must turn out to have been selling too high and the others too low. There are strong, if not conclusive, reasons for arguing that this point may have already been reached in 1940. The two possible points of weakness in the "good stocks" are paralleled by corresponding favorable possibilities in the others. The numerous issues selling below net current asset value, even in normal markets, are a powerful indication that Wall Street's favoritism has been overdone. Finally, if we carry the analysis further, we must realize that the smaller listed companies are representative of the hundreds of thousands of private enterprises, of all sizes, throughout the country. Wall Street is apparently predicting the continued decline of *all* business except the very largest, which is to flourish mightily. In our own opinion such a development appears neither economically probable nor politically possible.

Similar doubts may be voiced as to the stock market's emphasis on certain favored industries. This is something that, by the nature of the case, must always be overdone—since there are no quantitative checks on the public's enthusiasm for what it likes. Not only has the market invariably carried its optimism too far, but it has shown a surprising aptitude for favoring industries that soon turned out to be facing adverse developments. (Witness the baking stocks in 1925, the radio and refrigeration issues in 1927, the public utility and chain stores in 1928–1929, the liquor issues in 1933.) It is interesting to compare the "investor's" eagerness to buy Abbott Laboratories in 1939 and his comparative indifference to American Home Products—the one kind of pharmaceutical company being thought to have brilliant, and the other to have only mediocre, prospects in store. This distinction may prove to have been soundly and shrewdly drawn; but the student who remembers the market's not so remote enthusiasm for American Home Products itself and its companions (particularly Lambert) in 1927 can hardly be too confident of the outcome.[2]

Interest Rates. Coming now to the third point of importance, *viz.*, the relation between interest rates and common-stock prices, it is

---

[2] Data relating to these three companies are given in Appendix Note 1.

clear that if current low bond yields are permanent, they must produce a corresponding decline in average stock yields and an advance in the value of a dollar of expected earning power, as compared with the situation, say, in 1923–1925. The more liberal valuation of earnings in 1936–1938, as shown by the data relating to the Dow-Jones Industrial Average (found in the Introduction to the Second Edition), would thus appear to have been justified by the change in the long-term interest rate. The disconcerting question presents itself, however, whether or not the fall in interest rates is not closely bound up with the cessation of the secular expansion of business and with a decline in the average profitability of invested capital. If this is so, the debit factors in stock values generally may outweigh the credit influence of low interest rates, and a typical dollar of earning power in 1936–1938 may not really have been worth more than it should have been worth a decade and a half previously.

The Factor of Timing. Increasing importance has been ascribed in recent years to the desirability of buying and selling at the right time, as distinguished from the right price. In earlier periods, when the prices of investment issues did not usually fluctuate over a wide range, the time of purchase was not considered of particular importance. Between 1924 and 1929, a comfortable but quite misleading confidence developed in the unlimited future growth of sound stocks, so that any mistake in timing was sure to be rectified by the market's recovery to ever higher levels. The past decade has witnessed very wide fluctuations without a long-term upward trend, except in a relatively small number of issues. Under these conditions it is not surprising that successful investment seems, like successful speculation, to be bound up inescapably with the choice of the right moment to buy and to sell. We thus find that forecasting of the major market swings appears now to be an integral part of the art of investment in common stocks.

The validity of stock-market forecasting methods is a subject for extensive inquiry and perhaps vigorous controversy. At this point we must content ourselves with a summary judgment, which may reflect our own prejudices along with our investigations. It is our view that stock-market timing cannot be done, with general success, unless the time to buy is related to an attractive price level, as measured by analytical standards. Similarly, the investor must take his cue to sell primarily not from so-called technical market signals but from an advance in the price level beyond a point justified by objective standards of value. It may be that within these paramount limits there are refinements of stock-market technique that can make for better timing and more satisfactory over-all results. Yet we cannot avoid the conclusion that the most generally accepted principle of timing—*viz.*, that purchases should be made only *after* an upswing has definitely announced itself—is basically opposed to the essential nature of investment. Traditionally the investor has been the man with patience and the courage of his convictions who would buy when the harried or disheartened speculator was selling. If the investor is now to hold back until the market itself encourages him, how will he distinguish himself from the speculator, and wherein will he deserve any better than the ordinary speculator's fate?

Conclusion. Our search for definite investment standards for the common-stock buyer has been more productive of warnings than of concrete suggestions. We have been led to the old principle that the investor should wait for periods of depressed business and market levels to buy representative common stocks, since he is unlikely to be able to acquire them at other times except at prices that the future may cause him to regret. On the other hand, the thousands of so-called "secondary companies" should offer at least a moderate number of true investment opportunities under all conditions, except perhaps in the heydey of a bull market. This wide but quite unpopular field may present the more logical challenge to the interest of the bona fide investor and to the talents of the securities analyst.

PART I

Survey and Approach

Benjamin Graham—in His Time and Ours

by Roger Lowenstein

Of all the stocks Benjamin Graham bought over the course of his career, none were more influential than the odd lot of U.S. Steel purchased by his mother. Left a widow in 1904, she tried to keep up her husband's import business, then ran a boardinghouse; both efforts failed. In 1907, with bullish sentiment riding high, she purchased Steel on margin. Later that year, Wall Street succumbed to a panic, and her account was wiped out. Such was 13-year-old Ben's introduction to investing.

Graham was to learn the lesson more than once. His early history is important, because it was the source of his insight into investing. He grew up in New York City and managed to attend Columbia University despite his family's meager savings. Upon graduation, the deans of three departments (mathematics, philosophy, and English) offered him teaching jobs, but the dean of Columbia College[1] liked to send prize pupils downtown, to Wall Street. Graham went to work in 1914 in the bond department of Newburger, Henderson & Loeb, at $12 a week. World War I erupted months later. Although the war cast a pall on Wall Street, as it became clear that America was to provision

---

[1] The college dean was Frederick Paul Keppel. This account draws on Irving Kahn and Robert D. Milne, "Benjamin Graham: The Father of Financial Analysis," *Financial Analysts Research Foundation*, Occasional Paper No. 5.

Europe, the market turned bullish. Graham tackled securities with the same intellectual curiosity he had displayed in school. Corporate information in that preregulatory era was scarce. Investors in stocks were not truly investors; they were speculators betting on trends. Graham was different.

Almost from the first, he took to analyzing securities on the basis of their asset value, though obtaining information required considerable sleuthing. One early success was Guggenheim Exploration Company, which, as Graham divined, owned a collection of valuable mining stocks underappreciated by Wall Street. By 1916, the 22-year-old Graham, still on salary at Newburger, was also managing investments for one of his professors. Many of Graham's investments were arbitrages such as Guggenheim—objectively a bargain. This led him to feel secure. Alas, in the fall of 1916, stocks entered a prolonged decline. Despite his mother's example, Graham had purchased on margin. He was forced to sell at a loss and spent two painful years recouping the professor's capital.

Such cycles recurred throughout his career; indeed, they recur to this day. Graham grasped, at a remarkably young age, the cardinal distinction between investment and speculation, but even for him, good times loosened the strings of prudence. Before he was 30, he had left Newburger to run a money management venture, Grahar Corporation. His reputation for spotting arbitrage and hedging opportunities spread quickly. One example: DuPont, which owned a controlling interest in General Motors, was selling for no more than the value of its investment in GM, thus according *no* value to its chemical business. To Graham, that was low-hanging fruit. But Wall Street to him was more than a mathematical exercise. He had a knack for stripping complicated securities to their essence. He realized early on that value does not reside in the *form* of a security, but in the hierarchy and value of its claim on the underlying assets. While still at Newburger, he concluded that many convertible stocks offered the same potential profits as the common stock, but with less downside. He applied this insight to Consolidated Textile, acquiring its 7% convertible bond, which he judged to be safe, and selling short the common stock, a speculative favorite due to the allure of its various cotton mills. Ben warned a senior partner who owned the common that he was taking a risk, but the partner said he preferred an "active stock" to a stodgy bond. Within a year, the common plunged from 70 to 20 while the convertible was, soon, redeemed at a premium.

With fast-accumulating experience, Graham began to think of himself as a teacher as well as practitioner. By 1919, the precocious apprentice was writing pamphlets entitled "Lessons for Investors." In 1925, he decided to write a book imparting his investment knowledge. Fortunately, he later recalled, "I had the inspiration to learn more on the subject." Nothing he might have written then could have resembled the volume, now in your hands, that he was to write seven years later. That he did wait is, of course, what makes *Security Analysis* so relevant today.

The late 1920s were a heady time on Wall Street. The new era of stocks that did not go down, only up, was gathering momentum. Graham, instinctively, was cautious. He bought only those stocks that he judged (on the basis of laborious research) worth considerably more than their price. His renown also grew. In 1926, he traveled to Washington and discovered through reading obscure filings at the Interstate Commerce Commission that Northern Pipeline, a former part of the Standard Oil Trust, was sitting on $95 a share in securities such as railroad bonds. This was unknown to the public, and the stock foundered at 65. Graham, now operating a partnership with Jerry Newman, patiently bought 170,000 shares and pressured the company to divest the securities and pay a large dividend. When management resisted, he launched a proxy fight and won a board seat. Several distributions totaling $110 a share followed—a huge windfall.

Graham's pursuit of Northern, and of other former Standard Oil subsidiaries, brought him into contact with the eminent financier Bernard Baruch. Graham recommended ostensibly safe stocks and Baruch gobbled them up. As the bull market accelerated, Baruch and Graham each worried about the evident excess. Baruch observed that it was absurd for the Dow Jones Industrials to be yielding only 2% when short-term fixed-income securities were yielding 8%. Graham tellingly replied, "By the law of compensation, someday the reverse should happen." Yet Graham was not quite prepared. In 1928, his partnership, the Benjamin Graham Joint Account, gained 60%, besting even the 49%[2] rise in the Dow. Ben's share of the profits topped $600,000 (nearly 10 times what Babe Ruth was making at the time). Graham had also begun teaching an evening course at Columbia; many of his students were Wall Street pros eager for tips. Seemingly, Graham was on top of the world.

In October 1929, however, the market broke. In 1930, when Graham presumed the worst was over, the Joint Account invested heavily, again on margin. According to Irving Kahn, his assistant, Graham "did not realize that all operations involving borrowing, including his own," were at risk. The selling was far from over. By 1932, the depths of the Great Depression, the Joint Account had fallen 70%. Graham and Newman went five years without salary. Graham's wife returned to work as a dance instructor, and the family abandoned their posh Central Park duplex for a rear apartment.

It was then that Graham and Columbia's David Dodd signed with McGraw-Hill to write *Security Analysis*. (Although Dodd, then an

---

[2] Not including dividends.

assistant professor, was generously credited by Graham as coauthor, in fact he was Graham's assistant; Graham wrote the text and Dodd checked facts, offered suggestions, and so forth.) It was an extraordinary time to write an investment manual. A third of American industry was selling at less than its liquidation value. Many so-called experts discounted the notion of investing in stocks at all— any stock purchase, they asserted, was sheer speculation. Yet Graham had the courage to recognize a buying opportunity. Hard-won wisdom had honed his belief that the market trend was a fickle barometer. The stock market is not a *"weighing machine,"* he wrote; it was *"a voting machine"* in which countless individuals registered choices produced "partly of reason and partly of emotion." *Security Analysis* was written to help investors appraise a security's enduring value and divorce themselves from momentary passions. It breathes with the wisdom of the author's classical training. Graham turned to Horace, the Roman poet, for his epigraph: "Many shall be restored that now are fallen and many shall fall that are now in favor." The metaphor was almost too good; underlying values could not be judged on the basis of their price, for prices were as fleeting as the fates. "That enormous profits should have turned into still more colossal losses . . . that unlimited optimism should have been succeeded by the deepest despair," no longer struck Graham as surprising.[3] The serious investor, therefore, had to trust in the long-term values reflected not by the stock price or predictions about the price, but by the intrinsic corporate worth, to be discerned from the balance sheet, earnings reports, and other sources.

This insight is no less true today than it was in 1934, yet the majority of investors approach the market with little trace of the enlightenment that prior experience might have taught. The list of investment fads and bubbles in the late twentieth and early twenty-

---

[3] Benjamin Graham and David Dodd, "Introduction," in *Security Analysis* (New York, NY: McGraw-Hill, 1934), p. 3.

first century has become well too long to enumerate. From the vantage of 2022, investors were confronted by a pandemic that shuttered the economy, a deadly war in Europe, and a rapid revival of domestic inflation. The first was utterly outside the experience of contemporary investors; the other two seemed ghosts from a distant past. These multiple shocks were a reminder that, along with many calculable risks such as interest rate movements, investors face uncertainties that defy anticipation, much less arithmetic estimation. This argues for investors—even those in reputedly "safe" stocks—to build in a layer of protection, what Graham memorably termed a margin of safety.

It is tempting to wonder, "If Ben Graham were writing this book today, what would he be saying?" The question is unanswerable, but we can make a useful distinction. Although we cannot guess how he would assemble a portfolio, investors can still apply his *approach*. The axiom that market prices convey little about the future that is useful (or lasting) is as valid as ever. The truism that any trend is subject to reversal still suggests an urgent need for a margin of safety. Graham would not recognize software or digital apps, but he would, I suspect, find much familiar in the markets of 2007–2022, during which the Standard & Poor's 500 Index crashed three times, once by half and another time by a third, and yet overall rose a remarkable 11% per annum, with price-earnings ratios rising to levels close to those of 1929.[4]

On the recent fetish for so-called private equity, Graham, we imagine, would have pointed out that the distinction between such investments and traditional public stocks was chiefly superficial—one of form. Substantively, each consists of an ownership interest whose value ultimately depends on a business's performance. It is true that private equities, which are not quoted daily (or hourly) present a less-volatile

---

[4] 11% is the compounded rise from Dec. 31, 2007 (close to the top of the previous bull market) through August 2022; for the price-earnings ratio, see the Shiller P/E at https://www.multpl.com/shiller-pe.

surface, but the underlying businesses are subject to the same fundamental pressures. In 2022, these included rising interest rates, inflation, at least two consecutive quarters of declining GDP, volatile energy prices, labor shortages, persistent supply chain delays, and the war in Ukraine. Public shares fell 23% over the first half of the year, yet private equity managers were still touting past rosy returns. Beneath the surface, the $3.3 trillion in private equities, most of it invested at elevated prices, faced the same pressures. An index that mapped the public stock equivalents of private equity portfolios had fallen 37%.[5] To the extent that past performance of private equity benefitted from their considerably higher levels of debt, Graham would have shuddered. As he knew, debt is a double-edged sword; it magnifies returns on the way up, but imposes killer costs as interest rates rise or alternatively, as business slows. The U.S. economy was experiencing both, and slowdowns appeared to be underway in Europe, Britain, and China as well.

Graham would also have been mystified by the phenomenon known as meme stocks. In the early 2020s, these attracted considerable followings (and valuations) on the sole basis of social media promotion. The most celebrated of these, GameStop, a chain of video game stores operating at a loss, caught the attention of small investors who traded on a mobile trading app. The small investors trumpeted their lack of investing experience as a badge of honor; some asserted that their motive was less profit than to inflict losses on professional investors who had sold the stock short. In a matter of months, GameStop shares vaulted from single digits to $483, representing a total valuation of more than $30 billion. The retail investors were egged on by celebrity touts such as Jim Cramer, a television financial commentator, and billionaire Elon Musk, and encouraged by elected officials who imagined that they represented a populist crusade against

[5] "PE Lessons," *The Economist*, July 9, 2022.

Wall Street. One bestselling author portrayed the GameStop buying panic as a "millennial version of the French Revolution."[6] In the event, the stock plunged to a fraction of its peak, though as of late 2022 still considerably higher than before.

A more substantive phenomenon than meme stocks was the craze for special purpose acquisition vehicles (SPACs). We'll discuss SPACs at some length, not because they were truly "special," but rather they were so illustrative of the way that Wall Street, in Graham's day and in ours, goes off the rails: a clever if minor financial innovation is exploited by those with pecuniary interest and sold to investors whose desire for large and swift profits blinded them to the utter lack of a fundamental basis, that is, of a margin of safety. For a brief moment in 2020 and 2021, SPACs transformed the market for initial public offerings. As with private equity, the novelty of SPACs was one of *form*, not substance. Private companies have been raising capital via IPOs since the early days of Wall Street. What distinguished SPACs was a twist on the usual sequence. Normally, at some point after starting a business, insiders go to Wall Street and try to raise money. SPACs inverted the order. *First*, Wall Street raised the money; *then* the sponsors looked for a company in which to deploy it.

Even a novice to Wall Street—maybe *especially* a novice—will detect a certain illogic to this way of doing things. Perhaps in no area of recent finance was Ben Graham so sorely missed, because despite considerable press coverage (much of it fawning), the risks to investors in SPACs were widely overlooked.[7]

SPACs are paper corporations that sell shares in IPOs, customarily priced at $10 a share. Unlike a traditional IPO, a SPAC raises capital

---

[6] Ben Mezrich, *The Antisocial Network*.

[7] A singular, and praiseworthy, exception was Michael Klausner, Michael Ohlrogge, and Emily Ruan, "A Sober Look at SPACS," European Corporate Governance Institute, Working Paper, January 2022.

not for an operating business (it has none) but for a corporate shell that is obligated to purchase an operating business, generally within 18 or 24 months. If the SPAC is unable to complete an acquisition, the investors get their money back in full, and the SPAC is liquidated.

Moreover, when the SPAC agrees to acquire a target, investors have the option of redeeming for $10 a share, plus interest.[8] Those who do not redeem will own a share in the newly merged business. In other words, the SPAC investors get a free look. Actually, their situation is even better than that. Original investors in a SPAC not only get a share for their 10 bucks, they also get a fractional warrant. Since holders who redeem may keep the warrants, redeeming investors even retain some upside.

Clearly, there is a carrot for SPAC investors, but it is fair to ask, who is paying for this seemingly free lunch and why? SPACs do not materialize out of thin air; they are formed by a sponsor, generally an investor group or other financial operator. In return for organizing the SPAC, the sponsor takes a 20% slice of the SPAC essentially for free, although it does have to invest some millions in setting it up. Thus the sponsor has a powerful incentive to find a target company and execute a merger—otherwise, the SPAC liquidates and its investment is lost.

The free lunch for the SPAC investors serves as an inducement to attract capital and get the project going. And they are not the only ones getting lunch. The sponsor needs a Wall Street bank or banks to underwrite the initial sale of shares, and the investment bank charges a 2% fee on the underwriting and another 3.5% if the SPAC completes an acquisition. The SPAC is also subject to various advisory, legal, and other fees. Adding up these sundry expenses, it should be clear that the SPAC is burdened with considerable costs.

---

[8] IPO funds are put in trust, thus redemption is guaranteed.

Not surprisingly, in light of their complexity, SPACs were only a tiny outpost on Wall Street and not an especially reputable outpost. That SPACs existed at all is owed to the interests of a party we have not yet considered—the target company that the SPAC acquires. The targets were generally small private firms, often early start-ups. Many were too speculative to raise money in a conventional IPO. For this small niche of companies, SPACs offered a decided though unintended advantage.

In an ordinary IPO, the underwriters cannot offer forecasts of future earnings, revenue, and so forth without incurring great risk of litigation. This is for good reason. Insiders selling stock are anything but neutral parties. Their forecasts are naturally prone to optimism, and the company being private, the insiders are the *only* source of information. Since the public is effectively at their mercy, regulators do not grant IPOs the customary "safe harbor" to issue forward-looking statements.

In the case of a SPAC, however, due to an inadvertent loophole in securities regulation,[9] no such restraint exists. Recall that a SPAC's progress to maturity consists of two transactions. First, a corporate shell raises capital by selling shares. Technically, this is its IPO, but scrutiny is hardly an issue, because the SPAC has no assets to scrutinize. In the second stage, the SPAC purchases a private business. Although this purchase *has the effect of taking the target public*, the merger, technically, is not an IPO, because the SPAC has already gone public. Thus the process offers an end run around the normal IPO requirements; worrisomely, it deprives the public of regulatory protection.

For many years, SPACs were inconsequential. In 2016, only 13 SPACs went public, compared to 75 ordinary IPOs.[10] Then volume

[9] Klausner, et al., op. cit., pp. 52–54, 67, 71.
[10] Kristi Marvin, SPACInsider.

began to creep up. By 2019, Wall Street was minting a SPAC a week. Richard Branson was able to find a SPAC buyer—to the tune of $800 million—for equity in Virgin Galactic, a space tourism company with no revenue. Wall Street noticed (noticed the fees). In April 2020, DraftKings, a sports fantasy and betting company with a prior history of regulatory trouble, went public via a SPAC. Suddenly, SPACs were hot. When Covid-19 lockdowns put the economy into recession, and the Federal Reserve started pumping liquidity into markets, speculators armed with cheap money flocked to SPACs. According to Kristi Marvin, CEO of SPACInsider, "Everybody wanted one. Valuations went through the roof."

Traditionally, investors in SPAC IPOs were financial buyers such as hedge funds. The hedge funds either redeemed when an acquisition was announced or (if the price was favorable) sold to other investors. In 2020, interest broadened to retail buyers and institutions, sometimes denoted as "SPAC tourists." The question for whomever owned the stock was simple: post-merger, were the shares likely to trade above $10? If not, investors were better off redeeming. For them, exit was preferable to a bad deal.

The calculus for the sponsor was quite different. Financial structures in which incentives are misaligned often lead to trouble, and the incentives in SPACs were badly misaligned. The sponsor naturally hoped to acquire an attractive business at a favorable price. But for the sponsor, *even a bad deal was preferable to no deal at all.* Its shares would still be worth a good deal more than it had paid (which was zero), whereas if no deal transpired, it would lose the millions it had spent establishing the SPAC.

The possibility of redemption hung over each party like a sword, but in different ways. Redemptions weakened the capital structure and shrunk the base over which those hefty costs were spread. (If half the shares were redeemed, a 5.5% underwriting fee became equal to 11%

fee on the capital remaining.) Since each shareholder that redeemed *increased the burden on those that remained,* the SPAC structure spawned a potential race for the exits.

For the sponsor, having no exit option, the paramount goal was to minimize redemptions and retain as much cash as possible in the business. Some SPAC sponsors cut preferential, secretive deals with large shareholders in which the shareholders agreed *not* to redeem.[11] Sponsors also raised private capital—again on preferential terms—to replace the capital that was redeemed.

Sponsors went to great lengths to develop a public market for the shares so that exiting shareholders could sell rather than redeem. Practically, this meant persuading the public that the merged entity would trade above $10. This presented an almost insoluble problem: as a matter of math, SPAC shares, premerger, were clearly worth less than $10. After all, its only tangible assets consisted of the $10 per share raised in the IPO *less its considerable costs.* How could a merger elevate its value?

One solution would be to purchase a target company at a bargain price, so that the per-share value of the merged enterprise would be higher. But bargains do not grow on trees. The target shareholders, naturally, want to receive fair value for their business. In fact, target companies are in a position to demand *more* than fair value, because they know that sponsors need to do a deal. Another possibility was that merely taking the target company public would enhance its value—possible in theory, though not very likely in practice. Or perhaps, the expertise and talent of the sponsor executives (who commonly go on the company's board) is such that the target business will, under their tutelage, improve.

Investors, being impressionable, often simply assumed that sponsors were intelligent and working in the investors' interests.

---

[11] Klausner, et al., op. cit., pp. 12–13.

Disclosure was opaque, and few investors were aware of the total of embedded costs. According to a study of all SPACs that merged over an 18-month period when SPACs were hot, after accounting for the sponsor's interest, the investor warrants, the bankers' fees, and other fees, the median public investor's interest had been diluted to only $5.70 of the initial $10.[12] This amounted to a whopping 43% reduction in intrinsic value.[13] Not only were investors unaware of the expenses, many had believed that SPACs were cost-effective compared with conventional IPOs, when in fact they were considerably more expensive. Michael Klausner, a Stanford Law School professor who examined SPACs in detail, found that, "SPACs are far less transparent than they could be with respect to their embedded costs."[14]

Owing to the holes in applicable regulation, sponsors had the motive and the opportunity to aggressively promote their mergers. The sponsors conducted road shows to sell their deals, similar to road shows for conventional IPOS—except that SPACs were free to indulge in optimistic—at times, wildly optimistic—forecasts. Coinciding with the posteconomic stimulus market rally in the second half of 2021, Wall Street's eagerness to exploit this loophole was unrestrained.

Many SPACs were promoted by celebrities, such as the rapper Shawn "Jay-Z" Carter (for a cannabis company), investor and reality television personality Matt Higgins, home décor celebrity Martha Stewart, hedge fund titan Bill Ackman, quarterback Patrick Mahomes, and tennis star Serena Williams. SPACs were financed by the bluest chip underwriters, led by Citigroup, Goldman Sachs, and Credit Suisse.

---

[12] Klausner, et al., op. cit., abstract. Average net cash positions were even worse; that is, the average cash position of all SPACs in the study, before they merged, was only $4.10.

[13] According to Klausner (p. 10), post-merger SPAC results were "highly correlated" with net cash (SPACs with higher expenses did worse). Presumably, targets were aware of how much cash SPACs actually delivered and negotiated deals that allocated the expense burden entirely to the SPAC shareholders.

[14] Ibid., 8.

Promotion of SPAC mergers was unblushing. Nikola, an electric truck start-up, released a video of a truck barreling downhill, embedded in a tweet reading "Behold, the Nikola One in motion." According to the SEC, the video was posted on Nikola's corporate Twitter and Facebook accounts in early 2018 (prior to its May 2018 SPAC merger), and it remained posted and available to investors at least until September 2020. Investors thought they had found the next Tesla, and the stock soared to 73, making it more valuable than Ford, although it had yet to sell a single vehicle. According to an SEC cease-and-desist order issued 18 months after its SPAC merger, Nikola had made "scores of misrepresentations" to inflate its stock price. In particular, it omitted the detail that the truck in the video was not powered by a Nikola battery, or any Nikola part—it was rolling under the influence of gravity.[15] After the fraud was revealed, the stock crashed.[16] Although Nikola was an extreme case, it was common for SPACs to project sharply rising revenue and profits for targets that had little actual business. Dozens of SPAC deals subsequently (and quickly) missed their forecasts.[17] The CEO of Arrival SA, an electric bus company (electric vehicles were a hot sector for SPACs) forecast ahead of its March 2021 merger that revenue would surge from zero to $14 billion in three years. Later that year, the CEO said, simply and devastatingly, "We withdraw our long-term forecasts."[18] View, a company that made sunlight-sensitive windows, compared itself, in an

---

[15] SEC Administrative Proceeding File NO. 3-20687, "In the Matter of Nikola Corp.," December 21, 2021.

[16] Nikola founder Trevor Milton was convicted of securities fraud on October 14, 2022.

[17] Paul Kiernan, "SEC Proposes New Disclosure Requirements for SPACs," Wall Street Journal, March 30, 2022.

[18] Heather Somerville and Eliot Brown, "SPAC Startups Made Lofty Promises. They Aren't Working Out," *Wall Street Journal*, February 25, 2022.

investor presentation, to Tesla and Amazon. After its merger with a
SPAC, the happy talk ceased.[19]

In 2020, 248 SPACs raised $83 billion, an enormous sum (indeed,
more than in the entire previous decade). In 2021, 613 SPACs raised
$162 billion,[20] and more SPACs went public than traditional IPOs.
The mania reached such a fever that the average SPAC climbed to
$11.50 per share *prior to any merger announcement,* meaning that cash
held by a SPAC, though depleted by significant costs, was trading at a
15% premium to the cash in one's pocket.[21] Investors were giving
sponsors a blank check based on credulity or faith. Many reckoned, in
so many words, "They are smart people; they will find something." Of
course, each individual investor believed he or she was behaving
rationally. They had the comfort of the redemption option—the free
look. And if the stock was trading over 10, why should they redeem?

At the height of the mania, shares of SPACs postmerger
announcement soared to an average of $15.77 per share. Not
surprisingly, given the glorious returns, four of five SPAC investors
chose *not* to redeem.[22] Alas, in the spring of 2021, companies that had
merged with SPACs, now being public, were exposed for all to see,
and performances did not live up to expectations. The bubble cracked,
and SPAC prices tumbled. As enthusiasm wilted, more than half of
investors in forthcoming SPAC mergers chose to redeem.[23] Volume in
new SPAC issues withered. In July 2022, for the first month in five
years, not a single new SPAC went to market. Existing SPACs found it
increasingly hard to negotiate mergers acceptable to both target

---

[19] Eliot Brown, "SPACs Are Warning They May Go Bust," *Wall Street Journal,* May 27,
2022.

[20] SPACInsider.

[21] Klausner, et al., op. cit., 76–77.

[22] Ibid., 77, 79.

[23] Ibid., 79.

companies and to investors. Of the 613 SPACs that went public in 2021, more than 70% were, with increasing desperation, still searching for a target in September 2022.[24]

Many of those, presumably, will be forced to liquidate. Their investors will get their money back, but shareholders in completed mergers were not so fortunate. By September 2022, the average price of SPACs that had raised money in 2020 and 2021 and completed a merger had plummeted to a mere $5.03.[25] Not only had investors lost half their capital on average, but the losses were widely shared—of the hundreds of SPACs that completed a merger since the start of 2020, fewer than 15% were trading at the breakeven price of $10 a share.[26] More than 70 fell to less than $2.[27] Even in relative terms, SPACs significantly underperformed both the Nasdaq and conventional IPOs.[28]

In contrast to these losses, the sponsors made, on average, more than $100 million per deal. Even in deals that lost money for public investors, the sponsors typically cleared millions of dollars.[29] Wall Street was richly rewarded for enabling the bubble; from the start of 2020 through the third quarter of 2022, underwriters pocketed an estimated $8 billion in fees.[30] In March 2022—that is, after the bubble burst—the SEC belatedly proposed regulatory reforms that would tighten disclosure requirements and make it easier to sue when SPAC

---

[24] SPACInsider; Matthew Goldstein, "SPACS Were All the Rage. Now, Not So Much," *New York Times*, June 2, 2022.

[25] SPACInsider; data as of September 14, 2022. Jay Ritter, longtime IPO expert at University of Florida, calculated, alternatively, that an investor who purchased all 199 SPACs that completed mergers in 2021 had suffered a 63.8% loss by September 14, 2022.

[26] SPACInsider. The figures: As of September 14, 2022, 330 SPACs had completed mergers since January 1, 2020, of which 39 were trading above $10.

[27] Bailey Lipschultz, "SPCA Fire Sales Stick Investors with Deeply Discounted Buyouts," *Bloomberg*, June 9 2022.

[28] Klausner, et. al., op. cit., 35.

[29] Ibid., 11, 43.

[30] Jay Ritter.

projections missed the mark.[31] Goldman Sachs promptly reduced its footprint in the industry, citing the "changed regulatory environment."[32] On form, if SPACs could no longer mislead investors, Wall Street was no longer so game.

A backward glance at the bubble suggests that the only purpose of SPACs was to provide targets a backdoor to going public, which came at the considerable cost of sidestepping securities regulations and the attendant risk of capital misallocation (and investor losses). The majority of initial SPAC investors protected themselves by redeeming or selling. But the investors who took their places—those who chose not to redeem—wound up underwriting the various other parties, in particular the targets. Professor Klausner concluded, "SPAC shareholders that choose not to redeem . . . unwittingly subsidize the firms they bring public."[33]

The SPAC bubble, though instructive, was brief. It was overshadowed by the more enduring speculation in cryptocurrencies. While Graham would have blinked, uncomprehendingly, at Bitcoin, he would have recognized, almost as though reading a page from the roaring twenties, the self-interested promotion by Wall Street institutions and the herdlike credulity of small investors.

Bitcoin and other crypto assets were touted as an alternate currency, the currency of the future, apparently spawned by an ideological desire to create a currency free of government involvement. However, only El Salvador made Bitcoin its legal tender (a decision disclosed by its 40-year-old president while attending a Bitcoin conference in Miami). Investing in its new money, the Central American nation promptly incurred an unrealized loss of 50%. Even

---

[31] "SEC Proposes New Disclosure Requirements for SPACs."
[32] "SPACS Were All the Rage."
[33] Klausner et. al., op. cit., 7.

in El Salvador, virtually no one uses Bitcoin to pay for goods and services; they use, in fact, the U.S. dollar. In the United States, millions of people have purchased crypto, but similarly, it plays no role in the economy. People do not *think* of it as a currency or benchmark. They track the price of crypto *in dollars*, not the reverse. Bitcoin is transacted far too slowly to serve as a medium for electronic payments (Visa and Mastercard are thousands of times faster).[34] The blockchain platforms that support crypto are ingenious and might potentially serve some additional purposes. A few investment banks trade debt securities on blockchain networks. However—a fact often ignored— "investors" in cryptocurrency do not own a claim on the technology. They own a code to, and only to, their own coin. What Bitcoin *has* proved useful for is illicit transfers by drug cartels, kidnappers, pornographers, and the like. As Eswar Prasad, a Cornell University professor and digital expert, told this writer, Bitcoin remains a "pure speculative asset whose whole value is based on scarcity. The only reason it has value is everyone else thinks it has a value."

Few speculative vehicles have attained such widespread popularity. Scores of coins have been (digitally) minted, worth well over a trillion dollars at market prices. Yet no one has offered a definition, even an approach, to ascertaining any intrinsic value to these coins. They produce no revenue, dividends, or cash flow; they yield no earnings. Like the tulip mania in seventeenth-century Holland, they are purchased in the hope that other buyers will pay more. To borrow an example from the organizing editor of this volume and my fellow contributor, Seth Klarman, they are like the West Coast sardines whose price soared well beyond what any sane consumer would pay because, a speculator explained, these were not "eating sardines"; they were

---

[34] Ed Lin, "Bitcoin Can't Take a Bite out of Visa, Mastercard," Barrons.com, March 28, 2018, https://www.barrons.com/articles/bitcoin-cant-take-a-bite-out-of-visa-mastercard -1522238401.

"trading sardines." Tulip and sardine prices are anchored by the cost of other tangible goods—other flowers or other seafood. Crypto is untethered speculation. Over a six-month span in 2021 and 2022, Bitcoin traded above $67,000 and then collapsed to under $20,000. There is no rational way of determining if either price was correct, or that any price is; Bitcoins are for trading, not eating.

Leading investment firms once shunned crypto as speculative and risky, unsuitable for clients. Mimicking the behavior of brokers in the 1920s, they soon cashiered their so-called principles. The big investment banks established crypto departments to promote or enable speculative trading. Wall Street goes where the money is. Mathew McDermott, global head of digital assets at Goldman Sachs, proclaimed that Goldman would expand in crypto to meet investor demand. When crypto prices plunged, McDermott said, "Seeing moves like this in this environment doesn't come as a huge surprise."[35] It would be interesting to hear if Goldman's clients were surprised.

Fidelity Investments, broker to Main Street, pushed the Department of Labor in 2022 to muzzle the latter's "serious concerns" over plans, including those by Fidelity, to include Bitcoin as an option for 401(k) sponsors. If it ultimately succeeds, crypto will become part of the nest eggs set aside for workers' retirements. According to the federal pension statute ERISA, retirement plan sponsors, many of whom are Fidelity clients, must adhere to an exacting standard of professionalism, which requires that the investment options offered to participants are "prudent." Fidelity would not comment on whether cryptocurrency was prudent; if sponsors want it, they will sell it. On its

---

[35] James Rubin, "Goldman's Crypto Chief Worries About Fraud, but Not Cryptocurrency's Future," Coindesk.com, May 22, 2021, https://www.coindesk.com/markets/2021/05/22/goldmans-crypto-chief-worries-about-fraud-but-not-cryptocurrencys-future/, and Mathew McDermott and Allison Nathan, "Crypto Volatility: What's the Outlook for Digital Assets?" Exchanges at Goldman Sachs (podcast), https://www.goldmansachs.com/insights/podcasts/episodes/05-18-22-mathew-mcdermott-f/transcript.pdf.

website, Fidelity describes Bitcoin as an "aspirational store of value."
Perhaps it imagines that senior citizens will retire on their aspirations.

Not unlike the speculative markets in Graham's day, crypto has
been virtually unregulated. The field attracted huckstering reminiscent
of the salesmen in the 1920s. Back then, Charles E. Mitchell (a.k.a.
"Sunshine Charley"), the president of National City Bank, floated
hundreds of millions' worth of securities, including highly speculative
Peruvian bonds, to small investors. Come the crash, many were wiped
out. In the benighted modern era, Michael Saylor, CEO of
MicroStrategy, borrowed $2.4 billion and also issued shares, the
proceeds of which he plowed into more than $3 billion of Bitcoin.
Saylor urged disciples to "Take all your money and buy Bitcoin.
Then . . . figure out how to borrow more money to buy more Bitcoin."
Saylor's digital evangelism appealed to investors' faith, not their
reason. It was the polar opposite of Graham-and-Dodd fundamental
analysis. After Bitcoin's price fell by two-thirds, MicroStrategy stock
crashed and Saylor resigned.

Another promoter, Mike Novogratz, had run a hedge fund but
shuttered it after heavy losses, only to reemerge as CEO of Galaxy
Digital, selling crypto-investment funds. Novogratz became a
missionary at crypto conferences and on television and social media,
promoting digital currencies with born-again faith. He said at a
Bitcoin convention that his role was to preach without end,
explaining, "I can't stop." Galaxy made a large investment in a new
coin known as Luna, priced at less than $1. As investors, including
many small retail investors, jumped aboard, Luna surged to $100.
Novogratz triumphantly tweeted, "I'm officially a Lunatic!!!" The tweet
included a tattooed image of a wolf baying at the moon on his left
biceps. Months later, investors panicked, and Luna plunged by 99%.
Investors lost billions of dollars. After the crash, Novogratz insisted in
an interview that his ravings had included "words of caution," though

he conceded, "It's painful to me that too many people lost too much."[36]

Luna's collapse was part of a reckoning for so-called crypto banks, which offered very high yields to investors who deposited crypto assets. One such firm was Celsius Network, which paid 7% interest on loans of crypto coins (which it lent out at even higher rates). At the time, ordinary banks were yielding less than 1%. Critics questioned how such yields could be sustained. Another ersatz bank, Voyager Digital, misleadingly implied that investor deposits were FDIC insured. Its marketing material promised, "In the rare event your USD funds are compromised due to the company or our banking partner's failure, you are guaranteed a full reimbursement (up to $250,000)."[37] Voyager offered 9% yields and was flooded with deposits. It characterized its approach to asset management as "low-risk." Mark Cuban, owner of the NBA's Dallas Mavericks, made Voyager an official sponsor. He egged on fans to trade on the Voyager platform, assuring them that Voyager was "a perfect fit for our Mavs fans . . . as close to risk-free as you're going to get in the crypto universe."[38]

Voyager and Celsius each borrowed on the order of $5 billon. Some investors believed their "deposits" were safe. But crypto banks were not legally banks; they were not FDIC insured, and most were highly leveraged. Voyager had a ratio of assets to equity of 23:1; Celsius, 19:1. That was less than half the equity cushion of the median

[36] Gregory Zuckerman and Justin Baer, "Mike Novogratz's Crypto Comeback Faces a Trial by Fire," *Wall Street Journal*, June 4, 2022.

[37] Eliot Brown and Yifan Wang, "Crypto Meltdown Pushes Voyager into Bankruptcy," *Wall Street Journal*, July 6, 2022; David Benoit, "Customers Learn Crypto Accounts Not FDIC Insured," *Wall Street Journal*, July 8, 2022, and https://www.cbsnews.com/news/voyager-fdic-insurance-federal-reserve/.

[38] On Voyager: https://fortune.com/2022/08/11/mark-cuban-sued-voyager-digital-crypto-web3/ and https://www.youtube.com/watch?v=aB9GpBOroIw. On Celsius: https://www.wsj.com/articles/celsius-owes-users-more-than-4-7-billion-11657841826.

traditional bank. Nonetheless, Alex Mashinsky, the founder of Celsius, maintained that his firm offered a better deal for the customer. "For 700 years of banking," he said, "there was never an option." After those 700 years, the crypto market crashed, and investors withdrew funds en masse. Voyager and Celsius suspended withdrawals. Each filed for bankruptcy.

Crypto checked off almost every Graham test for speculation: utter reliance on the market trend, no discernible intrinsic value, high leverage. As in the 1920s, salesmen did not even discuss the issue of valuation. Rather, they touted crypto as the hallmark of a "New Era." Companies in the business of promoting and trading crypto proved adept at recruiting celebrity endorsers, such as NFL quarterback Tom Brady and comedian Larry David. Numerous retired government regulators joined the boards of crypto firms, giving the industry a patina of institutional stability. Coinbase, the largest U.S.-based crypto exchange, recruited to its board Kathryn Haun, formerly assistant U.S. attorney and digital currency coordinator at the U.S. Department of Justice. Coinbase went public in 2021 at a stratospheric price of 381, or $86 billion. After the IPO, four company insiders sold $1.2 billion of stock at prices ranging from 189 to 422. In 2022, the company's revenue plunged and the stock crashed to under 100.[39]

With a measure of Graham-like detachment, we can see that the crypto bubble is an offshoot of the rise of a technological elite. The impact of technology has been so profound that its experts have come to be regarded as modern priests, akin to the soothsayers of old, and its companies judged on a different standard—as if immune to the age-old test of price and value. The complexity of software, its opaqueness to the nonexpert, affords them an immunity to traditional measures of value, for who can appraise what they cannot

[39] Corrie Driebusch and Tom McGinty, "Coinbase Leaders Net $1.2 Billion in Share Sales," *Wall Street Journal*, May 27, 2022.

comprehend? The fact that many technology businesses grew at unusually high rates, and did so over long periods, nurtured a reasonable premise that these businesses were uncommonly valuable. Under the influence of persistently bullish trends, this premise was exchanged, at times unconsciously, for one that was far less reasonable—that high growth rates were a fixed fact of the industry, and that leading technology stocks were worthy investments at any price. This resembled the philosophy behind the "one-decision" stocks of the late 1960s and early 1970s (also known as the Nifty Fifty)—blue chips such as ITT, Avon, and Polaroid. These were supposedly "one decision" stocks that could be bought and held forever. But peak to trough, the Nifty Fifty would plunge 80%.

While the one-decision credo was less explicit in the digital era, its application was similar, with consequent inflation of share prices *even relative to digital's growing economic importance.* Over the early part of the century, the digital share of America's GDP rose by a third, to approximately 10%.[40] While that was impressive, it was outpaced by the action in the stock market, where technology's share of the S&P 500 was 28%.[41] A Graham-and-Dodd investor would hardly shirk technology, but he or she would be cognizant that prices will not trade without some relation to value, or not forever. Over the first eight months of 2022, the tech-heavy Nasdaq lost a quarter of its value. Many digital icons fell by more than half.

The market rout of 2022 was illustrative because it stemmed not from a shift in the speculative winds but rather from verities in the underlying economy. Technology had been treated as exceptional: it

---

[40] "The Era of Big-Tech Exceptionalism May Be Over," The Economist, July 27, 2022; see also https://www.statista.com/statistics/1239480/united-states-leading-states-by-tech -contribution-to-gross-product/#:~:text=In%202021%2C%20the%20United%20States,GDP %20has%20remained%20relatively%20consistent.

[41] As of March 30, 2022.

was seen as impervious to ordinary economic cycles. In 2022, however, one high-flying technology company after another reported slowing revenues and/or profits, increased competition, and pressure from the slowing economy and worldwide supply interruptions; in other words, all of the same pressures faced in other industries. *The Economist* magazine was moved to wonder whether the era "of big tech exceptionalism" was over.[42]

A Graham-and-Dodd investor would bet neither for nor against such a broad-brush proposition. The Graham discipline teaches bottom-up securities selection based on research into specific securities. Ultimately, what counts is prospective earnings and free cash flow deduced with a reliable margin of safety. Absent such assurance, Graham counseled, securities were not investments at all; they were speculations. Meme stocks, the excesses in private equity valuations, SPACs, crypto, and high-leverage lending by phony crypto banks, were all variations on this speculative theme. Perhaps securities markets, captive to some faulty wiring in human behavior, are bound forever to repeat such follies. Perhaps human society will be capable of making modest improvements. Until that day, the reader of this volume will profit no less than the reader in 1934. As the review of *Security Analysis* that appeared in the *New York Times* said: "On the assumption that despite the debacle of recent history there are still left people whose money burns a hole in their pockets, it is to be hoped that they will read this book. It is a full-bodied, mature, meticulous, and wholly meritorious outgrowth of scholarly probing and practical sagacity."[43]

---

[42] "The Era of Big-Tech Exceptionalism May Be Over."

[43] Louis Rich, "Sagacity and Securities," *New York Times*, December 2, 1934.

CHAPTER 1

The Scope and Limitations of Security Analysis. The Concept of Intrinsic Value

ANALYSIS CONNOTES the careful study of available facts with the attempt to draw conclusions therefrom based on established principles and sound logic. It is part of the scientific method. But in applying analysis to the field of securities we encounter the serious obstacle that investment is by nature not an exact science. The same is true, however, of law and medicine, for here also both individual skill (art) and chance are important factors in determining success or failure. Nevertheless, in these professions analysis is not only useful but indispensable, so that the same should probably be true in the field of investment and possibly in that of speculation.

In the last three decades the prestige of security analysis in Wall Street has experienced both a brilliant rise and an ignominious fall—a history related but by no means parallel to the course of stock prices. The advance of security analysis proceeded uninterruptedly until about 1927, covering a long period in which increasing attention was paid on all sides to financial reports and statistical data. But the "new era" commencing in 1927 involved at bottom the abandonment of the analytical approach; and while emphasis was still seemingly placed on facts and figures, these were manipulated by a sort of pseudo-analysis to support the delusions of the period. The market collapse in October 1929 was no surprise to such analysts as had kept their heads, but the extent of the business collapse which later developed, with its devastating effects on established earning power, again threw their calculations out of gear. Hence the ultimate result was that serious analysis suffered a double discrediting: the first—prior to the crash—due to the persistence of imaginary values, and the second—after the crash—due to the disappearance of real values.

The experiences of 1927–1933 were of so extraordinary a character that they scarcely provide a valid criterion for judging the usefulness of security analysis. As to the years since 1933, there is perhaps room for a difference of opinion. In the field of bonds and preferred stocks, we believe that sound principles of selection and rejection have justified themselves quite well. In the common-stock arena the partialities of the market have tended to confound the conservative viewpoint, and conversely many issues appearing cheap under analysis have given a disappointing performance. On the other hand, the analytical approach would have given strong grounds for believing representative stock prices to be too high in early 1937 and too low a year later.

THREE FUNCTIONS OF ANALYSIS:
1. DESCRIPTIVE FUNCTION

The functions of security analysis may be described under three headings: descriptive, selective, and critical. In its more obvious form, descriptive analysis consists of marshalling the important facts relating to an issue and presenting them in a coherent, readily intelligible manner. This function is adequately performed for the entire range of marketable corporate securities by the various manuals, the Standard Statistics and Fitch services, and others. A more penetrating type of description seeks to reveal the strong and weak points in the position of an issue, compare its exhibit with that of others of similar character, and appraise the factors which are likely to influence its future performance. Analysis of this kind is applicable to almost every corporate issue, and it may be regarded as an adjunct not only to investment but also to intelligent speculation in that it provides an organized factual basis for the application of judgment.

2. THE SELECTIVE FUNCTION OF SECURITY ANALYSIS

In its selective function, security analysis goes further and expresses specific judgments of its own. It seeks to determine whether a given issue should be bought, sold, retained, or exchanged for some other. What types of securities or situations lend themselves best to this more positive activity of the analyst, and to what handicaps or limitations is it subject? It may be well to start with a group of examples of analytical judgments, which could later serve as a basis for a more general inquiry.

Examples of Analytical Judgments. In 1928 the public was offered a large issue of 6% noncumulative preferred stock of St. Louis-San Francisco Railway Company priced at 100. The record showed that in no year in the company's history had earnings been equivalent to as much as 1$^1/_2$ times the fixed charges and preferred dividends combined. The application of well-established standards of selection to the facts in this case would have led to the rejection of the issue as insufficiently protected.

A contrasting example: In June 1932 it was possible to purchase 5% bonds of Owens-Illinois Glass Company, due 1939, at 70, yielding 11% to maturity. The company's earnings were many times the interest requirements—not only on the average but even at that time of severe depression. The bond issue was amply covered by current assets alone, and it was followed by common and preferred stock with a very large aggregate market value, taking their lowest quotations. Here, analysis would have led to the recommendation of this issue as a strongly entrenched and attractively priced investment.

Let us take an example from the field of common stocks. In 1922, prior to the boom in aviation securities, Wright Aeronautical Corporation stock was selling on the New York Stock Exchange at only $8, although it was paying a $1 dividend, had for some time been earning over $2 a share, and showed more than $8 per share in cash assets in the treasury. In this case analysis would readily have established that the intrinsic value of the issue was substantially above the market price.

Again, consider the same issue in 1928 when it had advanced to $280 per share. It was then earning at the rate of $8 per share, as against $3.77 in 1927. The dividend rate was $2; the net-asset value was less than $50 per share. A study of this picture must have shown conclusively that the market price represented for the most part the capitalization of entirely conjectural future prospects—in other words, that the intrinsic value was far less than the market quotation.

A third kind of analytical conclusion may be illustrated by a comparison of Interborough Rapid Transit Company First and Refunding 5s with the same company's Collateral 7% Notes, when both issues were selling at the same price (say 62) in 1933. The 7% notes were clearly worth considerably more than the 5s. Each $1,000 note was secured by deposit of $1,736 face amount of 5s; the principal of the notes had matured; they were entitled either to be paid off in full or to a sale of the collateral for their benefit. The annual interest received on the collateral was equal to about $87 on each 7% note (which amount was actually being distributed to the note holders), so that the current income on the 7s was considerably greater than that on the 5s. Whatever technicalities might be invoked to prevent the note holders from asserting their contractual rights promptly and completely, it was difficult to imagine conditions under which the 7s would not be intrinsically worth considerably more than the 5s.

A more recent comparison of the same general type could have been drawn between Paramount Pictures First Convertible Preferred selling at 113 in October 1936 and the common stock concurrently selling at 15 7/8. The preferred stock was convertible at the holders' option into seven times as many shares of common, and it carried accumulated dividends of about $11 per share. Obviously the preferred was cheaper than the common, since it would have to receive very substantial dividends before the common received anything, and it could also share fully in any rise of the common by reason of the conversion privilege. If a common stockholder had accepted this analysis and exchanged his shares for one-seventh as many preferred, he would soon have realized a large gain both in dividends received and in principal value.[1]

Intrinsic Value vs. Price. From the foregoing examples it will be seen that the work of the securities analyst is not without concrete results of considerable practical value, and that it is applicable to a wide variety of situations. In all of these instances he appears to be concerned with the intrinsic value of the security and more particularly with the discovery of discrepancies between the intrinsic value and the market price. We must recognize, however, that intrinsic value is an elusive concept. In general terms it is understood to be that value which is justified by the facts, *e.g.*, the assets, earnings, dividends, definite prospects, as distinct, let us say, from market quotations established by artificial manipulation or distorted by psychological excesses. But it is a great mistake to imagine that intrinsic value is as definite and as determinable as is the market price. Some time ago intrinsic value (in the case of a common stock) was thought to be about the same thing as "book value," *i.e.*, it was equal to the net assets of the business, fairly

---

[1] For the sequels to the six examples just given, see Appendix Note 2.

priced. This view of intrinsic value was quite definite, but it proved almost worthless as a practical matter because neither the average earnings nor the average market price evinced any tendency to be governed by the book value.

Intrinsic Value and "Earning Power." Hence this idea was superseded by a newer view, *viz.*, that the intrinsic value of a business was determined by its earning power. But the phrase "earning power" must imply a fairly confident expectation of certain future results. It is not sufficient to know what the past earnings have averaged, or even that they disclose a definite line of growth or decline. There must be plausible grounds for believing that this average or this trend is a dependable guide to the future. Experience has shown only too forcibly that in many instances this is far from true. This means that the concept of "earning power," expressed as a definite figure, and the derived concept of intrinsic value, as something equally definite and ascertainable, cannot be safely accepted as a *general premise* of security analysis.

Example: To make this reasoning clearer, let us consider a concrete and typical example. What would we mean by the intrinsic value of J. I. Case Company common, as analyzed, say, early in 1933? The market price was $30; the asset value per share was $176; no dividend was being paid; the average earnings for ten years had been $9.50 per share; the results for 1932 had shown a *deficit* of $17 per share. If we followed a customary method of appraisal, we might take the average earnings per share of common for ten years, multiply this average by ten, and arrive at an intrinsic value of $95. But let us examine the individual figures which make up this ten-year average. They are as shown in the table tht follows. The average of $9.50 is obviously nothing more than an arithmetical resultant from ten unrelated figures. It can hardly be urged that this average is in any way representative of *typical* conditions in the past or representative of what may be expected in the future. Hence any figure of "real" or intrinsic value derived from this average must be characterized as equally accidental or artificial.[2]

---

[2] Between 1933 and 1939 the earnings on Case common varied between a deficit of $14.66 and profits of $19.20 per share, averaging $3.18. The price ranged between 30 1/2 and 191 3/4, closing in 1939 at 73 3/4.

Earnings per Share of J.I. Case Common

1932	$17.40(d)
1931	2.90(d)
1930	11.00
1929	20.40
1928	26.90
1927	26.00
1926	23.30
1925	15.30
1924	5.90(d)
1923	2.10(d)
Average	$9.50

(d) Deficit.

The Role of Intrinsic Value in the Work of the Analyst. Let us try to formulate a statement of the role of intrinsic value in the work of the analyst which will reconcile the rather conflicting implications of our various examples. The essential point is that security analysis does not seek to determine exactly what is the intrinsic value of a given security. It needs only to establish either that the value is *adequate*—e.g., to protect a bond or to justify a stock purchase—or else that the value is considerably higher or considerably lower than the market price. For such purposes an indefinite and approximate measure of the intrinsic value may be sufficient. To use a homely simile, it is quite possible to decide by inspection that a woman is old enough to vote without knowing her age or that a man is heavier than he should be without knowing his exact weight.

This statement of the case may be made clearer by a brief return to our examples. The rejection of St. Louis-San Francisco Preferred did not require an exact calculation of the intrinsic value of this railroad system. It was enough to show, very simply from the earnings record, that the margin of value above the bondholders' and preferred stockholders' claims was too small to assure safety. Exactly the opposite was true for the Owens-Illinois Glass 5s. In this instance, also, it would undoubtedly have been difficult to arrive at a fair valuation of the business; but it was quite easy to decide that this value in any event was far in excess of the company's debt.

In the Wright Aeronautical example, the earlier situation presented a set of facts which demonstrated that the business was worth substantially more than $8 per share, or $1,800,000. In the later year, the facts were equally conclusive that the business did not have a reasonable value of $280 per share, or $70,000,000 in all. It would have been difficult for the analyst to determine whether Wright Aeronautical was actually worth $20 or $40 a share in 1922—or actually worth $50 or $80 in 1929. But fortunately it was not necessary to decide these points in order to conclude that the shares were attractive at $8 and unattractive, intrinsically, at $280.

The J. I. Case example illustrates the far more typical common-stock situation, in which the analyst cannot reach a dependable conclusion as to the relation of intrinsic value to market price. But even here, *if the price had been low or high enough*, a conclusion might have been warranted. To express the uncertainty of the picture, we might say that it was difficult to determine in early 1933 whether the intrinsic value of Case common was nearer $30 or $130. Yet if the stock had been selling at as low as $10, the analyst would undoubtedly have been justified in declaring that it was worth more than the market price.

Flexibility of the Concept of Intrinsic Value. This should indicate how flexible is the concept of intrinsic value as applied to security analysis. Our notion of the intrinsic value may be more or less distinct, depending on the particular case. The degree of indistinctness may be expressed by a very hypothetical "range of approximate value," which would grow wider as the uncertainty of the picture increased, e.g., $20 to $40 for Wright Aeronautical in 1922 as against $30 to $130 for Case in 1933. It would follow that even a very indefinite idea of the intrinsic value may still justify a conclusion if the current price falls far outside either the maximum or minimum appraisal.

More Definite Concept in Special Cases. The Interborough Rapid Transit example permits a more precise line of reasoning than any of the others. Here a given market price for the 5% bonds results in a very definite valuation for the 7% notes. If it were certain that the collateral securing the notes would be acquired for and distributed to the note holders, then the mathematical relationship—*viz.*, $1,736 of value for the 7s against $1,000 of value for the 5s—would eventually be established at this ratio in the market. But because of quasi-political complications in the picture, this normal procedure could not be expected with certainty. As a practical matter, therefore, it is not possible to say that the 7s are actually worth 74% more than the 5s, but it may be said with assurance that the 7s are worth *substantially more*—which is a very useful conclusion to arrive at when both issues are selling at the same price.

The Interborough issues are an example of a rather special group of situations in which analysis may reach more definite conclusions respecting intrinsic value than in the ordinary case. These situations may involve a liquidation or give rise to technical operations known as "arbitrage" or "hedging." While, viewed in the abstract, they are probably the most satisfactory field for the analyst's work, the fact that they are specialized in character and of infrequent occurrence makes them relatively unimportant from the broader standpoint of investment theory and practice.

Principal Obstacles to Success of the Analyst. *a. Inadequate or Incorrect Data.* Needless to say, the analyst cannot be right all the time. Furthermore, a conclusion may be logically right but work out badly in practice. The main obstacles to the success of the analyst's work are threefold, *viz.*, (1) the inadequacy or incorrectness of the data, (2) the uncertainties of the future, and (3) the irrational behavior of the market. The first of these drawbacks, although serious, is the least important of the three. Deliberate falsification of the data is rare; most of the misrepresentation flows from the use of accounting artifices which it is the function of the capable analyst to detect. Concealment is more common than misstatement. But the extent of such concealment has been greatly reduced as the result of regulations, first of the New York Stock Exchange and later of the S.E.C., requiring more complete disclosure and fuller explanation of accounting practices. Where information on an important point is still withheld, the analyst's experience and skill should lead him to note this defect and make allowance therefor—if, indeed, he may not elicit the facts by proper inquiry and pressure. In some cases, no doubt, the concealment will elude detection and give rise to an incorrect conclusion.

b. Uncertainties of the Future. Of much greater moment is the element of future change. A conclusion warranted by the facts and by the apparent prospects may be vitiated by new developments. This raises the question of how far it is the function of security analysis to anticipate changed conditions. We shall defer consideration of this point until our discussion of various factors entering into the processes of analysis. It is manifest, however, that future changes are largely unpredictable, and that security analysis must ordinarily proceed on the assumption that the past record affords at least a rough guide to the future. The more questionable this assumption, the less valuable is the analysis. Hence this technique is more useful when applied to senior securities (which are protected against change) than to common stocks; more useful when applied to a business of inherently stable character than to one subject to wide variations; and, finally, more useful when carried on under fairly normal general conditions than in times of great uncertainty and radical change.

   c. *The Irrational Behavior of the Market.* The third handicap to security analysis is found in the market itself. In a sense the market and the future present the same kind of difficulties. Neither can be predicted or controlled by the analyst, yet his success is largely dependent upon them both. The major activities of the investment analyst may be thought to have little or no concern with market prices. His typical function is the selection of high-grade, fixed-income-bearing bonds, which upon investigation he judges to be secure as to interest and principal. The purchaser is supposed to pay no attention to their subsequent market fluctuations, but to be interested solely in the question whether the bonds will continue to be sound investments. In our opinion this traditional view of the investor's attitude is inaccurate and somewhat hypocritical. Owners of securities, whatever their character, are interested in their market quotations. This fact is recognized by the emphasis always laid in investment practice upon *marketability.* If it is important that an issue be readily salable, it is still more important that it command a satisfactory price. While for obvious reasons the investor in high-grade bonds has a lesser concern with market fluctuations than has the speculator, they still have a strong psychological, if not financial, effect upon him. Even in this field, therefore, the analyst must take into account whatever influences may adversely govern the market price, as well as those which bear upon the basic safety of the issue.

   In that portion of the analyst's activities which relates to the discovery of undervalued, and possibly of overvalued securities, he is more directly concerned with market prices. For here the vindication of his judgment must be found largely in the ultimate market action of the issue. This field of analytical work may be said to rest upon a twofold assumption: first, that the market price is frequently out of line with the true value; and, second, that there is an inherent tendency for these disparities to correct themselves. As to the truth of the former statement, there can be very little doubt—even though Wall Street often speaks glibly of the "infallible judgment of the market" and asserts that "a stock is worth what you can sell it for—neither more nor less."

The Hazard of Tardy Adjustment of Price Value. The second assumption is equally true in theory, but its working out in practice is often most unsatisfactory. Undervaluations caused by neglect or prejudice may persist for an inconveniently long time, and the same applies to inflated prices caused by overenthusiasm or artificial stimulants. The particular danger to the analyst is that, because of such delay, new determining factors may supervene before the market price adjusts itself to the value as he found it. In other words, by the time the price finally does reflect the value, this value may have changed considerably and the facts and reasoning on which his decision was based may no longer be applicable.

The analyst must seek to guard himself against this danger as best he can: in part, by dealing with those situations preferably which are not subject to sudden change; in part, by favoring securities in which the popular interest is keen enough to promise a fairly swift response to value elements which he is the first to recognize; in part, by tempering his activities to the general financial situation—laying more emphasis on the discovery of undervalued securities when business and market conditions are on a fairly even keel, and proceeding with greater caution in times of abnormal stress and uncertainty.

The Relationship of Intrinsic Value to Market Price. The general question of the relation of intrinsic value to the market quotation may be made clearer by the following chart, which traces the various steps culminating in the market price. It will be evident from the chart that the influence of what we call analytical factors over the market price is both *partial* and *indirect*—partial, because it frequently competes with purely speculative factors which influence the price in the opposite direction; and indirect, because it acts through the intermediary of people's sentiments and decisions. In other words, the market is not a *weighing machine*, on which the value of each issue is recorded by an exact and impersonal mechanism, in accordance with its specific qualities. Rather should we say that the market is a *voting machine*, whereon countless individuals register choices which are the product partly of reason and partly of emotion.

Relationship of Intrinsic Value Factors to Market Price

I. *General market factors.*

II. *Individual factors.*

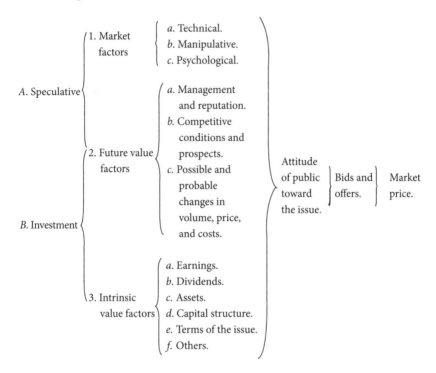

ANALYSIS AND SPECULATION

It may be thought that sound analysis should produce successful results in any type of situation, including the confessedly speculative, *i.e.*, those subject to substantial uncertainty and risk. If the selection of speculative issues is based on expert study of the companies' position, should not this approach give the purchaser a considerable advantage? Admitting future events to be uncertain, could not the favorable and unfavorable developments be counted on to cancel out against each other, more or less, so that the initial advantage afforded by sound analysis will carry through into an eventual average profit? This is a plausible argument but a deceptive one; and its over-ready acceptance has done much to lead analysts astray. It is worth while, therefore, to detail several valid arguments against placing chief reliance upon analysis in speculative situations.

In the first place, what may be called the mechanics of speculation involves serious handicaps to the speculator, which may outweigh the benefits conferred by analytical study. These disadvantages include the payment of commissions and interest charges, the so-called "turn of the market" (meaning the spread between the bid and asked price), and, most important of all, an inherent tendency for the average loss to exceed the average profit, unless a certain technique of trading is followed, which is opposed to the analytical approach.

The second objection is that the underlying analytical factors in speculative situations are subject to swift and sudden revision. The danger, already referred to, that the intrinsic value may change before the market price reflects that value, is therefore much more serious in speculative than in investment situations. A third difficulty arises from circumstances surrounding the unknown factors, which are necessarily left out of security analysis. Theoretically these unknown factors should have an equal chance of being favorable or unfavorable, and thus they should neutralize each other in the long run. For example, it is often easy to determine by comparative analysis that one company is selling much lower than another in the same field, in relation to earnings, although both apparently have similar prospects. But it may well be that the low price for the apparently attractive issue is due to certain important unfavorable factors which, though not disclosed, are known to those identified with the company—and *vice versa* for the issue seemingly selling above its relative value. In speculative situations, those "on the inside" often have an advantage of this kind which nullifies the premise that good and bad changes in the picture should offset each other, and which loads the dice against the analyst working with some of the facts concealed from him.[3]

The Value of Analysis Diminishes as the Element of Chance Increases.
The final objection is based on more abstract grounds, but, nevertheless, its practical importance is very great. Even if we grant that analysis can give the speculator a mathematical advantage, it does not assure him a profit. His ventures remain hazardous; in any individual case a loss may be taken; and after the operation is concluded, it is difficult to determine whether the analyst's contribution has been a benefit or a detriment.

---

[3] See Appendix Note 3 for the result of a study of the market behavior of "high price-earnings ratio stocks" as compared with "low price-earnings ratio stocks."

Hence the latter's position in the speculative field is at best uncertain and somewhat lacking in professional dignity. It is as though the analyst and Dame Fortune were playing a duet on the speculative piano, with the fickle goddess calling all the tunes.

By another and less imaginative simile, we might more convincingly show why analysis is inherently better suited to investment than to speculative situation. (In anticipation of a more detailed inquiry in a later chapter, we have assumed throughout this chapter that investment implies expected safety and speculation connotes acknowledged risk.) In Monte Carlo the odds are weighted 19 to 18 in favor of the proprietor of the roulette wheel, so that on the average he wins one dollar out of each 37 wagered by the public. This may suggest the odds against the untrained investor or speculator. Let us assume that, through some equivalent of analysis, a roulette player is able to reverse the odds for a limited number of wagers, so that they are now 18 to 19 in his favor. If he distributes his wagers evenly over all the numbers, then whichever one turns up he is certain to win a moderate amount. This operation may be likened to an investment program based upon sound analysis and carried on under propitious general conditions.

But if the player wagers all his money on a single number, the small odds in his favor are of slight importance compared with the crucial question whether chance will elect the number he has chosen. His "analysis" will enable him to win a little more if he is lucky; it will be of no value when luck is against him. This, in slightly exaggerated form perhaps, describes the position of the analyst dealing with essentially speculative operations. Exactly the same mathematical advantage which practically assures good results in the investment field may prove entirely ineffective where luck is the overshadowing influence.

It would seem prudent, therefore, to consider analysis as an *adjunct* or *auxiliary* rather than as a *guide* in speculation. It is only where chance plays a subordinate role that the analyst can properly speak in an authoritative voice and accept responsibility for the results of his judgments.

3. THE CRITICAL FUNCTION OF SECURITY ANALYSIS

The principles of investment finance and the methods of corporation finance fall necessarily within the province of security analysis. Analytical judgments are reached by applying standards to facts. The analyst is concerned, therefore, with the soundness and practicability of the standards of selection. He is also interested to see that securities, especially bonds and preferred stocks, be issued with adequate protective provisions, and—more important still—that proper methods of enforcement of these covenants be part of accepted financial practice.

It is a matter of great moment to the analyst that the facts be fairly presented, and this means that he must be highly critical of accounting methods. Finally, he must concern himself with all corporate policies affecting the security owner, for the value of the issue which he analyzes may be largely dependent upon the acts of the management. In this category are included questions of capitalization set-up, of dividend and expansion policies, of managerial compensation, and even of continuing or liquidating an unprofitable business.

On these matters of varied import, security analysis may be competent to express critical judgments, looking to the avoidance of mistakes, to the correction of abuses, and to the better protection of those owning bonds or stocks.

CHAPTER 2

Fundamental Elements in the Problem of Analysis. Quantitative and Qualitative Factors

IN THE PREVIOUS chapter we referred to some of the concepts and materials of analysis from the standpoint of their bearing on what the analyst may hope to accomplish. Let us now imagine the analyst at work and ask what are the broad considerations which govern his approach to a particular problem, and also what should be his general attitude toward the various kinds of information with which he has to deal.

FOUR FUNDAMENTAL ELEMENTS

The object of security analysis is to answer, or assist in answering, certain questions of a very practical nature. Of these, perhaps the most customary are the following: What securities should be bought for a given purpose? Should issue *S* be bought, or sold, or retained?

In all such questions, four major factors may be said to enter, either expressly or by implication. These are:

1. The security.
2. The price.
3. The time.
4. The person.

More completely stated, the second typical question would run, Should security *S* be bought (or sold, or retained) at price *P*, at this time *T*, by individual *I*? Some discussion of the relative significance of these four factors is therefore pertinent, and we shall find it convenient to consider them in inverse order.

The Personal Element. The personal element enters to a greater or lesser extent into every security purchase. The aspect of chief importance is usually the financial position of the intending buyer. What might be an attractive speculation for a business man should under no circumstances be attempted by a trustee or a widow with limited income. Again, United States Liberty 3¹/₂s should not have been purchased by those to whom their complete tax-exemption feature was of no benefit, when a considerably higher yield could be obtained from partially taxable governmental issues.[1]

Other personal characteristics that on occasion might properly influence the individual's choice of securities are his financial training and competence, his temperament, and his preferences. But however vital these considerations may prove at times, they are not ordinarily determining factors in analysis. Most of the conclusions derived from analysis can be stated in impersonal terms, as applicable to investors or speculators as a class.

The Time. The time at which an issue is analyzed may affect the conclusion in various ways. The company's showing may be better, or its outlook may seem better, at one time than another, and these changing circumstances are bound to exert a varying influence on the analyst's viewpoint toward the issue. Furthermore, securities are selected by the application of standards of quality and yield, and both of these—particularly the latter—will vary with financial conditions in general. A railroad bond of highest grade yielding 5% seemed attractive in June 1931 because the average return on this type of bond was 4.32%. But the same offering made six months later would have been quite unattractive, for in the meantime bond prices had fallen severely and the yield on this group had increased to 5.86%. Finally, nearly all security commitments are influenced to some extent by the current view of the financial and business outlook. In speculative operations these considerations are of controlling importance; and while conservative investment is ordinarily supposed to disregard these elements, in times of stress and uncertainty they may not be ignored.

Security analysis, as a study, must necessarily concern itself as much as possible with principles and methods which are valid at all times—or, at least, under all ordinary conditions. It should be kept in mind,

---

[1] In 1927 the yield on these 3¹/₂s was 3.39%, while U. S. Liberty 4¹/₄s, due about the same time, were yielding 4.08%.

however, that the practical applications of analysis are made against a background largely colored by the changing times.

The Price. The price is an integral part of every complete judgment relating to securities. In the selection of prime investment bonds, the price is usually a subordinate factor, not because it is a matter of indifference but because in actual practice the price is rarely unreasonably high. Hence almost entire emphasis is placed on the question whether the issue is adequately secured. But in a special case, such as the purchase of high-grade *convertible* bonds, the price may be a factor fully as important as the degree of security. This point is illustrated by the American Telephone and Telegraph Company Convertible $4^1/_2$s, due 1939, which sold above 200 in 1929. The fact that principal (at par) and interest were safe beyond question did not prevent the issue from being an extremely risky purchase *at that price*—one which in fact was followed by the loss of over half its market value.[2]

In the field of common stocks, the necessity of taking price into account is more compelling, because the danger of paying the wrong price is almost as great as that of buying the wrong issue. We shall point out later that the new-era theory of investment left price out of the reckoning, and that this omission was productive of most disastrous consequences.

The Security: Character of the Enterprise and the Terms of the Commitment. The roles played by the security and its price in an investment decision may be set forth more clearly if we restate the problem in somewhat different form. Instead of asking, (1) In what security? and (2) At what price? let us ask, (1) In what enterprise? and (2) On what terms is the commitment proposed? This gives us a more comprehensive and evenly balanced contrast between two basic elements in analysis. By the *terms* of the investment or speculation, we mean not only the price but also the provisions of the issue and its status or showing at the time.

---

[2] Annual price ranges for American Telephone and Telegraph Company Convertible $4^1/_2$s, due in 1939, were as follows:

Year	High	Low
1929	227	118
1930	$193^3/_8$	116
1931	135	95

Example of Commitment on Unattractive Terms. An investment in the soundest type of enterprise may be made on unsound and unfavorable terms. Prior to 1929 the value of urban real estate had tended to grow steadily over a long period of years; hence it came to be regarded by many as the "safest" medium of investment. But the purchase of a preferred stock in a New York City real estate development in 1929 might have involved *terms* of investment so thoroughly disadvantageous as to banish all elements of soundness from the proposition. One such stock offering could be summarized as follows:[3]

1. *Provisions of the Issue.* A preferred stock, ranking junior to a large first mortgage and without unqualified rights to dividend or principal payments. It ranked ahead of a common stock which represented no cash investment so that the common stockholders had nothing to lose and a great deal to gain, while the preferred stockholders had everything to lose and only a small share in the possible gain.

2. *Status of the Issue.* A commitment in a new building, constructed at an exceedingly high level of costs, with no reserves or junior capital to fall back upon in case of trouble.

3. *Price of the Issue.* At par the dividend return was 6%, which was much less than the yield obtainable on real-estate second mortgages having many other advantages over this preferred stock.[4]

Example of a Commitment on Attractive Terms. We have only to examine electric power and light financing in recent years to find countless examples of unsound securities in a fundamentally attractive industry. By way of contrast let us cite the case of Brooklyn Union Elevated

---

[3] The financing method described is that used by the separate owning corporations organized and sponsored by the Fred F. French Company and affiliated enterprises, with the exception of some of the later Tudor City units in the financing of which interest-bearing notes, convertible par for par into preferred stock at the option of the company, were substituted for the preferred stock in the financial plan. See *The French Plan* (10th ed., December 1928) published and distributed by the Fred F. French Investing Company, Inc. See also *Moody's Manual;* "Banks and Finance," 1933, pp. 1703–1707.

[4] The real-estate enterprise from which this example is taken gave a bonus of common stock with the preferred shares. The common stock had no immediate value, but it did have a potential value which, *under favorable conditions*, might have made the purchase profitable. From the investment standpoint, however, the preferred stock of this enterprise was subject to all of the objections which we have detailed. Needless to say, purchasers of these issues fared very badly in nearly every case.

Railroad First 5s, due 1950, which sold in 1932 at 60 to yield 9.85% to maturity. They are an obligation of the Brooklyn-Manhattan Transit System. The traction, or electric railway, industry has long been unfavorably regarded, chiefly because of automobile competition but also on account of regulation and fare-contract difficulties. Hence this security represents a comparatively unattractive *type* of enterprise. Yet the *terms* of the investment here might well make it a satisfactory commitment, as shown by the following:

1. *Provisions of the Issue.* By contract between the operating company and the City of New York, this was a first charge on the earnings of the combined subway and elevated lines of the system, both company and city owned, representing an investment enormously greater than the size of this issue.

2. *Status of the Issue.* Apart from the very exceptional specific protection just described, the bonds were obligations of a company with stable and apparently fully adequate earning power.

3. *Price of Issue.* It could be purchased to yield somewhat more than the Brooklyn-Manhattan Transit Corporation 6s, due 1968, which occupied a subordinate position. (At the low price of 68 for the latter issue in 1932, its yield was 9% against 9.85% for the Brooklyn Union Elevated 5s.[5])

Relative Importance of the Terms of the Commitment and the Character of the Enterprise. Our distinction between the character of the enterprise and the terms of the commitment suggests a question as to which element is the more important. Is it better to invest in an attractive enterprise on unattractive terms or in an unattractive enterprise on attractive terms? The popular view unhesitatingly prefers the former alternative, and in so doing it is instinctively, rather than logically, right. Over a long period, experience will undoubtedly show that less money has been lost by the great body of investors through paying too high a price for securities of the best regarded enterprises than by trying to secure a larger income or profit from commitments in enterprises of lower grade.

---

[5] By 1936 the price of the Brooklyn Union Elevated 5s had advanced to 115$^{1}/_{2}$. After 1937 the earnings of the B.M.T. declined, and the price of this issue fell to 59. In the purchase of the system by New York City in 1940, however, the strong position of this issue was recognized, and its price recovered again to 92.

From the standpoint of analysis, however, this empirical result does not dispose of the matter. It merely exemplifies a rule that is applicable to all kinds of merchandise, *viz.*, that the *untrained buyer* fares best by purchasing goods of the highest reputation, even though he may pay a comparatively high price. But, needless to say, this is not a rule to guide the expert merchandise buyer, for he is expected to judge quality by examination and not solely by reputation, and at times he may even sacrifice certain definite degrees of quality if that which he obtains is adequate for his purpose and attractive in price. This distinction applies as well to the purchase of securities as to buying paints or watches. It results in two principles of quite opposite character, the one suitable for the untrained investor, the other useful only to the analyst.

1. Principle for the untrained security buyer: *Do not put money in a low-grade enterprise on any terms.*
2. Principle for the securities analyst: *Nearly every issue might conceivably be cheap in one price range and dear in another.*

We have criticized the placing of exclusive emphasis on the choice of the enterprise on the ground that it often leads to paying too high a price for a good security. A second objection is that the enterprise itself may prove to be unwisely chosen. It is natural and proper to prefer a business which is large and well managed, has a good record, and is expected to show increasing earnings in the future. But these expectations, though seemingly well-founded, often fail to be realized. Many of the leading enterprises of yesterday are today far back in the ranks. Tomorrow is likely to tell a similar story. The most impressive illustration is afforded by the persistent decline in the relative investment position of the railroads as a class during the past two decades. The standing of an enterprise is in part a matter of fact and in part a matter of opinion. During recent years investment opinion has proved extraordinarily volatile and undependable. In 1929 Westinghouse Electric and Manufacturing Company was quite universally considered as enjoying an unusually favorable industrial position. Two years later the stock sold for much less than the net current assets alone, presumably indicating widespread doubt as to its ability to earn *any* profit in the future. Great Atlantic and Pacific Tea Company, viewed as little short of a miraculous enterprise in 1929, declined from 494 in that year to 36 in 1938. At the latter date the common sold for less than its cash assets, the preferred being amply covered by other current assets.

These considerations do not gainsay the principle that untrained investors should confine themselves to the best regarded enterprises. It should be realized, however, that this preference is enjoined upon them because of the greater risk for them in other directions, and not because the most popular issues are necessarily the safest. The analyst must pay respectful attention to the judgment of the market place and to the enterprises which it strongly favors, but he must retain an independent and critical viewpoint. Nor should he hesitate to condemn the popular and espouse the unpopular when reasons sufficiently weighty and convincing are at hand.

QUALITATIVE AND QUANTITATIVE FACTORS IN ANALYSIS

Analyzing a security involves an analysis of the business. Such a study could be carried to an unlimited degree of detail; hence practical judgment must be exercised to determine how far the process should go. The circumstances will naturally have a bearing on this point. A buyer of a $1,000 bond would not deem it worth his while to make as thorough an analysis of an issue as would a large insurance company considering the purchase of a $500,000 block. The latter's study would still be less detailed than that made by the originating bankers. Or, from another angle, a less intensive analysis should be needed in selecting a high-grade bond yielding 3% than in trying to find a well-secured issue yielding 6% or an *unquestioned bargain* in the field of common stocks.

Technique and Extent of Analysis Should Be Limited by Character and Purposes of the Commitment. The equipment of the analyst must include a sense of proportion in the use of his technique. In choosing and dealing with the materials of analysis he must consider not only inherent importance and dependability but also the question of accessibility and convenience. He must not be misled by the availability of a mass of data— *e.g.,* in the reports of the railroads to the Interstate Commerce Commission—into making elaborate studies of nonessentials. On the other hand, he must frequently resign himself to the lack of significant information because it can be secured only by expenditure of more effort than he can spare or the problem will justify. This would be true frequently of some of the elements involved in a complete "business analysis"—as, for example, the extent to which an enterprise is dependent upon patent protection or geographical advantages or favorable labor conditions which may not endure.

Value of Data Varies with Type of Enterprise. Most important of all, the analyst must recognize that the value of a particular kind of data varies greatly with the type of enterprise which is being studied. The five-year record of gross or net earnings of a railroad or a large chain-store enterprise may afford, if not a conclusive, at least a reasonably sound basis for measuring the safety of the senior issues and the attractiveness of the common shares. But the same statistics supplied by one of the smaller oil-producing companies may well prove more deceptive than useful, since they are chiefly the resultant of two factors, *viz.*, price received and production, both of which are likely to be radically different in the future than in the past.

Quantitative vs. Qualitative Elements in Analysis. It is convenient at times to classify the elements entering into an analysis under two headings: the quantitative and the qualitative. The former might be called the company's statistical exhibit. Included in it would be all the useful items in the income account and balance sheet, together with such additional specific data as may be provided with respect to production and unit prices, costs, capacity, unfilled orders, etc. These various items may be subclassified under the headings: (1) capitalization, (2) earnings and dividends, (3) assets and liabilities, and (4) operating statistics.

The qualitative factors, on the other hand, deal with such matters as the nature of the business; the relative position of the individual company in the industry; its physical, geographical, and operating characteristics; the character of the management; and, finally, the outlook for the unit, for the industry, and for business in general. Questions of this sort are not dealt with ordinarily in the company's reports. The analyst must look for their answers to miscellaneous sources of information of greatly varying dependability—including a large admixture of mere opinion.

Broadly speaking, the quantitative factors lend themselves far better to thoroughgoing analysis than do the qualitative factors. The former are fewer in number, more easily obtainable, and much better suited to the forming of definite and dependable conclusions. Furthermore the financial results will themselves epitomize many of the qualitative elements, so that a detailed study of the latter may not add much of importance to the picture. The typical analysis of a security—as made, say, in a broker-age-house circular or in a report issued by a statistical service—will treat the qualitative factors in a superficial or summary fashion and devote most of its space to the figures.

Qualitative Factors: Nature of the Business and Its Future Prospects. The qualitative factors upon which most stress is laid are the nature of the business and the character of the management. These elements are exceedingly important, but they are also exceedingly difficult to deal with intelligently. Let us consider, first, the nature of the business, in which concept is included the general idea of its future prospects. Most people have fairly definite notions as to what is "a good business" and what is not. These views are based partly on the financial results, partly on knowledge of specific conditions in the industry, and partly also on surmise or bias.

During most of the period of general prosperity between 1923 and 1929, quite a number of major industries were backward. These included cigars, coal, cotton goods, fertilizers, leather, lumber, meat packing, paper, shipping, street railways, sugar, woolen goods. The underlying cause was usually either the development of competitive products or services (*e.g.*, coal, cotton goods, tractions) or excessive production and demoralizing trade practices (*e.g.*, paper, lumber, sugar). During the same period other industries were far more prosperous than the average. Among these were can manufacturers, chain stores, cigarette producers, motion pictures, public utilities. The chief cause of these superior showings might be found in unusual growth of demand (cigarettes, motion pictures) or in absence or control of competition (public utilities, can makers) or in the ability to win business from other agencies (chain stores).

It is natural to assume that industries which have fared worse than the average are "unfavorably situated" and therefore to be avoided. The converse would be assumed, of course, for those with superior records. But this conclusion may often prove quite erroneous. Abnormally good or abnormally bad conditions do not last forever. This is true not only of general business but of particular industries as well. Corrective forces are often set in motion which tend to restore profits where they have disappeared, or to reduce them where they are excessive in relation to capital.

Industries especially favored by a developing demand may become demoralized through a still more rapid growth of supply. This has been true of radio, aviation, electric refrigeration, bus transportation, and silk hosiery. In 1922 department stores were very favorably regarded because of their excellent showing in the 1920–1921 depression; but they did not maintain this advantage in subsequent years. The public utilities were unpopular in the 1919 boom, because of high costs; they became speculative and investment favorites in 1927–1929; in 1933–1938 fear of inflation, rate regulation, and direct governmental competition again undermined the public's confidence in them. In 1933, on the other hand, the cotton-goods industry—long depressed—forged ahead faster than most others.

The Factor of Management. Our appreciation of the importance of selecting a "good industry" must be tempered by a realization that this is by no means so easy as it sounds. Somewhat the same difficulty is met with in endeavoring to select an unusually capable management. Objective tests of managerial ability are few and far from scientific. In most cases the investor must rely upon a reputation which may or may not be deserved. The most convincing proof of capable management lies in a superior comparative record over a period of time. But this brings us back to the quantitative data.

There is a strong tendency in the stock market to value the management factor twice in its calculations. Stock prices reflect the large earnings which the good management has produced, *plus* a substantial increment for "good management" considered separately. This amounts to "counting the same trick twice," and it proves a frequent cause of overvaluation.

The Trend of Future Earnings. In recent years increasing importance has been laid upon the *trend of earnings*. Needless to say, a record of increasing profits is a favorable sign. Financial theory has gone further, however, and has sought to estimate future earnings by projecting the past trend into the future and then used this projection as a basis for valuing the business. Because figures are used in this process, people mistakenly believe that it is "mathematically sound." But while a trend shown in the past is a fact, a "future trend" is only an assumption. The factors that we mentioned previously as militating against the maintenance of abnormal prosperity or depression are equally opposed to the indefinite continuance of an upward or downward trend. By the time the trend has become clearly noticeable, conditions may well be ripe for a change.

It may be objected that as far as the future is concerned it is just as logical to expect a past trend to be maintained as to expect a past average to be repeated. This is probably true, but it does not follow that the trend is more useful to analysis than the individual or average figures of the past. For security analysis does not assume that a past average will be repeated, but only that it supplies a *rough index* to what may be expected of the future. A trend, however, cannot be used as a rough index; it represents a definite prediction of either better or poorer results, and it must be either right or wrong.

This distinction, important in its bearing on the attitude of the analyst, may be made clearer by the use of examples. Let us assume that in 1929 a railroad showed its interest charges earned three times on the average during the preceding seven years. The analyst would have ascribed great weight to this point as an indication that its bonds were sound. This is a judgment based on quantitative data and standards. But it does not imply a prediction that the earnings in the next seven years will average three times interest charges; it suggests only that earnings are not likely to fall so much under three times interest charges as to endanger the bonds. In nearly every actual case such a conclusion would have proved correct, despite the economic collapse that ensued.

Now let us consider a similar judgment based primarily upon the trend. In 1929 nearly all public-utility systems showed a continued growth of earnings, but the fixed charges of many were so heavy—by reason of pyramidal capital structures—that they consumed nearly all the net income. Investors bought bonds of these systems freely on the theory that the small margin of safety was no drawback, since earnings were certain to continue to increase. They were thus making a clear-cut prediction as to the future, upon the correctness of which depended the justification of their investment. If their prediction were wrong—as proved to be the case—they were bound to suffer serious loss.

Trend Essentially a Qualitative Factor. In our discussion of the valuation of common stocks, later in this book, we shall point out that the placing of preponderant emphasis on the trend is likely to result in errors of overvaluation or undervaluation. This is true because no limit may be fixed on how far ahead the trend should be projected; and therefore the process of valuation, while seemingly mathematical, is in reality psychological and quite arbitrary. For this reason we consider the trend as a *qualitative* factor in its practical implications, even though it may be stated in quantitative terms.

Qualitative Factors Resist Even Reasonably Accurate Appraisal. The trend is, in fact, a statement of future prospects in the form of an exact prediction. In similar fashion, conclusions as to the nature of the business and the abilities of the management have their chief significance in their bearing on the outlook. These qualitative factors are therefore all of the same general character. They all involve the same basic difficulty for the analyst, *viz.*, that it is impossible to judge how far they may properly reflect themselves in the price of a given security. In most cases, if they are recognized at all, they tend to be overemphasized. We see the same influence constantly at work in the general market. The recurrent excesses of its advances and declines are due at bottom to the fact that, when values are determined chiefly by the outlook, the resultant judgments are not subject to any mathematical controls and are almost inevitably carried to extremes.

Analysis is concerned primarily with values which are supported by the facts and not with those which depend largely upon expectations. In this respect the analyst's approach is diametrically opposed to that of the speculator, meaning thereby one whose success turns upon his ability to forecast or to guess future developments. Needless to say, the analyst must take possible future changes into account, but his primary aim is not so much to *profit* from them as to *guard against* them. Broadly speaking, he views the business future as a hazard which his conclusions must encounter rather than as the source of his vindication.

Inherent Stability a Major Qualitative Factor. It follows that the qualitative factor in which the analyst should properly be most interested is that of *inherent stability*. For stability means resistance to change and hence greater dependability for the results shown in the past. Stability, like the trend, may be expressed in quantitative terms—as, for example, by stating that the earnings of General Baking Company during 1923–1932 were never less than ten times 1932 interest charges or that the operating profits of Woolworth between 1924 and 1933 varied only between $2.12 and $3.66 per share of common. But in our opinion stability is really a qualitative trait, because it derives in the first instance from the character of the business and not from its statistical record. A stable record suggests that the business is inherently stable, but this suggestion may be rebutted by other considerations.

Examples: This point may be brought out by a comparison of two preferred-stock issues as of early 1932, *viz.*, those of Studebaker (motors) and of First National (grocery) Stores, both of which were selling above par. The two exhibits were similar, in that both disclosed a continuously satisfactory margin above preferred-dividend requirements. The Studebaker figures were more impressive, however, as the following table will indicate:

Number of Times Preferred Dividend Was Covered

First National Stores		Studebaker	
Period	Times covered	Calendar year	Times covered
Calendar year, 1922	4.0	1922	27.3
Calendar year, 1923	5.1	1923	30.5
Calendar year, 1924	4.9	1924	23.4
Calendar year, 1925	5.7	1925	29.7
15 mos. ended Mar. 31, 1927	4.6	1926	24.8
Year ended Mar. 31, 1928	4.4	1927	23.0
Year ended Mar. 31, 1929	8.4	1928	27.3
Year ended Mar. 31, 1930	13.4	1929	23.3
Annual average	6.3		26.2

But the analyst must penetrate beyond the mere figures and consider the inherent character of the two businesses. The chain-store grocery trade contained within itself many elements of relative stability, such as stable demand, diversified locations, and rapid inventory turnover. A typical large unit in this field, provided only it abstained from reckless expansion policies, was not likely to suffer tremendous fluctuations in its earnings. But the situation of the typical automobile manufacturer was quite different. Despite fair stability in the industry as a whole, the individual units were subject to extraordinary variations, due chiefly to the vagaries of popular preference. The stability of Studebaker's earnings could not be held by any convincing logic to demonstrate that this company enjoyed a special and permanent immunity from the vicissitudes to which most of its competitors had shown themselves subject. The soundness of Studebaker Preferred rested, therefore, largely upon a stable statistical showing which was at variance with the general character of the industry, so far as its individual units were concerned. On the other hand, the satisfactory exhibit of First National Stores Preferred was in thorough accord with what was generally thought to be the inherent character of the business. The later consideration should have carried great weight with the analyst and should have made First National Stores Preferred appear intrinsically sounder as a fixed-value investment than Studebaker Preferred, despite the more impressive *statistical* showing of the automobile company.[6]

Summary. To sum up this discussion of qualitative and quantitative factors, we may express the dictum that the analyst's conclusions must always rest upon the figures and upon established tests and standards. These figures alone are not *sufficient;* they may be completely vitiated by qualitative considerations of an opposite import. A security may make a satisfactory statistical showing, but doubt as to the future or distrust of the management may properly impel its rejection. Again, the analyst is likely to attach prime importance to the qualitative element of *stability,* because its presence means that conclusions based on past results are not so likely to be upset by unexpected developments. It is also true that he will be far more confident in his selection of an issue if he can buttress an adequate quantitative exhibit with unusually favorable qualitative factors.

But whenever the commitment depends to a substantial degree upon these qualitative factors—whenever, that is, the price is considerably higher than the figures alone would justify—then the analytical basis of approval is lacking. In the mathematical phrase, a satisfactory statistical exhibit is a *necessary* though by no means a *sufficient condition* for a favorable decision by the analyst.

---

[6] First National Stores has since maintained its earning power with little change; the preferred stock was redeemed in 1934 and subsequently. Studebaker's earnings fell off sharply after 1930; a receiver was appointed in 1933; and the preferred stock lost nearly all its value.

CHAPTER 3

Sources of Information

It is impossible to discuss or even to list all the sources of information which the analyst may find it profitable to consult at one time or another in his work. In this chapter we shall present a concise outline of the more important sources, together with some critical observations thereon; and we shall also endeavor to convey, by means of examples, an idea of the character and utility of the large variety of special avenues of information.

DATA ON THE TERMS OF THE ISSUE

Let us assume that in the typical case the analyst seeks data regarding: (1) the terms of the specific issue, (2) the company, and (3) the industry. The provisions of the issue itself are summarized in the security manuals or statistical services. For more detailed information regarding a bond contract the analyst should consult the indenture (or deed of trust), a copy of which may be obtained or inspected at the office of the trustee. The terms of the respective stock issues of a company are set forth fully in the charter (or articles of incorporation), together with the by-laws. If the stock is listed, these documents are on file with the S.E.C. and also with the proper stock exchange. In the case of both bonds and stocks, the listing applications—which are readily obtainable—contain nearly all the significant provisions. Prospectuses of new issues also contain these provisions.

DATA ON THE COMPANY

Reports to Stockholders (Including Interim News Releases). Coming now to the *company*, the chief source of statistical data is, of course, the reports issued to the stockholders. These reports vary widely with respect to both frequency and completeness, as the following summary will show:

All important railroads supply *monthly* figures down to net after rentals (net railway operating income). Most carry the results down to the balance for dividends (net income). Many publish carloading figures *weekly*, and a few have published gross earnings weekly. The pamphlet annual reports publish financial and operating figures in considerable detail.[1]

The ruling policy of public-utility companies varies between *quarterly* and *monthly* statements. Figures regularly include gross, net after taxes, and balance for dividends. Some companies publish only a moving twelve-month total—e.g., American Water Works and Electric Company (monthly), North American Company (quarterly). Many supply *weekly* or *monthly* figures of kilowatt-hours sold.

Industrials. The practices followed by industrial companies are usually a matter of individual policy. In some industrial groups there is a tendency for most of the companies therein to follow the same course.

1. *Monthly Statements.* Most chain stores announce their monthly sales in dollars. Prior to 1931, copper producers regularly published their monthly output. General Motors publishes monthly sales in units.

Between 1902 and 1933, United States Steel Corporation published its unfilled orders each month, but in 1933 it replaced this figure by monthly deliveries in tons. Baldwin Locomotive Works has published monthly figures of shipments, new orders, and unfilled orders in dollars. The "Standard Oil Group" of pipeline companies publish monthly statistics of operations in barrels.

Monthly figures of net earnings are published by individual companies from time to time, but such practices have tended to be sporadic or temporary (*e.g.*, Otis Steel, Mullins Manufacturing, Alaska Juneau).[2] There is a tendency to inaugurate monthly statements during periods of improvement and to discontinue them with earnings decline. Sometimes figures by months are included in the quarterly statements—*e.g.*, United States Steel Corporation prior to 1932.

---

[1] Some railroads now send all stockholders a condensed annual statement but offer to send a more comprehensive report on request.

[2] The Alaska Juneau figures—somewhat abbreviated—have continued from about 1925 to the end of 1939. In 1938 Caterpillar Tractor began to publish monthly a complete income account and a balance sheet. This is not really so extraordinary, for most companies supply these data to their directors.

2. *Quarterly Statements.* Publication of results quarterly is considered as the standard procedure in nearly all lines of industry. The New York Stock Exchange has been urging quarterly reports with increasing vigor and has usually been able to make its demands effective in connection with the listing of new or additional securities. Certain types of businesses are considered—or consider themselves—exempt from this requirement, because of the seasonal nature of their results. These lines include sugar production, fertilizers, and agricultural implements. Seasonal fluctuations may be concealed by publishing quarterly a moving twelve-months' figure of earnings. This is done by Continental Can Company.[3]

It is not easy to understand why all the large cigarette manufacturers and the majority of department stores should withhold their results for a full year. It is inconsistent also for a company such as Woolworth to publish sales monthly but no interim statements of net profits. Many individual companies, belonging to practically every division of industry, still fail to publish quarterly reports. In nearly every case such interim figures are available to the management but are denied to the stockholders without adequate reason.

The data given in the quarterly statements vary from a single figure of net earnings (sometimes without allowance for depreciation or federal taxes) to a fully detailed presentation of the income account and the balance sheet, with president's remarks appended. General Motors Corporation is an outstanding example of the latter practice.

3. *Semiannual Reports.* These do not appear to be standard practice for any industrial group, except possibly the rubber companies. A number of individual enterprises report semiannually—*e.g.,* American Locomotive and American Woolen.

4. *Annual Reports.* Every listed company publishes an annual report of some kind. The annual statement is generally more detailed than those covering interim periods. It frequently contains remarks—not always illuminating—by the president or the chairman of the board, relating to the past year's results and to the future outlook. The distinguishing feature of the annual report, however, is that it invariably presents the balance-sheet position.

---

[3] In March 1936 the New York Stock Exchange suggested that all listed companies follow this procedure instead of publishing the usual quarterly earnings. This suggestion aroused great opposition and was withdrawn the next month.

The information given in the income account varies considerably in extent. Some reports give no more than the earnings available for dividends and the amount of dividends paid, *e.g.*, United States Leather Company.[4]

The Income Account. In our opinion an annual income account is not reasonably complete unless it contains the following items: (1) sales, (2) net earnings (before the items following), (3) depreciation (and depletion), (4) interest charges, (5) nonoperating income (in detail), (6) income taxes, (7) dividends paid, (8) surplus adjustments (in detail).

Prior to the passage of the Securities and Exchange Act it was unfortunately true that less than half of our industrial corporations supplied this very moderate quota of information. (By contrast, data relative to railroads and public utilities have long been uniformly adequate.) The S.E.C. regulations now require virtually all this information to be published in the original registration statement (Form 10) and the succeeding annual reports (Form 10-K). Quite a number of companies have requested the S.E.C. to keep their sales figures confidential, on the ground that publication would be detrimental to the enterprise. Most of these requests have been either withdrawn or denied.[5]

---

[4] Pocahontas Fuel Company appears to have been the only enterprise that, although listed on the New York Stock Exchange, published an annual balance sheet only and provided no income statement of any kind. Its bonds were removed from listing in October 1934.

The New York Curb dealings include a number of so called "unlisted issues"—dating from pre-S.E.C. days—which are not subject to requirements of the S.E.C. Among these are companies like American Book, which does not publish an income account, and New Jersey Zinc, which publishes an income account but no balance sheet.

Companies whose issues are dealt in "over-the-counter," and are thus not subject to S.E.C. regulation, generally publish annual reports only. They tend to be less detailed than the statements of listed companies, being especially prone to omit sales and depreciation figures. The great majority supply both a balance sheet and income account, but exceptions are fairly numerous. An amusing example is Dun & Bradstreet Corporation. This purveyor of financial information does not reveal its own earnings to its stockholders. Other companies omitting income accounts are Bemis Brothers' Bag, Joseph Dixon Crucible (since 1935), Glenwood Range, Goodman Manufacturing, Perfection Stove, Regal Shoe, etc.

[5] A few companies, *e.g.*, Celanese Corporation of America, succeeded in obtaining a confidential status for their sales figures in certain years prior to 1938. In some, possibly most, of the cases later requests were denied, and sales figures were subsequently published.

Our study of the 1938 reports of practically all the industrial companies listed on the New York Stock Exchange (648 enterprises) disclosed that only eight had failed to reveal their sales figures by the end of the following year. The S.E.C. advised that confidential treatment of the sales figure had been granted to one company (United Fruit) and that no

The standard of *reasonable completeness* for annual reports, suggested above, by no means includes all the information which might be vouchsafed to shareholders. The reports of United States Steel Corporation may be taken as a model of comprehensiveness. The data there supplied embrace, in addition to our standard requirements, the following items:

1. Production and sales in units. Rate of capacity operated.
2. Division of sales as between:
   Domestic and foreign.
   Intercompany and outsiders.
3. Details of operating expenses:
   Wages, wage rates, and number of employees.
   State and local taxes paid.
   Selling and general expense.
   Maintenance expenditures, amount and details.
4. Details of capital expenditures during the year.
5. Details of inventories.
6. Details of properties owned.
7. Number of stockholders.

The Balance Sheet. The form of the balance sheet is better standardized than the income account, and it does not offer such frequent grounds for criticism. Formerly a widespread defect of balance sheets was the failure to separate intangible from tangible fixed assets, but this is now quite rare in the case of listed issues. (Among the companies that since 1935 have disclosed the amount of good-will formerly included in their property accounts are American Steel Foundries, American Can, Harbison

---

decision had been reached with respect to the other seven (American Sumatra Tobacco, Bon Ami, Collins & Aikman, Mathieson Alkali, Mesta Machine, Sheaffer Pen, United Engineering and Foundry), as late as December 1939.

Various issues, *e.g.*, Trico Products Corporation, failed to register and were dropped from listing, presumably because of their unwillingness to supply sales figures. The withdrawal of Marlin Rockwell Corporation from listing in 1938 may be ascribed to the same reason. The stock exchanges have favored an amendment to the law requiring full disclosure in the case of over-the-counter issues, to remove what they regard as an unfair advantage.

Many companies still provide their stockholders in their annual reports with much less information than they file with the S.E.C. The Standard Statistics *Corporation Records Service*, however, regularly publishes the S.E.C. figures as supplementary data.

Walker Refractories, Loose-Wiles Biscuit, and United States Steel. In nearly all these cases the good-will was written off against surplus.)

Criticism may properly be voiced against the practice of a great many companies in stating only the *net* figure for their property account without showing the deduction for depreciation. Other shortcomings sometimes met are the failure to state the market value of securities owned—*e.g.*, Oppenheim Collins and Company in 1932; to identify "investments" as marketable or nonliquid—*e.g.*, Pittsburgh Plate Glass Company; to value the inventory at lower of cost or market—*e.g.*, Celanese Corporation of America in 1931; to state the nature of miscellaneous reserves—*e.g.*, Hazel-Atlas Glass Company; and to state the amount of the company's own securities held in the treasury—*e.g.*, American Arch Company.[6]

Periodic Reports to Public Agencies. Railroads and most public utilities are required to supply information to various federal and state commissions. Since these data are generally more detailed than the statements to shareholders, they afford a useful supplementary source of material. A few practical illustrations of the value of these reports to commissions may be of interest.

For many years prior to 1927 Consolidated Gas Company of New York (now Consolidated Edison Company of New York) was a "mystery stock" in Wall Street because it supplied very little information to its stockholders. Great emphasis was laid by speculators upon the undisclosed value of its interest in its numerous subsidiary companies. However, complete operating and financial data relating to both the company and its subsidiaries were at all times available in the annual reports of the Public Service Commission of New York. The same situation pertained over a long period with respect to the Mackay Companies, controlling Postal Telegraph and Cable Corporation, which reported no details to its stockholders but considerable information to the Interstate Commerce Commission. A similar contrast exists between the unilluminating reports of Fifth Avenue Bus Securities Company to its shareholders and the complete information filed by its operating subsidiary with the New York Transit Commission.

---

[6] Several of these points were involved in a protracted dispute between the New York Stock Exchange and Allied Chemical and Dye Corporation, which was terminated to the satisfaction of the Stock Exchange in 1933. But the annual reports of the company to shareholders are still inadequate in that they fail to furnish figures for sales, operating expenses, or depreciation.

Finally, we may mention the "Standard Oil Group" of pipeline companies, which have been extremely chary of information to their stockholders. But these companies come under the jurisdiction of the
Interstate Commerce Commission and are required to file circumstantial
annual reports at Washington. Examination of these reports several years
ago would have disclosed striking facts about these companies' holdings
of cash and marketable securities.

The voluminous data contained in the *Survey of Current Business*,
published monthly by the United States Department of Commerce, have
included sales figures for individual chain-store companies which were
not given general publicity—*e.g.*, Waldorf System, J. R. Thompson,
United Cigar Stores, Hartman Corporation, etc. Current statistical information regarding particular companies is often available in trade publications or services.

Examples: Cram's Auto Service gives weekly figures of production for
each motor-car company. Willett and Gray publish several estimates of
sugar production by companies during the crop year. The *Oil and Gas
Journal* often carries data regarding the production of important fields
by companies. The *Railway Age* supplies detailed information regarding
equipment orders placed. Dow, Jones and Company estimate weekly the
rate of production of United States Steel.

Listing Applications. In pre-S.E.C. days these were the most important
nonperiodic sources of information. The reports required by the New
York Stock Exchange, as a condition to admitting securities to its list, are
much more detailed than those usually submitted to the stockholders.
The additional data may include sales in dollars, output in units, amount
of federal taxes, details of subsidiaries' operations, basis and amount of
depreciation and depletion charges. Valuable information may also be
supplied regarding the properties owned, the terms of contracts, and the
accounting methods followed.

The analyst will find these listing applications exceedingly helpful. It
is unfortunate that they appear at irregular intervals, and therefore cannot be counted upon as a steady source of information.

Registration Statements and Prospectuses. As a result of the S.E.C. legislation and regulations, the information available regarding all listed securities and all *new* securities (whether listed or not) is much more
comprehensive than heretofore. These data are contained in registration

statements filed with the Commission in Washington and available for inspection or obtainable in copy upon payment of a fee. The more important information in the registration statement must be included in the prospectus supplied by the underwriters to intending purchasers of new issues. Similar registration statements must be filed with the S.E.C. under the terms of the Public Utility Act of 1935, which applies to holding companies, some of which might not come under the other legislation. Although it is true that the registration statements are undoubtedly too bulky to be read by the typical investor, and although it is doubtful if he is even careful to digest the material in the abbreviated prospectus (which still may cover more than 100 pages), there is no doubt that this material is proving of the greatest value to the analyst and through him to the investing public.

Miscellaneous Official Reports. Information on individual companies may be unearthed in various kinds of official documents. A few examples will give an idea of their miscellaneous character. The report of the United States Coal Commission in 1923 (finally printed as a Senate Document in 1925) gave financial and operating data on the anthracite companies which had not previously been published. Reports of the Federal Trade Commission have recently supplied a wealth of information heretofore not available concerning utility operating and holding companies, and natural-gas and pipe-line companies, unearthed in an elaborate investigation extending over a period of about nine years. In 1938 and 1939 the Commission published detailed reports on the farm implement and automobile manufacturers. In 1933 a comprehensive study of the pipe-line companies was published under the direction of the House Committee on Interstate and Foreign Commerce. Voluminous studies of the American Telephone and Telegraph System have emanated from the investigation carried on by the Federal Communications Commission pursuant to a Congressional resolution adopted in 1935.[7] Some of the opinions of the Interstate Commerce Commission have contained material of great value to the analyst. Trustees under mortgages may have

---

[7] These reports have been published respectively as Sen. Doc. 92, pts. 1–84D, 70th Congress, 1st Session (1928–1937); House Doc. 702, pts. 1 and 2, 75th Congress, 3d Session (1938); House Doc. 468, 76th Congress, 1st Session (1939); House Report No. 2192, pts. 1 and 2, 72d Congress, 2d Session (1933); House Doc. 340, 76th Congress, 1st Session (1939), together with supplementary reports mentioned on pp. 609–611 thereof; and Proposed Report, Telephone Investigation Pursuant to Public Resolution No. 8, 74th Congress (1938).

information required to be supplied by the terms of the indenture. These figures may be significant. For example, unpublished reports with the trustee of Mason City and Fort Dodge Railroad Company 4s, revealed that the interest on the bonds was not being earned, that payment thereof was being continued by Chicago Great Western Railroad Company as a matter of policy only, and hence that the bonds were in a far more vulnerable position than was generally suspected.

Statistical and Financial Publications. Most of the information required by the securities analyst in his daily work may be found conveniently and adequately presented by the various statistical services. These include comprehensive manuals published annually with periodic supplements (Poor's, Moody's); descriptive stock and bond cards, and manuals frequently revised (Standard & Poor's, Fitch); daily digests of news relating to individual companies (Standard Corporation Records, Fitch).[8] These services have made great progress during the past 20 years in the completeness and accuracy with which they present the facts. Nevertheless they cannot be relied upon to give all the data available in the various original sources above described. Some of these sources escape them completely, and in other cases they may neglect to reproduce items of importance. It follows therefore that in any thoroughgoing study of an individual company, the analyst should consult the original reports and other documents wherever possible, and not rely upon summaries or transcriptions.

In the field of financial periodicals, special mention must be made of *The Commercial and Financial Chronicle*, a weekly publication with numerous statistical supplements. Its treatment of the financial and industrial field is unusually comprehensive; and its most noteworthy feature is perhaps its detailed reproduction of corporate reports and other documents.

Requests for Direct Information from the Company. Published information may often be supplemented to an important extent by private inquiry of or by interview with the management. There is no reason why stockholders should not ask for information on specific points, and in many cases part at least of the data asked for will be furnished. It must never be forgotten that a stockholder is an *owner* of the business and an *employer* of its offi-

---

[8] During 1941 Poor's Publishing Company and Standard Statistics Company merged into Standard & Poor's Corp. The separate Poor's services have been discontinued.

cers. He is entitled not only to ask legitimate questions but also to have them answered, unless there is some persuasive reason to the contrary.

Insufficient attention has been paid to this all-important point. The courts have generally held that a bona fide stockholder has the same right to full information as a partner in a private business. This right may not be exercised to the detriment of the corporation, but the burden of proof rests upon the management to show an improper motive behind the request or that disclosure of the information would work an injury to the business.

Compelling a company to supply information involves expensive legal proceedings and hence few shareholders are in a position to assert their rights to the limit. Experience shows, however, that vigorous demands for legitimate information are frequently acceded to even by the most recalcitrant managements. This is particularly true when the information asked for is no more than that which is regularly published by other companies in the same field.

INFORMATION REGARDING THE INDUSTRY

Statistical data respecting industries as a whole are available in abundance. The *Survey of Current Business*, published by the United States Department of Commerce, gives monthly figures on output, consumption, stocks, unfilled orders, etc., for many different lines. Annual data are contained in the Statistical Abstract, the World Almanac, and other compendiums. More detailed figures are available in the Biennial Census of Manufactures.

Many important summary figures are published at frequent intervals in the various trade journals. In these publications will be found also a continuous and detailed picture of the current and prospective state of the industry. Thus it is usually possible for the analyst to acquire without undue difficulty a background of fairly complete knowledge of the history and problems of the industry with which he is dealing.

In recent years the leading statistical agencies have developed additional services containing basic surveys of the principal industrial groups, supplemented frequently by current data designed to keep the basic surveys up to date.[9]

---

[9] For description of these services see *Handbook of Commercial and Financial Services*, Special Libraries Association, New York, 1939.

CHAPTER 4

Distinctions Between Investment and Speculation

General Connotations of the Term "Investment." Investment or invest-ing, like "value" in the famous dictum of Justice Brandeis, is "a word of many meanings." Of these, three will concern us here. The first meaning, or set of meanings, relates to putting or having money in a business. A man "invests" $1,000 in opening a grocery store; the "return on invest-ment" in the steel industry (including bonded debt and retained profits) averaged 2.40% during 1929–1938.[1] The sense here is purely descriptive; it makes no distinctions and pronounces no judgments. Note, however, that it accepts rather than rejects the element of risk—the ordinary busi-ness investment is said to be made "at the risk of the business."

The second set of uses applies the term in a similar manner to the field of finance. In this sense all securities are "investments." We have invest-ment dealers or brokers, investment companies[2] or trusts, investment lists. Here, again, no real distinction is made between investment and other types of financial operations such as speculation. It is a convenient omnibus word, with perhaps an admixture of euphemism—i.e., a desire to lend a certain respectability to financial dealings of miscella-neous character.

Alongside of these two indiscriminate uses of the term "investment" has always been a third and more limited connotation—that of invest-ment as opposed to speculation. That such a distinction is a useful one

---

[1] *Dollars Behind Steel*, pamphlet of American Iron and Steel Institute, New York, 1939.

[2] Note that in October 1939 the S.E.C. listed under the title of "Investment Company" the offering of stock of "The Adventure Company, Ltd.," a new enterprise promoted by "The Discovery Company, Ltd." The fact that 1¢ par value stock was offered at $10 per share, although not really significant, has a certain appropriateness.

is generally taken for granted. It is commonly thought that investment, in this special sense, is good for everybody and at all times. Speculation, on the other hand, may be good or bad, depending on the conditions and the person who speculates. It should be essential, therefore, for anyone engaging in financial operations to know whether he is investing or speculating and, if the latter, to make sure that his speculation is a justifiable one.

The difference between investment and speculation, when the two are thus opposed, is understood in a general way by nearly everyone; but when we try to formulate it precisely, we run into perplexing difficulties. In fact something can be said for the cynic's definition that an investment is a successful speculation and a speculation is an unsuccessful investment. It might be taken for granted that United States government securities are an investment medium, while the common stock, say, of Radio Corporation of America—which between 1931 and 1935 had neither dividends, earnings, nor tangible assets behind it—must certainly be a speculation. Yet operations of a definitely speculative nature may be carried on in United States government bonds (*e.g.*, by specialists who buy large blocks in anticipation of a quick rise); and on the other hand, in 1929 Radio Corporation of America common was widely regarded as an investment, to the extent in fact of being included in the portfolios of leading "Investment Trusts."

It is certainly desirable that some exact and acceptable definition of the two terms be arrived at, if only because we ought as far as possible to know what we are talking about. A more forceful reason, perhaps, might be the statement that the failure properly to distinguish between investment and speculation was in large measure responsible for the market excesses of 1928–1929 and the calamities that ensued—as well as, we think, for much continuing confusion in the ideas and policies of would-be investors. On this account we shall give the question a more thorough-going study than it usually receives. The best procedure might be first to examine critically the various meanings commonly intended in using the two expressions, and then to endeavor to crystallize therefrom a single sound and definite conception of investment.

Distinctions Commonly Drawn Between the Two Terms. The chief distinctions in common use may be listed in the following table:

Investment	Speculation
1. In bonds.	In stocks.
2. Outright purchases.	Purchases on margin.
3. For permanent holding.	For a "quick turn."
4. For income.	For profit.
5. In safe securities.	In risky issues.

The first four distinctions have the advantage of being entirely definite, and each of them also sets forth a characteristic which is applicable to the *general run* of investment or speculation. They are all open to the objection that in numerous individual cases the criterion suggested would not properly apply.

1. Bonds vs. Stocks. Taking up the first distinction, we find it corresponds to a common idea of investing as opposed to speculating, and that it also has the weight of at least one authority on investment who insists that only bonds belong in that category.[3] The latter contention, however, runs counter to the well-nigh universal acceptance of high-grade preferred stocks as media of investment. Furthermore, it is most dangerous to regard the bond form as possessing inherently the credentials of an investment, for a poorly secured bond may not only be thoroughly speculative but the most unattractive form of speculation as well. It is logically unsound, furthermore, to deny investment rating to a strongly entrenched common stock merely because it possesses profit possibilities. Even the popular view recognizes this fact, since at all times certain especially sound common stocks have been rated as investment issues and their purchasers regarded as investors and not as speculators.

2 and 3. Outright vs. Marginal Purchases; Permanent vs. Temporary Holding. The second and third distinctions relate to the customary *method* and *intention*, rather than to the innate character of investment and speculative operations. It should be obvious that buying a stock outright does not *ipso facto* make the transaction an investment. In truth the

---

[3] Lawrence Chamberlain at p. 8 of *Investment and Speculation* by Chamberlain and William W. Hay, New York, 1931.

most speculative issues, *e.g.*, "penny mining stocks," *must* be purchased outright, since no one will lend money against them. Conversely, when the American public was urged during the war to buy Liberty Bonds with borrowed money, such purchases were nonetheless universally classed as investments. If strict logic were followed in financial operations—a very improbable hypothesis!—the common practice would be reversed: the safer (investment) issues would be considered more suitable for marginal purchase, and the riskier (speculative) commitments would be paid for in full.

Similarly the contrast between permanent and temporary holding is applicable only in a broad and inexact fashion. An authority on common stocks has defined an investment as any purchase made with the intention of holding it for a year or longer; but this definition is admittedly suggested by its convenience rather than its penetration.[4] The inexactness of this suggested rule is shown by the circumstance that *short-term investment* is a well-established practice. *Long-term speculation* is equally well established as a rueful fact (when the purchaser holds on hoping to make up a loss), and it is also carried on to some extent as an intentional undertaking.

4 and 5. Income vs. Profit; Safety vs. Risk. The fourth and fifth distinctions also belong together, and so joined they undoubtedly come closer than the others to both a rational and a popular understanding of the subject. Certainly, through many years prior to 1928, the typical investor had been interested above all in safety of principal and continuance of an adequate income. However, the doctrine that common stocks are the best long-term investments has resulted in a transfer of emphasis from current income to future income and hence inevitably to future enhancement of principal value. In its complete subordination of the income element to the desire for profit, and also in the prime reliance it places upon favorable developments expected in the future, the new-era style of investment—as exemplified in the general policy of the investment trusts—is practically indistinguishable from speculation. In fact this so-called "investment" can be accurately defined as speculation in the common stocks of strongly situated companies.

---

[4] Sloan, Laurence H., *Everyman and His Common Stocks*, pp. 8–9, 279 *ff.*, New York, 1931.

It would undoubtedly be a wholesome step to go back to the accepted idea of income as the central motive in investment, leaving the aim toward profit, or capital appreciation, as the typical characteristic of speculation. But it is doubtful whether the true inwardness of investment rests even in this distinction. Examining standard practices of the past, we find some instances in which current income was not the leading interest of a bona fide investment operation. This was regularly true, for example, of bank stocks, which until recent years were regarded as the exclusive province of the wealthy investor. These issues returned a smaller dividend yield than did high-grade bonds, but they were purchased on the expectation that the steady growth in earnings and surplus would result in special distributions and increased principal value. In other words, it was the earnings accruing to the stockholder's credit, rather than those distributed in dividends, which motivated his purchase. Yet it would not appear to be sound to call this attitude speculative, for we should then have to contend that only the bank stocks which paid out most of their earnings in dividends (and thus gave an adequate current return) could be regarded as investments, while those following the conservative policy of building up their surplus would therefore have to be considered speculative. Such a conclusion is obviously paradoxical; and because of this fact it must be admitted that an investment in a common stock might conceivably be founded on its earning power, without reference to current dividend payments

Does this bring us back to the new-era theory of investment? Must we say that the purchase of low-yielding industrial shares in 1929 had the same right to be called investment as the purchase of low-yielding bank stocks in prewar days? The answer to this question should bring us to the end of our quest, but to deal with it properly we must turn our attention to the fifth and last distinction in our list—that between safety and risk.

This distinction expresses the broadest concept of all those underlying the term *investment*, but its practical utility is handicapped by various shortcomings. If safety is to be judged by the result, we are virtually begging the question, and come perilously close to the cynic's definition of an investment as a successful speculation.[5] Naturally the safety must be posited in advance, but here again there is room for much that is indefinite

---

[5] For a *serious* suggestion along these lines see Felix I. Shaffner, *The Problem of Investment*, pp. 18–19, New York, 1936.

and purely subjective. The race-track gambler, betting on a "sure thing," is convinced that his commitment is safe. The 1929 "investor" in high-priced common stocks also considered himself safe in his reliance upon future growth to justify the figure he paid and more.

Standards of Safety. The concept of safety can be really useful only if it is based on something more tangible than the psychology of the purchaser. The safety must be assured, or at least strongly indicated, by the application of definite and well-established standards. It was this point which distinguished the bank-stock buyer of 1912 from the common-stock investor of 1929. The former purchased at price levels which he considered conservative in the light of experience; he was satisfied, from his knowledge of the institution's resources and earning power, that he was getting his money's worth in full. If a strong speculative market resulted in advancing the price to a level out of line with these standards of value, he sold his shares and waited for a reasonable price to return before reacquiring them.

Had the same attitude been taken by the purchaser of common stocks in 1928–1929, the term *investment* would not have been the tragic misnomer that it was. But in proudly applying the designation "blue chips" to the high-priced issues chiefly favored, the public unconsciously revealed the gambling motive at the heart of its supposed investment selections. These differed from the old-time bank-stock purchases in the one vital respect that the buyer did not determine that they were worth the price paid by the application of firmly established standards of value. The market made up new standards as it went along, by accepting the current price—however high—as the sole measure of value. Any idea of safety based on this uncritical approach was clearly illusory and replete with danger. Carried to its logical extreme, it meant that no price could possibly be too high for a good stock, and that such an issue was equally "safe" after it had advanced to 200 as it had been at 25.

A Proposed Definition of Investment. This comparison suggests that it is not enough to identify investment with expected safety; the expectation must be based on study and standards. At the same time, the investor need not necessarily be interested in current income; he may at times legitimately base his purchase on a return which is accumulating to his credit and realized by him after a longer or shorter wait. With these observations in mind, we suggest the following definition of investment as one in harmony with both the popular understanding of the term and the requirements of reasonable precision:

> *An investment operation is one which, upon thorough analysis, promises safety of principal and a satisfactory return. Operations not meeting these requirements are speculative.*

Certain implications of this definition are worthy of further discussion. We speak of an *investment operation* rather than an issue or a purchase, for several reasons. It is unsound to think always of investment character as inhering in an issue *per se.* The price is frequently an essential element, so that a stock (and even a bond) may have investment merit at one price level but not at another. Furthermore, an investment might be justified in a group of issues, which would not be sufficiently safe if made in any one of them singly. In other words, diversification might be necessary to reduce the risk involved in the separate issues to the minimum consonant with the requirements of investment. (This would be true, in general, of purchases of common stocks for investment.)

In our view it is also proper to consider as investment operations certain types of arbitrage and hedging commitments which involve the sale of one security against the purchase of another. In these operations the element of safety is provided by the combination of purchase and sale. This is an extension of the ordinary concept of investment, but one which appears to the writers to be entirely logical.

The phrases *thorough analysis, promises safety,* and *satisfactory return* are all chargeable with indefiniteness, but the important point is that their meaning is clear enough to prevent serious misunderstanding. By *thorough analysis* we mean, of course, the study of the facts in the light of established standards of safety and value. An "analysis" that recommended investment in General Electric common at a price forty times its highest recorded earnings merely because of its excellent prospects would be clearly ruled out, as devoid of all quality of thoroughness.

The *safety* sought in investment is not absolute or complete; the word means, rather, protection against loss under all normal or reasonably likely conditions or variations. A safe bond, for example, is one which could suffer default only under exceptional and highly improbable circumstances. Similarly, a safe stock is one which holds every prospect of being worth the price paid except under quite unlikely contingencies.

Where study and experience indicate that an appreciable chance of loss must be recognized and allowed for, we have a speculative situation.

A *satisfactory return* is a wider expression than *adequate income*, since it allows for capital appreciation or profit as well as current interest or dividend yield. "Satisfactory" is a subjective term; it covers any rate or amount of return, however low, which the investor is willing to accept, provided he acts with reasonable intelligence.

It may be helpful to elaborate our definition from a somewhat different angle, which will stress the fact that investment must always consider the *price* as well as the *quality* of the security. Strictly speaking, there can be no such thing as an "investment issue" in the absolute sense, *i.e.*, implying that it remains an investment regardless of price. In the case of high-grade bonds, this point may not be important, for it is rare that their prices are so inflated as to introduce serious risk of loss of principal. But in the common-stock field this risk may frequently be created by an undue advance in price—so much so, indeed, that in our opinion the great majority of common stocks of strong companies must be considered speculative during most of the time, simply because their price is too high to warrant safety of principal in any intelligible sense of the phrase. We must warn the reader that prevailing Wall Street opinion does not agree with us on this point; and he must make up his own mind which of us is wrong.

Nevertheless, we shall embody our principle in the following additional criterion of investment:

> *An investment operation is one that can be justified on* both *qualitative and quantitative grounds.*

The extent to which the distinction between investment and speculation may depend upon the underlying facts, including the element of price, rather than on any easy generalization, may be brought home in somewhat extreme fashion by two contrasting examples based upon General Electric Special (*i.e.*, Preferred) stock, which occurred in successive months.

Example 1: In December 1934 this issue sold at 12³/₄. It paid 6% on $10 par and was callable on any dividend date at 11. In spite of the preeminent quality of this issue, as far as safety of dividends was concerned, the buyer at 12³/₄ was *speculating* to the extent of more than 10% of his principal. He was virtually wagering that the issue would not be called for some years to come.[6] As it happened, the issue was called that very month for redemption at $11 per share on April 15, 1935.

Example 2: After the issue was called, the price promptly declined to 11. At that time the issue offered an unusual opportunity for profitable *short-term investment on margin.* Brokers buying the shares at 11 (without paying commission), say on January 15, 1935, could have borrowed $10 per share thereon at not more than 2% per annum. This operation would have netted a sure return at the rate of 40% per annum on the capital invested—as shown by the following calculation:

Cost of 1,000 shares at 11 net..$11,000
Redeemed Apr. 15, 1935, at 11 plus dividend...........................11,150
    Gross profit 150
Less 3 months' interest at 2% on $10,000..50
    Net profit..100

Net profit of $100 on $1,000 in 3 months is equivalent to annual return of 40%.

Needless to say, the safety, and the resultant *investment* character, of this unusual operation derived solely from the fact that the holder could count absolutely on the redemption of the shares in April 1935.

The conception of investment advanced above is broader than most of those in common use. Under it investment may conceivably—though not usually—be made in stocks, carried on margin, and purchased with the chief interest in a quick profit. In these respects it would run counter to the first four distinctions which we listed at the outset. But to offset this seeming laxity, we insist on a satisfactory assurance of safety based on adequate analysis. We are thus led to the conclusion that the viewpoint of analysis and the viewpoint of investment are largely identical in their scope.

---

[6] In recent years many United States Government short-term securities have been purchased at prices yielding less than nothing to maturity in the expectation that the holders would be given valuable exchange privileges into new issues. According to our definition all such purchases must be called speculative to the extent of the premium paid above par and interest to maturity.

OTHER ASPECTS OF INVESTMENT
AND SPECULATION

Relation of the Future to Investment and Speculation. It may be said, with some approximation to the truth, that investment is grounded on the past whereas speculation looks primarily to the future. But this statement is far from complete. Both investment and speculation must meet the test of the future; they are subject to its vicissitudes and are judged by its verdict. But what we have said about the analyst and the future applies equally well to the concept of investment. For investment, the future is essentially something to be guarded against rather than to be profited from. If the future brings improvement, so much the better; but investment as such cannot be founded in any important degree upon the expectation of improvement. Speculation, on the other hand, may always properly—and often soundly—derive its basis and its justification from prospective developments that differ from past performance.

Types of "Investment." Assuming that the student has acquired a fairly clear concept of investment in the distinctive sense that we have just developed, there remains the confusing effect of the prevalent use of the term in the broader meanings referred to at the beginning of this chapter. It might be useful if some descriptive adjective were regularly employed, when care is needed, to designate the particular meaning intended. Let us tentatively suggest the following:

1. Business investment	Referring to money put or held in a business.
2. Financial investment or investment generally	Referring to securities generally.
3. Sheltered investment	Referring to securities regarded as subject to small risk by reason of their prior claim on earnings or because they rest upon an adequate taxing power.
4. Analyst's investment	Referring to operations that, upon thorough study, promise safety of principal and an adequate return.

Evidently these different types of investment are not mutually exclusive. A good bond, for example, would fall under all four headings. Unless we specify otherwise, we shall employ the word "investment," and its relatives, in the sense of "analyst's investment," as developed in this chapter.

Types of Speculation. The distinction between speculation and gambling assumes significance when the activities of Wall Street are subjected to critical scrutiny. It is more or less the official position of the New York Stock Exchange that "gambling" represents the creation of risks not previously existing—e.g., race-track betting—whereas "speculation" applies to the taking of risks that are implicit in a situation and so must be taken by someone. A formal distinction between "intelligent speculation" and "unintelligent speculation" is no doubt open to strong theoretical objections, but we do think that it has practical utility. Thus we suggest the following:

1. Intelligent speculation	The taking of a risk that appears justified after careful weighing of the pros and cons.
2. Unintelligent speculation	Risk taking without adequate study of the situation.

In the field of general business most well-considered enterprises would belong in the class of intelligent speculations as well as representing "business investments" in the popular sense. If the risk of loss is very small—an exceptional occurrence—a particular business venture may qualify as an analyst's investment in our special sense. On the other hand, many ill-conceived businesses must be called unintelligent speculations. Similarly, in the field of finance, a great deal of common-stock buying is done with reasonable care and may be called intelligent speculation; a great deal, also, is done upon inadequate consideration and for unsound reasons and thus must be called unintelligent; in the exceptional case a common stock may be bought on such attractive terms, qualitative and quantitative, as to set the inherent risk at a minimum and justify the title of analyst's investment.

Investment and Speculative Components. A proposed purchase that cannot qualify as an "analyst's investment" automatically falls into the speculative category. But at times it may be useful to view such a purchase somewhat differently and to divide the price paid into an investment and a speculative component. Thus the analyst, considering General Electric common at its average price of $38 in 1939, might conclude that up to, say, $25 per share is justified from the strict standpoint of investment value. The remaining $13 per share will represent the stock market's average appraisal of the company's excellent long-term prospects, including therein, perhaps, a rather strong psychological bias in favor of this outstanding enterprise. On the basis of such a study, the analyst would declare that the price of $38 for General Electric includes an investment component of some $25 per share and a speculative component of about $13 per share. If this is sound, it would follow that at a price of 25 or less, General Electric common would constitute an "analyst's investment" completely; but above that price the buyer should recognize that he is paying something for the company's very real speculative possibilities.[7]

Investment Value, Speculative Value, and Intrinsic Value. The foregoing discussion suggests an amplification of what was said in Chap. 1 on the concept of "intrinsic value," which was there defined as "value justified by the facts." It is important to recognize that such value is by no means limited to "value for investment"—*i.e.,* to the investment component of total value—but may properly include a substantial component of speculative value, provided that such speculative value is intelligently arrived at. Hence the market price may be said to exceed intrinsic value only when the market price is clearly the reflection of unintelligent speculation.

Generally speaking, it is the function of the stock market, and not of the analyst, to appraise the speculative factors in a given common-stock picture. To this important extent the market, not the analyst, determines intrinsic value. The range of such an appraisal may be very wide, as illustrated by our former suggestion that the intrinsic value of J. I. Case common in 1933 might conceivably have been as high as 130 or as low as 30. At any point between these broad limits it would have been necessary to accept the market's verdict—changeable as it was from day to day—as representing the best available determination of the intrinsic value of this volatile issue.

---

[7] We have intentionally, and at the risk of future regret, used an example here of a highly controversial character. Nearly everyone in Wall Street would regard General Electric stock as an "investment issue" irrespective of its market price and, more specifically, would consider the average price of $38 as amply justified from the investment standpoint. But we are convinced that to regard investment quality as something independent of price is a fundamental and dangerous error. As to the point at which the investment value of General Electric ceases and its speculative value begins, there is naturally room for a fairly wide difference of opinion. Our figure is only illustrative.

CHAPTER 5

Classification of Securities

SECURITIES ARE CUSTOMARILY divided into the two main groups of bonds and stocks, with the latter subdivided into preferred stocks and common stocks. The first and basic division recognizes and conforms to the fundamental legal distinction between the creditors' position and the partners' position. The bondholder has a fixed and prior claim for principal and interest; the stockholder assumes the major risks and shares in the profits of ownership. It follows that a higher degree of safety should inhere in bonds as a class, while greater opportunity of speculative gain—to offset the greater hazard—is to be found in the field of stocks. It is this contrast, of both legal status and investment character, as between the two kinds of issues, which provides the point of departure for the usual textbook treatment of securities.

Objections to the Conventional Grouping: 1. Preferred Stock Grouped with Common. While this approach is hallowed by tradition, it is open to several serious objections. Of these the most obvious is that it places preferred stocks with common stocks, whereas, so far as investment practice is concerned, the former undoubtedly belong with bonds. The typical or standard preferred stock is bought for fixed income and safety of principal. Its owner considers himself not as a partner in the business but as the holder of a claim ranking ahead of the interest of the partners, *i.e.,* the common stockholders. Preferred stockholders are partners or owners of the business only in a technical, legalistic sense; but they resemble bondholders in the purpose and expected results of their investment.

2. Bond Form Identified with Safety. A weightier though less patent objection to the radical separation of bonds from stocks is that it tends to identify the *bond form* with the idea of safety. Hence investors are led to believe that the very name "bond" must carry some especial assurance against loss. This attitude is basically unsound, and on frequent occasions is responsible for serious mistakes and loss. The investor has been spared even greater penalties for this error by the rather accidental fact that fraudulent security promoters have rarely taken advantage of the investment prestige attaching to the bond form.[1] It is true beyond dispute that bonds as a whole enjoy a degree of safety distinctly superior to that of the average stock. But this advantage is not the result of any essential virtue of the bond form; it follows from the circumstance that the typical American enterprise is financed with some honesty and intelligence and does not assume fixed obligations without a reasonable expectation of being able to meet them. But it is not the obligation that creates the safety, nor is it the legal remedies of the bondholder in the event of default. *Safety depends upon and is measured entirely by the ability of the debtor corporation to meet its obligations.*

The bond of a business without assets or earning power would be every whit as valueless as the stock of such an enterprise. Bonds representing all the capital placed in a new venture are no safer than common stock would be, and are considerably less attractive. For the bondholder could not possibly get more out of the company by virtue of his fixed claim than he could realize if he owned the business in full, free and clear.[2] This simple principle seems too obvious to merit statement; yet because of the traditional association of the bond form with superior safety, the investor has often been persuaded that by the mere act of limiting his return he obtained an assurance against loss.

3. Failure of Titles to Describe Issues with Accuracy. The basic classification of securities into bonds and stocks—or even into three main classes of bonds, preferred stocks, and common stocks—is open to the third objection that in many cases these titles fail to supply an accurate description of the issue. This is the consequence of the steadily mounting per-

---

[1] For an example of fraudulent sales of bonds see Securities Act of 1933: Release No. 2112, dated Dec. 4, 1939, relating to conviction of various parties in connection with the sale of American Terminals and Transit Company bonds and Green River Valley Terminal Company notes.

[2] See Appendix Note 4 for a phase of the liquidation of the United States Express Company illustrating this point and for the more recent example of Court-Livingston Corporation.

centage of securities which do not conform to the standard patterns, but instead modify or mingle the customary provisions.

Briefly stated, these standard patterns are as follows:

I. The bond pattern comprises:
   A. The unqualified right to a fixed interest payment on fixed dates.
   B. The unqualified right to repayment of a fixed principal amount on a fixed date.
   C. No further interest in assets or profits, and no voice in the management.
II. The preferred-stock pattern comprises:
   A. A stated rate of dividend in priority to any payment on the common. (Hence full preferred dividends are mandatory if the common receives any dividend; but if nothing is paid on the common, the preferred dividend is subject to the discretion of the directors.)
   B. The right to a stated principal amount in the event of dissolution, in priority to any payments to the common stock.
   C. Either no voting rights, or voting power shared with the common.
III. The common-stock pattern comprises:
   A. A pro rata ownership of the company's assets in excess of its debts and preferred stock issues.
   B. A pro rata interest in all profits in excess of prior deductions.
   C. A pro rata vote for the election of directors and for other purposes.

Bonds and preferred stocks conforming to the above standard patterns will sometimes be referred to as *straight bonds* or *straight preferred stocks.*

Numerous Deviations from the Standard Patterns. However, almost every conceivable departure from the standard pattern can be found in greater or less profusion in the security markets of today. Of these the most frequent and important are identified by the following designations: *income* bonds; *convertible* bonds and preferred stocks; bonds and preferred stocks with *stock-purchase warrants* attached; *participating* preferred stocks; common stocks with *preferential features; nonvoting* common stock. Of recent origin is the device of making bond interest or preferred dividends payable either in cash or in common stock at the holder's *option.* The *callable feature* now found in most bonds may also be termed a lesser departure from the standard provision of fixed maturity of principal.

Of less frequent and perhaps unique deviations from the standard patterns, the variety is almost endless.[3] We shall mention here only the glaring instance of Great Northern Railway Preferred Stock which for many years has been in all respects a plain common issue; and also the resort by Associated Gas and Electric Company to the insidious and highly objectionable device of bonds convertible into preferred stock *at the option of the company* which are, therefore, not true bonds at all.

More striking still is the emergence of completely distinctive types of securities so unrelated to the standard bond or stock pattern as to require an entirely different set of names. Of these, the most significant is the option warrant—a device which during the years prior to 1929 developed into a financial instrument of major importance and tremendous mischief-making powers. The option warrants issued by a single company—American and Foreign Power Company—attained in 1929 an aggregate market value of more than a *billion dollars*, a figure exceeding our national debt in 1914. A number of other newfangled security forms, bearing titles such as allotment certificates and dividend participations, could be mentioned.[4]

The peculiarities and complexities to be found in the present day security list are added arguments against the traditional practice of pigeonholing and generalizing about securities in accordance with their *titles*. While this procedure has the merit of convenience and a certain rough validity, we think it should be replaced by a more flexible and accurate basis of classification. In our opinion, the criterion most useful for purposes of study would be the *normal behavior* of the issue after purchase—in other words its risk-and-profit characteristics as the buyer or owner would reasonably view them.

New Classification Suggested. With this standpoint in mind, we suggest that securities be classified under the following three headings:

---

[3] The reader is referred to Appendix Note 3 of the first edition of this work for a comprehensive list of these deviations, with examples of each. To save space that material is omitted from this edition.

[4] In June 1939 the S.E.C. set a salutary precedent by refusing to authorize the issuance of "Capital Income Debentures" in the reorganization of the Griess-Pfleger Tanning Company, on the ground that the devising of new types of hybrid issues had gone far enough. See S.E.C. Corporate Reorganization Release No. 13, dated June 16, 1939. Unfortunately, the court failed to see the matter in the same light and approved the issuance of the new security.

Class	Representative Issue
I. Securities of the fixed-value type.	A high-grade bond or preferred stock.
II. Senior securities of the variable-value type.	
A. Well-protected issues with profit possibilities.	A high-grade convertible bond.
B. Inadequately protected issues.	A lower-grade bond or preferred stock.
III. Common-stock type.	A common stock.

An approximation to the above grouping could be reached by the use of more familiar terms, as follows:

I.   Investment bonds and preferred stocks.
II. Speculative bonds and preferred stocks.
    A. Convertibles, etc.
    B. Low-grade senior issues.
III. Common stocks.

The somewhat novel designations that we employ are needed to make our classification more comprehensive. This necessity will be clearer, perhaps, from the following description and discussion of each group.

Leading Characteristics of the Three Types. The first class includes issues, of whatever title, in which prospective change of value may fairly be said to hold minor importance.[5] The owner's dominant interest lies in the safety of his principal and his sole purpose in making the commitment is to obtain a steady income. In the second class, prospective changes in the value of the principal assume real significance. In Type *A*, the investor hopes to obtain the safety of a straight investment, with an added possibility of profit by reason of a conversion right or some similar privilege. In Type *B*, a definite risk of loss is recognized, which is presumably offset

---

[5] The actual fluctuations in the price of long-term investment bonds since 1914 have been so wide (see "Introduction to the Second Edition") as to suggest that these price changes must surely be of more than minor importance. It is true, nonetheless, that the investor habitually acts as *if* they were of minor importance to him, so that, subjectively at least, our criterion and title are justified. To the objection that this is conniving at self-delusion by the investor, we may answer that on the whole he is likely to fare better by overlooking the price variations of high-grade bonds than by trying to take advantage of them and thus transforming himself into a trader.

by a corresponding chance of profit. Securities included in Group II*B* will differ from the common-stock type (Group III) in two respects: (1) They enjoy an effective priority over some junior issue, thus giving them a certain degree of protection. (2) Their profit possibilities, however substantial, have a fairly definite limit, in contrast with the unlimited percentage of possible gain theoretically or optimistically associated with a fortunate common-stock commitment.

Issues of the fixed-value type include all *straight* bonds and preferred stocks of high quality selling at a normal price. Besides these, there belong in this class:

1. Sound convertible issues where the conversion level is too remote to enter as a factor in the purchase. (Similarly for participating or warrant-bearing senior issues.)
2. Guaranteed common stocks of investment grade.
3. "Class *A*" or prior-common stocks occupying the status of a high-grade, straight preferred stock.

On the other hand, a bond of investment grade which happens to sell at any unduly low price would belong in the second group, since the purchaser might have reason to expect and be interested in an appreciation of its market value.

Exactly at what point the question of price fluctuation becomes material rather than minor is naturally impossible to prescribe. The price level itself is not the sole determining factor. A long-term 3% bond selling at 60 may have belonged in the fixed-value class (*e.g.*, Northern Pacific Railway 3s, due 2047 between 1922 and 1930), whereas a one-year maturity of any coupon rate selling at 80 would *not* because in a comparatively short time it must either be paid off at a 20-point advance or else default and probably suffer a severe decline in market value. We must be prepared, therefore, to find marginal cases where the classification (as between Group I and Group II) will depend on the personal viewpoint of the analyst or investor.

Any issue which displays the main characteristics of a common stock belongs in Group III, whether it is entitled "common stock," "preferred stock" or even "bond." The case, already cited, of American Telephone and Telegraph Company Convertible 4$^{1}/_{2}$s, when selling about 200, provides an apposite example. The buyer or holder of the bond at so high a level was to all practical purposes making a commitment in the common stock, for the bond and stock would not only advance together but also decline together over an exceedingly wide price range. Still more definite illustration of this point was supplied by the Kreuger and Toll Participating Debentures at the time of their sale to the public. The offering price was so far above the amount of their prior claim that their title had no significance at all, and could only have been misleading. *These "bonds" were definitely of the common-stock type.*[6]

The opposite situation is met when issues, senior in name, sell at such low prices that the junior securities can obviously have no real equity, *i.e.*, ownership interest, in the company. In such cases, the low-priced bond or preferred stock stands virtually in the position of a common stock and should be regarded as such for purposes of analysis. A preferred stock selling at 10 cents on the dollar, for example, should be viewed not as a preferred stock at all, but as a common stock. On the one hand it lacks the prime requisite of a senior security, *viz.*, that it should be followed by a junior investment of substantial value. On the other hand, it carries all the profit features of a common stock, since the amount of possible gain from the current level is for all practical purposes unlimited.

The dividing line between Groups II and III is as indefinite as that between Groups I and II. Borderline cases can be handled without undue difficulty however, by considering them from the standpoint of either category or of both. For example, should a 7% preferred stock selling at 30 be considered a low-priced senior issue or as the equivalent of a common stock? The answer to this question will depend partly on the exhibit of the company and partly on the attitude of the prospective buyer. If real value may conceivably exist in excess of the par amount of the preferred stock, the issue may be granted some of the favored status of a senior security. On the other hand, whether or not the buyer should consider it in the same light as a common stock may also depend on whether he would be amply satisfied with a possible 250% appreciation, or is looking for even greater speculative gain.[7]

---

[6] See Appendix Note 5 for the terms of this issue.

[7] There were many preferred stocks of this kind in 1932—*e.g.*, Interstate Department Stores Preferred which sold at an average price of about 30 in 1932 and 1933 and then advanced to 107 in 1936 and 1937. A similar remark applies to low-priced bonds, such as those mentioned in the table Chap. 26.

From the foregoing discussion the real character and purpose of our classification should now be more evident. Its basis is not the title of the issue, but the practical significance of its specific terms and status to the owner. Nor is the primary emphasis placed upon what the owner is legally entitled to demand, but upon what he is likely to get, or is justified in expecting, under conditions which appear to be probable at the time of purchase or analysis.

PART II

Fixed-Value
Investments

Unshackling Bonds

by Howard S. Marks

My first exposure to *Security Analysis* came in 1965. As a Wharton undergraduate, I was assigned readings from the masterwork of Benjamin Graham and David Dodd (by that time, joined by editor Sidney Cottle).

These were the early days, when a career in investment management mostly meant working for a bank, a trust company, or an insurance company. The first institutional investment boutique that I remember—Jennison Associates—was still a few years away from its founding. Common stock investors referenced the Dow Jones Industrial Average, not the Standard & Poor's 500 or the Russell 3000, and there was no ranking of investment managers' performance by percentile. In fact, it was just a few years earlier, at the University of Chicago's Center for Research in Security Prices, that stock prices since 1926 had been digitized manually, permitting calculation of the 9.2% historic return on equities.

The term "growth stock investing" was relatively new (and in its absence, there had been no need for the contrasting term "value investing"). Hedge funds had yet to become a topic of popular discourse, and I'm not sure the term even existed. No one had ever heard of a venture capital fund, a private equity fund, an index fund, a quant fund, or an emerging markets fund. Even "famous investor" was largely an oxymoron—Warren Buffett hadn't yet become a celebrity, for example, and only a small circle of investing cognoscenti recognized the name of his teacher at Columbia, Ben Graham.

The world of fixed income bore little resemblance to that of today. There was no way for bondholders to avoid uncertainty regarding the rate at which interest payments could be reinvested, because zero-coupon bonds had not been invented. Bonds rated below investment grade couldn't be issued as such (rating agency Moody's described a B-rated bond as "fails to possess the characteristics of a desirable investment"). The low-rated bonds that were outstanding were "fallen angels"—former investment-grade bonds whose issuers had gotten into trouble and been downgraded—and they had yet to be labeled "junk" or "high yield" bonds. Of course, there were no leveraged loans, mortgage-backed securities (MBSs), or collateralized bond, debt, and loan obligations. Today's bond professionals might give some thought to how their predecessors arrived at yields to maturity before the existence of computers, calculators, or Bloomberg terminals.

I'm lucky to have begun my studies in the mid-1960s, because the finance and investment theory I would go on to learn at the University of Chicago Graduate School of Business was new and hadn't yet spread broadly. Thus my time spent at Wharton didn't include exposure to the Efficient Market Hypothesis, which told the next few generations of students of finance that there was no use for *Security Analysis*: a guidebook to the impossible task of beating the market.

• • •

I learned a lot from this book, which was generally accepted in 1965 as "the bible of security analysis" and still is. Yet I came away with a negative reaction as well, feeling that it contained too much dogma and too many formulas incorporating numerical constants like "multiply by x" or "count only y years."

My recent rereading of the chapters on fixed-income securities in the 1940 edition of *Security Analysis* served to remind me of some of the rules I had found too rigid. But it also showed me the vast wealth of less quantitative and more flexible common sense the book contained, as well as some of the forward-looking insights.

To my mind, some of the most interesting aspects of the book—and of developments in the investment world over the last several decades—are seen in Graham and Dodd's perspective on the evolution of investment standards.

- At least through 1940, there were well-accepted and very specific criteria for what was proper and what was not, especially in fixed income. Laws, rules, and traditions governed the actions of fiduciaries and the things they could and could not do. In this environment, a fiduciary who lost money for beneficiaries in a nonqualifying investment could be "surcharged"—forced to make good the losses—without reference to how well they did their job overall or whether the whole portfolio made money. Understandably, these conditions caused a strong emphasis on excluding risky assets from fiduciary portfolios.

- Subsequently, the law accepted the concept of the "prudent man," based on a nineteenth-century court case. The test now was whether this was something a prudent person would do, judged in the light of the circumstances under which the decision was made and in the context of the portfolio as a whole. Thus individual losing investments need not give rise to penalties if the fiduciary's decisions and results were acceptable *in toto*. The prudent man rule was highly evolved in comparison to the outright ban on risk-taking that had preceded it.

- Harry Markowitz was a leading contributor to the finance theory we attribute to "Chicago School." In the 1950s, based on the risk presented by highly correlated assets, he pointed out that the addition of a "risky" asset to a portfolio can reduce the portfolio's overall riskiness by increasing its diversification.

- Finally, the ultimate contribution of the Chicago School came through the assertion that the "goodness" of an investment—and of a performance record—should be evaluated based on the relationship between its return and its risk. A safe investment is not necessarily a good investment, and a risky investment is not necessarily a bad investment. Good-enough performance prospects can compensate for the riskiness of a risky investment, rendering it both attractive and prudent.

Through this process, the practice of investing evolved from risk avoidance to risk management. Today we see few absolute rules of investing. In fact, it's hard to think of anything that's off-limits, and most investors will do almost anything to make a buck. The 1940 edition of *Security Analysis* marks an interesting turn toward what we would consider very modern thinking—it references some absolute standards, but dismisses many others and reflects an advanced attitude toward sensible fixed-income investing.

INVESTMENT ABSOLUTES

The 1940 edition certainly contains statements that seem inflexible. Here are some examples:

> Deficient safety cannot be compensated for by an abnormally high coupon rate. The selection of all bonds for investment should be subject to rules of exclusion and to specific quantitative tests. (Chap. 6)

> If a company's junior bonds are not safe, its first-mortgage bonds are not a desirable fixed-value investment. For if the second mortgage is unsafe, the company itself is weak, and generally speaking there can be no high-grade obligations of a weak enterprise. (Chap. 6)

Bonds of smaller industrial companies are not well qualified for consideration as fixed-value investments. (Chap. 7)

When I began to manage high yield bonds in 1978, most institutional portfolios were governed by rules that limited bond holdings to either "investment grade" (rated triple-B or better) or "A or better." Rules like these, which put certain securities off-limits to most buyers regardless of price, had the effect of making bargains available to the few of us who weren't so restricted. At first glance, Graham and Dodd's proscriptions would seem to be among those rules.

INVESTMENT VERSUS SPECULATION

As I reread the chapters in this edition, I came across several statements like these, to the effect that some bond is or is not appropriate for investment. No mention of price or yield; just yes or no . . . good or bad. To someone whose career in portfolio management has dealt almost exclusively with below-investment-grade assets, this would seem to rule out whole sections of the investment universe. The ideas that potential return can compensate for risk, and that the debt of a financially troubled company can become so cheap that it's a screaming buy, appear to fight the authors' principles.

Then I looked again, and it dawned on me that Graham and Dodd were saying one thing and I was reading another—and that a good deal of the gap was a matter of language. Graham and Dodd didn't mean that something shouldn't be bought, but rather that it shouldn't be bought, to use their phrase, "on an investment basis." That was an important distinction 80 years ago. Today people attach the word "investment" to anything purchased for the purpose of financial gain, as opposed to something bought for use or consumption. People invest today in not just stocks and bonds, but also in jewelry, vacation-home timeshares, collectibles, art, and cryptocurrencies. But 80 years ago, "investing" meant something very different: the purchase of financial assets that by their intrinsic nature satisfied the requirements of conservatism, prudence, and above all, safety. In particular, investing was differentiated from "speculating," a word we rarely hear these days.

Among the online definitions for "speculation," I found secondary definitions like this one: "to engage in any business transaction involving considerable risk or the chance of large gains, especially to buy and sell commodities, stocks, etc., in the expectation of a quick or very large profit" (dictionary.com). To me, that definition doesn't provide a sufficient sense for what distinguishes speculating from investing. I think it's more helpful to look to primary definitions for "speculation" that aren't confined to the word's application in investing: "to think about something and make guesses about it: to form ideas or theories about something usually when there are many things not known about it" (https://www.britannica.com/dictionary) and "reasoning based on inconclusive evidence; conjecture or supposition" (thefreedictionary.com). Perhaps a full appreciation for the word can best be derived from some of the synonyms offered by Merriam-Webster: "chance," "gamble," "flier," and "crapshoot."

In Graham and Dodd's day, securities qualified for investment on the basis of quality, not prospective return. They either were of high-enough quality to be eligible for investment or they weren't. In the extreme, there were hard-and-fast rules, such as those promulgated by each of the states for its savings banks. In New York, for example, savings banks could buy railroad, gas, and electric bonds, but not the bonds of streetcar railway or water companies. Bonds secured by first mortgages on real estate qualified as investments, but—startlingly— industrial bonds did not.

Investments that hewed to the accepted standards were considered "safe" (and probably litigation-proof for the fiduciary who bought them), while speculating was chancy. It was this rigid, exclusionary, black-and-white attitude toward investment propriety that likely led John Maynard Keynes to his trenchant observation that "a speculator is one who runs risks of which he is aware, and an investor is one who runs risks of which he is unaware."[1]

A more modern attitude—and, like Keynes's, well ahead of its time—would be based on the notion that virtually any asset can be a good investment if bought knowledgeably and at a low-enough price. The opposite is also something that I insist is true: there is no asset so good that it can't be a bad investment if bought at too high a price. Everyone now realizes that membership on a list of "acceptable investments" certainly doesn't provide protection against loss. If you don't agree with that statement, try looking for the 40 or so corporate bonds that were rated AAA when I was in college. or the enormous numbers of tranched mortgage-backed securities that received AAA ratings in the lead-up to the Global Financial Crisis of 2007–2009, but were downgraded and eventually recovered less than par.

In *Security Analysis*, the principle is developed and reiterated that "a high coupon rate is not adequate compensation for the assumption of substantial risk of principal." (Chap. 9) This statement would seem to rule out investing in high yield bonds, which has been successfully pursued over the last 45 years with absolute and risk-adjusted returns well above those on investment-grade bonds. A more thorough reading, however, shows that securities that the authors say should not be purchased "on an investment basis" can still be considered "for speculation." Nevertheless, today Graham and Dodd's blanket statement certainly seems doctrinaire—especially in that it implements a distinction that has almost entirely ceased to exist. The statement that certain assets either are or are not appropriate for purchase on an investment basis is probably one of the dicta to which I reacted

---

[1] John Maynard Keynes, *The General Theory of Employment, Interest and Money*, London: Macmillan, 1936, p. 153.

negatively 57 years ago. But now, in this rereading, I was able to see further.

INVESTMENT REALISM

Over the last five or six decades, the investment world has seen the development of what could be described as a much more pragmatic approach to making money: judging investment merit not on absolute notions of quality and safety—or on descriptions such as "investment grade" or "speculative"—but rather on the relationship between expected return and expected risk. Alternatively, of course, this could be described as a lowering of standards; what ever happened to concepts like fiduciary duty and preservation of capital?

Graham and Dodd seem to operate in a middle ground. They propound absolute requirements for purchases on an investment basis, but they also admit that apparent quality and safety alone shouldn't be expected to make some things successful investments or rule out others. Here are several examples:

> [Given that fixed-income securities lack the upside potential of equities,] "the essence of proper bond selection consists, therefore, in obtaining specific and convincing factors of safety in compensation for the surrender of participation in profits." (Chap. 6) [Fixed-income investing can't be expected to work if creditworthiness isn't there.]

> "The conception of a mortgage lien as a guaranty of protection independent of the success of the business itself is in most cases a complete fallacy. . . . The established practice of stating the original cost or appraised value of the pledged property as an inducement to purchase bonds is entirely misleading." (Chap. 6) [To be creditworthy, securities must be backed by cash flows or assets with real current value.]

> "The debentures [unsecured bonds] of a strong enterprise are undoubtedly sounder investments than the mortgage issues of a weak company." (Chap. 6) [Labels alone mean nothing.]

"It is clear . . . that the investor who favors the Cudahy first-lien 5s
[yielding 5½ versus the junior 5½'s yielding over 20%] is paying a
premium of about 15% per annum (the difference in yield) for only a
partial insurance against loss. On this basis he is undoubtedly giving up
too much for what he gets in return. . . . [On the other hand,] where
the first-mortgage bond yields only slightly less, it is undoubtedly wise
to pay the small insurance premium for protection against unexpected
trouble." (Chap. 6) [What matters is the relationship between the risk
borne and the potential return to be received.]

[In reviewing bond collapses among railroads between 1931 and 1933,]
"the fault appears to be that the stability of the transportation industry
was overrated, so that investors were satisfied with a margin of
protection which proved insufficient. *It was not a matter of imprudently
disregarding old established standards of safety . . . but of being content
with old standards when conditions called for more stringent
requirements.* . . . If [the investor] had required his railroad bonds to
meet the same tests that he applied to industrial issues, he would have
been compelled to confine his selection to a relatively few of the strongly
situated lines. As it turned out, nearly all of these have been able to
withstand the tremendous loss of traffic since 1929 without danger to
their fixed charges." (Chap. 7, emphasis added) [Issuers can't be
assumed to be stable and unchanging; the potential for deterioration
and disruption must be considered (certainly now more than ever).]

It is clear that Graham and Dodd are insistent on substance over
form, and on logic rather than rules. Credit standards must not be
fixed but instead must change as the world changes. It's how likely a
bond is to pay that matters, not what it's labeled. Mortgages are not
automatically better than unsecured debentures. Senior bonds are not
necessarily better buys than their juniors. Superior yield *can* render
riskier issues more attractive than ostensibly safer ones.

Although the stilted language of 80 years ago initially masks this
point, a thorough reading makes it clear that Graham and Dodd are
true investment pragmatists. More echoing Keynes than diverging

from him, they argue for in-depth analysis followed by intelligent risk bearing (as opposed to knee-jerk risk avoidance).

OUR METHODOLOGY FOR BOND INVESTING

To examine the relevance of *Security Analysis* to fixed-income investments, I reviewed Graham and Dodd's process for bond investing, and I compared their approach to the one applied by my firm, Oaktree Capital Management, L.P. The bottom line is that, while Graham and Dodd's thoughts may be expressed differently, most are highly applicable to today's investment world. In fact, they strongly parallel the approach and methodology developed and applied in the area of high yield bonds over the last 45 years by my partner, Sheldon Stone, and me.

1. *Our entire approach is based on recognition of the asymmetry that underlies all non-distressed bond investing.* Gains on fixed-income securities are limited to the promised yield plus perhaps a few points of appreciation, while credit losses can cause most or all of one's principal to be lost. The key to success lies in avoiding losers, not in searching for winners. As Graham and Dodd note:

   Instead of associating bonds primarily with the presumption of *safety* . . . it would be sounder to start with what is not presumption but fact, *viz.*, that a (straight) bond is an investment with *limited return.* . . .
   Our primary conception of the bond as a commitment with limited return leads us to another important viewpoint toward bond investment. Since the chief emphasis must be placed on avoidance of loss, bond selection is primarily a negative art. It is a process of exclusion and rejection, rather than of search and acceptance. (Chap. 6)

2. *Our high yield bond portfolios are tightly focused.* We work mostly in that part of the curve that we consider the "sweet spot," centered around B-rated bonds, where healthy yields can be earned, and the

risk of default is limited. For us, higher-rated bonds don't have enough yield, and lower-rated bonds have too much uncertainty. This single-B zone is where our clients expect us to operate. (Of course, we have to be ready to alter our focus should risk/return relationships change.)

It would be sounder procedure to start with minimum standards of safety, which all bonds must be required to meet . . . Essentially, bond selection should consist of working upward from definite minimum standards rather than working downward in haphazard fashion from some ideal but overly restrictive level of maximum security. (Chap. 7)

3. *Credit risk stems primarily from the quantum of leverage and the firm's basic instability, the interaction of which in tough times can erode the margin by which interest coverage exceeds debt service requirements.* A company with very stable cash flows can support high leverage and heavy debt service. By the same token, a company with limited leverage and modest debt service requirements can survive severe fluctuations in its cash flow. But the combination of high leverage and undependable cash flow can result in a failure to service debt, as investors are reminded painfully from time to time. Graham and Dodd cite the very same elements.

Studying the 1931–1933 record, we note that price collapses [among industrial bonds] were not due primarily to unsound financial structures, as in the case of utility bonds, nor to a miscalculation by investors as to the margin of safety needed, as in the case of railroad bonds. We are confronted in many cases by a sudden disappearance of earning power, and a disconcerting question as to whether the business can survive. (Chap. 7)

4. *Analysis of individual issues calls for a multifaceted approach.* Since 1985, my team of analysts has applied an eight-factor credit analysis process developed by Sheldon Stone. Most of the elements are reflected in—perhaps ultimately were inspired by—aspects of

Graham and Dodd's thinking. Our concerns are with industry, company standing within the industry, quality of management, interest coverage, capital structure, alternative sources of liquidity, liquidation value, and covenants. *Security Analysis* reflects many of these same concerns.

> *On company standing:* "The experience of the past decade indicates that dominant or at least substantial size affords an element of protection against the hazards of instability." (Chap. 7)
>
> *On interest coverage:* "The present-day investor is accustomed to regard the ratio of earnings to interest charges as the most important specific test of safety." (Chap. 9)
>
> *On capital structure:* "The biggest company may be the weakest if its bonded debt is disproportionately large." (Chap. 7)

5. *"Buy-and-hold" investing is inconsistent with the responsibilities of the professional investor, and the creditworthiness of every issuer represented in the portfolio must be revisited no less than quarterly.*

Even before the market collapse of 1929, the danger ensuing from neglect of investments previously made, and the need for periodic scrutiny or supervision of all holdings, had been recognized as a new canon in Wall Street. This principle, directly opposed to the former practice, is frequently summed up in the dictum, "There are no permanent investments." (Chap. 21)

6. *Don't engage in market timing based on economic and interest rate forecasts.* Instead, we confine our efforts to "knowing the knowable," which can result only from superior efforts to understand industries, companies, and securities.

It is doubtful if trading in bonds, to catch the market swings, can be carried on successfully by the investor. . . . We are sceptical of the ability of any paid agency to provide reliable forecasts of the market action of either bonds or stocks. Furthermore we are convinced that any combined effort to advise upon the choice of individual high-grade investments and upon the course of bond *prices* is fundamentally illogical and confusing. Much as the investor would like to be able to buy at just the right time and to sell out when prices are about to fall, experience shows that he is not likely to be brilliantly successful in such efforts and that by injecting the trading element into his investment operations he will . . . inevitably shift his interest into speculative directions. (Chap. 21)

7. *Despite our best efforts, defaults will creep into our portfolios, whether due to failings in credit analysis or bad luck.* For the incremental yield gained from taking risks to regularly exceed the losses incurred as a result of defaults, individual holdings must be small enough so that a single default won't dissipate a large amount of the portfolio's capital. We have always thought of our approach to risk as being akin to that of an insurance company. In order for the actuarial process to work, the risk must be spread over many small holdings and the expected return given a chance to prove out. Thus you should not invest in high yield bonds unless your portfolio can be thoroughly diversified.

The [individual] investor cannot prudently turn himself into an insurance company and incur risks of losing his principal in exchange for annual premiums in the form of extra-large interest coupons. One objection to such a policy is that sound insurance practice requires a very wide distribution of risk, in order to minimize the influence of luck and to allow maximum play to the law of probability. The investor may endeavor to attain this end by diversifying his holdings, but as a practical matter, he cannot approach the division of risk attained by an insurance company. (Chap. 7)

To wrap up the subject of investment approach, we feel the successful assumption of credit risk in the fixed-income universe depends on the successful assessment of the company's future ability to service its debts. Extensive financial statement analysis is not nearly as important as a few skilled judgments regarding the company's prospects.

> The selection of a fixed-value security for limited-income return should be, relatively, at least, a simple operation. The investor must make certain by quantitative tests that the income has been amply above the interest charges and that the current value of the business is well in excess of its debts. In addition, he must be satisfied in his own judgment that the character of the enterprise is such as to promise continued success in the future, or more accurately speaking, to make failure a highly unlikely occurrence. (Chap. 12)

In the end, though, we diverge from Graham and Dodd in one important way. In selecting bonds for purchase, we make judgments about the issuers' prospects, and here's why: when I began to analyze and manage high yield bonds in 1978, the widely held view was that investing in bonds and assessing the future are fundamentally incompatible, and that prudent bond investing must be based on solid inferences drawn from past and present data, as opposed to "speculation" regarding future events. But credit risk is prospective, and thus substantial credit risk can be borne intelligently only on the basis of skilled judgments about the future.

In large part, the old position represented a prejudice: that buying stocks—an inherently riskier proposition—can be done intelligently on the basis of judgments regarding the future, but depending on those same judgments in the more conservative world of bond investing just isn't right. Some of the greatest—and most profitable—market inefficiencies I have encountered have been the result of prejudices that walled off certain opportunities from "proper investing," and thus left them for flexible investors to pick off at prices far below their fair value. This seems to be one of these prejudices.

One of the reasons I was chosen to start First National City Bank's high yield bond operation in 1978 was my immediately prior experience as the bank's director of research for equities. All I had to do, then, was apply the future-oriented process for analyzing common stocks to the universe of bonds rated below triple-B. Few walls still stand in the investment world today, and it is widely understood that forward-looking analysis can be profitably applied to instruments of all sorts. That lesson remained to be learned in 1940.

COMMON SENSE

Much of the value of *Security Analysis* lies not in its specific instructions, but in its common sense. Several of its lessons have specific relevance to the present. More important, Graham and Dodd's insight and thought process show how investors should try to dig beneath customary, superficial answers to investment questions.

> "Security prices and yields are not determined by any exact mathematical calculation of the expected risk, but they depend rather upon the popularity of the issue." (Chap. 7) [Markets are not clinically efficient.]

> "It may be pointed out further that the supposed actuarial computation of investment risks is out of the question theoretically as well as in practice. There are no experience tables available by which the expected "mortality" of various types of issues can be determined. Even if such tables were prepared, based on long and exhaustive studies of past records, it is doubtful whether they would have any real utility for the future. In life insurance, the relation between age and mortality rate is well defined and changes only gradually. The same is true, to a much lesser extent, of the relation between the various types of structures and the fire hazard attaching to them. But the relation between different types of investments and the risk of loss is entirely too indefinite, and too variable with changing conditions, to permit of sound mathematical formulation. This is particularly true because investment losses are not distributed fairly evenly in

point of time, but tend to be concentrated at intervals, *i.e.*, during periods of general depression. Hence the typical investment hazard is roughly similar to the conflagration or epidemic hazard, which is the exceptional and incalculable factor in fire or life insurance." (Chap. 7, emphasis added) [So much for assessing risk and the adequacy of return on the basis of supposedly reliable quantitative models.]

"Among [the aspects of the earnings picture to which the investor would do well to pay attention] are the *trend*, the *minimum* figure, and the *current* figure. The importance of each of these cannot be gainsaid, but they do not lend themselves effectively to the application of hard and fast rules." (Chap. 9)

"The investor . . . will be *attracted* by: (a) a rising trend in profits; (b) an especially good current showing; and (c) a satisfactory margin over interest charges in *every* year during the period studied. If a bond is deficient in any one of these three aspects, the result should not necessarily be to condemn the issue but rather to exact an average earnings coverage well in excess of the minimum and to require closer attention to the general or qualitative elements in the situation." (Chap. 9)

"If [a ratio of] $1 of stock to $1 of bonds is taken as the 'normal' requirement for an industrial company, would it not be sound to demand, say, a $2-to-$1 ratio when stock prices are inflated, and conversely to be satisfied with a 50-cent-to-$1 ratio when quotations are far below intrinsic values? But this suggestion is impracticable for two reasons, the first being that it implies that the bond buyer can recognize an unduly high or low level of stock prices, which is far too complimentary an assumption. The second is that it would require bond investors to act with especial caution when things are booming and with greater confidence when times are hard. This is a counsel of perfection which it is not in human nature to follow. Bond buyers are people, and they cannot be expected to escape entirely either the enthusiasm of bull markets or the apprehensions of a severe depression." (Chap. 11)

"In the purely speculative field the objection to paying for advice is that if the adviser *knew* whereof he spoke he would not need to bother with a consultant's duties." (Chap. 21) [This isn't much different from Warren Buffett's observation that "Wall Street is the only place that people ride to in a Rolls-Royce to get advice from those who take the subway."[2]]

There are many instances in which Graham and Dodd offer commonsense advice or even more interestingly, in which they refute existing rules of investing, substituting common sense for "accepted wisdom," that great oxymoron. To me, this represents the greatest strength of the section on fixed-income securities. In the end, Graham and Dodd remind us, "Investment theory should be chary of easy generalizations." (Chap. 8)

SECURITY ANALYSIS THROUGH THE YEARS

Many of Graham and Dodd's specific ideas have withstood the test of time and in fact been picked up and carried forward by others.

- Their observation that "an investor may reject any number of good bonds with virtually no penalty at all" (Chap. 6) may have inspired Warren Buffett, who draws a very apt comparison to batters in baseball. Buffett reportedly commented that a baseball hitter will be called out if he fails to swing at three pitches in the strike zone, while an investor can let any number of investment opportunities go by without being penalized.

- Likewise, Graham and Dodd submitted that "the best criterion that we are able to offer [for the purpose of assessing the margin of assets over indebtedness] is the ratio of the *market value* of the capital stock to the total funded debt." (Chap. 11) This was paralleled by the market-adjusted debt (MAD) ratios popularized by Michael Milken, when he pioneered the issuance of high yield

---

[2] *Los Angeles Times Magazine*, April 7, 1991.

bonds at Drexel Burnham Lambert in the 1970s and 1980s. Market values are far from perfect, but accounting data are purely historical and are often out-of-date at best and irrelevant at worst.

- Importantly, Graham and Dodd highlight the importance of cash flow stability in a company's ability to service its debts in an adverse environment. "Once it is admitted—as it always must be—that the industry can suffer *some* reduction in profits, then the investor is compelled to estimate the possible extent of the shrinkage and compare it with the surplus above the interest requirements. He thus finds himself . . . vitally concerned with the ability of the company to meet the vicissitudes of the future." (Chap. 7) This consideration contributed to the fact that, in its infancy in the mid-1970s, the leveraged buyout industry restricted its purchases to noncyclical companies and avoided high-tech firms. Like all important investment principles, this one is often ignored in bullish periods, as enthusiasm and optimism gain sway and the stable-cash-flow rule can be easily forgotten.

ADDITIONAL THOUGHTS

In considering the relevance 83 years later of the 1940 edition of *Security Analysis*, a number of additional observations deserve to be made.

First, most of the timing that interested Graham and Dodd concerned "depressions" and their impact on creditworthiness. They cite three depressions—1920 to 1922, 1930 to 1933, and 1937 to 1938—whereas we talk today about there having been only one in the twentieth century: the Great Depression. Clearly, Graham and Dodd included under this heading what we call "recessions."

Second, they were not concerned with predicting interest rate fluctuations. The primary reason for this may be that interest rates didn't fluctuate as much in those days. A table in Chap. 6 shows, for example, that in the 13 years from 1926 to 1938—a period that sandwiched a famous boom between two "depressions"—the yield on 40 utility bonds moved only between 3.9% and 6.3%. At the time the 1940 edition was published, interest rates had been low and fairly steady for years.

Third, it is important to note that several of Graham and Dodd's warnings against risk taking are directed not at professionals, but at the individual investors who appear to have been the authors' target audience.

"As a practical matter it is not so easy to distinguish in advance between the underlying bonds that come through reorganization unscathed and those which suffer drastic treatment. Hence the ordinary investor may be well advised to leave such issues out of his calculations and stick to the rule that only strong companies have strong bonds." (Chap. 6)

"The individual is not qualified to be an insurance underwriter. It is not his function to be paid for incurring risks; on the contrary it is to his interest to pay others for insurance against loss. . . . Even assuming that the high coupon rates [on higher yielding securities] will, in the great aggregate, more than compensate on an *actuarial* basis for the risks accepted, such bonds are still undesirable investments from the *personal* standpoint of the average investor." (Chap. 7)

Thus concern for the safety of nonprofessional investors appears to be at the root of many of *Security Analysis*'s most rigid dicta. I would not differ with the proposition that direct investment in distressed debt and high yield bonds should be left to professionals. If they want exposure to this market sector—as well as to many others—people lacking the necessary expertise would be best off investing in diversified high yield bond ETFs or some other vehicle for investing passively.

AN EVOLVING MARKET

The investing world is mainly about money, of course. Companies need financing to operate, and in obtaining it they look to minimize cost and maximize flexibility. Investment bankers are in business to aid in that process, for a fee. Investors supply the needed capital, and they look to earn returns and outperform other investors. Investment managers invest the capital of their clients, also for a fee. All parties are financially motivated.

The human mind is a creative organ, always looking for something better, faster, and more profitable. Given the high level of motivation, considerable brainpower is applied to financial challenges, and the result is financial innovation. Wall Street constantly invents new securities and techniques, which are regularly heralded as seminal advances and surefire solutions. Some prove out when tested in hostile economic environments, and some are defrocked.

Because of this tendency toward evolution, the fixed-income market of today is nearly unrecognizable from what it looked like when the 1940 edition of *Security Analysis* was written. Even in just the period since 2009, when I first updated the section on "fixed-value" investing for a new edition, our markets have continued to evolve. For those who are intellectually curious and interested in new subjects to conquer, this is one of the great benefits of being an investor.

I described the transition of investing from the rules-bound pursuit of quality and safety to the flexible maximization of risk-adjusted returns, and thus from risk avoidance to the intelligent bearing of risk for profit. These developments have contributed to substantial change in the fixed-income markets, in ways Graham and Dodd could never have foreseen. I want to close this section by describing some of them.

"Fixed-value" is the term Graham and Dodd used to describe investing in debt securities. Over time, that morphed into "fixed income." Even that latter term is heard less often these days, perhaps because the popularity of floating rate securities and the importance of changes in creditworthiness have rendered our turf much less "fixed."

Today, the term we hear more often is "credit," which refers to all fixed-income securities other than debt of governments. The term "credit" might be viewed as shorthand for "debt where the issuer's creditworthiness matters," a reminder that repayment is less than 100% certain in nongovernment securities—more so in some cases than others.

When I joined First National City Bank in 1969, the fixed-income securities we heard about most were bonds. They were overseen there by two bond veterans; their area became a backwater as equities soared, and they ceased publishing bond data when their readership disappeared in the 1970s. Investment-grade bonds were paid little attention over the next few decades.

Attention was paid, however, to the high yield, or sub-investment grade, bonds that began to be issued around 1977–1978. These securities offered yields well above those on investment-grade bonds, they financed a new industry in leveraged buyouts (now called "private equity"), and they exemplified the practice of buying risky securities if they appear to offer more-than-commensurate returns.

Prior to the turn of the century, the word "loans" mostly meant "bank loans," which the lead bank originated and perhaps syndicated to (i.e., shared with) a few other banks. Publicly issued "senior loans," "leveraged loans," or "floating rate loans" began to appear in the early 2000s. These new debt securities are issued by non-investment-grade companies just like high yield bonds; are senior in rank, not subordinated; provide yields that are slightly below those on high yield bonds (due to their seniority); and are characterized by interest rates that float, tied to benchmarks such as LIBOR or SOFR.

Most banks were chastened in the Global Financial Crisis and tightly regulated afterward, such that they were less willing to lend money. This created a vacuum, which nonbank lenders began to fill around 2011. As a result, "private debt" or "direct lending" has become an important asset class, entailing illiquidity, but also higher interest rates in compensation therefore.

Many of the innovations in credit brought hopes for increased absolute returns or risk-adjusted returns. However, many of those perceived improvements were accompanied by declines in marketability or liquidity. In times of market upset, selling lower-grade debt securities is more difficult and entails accepting big discounts from the previous price. Private debt is, by definition, salable only in off-market transactions, which can become hard to engineer in tough times.

In the past, bonds were considered more prone to price fluctuation the more time remaining to maturity. More recently, bond investors' focus has shifted from maturity to "duration," or the number of years until half the discounted value of the future cash flows will have been realized. Because bondholders must wait longer on average to get cash from a 2% 10-year bond than from a 10% 10-year bond, for example, the 2% bond has a longer duration and is expected to fluctuate more in response to a given change in interest rates, even though its maturity is the same.

Because of the role of the ups and downs of interest rates in causing bond depreciation and appreciation, until 20 to 30 years ago many bond investors were "interest rate anticipators," predicting interest rate movements based on the business cycle. Now, they pay more attention the actions of the Federal Reserve and to corporate developments (because more debt securities come from low-grade companies and thus are greatly affected by changes in their issuers' creditworthiness).

In the distant past, bonds were bought primarily to diversify portfolios and provide steady income. Today many people buy them for total return and/or trade them actively for short-term profits, just as with equities.

Today, given that investors care about total return, the distinction between income and appreciation is accorded less importance. People are perfectly happy spending some of the appreciation on securities that don't provide income, and income is often retained in the hope of generating subsequent appreciation.

These days, debt securities aren't only purchased, but also sold short to bet on negative developments, or arbitraged to take advantage of price anomalies.

Today, an investor can place bets on the future direction of interest rates, the broad debt market, or subsets of the market without ever transacting in debt securities themselves. Rather, investment banks are happy to sell derivatives, baskets, and synthetics that mirror the performance of the assets in question.

Recent decades have brought the creation of "structured," or "tranched," debt securities. These include securities backed by mortgages on residential or commercial properties; asset-backed securities collateralized by things such as credit card receivables; and collateralized loan obligations backed by portfolios of senior loans. The various tranches of these securities have repayment priorities ranging from senior to junior, and thus varying levels of riskiness. The assets backing the junior tranches render the seniors overcollateralized, and the capital from buyers of the lower-yielding senior tranches levers up the potential returns to the holders of the junior tranches. (These structured debt securities are particularly complex, and it was mostly underestimation of the riskiness of sub-prime mortgage-backed securities that led to the Global Financial Crisis.)

When below-investment-grade bonds began to be publicly issued in the 1970s, they usually carried "covenants": representations from (or limitations on) the issuers that would protect bondholders from potentially deleterious actions on the issuers' part. But investors became more comfortable with risky debt over the years, and more recently heavy inflows of capital created a seller's market in which investors were forced to compete for the opportunity to provide financing by accepting lower yields or increased risk. In the process, covenants are mostly gone from new loans, meaning lenders came to enjoy less protection.

Before I leave the topic of changes we've seen, I want to mention one of the most significant: the downtrend in interest rates that has prevailed over the working lives of most of today's investors. In the 1970s, I took out a personal loan from a bank at "three-quarters over prime," and I've framed the slip from 1980 notifying me that the interest rate had risen to 22¼%. Forty years later, in 2020, I was able to borrow at 2%. The 2,000-basis-point decline in rates was the result of the low level of inflation over the period. Because lower rates mean higher discounted values for future cash flows—and less competition from bonds against other assets, enhancing the value of the latter—this rate decline was a massive tailwind behind the returns enjoyed by all investors, not just those in fixed income. We saw the return of inflation in 2021–2022, and corresponding drops in the prices of bonds and most other assets. Readers in future years will know more about the continuation of this trend and its ramifications than I do as of this writing.

Finally, if you've wanted to keep abreast of the fixed–income markets, you had to constantly learn new terminology. I'm confident Graham and Dodd would have no idea what today's investors are saying:

"I'm long duration," meaning "The duration of my portfolio is longer than average, meaning I'm betting that interest rates will fall and bond prices will rise."

"I'm short spreads," meaning "I believe the spread by which the yield on high yield bonds exceeds the yield on Treasury bonds—which results from perceived corporate credit risk—will increase in the future. That means the prices of risky bonds will fall."

"I'm long credit," meaning "My bond portfolio is overweighted in corporate bonds relative to government bonds, meaning I think positive trends in economic growth and corporate profits will cause corporates to outperform."

"I trade rates," meaning "I deal in government debt and anything related to it, such as inflation-indexed bonds, futures, forwards, options, swaps, and swaptions [don't ask]."

LOOKING BACK

I was exceptionally fortunate to participate in the credit markets over the last 45 years and to have benefited, first from the emergence of markets most others failed to capitalize on, and second from the popularization of these markets after I found them and staked my position. The result has been steady employment and untold intellectual satisfaction.

In dealing with these emergent markets, with their appearance of riskiness, my Oaktree partners and I chose to build a firm that would emphasize risk control, consistency, long-term investment, and limits on the amount of capital we would manage. We also insisted on creating a culture that would emphasize these things. In sum, we tried to offer a "low-risk option," giving clients a way to participate with less-than-full risk. Our motto at Oaktree's founding was "if we avoid the losers, the winners will take care of themselves," and that remains our lodestar, putting a high priority on risk consciousness even now that we've added a number of "aspirational" strategies that demand that winners be found.

We've made only modest claims regarding what our results would be in good times. After all, everyone makes a lot of money in good times, and I've never understood the need for outperformance in good times (given that pursuing it usually requires an investor to carry above-average risk). Instead, we've emphasized outperformance in bad times: it's really then that outperformance is essential. It's also in bad times—usually marked by large number of defaults—that selectivity and highly proficient credit research can best add value through the avoidance of holdings that are negatively affected.

Another way in which I've been fortunate was to have been an investor in credit over the course of the 40-year, 2,000-basis-point decline of interest rates and the resulting bull market in credit assets. I didn't do anything to produce that bull market, and I didn't foresee it; I was merely in the right market at the right time. But the salutary impact of declining interest rates must not be underestimated or the resulting returns misattributed.

When I look back at the period in which my partners and I have invested, we could have been more aggressive than we were. We could have taken more risk. We could have actively pursued more winners and taken a chance on more iffy credits. We could have put more faith in the Fed to keep the economy growing and the markets aloft. Given how benign the investment climate turned out to be in this period overall, doing these things may well have led to higher returns. I'm unlikely to get a chance to find out if they will constitute a winning approach for the years ahead, however, as Oaktree isn't likely to change its spots in this regard.

Prevailing conditions truly have combined to make the last 45 years in the credit market the "best of times." Credit investors have benefited from economic growth, declining default rates, low inflation, the downtrend in interest rates, and the increased popularity of credit assets. Will the coming years be as kind? There's no way to know. But I think we can all agree that we're unlikely to see much more in the way of interest rate declines, given today's historic lows, meaning there won't be a significant tailwind from that source. In addition, the credit market, like most others, is now much more "efficient," meaning it'll be harder to find as many bargains as we did in the past. As I say in response to most questions about the macro future, "We'll see."

• • •

The market for debt securities, like all aspects of investing—and, in fact, most areas of human endeavor—has evolved greatly and is sure to continue to do so. How-to books written to treat the questions of the day may be immediately helpful, but they're unlikely to remain relevant for long. On the other hand, the 1940 edition of *Security Analysis* contains wisdom for the ages, applicable at the time it was written as well as today and tomorrow. Importantly, it shows the reader how to think about investing, which is more valuable than what to think. I'm sure it will remain a bible of investing for years to come.

CHAPTER 6

The Selection of
Fixed-Value Investments

HAVING SUGGESTED a classification of securities by character rather than
by title, we now take up in order the principles and methods of selection
applicable to each group. We have already stated that the fixed-value
group includes:

1. High-grade straight bonds and preferred stocks.
2. High-grade privileged issues, where the value of the privilege is too
   remote to count as a factor in selection.
3. Common stocks which through guaranty or preferred status
   occupy the position of a high-grade senior issue.

Basic Attitude Toward High-Grade Preferred Stocks. By placing gilt-
edged preferred stocks and high-grade bonds in a single group, we indicate that the same investment attitude and the same general method of
analysis are applicable to both types. The very definite inferiority of the
preferred stockholders' legal claim is here left out of account, for the logical reason that the soundness of the best investments must rest not upon
legal rights or remedies but upon ample financial capacity of the enterprise. Confirmation of this viewpoint is found in the investor's attitude
toward such an issue as National Biscuit Company Preferred, which for
nearly 40 years has been considered as possessing the same *essential
investment character* as a good bond.[1]

**Preferred Stocks Not Generally Equivalent to Bonds in Investment
Merit.** But it should be pointed out immediately that issues with the history and standing of National Biscuit Preferred constitute a very small

---

[1] See Appendix Note 6 for supporting data.

percentage of all preferred stocks. Hence, we are by no means asserting the investment equivalence of bonds and preferred stocks *in general*. On the contrary, we shall in a later chapter be at some pains to show that the *average* preferred issue deserves a lower rank than the average bond, and furthermore that preferred stocks have been much too readily accepted by the investing public. The majority of these issues have not been sufficiently well protected to assure continuance of dividends *beyond any reasonable doubt*. They belong properly, therefore, in the class of variable or speculative senior issues (Group II), and in this field the contractual differences between bonds and preferred shares are likely to assume great importance. A sharp distinction must, therefore, be made between the typical and the exceptional preferred stock. It is only the latter which deserves to rank as a fixed-value investment and to be viewed in the same light as a good bond. To avoid awkwardness of expression in this discussion we shall frequently use the terms "investment bonds" or merely "bonds" to represent all securities belonging to the fixed-value class.

Is Bond Investment Logical? In the 1934 edition of this work we considered with some seriousness the question whether or not the extreme financial and industrial fluctuations of the preceding years had not impaired the fundamental logic of bond investment. Was it worth while for the investor to limit his income return and to forego all prospect of speculative gain, if despite these sacrifices he must still subject himself to serious risk of loss? We suggested in reply that the phenomena of 1927–1933 were so completely abnormal as to afford no fair basis for investment theory and practice. Subsequent experience seems to have borne us out, but there are still enough uncertainties facing the bond buyer to banish, perhaps for a long time, his old sense of complete security. The combination of a record high level for bonds (in 1940) with a history of two catastrophic price collapses in the preceding twenty years and a major war in progress is not one to justify airy confidence in the future.

Bond Form Inherently Unattractive: Quantitative Assurance of Safety Essentials. This situation clearly calls for a more critical and exacting attitude towards bond selection than was formerly considered necessary by investors, issuing houses, or authors of textbooks on investment. Allusion has already been made to the dangers inherent in the acceptance of the bond *form* as an assurance of safety, or even of smaller risk than is found in stocks. Instead of associating bonds primarily with the presumption of *safety* as has long been the practice—it would be sounder to start with what is not presumption but fact, *viz.*, that a (straight) bond is an investment with *limited return*. In exchange for limiting his participation in future profits, the bondholder obtains a prior claim and a definite promise of payment, while the preferred stockholder obtains only the priority, without the promise. But neither priority nor promise is itself an *assurance* of payment. This assurance rests in the ability of the enterprise to fulfill its promise, and must be looked for in its financial position, record, and prospects. The essence of proper bond selection consists, therefore, in obtaining specific and convincing factors of safety in compensation for the surrender of participation in profits.

Major Emphasis on Avoidance of Loss. Our primary conception of the bond as a commitment with limited return leads us to another important viewpoint toward bond investment. Since the chief emphasis must be placed on avoidance of loss, bond selection is primarily a negative art. It is a process of exclusion and rejection, rather than of search and acceptance. In this respect the contrast with common-stock selection is fundamental in character. The prospective buyer of a given common stock is influenced more or less equally by the desire to avoid loss and the desire to make a profit. The penalty for mistakenly rejecting the issue may conceivably be as great as that for mistakenly accepting it. But an investor may reject any number of good bonds with virtually no penalty at all, provided he does not eventually accept an unsound issue. Hence, broadly speaking, there is no such thing as being unduly captious or exacting in the purchase of fixed-value investments. The observation that Walter Bagehot addressed to commercial bankers is equally applicable to the selection of investment bonds. "If there is a difficulty or a doubt the security should be declined."[2]

Four Principles for the Selection of Issues of the Fixed-Value Type. Having established this general approach to our problem, we may now

---

[2] *Lombard Street*, p. 245, New York, 1892.

state four additional principles of more specific character which are applicable to the selection of individual issues:

I. *Safety is measured not by specific lien or other contractual rights, but by the ability of the issuer to meet all of its obligations.*[3]

II. *This ability should be measured under conditions of depression rather than prosperity.*

III. *Deficient safety cannot be compensated for by an abnormally high coupon rate.*

IV. *The selection of all bonds for investment should be subject to rules of exclusion and to specific quantitative tests corresponding to those prescribed by statute to govern investments of savings banks.*

A technique of bond selection based on the above principles will differ in significant respects from the traditional attitude and methods. In departing from old concepts, however, this treatment represents not an innovation but the recognition and advocacy of viewpoints which have been steadily gaining ground among intelligent and experienced investors. The ensuing discussion is designed to make clear both the nature and the justification of the newer ideas.[4]

I. SAFETY NOT MEASURED BY LIEN BUT BY ABILITY TO PAY

The basic difference confronts us at the very beginning. In the past the primary emphasis was laid upon the specific security, *i.e.*, the character and supposed value of the property on which the bonds hold a lien. From our standpoint this consideration is quite secondary; the dominant element must be the strength and soundness of the obligor enterprise. There is here a clearcut distinction between two points of view. On the one hand the bond is regarded as a claim against *property*; on the other hand, as a claim against a *business*.

The older view was logical enough in its origin and purpose. It desired to make the bondholder independent of the risks of the business by

---

[3] This is a general rule applicable to the majority of bonds of the fixed-value type, but it is subject to a number of exceptions which are discussed later.

[4] These ideas are neither so new nor so uncommon in 1940 as they were in 1934, but we doubt whether they may be considered standard as yet.

giving him ample security on which to levy in the event that the enterprise proved a failure. If the business became unable to pay his claim, he could take over the mortgaged property and pay himself out of that. This arrangement would be excellent if it worked, but in practice it rarely proves to be feasible. For this there are three reasons:

1. The shrinkage of property values when the business fails.
2. The difficulty of asserting the bondholders' supposed legal rights.
3. The delays and other disadvantages incident to a receivership.

Lien Is No Guarantee Against Shrinkage of Values. The conception of a mortgage lien as a guaranty of protection independent of the success of the business itself is in most cases a complete fallacy. In the typical situation, the value of the pledged property is vitally dependent on the earning power of the enterprise. The bondholder usually has a lien on a railroad line, or on factory buildings and equipment, or on power plants and other utility properties, or perhaps on a bridge or hotel structure. These properties are rarely adaptable to uses other than those for which they were constructed. Hence if the enterprise proves a failure its fixed assets ordinarily suffer an appalling shrinkage in realizable value. For this reason the established practice of stating the original cost or appraised value of the pledged property as an inducement to purchase bonds is entirely misleading. The value of pledged assets assumes practical importance only in the event of default, and in any such event the book figures are almost invariably found to be unreliable and irrelevant. This may be illustrated by Seaboard-All Florida Railway First Mortgage 6s, selling in 1931 at 1 cent on the dollar shortly after completion of the road.[5]

Impracticable to Enforce Basic Legal Rights of Lien Holder. In cases where the mortgaged property is actually worth as much as the debt, the bondholder is rarely allowed to take possession and realize upon it. It must be recognized that the procedure following default on a corporation bond has come to differ materially from that customary in the case of a mortgage on privately owned property. The basic legal rights of the lien holder are supposedly the same in both situations. But in practice we find a very definite disinclination on the part of the courts to permit corporate bondholders to take over properties by foreclosing on their

---

[5] See Appendix Note 7 for supporting data.

liens, if there is any possibility that these assets may have a fair value in excess of their claim.[6] Apparently it is considered unfair to wipe out stockholders or junior bondholders who have a potential interest in the property but are not in a position to protect it. As a result of this practice, bondholders rarely, if ever, come into actual possession of the pledged property unless its value at the time is substantially less than their claim. In most cases they are required to take new securities in a reorganized company. Sometimes the default in interest is cured and the issue rein-stated.[7] On exceedingly rare occasions a defaulted issue may be paid off in full, but only after a long and vexing delay.[8]

Delays Are Wearisome. This delay constitutes the third objection to relying upon the mortgaged property as protection for a bond invest-ment. The more valuable the pledged assets in relation to the amount of the lien, the more difficult it is to take them over under foreclosure, and the longer the time required to work out an "equitable" division of interest among the various bond and stock issues. Let us consider the most favorable kind of situation for a bondholder in the event of receivership. He would hold a comparatively small first mortgage fol-lowed by a substantial junior lien, the requirements of which have made the company insolvent. It may well be that the strength of the first-mortgage bondholder's position is such that at no time is there any real chance of eventual loss to him. Yet the financial difficulties of the com-pany usually have a depressing effect on the market price of all its secu-rities, even those presumably unimpaired in real value. As the receivership drags on, the market decline becomes accentuated, since investors are constitutionally averse to buying into a troubled situation. Eventually the first-mortgage bonds may come through the reorgani-zation undisturbed, but during a wearisome and protracted period the owners have faced a severe impairment in the quoted value of their holdings and at least some degree of doubt and worry as to the out-come. Typical examples of such an experience can be found in the case of Missouri, Kansas and Texas Railway Company First 4s and Brooklyn

---

[6] The failure to foreclose on Interborough Rapid Transit Secured 7s for seven years after default of principal (Appendix Note 2) well illustrates this point.

[7] See Appendix Note 8 for supporting data.

[8] See Appendix Note 9 for supporting data.

Union Elevated Railroad First 5s.[9] The subject of receivership and reorganization practice, particularly as they affect the bondholder, will receive more detailed consideration in a later chapter.

Basic Principle Is to Avoid Trouble. The foregoing discussion should support our emphatic stand that the primary aim of the bond buyer must be to avoid trouble and not to protect himself in the event of trouble. Even in the cases where the specific lien proves of real advantage, this benefit is realized under conditions which contravene the very meaning of *fixed-value* investment. In view of the severe decline in market price almost invariably associated with receivership, the mere fact that the investor must have recourse to his indenture indicates that his investment has been unwise or unfortunate. The protection that the mortgaged property offers him can constitute at best a mitigation of his mistake.

Corollaries from This First Principle. 1. *Absence of Lien of Minor Consequence.* From Principle I there follow a number of corollaries with important practical applications. Since specific lien is of subordinate importance in the choice of high-grade bonds, the absence of lien is also of minor consequence. The debenture,[10] *i.e.*, unsecured, obligations of a

---

[9] See Appendix Note 10 for supporting data. On the subject of delays in enforcing bondholders' claims, it should be pointed out that, with up to one-third of the country's railroad mileage in bankruptcy, not a single road emerged from trusteeship in the six years following passage of the Sec. 77 amendment to the Bankruptcy Act in 1933—a step designed to *accelerate* reorganization.

[10] The term "debenture" in American financial practice has the accepted meaning of "unsecured bond or note." For no good reason, the name is sometimes given to other kinds of securities without apparently signifying anything in particular. There have been a number of "secured debentures," *e.g.*, Chicago Herald and Examiner Secured Debenture 6 1/2s, due 1950, and Lone Star Gas Debenture 3 1/2s, due 1953. Also, a number of preferred issues are called debenture preferred stock or merely debenture stock, *e.g.*, Du Pont Debenture Stock (called in 1939); General Cigar Company Debenture Preferred (called in 1927).

Sometimes debenture issues, properly so entitled because originally unsecured, later acquire specific security through the operation of a protective covenant, *e.g.*, New York, New Haven and Hartford Railroad Company Debentures, discussed in Chap. 19. Another example was the Debenture 6 1/2s of Fox New England Theaters, Inc., reorganized in 1933. These debentures acquired as security a block of first-mortgage bonds of the same company, which were surrendered by the vendor of the theaters because it failed to meet a guarantee of future earnings.

Observe that there is no clear-cut distinction between a "bond" and a "note" other than the fact that the latter generally means a relatively short-term obligation, *i.e.*, one maturing not more than, say, ten years after issuance.

strong corporation, amply capable of meeting its interest charges, may qualify for acceptance almost as readily as a bond secured by mortgage. Furthermore the debentures of a strong enterprise are undoubtedly sounder investments than the mortgage issues of a weak company. No first-lien bond, for example, enjoys a better investment rating than Standard Oil of New Jersey Debenture 3s, due 1961. An examination of the bond list will show that the debenture issues of companies having no secured debt ahead of them will rank in investment character at least on a par with the average mortgage bond, because an enterprise must enjoy a high credit rating to obtain funds on its unsecured long-term bond.[11]

2. *The Theory of Buying the Highest Yielding Obligation of a Sound Company.* It follows also that if any obligation of an enterprise deserves to qualify as a fixed-value investment, then all its obligations must do so. Stated conversely, if a company's junior bonds are not safe, its first-mortgage bonds are not a desirable fixed-value investment. For if the second mortgage is unsafe the company itself is weak, and generally speaking there can be no high-grade obligations of a weak enterprise. The theoretically correct procedure for bond investment, therefore, is first to select a company meeting every test of strength and soundness, and then to purchase its highest yielding obligation, which would usually mean its junior rather than its first-lien bonds. Assuming no error were ever made in our choice of enterprises, this procedure would work out perfectly well in practice. The greater the chance of mistake, however, the more reason to sacrifice yield in order to reduce the potential loss in capital value. But we must recognize that in favoring the lower yielding first-mortgage issue, the bond buyer is in fact expressing a lack of confidence in his own judgment as to the soundness of the business—which, if carried far enough, would call into question the advisability of his making an investment in *any* of the bonds of the particular enterprise.

Example: As an example of this point, let us consider the Cudahy Packing Company First Mortgage 5s, due 1946, and the Debenture 5¹/₂s of the same company, due 1937. In June 1932 the First 5s sold at 95 to yield about 5¹/₂%, whereas the junior 5¹/₂s sold at 59 to yield over 20%

---

[11] This point is strikingly substantiated by the industrial bond financing between 1935 and 1939. During these years, when only high-grade issues could be sold, by far the greater part of the total was represented by *debentures.*

to maturity. The purchase of the 5% bonds at close to par could only be justified by a confident belief that the company would remain solvent and reasonably prosperous, for otherwise the bonds would undoubtedly suffer a severe drop in market price. But if the investor has confidence in the future of Cudahy, why should he not buy the debenture issue and obtain an enormously greater return on his money? The only answer can be that the investor wants the superior protection of the first mortgage in the event his judgment proves incorrect and the company falls into difficulties. In that case he would probably lose less as the owner of the first-mortgage bonds than through holding the junior issue. Even on this score it should be pointed out that if by any chance Cudahy Packing Company were to suffer the reverses that befell Fisk Rubber Company, the loss in market value of the first-mortgage bonds would be fully as great as those suffered by the debentures; for in April 1932 Fisk Rubber Company First 8s were selling as low as 17 against a price of 12 for the unsecured $5^{1}/_{2}$% Notes. It is clear, at any rate, that the investor who favors the Cudahy first-lien 5s is paying a premium of about 15% per annum (the difference in yield) for only a *partial* insurance against loss. On this basis he is undoubtedly giving up too much for what he gets in return. The conclusion appears inescapable either that he should make no investment in Cudahy bonds or that he should buy the junior issue at its enormously higher yield.[12] This rule may be laid down as applying to the general case where a first-mortgage bond sells at a fixed-value price (*e.g.*, close to par) and junior issues of the same company can be bought to yield a much higher return.[13]

3. *Senior Liens Are to Be Favored, Unless Junior Obligations Offer a Substantial Advantage.* Obviously a junior lien should be preferred only if the advantage in income return is substantial. Where the first-mortgage bond yields only slightly less, it is undoubtedly wise to pay the small insurance premium for protection against unexpected trouble.

Example: This point is illustrated by the relative market prices of Atchison Topeka and Santa Fe Railway Company General (first) 4s and Adjustment (second mortgage) 4s, both of which mature in 1995.

---

[12] Both of the Cudahy issues were retired at $102^{1}/_{2}$ in 1935.

[13] Exceptions to this rule may be justified in rare cases where the senior security has an unusually preferred status—*e.g.*, a very strongly entrenched underlying railroad bond. (Chap. 6)

Price of Atchison General 4s and Adjustment 4s at Various Dates

Date	Price of General 4s	Price of Adjustment 4s	Spread
Jan. 2, 1913	97$^1/_2$	88	9$^1/_2$
Jan. 5, 1917	95$^1/_2$	86$^3/_4$	8$^3/_4$
May 21, 1920	70$^1/_4$	62	8$^1/_4$
Aug. 4, 1922	93$^1/_2$	84$^1/_2$	9
Dec. 4, 1925	89$^1/_4$	85$^1/_4$	4
Jan. 3, 1930	93$^1/_4$	93	$^1/_4$
Jan. 7, 1931	98$^1/_2$	97	1$^1/_2$
June 2, 1932	81	66$^1/_2$	14$^1/_2$
June 19, 1933	93	88	5
Jan. 9, 1934	94$^1/_4$	83	11$^1/_4$
Mar. 6, 1936	114$^5/_8$	113$^1/_2$	1$^1/_8$
Apr. 26, 1937	103$^1/_2$	106$^3/_4$	3$^1/_4$
Apr. 14, 1938	99$^1/_4$	75$^1/_4$	24
Dec. 29, 1939	105$^3/_4$	85$^1/_4$	20$^1/_2$

Prior to 1924 the Atchison General 4s sold usually at about 7 to 10 points above the Adjustment 4s and yielded about $^1/_2$% less. Since both issues were considered safe without question, it would have been more logical to purchase the junior issue at its 10% lower cost. After 1923 this point of view asserted itself, and the price difference steadily narrowed. During 1930 and part of 1931 the junior issue sold on numerous occasions at practically the same price as the General 4s. This relationship was even more illogical than the unduly wide spread in 1922–1923, since the advantage of the Adjustment 4s in price and yield was too negligible to warrant accepting a junior position, even assuming unquestioned safety for both liens.

Within a very short time this rather obvious truth was brought home strikingly by the widening of the spread to over 14 points during the demoralized bond-market conditions of June 1932. As the record appeared in 1934, it could be inferred that a reasonable differential between the two issues would be about 5 points and that either a substantial widening or a virtual disappearance of the spread would present an opportunity for a desirable exchange of one issue for another. Two such opportunities did in fact appear in 1934 and 1936, as shown in our table.

But this example is of further utility in illustrating the all-pervasive factor of change and the necessity of taking it into account in bond analysis. By 1937 the failure of Atchison's earnings to recover within striking distance of its former normal, and the actual inadequacy of the margin above interest requirements as judged by conservative standards, should have warned the investor that the "adjustment" (*i.e.*, contingent) element in the junior issue could not safely be ignored. Thus a price relationship that was logical at a time when safety of interest was never in question could not be relied upon under the new conditions. In 1938 the poor earnings actually compelled the road to defer the May 1 interest payment on the adjustment bonds, as a result of which their price fell to 75$\frac{1}{4}$ and the spread widened to 24 points. Although the interest was later paid in full and the price recovered to 96 in 1939, it would seem quite unwise for the investor to apply pre-1932 standards to this bond issue.

A junior lien of Company *X* may be selected in preference to a first-mortgage bond of Company *Y*, on one of two bases:

1. The protection for the total debt of Company *X* is adequate and the yield of the junior lien is substantially higher than that of the Company *Y* issue; or
2. If there is no substantial advantage in yield, then the indicated protection for the total debt of Company *X* must be considerably better than that of Company *Y*.

Example of 2:

Issue	Price in 1930	Fixed charges earned, 1929*
Pacific Power and Light Co. First 5s, due 1955	101	1.53 times
American Gas and Electric Co. Debenture 5s, due 2028	101	2.52 times

* Average results approximately the same.

The appreciably higher coverage of total charges by American Gas and Electric would have justified preferring its junior bonds to the first-mortgage issue of Pacific Power and Light, when both were selling at about the same price.[14]

---

[14] In 1937 the low price of Pacific Power and Light 5s was 51, against a low of 104 for the American Gas and Electric Debentures.

Special Status of "Underlying Bonds." In the railroad field an especial investment character is generally supposed to attach to what are known as "underlying bonds." These represent issues of relatively small size secured by a lien on especially important parts of the obligor system, and often followed by a series of "blanket mortgages." The underlying bond usually enjoys a first lien, but it may be a second- or even a third-mortgage issue, provided the senior issues are also of comparatively small magnitude.

Example: New York and Erie Railroad Third Mortgage Extended $4^1/2$s, due 1938, are junior to two small prior liens covering an important part of the Erie Railroad's main line. They are followed by four successive blanket mortgages on the system, and they have regularly enjoyed the favored status of an underlying bond.

Bonds of this description have been thought to be entirely safe, regardless of what happens to the system as a whole. They have almost always come through reorganization unscathed; and even during a receivership interest payments are usually continued as a matter of course, largely because the sum involved is proportionately so small. They are not exempt, however, from fairly sharp declines in market value if insolvency overtakes the system.

Examples: In the case of New York and Erie Third $4^1/2$s (which had been voluntarily extended on maturity in 1923 and again in 1933), principal and interest were defaulted in March 1938, following the bankruptcy of the Erie two months earlier. The bid price declined to as low as 61. However, the various reorganization plans filed to the end of 1939 all provided for the payment of principal and interest in full on this issue.

Chicago and Eastern Illinois Consolidated 6s, due 1934, were finally paid off in full in 1940, with further interest at 4%—but not until their price had fallen as low as 32 in 1933.

Pacific Railway of Missouri First 4s and Second 5s and Missouri Pacific Railway Third 4s, all extended from their original maturities to 1938, are underlying bonds of the Missouri Pacific system. They continued to receive interest and were left undisturbed in the receivership of 1915. Following the second bankruptcy in 1933, they continued to receive interest until their maturity date. At that time payment of principal was defaulted, but interest payments were continued through 1939. The various reorganization plans virtually provided for these bonds in full, by offering them prior-lien, fixed-interest obligations of the new company. But since 1931, the price of these three issues has been as low as 65, 60, and 53, respectively.

Other bonds, however, once regarded as underlying issues, have not fared so well following insolvency.

Example: Milwaukee, Sparta and Northwestern First 4s, due 1947, ranked as an underlying bond of the Chicago and North Western Railway, and for many years their price was not far below that of the premier Union Pacific First 4s, due the same year. Yet the receivership of the Chicago and North Western was followed by default of interest on this issue in 1935 and collapse of its price to the abysmal low of $8^{1}/8$ as late as 1939.

From the foregoing it would appear that *in some cases* underlying bonds may be viewed as exceptions to our rule that a bond is not sound unless the company is sound. For the most part such bonds are owned by institutions or large investors. (The same observations may apply to certain first-mortgage bonds of operating subsidiaries of public-utility holding-company systems.)

In railroad bonds of this type, the location and strategic value of the mileage covered are of prime importance. First-mortgage bonds on nonessential and unprofitable parts of the system, referred to sometimes as "divisional liens," are not true underlying bonds in the sense that we have just used the term. Divisional first liens on poorly located mileage may receive much less favorable treatment in a reorganization than blanket mortgage bonds ostensibly junior to them.

Example: Central Branch Union Pacific Railway First 4s, due 1938, were said to "underly" the Missouri Pacific First and Refunding mortgage, which provided for their retirement. Yet the reorganization plans presented to the end of 1939 all offered better treatment for the Missouri Pacific First and Refunding 5s than for the ostensibly senior Central Branch bonds.

As a practical matter it is not so easy to distinguish in advance between the underlying bonds that come through reorganization unscathed and those which suffer drastic treatment. Hence the ordinary investor may be well advised to leave such issues out of his calculations and stick to the rule that only strong companies have strong bonds.

CHAPTER 7

The Selection of Fixed-Value Investments: Second and Third Principles

II. BONDS SHOULD BE BOUGHT ON A DEPRESSION BASIS

The rule that a sound investment must be able to withstand adversity seems self-evident enough to be termed a truism. Any bond can do well when conditions are favorable; it is only under the acid test of depression that the advantages of strong over weak issues become manifest and vitally important. For this reason prudent investors have always favored the obligations of old-established enterprises which have demonstrated their ability to come through bad times as well as good.

Presumption of Safety Based upon Either the Character of the Industry or the Amount of Protection. Confidence in the ability of a bond issue to weather depression may be based on either of two different reasons. The investor may believe that the particular business will be immune from a drastic shrinkage in earning power, or else that the margin of safety is so large that it can undergo such a shrinkage without resultant danger. The bonds of light and power companies have been favored principally for the first reason, the bonds of United States Steel Corporation subsidiaries for the second. In the former case it is the *character* of the industry, in the latter it is the *amount* of protection, which justifies the purchase. Of the two viewpoints, the one which tries to avoid the perils of depression appeals most to the average bond buyer. It seems much simpler to invest in a depression-proof enterprise than to have to rely on the company's financial strength to pull its bonds through a period of poor results.

No Industry Entirely Depression-Proof. The objection to this theory of investment is, of course, that there is no such thing as a depression-proof industry, meaning thereby one that is immune from the danger of *any* decline in earning power. It is true that the Edison companies have shown themselves subject to only minor shrinkage in profits, as compared, say, with the steel producers. But even a small decline may prove fatal if the business is bonded to the limit of prosperity earnings. Once it is admitted—as it always must be—that the industry can suffer *some* reduction in profits, then the investor is compelled to estimate the possible extent of the shrinkage and compare it with the surplus above the interest requirements. He thus finds himself in the same position as the holder of any other kind of bond, vitally concerned with the ability of the company to meet the vicissitudes of the future.[1]

The distinction to be made, therefore, is not between industries which are *exempt* from and those which are *affected* by depression, but rather between those which are more and those which are less subject to fluctuation. The more stable the type of enterprise, the better suited it is to bond financing and the larger the portion of the supposed normal earning power which may be consumed by interest charges. As the degree of instability increases, it must be offset by a greater margin of safety to make sure that interest charges will be met; in other words, a smaller portion of total capital may be represented by bonds. If there is such a lack of inherent stability as to make survival of the enterprise doubtful under continued unfavorable conditions (a question arising frequently in the case of industrial companies of secondary size), then the bond issue cannot meet the requirements of fixed-value investment, even though the margin of safety—measured by past performance—may be exceedingly large. Such a bond will meet the quantitative but not the qualitative test, but both are essential to our concept of investment.[2]

---

[1] Note that a large number of utility holding-company issues (and even some overbonded operating companies) defaulted in 1931–1932, whereas the subsidiary bonds of the United States Steel Corporation maintained a high investment rating despite the exceedingly bad operating results.

[2] For examples of this important point, see our discussion of Studebaker Preferred stock in Chap. 2 and of Willys-Overland Company First $6^1/_2$s in Appendix Note 34.

Investment Practice Recognizes Importance of Character of the Industry. This conception of diverse margins of safety has been solidly grounded in investment practice for many years. The threefold classification of enterprises—as railroads, public utilities, or industrials—was intended to reflect inherent differences in relative stability and consequently in the coverage to be required above bond interest requirements. Investors thought well, for example, of any railroad which earned its bond interest twice over, but the same margin in the case of an industrial bond was ordinarily regarded as inadequate. In the decade between 1920 and 1930, the status of the public-utility division underwent some radical changes. A sharp separation was introduced between light, heat, and power services on the one hand, and street-railway lines on the other, although previously the two had been closely allied. The trolley companies, because of their poor showing, were tacitly excluded from the purview of the term "public utility," as used in financial circles, and in the popular mind the name was restricted to electric, gas, water, and telephone companies. (Later on, promoters endeavored to exploit the popularity of the public utilities by applying this title to companies engaged in all sorts of businesses, including natural gas, ice, coal, and even storage.) The steady progress of the utility group, even in the face of the minor industrial setbacks of 1924 and 1927, led to an impressive advance in its standing among investors, so that by 1929 it enjoyed a credit rating fully on a par with the railroads. In the ensuing depression, it registered a much smaller shrinkage in gross and net earnings than did the transportation industry, and its seems logical to expect that bonds of soundly capitalized light and power companies will replace high-grade railroad bonds as the premier type of corporate investment. (This seems true to the authors despite the distinct recession in the popularity of utility bonds and stocks since 1933, due to a combination of rate reductions, governmental competition and threatened dangers from inflation.)

Depression Performance as a Test of Merit. Let us turn our attention now to the behavior of these three investment groups in the two recent depression tests—that of 1931–1933 and that of 1937–1938. Of these, the former was of such unexampled severity that it may seem unfair and impractical to ask that any investment now under consideration should be measured by its performance in those disastrous times. We have felt, however, that the experiences of 1931–1933 may be profitably viewed as

Comparison of Railroad and Public-utility Gross and Net with the Average Yield
on High-Grade Railroad and Utility Bonds, 1926–1938 (Unit $1,000,000)

	Railroads			Public utilities		
Year	Gross[1]	Net railway operating income[2]	Yield on railroad bonds, %[3]	Gross[4]	Net[5] (index %)	Yield on public-utility bonds, %[3]
1926	$6,383	$1,213	5.13	$1,520	100.0	5.11
1927	6,136	1,068	4.83	1,661	106.8	4.96
1928	6,112	1,173	4.85	1,784	124.0	4.87
1929	6,280	1,252	5.18	1,939	142.5	5.14
1930	5,281	869	4.96	1,991	127.7	5.05
1931	4,188	526	6.09	1,976	123.5	5.27
1932	3,127	326	7.61	1,814	96.6	6.30
1933	3,095	474	6.09	1,755	98.2	6.25
1934	3,272	463	4.96	1,832	88.1	5.40
1935	3,452	500	4.95	1,912	92.9	4.43
1936	4,053	667	4.24	2,045	120.7	3.88
1937	4,166	590	4.34	2,181	125.8	3.93
1938	3,565	373	5.21	2,195	106.0	3.87

[1] Railway operating revenues for all Class I railroads in the United States (I.C.C.).
[2] Net railway operating income for the same roads (I.C.C.).
[3] Average yields on 40 rail and 40 utility bonds, respectively, as compiled by Moody's.
[4] Revenues from the sale of electric power to ultimate consumers, compiled by Edison Electric Institute. Data from 90% of the industry are adjusted to cover 100% of the industry (*Survey of Current Business*).
[5] Index of corporate profits of 15 public utilities, compiled by Standard Statistics Company, Inc. Figures are annual averages of quarterly relatives in which 1926 is the base year.

a "laboratory test" of investment standards, involving degrees of stress not to be expected in the ordinary vicissitudes of the future. Even though the conditions prevalent in those years may not be duplicated, the behavior of various types of securities at the time should throw a useful light on investment problems.

Various Causes of Bond Collapses. 1. *Excessive Funded Debt of Utilities.* If we study the bond issues which suffered collapse in the post-bubble period, we shall observe that different causes underlay the troubles of each group. The public-utility defaults were caused not by a disappearance of earnings but by the inability of overextended debt structures to withstand a relatively moderate setback. Enterprises capitalized on a

reasonably sound basis, as judged by former standards, had little difficulty in meeting bond interest. This did not hold true in the case of many
holding companies with pyramided capital structures which had
absorbed nearly every dollar of peak-year earnings for fixed charges and
so had scarcely any margin available to meet a shrinkage in profits. The
widespread difficulties of the utilities were due not to any weakness in
the light and power *business*, but to the reckless extravagance of its
financing methods. The losses of investors in public-utility bonds could
for the most part have been avoided by the exercise of ordinary prudence
in bond selection. Conversely, the unsound financing methods employed
must eventually have resulted in individual collapses, even in the ordinary course of the business cycle. In consequence, the theory of investment in sound public-utility bonds appears in no sense to have been
undermined by 1931–1933 experience.

2. *Stability of Railroad Earnings Overrated.* Turning to the railroads,
we find a somewhat different situation. Here the fault appears to be that
the stability of the transportation industry was overrated, so that investors
were satisfied with a margin of protection which proved insufficient. It
was not a matter of imprudently disregarding old established standards
of safety, as in the case of the weaker utilities, but rather of being content
with old standards when conditions called for more stringent requirements. Looking back, we can see that the failure of the carriers generally
to increase their earnings with the great growth of the country since prewar days was a sign of a weakened relative position, which called for a
more cautious and exacting attitude by the investor. If he had required
his railroad bonds to meet the same tests that he applied to industrial
issues, he would have been compelled to confine his selection to a relatively few of the strongly situated lines.[3] As it turned out, nearly all of these
have been able to withstand the tremendous loss of traffic since 1929 without danger to their fixed charges. Whether or not this is a case of wisdom

---

[3] If, for example, the investor had restricted his attention to bonds of roads which in the
prosperous year 1928 covered their fixed charges $2^1/2$ times or better, he would have confined his selections to bonds of: Atchison; Canadian Pacific; Chesapeake and Ohio; Chicago,
Burlington and Quincy; Norfolk and Western; Pere Marquette; Reading; and Union Pacific.
(With the exception of Pere Marquette, the bonds of these roads fared comparatively well in
the depression. Note, however, that the foregoing test may be more stringent than the one
we propose later on: *average* earnings = twice fixed charges.)

after the event is irrelevant to our discussion. Viewing past experience as a lesson for the future, we can see that *selecting railroad bonds on a depression basis* would mean requiring a larger margin of safety in normal times than was heretofore considered necessary.

The 1937–1938 Experience. These conclusions with respect to railroad and utility bonds are supported by the behavior of the two groups in the 1937–1938 recession. Nearly all issues which met reasonably stringent quantitative tests at the beginning of 1937 came through the ensuing slump with a relatively small market decline and no impairment of inherent position. On the other hand, bonds of both groups showing a substandard earnings coverage for 1936 suffered in most cases a really serious loss of quoted value, which in some instances proved the precursor of financial difficulties for the issuer.[4]

3. *Depression Performance of Industrial Bonds.* In the case of industrial obligations, the 1937–1938 pattern and the 1931–1933 pattern are appreciably different, so that the investor's attitude toward this type of security may depend somewhat on whether he feels it necessary to guard against the more or the less serious degree of depression. Studying the 1931–1933 record, we note that price collapses were not due primarily to unsound financial structures, as in the case of utility bonds, nor to a miscalculation by investors as to the margin of safety needed, as in the case of railroad bonds. We are confronted in many cases by a sudden disappearance of earning power, and a disconcerting question as to whether the business can survive. A company such as Gulf States Steel, for example, earned its 1929 interest charges at least $3^{1}/_{2}$ times in every year from 1922 to 1929. Yet in 1930 and 1931 operating losses were so large as to threaten its solvency.[5] Many basic industries, such as the Cuban sugar producers and our own coal mines, were depressed prior to the 1929 debacle. In the past, such eclipses had always proven to be temporary, and investors felt justified in holding the bonds of these companies in the expectation of a speedy recovery. But in this instance the continuance of adverse conditions beyond all previous experience defeated their calculations and destroyed the values behind their investment.

---

[4] See Appendix Note 11 for a summary of the performance of representative railroad and utility bonds in 1937–1938, as related to earnings coverage for 1936.

[5] See Appendix Note 12 for supporting data and other examples.

From these cases we must conclude that even a high margin of safety in good times may prove ineffective against a succession of operating losses caused by prolonged adversity. The difficulties that befell industrial bonds, therefore, cannot be avoided in the future merely by more stringent requirements as to bond-interest coverage in normal years.

If we examine more closely the behavior of the industrial bond list in 1932–1933 (taking all issues listed on the New York Stock Exchange), we shall note that the fraction that maintained a price reflecting reasonable confidence in the safety of the issue was limited to only 18 out of some 200 companies.[6]

The majority of these companies were of outstanding importance in their respective industries. This point suggests that *large size* is a trait of considerable advantage in dealing with exceptionally unfavorable developments in the industrial world, which may mean in turn that industrial investments should be restricted to major companies. The evidence, however, may be objected to on the ground of having been founded on an admittedly abnormal experience. The less drastic test of 1937–1938 points rather towards the conventional conclusion that issues strongly buttressed by past earnings can be relied on to withstand depressions.[7] If, however, we go back over a longer period—say, since 1915—we shall find perennial evidence of the instability of industrial earning power. Even in the supposedly prosperous period between 1922 and 1929, the bonds of smaller industrial enterprises did not prove a dependable medium of investment. There were many instances wherein an apparently well-established earning power suffered a sudden disappearance.[8] In fact these unpredictable variations were sufficiently numerous to suggest the conclusion that there is an inherent lack of stability in the small

---

[6] These companies were: American Machine and Foundry, American Sugar Refining Company, Associated Oil Company, Corn Products Refining Company, General Baking Company, General Electric Company, General Motors Acceptance Corporation, Humble Oil and Refining Company, International Business Machine Corporation, Liggett and Myers Tobacco Company, P. Lorillard Company, National Sugar Refining Company, Pillsbury Flour Mills Company, Smith (A.O.) Corporation, Socony-Vacuum Corporation, Standard Oil Company of Indiana, Standard Oil Company of New Jersey and United States Steel Corporation.

[7] Appendix Note 13 summarizes the performance of industrial bonds in 1937–1938, as related to earnings for a period ended in 1936.

[8] See Appendix Note 14 for examples.

or medium-sized industrial enterprise, which makes them ill-suited to bond financing. A tacit recognition of this weakness has been responsible in part for the growing adoption of conversion and subscription-warrant privileges in connection with industrial-bond financing.[9] To what extent such embellishments can compensate for insufficient safety will be discussed in our chapters on Senior Securities with Speculative Features. But in any event the widespread resort to these profit-sharing artifices seems to confirm our view that bonds of smaller industrial companies are not well qualified for consideration as fixed-value investments.

Unavailability of Sound Bonds No Excuse for Buying Poor Ones. However, if we recommend that straight bond investment in the industrial field be confined to companies of dominant size, we face the difficulty that such companies are few in number and many of them have no bonds outstanding. It may be objected further that such an attitude would severely handicap the financing of legitimate businesses of secondary size and would have a blighting effect on investment-banking activities. The answer to these remonstrances must be that no consideration can justify the purchase of unsound bonds at an investment price. The fact that no good bonds are available is hardly an excuse for either issuing or accepting poor ones. Needless to say, the investor is never forced to buy a security of inferior grade. At some sacrifice in yield he can always find issues that meet his requirements, however stringent; and, as we shall point out later, attempts to increase yield at the expense of safety are likely to prove unprofitable. From the standpoint of the corporations and their investment bankers, the conclusion must follow that if their securities cannot properly qualify as straight investments, they must be given profit-making possibilities sufficient to compensate the purchaser for the risk he runs.

Conflicting Views on Bond Financing. In this connection, observations are in order regarding two generally accepted ideas on the subject of bond financing. The first is that bond issues are an element of weakness in a company's financial position, so that the elimination of funded debt is always a desirable object. The second is that when companies are unable to finance through the sale of stock it is proper to raise money by

---

[9] See Chap. 22 Note 3.

means of bond issues. In the writers' view both of these widespread notions are quite incorrect. Otherwise there would be no really sound basis for any bond financing. For they imply that only weak companies should be willing to sell bonds—which, if true, would mean that investors should not be willing to buy them.

Proper Theory of Bond Financing. The proper theory of bond financing, however, is of quite different import. A reasonable amount of funded debt is of advantage to a prosperous business, because the stockholders can earn a profit above interest charges through the use of the bondholders' capital. It is desirable for both the corporation and the investor that the borrowing be limited to an amount which can safely be taken care of under all conditions. Hence, from the standpoint of sound finance, there is no basic conflict of interest between the strong corporation which floats bonds and the public which buys them. On the other hand, whenever an element of unwillingness or compulsion enters into the creation of a bond issue by an enterprise, these bonds are *ipso facto* of secondary quality and it is unwise to purchase them on a straight investment basis.

Unsound Policies Followed in Practice. Financial policies followed by corporations and accepted by the public have for many years run counter to these logical principles. The railroads, for example, have financed the bulk of their needs through bond sales, resulting in an overbalancing of funded debt as against stock capital. This tendency has been repeatedly deplored by all authorities, but accepted as inevitable because poor earnings made stock sales impracticable. But if the latter were true, they also made bond purchases inadvisable. It is now quite clear that investors were imprudent in lending money to carriers which themselves complained of the necessity of having to borrow it.

While investors were thus illogically lending money to weak borrowers, many strong enterprises were paying off their debts through the sale of additional stock. But if there is any thoroughly sound basis for corporate borrowing, then this procedure must also be regarded as unwise. If a reasonable amount of borrowed capital, obtained at low interest rates, is advantageous to the stockholder, then the replacement of this debt by added stock capital means the surrender of such advantage. The elimination of debt will naturally simplify the problems of the management, but surely there must be some point at which the return to the stockholders must also be considered. Were this not so, corporations would be constantly raising money from their owners and they would never pay any part of it back in dividends. It should be pointed out that the mania for debt retirement in 1927–1929 has had a disturbing effect upon our banking situation, since it eliminated most of the good commercial borrowers and replaced them by second-grade business risks and by loans on stock collateral, which were replete with possibilities of harm.

Significance of the Foregoing to the Investor. The above analysis of the course of industrial bond borrowing in the last 15 years is not irrelevant to the theme of this chapter, *viz.*, the application of depression standards to the selection of fixed-value investments. Recognizing the necessity of ultra-stringent criteria of choice in the industrial field, the bond buyer is faced by a further narrowing of eligible issues due to the elimination of funded debt by many of the strongest companies. Clearly his reaction must not be to accept the issues of less desirable enterprises, in the absence of better ones, but rather to refrain from any purchases on an investment basis if the suitable ones are not available. It appears to be a financial axiom that whenever there is money to invest, it is invested; and if the owner cannot find a good security yielding a fair return, he will invariably buy a poor one. But a prudent and intelligent investor should be able to avoid this temptation, and reconcile himself to accepting an unattractive yield from the best bonds, in preference to risking his principal in second-grade issues for the sake of a large coupon return.

Summary. The rule that bonds should be bought on the basis of their ability to withstand depression has been part of an old investment tradition. It was nearly lost sight of in the prosperous period culminating in 1929, but its importance was made painfully manifest during the following collapse and demonstrated again in the 1937–1938 recession. The bonds of reasonably capitalized electric and gas companies have given a satisfactory account of themselves during this decade and the same is true—to a lesser degree—of the relatively few railroads which showed a large margin above interest charges prior to 1930. In the industrial list, however, even an excellent past record has in many cases proved undependable, especially where the company is of small or moderate size. For this reason, the investor would seem to gain better protection against adverse developments by confining his industrial selections to companies which meet the two requirements of (1) dominant size and (2) substantial margin of earnings over bond interest.

III. THIRD PRINCIPLE: UNSOUND TO SACRIFICE SAFETY FOR YIELD

In the traditional theory of bond investment a mathematical relationship is supposed to exist between the interest rate and the degree of risk incurred. The interest return is divided into two components, the first constituting "pure interest"—*i.e.*, the rate obtainable with *no* risk of loss—and the second representing the premium obtained to compensate for the risk assumed. If, for example, the "pure interest rate" is assumed to be 2%, then a 3% investment is supposed to involve one chance in a hundred of loss, while the risk incurred in an 7% investment would be five times as great, or 1 in 20. (Presumably the risk should be somewhat less than that indicated, to allow for an "insurance profit.")

This theory implies that bond-interest rates are closely similar to insurance rates, and that they measure the degree of risk on some reasonably precise actuarial basis. It would follow that, by and large, the return from high-and low-yielding investments should tend to equalize, since what the former gain in income would be offset by their greater percentage of principal losses, and *vice versa*.

No Mathematical Relationship Between Yield and Risk. This view, however, seems to us to bear little relation to the realities of bond investment. Security prices and yields are not determined by any exact mathematical calculation of the expected risk, but they depend rather upon the *popularity* of the issue. This popularity reflects in a general way the investors' view as to the risk involved, but it is also influenced largely by other factors, such as the degree of familiarity of the public with the company and the issue (seasoning) and the ease with which the bond can be sold (marketability).

It may be pointed out further that the supposed actuarial computation of investment risks is out of the question theoretically as well as in practice. There are no experience tables available by which the expected "mortality" of various types of issues can be determined. Even if such tables were prepared, based on long and exhaustive studies of past records, it is doubtful whether they would have any real utility for the future. In life insurance the relation between age and mortality rate is well defined and changes only gradually. The same is true, to a much lesser extent, of the relation between the various types of structures and the fire hazard attaching to them. But the relation between different kinds of investments and the risk of loss is entirely too indefinite, and too variable with changing conditions, to permit of sound mathematical formulation. This is particularly true because investment losses are not distributed fairly evenly in point of time, but tend to be concentrated at intervals, *i.e.*, during periods of general depression. Hence the typical investment hazard is roughly similar to the conflagration or epidemic hazard, which is the exceptional and incalculable factor in fire or life insurance.

Self-Insurance Generally Not Possible in Investment. If we were to assume that a precise mathematical relationship does exist between yield and risk, then the result of this premise should be inevitably to recommend the lowest yielding—and therefore the safest—bonds to all investors. For the individual is not qualified to be an insurance underwriter. It is not his function to be paid for incurring risks; on the contrary it is to his interest to pay others for insurance against loss. Let us assume a bond buyer has his choice of investing $1,000 for $20 per annum without risk, or for $70 per annum with 1 chance out of 20 each year that his principal would be lost. The $50 additional income on the second investment is mathematically equivalent to the risk involved. But in terms of *personal requirements*, an investor cannot afford to take even a small chance of losing $1,000 of principal in return for an extra $50 of income. Such a procedure would be the direct opposite of the standard procedure of *paying* small annual sums to protect property values against loss by fire and theft.

The Factor of Cyclical Risks. The investor cannot prudently turn himself into an insurance company and incur risks of losing his principal in exchange for annual premiums in the form of extra-large interest coupons. One objection to such a policy is that sound insurance practice requires a very wide distribution of risk, in order to minimize the influence of luck and to allow maximum play to the law of probability. The investor may endeavor to attain this end by diversifying his holdings, but as a practical matter he cannot approach the division of risk attained by an insurance company. More important still is the danger that many risky investments may collapse together in a depression period, so that the investor in high-yielding issues will find a period of large income (which he will probably spend) followed suddenly by a deluge of losses of principal.

It may be contended that the higher yielding securities on the whole return a larger premium above "pure interest" than the degree of risk requires; in other words, that in return for taking the risk, investors will in the long run obtain a *profit* over and above the losses in principal suffered. It is difficult to say definitely whether or not this is true. But even assuming that the high coupon rates will, in the great aggregate, more than compensate on an *actuarial* basis for the risks accepted, such bonds are still undesirable investments from the *personal* standpoint of the average investor. Our arguments against the investor turning himself into an insurance company remain valid even if the insurance operations all told may prove profitable. The bond buyer is neither financially nor psychologically equipped to carry on extensive transactions involving the setting up of reserves out of regular income to absorb losses in substantial amounts suffered at irregular intervals.

Risk and Yield Are Incommensurable. The foregoing discussion leads us to suggest the principle that income return and risk of principal should be regarded as *incommensurable*. Practically speaking, this means that acknowledged risks of losing principal should not be offset merely by a high coupon rate, but can be accepted only in return for a corresponding opportunity for enhancement of principal, *e.g.*, through the purchase of bonds at a substantial discount from par, or possibly by obtaining an unusually attractive conversion privilege. While there may be no real *mathematical* difference between offsetting risks of loss by a higher income or by a chance for profit, the *psychological* difference is very important. The purchaser of low-priced bonds is fully aware of the risk he is running; he is more likely to make a thorough investigation of the issue and to appraise carefully the chances of loss and of profit; finally— most important of all—he is prepared for whatever losses he may sustain, and his profits are in a form available to meet his losses. Actual investment experience, therefore, will not favor the purchase of the typical high-coupon bond offered at about par, wherein, for example, a 7% interest return is imagined to compensate for a distinctly inferior grade of security.[10]

Fallacy of the "Business Man's Investment." An issue of this type is commonly referred to in the financial world as a "business man's investment" and is supposedly suited to those who can afford to take some degree of risk. Most of the foreign bonds floated between 1923 and 1929 belonged in that category. The same is true of the great bulk of straight preferred stock issues. According to our view, such "business man's investments" are an illogical type of commitment. The security buyer who can afford to take some risk should seek a commensurate opportunity of enhancement in price and pay only secondary attention to the income obtained.

Reversal of Customary Procedure Recommended. Viewing the matter more broadly, it would be well if investors reversed their customary attitude toward income return. In selecting the grade of bonds suitable to their situation, they are prone to start at the top of the list, where maximum safety is combined with lowest yield, and then to calculate how great a concession from ideal security they are willing to make for the sake of a more attractive income rate. From this point of view, the ordinary investor becomes accustomed to the idea that the type of issue suited to his needs must rank somewhere below the very best, a frame of mind which is likely to lead to the acceptance of definitely unsound bonds, either because of their high income return or by surrender to the blandishments of the bond salesman.

It would be sounder procedure to start with minimum standards of safety, which all bonds must be required to meet in order to be eligible for further consideration. Issues failing to meet these minimum requirements should be automatically disqualified as straight investments, regardless of high yield, attractive prospects, or other grounds for partiality. Having thus delimited the field of eligible investments, the buyer may then apply such further selective processes as he deems appropriate. He may desire elements of safety far beyond the accepted minima, in

---

[10] In an exceptional year such as 1921 strongly entrenched bonds were offered bearing a 7% coupon, due to the prevailing high money rates.

which case he must ordinarily make some sacrifice of yield. He may also indulge his preferences as to the nature of the business and the character of the management. But, essentially, bond selection should consist of working upward from definite minimum standards rather than working downward in haphazard fashion from some ideal but unacceptable level of maximum security.

CHAPTER 8

Specific Standards
for Bond Investment

IV. FOURTH PRINCIPLE: DEFINITE STANDARDS
OF SAFETY MUST BE APPLIED

Since the selection of high-grade bonds has been shown to be in good
part a process of exclusion, it lends itself reasonably well to the application of definite rules and standards designed to disqualify unsuitable
issues. Such regulations have in fact been set up in many states by legislative enactment to govern the investments made by savings banks and
by trust funds. In most such states, the banking department prepares
each year a list of securities which appear to conform to these regulations and are therefore considered "legal," *i.e.*, eligible for purchase
under the statute.

It is our view that the underlying idea of fixed standards and minima
should be extended to the entire field of straight investment, *i.e.*, investment for income only. These legislative restrictions are intended to promote a high average level of investment quality and to protect depositors
and beneficiaries against losses from unsafe securities. If such regulations
are desirable in the case of institutions, it should be logical for individuals
to follow them also. We have previously challenged the prevalent idea
that the ordinary investor can afford to take greater investment risks than
a savings bank, and need not therefore be as exacting with respect to
the soundness of his fixed-value securities. The experience since 1928
undoubtedly emphasizes the need for a general tightening of investment
standards, and a simple method of attaining this end might be to confine all straight-bond selections to those which meet the legal tests
of eligibility for savings banks or trust funds. Such a procedure would
appear directly consonant with our fundamental principle that straight

investments should be made only in issues of unimpeachable soundness, and that securities of inferior grade must be bought only on an admittedly speculative basis.

New York Savings-Bank Law as a Point of Departure. As a matter of *practical policy*, an individual bond buyer is likely to obtain fairly satisfactory results by subjecting himself to the restrictions which govern the investment of savings banks' funds. But this procedure cannot be seriously suggested as a *general principle of investment*, because the legislative provisions are themselves far too imperfect to warrant their acceptance as the best available theoretical standards. The acts of the various states are widely divergent; most of them are antiquated in important respects; none is entirely logical or scientific. The legislators did not approach their task from the viewpoint of establishing criteria of sound investments for universal use; consequently they felt free to impose arbitrary restrictions on savings-bank and trust funds, which they would have hesitated to prescribe for investors generally. The New York statute, generally regarded as the best of its class, is nevertheless marred by a number of evident defects. In the formulation of comprehensive investment standards, the New York legislation may best be used, therefore, as a guide or point of departure, rather than as a final authority. The ensuing discussion will follow fairly closely the pattern set forth in the statutory provisions (as they existed in 1939); but these will be criticized, rejected, or amplified, whenever such emendation appears desirable.

GENERAL CRITERIA PRESCRIBED
BY THE NEW YORK STATUTE

The specific requirements imposed by the statute upon bond investments may be classified under seven heads, which we shall proceed to enumerate and discuss:

1. The *nature* and *location* of the business or government.
2. The *size* of the enterprise, or the issue.
3. The *terms* of the issue.
4. The *record* of solvency and dividend payments.
5. The relation of *earnings* to interest requirements.
6. The relation of the *value* of the property to the funded debt.
7. The relation of *stock* capitalization to the funded debt.

NATURE AND LOCATION

The most striking features of the laws governing savings-bank investments is the complete exclusion of bonds in certain broad categories. The New York provisions relative to permitted and prohibited classes may be summarized as follows (subject to a 1938 amendment soon to be discussed):

Admitted	Excluded
United States government, state and municipal bonds.	Foreign government and foreign corporation bonds.
Railroad bonds and electric, gas and telephone mortgage bonds.	Street railway and water bonds. Debentures of public utilities.
Bonds secured by first mortgages on real estate.	All industrial bonds.
	Bonds of financial companies (investment trusts, credit concerns, etc.).

The Fallacy of Blanket Prohibitions. The legislature was evidently of the view that bonds belonging to the excluded categories are essentially too unstable to be suited to savings-bank investment. If this view is entirely sound, it would follow from our previous reasoning that all issues in these groups are unsuited to conservative investment generally. Such a conclusion would involve revolutionary changes in the field of finance, since a large part of the capital now regularly raised in the investment market would have to be sought on an admittedly speculative basis.

In our opinion, a considerable narrowing of the investment category is in fact demanded by the unsatisfactory experience of bond investors over a fairly long period. Nevertheless, there are strong objections to the application of blanket prohibitions of the kind now under discussion. Investment theory should be chary of easy generalizations. Even if full recognition is given, for example, to the unstable tendencies of industrial bonds, as discussed in Chap. 7, the elimination of this entire major group from investment consideration would seem neither practicable nor desirable. The existence of a fair number of industrial issues (even though a small percentage of the total) which have maintained an undoubted investment status through the severest tests, would preclude investors generally from adopting so drastic a policy. Moreover, the confining of investment demand to a few eligible types of enterprise is likely to make for scarcity, and hence for the acceptance of inferior issues merely because they fall within these groups. This has in fact been one of the unfortunate results of the present legislative restrictions.

Individual Strength May Compensate for Inherent Weakness of a Class. It would seem a sounder principle, therefore, to require a stronger exhibit by the *individual* bond to compensate for any weakness supposedly inherent in its *class*, rather than to seek to admit all bonds of certain favored groups and to exclude all bonds of others. An industrial bond may properly be required to show a larger margin of earnings over interest charges and a smaller proportion of debt to going-concern value than would be required of an obligation of a gas or electric enterprise. The same would apply in the case of traction bonds. In connection with the exclusion of *water-company bonds* by the New York statute, it should be noted that this group is considered by most other states to be on a par with gas, electric, and telephone obligations. There seems to be no good reason for subjecting them to more stringent requirements than in the case of other types of public-service issues.

The 1938 Amendment to the Banking Law. In 1938 the New York legislature, recognizing the validity of these objections to categorical exclusions, proceeded to relieve the situation in a rather peculiar manner. It decreed that the Banking Board could authorize savings banks to invest in interest-bearing obligations not otherwise eligible for investment, provided application for such authorization shall have been made by not less than 20 savings banks, or by a trust company, all of the capital stock of which is owned by not less than 20 savings banks. (This meant the Savings Bank Trust Company of New York.)

Clearly this amendment goes much farther than a mere widening of the categories of savings-bank investment. What it does, in fact, is to supersede—potentially, at least—all the specific requirements of the law (other than the primary insistence on interest-paying bonds) by the combined judgment of the savings banks themselves and the Banking Board. This means that, in theory, all seven of the criteria imposed by the law may be set aside by agreement of the parties. Obviously there is no practical danger that the legislative wisdom of the statute will be completely flouted. In fact, investments authorized by virtue of this new provision up to the end of 1939 are all unexceptionable in character. They include previously ineligible debenture issues of very strong telephone and industrial companies. (Curiously enough, no industrial mortgage bond has as yet been approved, but this may serve to confirm our previous statement that good industrial bonds are likely to be debentures.)

The action to date under the 1938 amendment has represented a praiseworthy departure from the unduly narrow restrictions of the statute itself, which we have criticized above. We are by no means convinced, however, that the legislation as it now stands is in really satisfactory form. There seems to be something puerile about enacting a long list of rules and then permitting an administrative body to waive as many of them as it sees fit. Would it not be better to prescribe a few really important criteria, which must be followed in every instance, and then give the Banking Board discretionary power to *exclude* issues that meet these minimum requirements but still are not sound enough in its conservative judgment?

Obligations of Foreign Governments. We have argued against any broad exclusions of entire categories of bonds. But in dealing with foreign-government debts, a different type of reasoning may conceivably be justified. Such issues respond in but small degree to financial analysis, and investment therein is ordinarily based on general considerations, such as confidence in the country's economic and political stability and the belief that it will faithfully endeavor to discharge its obligations. To a much greater extent, therefore, than in the case of other bonds, an opinion may be justified or even necessitated as to the *general desirability* of foreign-government bonds for fixed-value investment.

The Factor of Political Expediency. Viewing objectively the history of foreign-bond investment in this country since it first assumed importance during the World War, it is difficult to escape an unfavorable conclusion on this point. In the final analysis, a foreign-government debt is an unenforceable contract. If payment is withheld, the bondholder has no direct remedy. Even if specific revenues or assets are pledged as security, he is practically helpless in the event that these pledges are broken.[1] It follows

---

[1] Among the numerous examples of this unhappy fact we may mention the pledge of specific revenues behind the Dawes Loan (German government) 7s, due 1949, and the Sao Paulo Secured 7s, due 1956. Following default of service of these two loans in 1934 and 1932, respectively, nothing whatever was done, or could have been done, to enforce the claim against the pledged revenues.

that while a foreign-government obligation is in theory a claim against the entire resources of the nation, the extent to which these resources are actually drawn upon to meet the external debt burden is found to depend in good part on political expediency. The grave international dislocations of the postwar period made some defaults inevitable, and supplied the pretext for others. In any event, because nonpayment has become a familiar phenomenon, its very frequency has removed much of the resultant obloquy. Hence the investor has, seemingly less reason than of old to rely upon herculean efforts being made by a foreign government to live up to its obligations during difficult times.

The Foreign-Trade Argument. It is generally argued that a renewal of large-scale international lending is necessary to restore world equilibrium. More concretely, such lending appears to be an indispensable adjunct to the restoration and development of our export trade. But the investor should not be expected to make unsound commitments for idealistic reasons or to benefit American exporters. As a *speculative operation*, the purchase of foreign obligations at low prices, such as prevailed in 1932, might prove well justified by the attendant possibilities of profit; but these tremendously depreciated quotations are in themselves a potent argument against later purchases of new foreign issues at a price close to 100% of face value, no matter how high the coupon rate may be set.

The Individual-Record Argument. It may be contended, however, that investment in foreign obligations is essentially similar to any other form of investment in that it requires discrimination and judgment. Some nations deserve a high credit rating based on their past performance, and these are entitled to investment preference to the same degree as are domestic corporations with satisfactory records. The legislatures of several states have recognized the superior standing of Canada by authorizing savings banks to purchase its obligations, and Vermont has accepted also the dollar bonds of Belgium, Denmark, Great Britain, Holland, and Switzerland.

A strong argument in the contrary direction is supplied by the appended list of the various countries having debts payable in dollars, classified according to the credit rating indicated by the market action of their bonds during the severe test of 1932.

1. Countries whose bonds sold on an investment basis: Canada, France, Great Britain, Netherlands, Switzerland.

2. Countries whose bonds sold on a speculative basis: Argentina, Australia, Austria, Bolivia, Brazil, Bulgaria, Chile, China, Colombia, Costa Rica, Cuba, Czecho-Slovakia, Denmark, Dominican Republic, Esthonia, Finland, Germany, Guatemala, Greece, Haiti, Hungary, Japan, Jugoslavia, Mexico, Nicaragua, Panama, Peru, Poland, Rumania, Russia, Salvador, Uruguay.

3. Borderline countries: Belgium, Ireland, Italy, Norway, Sweden.

Of the five countries in the first or investment group, the credit of two, *viz.*, France and Great Britain, was considered speculative in the preceding depression of 1921–1922. Out of 42 countries represented, therefore, only three (Canada, Holland, and Switzerland) enjoyed an unquestioned investment rating during the twelve years ending in 1932.

Twofold Objection to Purchase of Foreign-Government Bonds. This evidence suggests that the purchase of foreign-government bonds is subject to a twofold objection of *generic* character: theoretically, in that the basis for credit is fundamentally intangible; and practically, in that experience with the foreign group has been preponderantly unsatisfactory. Apparently it will require a considerable betterment of world conditions, demonstrated by a fairly long period of punctual discharge of international obligations, to warrant a revision of this unfavorable attitude toward foreign bonds as a class.

Canadian issues may undoubtedly be exempted from this blanket condemnation, both on their record and because of the closeness of the relationship between Canada and the United States. Individual investors, for either personal or statistical reasons, may be equally convinced of the high credit standing of various other countries, and will therefore be ready to purchase their obligations as high-grade investments. Such commitments may prove to be fully justified by the facts; but for some years, at least, it would be well if the investor approached them in the light of *exceptions* to a general rule of avoiding foreign bonds, and required them accordingly to present exceptionally strong evidence of stability and safety.[2]

---

[2] The foregoing section relating to foreign-government bonds is reproduced without change from the 1934 edition of this work. War conditions existing in 1940 add emphasis to our conclusions. Note that at the end of 1939 the dollar bonds of only Argentina, Canada, and Cuba were selling on better than a 6% basis in our markets. (Certain Cuban bonds were selling to yield over 6%. Note also that Great Britain, Netherlands, Sweden, and Switzerland had no dollar bonds outstanding.) For data concerning foreign-bond defaults see various news releases and reports of Foreign Bondholders' Protective Council, Inc.

Bonds of Foreign Corporations. In *theory*, bonds of a corporation, however prosperous, cannot enjoy better security than the obligations of the country in which the corporation is located. The government, through its taxing power, has an unlimited prior claim upon the assets and earnings of the business; in other words, it can take the property away from the private bondholder and utilize it to discharge the national debt. But in actuality, distinct limits are imposed by political expediency upon the exercise of the taxing power. Accordingly we find instances of corporations meeting their dollar obligations even when their government is in default.[3]

Foreign-corporation bonds have an advantage over governmental bonds in that the holder enjoys specific legal remedies in the event of nonpayment, such as the right of foreclosure. Consequently it is probably true that a foreign company is under greater *compulsion* to meet its debt than is a sovereign nation. But it must be recognized that the conditions resulting in the default of government obligations are certain to affect adversely the position of the corporate bondholder. Restrictions on the transfer of funds may prevent the payment of interest in dollars even though the company may remain amply solvent.[4] Furthermore, the distance separating the creditor from the property, and the obstacles interposed by governmental decree, are likely to destroy the practical value of his mortgage security. For these reasons the unfavorable conclusions reached with respect to foreign-government obligations as fixed-value investments must be considered as applicable also to foreign-corporation bonds.

SIZE

The bonds of very small enterprises are subject to objections which disqualify them as media for conservative investment. A company of relatively minor size is more vulnerable than others to unexpected happenings, and it is likely to be handicapped by the lack of strong banking connections or of technical resources. Very small businesses, therefore, have never been able to obtain public financing and have depended on private capital, those supplying the funds being given the double induce-

---

[3] See Appendix Note 15 for examples.

[4] See Appendix Note 16 for examples.

ment of a share in the profits and a direct voice in the management. The objections to bonds of undersized corporations apply also to tiny villages or microscopic townships, and the careful investor in municipal obligations will ordinarily avoid those below a certain population level.

The establishment of such minimum requirements as to size necessarily involves the drawing of arbitrary lines of demarcation. There is no mathematical means of determining exactly at what point a company or a municipality becomes large enough to warrant the investor's attention. The same difficulty will attach to setting up any other quantitative standards, as for example the margin of earnings above interest charges, or the relation of stock or property values to bonded debt. It must be borne in mind, therefore, that all these "critical points" are necessarily rule-of-thumb decisions, and the investor is free to use other amounts if they appeal to him more. But however arbitrary the standards selected may be, they are undoubtedly of great practical utility in safeguarding the bond buyer from inadequately protected issues.

Provisions of New York Statute. The New York statute has prescribed various standards as to minimum size in defining investments eligible for savings banks. As regards municipal bonds, a population of not less than 10,000 is required for states adjacent to New York, and of 30,000 for other states. Railroads must either own 500 miles of standard-gauge line or else have operating revenues of not less than $10,000,000 per annum. Unsecured and income bonds of railroad companies are admitted only if (among other special requirements) the *net income* available for dividends amounts to $10,000,000. For gas and electric companies, gross revenues must have averaged $1,000,000 per year during the preceding five years; but in the case of telephone bonds, this figure must be $5,000,000. There are further provisions to the effect that the size of the bond issue itself must be not less than $1,000,000 for gas and electric companies, and not less than $5,000,000 in the case of telephone obligations.

Some Criticisms of These Requirements. The figures of minimum gross receipts do not appear well chosen from the standpoint of bond investment in general. The distinctions as to population requirements would scarcely appeal to investors throughout the country. The alternative tests for railroads, based on either mileage or revenues, are confusing and unnecessary. The $10,000,000-gross requirement by itself is too high; it would have eliminated, for example, the Bangor and Aroostook

Railroad, one of the few lines to make a satisfactory exhibit during the 1930–1933 depression as well as before. Equally unwarranted is the requirement of $5,000,000 gross for telephone concerns, as against only $1,000,000 for gas and electric utilities. This provision would have ruled out the bonds of Tri-State Telephone and Telegraph Company prior to 1927, although they were then (and since) obligations of unquestioned merit. We believe that the following proposed requirements for minimum size, although by necessity arbitrarily taken, are in reasonable accord with the realities of sound investment:

	Minimum Requirement of Size
Municipalities	10,000 population
Public-utility enterprises	$2,000,000 gross
Railroad systems	$3,000,000 gross
Industrial companies	$5,000,000 gross

Industrial Bonds and the Factor of Size. Since industrial bonds are not eligible for savings banks under the New York law, no minimum size is therein prescribed. We have expressed the view that industrial obligations may be included among high-grade investments provided they meet stringent tests of safety. The experience of the past decade indicates that dominant or at least substantial size affords an element of protection against the hazards of instability to which industrial enterprises are more subject than are railroads or public utilities. A cautious investor, seeking to profit from recent lessons, would apparently be justified in deciding to confine his purchases of fixed-value bonds to perhaps the half dozen leading units in each industrial group, and also perhaps in adding the suggested minimum requirement of $5,000,000 annual sales.

Such minimum standards may be criticized as unduly stringent, in that if they were universally applied (which in any event is unlikely) they would make it impossible for sound and prosperous businesses of moderate size to finance themselves through straight bond issues. It is conceivable that a general stabilization of industrial conditions in the United States may invalidate the conclusions derived from the extreme variations of the past ten years. But until such a tendency in the direction of stability has actually demonstrated itself, we should favor a highly exacting attitude toward the purchase of industrial bonds *at investment levels.*

Large Size Alone No Guarantee of Safety. These recommendations on the subject of minimum size do not imply that enormous dimensions are in themselves a guarantee of prosperity and financial strength. The biggest company may be the weakest if its bonded debt is disproportionately large. Moreover, in the railroad, public-utility, and municipal groups, no practical advantage attaches to the very largest units as compared with those of medium magnitude. Whether the gross receipts of an electric company are twenty millions or a hundred millions has, in all probability, no material effect on the safety of its bonds; and similarly a town of 75,000 inhabitants may deserve better credit than would a city of several millions. It is only in the industrial field that we have suggested that the bonds of a very large enterprise may be inherently more desirable than those of middle-sized companies; but even here a thoroughly satisfactory statistical showing on the part of the large company is necessary to make this advantage a dependable one.

Other Provisions Rejected. The New York statute includes an additional requirement in respect to unsecured railroad bonds, *viz.*, that the *net* earnings after interest charge must equal $10,000,000. This does not appear to us to be justified, since we have previously argued against attaching particular significance to the possession or lack of mortgage security. There is a certain logical fallacy also in the further prescription of a minimum size for the bond issue itself in the case of public utilities. If the enterprise is large enough as measured by its gross business, then the smaller the bond issue the easier it would be to meet interest and principal requirements. The legislature probably desired to avoid the inferior marketability associated with very small issues. In our view, the element of marketability is generally given too much stress by investors; and in this case we do not favor following the statutory requirement with respect to the size of the issue as a general rule for bond investment.

See Chapter 9, "Specific Standards for Bond Investment (*Continued*)" online at www.mhprofessional.com/SecurityAnalysis7.

CHAPTER 10

Specific Standards for Bond Investment (*Continued*)

THE RELATION OF THE VALUE OF THE PROPERTY TO THE FUNDED DEBT

In our earlier discussion (Chap. 6) we pointed out that the soundness of the typical bond investment depends upon the ability of the obligor corporation to take care of its debts, rather than upon the value of the property on which the bonds have a lien. This broad principle naturally leads directly away from the establishment of any *general* tests of bond safety based upon the value of the mortgaged assets, where this value is considered apart from the success or failure of the enterprise itself.

Stating the matter differently, we do not believe that in the case of the ordinary corporation bond—whether railroad, utility, or industrial—it would be advantageous to stipulate any minimum relationship between the value of the physical property pledged (taken at either original or reproduction cost) and the amount of the debt. In this respect we are in disagreement with statutory provisions in many states (including New York) which reflect the traditional emphasis upon property values. The New York law, for example, will not admit as eligible a gas, electric, or telephone bond, unless it is secured by property having a value $66^2/3\%$ in excess of the bond issue. This value is presumably book value, which either may be the original dollar cost less depreciation or may be some more or less artificial value set up as a result of transfer or reappraisal.

Special Types of Obligations: 1. Equipment Obligations. It is our view that the book value of public-utility properties—and of railroads and the typical industrial plant as well—is no guidance in determining the safety of the bond issues secured thereon. There are, however, various *special* types of obligations, the safety of which is in great measure dependent upon the assets securing them, as distinguished from the going-concern value of the enterprise as a whole. The most characteristic of these, perhaps, is the railroad-equipment trust certificate, secured by title to locomotives, freight cars, or passenger cars, and by the pledge of the lease under which the railroad is using the equipment. The investment record of these equipment obligations is very satisfactory, particularly because until recently even the most serious financial difficulties of the issuing road have very rarely prevented the prompt payment of interest and principal.[1] The primary reason for these good results is that the specific property pledged is removable and usable by other carriers. Consequently it enjoys an independent salable value, similar to automobiles, jewelry, and other chattels on which personal loans are made. Even where there might be great difficulty in actually selling the rolling stock to some other railroad at a reasonable price, this mobility still gives the equipment obligation a great advantage over the mortgages on the railroad itself. Both kinds of property are essential to the operation of the line, but the railroad bondholder has no alternative save to permit the receiver to operate his property, while the holder of the equipment lien can at least threaten to take the rolling stock away. It is the possession of this *alternative* which in practice has proved of prime value to the owner of equipment trusts because it has virtually compelled the holders even of the first mortgages on the road itself to subordinate their claim to his.

It follows that the holder of equipment-trust certificates has two separate sources of protection, the one being the credit and success of the borrowing railway, the other being the value of the pledged rolling stock. If the latter value is sufficiently in excess of the money loaned against it, he may be able to ignore the first or credit factor entirely, in the same way as a pawn-broker ignores the financial status of the individual to whom he lends money and is content to rely exclusively on the pledged property.

The conditions under which equipment trusts are usually created supply a substantial degree of protection to the purchaser. The legal forms are designed to facilitate the enforcement of the lienholder's rights in the event of nonpayment. In practically all cases at least 20% of the cost of the equipment is provided by the railway, and consequently the amount of the equipment obligations is initially not more than 80% of

---

[1] See Appendix Note 17 for information on the investment record of such issues.

the value of the property pledged behind them. The principal is usually repayable in 15 equal annual installments, beginning one year from issuance, so that the amount of the debt is reduced more rapidly than ordinary depreciation would require.

The protection accorded the equipment-trust holder by these arrangements has been somewhat diminished in recent years, due partly to the drop in commodity prices which has brought reproduction (and therefore, salable) values far below original cost, and also to the reduced demand for equipment, whether new or used, because of the smaller traffic handled. Since 1930 certain railroads in receivership (*e.g.*, Seaboard Air Line and Wabash) have required holders of maturing equipment obligations to extend their maturities for a short period or to exchange them for trustee's or receiver's certificates carrying a lower coupon. In the unique case of one Florida East Coast Railway issue (Series "D") the receivers permitted the equipment-trust holders to take over and sell the pledged equipment, which seemed to have been less valuable than that securing other series. In this instance the holders realized only 43 cents on the dollar from the sale and have a deficiency judgment (of doubtful value) against the road for the balance. These maneuvers and losses suggest that the claim of "almost absolute safety" frequently made in behalf of equipment issues will have to be moderated; but it cannot be denied that this form of investment enjoys a positive and substantial advantage through the realizability of the pledged assets.[2] (This conclusion may be supported by a concrete reference to the sale in November 1939 of Chicago and North Western new Equipment Trust $2^{1}/_{2}$s, due 1940–1949, at prices to yield only from 0.45 to 2.35%, despite the fact that all the mortgage issues of that road were then in default.)

2. Collateral-Trust Bonds. Collateral-trust bonds are obligations secured by the pledge of stocks or other bonds. In the typical case, the collateral consists of bonds of the obligor company itself, or of the bonds or stocks of subsidiary corporations. Consequently the realizable value of the collateral is usually dependent in great measure on the success of the enterprise as a whole. But in the case of the collateral-trust issues of investment companies, a development of recent years, the holder may be said to have a primary interest in the market value of the pledged securities, so that

---

[2] See Appendix Note 18 for comment and supporting data.

it is quite possible that by virtue of the protective conditions in the indenture, he may be completely taken care of under conditions which mean virtual extinction for the stockholders. This type of collateral-trust bond may therefore be ranked with equipment-trust obligations as exceptions to our general rule that the bond buyer must place his chief reliance on the success of the enterprise and not on the property specifically pledged.

Going behind the form to the substance, we may point out that this characteristic is essentially true also of investment-trust *debenture* obligations. For it makes little practical difference whether the portfolio is physically pledged with a trustee, as under a collateral-trust indenture, or whether it is held by the corporation subject to the claim of the debenture bondholders. In the usual case the debentures are protected by adequate provisions against increasing the debt, and frequently also by a covenant requiring the market price of the company's assets to be maintained at a stated percentage above the face amount of the bonds.

Example: The Reliance Management Corporation Debenture 5s, due 1954, are an instance of the working of these protective provisions. The enterprise as a whole was highly unsuccessful, as is shown vividly by a decline in the price of the stock from 69 in 1929 to 1 in 1933. In the case of the ordinary bond issue, such a collapse in the stock value would have meant almost certain default and large loss of principal. But here the fact that the assets could be readily turned into cash gave significance to the protective covenants behind the debentures. It made possible and compelled the repurchase by the company of more than three-quarters of the issue, and it even forced the stockholders to contribute additional capital to make good a deficiency of assets below the indenture requirements. This resulted in the bonds selling as high as 88 in 1932 when the stock sold for only $2^1/_2$. The balance of the issue was called at $104^1/_4$ in February 1937.

In Chap. 18, devoted to protective covenants, we shall refer to the history of a collateral-trust bond issue of an investment company (Financial Investing Company), and we shall point out that the intrinsic strength of such obligations is often impaired—unnecessarily, in our opinion—by hesitation in asserting the bondholders' rights.

3. Real Estate Bonds. Of much greater importance than either of the two types of securities just discussed is the large field of real estate mortgages and real estate mortgage bonds. The latter represent participations of convenient size in large individual mortgages. There is no doubt that in the case of such obligations the value of the pledged land and buildings is of paramount importance. The ordinary real estate loan made by an experienced investor is based chiefly upon his conclusions as to the fair value of the property offered as security. It seems to us, however, that in a broad sense the values behind real estate mortgages are *going-concern values; i.e.,* they are derived fundamentally from the earning power of the property, either actual or presumptive. In other words, the value of the pledged asset is not something *distinct* from the success of the enterprise (as is possibly the case with a railroad-equipment trust certificate), but is rather *identical* therewith.

This point may be made clearer by a reference to the most typical form of real estate loan, a first mortgage on a single-family dwelling house. Under ordinary conditions a home costing $10,000 would have a rental value (or an equivalent value to an owner-tenant) of some $1,200 per year, and would yield a net income of about $800 after taxes and other expenses. A 5% first-mortgage loan on the savings-bank basis, *i.e.,* 60% of value, or $6,000, would therefore be protected by a normal *earning power* of over twice the interest requirements. Stated differently, the rental value could suffer a reduction of over one-third before the ability to meet interest charges would be impaired. Hence the mortgagee reasons that regardless of the ability of the then owner of the house to pay the carrying charges, he could always find a tenant or a new purchaser who would rent or buy the property on a basis at least sufficient to cover his 60% loan. (By way of contrast, it may be pointed out that a typical *industrial plant,* costing $1,000,000 and bonded for $600,000, could not be expected to sell or rent for enough to cover the 5% mortgage if the issuing company went into bankruptcy.)

Property Values and Earning Power Closely Related. This illustration shows that under normal conditions obtaining in the field of *dwellings, offices,* and *stores,* the property values and the rental values go hand in hand. In this sense it is largely immaterial whether the lender views mortgaged property of this kind as something with salable value or as something with an earning power, the equivalent of a going concern. To some extent this is true also of vacant lots and unoccupied houses or stores, since the market value of these is closely related to the *expected* rental when improved or let. (It is emphatically not true, however, of buildings erected for a special purpose, such as factories, etc.)

Misleading Character of Appraisals. The foregoing discussion is important in its bearing on the correct attitude that the intending investor in real estate bonds should take towards the property values asserted to exist behind the issues submitted to him. During the great and disastrous development of the real estate mortgage-bond business between 1923 and 1929, the only datum customarily presented to support the usual bond offering—aside from an estimate of future earnings—was a statement of the *appraised value* of the property, which almost invariably amounted to some $66^2/3\%$ in excess of the mortgage issue. If these appraisals had corresponded to the market values which experienced buyers of or lenders on real estate would place upon the properties, they would have been of real utility in the selection of sound real estate bonds. But unfortunately they were purely artificial valuations, to which the appraisers were willing to attach their names for a fee, and whose only function was to deceive the investor as to the protection which he was receiving.

The method followed by these appraisals was the capitalization on a liberal basis of the rental expected to be returned by the property. By this means, a typical building which cost $1,000,000, including liberal financing charges, would immediately be given an "appraised value" of $1,500,000. Hence a bond issue could be floated for almost the entire cost of the venture so that the builders or promoters retained the equity (*i.e.*, the ownership) of the building, without a cent's investment, and in many cases with a goodly cash profit to boot.[3] This whole scheme of real estate financing was honeycombed with the most glaring weaknesses, and it is sad commentary on the lack of principle, penetration, and ordinary common sense on the part of all parties concerned that it was permitted to reach such gigantic proportions before the inevitable collapse.[4]

---

[3] The 419–4th Avenue Corporation (Bowker Building) floated a $1,230,000 bond issue in 1927 with a paid-in capital stock of only $75,000. (By the familiar process, the land and building which cost about $1,300,000 were appraised at $1,897,788.) Default and receivership in 1931–1932 were inevitable.

[4] See Appendix Note 19 for a report of Real Estate Securities Committee of the Investment Bankers Association of America commenting on defaults in this field.

Abnormal Rentals Used as Basis of Valuation. It was indeed true that the scale of rentals prevalent in 1928–1929 would yield an abundantly high rate of income on the cost of a new real estate venture. But this condition could not properly be interpreted as making a new building immediately worth 50% in excess of its actual cost. For this high income return was certain to be only temporary, since it could not fail to stimulate more and more building, until an oversupply of space caused a collapse in the scale of rentals. This overbuilding was the more inevitable because it was possible to carry it on without risk on the part of the owner, who raised all the money needed from the public.

Debt Based on Excessive Construction Costs. A collateral result of this overbuilding was an increase in the cost of construction to abnormally high levels. Hence even an apparently conservative loan made in 1928 or 1929, in an amount not exceeding two-thirds of *actual cost*, did not enjoy a proper degree of protection, because there was the evident danger (subsequently realized) that a sharp drop in construction costs would reduce fundamental values to a figure below the amount of the loan.

Weakness of Specialized Buildings. A third general weakness of real estate-bond investment lay in the entire lack of discrimination as between various types of building projects. The typical or standard real estate loan was formerly made on a home, and its peculiar virtue lay in the fact that there was an indefinitely large number of prospective purchasers or tenants to draw upon, so that it could always be disposed of at some moderate concession from the current scale of values. A fairly similar situation is normally presented by the ordinary apartment house, or store, or office building. But when a structure is built for some *special* purpose, such as a hotel, garage, club, hospital, church, or factory, it loses this quality of rapid disposability, and *its value becomes bound up with the success of the particular enterprise for whose use it was originally intended.* Hence mortgage bonds on such structures are not actually real estate bonds in the accepted sense, but rather *loans extended to a business;* and consequently their safety must be judged by all the stringent tests surrounding the purchase of an industrial obligation.

This point was completely lost sight of in the rush of real estate financing preceding the collapse in real estate values. Bonds were floated to build hotels, garages, and even hospitals, on very much the same basis as loans made on apartment houses. In other words, an appraisal showing a "value" of one-half to two-thirds in excess of the bond issue was considered almost enough to establish the safety of the loan. It turned out, however, that when such new ventures proved commercially unsuccessful and were unable to pay their interest charges, the "real estate" bondholders were in little better position than the holders of a mortgage on an unprofitable railroad or mill property.[5]

Values Based on Initial Rentals Misleading. Another weakness should be pointed out in connection with apartment-house financing. The rental income used in determining the appraised value was based on the rentals to be charged at the outset. But apartment-house tenants are accustomed to pay a substantial premium for space in a new building, and they consider a structure old, or at least no longer especially modern and desirable, after it has been standing a very few years. Consequently, under normal conditions the rentals received in the first years are substantially larger than those which can conservatively be expected throughout the life of the bond issue.

Lack of Financial Information. A defect related to those discussed above, but of a different character, was the almost universal failure to supply the bond buyer with operating and financial data after his purchase. This drawback applies generally to companies that sell bonds to the public but whose stock is privately held—an arrangement characteristic of real estate financing. As a result, not only were most bondholders unaware of the poor showing of the venture until default had actually taken place, but—more serious still—at that time they frequently found that large unpaid taxes had accrued against the property while the owners were "milking" it by drawing down all available cash.

Suggested Rules of Procedure. From this detailed analysis of the defects of real estate bond financing in the past decade, a number of specific rules of procedure may be developed to guide the investor in the future.

In the case of single-family dwellings, loans are generally made directly by the mortgage holder to the owner of the home, *i.e.*, without the intermediary of a real estate mortgage *bond* sold by a house of issue. But an extensive business has also been transacted by mortgage companies (*e.g.*, Lawyers Mortgage Company, Title Guarantee and Trust Company) in

---

[5] See Appendix Note 20 for an example (Hudson Towers).

guaranteed mortgages and mortgage-participation certificates, secured on such dwellings.[6]

Where investments of this kind are made, the lender should be certain: (*a*) that the amount of the loan is not over 66²/₃% of the value of the property, as shown either by actual recent cost or by the amount which an experienced real estate man would consider a fair price *to pay* for the property; and (*b*) that this cost or fair price does not reflect recent speculative inflation and does not greatly exceed the price levels existing for a long period previously. If so, a proper reduction must be made in the maximum relation of the amount of mortgage debt to the current value.

The more usual real estate mortgage *bond* represents a participation in a first mortgage on a new apartment house or office building. In considering such offerings the investor should ignore the conventional "appraised values" submitted and demand that the actual cost, fairly presented, should exceed the amount of the bond issue by at least 50%. Secondly, he should require an estimated income account, conservatively calculated to reflect losses through vacancies and the decline in the rental scale as the building grows older. This income account should forecast a margin of at least 100% over interest charges, after deducting from earnings a depreciation allowance to be actually expended as a sinking fund for the gradual retirement of the bond issue. The borrower should agree to supply the bondholders with regular operating and financial statements.

Issues termed "first-*leasehold* mortgage bonds" are in actuality second mortgages. They are issued against buildings erected on leased land and the ground rent operates in effect as a first lien or prior charge against the entire property. In analyzing such issues the ground rent should be added to the bond-interest requirements to arrive at the total interest charges of the property. Furthermore, it should be recognized that in the field of real estate obligations the advantage of a first mortgage over a junior lien is much more clean-cut than in an ordinary business enterprise.[7]

---

[6] Since 1933 real estate financing on single-family homes has been taken over so substantially by the Federal government, through the Federal Housing Administration (F.H.A.), that practically no real estate bonds of this type have been sold to investors. Financing on larger buildings has been greatly restricted. Practically all of it has been provided by financial institutions (insurance companies, etc.), and there have been virtually no sales of real estate securities to the general public (to the end of 1939).

[7] See Appendix Note 21 for examples and comment.

In addition to the above quantitative tests, the investor should be satisfied in his own mind that the location and type of the building are such as to attract tenants and to minimize the possibility of a large loss of value through unfavorable changes in the character of the neighborhood.[8]

Real estate loans should not be made on buildings erected for a special or limited purpose, such as hotels, garages, etc. Commitments of this kind must be made in the venture itself, considered as an individual business. From our previous discussion of the standards applicable to a high-grade industrial-bond purchase, it is difficult to see how any bond issue on a new hotel, or the like, could logically be bought on a straight investment basis. All such enterprises should be financed at the outset by private capital, and only after they can show a number of years of successful operation should the public be offered either bonds or stock therein.[9]

---

[8] Footnote to 1934 edition: "One of the few examples of a conservatively financed real estate-bond issue extant in 1933 is afforded by the Trinity Buildings Corporation of New York First 5^1/$_2$s, due 1939, secured on two well-located office buildings in the financial district of New York City. This issue was outstanding in the amount of $4,300,000, and was secured by a first lien on land and buildings assessed for taxation at $13,000,000. In 1931, gross earnings were $2,230,000 and the net after depreciation was about six times the interest on the first-mortgage bonds. In 1932, rent income declined to $1,653,000, but the balance for first-mortgage interest was still about 3^1/$_2$ times the requirement. In September 1933 these bonds sold close to par."

This footnote and the sequel well illustrate the importance of the location factor referred to in the text. Despite the improvement in general business conditions since 1933, the lessened activity in the financial district resulted in a loss of tenants and a severe decline in rental rates. The net earnings of Trinity Building Corporation failed even to cover depreciation charges in 1938 and were less than interest charges, even ignoring depreciation; principal and interest were defaulted at maturity in 1939; the guarantee by United States Realty and Improvement Company, the parent enterprise, proved inadequate; and the holders were faced with the necessity of extending their principal and accepting a reduction in the fixed coupon rate. In this instance an undoubtedly conservative financial set-up (a *quantitative* factor) did not prove strong enough to offset a decline in the rental value of the neighborhood (a *qualitative* factor).

[9] The subject of guaranteed real estate mortgage issues is treated in Chap. 17.

See Chapter 11, "Specific Standards for Bond Investment *(Continued)*"; Chapter 12, "Special Factors in the Analysis of Railroad and Public-Utility Bonds"; Chapter 13, "Other Special Factors in Bond Analysis"; Chapter 14, "The Theory of Preferred Stocks."; Chapter 15, "Technique of Selecting Preferred Stocks for Investment"; and Chapter 16, "Income Bonds and Guaranteed Securities" online at www.mhprofessional.com/SecurityAnalysis7.

CHAPTER 17

Guaranteed Securities (*Continued*)

GUARANTEED REAL ESTATE MORTGAGES AND MORTGAGE BONDS

The practice of guaranteeing securities reached its widest development in the field of real estate mortgages. These guarantees are of two different types: the first being given by the corporation engaged in the sale of the mortgages or mortgage participations (or by an affiliate); the second and more recent form being the guaranty given by an independent surety company, which assumes the contingent liability in return for a fee.

The idea underlying real estate mortgage guarantees is evidently that of insurance. It is to the mortgage holder's advantage to protect himself, at some cost in income return, against the possibility of adverse developments affecting his particular property (such as a change in the character of the neighborhood). It is within the province of sound insurance practice to afford this protection in return for an adequate premium, provided of course, that all phases of the business are prudently handled. Such an arrangement will have the best chance of success if:

1. The mortgage loans are conservatively made in the first instance.
2. The guaranty or surety company is large, well managed, independent of the agency selling the mortgages, and has a diversification of business in fields other than real estate.
3. Economic conditions are not undergoing fluctuations of abnormal intensity.

The collapse in real estate values after 1929 was so extreme as to contravene the third of these conditions. Accordingly the behavior of real estate mortgage guarantees during this period may not afford a really fair guide to their future value. Nevertheless, some of the characteristics which they revealed are worthy of comment.

This Business Once Conservatively Managed. In the first place a striking contrast may be drawn between the way in which the business of guaranteeing mortgages had been conducted prior to about 1924 and the lax methods which developed thereafter, during the very time that this part of the financial field was attaining its greatest importance.

If we consider the policies of the leading New York City institutions which guaranteed real estate mortgages (*e.g.*, Bond and Mortgage Guarantee Company, Lawyers Mortgage Company), it is fair to say that for many years the business was conservatively managed. The amount of each mortgage was limited to not more than 60% of the value, carefully determined; large individual mortgages were avoided; and a fair diversification of risk, from the standpoint of location, was attained. It is true that the guarantor companies were not independent of the selling companies, nor did they have other types of surety business. It is true also that the general practice of guaranteeing mortgages due only three to five years after their issuance contained the possibility, later realized, of a flood of maturing obligations at a most inconvenient time. Nevertheless, the prudent conduct of their activities had enabled them successfully to weather severe real estate depressions such as occurred in 1908 and 1921.

New and Less Conservative Practices Developed. The building boom which developed during the "new era" was marked by an enormous growth of the real estate mortgage business and of the practice of guaranteeing obligations of this kind. New people, new capital, and new methods entered the field. Several small local concerns which had been in the field for a long period were transformed into highly aggressive organizations doing a gigantic and nation-wide business. Great emphasis was laid upon the long record of success in the past, and the public was duly impressed— not realizing that the size, the methods, and the personnel were so changed that they were in fact dealing with a different institution. In a previous chapter we pointed out how recklessly unsound were the methods of financing real estate ventures during this period. The weakness of the mortgages themselves applied equally to the guarantees which were frequently attached thereto for an extra consideration. The guarantor companies were mere subsidiaries of the sellers of the bonds. Hence, when the crash came, the value of the properties, the real estate bond company, and the affiliated guarantor company all collapsed together.

Evil Effects of Competition and Contagion. The rise of the newer and more aggressive real estate bond organizations had a most unfortunate effect upon the policies of the older concerns. By force of competition they were led to relax their standards of making loans. New mortgages were granted on an increasingly liberal basis, and when old mortgages matured, they were frequently renewed in a larger sum. Furthermore, the face amount of the mortgages guaranteed rose to so high a multiple of the capital of the guarantor companies that it should have been obvious that the guaranty would afford only the flimsiest of protection in the event of a general decline in values.

When the real estate market broke in 1931, the first consequence was the utter collapse of virtually every one of the newer real estate bond companies and their subsidiary guarantor concerns. As the depression continued, the older institutions gave way also. The holders of guaranteed mortgages or participations therein (aggregating about $3,000,000,000 guaranteed by New York title and mortgage companies alone) found that the guaranty was a mere name and that they were entirely dependent upon the value of the underlying properties. In most cases these had been mortgaged far more heavily than reasonable prudence would have permitted. Apparently only a very small fraction of the mortgages outstanding in 1932 were created under the conservative conditions and principles that had ruled up to, say, eight years previously.

Guarantees by Independent Surety Companies. During the 1924–1930 period several of the independent surety and fidelity companies extended their operations to include the guaranteeing of real-estate mortgages for a fee or premium. Theoretically, this should have represented the soundest method of conducting such operations. In addition to the strength and general experience of the surety company there was the important fact that such a guarantor, being entirely independent, would presumably be highly critical of the issues submitted for its guaranty. But this theoretical advantage was offset to a great extent by the fact that the surety companies began the practice of guaranteeing real estate mortgage bonds only a short time prior to their debacle, and they were led by the general overoptimism then current to commit serious errors in judgment. In most cases the resultant losses to the guarantor were greater than it could stand; several of the companies were forced into receivership (notably

National Surety Company), and holders of bonds with such guarantees failed to obtain full protection.[1]

LEASEHOLD OBLIGATIONS EQUIVALENT TO GUARANTEES

The property of one company is often leased to another for a fixed annual rental sufficient to pay interest and dividends on the former's capital issues. Frequently the lease is accompanied by a specific guaranty of such interest and dividend payments, and in fact the majority of guaranteed corporate issues originate in this fashion.[2] But even if there is no explicit guaranty, a lease or other contract providing fixed annual payments will supply the equivalent of a guaranty on the securities of the lessee company.

Examples: An excellent instance of the value of such an arrangement is afforded by the Westvaco Chlorine Products Corporation 5$1/2$s, issued in 1927 and maturing in 1937. The Westvaco Company agreed to sell part of its output to a subsidiary of Union Carbide and Carbon Corporation, and the latter enterprise guaranteed that monthly payments would be made to the trustee sufficient to take care of the interest and retirement of the 5$1/2$% bonds. In effect this arrangement was a guaranty of interest and principal of the Westvaco issue by Union Carbide and Carbon, a very strong concern. By reason of this protection and the continuous purchases for redemption made thereunder, the price of the issue was maintained at 99 or higher throughout 1932–1933. This contrasts with a decline in the price of Westvaco common stock from 116$1/2$ in 1929 to 3 in 1932. (The entire bond issue was called at 100$1/2$ in September 1935.)

Another interesting example is supplied by the Tobacco Products Corporation of New Jersey 6$1/2$s, due 2022. The properties of this com-

---

[1] But in the case of the independent surety companies the guarantees proved of substantial, if only partial, value. The bankruptcy estate of National Surety Company yielded a large cash payment to holders of bonds bearing its guarantee. Some of the other companies managed to remain solvent by affecting a kind of composition with bondholders, involving the issuance of new bonds carrying a guarantee of interest at rather low rates, though not of principal. *Examples:* Metropolitan Casualty Company, Maryland Casualty Company, United States Fidelity and Guaranty Company.

[2] For example Pittsburgh, Fort Wayne and Chicago Railway Company Preferred and Common receive 7% dividends under a 999-year lease to the Pennsylvania Railroad Company. These dividends are also guaranteed by the Pennsylvania.

pany were leased to American Tobacco Company under a 99-year contract, expiring also in 2022, providing for annual payments of $2,500,000
(with the privilege to the lessee to settle by a lump-sum payment equivalent to the then present value of the rental, discounted at 7% per annum).
By means of a sinking-fund arrangement these rental payments were calculated to be sufficient to retire the bond issue in full prior to maturity, in
addition to taking care of the interest. These Tobacco Products 6$^{1}/_{2}$s were
the equivalent of fixed obligations of American Tobacco Company. As
such they ranked ahead of American Tobacco Preferred, dividends on
which, of course, are not a fixed charge. When the bonds were created in
1931 the investing public was either sceptical of the validity of the lease
or—more probably—was not familiar with this situation, for American
Tobacco Preferred sold at a much higher relative price than the Tobacco
Products bonds. At the low price of 73 in 1932 the bonds yielded 8.90%,
while American Tobacco preferred was selling at 95, to yield 6.32%. In
January 1935 the lease was commuted by a lump-sum payment resulting
in the redemption of the Tobacco Products 6$^{1}/_{2}$s at par.

Specific Terms of Lease Important.

Example: As in the case of guaranteed issues, the details of the lease
arrangement may have a vital bearing on the status of the issue benefiting
therefrom. Some of the elements here involved are illustrated by the following example:

Georgia Midland Railway First 3s, due 1946. Not guaranteed, but
property leased to Southern Railway until 1995, at a rental equal to present bond interest. (Price in January 1939, 35.)

In this case the lease agreement is fully equivalent to a guarantee of
interest up to and far beyond the maturity date. The value of the guaranty
itself depends upon the solvency of the Southern Railway. The status of
the bond issue at maturity in 1946 will depend, however, on a number
of other factors as well, *e.g.*:

1. The market value of a long-term rental obligation of Southern
Railway. If interest rates are low enough, and the credit of Southern
Railway high enough, the issue could be refunded at the same 3% interest
rate into a longer maturity. (This would seem far from probable in 1939.)

2. The value of the Georgia Midland mileage. If this mileage actually
earns substantially more than the rental paid, then Southern Railway
could be expected to make a special effort to pay the bonds at maturity,

for fear of otherwise losing control of the property. This would involve an agreement to pay such higher rental (*i.e.*, interest rate) as may be necessary to permit extension or refunding of the bond maturity. (However, traffic-density data in private hands in 1939 indicated that this mileage was not a valuable part of the Southern Railway System.)

3. Possible payment on grounds of convenience, etc. If the Southern Railway is prosperous in 1946, it may take care of this maturity merely to avoid insolvency for part of the system. There is also the technical possibility that by the terms of its own "blanket" Development and General Mortgage (under which sufficient bonds are reserved to refund the Georgia Midland 3s at maturity), it may be considered to have an obligation to provide for payment of these bonds in 1946. (Here also, as in the two previous paragraphs, the bondholder in 1939 could not be too confident of the strength of his position).

The foregoing discussion will perhaps adequately explain the low price of the Georgia Midland 3s at the beginning of 1939. It is interesting to note, as an element of security analysis, that the key fact in this situation—the unprofitable character of the mileage covered—was not a matter of public record but required a check into supplementary sources of information.

Guaranteed Issues Frequently Undervalued. The Tobacco Products example illustrates the fairly frequent undervaluation of guaranteed or quasi-guaranteed issues as compared with other securities of the guarantor enterprise. A well-known instance was that of San Antonio and Aransas Pass Railway Company First 4s, due 1943, guaranteed as to principal and interest by Southern Pacific Company. Although these enjoyed a mortgage security in addition to the guaranty they regularly sold at prices yielding higher returns than did the unsecured obligations of the Southern Pacific.[3]

---

[3] A. S. Dewing, in his *A Study of Corporation Securities*, pp. 293–297, New York, 1934, makes the following statements with respect to guaranteed bonds:

"There may be, however, instances in which a holding or controlling corporation will maintain the interest or rental on an unprofitable subsidiary's bonds for strategic reasons." (Here follow examples, including details concerning San Antonio and Aransas Pass First 4s, due 1943, showing failure of the issuer to earn its charges in most years.) "Yet its [San Antonio and Aransas Pass Railway's] importance to the Southern Pacific Company's lines is such that the guarantor company very wisely meets the bond interest deficit… In spite of such instances, the rule holds good almost always that the strength of a guaranteed bond is no greater than that of the corporation issuing it and the earning capacity of the property directly covered by it."

Examples: A more striking contrast was afforded by the price of Barnhart Bros. and Spindler Company First and Second Preferred (both guaranteed as to principal and dividends by American Type Founders Company) in relation to the price of the guarantor's own preferred stock which was not a fixed obligation. Additional examples of this point are afforded by the price of Huyler's of Delaware, Inc., Preferred, guaranteed by Schulte Retail Stores Corporation, as compared with the price of Schulte Preferred; and by the price of Armour and Company of Delaware guaranteed preferred, as compared with the preferred stock of the guarantor company, Armour and Company of Illinois. Some comparative quotations relating to these examples are given below.

**Comparative Prices and Yields of Guaranteed Securities
and Securities of the Guarantor***

Issue	Date	Price	Yield, %
San Antonio & Aransas Pass 1st 4s/1943 (GTD)	Jan. 2, 1920	56¼	8.30
Southern Pacific Co. Debenture 4s/1929	Jan. 2, 1920	81	6.86
Barnhart Bros. & Spindler 7% 1st Pfd. (GTD)	1923 low price	90	7.78
Barnhart Bros. & Spindler 7% 2d Pfd. (GTD)	1923 low price	80	8.75
American Type Founders 7% Pfd	1923 low price	95	7.37
Huyler's of Delaware 7% Pfd. (GTD)	April 11, 1928	102½	6.83
Schulte Retail Stores 8% Pfd.	April 11, 1928	129	6.20
Armour of Delaware 7% Pfd. (GTD)	Feb. 13, 1925	95⅛	7.36
Armour of Illinois 7% Pfd.	Feb. 13, 1925	92⅞	7.54

* If the reader traces the subsequent history of the various issues in this table, he will find a great variety of developments, including assumption through merger (San Antonio and Aransas Pass Railroad), redemption (Barnhart Brothers and Spindler), and default (Huylers of Delaware, Inc.). But the fact that the guaranteed issues were *relatively* undervalued is demonstrated by the sequel in each case.

It is obvious that in cases of this sort advantageous exchanges can be made from the lower yielding into the higher yielding security with no

---

It seems clear to us that these statements misinterpret the essential character of the obligation under a guarantee. Southern Pacific met the San Antonio and Aransas Pass bond interest deficit, not out of "wisdom" but by compulsion. The strength of a guaranteed bond *may be very much greater than* that of the corporation issuing it, because that strength rests upon the dual claim of the holder against *both* the issuing corporation and the guarantor.

impairment of safety; or else into a much better secured issue with little sacrifice of yield, and sometimes with an actual gain.[4]

INCLUSION OF GUARANTEES AND RENTALS IN THE CALCULATION OF FIXED CHARGES

All obligations equivalent to bond interest should be included with a company's interest charges when calculating the coverage for its bond issues. This point has already been explained in some detail in connection with railroad fixed charges, and it was touched upon briefly in our discussion of public-utility bonds. The procedure in these groups offers no special difficulties. But in the case of certain types of industrial companies, the treatment of rentals and guarantees may offer confusing variations. This question is of particular moment in connection with retail enterprises, theater companies, etc., in which rent or other obligations related to buildings occupied may be an important element in the general picture. Such a building may be owned by the corporation and paid for by a bond issue, in which case the obligation will be fully disclosed in both the balance sheet and the income account. But if another company occupies a similar building under long-term lease, no separate measure of the rental obligation appears in the income account and no indication thereof can be found in the balance sheet. The second company may *appear* sounder than the first, but that is only because its obligations are undisclosed; essentially, both companies are carrying a similar burden. Conversely, the outright ownership of premises free and clear carries an important advantage (from the standpoint of preferred stock, particularly) over operation under long-term lease, although the capitalization set-up will not reveal this advantage.

Examples: If Interstate Department Stores Preferred had been compared with The Outlet Company Preferred in 1929 the two exhibits might have appeared closely similar; the earnings coverage averaged about the same, and neither company showed any bond or mortgage liability. But Outlet's position was in actuality by far the stronger, because it owned its land and buildings while those of Interstate (with a minor exception) were

---

[4] In Appendix Note 31will be found a concise discussion of certain interesting phases of guarantees and rentals, as illustrated by the N.Y. and Harlem Railroad and the Mobile and Ohio Railroad situations.

held under lease. The real effect of this situation was to place a substantial fixed obligation ahead of Interstate Department Stores Preferred which did not exist in the case of Outlet. In the chain-store field a similar observation would apply to a comparison of J. C. Penney Preferred and S. H. Kress Preferred in 1932; for the latter company owned more than half of its store properties, while nearly all the Penney locations were leased.

Lease Liabilities Generally Overlooked. The question of liability under long-term leases received very little attention from the financial world until its significance was brought home rudely in 1931 and 1932, when the high level of rentals assumed in the preceding boom years proved intolerably burdensome to many merchandising companies.

Example: The influence of this factor upon a supposed investment security is shown with striking force in the case of United Cigar Stores Preferred. This issue, and its predecessor, had for many years shown every sign of stability and had sold accordingly at a consistently high level. For 1928 the company reported "no funded debt" and earnings equal to about seven times the preferred dividend. Yet so crushing were the liabilities under its long-term leases (and to carry properties acquired by subsidiaries), that in 1932 bankruptcy was resorted to and the preferred stock was menaced with extinction.

Such Liabilities Complicated Analysis. It must be admitted that in the case of companies where the rental factor is important, its obtrusion has badly complicated the whole question of bond or preferred stock analysis. Fortunately the investor now has some data as to the extent of such leasehold obligations, since they are now required to be summarized in registration statements filed with the S.E.C., and the actual rent payments must be stated each year (on Form 10-K).[5] But the problem remains whether or not these rentals should be treated, in whole or in part, as the equivalent of fixed charges. To some extent, certainly, they are identical rather with fixed "overhead"—e.g., depreciation, taxes, general expense—which it has not been found feasible to add in with bond interest for the purpose of figuring a margin of safety. One type of solution is obvious: If the company meets the earnings test, even after adding rents paid to bond interest, the rent situation need not worry the investor.

---

[5] The S.E.C. forms group "rents and royalties" together, but in the typical case this entire item relates to rents and can be treated as such.

Example:

Swift and Company 3³/₄s, Due 1950

1934–1938 Average Results

Balance for dividends	$8,630,000
Interest paid	2,107,000
Rentals paid	996,000
Interest earned	5.1 times
Interest and rentals earned	3.8 times

We feel, however, that it would be neither fair nor practicable to require every company to meet a test so severe. A compromise suggestion based on some study of actual exhibits may be hazarded, *viz.:* (1) that one-third the annual rentals (for building space) be included with fixed charges (and preferred dividends), to compute the earnings coverage; and (2) that in the case of retail establishments (chain stores, department stores) the minimum coverage required for interest plus one-third of rentals be reduced from 3 to 2. This reduction would recognize the relative stability of retail business, after allowance is made for the special burden attaching to the rental factor. The corresponding coverage required for a retail company's preferred stock would be reduced from 4 to 2¹/₂.

Examples:

(A) Nonretail Bond Issue Loew's, Inc., 3¹/₂s, Due 1946

August 1934–August 1938 Average Results

Balance for dividends	$10,097,000
Interest (and subsid. preferred dividends) paid.	2,614,000
One-third of rentals paid	1,107,000
Interest, etc., earned	4.86 times
Interest and one-third of rentals earned	3.71 times

(B) Retail Enterprise Preferred Stock

1934–1938 Average Results

	McCrory Stores Corp. 6% Preferred	McLellan Stores Co. 6% Preferred
Balance for common stock	$1,682,000	$1,148,000
Interest on bonds	abt. 200,000	
One-third of rentals	770,000*	434,000
Preferred dividends	300,000	180,000
Preferred dividend (and interest earned)		4.36 times
7.38 times		
Preferred dividend, interest and ¹/₃ of rentals earned	2.33 times	2.87 times

* 1935–1938 average.

Conclusions: Loew's 3¹/2s pass our quantitative test for nonretail bond issues. McLellan Preferred does, but McCrory Preferred does not, pass our suggested test for retail-store preferred stocks.

The four preceding examples illustrate a simplified technique for earnings coverage. Instead of first computing the amount available for the charges, we divide the charges (and preferred dividends) into the balance *after* charges (and preferred dividends) and add 1 to the quotient.

The reader is warned that these suggested standards and the calculations illustrating them are submitted with considerable hesitation. They represent a new departure in analytical method; the data for rentals paid are available only at some effort; most serious of all, the arithmetical standards proposed are arbitrary and perhaps not the best that can be devised. We might point out, further, that the new test may yield some unexpected results. Note that McLellan Preferred has sold (in 1939) at a lower price than McCrory Preferred—a point that *may* be justified by other factors. Note, further, that if the same calculation as above is applied to W. T. Grant 5% Preferred—a high-priced issue, which earned its dividend nearly ten times over in 1934–1938—we should find that the preferred dividend plus one-third of rentals was covered not quite 2¹/2 times.[6]

Status of Guaranteed Obligations. Some additional observations may properly be made as to the computation of earnings coverage in the case of guaranteed obligations. In the typical case the properties involved in the guarantee form part of the whole enterprise; hence both the earnings therefrom and the guaranteed payments are included in a single income statement.

Example: Neisner Realty Corporation 6s, due 1948, are guaranteed by Neisner Brothers, Inc. The corporation's operations and interest charges are included in the parent company's consolidated statement.

When the guaranteed security is outstanding against a separately operated property, its standing may depend either on its own results or on those of the guarantor. Hence the issue need be required to pass only one of three alternative tests, based on (1) earnings of issuing company, independent of the guarantee; or (2) combined earnings and charges of the issuing and guarantor companies; or (3) earnings of guarantor company applied to its own charges plus its guarantees.

---

[6] This stock, par 20, sold at 25 in 1939 although callable at 22.

Examples: a. Indiana Harbor Belt Railway General 4s and 4¹/₂s, due 1957. Guaranteed as to principal and interest by New York Central Railroad and an important subsidiary. The Standard Statistics Bond Guide gives as the interest coverage that of the guarantor, the New York Central System. But the showing of the company itself is much better, *e.g.*:

	Charges earned	
	N.Y. Central System	Indiana Harbor Belt
1938	0.59 times	2.98 times
1937	1.12 times	3.81 times

b. This is the typical situation, in which coverage is calculated from a consolidated income account, including operations of both the parent (guarantor) company and its guaranteed subsidiaries.

c. Minneapolis, St. Paul and Sault Sainte Marie 5¹/₂s, due 1978, guaranteed as to interest by Canadian Pacific Railway. The "Soo line" shows earnings of only a small part of total interest charges. Coverage for this issue might best be computed by applying earnings of Canadian Pacific Railway to the total of its own interest charges plus the guaranteed interest on these and other bonds guaranteed by Canadian Pacific Railway.

SUBSIDIARY COMPANY BONDS

The bonds of a subsidiary of a strong company are generally regarded as well protected, on the theory that the parent company will take care of all its constituents' obligations. This viewpoint is encouraged by the common method of setting up consolidated income accounts, under which all the subsidiary bond interest appears as a charge against all the combined earnings, ranking ahead of the parent company's preferred and common stocks. If, however, the parent concern is not contractually responsible for the subsidiary bonds, by guaranty or lease (or direct assumption), this form of statement may prove to be misleading. For if a particular subsidiary proves unprofitable, its bond interest may conceivably not be taken care of by the parent company, which may be willing to lose its investment in this part of its business and turn it over to the subsidiary's bondholders. Such a development is unusual, but the possibility thereof was forcibly demonstrated in 1932–1933 by the history of United Drug Company 5s, due 1953.

Examples: United Drug was an important subsidiary of Drug, Inc., which had regularly earned and paid large dividends, gained chiefly from the manufacture of proprietary medicines and other drugs. In the first half of 1932, the consolidated income account showed earnings equal to ten times the interest on United Drug 5s, and the record of previous years was even better. While this issue was not assumed or guaranteed by Drug, Inc., investors considered the combined showing so favorable as to assure the safety of the United Drug 5s beyond question. But United Drug owned, as part of its assets and business, the stock of Louis K. Liggett Company, which operated a large number of drug stores and which was burdened by a high-rental problem similar to that of United Cigar Stores. In September 1932 Liggett's notified its landlords that unless rents were reduced it would be forced into bankruptcy.

This announcement brought rudely home to investors the fact that the still prosperous Drug, Inc., was not assuming responsibility for the liabilities of its (indirect) subsidiary, Liggett's, and they immediately became nervously conscious of the fact that Drug, Inc., was not responsible for interest payments on United Drug 5s either. Sales of these bonds resulting from this discovery depressed the price from 93 earlier in the year down to 42. At the latter figure, the $40,000,000 of United Drug 5s were quoted at only $17,000,000, although the parent company's stock was still selling for more than $100,000,000 (3,500,000 shares at about 30). In the following year the "Drug, Inc., System" was voluntarily dissolved into its component parts—an unusual development—and the United Drug Co. resumed its entirely separate existence. (It has since shown an inadequate coverage for the 5% bonds.)

Consolidated Traction Company of New Jersey First 5s were obligations of a large but unprofitable subsidiary of Public Service Corporation of New Jersey. The bonds were not guaranteed by the parent company. When they matured in 1933 many of the holders accepted an offer of 65 for their bonds made by the parent company.

Saltex Looms, Inc., 1st 6s, due 1954, were obligations of a subsidiary of Sidney Blumenthal & Co., Inc., but in no way guaranteed by the parent company. The consolidated earning statements of Blumenthal regularly deducted the Saltex bond interest before showing the amount available for its own preferred stock. Interest on the bonds was defaulted, however, in 1939; and in 1940 the bonds sold at 7 while Blumenthal preferred was quoted above 70.

Separate Analysis of Subsidiary Interest Coverage Essential. These examples suggest that just as investors are prone to underestimate the value of a guaranty by a strong company, they sometimes make the opposite mistake and attach undue significance to the fact that a company is controlled by another. From the standpoint of fixed-value investment, nothing of importance may be taken for granted. Hence a subsidiary bond should not be purchased on the basis of the showing of its parent company, unless the latter has assumed direct responsibility for the bond in question. In other cases the exhibit of the subsidiary itself can afford the only basis for the acceptance of its bond issues.[7]

If the above discussion is compared with that in Chap. 13, it will be seen that investors in bonds of a *holding company* must insist upon a consolidated income account, in which the subsidiary interest—whether guaranteed or not—is shown as a prior charge; but that purchasers of unguaranteed *subsidiary* bonds cannot accept such consolidated reports as a measure of their safety, and must require a statement covering the subsidiary alone. These statements may be obtainable only with some difficulty, as was true in the case of United Drug 5s, but they must nevertheless be insisted upon.

---

[7] As a practical matter, the financial interest of the parent company in its subsidiary, and other business reasons, may result in its protecting the latter's bonds even though it is not obligated to do so. This would be a valid consideration, however, only in deciding upon a purchase on a *speculative* basis (*i.e.*, carrying a chance of principal profit), but would not justify buying the bond at a full investment price. Concretely stated, it might have made United Drug 5s an excellent speculation at 45, but they were a poor investment at 93.

CHAPTER 18

Protective Covenants and Remedies of Senior Security Holders

IN THIS AND the two succeeding chapters we shall consider the provisions usually made to protect the rights of bond owners and preferred stockholders against impairment, and the various lines of action which may be followed in the event of nonfulfillment of the company's obligations. Our object here, as throughout this book, is not to supply information of a kind readily available elsewhere, but rather to subject current practices to critical examination and to suggest feasible improvements therein for the benefit of security holders generally. In this connection a review of recent developments in the field of reorganization procedure may also be found of value.

Indenture or Charter Provisions Designed to Protect Holder of Senior Securities. The contract between a corporation and the owners of its bonds is contained in a document called the *indenture or deed of trust.* The corresponding agreements relating to the rights of preferred stockholders are set forth in the Articles, or Certificate, of Incorporation. These instruments usually contain provisions designed to prevent corporate acts injurious to senior security holders and to afford remedies in case of certain unfavorable developments. The more important occurrences for which such provision is almost always made may be listed under the following heads:

1. In the case of bonds:
   a. Nonpayment of interest, principal, or sinking fund.
   b. Default on other obligations, or receivership.
   c. Issuance of new secured debt.
   d. Dilution of a conversion (or subscription) privilege.

2. In the case of preferred stocks:
   a. Nonpayment of (cumulative) preferred dividends for a period of time.
   b. Creation of funded debt or a prior stock issue.
   c. Dilution of a conversion (or subscription) privilege.

A frequent, but less general, provision requires the maintenance of working capital at a certain percentage of the bonded debt of industrial companies. (In the case of investment-trust or holding-company bonds it is the *market value* of all the assets which is subject to this provision.)

The remedies provided for bondholders in cases falling under 1*a* and 1*b* above are fairly well standardized. Any one of these untoward developments is designated as an "event of default" and permits the trustee to declare the principal of the bond issue due and payable in advance of the specified maturity date. The provisions therefor in the indenture are known as "acceleration clauses." Their purpose in the main is to enable the bondholders to assert the full amount of their claim in competition with the other creditors.

Contradictory Aspects of Bondholders' Legal Rights. In considering these provisions from a critical standpoint, we must recognize that there are contradictory aspects to the question of the bondholders' legal rights. Receivership[1] is a dreaded word in Wall Street; its advent means ordinarily a drastic shrinkage in the price of all the company's securities, including the bonds for the "benefit" of which the receivership was instituted. As we pointed out in a former chapter, the market's appraisal of a bond in default is no higher on the whole, and perhaps lower, than that of a non-dividend-paying preferred stock of a solvent company.

The question arises, therefore, whether the bondholders might not be better off if they did not have any enforceable claim to principal or interest payments *when conditions are such as to make prompt payment impossible.* For at such times the bondholder's legal rights apparently suc-

---

[1] "Receivership" was formerly a convenient term, applying to all kinds of financial difficulties that involved court action. As a result of the Chandler Act (Bankruptcy Act of 1938), receivers have been largely replaced by trustees. No doubt the word "receivership" will continue to be used—for a while at least—because the terms "trusteeship" and "bankruptcy" are not quite satisfactory, the former being somewhat ambiguous, the latter having an overdrastic connotation. "Insolvency" is a suitable word but awkward to use at times.

So-called "equity receivers" will still be appointed in the future in connection with stockholder's suits, voluntary liquidations, and other special matters.

ceed only in ruining the corporation without benefiting the bondholder. As long as the interest or principal is not going to be paid anyway, would it not be to the interest of the bondholders themselves to postpone the date of payment and keep the enterprise out of the courts?

Corporate Insolvency and Reorganization. This question leads into the broad field of corporate insolvency and reorganization. We must try, within as brief a space as possible, first, to describe the procedure followed prior to the amendatory legislation beginning in 1933; secondly, to summarize the changes brought about by the recent statutes; and, finally, to evaluate the bondholder's position as it now appears. (The latter will be especially difficult, since the new laws have not yet had time to prove their merits or deficiencies in actual practice.)

The old pattern for corporate reorganization went usually as follows: Inability to pay interest or principal of indebtedness led to an application by the corporation itself for a receiver.[2] It was customary to select a "friendly" court; the receiver was generally the company's president; the bondholders' interests were represented by protective committees ordinarily formed by the investment banking houses that had floated the issues. A reorganization plan was agreed upon by the committees and then approved by the court. The plan usually represented a compromise of the conflicting interests of the various ranks of security holders, under which, generally speaking, everyone retained *some* interest in the new company and everyone made some sacrifice. (In numerous cases, however, small and well-entrenched issues at the top were paid off or left undisturbed; and in hopeless situations stock issues were sometimes completely wiped out.) The actual mechanics of reorganization was through a foreclosure or bankruptcy sale. The properties were bought in in behalf of the assenting security holders; and creditors who refused to participate received in cash their pro rata share, if any, of the sale price. This price was usually set so low that everyone was better off to join in the plan and take new securities rather than to stay out and take cash.

Between 1933 and 1939 this procedure was completely transformed by a series of remedial laws, the most important of which was the

---

[2] Other "events of default"—*e.g.*, failure to meet sinking-fund or working-capital requirements—rarely resulted in receivership. Almost always bondholders preferred to overlook, or negotiate over, these matters rather than harm themselves by throwing the company in the

Chandler Act. The defects for which a cure was desired were of two kinds: On the one hand the necessity for paying nonassenting bondholders had developed into a dilemma; because unduly low "upset," or minimum, foreclosure-sale prices were being frowned on by the courts, whereas payment of a fair price involved often an insuperable problem of finding the cash. More serious was the fact that the whole mechanics of reorganization tended to keep complete dominance of the situation in the hands of the old controlling group—who may have been inefficient or even dishonest, and who certainly had special interests to serve.

Beginning with the 1933 changes, a reorganization technique was set up under which a plan accepted by two-thirds of the creditors and a majority of the stockholders (if they had some "equity"), and approved by the court, was made binding on all the security holders. This has done away with the cumbersome and otherwise objectionable device of the foreclosure sale. As perfected by the Chandler Act and the Trust Indenture Act of 1939, the new procedure for other than railroad companies includes the following additional important points:[3]

1. The company must be turned over to at least one disinterested trustee. This trustee must decide whether any claims should be asserted against the old management and also whether or not the business is worth continuing.

2. Actual responsibility for devising a reorganization plan devolves on three disinterested agencies: (1) the trustee, who must present the plan in the first instance; (2) the S.E.C. (when the liabilities exceed $3,000,000), who may submit an advisory opinion thereon; (3) and the judge, who must officially approve it. Although the security holders and their protective committees may make suggestions, their acceptance is not asked for until the disinterested agencies have done their work. Furthermore, apparently wide powers are now given the court to force acceptance upon

---

[3] Provisions 1 to 4 appear in Chap. X of the Chandler Act, an outgrowth of the famous Sec. 77B, which was added to the old bankruptcy act in 1933. Railroad reorganizations are governed by Sec. 77, which was carried over into the Chandler Act intact, and by Chap. XV, added in 1939 (see footnote 12, p. 238). There is also a Chap. XI proceeding under the Chandler Act, relating to "arrangements" of unsecured indebtedness only. Note resort to such proceedings by Haytian Corporation in 1938 and by United States Realty and Improvement Company in 1939. In the latter case the only matter affected was its guarantee of Trinity Buildings Corporation $5^1/2$s, the company seeking to keep its own structure unchanged. Difficulties developed, and the proceedings were replaced by others.

classes of holders who have failed to approve in the requisite percentage; but the exact extent of these powers is still uncertain.

3. The reorganization plan must meet a number of standards of fairness prescribed in the statute, including provisions relating to voting power, publication of reports, etc. The court must specifically approve the new management.

4. The activities of protective committees are subject to close scrutiny and supervision. Reorganization costs of all kinds, including compensation to all and sundry, must receive court sanction.

5. As distinct from reorganization procedure proper, the Trust Indenture Act prescribes a number of requirements for trustees acting under bond indentures. These are designed both to obviate certain conflicts in interest that have caused considerable complaint and also to insure a more active attitude by the trustee in behalf of the bondholders.

There is no doubt at all in our minds that in the typical case the recent legislation[4] will prove highly beneficial. It should eliminate a number of the abuses formerly attaching to receiverships and reorganizations. It should also speed up materially the readjustment process. This should be true, especially, after more definite standards of fairness in reorganization plans have come to be established, so that there will not be so much room as heretofore for protracted disputes between the different ranks of security holders.[5]

---

[4] Legislation analogous to the mechanics of the 77B and Chandler Act provisions was applied to real estate readjustments in the Schackno and Burchill Acts passed by the New York State Legislature in 1933. In the same year The Companies' Creditors Arrangement Act, adopted in Canada, provided that insolvent Canadian Companies might escape proceedings under the Bankruptcy Act and work out compromises with creditors with the sanction of the court. When properly approved, such compromises are binding on minority groups. See W. S. Lighthall, *The Dominion Companies Act* 1934, *annotated*, pp. 289, 345 *ff.*, Montreal, 1935.

[5] The tendency of the S.E.C. advisory opinions, as well as the findings of the I.C.C. in railroad reorganizations, has been strongly in the direction of eliminating stockholders when there appears to be no chance that earnings will cover former interest charges. For a discussion of this point by one of the authors, see Benjamin Graham, "Fair Reorganization Plans under Chapter X of the Chandler Act," *Brooklyn Law Review*, December 1938.

Despite the improvements in the law, railroad reorganizations have been subject to extraordinary delays since 1933. In our opinion, however, this was due not so much to weaknesses remaining in the statute as it was to the extraordinary problem of devising fair plans for extremely complicated corporate structures when the question of future earning power was both highly controversial and of critical importance.

Alternative Remedy Suggested. Despite these undoubted reforms in reorganization technique, we shall be bold enough to venture the assertion that the ideal protective procedure for bondholders may often be found along other and simpler lines. In our opinion—given a sufficiently simple debt structure—the best remedy for all injuries suffered by bondholders is the immediate vesting in them of voting control over the corporation, together with an adequate mechanism to assure the intelligent exercise of such control. In many cases the creditors would then be able to marshal the company's resources and earnings for their own protection in such a way as to avoid recourse to expensive and protracted judicial proceedings.

Our suggestion falls into two parts: First, voting control by bondholders would, by the terms of the indenture, constitute the sole immediate remedy for any event of default, including nonpayment of interest or principal. During such control, unpaid interest or principal would be considered subject to a grace period. But the directors representing the bondholders should have the right to apply for a trusteeship under the Chandler Act, if they feel that comprehensive reorganization is preferable to an indefinite continuance of the moratorium plus control. Secondly, this voting control could best be implemented through the indenture trustee—a large and financially experienced institution, which is competent to represent the bondholders generally and to recommend to them suitable candidates for the controlling directorships. Stockholder's interests should continue to be represented on the board by minority directors.

What this arrangement would mean in effect is the turning of a fixed-interest bond into an income bond during the period of bondholders' control; and the postponement of maturing debt until voluntary extension or refinancing becomes feasible or else until liquidation or sale is found to be the desirable course. It should also be feasible to extend the basic technique and principle of voluntary recapitalization by statute (now applying only to the various stock issues) to include a bond issue as well, when the plan emanates from bondholders' representatives who have the alternative of keeping control and merely waiting.

Obviously, however, control cannot well be vested in creditors when they belong to several classes with conflicting interests. In such cases Chandler Act proceedings would seem necessary to cut the Gordian knot. But, theoretically at least, a voting-control arrangement is possible with a simple senior and a simple junior lien. If default should occur only with respect to the junior lien, voting control would pass to that issue. If the senior lien is defaulted, it would take control as a single class.

Although these suggestions may inspire doubt because of their novelty, it should be pointed out that the idea of voting by bondholders is both an old one and growing in vogue. Although in the past it was an exceptional arrangement, we now find that many reorganization plans, providing for issuance of income bonds, give voting powers to these securities, generally calling for control of the board of directors until all or most of the issue is retired or if interest is not paid in full.[6] Furthermore, many indentures covering fixed-interest bonds now provide for a vote by bondholders on amendments to the indenture.[7] It is also common for Canadian trust indentures to provide for meetings of bondholders in order to amend the terms of the indenture, including even the postponement or change of interest or principal payments.[8] Such meetings may be called by the trustee, by a stated proportion of the bondholders, or in certain instances by the company itself.

It may be objected that the suggested arrangement would really give a bondholder no better legal rights than a preferred stockholder and would thus relegate him to the unsatisfactory position of having both a

---

[6] *Examples:* The reorganization plan of New York State Railways (Syracuse System), dated February 1939, provides that the holders of the new income notes shall be entitled to elect two-thirds of the directors until at least 80% of the notes have been retired. Commercial Mackay Corporation Income Debentures, due 1967, elect one-third of the directors until all bonds are retired.

National Hotel of Cuba Income 6s, due 1959 (issued in 1929), were given voting control in the event of default of one year's interest. Older examples of voting rights given to bondholders include Erie Railroad Prior Lien 4s and General 4s, Mobile and Ohio Railroad General 4s, Third Avenue Railway Adjustment 5s.

The 1934 reorganization of Maple Leaf Milling Company, Ltd. (Canada), provided that the Indenture Trustee of the 5$1/2$s due 1949 (later extended to 1958) would exercise effective control of the company by ownership (in trust) of 2 out of 3 management or voting shares.

[7] Generally excluded from this provision are changes in maturity dates of principal or interest, the rate of interest, the redemption price and the conversion rate. *Examples:* Richfield Oil Corporation Debenture 4s, due 1952. The Industrial Rayon First 4$1/2$s, due 1948, are unusual in that the indenture permits a two-thirds vote of bondholders to postpone interest payments. However, the New York Stock Exchange required an undertaking not to invoke this clause, as a condition of listing the issue.

[8] See the S.E.C. *Report on the Study and Investigation of the Work, Activities, Personnel and Functions of Protective and Reorganization Committees,* Pt. VI, pp. 135–177, especially pp. 138–143, 164–177, Washington, 1936.

limited interest and an unenforceable claim. Our answer must be that, if the control device can be developed properly, it would provide an adequate remedy for both bondholders and preferred stockholders. In that case the basic contractual advantage of bonds over preferred shares would vanish, except to the extent of the right of bonds to repayment at a fixed date. We repeat, in conclusion, the point made in our discussion of the theory of preferred stocks (Chap. 14) that the contractual disadvantage of preferred shares is, at bottom, not so much a matter of inherent legal rights as it is of practical corporate procedure and of the investor's own shortcomings.

Tendency of Securities of Insolvent Companies to Sell Below Their Fair Value. Some additional aspects of the corporate-reorganization question deserve attention. The first relates to the market action of securities of insolvent companies. Receiverships in the past have been productive generally of a vast and pervasive uncertainty, which threatens extinction to the stockholders but fails to promise anything specific to the bondholders. As a result there has been a tendency for the securities of companies in receivership to sell below their fair value in the aggregate; and also a tendency for illogical relationships to be established between the price of a bond issue in default and the price of the junior stock issues.

Examples: The Fisk Rubber Company case is an excellent example of the former point; the Studebaker Corporation situation in September 1933 illustrates the latter.

Market Value of Fisk Rubber Securities in April 1932

$7,600,000 First 8s @ 16	$ 1,200,000
8,200,000 Debenture 5^1/2s @ 11	900,000
Stock issues	Nominal
Total market value of the company	$ 2,100,000

Balance Sheet, June 30, 1932

Cash	$ 7,687,000
Receivables (less reserve of $1,425,000)	4,838,000
Inventories (at lower of cost or market)	3,216,000
	$15,741,000
Accounts Payable	363,000
Net current assets	$15,378,000
Fixed assets (less $8,400,000 depreciation)	23,350,000

The company's securities were selling together for less than one-third of the cash alone, and for only one-seventh of the net current assets, allowing nothing for the fixed property.[9]

Studebaker Corporation, September 1933

Issue	Face amount	Market price	Market value
10-year 6% notes and other claims	$22,000,000	40	$8,800,000
Preferred stock	5,800,000	27	$1,500,000
Common stock (2,464,000 shares)		6	14,700,000
Total value of stock issues			$16,200,000

The company's debt, selling at 40 cents on the dollar, was entitled to *prompt payment in full* before the stockholder received anything. Nevertheless, the market placed a much larger value upon the stock issues than upon the prior debt.

Voluntary Readjustment Plans. Realization of the manifest disadvantages of receivership has often led bondholders to accept suggestions emanating from the management for a voluntary reduction of their contractual claims. Arrangements of this kind have varied from the old-fashioned type of "composition" (in which creditors extended or even curtailed their claims, while the stockholders retained their interest intact) to cases where the bondholders received a substantial part of the stock equity.

Examples: At the end of 1931 Radio-Keith-Orpheum Corporation, needing funds to meet pressing obligations, found ordinary financing impossible. The stockholders ratified a plan under which in effect they surrendered 75% of their stock interest, which was given in turn as a bonus to those who supplied the $11,600,000 required by purchasing debenture notes. (Continued large losses, however, forced the company into receivership a year later.)

In 1933 Fox Film Corporation effected a recapitalization of the same general type. The stockholders gave up over 80% of their holdings, and this stock was in turn *exchanged* for nearly all of approximately $40,000,000 of 5-year notes and bank debt.

---

[9] As pointed out in Chap. 50, below, the Fisk Rubber 8s later proved to be worth close to 100 and the 5^{1}/2s more than 70.

The Kansas City Public Service Company readjustment plan, also consummated in 1933, was designed to meet the simpler problem of reducing interest charges during a supposedly temporary period of subnormal earnings. It provided that the coupon rate on the 6% first-mortgage bonds should be reduced to 3% during the four years 1933–1936, restored to 6% for 1937–1938, and advanced to 7% for 1939–1951, thus making up the 12% foregone in the earlier years. A substantial sinking fund, contingent upon earnings; was set up to retire the issue gradually and to improve its market position.

It was obvious that the Kansas City Public Service bondholders were better off to accept temporarily the 3% which could be paid rather than to insist on 6% which could not be paid and thereby precipitate a receivership. (The previous receivership of the enterprise, terminated in 1926, had lasted six years.) In this case the stockholders were not required to give up any part of their junior interest to the bondholders in return for the concessions made. While theoretically some such sacrifice and transfer would be equitable, it was not of much practical importance here because any stock bonus given to the bondholders would have had a very slight market value.[10] It should be recognized as a principle, however, that the waiving of any important right by the bondholders entitles them to some *quid pro quo* from the stockholders—in the form either of a contribution of cash to the enterprise or of a transfer of some part of their claim on future earnings to the bondholders.[11]

In 1939 additional legislation of a temporary nature was adopted, designed to facilitate so-called "voluntary reorganizations" of railroads by making them binding on all security holders.[12] This statute was

---

[10] In 1936 the company effected a second voluntary rearrangement, under which the interest rate was fixed at 4%, and the bondholders received a rather nugatory bonus of common stock. In 1939 still a third voluntary modification was accepted, in which bondholders took 30% in cash and 70% in preferred stock for their bonds—the money being advanced as a loan by the R.F.C.

[11] The reorganization of Industrial Office Building Company in 1932–1933 is a remarkable example of the conversion of fixed-interest bonds into income bonds without sacrifice of any kind by the stockholders. A detailed discussion of this instance is given in Appendix Note 32.

[12] This is the Chandler Railroad Readjustment Act of 1939, which actually adds a new Chap. XV to the Bankruptcy Act. Action thereunder must be begun before July 31, 1940, and must be substantially concluded within a year after its initiation. As far as the reorganization technique

intended specifically to aid the Baltimore and Ohio and Lehigh Valley roads, which had previously proposed voluntary reorganization plans. These were designed to reduce fixed-interest charges and to extend current and near maturities. The stockholders, in each case, were to retain their interests intact.

As we have previously stated, it is our opinion that voluntary readjustment plans are desirable in themselves, but they should be proposed *after* voting control over the corporation has passed to the bondholders, and they are in a position to choose between alternative courses of action.

Change in the Status of Bond Trustees. Not the least important of the remedial legislation enacted since 1933 is the "Trust Indenture Act of 1939." This undertakes to correct a number of inadequacies and abuses in the administration of their duties by bond trustees. The chief criticism of the behavior of indenture trustees in the past is that they did not act as trustees at all but merely as agents of the bondholders. This meant that as a general rule they took no action on their own initiative but only when directed to do so and were fully indemnified by a certain percentage of the bondholders.[13] Indentures have said practically nothing about the duties of a trustee but a great deal about his immunities and indemnification.

The 1939 statute aims directly at this unsatisfactory situation by including the following provision (in Section 315):

Duties of the Trustee in Case of Default

(c) The indenture to be qualified shall contain provisions requiring the indenture trustee to exercise in case of default (as such term is defined in the indenture) such of the rights and powers vested in it by such indenture, and to use the same degree of care and skill in their exercise, as a prudent man would exercise or use under the circumstances in the conduct of his own affairs.

There are further provisions limiting the use of so-called "exculpatory clauses," which in the past made it impossible to hold a trustee to account

---

is concerned, it is not significantly different from that provided in Section 77. In both cases approval of the I.C.C., of a court, and of a suitable percentage of security holders is required. The important difference is that under the new Chap. XV there is no bankruptcy in the involved legal sense. The company continues to administer its own affairs, and no contracts or other obligations are affected except those specifically included in the plan of readjustment.

[13] See Appendix Note 33 for further discussion and an example on this point appearing in the first edition of this work.

for anything except provable fraud or else negligence so gross as to be equivalent thereto.

A further cause of complaint arose from the fact that the indenture trustee has frequently been a creditor of the obligor (*e.g.*, a trust company holding its promissory notes) or else has been controlled by the same interests. These situations have created conflicts of interest, or an unwillingness to act impartially and vigorously, which have militated strongly against the bondholders. The Trust Indenture Act of 1939 contains stringent provisions designed to terminate these abuses.[14]

The Problem of the Protective Committee. Reform in the status of indenture trustees may lead to a solution of the vexing problem of the protective committee. Since 1929 the general status of protective committees has become uncertain and most unsatisfactory. Formerly it was taken for granted that the investment bankers who floated the issue would organize a protective committee in the event of default. But in recent years there has been a growing tendency to question the propriety or desirability of such action. Bondholders may lack faith in the judgment of the issuing house, or they may question its ability to represent them impartially because of other interests in or connections with the enterprise; or they may even consider the underwriters as legally responsible for the losses incurred. The arguments in favor of *competent* representation by agencies *other* than the houses of issue are therefore quite convincing. The difficulty lies however, in securing such competent representation. With the original issuing houses out of the picture, anybody can announce himself as chairman of a protective committee and invite deposits. The whole procedure has become unstandardized and open to serious abuses. Duplicate committees often appear; an undignified scramble for deposits takes place; persons with undesirable reputations and motives can easily inject themselves into the situation.

The new bankruptcy legislation of 1938 introduced some improvement into this situation by subjecting the activities and compensation

---

[14] The remedial legislation was an outgrowth of a trust indenture study made by the S.E.C. and was greatly stimulated by the opinion delivered by Judge Rosenman in 1936 denying the claims of holders of National Electric Power (secured) debentures to hold the trustee of the issue accountable for the huge losses suffered by them. The judge held that the exculpatory clauses saved the trustee in this case but that the whole system of indenture trusteeship was in need of radical reform.

of protective committees to court scrutiny. (In the case of railroads a committee cannot take part in a proceeding without prior permission from the I.C.C.) Further legislation will probably be enacted regulating in more detail the formation as well as the subsequent conduct of protective committees.

A Recommended Reform. The whole procedure might readily be clarified and standardized now that the trustee under the indenture is expected to assume the duty of *actively* protecting the bond issue. The large institutions which hold these positions have the facilities, the experience, and the standing required for the successful discharge of such a function. There seems no good reason, in the ordinary case, why the trustee should not itself organize the protective committee, with one of its executive officers as chairman and with the other members selected from among the larger bondholders or their nominees. The possible conflict of interest between the trustee as representative of all the bondholders and the protective committee as representative of the depositing holders only will be found on analysis rarely to be of more than technical and minor consequence. Such a conflict, if it should arise, could be solved by submission of the question to the court. There is no difficulty about awarding sufficient compensation to the trustee and its counsel for their labors and accomplishment on behalf of the bondholders.

This arrangement envisages effective cooperation between the trustee and a group of bondholders who in the opinion of the trustee are qualified to represent the issue as a whole. The best arrangement might be to establish this bondholders' group at the time the issue is sold, *i.e.*, without waiting for an event of default to bring it into being, in order that there may be from the very start some responsible and interested agency to follow the affairs of the corporation from the bondholders' standpoint, and to make objections, if need be, to policies which may appear to threaten the safety of the issue. Reasonable compensation for this service should be paid by the corporation. This would be equivalent in part to representation of the bondholders on the board of directors. If the time were to arrive when the group would have to act as a protective committee on behalf of the bondholders, their familiarity with the company's affairs should prove of advantage.

CHAPTER 19

Protective Covenants *(Continued)*

Prohibition of Prior Liens. A brief discussion is desirable regarding certain protective provisions other than those dealing with the ordinary events of default. (The matter of safeguarding conversion and other participating privileges against dilution will be covered in the chapters dealing with Senior Securities with Speculative Features.) Dealing first with mortgage bonds, we find that indentures almost always prohibit the placing of any new prior lien on the property. Exceptions are sometimes made in the case of bonds issued under a reorganization plan, when it is recognized that a prior mortgage may be necessary to permit raising new capital in the future.

Example: In 1926 Chicago, Milwaukee, St. Paul, and Pacific Railroad Company issued $107,000,000 of Series *A* Mortgage 5% bonds and, junior thereto, $185,000,000 of Convertible Adjustment Mortgage 5s, in exchange for securities of the bankrupt Chicago, Milwaukee, and St. Paul Railway Company. The indentures permitted the later issuance of an indefinite amount of First and Refunding Mortgage Bonds, which would rank ahead of the Series *A* Mortgage 5s.[1]

Equal-and-Ratable Security Clause. When a bond issue is unsecured it is almost always provided that it will share equally in any mortgage lien later placed on the property.

Example: The New York, New Haven, and Hartford Railroad Company sold a number of debenture issues between 1897 and 1908. These bonds were originally unsecured, but the indentures provided that they should be equally secured with any mortgage subsequently placed upon the property. In 1920 a first and refunding mortgage was author-

---

[1] In 1933 the St. Paul was granted permission to issue some of the new first and refunding bonds, to be held as collateral for short-term loans made by the United States government.

ized by the stockholders; consequently the earlier issues have since been equally secured with bonds issued under the new mortgage. They still carry the title of "debentures," but this is now a misnomer. There is, however, an issue of 4% debentures, due in 1957, which did not carry this provision and hence are unsecured. In 1939 the (unsecured) debenture 4s, due 1957, sold at one-third the price of the (secured) debenture 4s, due 1956, *e.g.*, 5 vs. 16.[2]

Purchase-Money Mortgages. It is customary to permit without restriction the assumption of *purchase-money mortgages*. These are liens attaching only to new property subsequently acquired, and their assumption is not regarded as affecting the position of the other bondholders. The latter supposition is not necessarily valid, of course, since it is possible thereby to increase the ratio of total debt of the enterprise to the total shareholder's equity in a manner which might jeopardize the position of the existing bondholders.

Subordination of Bond Issues to Bank Debt in Reorganization. In the case of bonds or notes issued under a reorganization plan it is sometimes provided that their claim shall be junior to that of present or future bank loans. This is done to facilitate bank borrowings which otherwise could be effected only by the pledging of receivables or inventories as security. An example of this arrangement is afforded by Aeolian Company Five-year Secured 6% Notes, due in 1937, which were issued under a capital readjustment plan in partial exchange for the Guaranteed 7% Preferred Stock of the company. The notes were subordinated to $400,000 of bank loans, which were later paid.

Safeguards Against Creation of Additional Amounts of the Same Issue. Nearly all bonds or preferred issues enjoy adequate safeguards in respect to the creation of additional amounts of the issue. The customary provisions require a substantial margin of earnings above the requirements of the issue as thus enlarged. For example, additional New York Edison

---

[2] In exceptional cases, debenture obligations are entitled to a *prior lien* on the property in the event that a subsequent mortgage is placed thereon. *Example:* National Radiator Corporation Debenture 6¹/₂s, due 1947, and the successor corporation's income debenture 5s, due 1946. In a second reorganization, effected in 1939, these debentures were replaced by stock. Here is an excellent example of the relative unimportance of protective provisions, as compared with profitable operations.

Company First Lien and Refunding Mortgage Bonds may not be issued, except for refunding purposes, unless consolidated net earnings for a recent 12-month period have been at least $1^3/_4$ times the annual interest charges on the aggregate bonded indebtedness of the company, including those to be issued. In the case of Wheeling Steel Corporation First Mortgage bonds the required ratio is 2 times.[3]

Provisions of this kind with reference to earnings-coverage are practically nonexistent in the railroad field, however. Railroad bonds of the blanket-mortgage type more commonly restrict the issuance of additional bonds through a provision that the total funded indebtedness shall not exceed a certain ratio to the capital stock outstanding, and by a limitation upon the emission of new bonds to a certain percentage of the *cost* or *fair value* of newly acquired property. (See, for example, the Baltimore and Ohio Railroad Company Refunding and General Mortgage Bonds and the Northern Pacific Railway Company Refunding and Improvement Bonds.) In the older bond issues it was customary to close the mortgage at a relatively small fixed amount, thus requiring that additional funds be raised by the sale of junior securities. This provision gave rise to the favorably situated "underlying bonds" to which reference was made in Chap. 6.

In the typical case additional issues of mortgage bonds may be made only against pledge of new property worth considerably more than the increase in debt. (See, for examples: Youngstown Sheet and Tube Company First Mortgage, under which further bonds may be issued to finance 75% of the cost of additions or improvements to the mortgaged properties; New York Edison Company, Inc., First Lien and Refunding Mortgage, under which bonds may be issued in further amounts to finance additions and betterments up to 75% of the actual and reasonable expenditure therefor; Pere Marquette Railway Company First-mortgage bonds, which may be issued up to 80% of the cost or fair value, whichever is the lower, of newly constructed or acquired property.)

These safeguards are logically conceived and almost always carefully observed. Their practical importance is less than might appear, however, because in the ordinary instance the showing stipulated would be needed anyway in order to attract buyers for the additional issue.

---

[3] For similar provisions in the case of preferred stocks see Consolidated Edison Company of New York $5 Preferred, General Foods Corporation $4.50 Preferred and Gotham Silk Hosiery Company 7% Preferred.

Working-Capital Requirements. The provisions for maintaining working capital at a certain percentage of bonded debt, and for a certain ratio of current assets to current liabilities, are by no means standardized. They appear only in industrial bond indentures.[4]

The required percentages vary, and the penalties for nonobservance vary also. In most cases the result is merely the prohibition of dividends until the proper level or ratio of working capital is restored. In a few cases the principal of the bond issue may be declared due.

Examples: 1. *Sole penalty, prohibition of dividends.* B. F. Goodrich First 4$^1/$4s, due 1956, and Wilson and Company First 4s, due 1955, require current assets to equal total indebtedness, *i.e.*, net quick assets to equal funded debt. In the case of West Virginia Pulp and Paper First 4$^1/$2s, due 1952, subsidiary preferred stocks are included with funded debt.

The provisions of Fairbanks, Morse and Company Debenture 4s, due 1956, require that current assets equal (*a*) 110% of total liabilities and (*b*) 200% of current liabilities. In the case of Wheeling Steel First 4$^1/$2s, due 1966, and Republic Steel General 4$^1/$2s, due 1956, current assets must equal 300% of current liabilities, and net current assets must equal 50% of the funded debt.

2. *Failure to meet requirement is an event of default.* Skelly Oil Debenture 4s, due 1951, and Serial Notes, due 1937–1941. Here the company agrees to maintain current assets equal to at least 200% of current liabilities.

In the case of Continental Steel 4$^1/$2s, due 1946, the required ratio is 115%.

Among former examples may be cited American Machine and Foundry 6s, due 1939, which had a twofold provision: the first prohibiting dividends unless net current assets equal 150% of the outstanding bond issue, and the second requiring unconditionally that the net current assets be maintained at 100% of the face value of outstanding bonds. In the case of United States Radiator Corporation 5s, due 1938, the company agreed at all times to maintain net working capital equal to 150% of the outstanding funded debt.

It would appear to be sound theory to require regularly some protective provisions on the score of working capital in the case of industrial

---

[4] Ashland Home Telephone First 4$^1/$2s, due 1961, are a *public-utility* issue with a peculiar, and rather weak, provision relating to net current assets.

bonds. We have already suggested that an adequate ratio of net current assets to funded debt be considered as one of the specific criteria in the selection of industrial bonds. This criterion should ordinarily be set up in the indenture itself, so that the bondholder will be entitled to the *maintenance* of a satisfactory ratio throughout the life of the issue and to an adequate remedy if the figure declines below the proper point.

The prohibition of dividend payments under such conditions is sound and practicable. But the more stringent penalty, which terms a deficiency of working capital "an event of default," is not likely to prove effective or beneficial to the bondholder. The objection that receivership harms rather than helps the creditors applies with particular force in this connection. Referring to the United States Radiator 5s, mentioned above, we may point out that the balance sheet of January 31, 1933, showed a default in the 150% working-capital requirement. (The net current assets were $2,735,000, or only 109% of the $2,518,000 bond issue.) Nevertheless, the trustee took no steps to declare the principal due, nor was it asked to do so by the required number of bondholders. In all probability a receivership invoked for this reason would have been considered as highly injurious to the bondholders' interests. But this attitude would mean that the provision in question should never have been included in the indenture.[5]

Voting Control as a Remedy. We have previously advanced and discussed the suggestion that the bondholders' right to the appointment of trustees in the event of any default might well be replaced by a right to receive *voting control* over the enterprise. Whatever the reader's view as to the soundness of this suggestion as applied to default in payment of interest or principal, we imagine that he will agree with us that it has merit in the case of "secondary" defaults, *e.g.*, failure to maintain working capital as agreed or to make sinking-fund payments; for the present alternatives—either to precipitate insolvency or to do nothing at all—are alike completely unsatisfactory.

---

[5] Similar situations existed in 1933 with respect to G. R. Kinney (shoe) Company $7^1/2$s, due 1936, and Budd Manufacturing Company First 6s, due 1935. Early in 1934, the United States Radiator Corporation asked the debenture holders to modify the provisions respecting both working-capital maintenance and sinking-fund payments. No substantial *quid pro quo* was offered for these concessions. Characteristically, the reason given by the company itself for this move was not that the bondholders were entitled to some remedial action but that the "technical default under the indenture" interfered with projected bank borrowings by the company.

Protective Provisions for Investment-Trust Issues. Investment-trust bonds belong in a special category, we believe, because by their nature they lend themselves to the application of stringent remedial provisions. Such bonds are essentially similar to the collateral loans made by banks on marketable securities. As a protection for these bank loans, it is required that the market value of the collateral be maintained at a certain percentage in excess of the amount owed. In the same way the lenders of money to an investment trust should be entitled to demand that the value of the portfolio continuously exceed the amount of the loans by an adequate percentage, *e.g.*, 25%. If the market value should decline below this figure, the investment trust should be required to take the same action as any other borrower against marketable securities. It should either put up more money (*i.e.*, raise more capital from the stockholders) or sell out securities and retire debt with the proceeds, in an amount sufficient to restore the proper margin.

The disadvantages that inhere in bond investment generally justify the bond buyer in insisting upon every possible safeguard. In the case of investment-trust bonds, a very effective measure of protection may be assured by means of the covenant to maintain the market value of the portfolio above the bonded debt. Hence investors in investment-trust issues should demand this type of protective provision, and—what is equally important—they should require its strict enforcement. Although this stand will inflict hardship upon the stockholders when market prices fall, this is part of the original bargain, in which the stockholders agreed to take most of the risk in exchange for the surplus profits.[6]

A survey of bond indentures of investment trusts discloses a signal lack of uniformity in the matter of these protective provisions. Most of them do require a certain margin of asset value over debt as a condition to the sale

---

[6] If the market value of the assets falls below 100% of the funded debt, a condition of insolvency would seem to be created which entitles the bondholders to insist upon immediate remedial action. For otherwise the stockholders would be permitted to speculate on the future with what is entirely the bondholders' capital. But even this apparently simple point is not without its difficulties. In 1938, holders of Reynolds Investing Company 5s endeavored to have a trustee appointed on grounds of insolvency, but stockholders claimed that the market price of certain large security holdings was less than their real value. After considerable delay, trustees were appointed, pursuant to an agreement among the various interests. Note that Guardian Investors Corporation 5s, due 1948, have been "under water" nearly all the time since 1932 and sold as low as 24, without any remedial steps being taken.

of additional bonds. The required ratio of net assets to funded debt varies from 120% (*e.g.*, General American Investors) to 250% (*e.g.*, Niagara Shares Corporation). The more usual figures are 125 or 150%. A similar restriction is placed upon the payment of cash dividends. The ratio required for this purpose varies from 125% (*e.g.*, Domestic and Foreign Investors) to 175% (which must be shown to permit cash dividends on Central States Electric Corporation common). The modal figure is probably 140 or 150%.

But the majority of issues do not require at all times and unconditionally the maintenance of a minimum excess of asset value above bonded indebtedness. Examples of such a covenant may indeed be given, *e.g.*, General Public Service Corporation Convertible Debenture 5s, due 1953; American European Securities Company Collateral 5s, due 1958; and Affiliated Fund, Inc., Secured Convertible Debenture $4^1/2$s and 4s, due 1949, all of which require maintenance of a 125% ratio of asset value at market to funded debt. In the case of Affiliated Fund, the remedy provided is the immediate sale by the trustee of pledged collateral and the retirement of bonds until the required ratio is restored. In the other cases more elaborate machinery is invoked to declare the entire issue due and payable. We would suggest that provisions of this type—preferably those most simple of application—be a standard requirement for investment-trust bond issues.[7]

SINKING FUNDS

In its modern form a sinking fund provides for the periodic retirement of a certain portion of a senior issue through payments made by the corporation. The sinking fund acquires the security by call, by means of sealed tenders, or by open-market purchases made by the trustee or the corporation. In the latter case the corporation turns in the bonds to the sinking fund in lieu of cash. The sinking fund usually operates once or

---

[7] Another type of remedy appeared in the indenture securing the Reynolds Investing Company 5s, which provided that if at any time the net value of the assets should fall below 110% of the bond issue, the latter should be due and payable on the next interest date. The same difficulty arose in applying this provision as in the case of the solvency question discussed above.

Note also the case of Alleghany Corporation Collateral Trust 5s, due 1949. The offering circular indicated that a coverage of 150% would be compulsory. Yet the indenture provided that failure to maintain this margin would not constitute an event of default but would result only in the prohibition of dividends and in the impounding by the trustee of the income from the pledged collateral.

twice a year, but provisions for quarterly and even monthly payments are by no means unusual. In the case of many bond issues, the bonds acquired by the sinking fund are not actually retired but are "kept alive," *i.e.*, they draw interest, and these interest sums are also used for sinking-fund purchases, thus increasing the latter at a compounded rate.

Example: An important instance of this arrangement was supplied by the two issues of United States Steel Sinking Fund 5s, originally totaling $504,000,000. Bonds of the junior issue, listed on the New York Stock Exchange, were familiarly known in the bond market as "Steel Sinkers." By adding the interest on bonds in the fund, the annual payments grew from $3,040,000 in 1902 to $11,616,000 in 1928. (The following year the entire outstanding amounts of these issues were retired or provided for.)

Benefits.   The benefits of a sinking fund are of a twofold nature. The continuous reduction in the size of the issue makes for increasing safety and the easier repayment of the balance at maturity. Also important is the support given to the market for the issue through the repeated appearance of a substantial buying demand. Nearly all industrial bond issues have sinking funds; the public-utility group shows about as many with as without; in the railroad list sinking funds are exceptional. But in recent years increasing emphasis has been laid upon the desirability of a sinking fund, and few long-term senior issues of any type are now offered without such a provision.[8]

Indispensable in Some Cases.   Under some circumstances a sinking fund is absolutely necessary for the protection of a bond. This is true in general when the chief backing of the issue consists of a wasting asset. Bonds on mining properties invariably have a sinking fund, usually of substantial proportions and based upon the tonnage mined. A sinking fund of smaller relative size is regularly provided for real estate mortgage bonds. In all these cases the theory is that the annual depletion or depreciation allowances should be applied to the reduction of the funded debt.

Examples: A special example of importance was the large Interborough Rapid Transit Company First and Refunding 5% issue, due 1966, which was secured mainly by a lease on properties that belong to

---

[8] During 1933 the Interstate Commerce Commission strongly recommended that railways adopt sinking funds to amortize their existing debt. The Chicago and North Western Railway thereupon announced a plan of this kind, the details of which were not particularly impres-

the City of New York. Obviously it was essential to provide through a sinking fund for the retirement of the entire issue by the time the lease expired in 1967, since the corporation would then be deprived of most of its assets and earning power. Similarly with Tobacco Products 6^1/2s, due in 2022, which depended for their value entirely upon the annual payments of $2,500,000 made by American Tobacco Company under a lease expiring in 2022.

The absence of a sinking fund under conditions of this kind invariably leads to trouble.

Examples: Federal Mining and Smelting Company supplied the unusual spectacle of a mining enterprise with a large preferred-stock issue ($12,000,000); and furthermore the preferred stock had no sinking fund. Declaration of a $10 dividend on the common in 1926 led to court action to protect the preferred stock against the threatened breakdown of its position through depletion of the mines coupled with the distribution of cash earnings to the junior shares. As a result of the litigation the company refrained from further common dividends until 1937 and devoted its surplus profits to reducing the preferred issue, which was completely retired in 1939.

Iron Steamboat Company General Mortgage 4s, due 1932, had no sinking fund, although the boats on which they were a lien were obviously subject to a constant loss in value. These bonds to the amount of $500,000 were issued in 1902 and were a second lien on the entire property of the company (consisting mainly of seven small steamboats operating between New York City and Coney Island), junior to $100,000 of first-mortgage bonds. During the years 1909 to 1925, inclusive, the company paid dividends on the common stock aggregating in excess of $700,000 and by 1922 had retired all of the first-mortgage bonds through the operation of the sinking fund for that issue. At this point the 4s, due 1932, became a first lien upon the entire property. In 1932, when the company went into bankruptcy, the entire issue was still outstanding. The mortgaged property was sold at auction in February 1933 for $15,050, a figure resulting in payment of less than 1 cent on the dollar to the bondholders. An adequate sinking fund might have retired the entire issue out of the earnings which were distributed to the stockholders.

When the enterprise may be regarded as permanent, the absence of a sinking fund does not necessarily condemn the issue. This is true not only of most high-grade railroad bonds and of many high-grade utility bonds but also of most of the select group of old-line industrial preferred stocks that merit an investment rating, *e.g.*, National Biscuit Preferred, which has no sinking fund. From the broader standpoint, therefore, sinking funds may be characterized as invariably desirable and sometimes but not always indispensable.

Serial Maturities as an Alternative. The general object sought by a sinking fund may be obtained by the use of serial maturities. The retirement of a portion of the issue each year by reason of maturity corresponds to the reduction by means of sinking-fund purchases. Serial maturities are relatively infrequent, their chief objection resting probably in the numerous separate market quotations that they entail. In the equipment-trust field, however, they are the general rule. This exception may be explained by the fact that insurance companies and other financial institutions are the chief buyers of equipment obligations, and for their special needs the variety of maturity dates proves a convenience. Serial maturities are also frequently employed in state and municipal financing.

Problems of Enforcement. The enforcement of sinking-fund provisions of a bond issue presents the same problem as in the case of covenants for the maintenance of working capital. Failure to make a sinking-fund payment is regularly characterized in the indenture as an event of default, which will permit the trustee to declare the principal due and thus bring about receivership. The objections to this "remedy" are obvious, and we can recall no instance in which the omission of sinking-fund payments, unaccompanied by default of interest, was actually followed by enforcement of the indenture provisions. When the company continues to pay interest but claims to be unable to meet the sinking fund, it is not unusual for the trustee and the bondholders to withhold action and merely to permit arrears to accumulate. More customary is the making of a formal request to the bondholders by the corporation for the postponement of the sinking-fund payments. Such a request is almost invariably acceded to by the great majority of bondholders, since the alternative is always pictured as insolvency. This was true even in the case of Interborough Rapid Transit 5s, for which—as we have pointed out—the sinking fund was an essential element of protection.[9]

---

[9] The plan of voluntary readjustment proposed in 1922 postponed sinking-fund payments on these bonds for a five-year period. About 75% of the issue accepted this modification.

The suggestion made in respect to the working-capital covenants, *viz.*, that voting control be transferred to the bondholders in the event of default, is equally applicable to the sinking-fund provision. In our view that would be distinctly preferable to the present arrangement under which the bondholder must either do nothing to protect himself or else take the drastic and calamitous step of compelling bankruptcy.

The emphasis we have laid upon the proper kind of protective provisions for industrial bonds should not lead the reader to believe that the presence of such provisions carries an assurance of safety. This is far from the case. The success of a bond investment depends primarily upon the success of the enterprise and only to a very secondary degree upon the terms of the indenture. Hence the seeming paradox that the senior securities that have fared best in the depression have on the whole quite unsatisfactory indenture or charter provisions. The explanation is that the best issues as a class have been the oldest issues, and these date from times when less attention was paid than now to protective covenants.

In Appendix Note 34, we present two examples of the opposite kind (Willys-Overland Company First $6^{1}/_{2}$s, due 1933, and Berkey and Gay Furniture Company First 6s, due 1941) wherein a combination of a strong statistical showing with all the standard protective provisions failed to safeguard the holders against a huge subsequent loss. But while the protective covenants we have been discussing do not *guarantee* the safety of the issue, they nevertheless *add* to the safety and are therefore worth insisting upon.

Sinking-fund payments have been suspended without penalty in the case of numerous real estate issues, under the provisions of various state mortgage moratorium laws. *Example:* Harriman Building First 6s, due 1951. No sinking-fund payments were made between 1934 and 1939 by virtue of the New York Moratorium Law.

See Chapter 20, "Preferred-Stock Protective Provisions. Maintenance of Junior Capital" online at www.mhprofessional.com/SecurityAnalysis7.

CHAPTER 21

Supervision of
Investment Holdings

Traditional Concept of "Permanent Investment." A generation ago "permanent investment" was one of the stock phrases of finance. It was applied to the typical purchase by a conservative investor and may be said to have embraced three constituent ideas: (1) intention to hold for an indefinite period; (2) interest solely in annual income, without reference to fluctuations in the value of principal; and (3) freedom from concern over future developments affecting the company. A sound investment was by definition one that could be bought, put away, and forgotten except on coupon or dividend dates.

This traditional view of high-grade investments was first seriously called into question by the unsatisfactory experiences of the 1920–1922 depression. Large losses were taken on securities that their owners had considered safe beyond the need of examination. The ensuing seven years, although generally prosperous, affected different groups of investment issues in such divergent ways that the old sense of complete security—with which the term "gilt-edged securities" was identified—suffered an ever-increasing impairment. Hence even before the market collapse of 1929, the danger ensuing from neglect of investments previously made, and the need for periodic scrutiny or supervision of all holdings, had been recognized as a new canon in Wall Street. This principle, directly opposed to the former practice, is frequently summed up in the dictum, "There are no permanent investments."

Periodic Inspection of Holdings Necessary—but Troublesome. That the newer view is justified by the realities of fixed-value investment can scarcely be questioned. But it must be frankly recognized also that this same necessity for supervision of all security holdings implies a rather serious indictment of the whole concept of fixed-value investment. If risk of loss can be minimized only by the exercise of constant supervisory care, in addition to the painstaking process of initial choice, has not such investment become more trouble than it is worth? Let it be assumed that the typical investor, following the conservative standards of selection herein recommended, will average a yield of $3^1/2$% on a diversified list of corporate securities. This $3^1/2$% return appears substantially higher than the $2^1/2$% obtainable from long-term United States government bonds and also more attractive than the 2 or $2^1/2$% offered by savings banks. Nevertheless, if we take into account not only the effort required to make a proper selection but also the greater efforts entailed by the subsequent repeated check-ups, and if we then add thereto the still inescapable risk of depreciation or definite loss, it must be confessed that a rather plausible argument can be constructed against the advisability of fixed-value investments in general. The old idea of permanent, trouble-free holdings was grounded on the not illogical feeling that if a limited-return investment could not be regarded as trouble-free it was not worth making at all.

Superiority of United States Savings Bonds. Objectively considered, investment experience of the last decade undoubtedly points away from the fixed-value security field and into the direction of (1) United States government bonds or savings-bank deposits; or (2) admittedly speculative operations, with endeavors to reduce risk and increase profits by means of skillful effort; or (3) a search for the exceptional combination of safety of principal with a chance for substantial profit. For all people of moderate means United States Savings Bonds undoubtedly offer the most suitable medium for fixed-value investment. In fact we are inclined to state categorically that, on the basis of 1940 interest yields, their superiority to other issues makes them the *only* sensible purchase of this type. The reason is, of course, that it is not possible to obtain a significantly higher return on investment issues (save for a few obscure exceptions) without injecting an element of principal risk which makes the commitment unsound. In addition the holder's redemption right before maturity is a very valuable feature of the bonds. If only small investors as a class would resolutely reject the various types of "savings plans," with their multifarious titles, now being offered to them with an ostensible "sure income return" of 4 to 6%, and thankfully take advantage of the 2.90% available on United States Savings Bonds, we are convinced that they would save in the aggregate an enormous amount of money, trouble and heartbreak.

But even if the ordinary investment problems of most investors could be thus simply disposed of, many investors would remain who must consider other types of fixed-value investment. These include: (1) institutional investors of all kinds, *e.g.*, savings and commercial banks, insurance companies, educational and philanthropic agencies; (2) other large investors, *e.g.*, corporations and wealthy individuals; (3) those with moderate income derived wholly from investments, since the maximum annual return ultimately obtainable from United States Savings Bonds is limited to $2,500 per annum.[1] It is true also that many smaller investors will for one reason or another prefer to place part of their funds in other types of fixed-value investment.

The second alternative, *viz.*, to speculate instead of investing, is entirely too dangerous for the typical person who is building up his capital out of savings or business profits. The disadvantages of ignorance, of human greed, of mob psychology, of trading costs, of weighting of the dice by insiders and manipulators,[2] will in the aggregate far overbalance the purely theoretical superiority of speculation in that it offers profit possibilities in return for the assumption of risk. We have, it is true, repeatedly argued against the acceptance of an admitted risk to principal without the presence of a compensating chance for profit. In so doing, however, we have not advocated speculation in place of investment but only intelligent speculation in preference to obviously unsound and ill-advised forms of investment. We are convinced that the public generally will derive far better results from fixed-value investments, if selected with exceeding care, than from speculative operations, even though these may be aided by considerable education in financial matters. It may well be that the results of investment will prove disappointing; but if so, the results of speculation would have been disastrous.

The third alternative—to look for investment merit combined with an opportunity for profit—presents, we believe, a suitable field for the talents of the securities analyst. But it is a dangerous objective to hold before the untrained investor. He can readily be persuaded that safety

---

[1] This is based on the maximum $7,500 permitted each year to one individual. After the tenth year of continued investment, an annual income of $2,500 would accrue via the maturity of a $10,000 unit each year and its replacement by a new $7,500 subscription.

[2] This factor has been greatly reduced by the operation of the Securities Exchange Act of 1934.

exists where there is only promise or, conversely, that an attractive statistical showing is alone sufficient to warrant purchase.

Having thus considered the three alternative policies open to those with capital funds, we see that fixed-value investment in the traditional field of high-grade bonds and preferred stocks remains a necessary and desirable activity for many individuals and corporate bodies. It is quite clear also that periodic reexamination of investment holdings is necessary to reduce the risk of loss. What principles and practical methods can be followed in such supervision?

Principles and Problems of Systematic Supervision; Switching. It is generally understood that the investor should examine his holdings at intervals to see whether or not all of them may still be regarded as entirely safe and that if the soundness of any issue has become questionable, he should exchange it for a better one. In making such a "switch" the investor must be prepared to accept a moderate loss on the holding he sells out, which loss he must charge against his aggregate investment income.

In the early years of systematic investment supervision, this policy worked out extremely well. Seasoned securities of the high-grade type tended to cling rather tenaciously to their established price levels and frequently failed to reflect a progressive deterioration of their intrinsic position until some time after this impairment was discoverable by analysis. It was possible, therefore, for the alert investor to sell out such holdings to some heedless and unsuspecting victim, who was attracted by the reputation of the issue and the slight discount at which it was obtainable in comparison with other issues of its class. The impersonal character of the securities market relieves this procedure of any ethical stigma, and it is considered merely as establishing a proper premium for shrewdness and a deserved penalty for lack of care.

Increased Sensitivity of Security Prices. In more recent years, however, investment issues have lost what may have been called their "price inertia," and their quotations have come to reflect promptly any materially adverse development. This fact creates a serious difficulty in the way of effective switching to maintain investment quality. By the time that any real impairment of security is manifest, the issue may have fallen in price not only to a speculative level but to a level even lower than the decline in earnings would seem to justify.[3] (One reason for this excessive price decline is that an unfavorable apparent *trend* has come to influence prices even more severely than the absolute earnings figures.) The owner's natural reluctance to accept a large loss is reinforced by the reasonable belief that he would be selling the issue at an unduly low price, and he is likely to find himself compelled almost unavoidably to assume a speculative position with respect to that security.

Exceptional Margins of Safety as Insurance Against Doubt. The only effective means of meeting this difficulty lies in following counsels of perfection in making the original investment. The degree of safety enjoyed by the issue, as shown by quantitative measures, must be so far in *excess* of the minimum standards that a large shrinkage can be suffered before its position need be called into question. Such a policy should reduce to a very small figure the proportion of holdings about which the investor will subsequently find himself in doubt. It would also permit him to make his exchanges when the showing of the issue is still comparatively strong and while, therefore, there is a better chance that the market price will have been maintained.

Example and Conclusion. As a concrete example, let us assume that the investor buys an issue such as the Liggett and Myers Tobacco Company Debenture 5s, due 1951, which earned their interest an average of nearly twenty times in 1934–1938, as compared with the minimum requirement of three times. If a decline in profits should reduce the coverage to four times, he might prefer to switch into some other issue (if one can be found) that is earning its interest eight to ten times. On these assumptions he would have a fair chance of obtaining a full price for the Liggett and Myers issue, since it would still be making an impressive exhibit. But if the influence of the downward trend of earnings has depressed the quotation to a large discount, then he could decide to retain the issue rather than accept an appreciable loss. In so doing he would have the great advantage of being able to feel that the safety of investment was still not in any real danger.

---

[3] Many railroad bonds have proved an exception to this statement since 1933. Note, for example, that Baltimore and Ohio Railroad First 4s, due 1948, sold at $109^{1}/_{2}$ in 1936, although the margin over total interest charges had long been much too small. In 1938 these bonds sold at $34^{1}/_{4}$.

Such a policy of demanding very high safety margins would obviously prove especially beneficial if a period of acute depression and market unsettlement should supervene. It is not practicable, however, to recommend this as a standard practice for all investors, because the supply of such strongly buttressed issues is too limited, and because, further, it is contrary to human nature for investors to take *extreme* precautions against future collapse when current conditions make for optimism.[4]

Policy in Depression. Assuming that the investor has exercised merely reasonable caution in the choice of his fixed-value holdings, how will he fare and what policy should he follow in a period of depression? If the depression is a moderate one, his investments should be only mildly affected marketwise and still less in their intrinsic position. If conditions should approximate those of 1930–1933, he could not hope to escape a severe shrinkage in the quotations and considerable uneasiness over the safety of his holdings. But any reasoned policy of fixed-value investment requires the assumption that disturbances of the 1930–1933 amplitude are nonrecurring in their nature and need not be specifically guarded against in the future. If the 1921–1922 and the 1937–1938 experiences are accepted instead as typical of the "recurrent severe depression," a carefully selected investment list should give a reasonably good account of itself in such a period. The investor should not be stampeded into selling out holdings with a strong past record because of a current decline in earnings. He is likely, however, to pay more attention than usual to the question of improving the quality of his securities, and in many cases it should be possible to gain some benefits through carefully considered switches.

The experiences of the 1937–1938 "recession" offer strong corroboration of the foregoing analysis. Practically all senior securities that would have met our stringent requirements at the end of 1936 came through the ensuing setback without serious damage marketwise. But bonds that have sold at high levels despite an inadequate over-all earnings coverage—particularly a large number of railroad issues—suffered an enormous shrinkage in value. (See our discussion in Chap. 7 and also Appendix Notes 11 and 13.)

---

[4] We must caution the reader, however, against assuming that very large coverage of interest charges is, in itself, a complete assurance of safety. An operating loss eliminates the margin of safety, however high it may have been. Hence, inherent stability is an essential requirement, as we emphasize in our Studebaker example given in Chap. 2.

Sources of Investment Advice and Supervision. Supervision of securities involves the question of who should do it as well as how to do it. Investors have the choice of various agencies for this purpose, of which the more important are the following:

1. The investor himself.
2. His commercial bank.
3. An investment banking (or underwriting) house.
4. A New York Stock Exchange firm.
5. The advisory department of a large trust company.
6. Independent investment counsel or supervisory service.

The last two agencies charge fees for their service, whereas the three preceding supply advice and information gratis.[5]

Advice from Commercial Bankers. The investor should not be his own sole consultant unless he has training and experience sufficient to qualify him to advise others professionally. In most cases he should at least supplement his own judgment by conference with others. The practice of consulting one's bank about investments is widespread, and it is undeniably of great benefit, especially to the smaller investor. If followed consistently it would afford almost complete protection against the hypnotic wiles of the high-pressure stock salesman and his worthless "blue sky" flotations.[6] It is doubtful, however, if the commercial banker is the most suitable adviser to an investor of means. Although his judgment is usually sound, his knowledge of securities is likely to be somewhat superficial, and he cannot be expected to spare the time necessary for a thoroughgoing analysis of his clients' holdings and problems.

Advice from Investment Banking Houses. There are objections of another kind to the advisory service of an investment banking house. An institution with securities of its own to sell cannot be looked to for entirely impartial guidance. However ethical its aims may be, the compelling force of self-interest is bound to affect its judgment. This is particularly true when

---

[5] A growing number of Stock Exchange firms now supply investment advice on a fee basis.

[6] Under S.E.C. supervision the "blue-sky flotation" of the old school has largely disappeared from interstate commerce, its place being taken by small but presumably legitimate enterprises which are sold to the public at excessively high prices. Numerous other types of fraud are still fairly prevalent, as can be seen from the 1938 report of the Better Business Bureau of New York City.

the advice is supplied by a bond salesman whose livelihood depends upon persuading his customers to buy the securities that his firm has "on its shelves." It is true that the reputable underwriting houses consider themselves as bound in some degree by a fiduciary responsibility toward their clients. The endeavor to give them sound advice and to sell them suitable securities arises not only from the dictates of good business practice but more compellingly from the obligations of a professional code of ethics.

Nevertheless, the sale of securities is not a profession but a business and is necessarily carried on as such. Although in the typical transaction it is to the advantage of the seller to give the buyer full value and satisfaction, conditions may arise in which their interests are in serious conflict. Hence it is impracticable, and in a sense unfair, to require investment banking houses to act as impartial advisers to buyers of securities; and, broadly speaking, it is unwise for the investor to rely primarily upon the advice of sellers of securities.

Advice from New York Stock Exchange Firms. The investment departments of the large Stock Exchange firms present a somewhat different picture. Although they also have a pecuniary interest in the transactions of their customers, their advice is much more likely to be painstaking and thoroughly impartial. Stock Exchange houses do not ordinarily own securities for sale. Although at times they participate in selling operations, which carry larger allowances than the ordinary market commission, their interest in pushing such individual issues is less vital than that of the underwriting houses who actually own them. At bottom, the investment business or bond department of Stock Exchange firms is perhaps more important to them as a badge of respectability than for the profits it yields. Attacks made upon them as agencies of speculation may be answered in part by pointing to the necessary services that they render to conservative investors. Consequently, the investor who consults a large Stock Exchange firm regarding a small bond purchase is likely to receive time and attention out of all proportion to the commission involved. Admittedly this practice is found profitable in the end, as a cold business proposition, because a certain proportion of the bond customers later develop into active stock traders. In behalf of the Stock Exchange houses it should be said that they make no effort to persuade their bond clients to speculate in stocks, but the atmosphere of a brokerage office is perhaps not without its seductive influence.

Advice from Investment Counsel. Although the idea of giving investment advice on a fee basis is not a new one, it has only recently developed into an important financial activity. The work is now being done by special departments of large trust companies, by a division of the statistical services, and by private firms designating themselves as investment counsel or investment consultants. The advantage of such agencies is that they can be entirely impartial, having no interest in the sale of any securities or in any commission on their client's transactions. The chief disadvantage is the cost of the service, which averages about $1/2\%$ per annum on the principal involved. As applied strictly to investment funds this charge would amount to about $1/7$ or $1/8$ of the annual income, which must be considered substantial.

In order to make their fees appear less burdensome, some of the private investment consultants endeavor to forecast the general course of the bond market and to advise their clients as to when to buy or sell. It is doubtful if trading in bonds, to catch the market swings, can be carried on successfully by the investor. If the course of the bond market can be predicted, it should be possible to predict that of the stock market as well, and there would be undoubted technical advantages in trading in stocks rather than in bonds. We are sceptical of the ability of any paid agency to provide reliable forecasts of the market action of either bonds or stocks. Furthermore we are convinced that any combined effort to advise upon the choice of individual high-grade investments and upon the course of bond *prices* is fundamentally illogical and confusing. Much as the investor would like to be able to buy at just the right time and to sell out when prices are about to fall, experience shows that he is not likely to be brilliantly successful in such efforts and that by injecting the trading element into his investment operations he will disrupt the income return on his capital and inevitably shift his interest into speculative directions.

It is not clear as yet whether or not advice on a fee basis will work out satisfactorily in the field of standard high-grade investments, because of their relatively small income return. In the purely speculative field the objection to paying for advice is that if the adviser *knew* whereof he spoke he would not need to bother with a consultant's duties. It may be that the profession of adviser on securities will find its most practicable field in the intermediate region, where the adviser will deal with problems arising from depreciated investments, and where he will propose advantageous exchanges and recommend bargain issues selling considerably below their intrinsic value.

PART III

Senior Securities with Speculative Features

Investing in Distressed Credit

by Dominique Mielle

Thereis a certain gravity to Graham and Dodd. The book in your hands feels heavy and substantial, the spine is extra wide. There is a sense of the Establishment in the authors' names, sounding like something straight out of a *Great Gatsby* guestlist. Their vocabulary tickles with evocative flourishes. Call me dull, but I never thought anything in my job could "easily prove a costly snare to the unwary." (Chap. 22) You flinch at the allegory of "Mr. Market" created by Benjamin Graham, because it is too apt a description of the people in the industry.

This, according to the *Wall Street Journal*, is the urtext of modern value investing.[1] Yes, I too had to look up this word.

Thus it would not be entirely illogical for Generation Z to conclude that the best use of *Security Analysis* is to prop up their laptop for a Zoom call. And you would be correct in assessing that this remarkable book, among many benefits, will put the camera exactly at your eye level, which is undeniably the most attractive video angle.

Having propelled the founding fathers of value investing into acute twenty-first century relevance, let me set the record straight on Benjamin

---

[1] "Graham's 1934 book, *Security Analysis*, with David Dodd, is widely viewed as the urtext of modern value investing." Ari Weinburg, "Can an Index Fund Deliver the 'Value'?" *Wall Street Journal*, September 8, 2015, https://www.wsj.com/amp/articles/can-an-index-fund -deliver-the-value-1441764704.

Graham, for there is more to him than meets the eye. First, Graham was born Gròssbaum, a poor Jewish immigrant whose family name was changed to assimilate into American society and avoid antisemitism. Second, he was apparently fond of the axiom that he wished "every day to do something foolish, something creative, and something generous." I suspect we would attract a different crowd to asset management with that subtitle on the cover. Indeed, it is an endearing and relatable motto, well-suited to some spectacularly successful investors. I am looking at you, Warren Buffett, zipping around on the back of a golf cart at 91 years old, having pledged 99% of your fortune and still leading one of the most valuable companies on earth. Not to mention Seth Klarman, the Oracle of Boston, who incidentally invited me to write this introduction, thereby checking off *generous* and *foolish* in a single stroke. Last, Graham could quote Kierkegaard (note to my fellow hedge fund managers: this is not the name of an artisanal beer). Here is the first lesson from Graham and Dodd: don't rely on appearances, don't trust first impressions, don't jump to conclusions.

But I digress. Imagine my reaction when asked to write an introduction to the investing in distressed credit section of *Security Analysis*: "I don't belong," I thought, and not in the least because I'm French, female, and funny. Consider the intellectual context: two clans have battled to gain control of the investing theory landscape over the last 80-odd years. The Graham and Dodd gang, defenders of the value investing credo, who call New York's Columbia Business School their turf, posit that financial instruments—stocks in particular—have an intrinsic value that is separate and different from their trading value. Investing consists of buying stocks where the latter is below the former by a considerable "margin of safety" (*i.e.*, undervalued stocks), and cashing in when inevitably albeit not necessarily swiftly, their trading value approaches intrinsic value. Their rivals, the Modern Portfolio clan from the mean streets of Chicago, led by Markowitz and

Sharpe, start with the Efficient Market Theory that every stock price reflects all available information. There is no other value than the trading value—in other words, the intrinsic value *is* the trading value. Investing is therefore not about selecting undervalued stocks; it's about building a portfolio of securities that optimize expected return for a given level of risk. While the Chicago School equates volatility with risk, value investors tend to view volatility as a source of opportunity.

I know what you are thinking. How did Steven Spielberg miss this perfect reboot for his *West Side Story* movie: dancing fund managers in Patagonia vests and singing Nobel Prize winners in corduroy pants duking it out over the shape of the Efficient Frontier?

I was raised on the wrong side of the rumble for this book. Not only did I not go to Columbia Business School, I attended Stanford, where I was taught by Bill Sharpe himself. As I started writing this essay, a recollection of his first lecture resurfaced—I hadn't given it a thought in 25 years. Professor Sharpe considered the probability of two students in class sharing the same day and month for their birthday. Contrary to everyone's instinct, we calculated a nontrivial percentage and not two but three of us qualified. He proceeded to tell us that these odds are roughly the same as an investor beating the market 15 years in a row. For any one investor, those odds are infinitesimally low. But given the vast number of investors, it is reasonably likely that *someone* will do it. That turned out to be the case for Bill Miller, portfolio manager at Legg Mason, a staunch proponent and practitioner of value investing. According to Professor Sharpe, Miller's streak of outperformance was not a validation of the value investing method; he was simply a dot on a normal distribution curve of outcomes. Somebody had to be. In my naiveté, I registered the fact as a tidbit of statistics. Not so: Bill Sharpe was proselytizing, and his class, Portfolio Management, had an indelible effect on my thinking.

The idea of a "true value" has always struck me as nebulous at best and mystical at worse. Graham and Dodd themselves appeared conflicted on the matter, explaining that intrinsic value "is that value, which is justified by the facts, *e.g.*, the assets, earnings, dividends, and definite prospects, as distinct, let us say, from market quotations established by market manipulation or distorted by psychological excesses." (Chap. 1) But they also warned that "it must always be remembered that the truth that the analyst uncovers is first of all not the whole truth and, secondly, not the immutable truth." (Chap. 31) Elsewhere they admit that "intrinsic value is an elusive concept" but can be approximated, just like "it is quite possible to decide by inspection that a woman is old enough to vote without knowing her age or that a man is heavier than he should be without knowing his weight." I don't know about you, but I've had a tough time estimating women's ages since my Beverly Hills orthodontist diversified into Botox, and I most definitely wouldn't pass judgment on a man's weight, at least not to his face. I believe deeply that "security analysis cannot presume to lay down general rules as to the 'proper value' of any given common stock. Practically speaking, there is no such thing." (Chap. 39)

My former employer, where I invested for 20 years as a portfolio manager, was a multi-asset class manager, a value-oriented and event-driven hedge fund. However, of all the partners' portfolios, mine was consistently the lightest in public equities, rarely having any exposure at all. Plainly, I am not a stock picker; blame it on my upbringing. If you described me as a Bond girl, I bet no one would bat an eye.

My supreme luck, however, was to discover that in a corner of the corporate bond market, distressed investing, lay the extraordinary opportunity to fuse both schools of thought to form a glorious ménage à trois—building a career along the way. Stressed and distressed investing entails buying the bonds or the loans of a company under severe operational or financial duress, either within bankruptcy or on the verge of filing for it. A bond has a contractual value, even a distressed bond selling at a deep discount to par. Thus I could do away with the nebulous concept of a "true value." I knew what I would recover if the value of the assets or business covered the face value of my claims. Second, the Efficient Market Hypothesis starts with the important assumption of perfect liquidity, meaning that there are always willing buyers and sellers. While liquidity is, if not perfect, excellent for large capitalization stocks, distressed assets are liquid as quicksand and forced sellers abound. This means that I could ignore the debilitating notion that securities are perfectly priced. The distressed investor is left with the challenge of evaluating what payment is available and how to get it. In that respect, Graham and Dodd are the messiahs of distressed investing, their method highly relevant and oftentimes prescient, their book a terrific recipe for long-term investment success.

The first commandment of the distressed investor is to focus on the downside. That is my read of Graham and Dodd's "margin of safety" concept: not the distance to the promised land of an intrinsic value, but how much further a bond will drop if things go wrong, which, for a distressed company, is quite probable. When reading "the primary aim of the bond buyer must be to avoid trouble and not to protect himself in the event of trouble," you may chuckle: aren't we already in trouble with distressed companies? (Chap. 6) Trust me, things can always get uglier. Repeat 100 times until memorized: "The purchaser of low-priced bonds is fully aware of the risk he is running; he is more likely to make a thorough investigation of the issue and to appraise carefully the chances of loss and of profit; finally—most important of all—he is prepared for whatever losses he may sustain, and his profits are in a form available to meet his losses." (Chap. 7)

How, pray, will this purchaser make a thorough investigation? Why, they will look not only at the income statement, but also at the balance sheet. "We have expressed our conviction that the balance sheet deserves more attention than Wall Street has been willing to accord it for many years past." (Chap. 42) I cherish Graham and Dodd's description of the "attention" that was my work for 20 years, less for their quantitative accuracy than their evocative quality. "There are unbounded opportunities for shrewd detective work, for critical comparisons, for discovering and pointing out a state of affairs quite different from that indicated by the publicized per-share earnings." (Chap. 31) *That* is the joy of distressed investing as I saw it: the thrilling investigations, the exciting discoveries, the creative and strategic thinking (the *creative* word again!) that deliver unique insights. A corporate indebtedness, being a private contract, has infinite variations. Even in the well-established U.S. leveraged loan and junk bond markets, there are differences in covenants, seniority, security, callability—sometimes extremely subtle and often highly controversial—that can make the difference between a losing trade and a winning one. As a company slides into trouble, conflicts arise over how to divide the corporate value pie among creditors, be it between secured and unsecured lenders, junior and senior bondholders, revolver and term loan bankers, first lien and second lien creditors—and all of them at once in an epic creditor battle. A good distressed investor is indeed a shrewd detective and a chess master, an army general and a diplomat, studying scenarios, positioning their bets, anticipating each stakeholder's next move. Scores of distressed investments have the twists and turns of the best TV drama, with colorful protagonists and supporting characters, dark hours and hopeful dawns, spells of luck and misfortune, good and bad endings. It's *Game of Thrones* and you're Daenerys, Mother of Dragons.

A prescient recommendation from Graham and Dodd is to avoid analyzing the balance sheet or the income statement separately because these can be incomplete and manipulated, focusing instead on their relationship, like pieces of a puzzle that form a corporate picture.

Fifty years ahead of their time, they foresaw the imperative of the cash flow statement. They also described the frauds and accounting manipulations that led to many of the largest ever corporate bankruptcies around 2001. These, helped along by the telecom and dot-com debacle in the early aughts, launched distressed investing as a lucrative branch of the hedge fund industry.

Graham and Dodd insisted that the connection between the financial statements is more informative than the static study of each, highlighting "the necessity of *relating* an analysis of income accounts to an examination of the appurtenant balance sheets" (emphasis mine). (Chap. 33) "The meaning of any income statement cannot properly be understood except with reference to the balance sheet at the beginning and at the end of the period." (Chap. 31) The cash flow statement is the report that neatly links the frozen picture of the balance sheet to the dynamic but mostly noncash, manipulable income statement. Not until 1987 did SFAS Statement No. 95 mandate that firms provide a cash flow statement, a disclosure that present-day distressed investors rely on extensively.

In the subsequent chapters of the "Analysis of the Income Account" section, Graham and Dodd proceed to describe accounting tricks and schemes on the income statement, from slightly deceptive to outright fraudulent. The current distressed investor would do well to study them, as "those who do not remember the past are condemned to repeat it."[2] The prehistory of distressed investing is in there. Manipulation of depreciation reserve? WorldCom is exhibit A. "Padding income by including items in earnings that have no real existence"? (Chap. 33) I give you Global Crossing. "Depreciating 609 often an issue in mergers"? (Chap. 31) Ask Tyco. "Earnings subject in extraordinary degree to arbitrary determination and manipulation"? (Chap. 31) Here's Enron.

---

[2] Benjamin Graham, *The Intelligent Investor*, 1949, Harper & Brothers.

I glibly described distressed investing as buying troubled companies' debt, but buying it is only the beginning, not the end game. A phenomenal amount of work is required to achieve a favorable outcome. This debt may be worthless unless and until we manage to clean up the company through a capital restructuring, or an operational turnaround, or more likely, both. The goal is to make the company viable and profitable again with a sustainable financing plan, thereby increasing the value of its securities. In short, the distressed investor is an *activist*. That term is often used for shareholders these days, but it is applicable in a bankruptcy to creditors, who stand to be the new owners. Our authors devote an entire chapter to stockholders-management relationships, in which they denounce the "notorious fact that the typical American stockholder is the most docile and apathetic animal in captivity." (Chap. 44) They list potential conflicts between shareholders and management, including expansion, compensation, dividend policy, information, even business continuation. They urge action: "Alert shareholders will not surrender their right that a corporation should operate in their sole interest!" That is music to the distressed investor's ears; it is their job to design and implement a restructuring plan that redresses the issues that led to failure—and collect a hefty return in so doing. Overleveraged balance sheet, hasty expansion, unprofitable acquisitions, excessive dividends, incompetent management team—all of it needs to be creatively and rigorously addressed in a plan ultimately approved by the bankruptcy judge and creditors.

The writers predicted the immense profit potential of the discipline, highlighting discrepancies between prices and values in receivership, as "obligations sold at a ridiculously low price compared with the current assets available to them." (Chap. 50) This had "previously led us to advise strongly against buying at investment levels *any* securities of a company that is likely to fall into financial difficulties; it now leads us to suggest *that* after these difficulties have arisen, they may produce attractive analytical opportunities" (emphasis their own). (Chap. 50) Our perceptive duo points out that "investors are constitutionally averse to buying into a troubled situation" (Chap. 6); not only constitutionally, one might add, but in many cases also institutionally, which confers a formidable edge to the distressed investor able to buy and hold securities that others must dump at inefficient prices.

The killer app (what previous generations called a "mouse trap") of the book resides under "Price Patterns Produced by Insolvency." Consider this prophetic sentence: "a profitable field of analytical activity should be found therefore in keeping in close touch with such situations, endeavoring to discover securities that appear to be selling far under their intrinsic values and to determine approximately the best time for making a commitment in them." (Chap. 50)

Alas, there is little elaboration on this promising topic; there is no example that considers receivership from the point of view of buying—only from selling or "switching" (upgrading a portfolio). There is, shockingly, no chapter on distressed analysis in the 800-some pages of the *Security Analysis* bible. Why? This omission baffled me until I looked back at the edition dates. Plainly, in the original Graham and Dodd world, there was no adequate process to make money in bankruptcy. Until the 1930s, bankruptcy generally meant liquidation, and bankruptcy courts dealt primarily with foreclosure of a firm's assets—hardly a way to make a profit for a bondholder when "in practice we find a very definite disinclination on the part of the courts to permit corporate bondholders to take over properties by foreclosing on their liens if there is any possibility that these assets may have a fair value in excess of their claim." (Chap. 6)

However, the Corporate Reorganization Act, followed by the Chandler Act and the Trust Indenture Act of 1939, introduced corporate reorganization rules with the purpose of keeping businesses alive and giving them a chance to emerge rather than dismantling them. While it was obviously a response to the crash of 1929 and the dire economic conditions of the 1930s, the charter of the bill was to be of "permanent helpful assistance to distressed corporations," providing "the opportunity for amicable adjustment by debtor and creditors, under the supervision and protection of the bankruptcy courts, and for holding the property of the debtor intact with its operation disturbed as little as practicable."[3]

Bankruptcy as we know it today, particularly Chapter 11 of the bankruptcy code, emerged from the 1978 reform, furthering the goal to maintain corporate operations, save jobs, and attract new sources of credit, while freezing pre-petition debt collection until it could be sorted out over time. As described by Professor Charles J. Tabb, a leading bankruptcy scholar, "the most often repeated justification for chapter 11 is to maximize the value of the debtor firm. The operative assumption is that there is a going-concern surplus for a reorganized firm over and above its liquidation value. In short, the most fundamental reason for having a corporate rescue procedure such as chapter 11 is to maximize value for the benefit of all stakeholders in the enterprise. More money is better than less."[4] Voila! Distressed investing could begin in earnest. Graham and Dodd indeed presumed that the process would be beneficial, but "the new laws have not yet had time to prove their merits or deficiencies in actual practices." (Chap. 18) Our scribes were, simply put, too early.

Nevertheless, they managed to give me a career. It's true! My big breakthrough as an investor finds its origin in *Security Analysis*, deep

---

[3] U.S. Congress, House of Representatives, Committee on the Judiciary, *Bankruptcy Act Revision: Hearings Before the Subcommittee on Civil and Constitutional Rights*, 94th Congress, 2nd session, 1976, p. 374, https://books.google.fr/books/about/Bankruptcy_Act_Revision.html?id=7IG3cVV9aY8C&redir_esc=y.

[4] Charles Jordan Tabb, "What's Wrong with Chapter 11?," University of Illinois College of Law Legal Studies Research Paper No. 19–15, March 13, 2019, https://ssrn.com/abstract=3352137 or http://dx.doi.org/10.2139/ssrn.3352137.

in an obscure section on "Special Types of Obligations" (Chap. 10) that describes railroad equipment certificates, bonds secured by title to locomotives, freight, or passenger cars, and by the pledge of the lease under which the railroad is using the equipment. According to our exacting authors, "the investment record of these equipment obligations is very satisfactory, particularly because until recently even the most serious financial difficulties of the issuing road have very rarely prevented the prompt payment of interest and principal." (Chap. 10) They continue, "the holder of the equipment lien can threaten to take the rolling stock away. It is the possession of this *alternative* which in practice has proved of prime value to the owner of equipment trusts." (Chap. 10) Little did Graham and Dodd know that decades later, bankers would ingeniously use this basic structure to finance commercial aircraft. They enhanced it by making EETC bonds (Enhanced Equipment Trust Certificates) bankruptcy-remote, tranched in senior and junior layers, and strengthened by a liquidity facility that enabled interest payments even if the airline went bankrupt. Thus EETC bonds were safer than regular airline corporate bonds, rated higher by rating agencies, and purchased by investment grade investors. Northwest Airlines was the first to issue an EETC in 1994. Gaining widespread acceptance, issuance ballooned to $15 billion as we entered 2001, and promised continued exponential growth. These were bulletproof bonds "which could suffer default only under exceptional and highly improbable circumstances." (Chap. 4)

Unfortunately, the exceptional and improbable and tragic did happen. After the terror attacks of September 11, 2001, EETCs plunged in price. The next day, I was tapped to cover the sector.

The entire U.S. airline industry teetered on insolvency. Carriers were promptly downgraded, and all but one filed for bankruptcy within five years. Aircraft prices cratered. We were in uncharted territory, with a new financial instrument that was still untried in a downside scenario, and holders who had been attracted to its safety and investment-grade rating and lacked any mandate or expertise in distressed investing. They stampeded for the exit, forcefully selling for whatever they could get. Suddenly bonds traded at prices below the value of the aircraft that served as collateral—sometimes even below their scrap value! Under a specific section of the bankruptcy code, bondholders could—as in the old railroad equipment bonds— repossess or threaten to repossess the aircraft, thereby gaining considerable leverage over the estate and other creditors while securing the ability to realize the bonds' intrinsic value.

It was a textbook Graham and Dodd setup, the mother of all value investments. United, the largest EETC issuer, stayed in bankruptcy for over three years, during which I scrambled to become an airline and aircraft expert. Until then, my knowledge of the industry consisted of buying a ticket, preferably in business class. By the time United emerged from its bankruptcy, Northwest and Delta were getting ready to file and provide new investment opportunities. Aircraft and airline bonds had developed into a profitable mainstay of our fund, and I had become a portfolio manager.

Now, it will come as a shock to my admirers, but I've had lousy investments in my days. A good many could have been avoided with a careful rereading of *Security Analysis*. One is particularly searing. Years after my first airline investment, I sought to expand my success in airlines to shipping: both transportation businesses with a high fixed-cost structure and volatile input (fuel), supported by long-life assets that can be traded worldwide, and first mortgage debt that could sometimes be purchased at a discount—how different could it be? Not at all, it turned out, except for the minus instead of the plus sign in front of my return. Financiers of ships do not benefit from the same ability to seize their collateral upon a default or a bankruptcy. First, it is exceedingly difficult to arrest a vessel. Second, even first lien debt is subordinated to maritime liens such as crew wages or unpaid freight, fuel, or port charges. In other words, you lack the "positive and substantial advantage of the realizability of the pledged assets." (Chap. 10) Last, shipping commands no customer loyalty, no brand value or corporate differentiation, hair-raisingly volatile rates, and low geographic arbitrage availability. You can repossess a plane from a distressed U.S. carrier and sell it to a thriving Brazilian domestic airline for a profitable route—not so in shipping. It would have been handy to realize in 2013 when I invested in Eagle Bulk Shipping that "the conception of a mortgage lien as a guaranty of protection independent of the success of the business itself is in most cases a complete fallacy." (Chap. 6) Yet Eagle Bulk started as a successful restructuring, smoothly navigating through the bankruptcy process (dare I say "sailing") with the support of lenders—including yours truly. Business continued uninterrupted, new financing was obtained, obligations to customers and employees were fulfilled, and the company emerged within six months with a brand spanking new capital structure and bright business prospects. Within months, shipping rates plummeted, and even the restructured first lien blew up. The illiquidity of the loan exacerbated the drop in price. The mortgaged assets provided no floor value. "Safety is not measured by lien but by the ability to pay" (Chap. 6) was the lesson. The proverbial Eagle had landed . . . but it was an emergency descent into distressed land again.

A lot has muddled the craft of distressed investing since my EETC encounter and shipping debacle. In chronological order, I would cite three seismic shifts. The first is that investing in distressed debt has become mainstream and institutionalized since the telecom crisis of 2001. Back then, the Callan Periodic Tables estimated distressed hedge funds at $24 billion in assets under management and multi-strategy hedge funds at $66 billion. While it would be arduous to circle a total number because most funds straddle multiple strategies, the largest 25 distressed players alone managed around $600 billion in 2022. Restructurings are increasingly imposed by and designed to maximize recovery for the megafunds. Anyone else (vendor, junior creditor, labor) is, as Iggy Pop used to say, a passenger who rides and who rides. Creditor-on-creditor violence is real, or as one expressive lawyer put it, the "cannibalistic assault by one group of lenders in a syndicate against another." Is the laudable goal of Chapter 11 to maximize the value of the debtor for all creditors and distribute it fairly and equitably, let alone amicably, ancient history? I don't believe so.

It's worth noting that distressed investing is not graveyard dancing; it's rebuilding, which is in the best interest of all constituencies. Through a capital restructuring, or an operational turnaround, or most likely both, a company can become viable again, with employees and vendors paid on time and growth prospects supported by sustainable financing sources.

The second tsunami is the Federal Reserve's intervention in the capital markets, including corporate debt. This is a new phenomenon that neither the value investing creators nor the Chicago School academics envisioned. After all, quantitative easing (QE) was introduced in the United States only in 2008. It made sense then: the Great Financial Recession was a liquidity and solvency crisis. How do you combat it? By injecting liquidity. Subsequent crises were neither, yet the Fed has used more versions of QE than there are sequels of *The Matrix* (QE 1, 2, 3 and 4, and Operation Twist between 2008 and 2014). As a result of the Covid-19 crisis, it deployed an even greater-reaching program, dipping its toes into purchasing high-yield bonds. One of many direct results is that episodes of debt dislocation have dramatically shortened, and supply of distressed bonds has become disappointingly shallow. While the peak-to-trough distressed bout persisted for over a year during the Global Financial Crisis and the telecom crisis, it shortened to barely three months through the taper tantrum of 2013, the energy price crunch of 2016, and the pandemic catastrophe of 2020. Simply put, the Fed has learned to act fast, wide, and decisively; it's the Grinch Who Stole Distressed.

The third revolution comes from mass retail online investing, an interesting phenomenon in the lenses of both value investing and efficient market theories. Our neoclassical investors probably wouldn't classify the actions of Robinhood, Reddit, or WallStreetBets users as investing, because I doubt Graham would define reading a tweet as "thorough analysis." But whether you call it speculation, gamification of stocks, or democratization of trading, it has become a critical market force with deep and sometimes lasting consequences, capable of bringing a large institutional fund to its knees and driving a large bankruptcy process to a specific outcome. It is well beyond the temporary yo-yo moves on "meme" stocks and "stonks." Ask Melvin Capital, the $12.5 billion hedge fund that required a capital infusion rescue after a devastating loss inflicted by the whiplash on GameStop and was still shut down a few months later. Or look at Hertz, where two successive restructuring plans initially left the equity for dead. A pop in the stock, unexplainable but for retail gambling in penny stocks, led first to a failed equity raise, then to a legal objection against restructuring plans that wiped out the equity, and finally to a 36-hour bidding auction that ascribed meaningful recovery to prebankruptcy equity holders.

Maybe the phenomenon is mere senseless mob speculation. But maybe, if we want to use the Graham and Dodd framework, the intrinsic value of some securities exceeds their economic utility because they deliver something more: entertainment value and membership in a community of holders. And maybe Markowitz and Sharpe would posit that this community holds a tool that is illegal for institutional investors, unfathomable until the era of social media, and antithetical to the Efficient Market Hypothesis: the ability to act as a group.

From these developments we would conclude that the imperative for distressed investing is to be as big as an elephant, quick as a bunny, and clever as a Roaring Kitty.[5] In other words: it's complicated. To the young and impetuous distressed investors of tomorrow, I say, fear not! For the answers are here, in the wise prose of Graham and Dodd. First, the capital advice, disregarded by many an esteemed colleague over the years yet reliably valuable in my experience: "We ought as far as possible to know what we are talking about." (Chap. 4) Second, if all else fails, remember this: "As the Danish philosopher Soren Kierkegaard noted, life can only be understood backward—but it must be lived forward."[6]

---

[5] Roaring Kitty is the Twitter name of Keith Patrick Gill, an American financial analyst and investor, whose posts on social media were cited as a driving factor in the GameStop short squeeze of January 2021.

[6] Benjamin Graham, *The Intelligent Investor.*

CHAPTER 22

Privileged Issues

WE COME now to the second major division of our revised classification of securities, *viz.*, bonds and preferred stocks presumed by the buyer to be subject to substantial change in principal value. In our introductory discussion (Chap. 5) we subdivided this group under two heads: those issues which are speculative because of inadequate safety, and those which are speculative because they possess a conversion or similar privilege which makes possible substantial variations in market price.[1]

SENIOR ISSUES WITH SPECULATIVE PRIVILEGES

In addition to enjoying a prior claim for a fixed amount of principal and income, a bond or preferred stock may also be given the right to share in benefits accruing to the common stock. These privileges are of three kinds, designated as follows:

1. Convertible—conferring the right to exchange the senior issue for common stock on stipulated terms.

2. Participating—under which additional income may be paid to the senior security holder, dependent usually upon the amount of common dividends declared.

3. Subscription—by which holders of the bond or preferred stock may purchase common shares, at prices, in amounts, and during periods, stipulated.[2]

---

[1] In the 1934 edition we had here a section on investment-quality senior issues obtainable at bargain levels. Although these were plentiful in the 1931–1933 period, they have since grown very scarce—even in the market decline of 1937–1938. To save space, therefore, we are now omitting this section.

[2] There is still a fourth type of profit-sharing arrangement, of less importance than the three just described, which made its first appearance in the 1928–1929 bull market. This is the so-called "optional" bond or preferred stock. The option consists of taking interest or dividend payments in a fixed amount of common stock (*i.e.*, at a fixed price per share) in lieu of cash.

Since the conversion privilege is the most familiar of the three, we shall frequently use the term "convertible issues" to refer to privileged issues in general.

Such Issues Attractive in Form. By means of any one of these three provisions a senior security can be given virtually all the profit possibilities that attach to the common stock of the enterprise. Such issues must therefore be considered as the most attractive of all in point of *form*, since they permit the combination of maximum safety with the chance of unlimited appreciation in value. A bond that meets all the requirements of a sound investment and in addition possesses an interesting conversion privilege would undoubtedly constitute a highly desirable purchase.

Their Investment Record Unenviable: Reasons. Despite this impressive argument in favor of privileged senior issues as a *form* of investment, we must recognize that actual experience with this class has not been generally satisfactory. For this discrepancy between promise and performance, reasons of two different kinds may be advanced.

The first is that only a small fraction of the privileged issues have actually met the rigorous requirements of a sound investment. The conversion feature has most often been offered to compensate for inadequate security.[3] This weakness was most pronounced during the period of great-

---

For example, Commercial Investment Trust $6 Convertible Preference, Optional Series of 1929, gave the holder the option to take his dividend at the annual rate of one-thirteenth share of common instead of $6 in cash. This was equivalent to a price of $78 per share for the common, which meant that the option would be valuable whenever the stock was selling above 78. Similarly, Warner Brothers Pictures, Inc., Optional 6% Convertible Debentures, due 1939, issued in 1929, gave the owner the option to take his interest payments at the annual rate of one share of common stock instead of $60 in cash.

It may be said that this optional arrangement is a modified form of conversion privilege, under which the interest or dividend amounts are made separately convertible into common stock. In most, possibly all, of these issues, the principal is convertible as well. The separate convertibility of the income payments adds somewhat, but not a great deal, to the attractiveness of the privilege.

[3] The *Report of the Industrial Securities Committee of the Investment Bankers Association of America* for 1927 quotes, presumably with approval, a suggestion that since a certain percentage of the senior securities of moderate-sized industrial companies "are liable to show substantial losses over a period of five or ten years," investors therein should be given a participation in future earnings through a conversion or other privilege to compensate for this risk. See *Proceedings of the Sixteenth Annual Convention of the Investment Bankers Association of America*, pp. 144–145, 1927.

est vogue for convertible issues, between 1926 and 1929.[4] During these years it was broadly true that the strongly entrenched industrial enterprises raised money through sales of common stock, whereas the weaker—or weakly capitalized—undertakings resorted to privileged senior securities.

The second reason is related to the conditions under which profit may accrue from the conversion privilege. Although there is indeed no upper limit to the price that a convertible bond may reach, there is a very real limitation on the amount of profit that the holder may realize while still maintaining an *investment position*. After a privileged issue has advanced with the common stock, its price soon becomes dependent *in both directions* upon changes in the stock quotation, and to that extent the continued holding of the senior issue becomes a *speculative* operation. An example will make this clear:

Let us assume the purchase of a high-grade $3^{1}/_{2}$% bond at par, convertible into two shares of common for each $100 bond (*i.e.*, convertible into common stock at 50). The common stock is selling at 45 when the bond is bought.

First Stage: (1) If the stock declines to 35, the bond may remain close to par. This illustrates the pronounced technical advantage of a convertible issue over the common stock. (2) If the stock advances to 55, the price of the bond will probably rise to 115 or more. (Its "immediate conversion value" would be 110, but a premium would be justified because of its advantage over the stock.) This illustrates the undoubted speculative possibilities of such a convertible issue.

Second Stage: The stock advances further to 65. The conversion value of the bond is now 130, and it will sell at that figure, or slightly higher. At this point the original purchaser is faced with a problem. Within wide limits, the future price of his bond depends entirely upon the course of the common stock. In order to seek a larger profit he must risk the loss of the profit in hand, which in fact constitutes a substantial part of the

---

[4] Prior to the appearance on Feb. 16, 1939, of *Release No.* 208 (*Statistical Series*) of the S.E.C., no comprehensive compilation of the dollar volume of privileged issues has been made and regularly maintained. That release gave data on a quarterly basis for the period from Apr. 1, 1937, through Dec. 31, 1938, and additional data have since been published quarterly by the S.E.C. Further evidence of the volume of this type of financing over a much longer period is presented in Appendix Note 35.

present market value of his security. (A drop in the price of the common could readily induce a decline in the bond from 130 to 110.) If he elects to hold the issue, he places himself to a considerable degree in the position of the stockholders, and this similarity increases rapidly as the price advances further. If, for example, he is still holding the bond at a level say of 180 (90 for the stock), he has for all practical purposes assumed the status and risks of a stockholder.

Unlimited Profit in Such Issues Identified with Stockholder's Position. The unlimited profit possibilities of a privileged issue are thus in an important sense illusory. They must be identified not with the ownership of a bond or preferred stock but with the assumption of a common stockholder's position—which any holder of a nonconvertible may effect by exchanging his bond for a stock. Practically speaking, the range of profit possibilities for a convertible issue, *although still maintaining the advantage of an investment holding*, must usually be limited to somewhere between 25 and 35% of its face value. For this reason original purchasers of privileged issues do not ordinarily hold them for more than a small fraction of the maximum market gains scored by the most successful among them, and consequently they do not actually realize these very large possible profits. Thus the profits taken may not offset the losses occasioned by unsound commitments in this field.

Examples of Attractive Issues. The two objections just discussed must considerably temper our enthusiasm for privileged senior issues as a class, but they by no means destroy their inherent advantages nor the possibilities of exploiting them with reasonable success. Although *most* new convertible offerings may have been inadequately secured,[5] there are fairly frequent exceptions to the rule, and these exceptions should be of prime interest to the alert investor. We append three leading examples of such opportunities, taken from the utility, the railroad, and the industrial fields.

1. *Commonwealth Edison Company Convertible Debenture 3½s, Due 1958.* These bonds were offered to shareholders in June and September 1938 at par. The statistical exhibit of the company gave every assurance that the debentures were a sound commitment at that price. They were convertible into 40 shares of common stock until maturity or prior redemption.

---

[5] This criticism does not apply to convertible bonds issued from 1933 to date, the majority of which meet our investment standards.

In September 1938 the debentures could have been bought on the New York Stock Exchange at par when the stock was selling at 24$^{1}/_{2}$. At these prices the bonds and stock were selling very close to a parity, and a slight advance in the price of the stock would enable the holder of the bond to sell at a profit. Less than a year later (July 1939) the stock had risen to 31$^{3}/_{8}$, and the bonds to 124$^{3}/_{4}$.

2. *Chesapeake and Ohio Railway Company Convertible 5s, Due 1946.* These bonds were originally offered to shareholders in June 1916. They were convertible into common stock at 75 until April 1, 1920; at 80 from the latter date until April 1, 1923; at 90 from the latter date until April 1, 1926; and at 100 from the latter date until April 1, 1936.

Late in 1924 they could have been bought on a parity basis (*i.e.*, without payment of a premium for the conversion privilege) at prices close to par. Specifically, they sold on November 28, 1924, at 101 when the stock sold at 91. At that time the company's earnings were showing continued improvement and indicated that the bonds were adequately secured. (Fixed charges were covered twice in 1924.) The value of the conversion privilege was shown by the fact that the stock sold at 131 in the next year, making the bonds worth 145.

3. *Rand Kardex Bureau, Inc., 5$^{1}/_{2}$s, Due 1931.* These bonds were originally offered in December 1925 at 99$^{1}/_{2}$. They carried stock-purchase warrants (detachable after January 1, 1927) entitling the holder to purchase 22$^{1}/_{2}$ shares of Class A common at $40 per share during 1926, at $42.50 per share during 1927, at $45 per share during 1928, at $47.50 per share during 1929, and at $50 per share during 1930. (The Class A stock was in reality a participating preferred issue.) The bonds could be turned in at par in payment for the stock purchased under the warrants, a provision that virtually made the bonds convertible into the stock.

The bonds appeared to be adequately secured. The previous exhibit (based on the earnings of the predecessor companies) showed the following coverage for the interest on the new bond issue:

Year	Number of Times Interest Covered
1921 (depression year)	1.7
1922 (depression year)	2.3
1923	6.7
1924	7.2
1925 (9 months)	12.2

Net current assets exceed twice the face value of the bond issue.

When the bonds were offered to the public, the Class A stock was quoted at about 42, indicating an immediate value for the stock-purchase warrants. The following year the stock advanced to 53, and the bonds to 130$^{1}/_{2}$. In 1927 (when Rand Kardex merged with Remington Typewriter) the stock advanced to 76, and the bonds to 190.

Example of an Unattractive Issue. By way of contrast with these examples we shall supply an illustration of a superficially attractive but basically unsound convertible offering, such as characterized the 1928–1929 period.

National Trade Journals, Inc., 6% Convertible Notes, Due 1938. The company was organized in February 1928 to acquire and publish about a dozen trade journals. In November 1928 it sold $2,800,000 of the foregoing notes at 97$^{1}/_{2}$. The notes were initially convertible into 27 shares of common stock (at $37.03 per share) until November 1, 1930; into 25 shares (at $40 a share) from the latter date until November 1, 1932; and at prices that progressively increased to $52.63 a share during the last two years of the life of the bonds.

These bonds could have been purchased at the time of issuance and for several months thereafter at prices only slightly above their parity value as compared with the market value of the equivalent stock. Specifically, they could have been bought at 97$^{1}/_{2}$ on November 30, when the stock sold at 34$^{1}/_{8}$, which meant that the stock needed to advance only two points to assure a profit on conversion.

However, at no time did the bonds appear to be adequately secured, despite the attractive picture presented in the offering circular. The circular exhibited "estimated" earnings of the predecessor enterprise based on the 3$^{1}/_{2}$ years preceding, which averaged 4.16 times the charges on the bond issue. But close to half of these estimated earnings were expected to be derived from economies predicted to result from the consolidation in the way of reduction of salaries, etc. The conservative investor would not be justified in taking these "earnings" for granted, particularly in a hazardous and competitive business of this type, with a relatively small amount of tangible assets.

Eliminating the estimated "earnings" mentioned in the preceding paragraph the exhibit at the time of issuance and thereafter was as follows:

Year	Price range of bonds	Price range of stock	Prevailing conversion price	Times interest earned	Earned per share on common
1925				1.73*	$0.78*
1926				2.52*	1.84*
1927				2.80*	2.20*
1928	100 −97¹/₂	35⁷/₈−30	$37.03	1.69†	1.95
1929	99 −50	34⁵/₈− 5	37.03	1.86†	1.04
1930	42 −10	6³/₈− ¹/₂	37.03−$40	0.09†	1.68(d)
1931	10¹/₂ − 5	1	40.00	Receivership	

* Predecessor enterprise. Pre-share figures are after estimating federal taxes.
† Actual earnings for last 10 months of 1928 and succeeding calendar years.

Receivers were appointed in June 1931. The properties were sold in August of that year, and bondholders later received about 8¹/₂ cents on the dollar.

Principle Derived. From these contrasting instances an investment principle may be developed that should afford a valuable guide to the selection of privileged senior issues. The principle is as follows: *A privileged senior issue, selling close to or above face value, must meet the requirements either of a straight fixed-value investment or of a straight common-stock speculation, and it must be bought with one or the other qualification clearly in view.*

The alternative given supplies two different approaches to the purchase of a privileged security. It may be bought as a sound investment with an *incidental* chance of profit through an enhancement of principal, or it may be bought *primarily* as an attractive form of speculation in the common stock. Generally speaking, there should be no middle ground. The *investor* interested in safety of principal should not abate his requirements in return for a conversion privilege; the *speculator* should not be attracted to an enterprise of mediocre promise because of the pseudo-security provided by the bond contract.

Our opposition to any compromise between the purely investment and the admittedly speculative attitude is based primarily on subjective grounds. Where an intermediate stand is taken, the result is usually confusion, clouded thinking, and self-deception. The investor who relaxes his safety requirements to obtain a profit-sharing privilege is frequently not prepared, financially or mentally, for the inevitable loss if fortune should frown on the venture. The speculator who wants to reduce his risk by operating in convertible issues is likely to find his primary interest divided between the enterprise itself and the terms of the privilege, and he will probably be uncertain in his own mind as to whether he is at bottom a stockholder or a bondholder. (Privileged issues *selling at substantial discounts from par* are not in general subject to this principle, since they belong to the second category of speculative senior securities to be considered later.)

Reverting to our examples, it will be seen at once that the Commonwealth Edison 3$^1/2$s could properly have been purchased as an investment without any regard to the conversion feature. The strong possibility that this privilege would be of value made the bond almost uniquely attractive at the time of issuance. Somewhat similar statements could be made with respect to the Chesapeake and Ohio and the Rand Kardex bonds. Any of these three securities should also have been attractive to a speculator who was persuaded that the related common stock was due for an advance in price.

On the other hand the National Trade Journals Debentures could not have passed stringent qualitative and quantitative tests of safety. Hence they should properly have been of interest only to a person who had full confidence in the future value of the stock. It is hardly likely, however, that most of the buying of this issue was motivated by the primary desire to invest or speculate in the National Trade Journals common stock, but it was based rather on the attractive terms of the conversion privilege and on the feeling that the issue was "fairly safe" as a bond investment. It is precisely this compromise between true investment and true speculation that we disapprove, chiefly because the purchaser has no clear-cut idea of the purpose of his commitment or of the risk that he is incurring.

Rules Regarding Retention or Sale. Having stated a basic principle to guide the *selection* of privileged issues, we ask next what rules can be established regarding their subsequent retention or sale. Convertibles bought primarily as a form of commitment in the common stock may be held for a larger profit than those acquired from the investment standpoint. If a bond of the former class advances from 100 to 150, the large premium need not in itself be a controlling reason for selling out; the owner must be guided rather by his views as to whether or not the common stock has advanced enough to justify taking his profit. But when the purchase is made primarily as a safe bond investment, then the limitation on the amount of profit that can conservatively be waited for comes directly into play. For the reasons explained in detail above, the conservative buyer of privileged issues will not ordinarily hold them for more than a 25 to 35% advance. This means that a really successful investment operation in the convertible field does not cover a long period of time. Hence such issues should be bought with the *possibility* of long-term holding in mind but with the *hope* that the potential profit will be realized fairly soon.

The foregoing discussion leads to the statement of another investment rule, *viz.*:

> In the typical case, a convertible bond should not be converted by the investor. It should be either held or sold.

It is true that the object of the privilege is to bring about such conversion when it seems advantageous. If the price of the bond advances substantially, its current yield will shrink to an unattractive figure, and there is ordinarily a substantial gain in income to be realized through the exchange into stock. Nevertheless when the investor does exchange his bond into the stock, he abandons the priority and the unqualified claim to principal and interest upon which the purchase was originally premised. If after the conversion is made things should go badly, his shares may decline in value far below the original cost of his bond, and he will lose not only his profit but part of his principal as well.

Moreover he is running the risk of transforming himself—generally, as well as in the specific instances—from a bond investor into a stock speculator. It must be recognized that there is something insidious about even a good convertible bond; it can easily prove a costly snare to the unwary. To avoid this danger the investor must cling determinedly to a conservative viewpoint. When the price of his bond has passed out of the investment range, he must sell it; most important of all, he must not consider his judgment impugned if the bond subsequently rises to a much higher level. The market behavior of the issue, once it has entered the speculative range, is no more the investor's affair than the price gyrations of any speculative stock about which he knows nothing.

If the course of action here recommended is followed by investors generally, the conversion of bonds would be brought about only through their purchase for this specific purpose by persons who have decided independently to acquire the shares for either speculation or supposed investment.[6] The arguments against the investor's converting convertible issues apply with equal force against his exercising stock-purchase warrants attached to bonds bought for investment purposes.

A continued policy of investment in privileged issues would, under favorable conditions, require rather frequent taking of profits and replacement by new securities not selling at an excessive premium. More concretely, a bond bought at 100 would be sold, say, at 125 and be replaced by another good convertible issue purchasable at about par. It is not likely that satisfactory opportunities of this kind will be continuously available or that the investor would have the means of locating all those that are at hand. But the trend of financing in recent years offers some promise that a fair number of really attractive convertibles may again make their appearance. Following the 1926–1929 period, marked by a flood of privileged issues generally of poor quality, and the 1930–1934 period, in which the emphasis on safety caused the virtual disappearance of conversion privileges from new bond offerings, there has been a definite swing of the pendulum towards a middle point, where participating features are at times employed to facilitate the sale of sound bond offerings.[7] Most of those sold between 1934 and 1939 either carried very low coupon rates or immediately jumped to a prohibitive premium. But we incline to the view that the discriminating and careful investor is again likely to find a reasonable number of attractive opportunities presented in this field.

---

[6] In actual practice, conversions often result also from arbitrage operations involving the purchase of the bond and the simultaneous sale of the stock at a price slightly higher than the "conversion parity."

[7] For data regarding the relative frequency of privilege issues between 1925 and 1938, see Appendix Note 35 and the S.E.C. statistical releases referred to in Chap. 22, Note 4.

CHAPTER 23

Technical Characteristics of Privileged Senior Securities

IN THE PRECEDING chapter privileged senior issues were considered in their relationship to the broader principles of investment and speculation. To arrive at an adequate knowledge of this group of securities from their practical side, a more intensive discussion of their characteristics is now in order. Such a study may conveniently be carried on from three successive viewpoints: (1) considerations common to all three types of privilege—conversion, participation, and subscription (*i.e.*, "warrant"); (2) the relative merits of each type, as compared with the others; (3) technical aspects of each type, considered by itself.[1]

CONSIDERATIONS GENERALLY APPLICABLE TO PRIVILEGED ISSUES

The attractiveness of a profit-sharing feature depends upon two major but entirely unrelated factors: (1) the *terms* of the arrangement and (2) the *prospects* of profits to share. To use a simple illustration:

Company *A*	Company *B*
4% bond selling at 100	4% bond selling at 100
Convertible into stock at 50 (*i.e.*, two shares of stock for a $100 bond)	Convertible into stock at 33$^1/_3$ (*i.e.*, three shares of stock for a $100 bond)
Stock selling at 30	Stock selling at 30

---

[1] This subject is treated at what may appear to be disproportionate length because of the growing importance of privileged issues and the absence of thoroughgoing discussion thereof in the standard descriptive textbooks.

Terms of the Privilege vs. Prospects for the Enterprise. The *terms* of the conversion privilege are evidently more attractive in the case of Bond *B*; for the stock need advance only a little more than 3 points to assure a profit, whereas Stock *A* must advance over 20 points to make conversion profitable. Nevertheless, it is quite possible that Bond *A* may turn out to be the more advantageous purchase. For conceivably Stock *B* may fail to advance at all while Stock *A* may double or triple in price.

As between the two factors, it is undoubtedly true that it is more profitable to select the right *company* than to select the issue with the most desirable *terms*. There is certainly no mathematical basis on which the attractiveness of the enterprise may be offset against the terms of the privilege, and a balance struck between these two entirely dissociated elements of value. But in analyzing privileged issues of the investment grade, the *terms* of the privilege must receive the greater attention, not because they are more important but because they can be more definitely dealt with. It may seem a comparatively easy matter to determine that one enterprise is more promising than another. But it is by no means so easy to establish that one common stock at a given price is clearly preferable to another stock at its current price.

Reverting to our example, if it were quite certain, or even reasonably probable, that Stock *A* is more likely to advance to 50 than Stock *B* to advance to 33, then both issues would not be quoted at 30. Stock *A*, of course, would be selling higher. The point we make is that the market price in general *reflects already* any superiority that one enterprise has demonstrated over another. The investor who prefers Bond *A* because he expects its related stock to rise a great deal faster than Stock *B*, is exercising independent judgment in a field where certainty is lacking and where mistakes are necessarily frequent. For this reason we doubt that a successful policy of buying privileged issues *from the investment approach* can be based primarily upon the purchaser's view regarding the future expansion of the profits of the enterprise. (In stating this point we are merely repeating a principle previously laid down in the field of fixed-value investment.)

Where the speculative approach is followed, *i.e.*, where the issue is bought primarily as a desirable method of acquiring an interest in the stock, it would be quite logical, of course, to assign dominant weight to the buyer's judgment as to the future of the company.

Three Important Elements. *1. Extent of the Privilege.* In examining the *terms* of a profit-sharing privilege, three component elements are seen to enter. These are:

a. The *extent* of the profit-sharing or speculative interest per dollar of investment.
b. The *closeness* of the privilege to a realizable profit at the time of purchase.
c. The *duration* of the privilege.

The amount of speculative interest attaching to a convertible or warrant-bearing senior security is equal to the current market value of the number of shares of stock covered by the privilege. Other things being equal, the larger the amount of the speculative interest per dollar of investment the more attractive the privilege.

Examples: Rand Kardex 5^1/$_2$s, previously described, carried warrants to buy 22^1/$_2$ shares of Class *A* stock initially at 40. Current price of Class *A* stock was 42. The "speculative interest" amounted to 22^1/$_2$ x 42, or $945 per $1,000 bond.

Reliable Stores Corporation 6s, offered in 1927, carried warrants to buy only 5 shares of common stock initially at 10. Current price of the common was 12. Hence the "speculative interest" amounted to 5 x 12, or only $60 per $1,000 bond.

Intercontinental Rubber Products Co. 7s offered an extraordinary example of a large speculative interest attaching to a bond. As a result of peculiar provisions surrounding their issuance in 1922, each $1,000 note was convertible into 100 shares of stock and also carried the right to purchase 400 additional shares at 10. When the stock sold at 10 in 1925, the speculative interest per $1,000 note amounted to 500 x 10, or $5,000. If the notes were then selling, say, at 120, the speculative interest would have equalled 417% of the bond investment—or 70 *times* as great as in the case of the Reliable Stores offering.

The practical importance of the amount of speculative interest can be illustrated by the following comparison, covering the three examples above given.

Item	Reliable Stores 6s	Rand Kardex 5$^1/2$s	Intercontinental Rubber 7s
Number of shares covered by each $1,000 bond	5	22$^1/2$	500
Base price	$10.00	$40.00	$10.00
Increase in value of bond when stock advances:			
25% above base price	12.50	225.00	1,250.00
50% above base price	25.00	450.00	2,500.00
100% above base price	50.00	900.00	5,000.00

In the case of convertible bonds the speculative interest always amounts to 100% of the bond at par when the stock sells at the conversion price. Hence in these issues our first and second component elements express the same fact. If a bond selling at par is convertible into stock at 50, and if the stock sells at 30, then the speculative interest amounts to 60% of the commitment, which is the same thing as saying that the current price of the stock is 60% of that needed before conversion would be profitable. Stock-purchase-warrant issues disclose no such fixed relationship between the amount of the speculative interest and the proximity of this interest to a realizable profit. In the case of the Reliable Stores 6s, the speculative interest was very small, but it showed an actual profit at the time of issuance, since the stock was selling *above* the subscription price.

Significance of Call on Large Number of Shares at Low Price. It may be said parenthetically that a speculative interest in a large number of shares selling at a low price is technically more attractive than one in a smaller number of shares selling at a high price. This is because low-priced shares are apt to fluctuate over a wider range *percentagewise* than higher priced stocks. Hence if a bond is both well secured and convertible into many shares at a low price, it will have an excellent chance for very large profit without being subject to the offsetting risk of greater loss through a speculative dip in the price of the stock.

For example, as a matter of *form* of privilege, the Ohio Copper Company 7s, due 1931, convertible into 1,000 shares of stock selling at $1, had better possibilities than the Atchison, Topeka and Santa Fe Convertible 4$^1/2$s, due 1948, convertible into 6 shares of common, selling at 166$^2/_3$, although in each case the amount of speculative interest equalled $1,000 per bond. As it turned out, Ohio Copper stock advanced from less than $1 a share in 1928 to 4$^7/_8$ in 1929, making the bond worth close to 500% of par. It would have required a rise in the price of Atchison from 166 to 800 to yield the same profit on the convertible 4$^1/_2$s, but the highest price reached in 1929 was under 300.

In the case of *participating issues*, the extent of the profit-sharing interest would ordinarily be considered in terms of the amount of extra income that may conceivably be obtained as a result of the privilege. A limited extra payment (*e.g.*, Bayuk Cigars, Inc., 7% Preferred, which may receive not more than 1% additional) is of course less attractive than an unlimited participation (*e.g.*, White Rock Mineral Springs Company 5% Second Preferred, which received a total of 26$^1/_4$% in 1930).

2 and 3. Closeness and Duration of the Privilege. The implications of the second and third factors in valuing a privilege are readily apparent. A privilege having a long period to run is in that respect more desirable than one expiring in a short time. The nearer the current price of the stock to the level at which conversion or subscription becomes profitable the more attractive does the privilege become. In the case of a participation feature, it is similarly desirable that the current dividends or earnings on the common stock should be close to the figure at which the extra distribution on the senior issue commences.

By "conversion price" is meant the price of the common stock equivalent to a price of 100 for the convertible issue. If a preferred stock is convertible into 1$^2/_3$ as many shares of common, the conversion price of the common is therefore 60. The term "conversion parity," or "conversion level," may be used to designate that price of the common which is equivalent to a given quotation for the convertible issue, or *vice versa*. It can be found by multiplying the price of the convertible issue by the conversion price of the common. If the preferred stock just mentioned is selling at 90, the conversion parity of the common becomes 60 x 90% = 54. This means that to a buyer of the preferred at 90 an advance in the common above 54 will create a realizable profit. Conversely, if the common sold at 66, one might say that the conversion parity of the preferred is 110.

The "closeness" of the privilege may be stated arithmetically as the ratio between the market price and the conversion parity of the common stock. In the foregoing example, if the common is selling at 54 and the preferred at 110 (equivalent to 66 for the common), the "index of close-ness" becomes 54 ÷ 66, or 0.82.

COMPARATIVE MERITS OF
THE THREE TYPES OF PRIVILEGES

From the theoretical standpoint, a participating feature—unlimited in time and possible amount—is the most desirable type of profit-sharing privilege. This arrangement enables the investor to derive the specific benefit of participation in profits (*viz.*, increased income) without modifying his original position as a senior-security holder. These benefits may be received over a long period of years. By contrast, a conversion privilege can result in higher income only through actual exchange into the stock and consequent surrender of the senior position. Its real advantage consists, therefore, only of the opportunity to make a profit through the sale of the convertible issue at the right time. Similarly the benefits from a subscription privilege may conservatively be realized only through sale of the warrants (or by the subscription to and prompt sale of the stock). If the common stock is purchased and held for permanent income, the operation involves the risking of additional money on a basis entirely different from the original purchase of the senior issue.

Example of Advantage of Unlimited Participation Privilege. An excellent practical example of the theoretical advantages attaching to a well-entrenched participating security is afforded by Westinghouse Electric and Manufacturing Company Preferred. This issue is entitled to cumulative prior dividends of $3.50 per annum (7% on $50 par) and in addition participates equally per share with the common in any dividends paid on the latter in excess of $3.50. As far back as 1917 Westinghouse Preferred could have been bought at $52^1/_2$, representing an attractive straight investment with additional possibilities through its participating feature. In the ensuing 15 years to 1932 a total of about $7 per share was disbursed in extra dividends above the basic 7%. In the meantime an opportunity arose to sell out at a large profit (the high price being 284 in 1929), which corresponded to the enhancement possibilities of a convertible or subscription-warrant issue. If the stock was not sold, the profit was naturally lost in the ensuing market decline. But the investor's original position remained unimpaired, for at the low point of 1932 the issue was still paying the 7% dividend and selling at 52 $^1/_2$—although the common had passed its dividend and had fallen to 15 $^5/_8$.

In this instance the investor was able to participate in the surplus profits of the common stock in good years while maintaining his preferred position, so that, when the bad years came, he lost only his temporary *profit*. Had the issue been convertible instead of participating, the investor could have received the higher dividends only through converting and would later have found the dividend omitted on his common shares and their value fallen far below his original investment.

Participating Issues at Disadvantage, Marketwise. Although from the standpoint of long-pull-investment holding, participating issues are theoretically the most desirable, they may behave somewhat less satisfactorily in a major market upswing than do convertible or subscription-warrant issues. During such a period a participating senior security may regularly sell below its proper comparative price. In the case of Westinghouse Preferred, for example, its price during 1929 was usually from 5 to 10 points lower than that of the common, although its intrinsic value per share could not be less than that of the junior stock.[2]

The reason for this phenomenon is as follows: The price of the common stock is made largely by speculators interested chiefly in quick profits, to secure which they need an active market. The preferred stock, being closely held, is relatively inactive. Consequently the speculators are willing to pay several points more for the inferior common issue simply because it can be bought and sold more readily and because other speculators are likely to be willing to pay more for it also.

The same anomaly arises in the case of closely held common stocks with voting power, compared with the more active nonvoting issue of the same company. American Tobacco *B* and Liggett and Myers Tobacco *B* (both nonvoting) have for years sold higher than the voting stock. A similar situation formerly existed in the two common issues of Bethlehem

---

[2] A much greater price discrepancy of this kind existed in the case of White Rock Mineral Springs Participating Preferred and common during 1929 and 1930. Because of this market situation, holders of nearly all the participating preferred shares accepted an offer to exchange into common stock, although this meant no gain in income and the loss of their senior position.

Steel, Pan American Petroleum and others.[3] The paradoxical principle holds true for the securities market generally that *in the absence of a special demand* relative scarcity is likely to make for a lower rather than a higher price.

In cases such as Westinghouse and American Tobacco the proper corporate policy would be to extend to the holder of the intrinsically more valuable issue the privilege of exchanging it for the more active but intrinsically inferior issue. The White Rock company actually took this step. Although the holders of the participating preferred might make a mistake in accepting such an offer, they cannot object to its being made to them, and the common stockholders may gain but cannot lose through its acceptance.

Relative Price Behavior of Convertible and Warrant-Bearing Issues. From the standpoint of price behavior under favorable market conditions the best results are obtained by holders of senior securities with detachable stock-purchase warrants.

To illustrate this point we shall compare certain price relationships shown in 1929 between four privileged issues and the corresponding common stocks. The issues are as follows:

1. Mohawk Hudson Power Corporation 7% Second Preferred, carrying warrants to buy 2 shares of common at 50 for each share of preferred.

2. White Sewing Machine Corporation 6% Debentures, due 1936, carrying warrants to buy $2^1/_2$ shares of common stock for each $100 bond.

3. Central States Electric Corporation 6% Preferred, convertible into common stock at $118 per share.

4. Independent Oil and Gas Company Debentures 6s, due 1939, convertible into common stock at $32 per share.

The following table shows in striking fashion that in speculative markets issues with purchase warrants have a tendency to sell at large premiums in relation to the common-stock price and that these premiums are much greater than in the case of similarly situated convertible issues.

---

[3] The persistently wide spread between the market prices for R. J. Reynolds Tobacco Company common and Class *B* stocks rests on the special circumstance that officers and employees of the company who own the common stock enjoy certain profit-sharing benefits not accorded to holders of the Class *B* stock. The New York Stock Exchange will no longer list nonvoting common stocks, nor are these permitted to be issued in reorganizations effected under Chap. X of the 1938 Bankruptcy Act.

Senior issue	Market price of common	Conversion or subscrip- tion price of common	Price of senior issue	Realizable value of senior issue based on privilege (conversion or subscrip- tion parity)	Amount by which senior issue sold above parity, ("pre- mium"), points
Mohawk Hudson 2d Pfd	52$^1/_2$	50	163*	105	58
White Sewing Machine 6s	39	40	123$^1/_2$†	97$^1/_2$	26
Central States Electric Pfd	116	118	97	98	−1
Independent Oil & Gas 6s	31	32	105	97	8

* Consisting of 107 for the preferred stock, ex-warrants, plus 56 for the warrants.
† Consisting of 98$^1/_2$ for the bonds, ex-warrants, plus 25 for the warrants.

Advantage of Separability of Speculative Component.

This advantage of subscription-warrant issues is due largely to the fact that their speculative component (*i.e.*, the subscription warrant itself) can be entirely separated from their investment component (*i.e.*, the bond or preferred stock ex-warrants). Speculators are always looking for a chance to make large profits on a small cash commitment. This is a distinguishing characteristic of stock option warrants, as will be shown in detail in our later discussion of these instruments. In an advancing market, therefore, speculators bid for the warrants attached to these privileged issues, and hence they sell separately at a substantial price even though they may have no immediate exercisable value. These speculators greatly prefer buying the option warrants to buying a corresponding *convertible bond*, because the latter requires a much larger cash investment per share of common stock involved.[4] It follows, therefore, that the separate market values of the

---

[4] Note that the Independent Oil and Gas bonds represented a commitment of $33.60 per share of common, whereas the White Sewing Machine warrants involved a commitment of only $10 per share of common. But the former meant *ownership* of either a fixed claim or a share of stock, whereas the latter meant only the *right to buy* a share of stock at a price above the market.

bond plus the option warrant (which combine to make the price of the bond "with warrants") may considerably exceed the single quotation for a closely similar convertible issue.

Second Advantage of Warrant-Bearing Issues. Subscription-warrant issues have a second point of superiority, in respect to callable provisions. A right reserved by the corporation to redeem an issue prior to maturity must in general be considered as a disadvantage to the holder; for presumably it will be exercised only when it is to the benefit of the issuer to do so, which means usually that the security would otherwise sell for more than the call price.[5] A callable provision, unless at a very high premium, might entirely vitiate the value of a participating privilege. For with such a provision there would be danger of redemption as soon as the company grew prosperous enough to place the issue in line for extra distributions.[6] In some cases participating issues that are callable are made convertible as well, in order to give them a chance to benefit from any large advance in the market price of the common that may have taken place up to the time of call. (See for examples: National Distillers Products Corporation $2.50 Cumulative Participating Convertible Preferred;[7] Kelsey-Hayes Wheel Company $1.50 Participating Convertible Class A stock.) Participating *bonds* are generally limited in their right to participate in surplus earnings and are commonly callable. (See White Sewing Machine Corporation Participating Debenture 6s, due 1940; United Steel Works

---

[5] The callable feature may be—and recently has been—an unfavorable element of great importance even in "straight" nonconvertible bonds.

In a few cases a callable feature works out to the advantage of the holder, by facilitating new financing which involves the redemption of the old issue at a price above the previous market. But the same result could be obtained, if there were no right to call, by an offer to "buy in" the security. This was done in the case of United States Steel Corporation 5s, due 1951, which were not callable but were bought in at 110.

[6] Dewing cites the case of Union Pacific Railroad—Oregon Short Line Participating 4s, issued in 1903, which were secured by the pledge of Northern Securities Company stock. The bondholders had the right to participate in any dividends in excess of 4% declared on the deposited collateral. The bonds were called at $102\frac{1}{2}$ just at the time when participating distributions seemed likely to occur. See Arthur S. Dewing, *A Study of Corporation Securities*, p. 328, New York, 1934.

[7] Coincident with the rise of the common stock from $16\frac{7}{8}$ to $124\frac{7}{8}$ in 1933, all the National Distillers Preferred Stock was converted in that year. Nearly all the conversions were precipitated by a change in the conversion rate after June 30, 1933. The small balance was converted as a result of the calling of issue at 40 and dividend in August.

Corporation Participating $6^1/2$s, Series *A*, due 1947; neither of which is convertible.) Sometimes participating issues are protected against loss of the privilege through redemption by setting the call price at a very high figure. Something of this sort was apparently attempted in the case of San Francisco Toll-Bridge Company Participating 7s, Due 1942, which were callable at 120 through November 1, 1933, and at lower prices thereafter. Celluloid Corporation Participating Second Preferred is callable at 150, whereas Celanese Corporation Participating First Preferred is noncallable.

Another device to prevent vitiating the participating privilege through redemption is to make the issue callable at a price that may be directly dependent upon the value of the participating privilege. For example, Siemens and Halske Participating Debentures, due in 2930, are callable after April 1, 1942, *at the average market price for the issue during the six months preceding notice of redemption but at not less than the original issue price* (which was over 230% of the par value). The Kreuger and Toll 5% Participating Debentures had similar provisions.

Even in the case of a *convertible* issue a callable feature is technically a serious drawback because it may operate to reduce the duration of the privilege. Conceivably a convertible bond may be called just when the privilege is about to acquire real value.[8]

But in the case of issues with stock-purchase warrants, the subscription privilege almost invariably runs its full time even though the senior issue itself may be called prior to maturity. If the warrant is detachable, it simply continues its separate existence until its own expiration date. Frequently, the subscription privilege is made "nondetachable"; *i.e.*, it can be exercised only by presentation of the senior security. But even in

---

[8] This danger was avoided in the case of Atchison, Topeka and Santa Fe Railway Convertible $4^1/2$s, due 1948, by permitting the issue to be called only after the conversion privilege expired in 1938. (On the other hand, Affiliated Fund Secured Convertible Debentures are callable at par at any time on 30 days' notice, in effect allowing the company to destroy any chance of profiting from the conversion privilege.)

Another protective device recently employed is to give the holder of a convertible issue a stock-purchase warrant, at the time the issue is redeemed, entitling the holder to buy the number of shares of common stock that would have been received upon conversion if the senior issue had not been redeemed. See Freeport Texas Company 6% Cumulative Convertible Preferred, issued in January 1933. United Biscuit 7% Preferred, convertible into $2^1/2$ shares of common, is callable at 110; but if called before Dec. 31, 1935, the holder had the option to take $100 in cash, plus a warrant to buy $2^1/2$ shares of common at 40 until Jan. 1,

these instances, if the issue should be redeemed prior to the expiration of the purchase-option period, it is customary to give the holder a separate warrant running for the balance of the time originally provided.

Example: Prior to January 1, 1934, United Aircraft and Transport Corporation had outstanding 150,000 shares of 6% Cumulative Preferred stock. These shares carried nondetachable warrants for one share of common stock at $30 a share for each two shares of preferred stock held. The subscription privilege was to run to November 1, 1938, and was protected by a provision for the issuance of a detached warrant evidencing the same privilege per share in case the preferred stock was redeemed prior to November 1, 1938. Some of the preferred stock was called for redemption on January 1, 1933, and detached warrants were accordingly issued to the holders thereof. (A year later the remainder of the issue was called and additional warrants issued.)

Third Advantage of Warrant-Bearing Issues. Subscription-warrant issues have still a third advantage over other privileged securities, and this is in a practical sense probably the most important of all. Let us consider what courses of conduct are open to holders of each type in the favorable event that the company prospers, that a high dividend is paid on the common, and that the common sells at a high price.

1. Holder of a participating issue:
   a. May sell at a profit.
   b. May hold and receive participating income.
2. Holder of a convertible issue:
   a. May sell at a profit.
   b. May hold but will receive no benefit from high common dividend.
   c. May convert to secure larger income but sacrifices his senior position.
3. Holder of an issue with stock-purchase warrants:
   a. May sell at a profit.
   b. May hold but will receive no benefit from high common dividend.
   c. May subscribe to common to receive high dividend. He may invest new capital, or he may sell or apply his security ex-warrants to provide funds to pay for the common. In either case he undertakes the risks of a common stockholder in order to receive the high dividend income.

d. May dispose of his warrants at a cash profit and retain his original security, ex-warrants. (The warrant may be sold directly, or he may subscribe to the stock and immediately sell it at the current indicated profit.)

The fourth option listed above is peculiar to a subscription-warrant issue and has no counterpart in convertible or participating securities. It permits the holder to cash his profit from the speculative component of the issue and still maintain his original *investment* position. Since the typical buyer of a privileged senior issue should be interested primarily in making a sound investment—with a secondary opportunity to profit from the privilege—this fourth optional course of conduct may prove a great convenience. He is not under the necessity of selling the entire commitment, as he would be if he owned a convertible, which would then require him to find some new medium for the funds involved. The reluctance to sell one good thing and buy another, which characterizes the typical investor, is one of the reasons that holders of high-priced convertibles are prone to convert them rather than to dispose of them. In the case of participating issues also, the owner can protect his *principal* profit only by selling out and thus creating a reinvestment problem.

Example: The theoretical and practical advantage of subscription-warrant issues in this respect may be illustrated in the case of Commercial Investment Trust Corporation 6¹/₂% Preferred. This was issued in 1925 and carried warrants to buy common stock at an initial price of $80 per share. In 1929 the warrants sold as high as $69.50 per share of preferred. The holder of this issue was therefore enabled to sell out its speculative component at a high price and to retain his original preferred-stock commitment, which maintained an investment status throughout the depression until it was finally called for redemption at 110 on April 1, 1933. At the time of the redemption call the common stock was selling at the equivalent of about $50 per old share. If the preferred stock had been convertible, instead of carrying warrants, many of the holders would undoubtedly have been led to convert and to retain the common shares. Instead of netting a large profit they would have been faced with a substantial loss.

Summary. To summarize this section, it may be said that, for *long-pull holding*, a sound participating issue represents the best form of profit-sharing privilege. From the standpoint of maximum *price advance* under favorable market conditions, a senior issue with detachable stock-purchase warrants is likely to show the best results. Furthermore, subscription-warrant issues as a class have definite advantages in that the privilege is ordinarily not subject to curtailment through early redemption of the security, and they permit the realization of a speculative profit while retaining the original investment position.

CHAPTER 24

Technical Aspects of Convertible Issues

THE THIRD DIVISION of the subject of privileged issues relates to technical aspects of each type, separately considered. We shall first discuss convertible issues.

The effective terms of a conversion privilege are frequently subject to change during the life of the issue. These changes are of two kinds: (1) a decrease in the conversion price, to protect the holder against "dilution"; and (2) an increase in the conversion price (in accordance usually with a "sliding-scale" arrangement) for the benefit of the company.

Dilution, and Antidilution Clauses. The value of a common stock is said to be diluted if there is an increase in the number of shares without a corresponding increase in assets and earning power. Dilution may arise through split-ups, stock dividends, offers of subscription rights at a low price, and issuance of stock for property or services at a low valuation per share. The standard "antidilution" provisions of a convertible issue endeavor to reduce the conversion price proportionately to any decrease in the per-share value arising through any act of dilution.

The method may be expressed in a formula, as follows: Let C be the conversion price, O be the number of shares now outstanding, N be the number of new shares to be issued, and P be the price at which they are to be issued.

Then

$$C' \text{ (the new conversion price)} = \frac{CO + NP}{O + N}$$

The application of this formula to Chesapeake Corporation Convertible Collateral 5s, due 1947, is given in Appendix Note 36. A simpler example of an antidilution adjustment is afforded by the Central States Electric

Corporation 6% Convertible Preferred previously referred to (Chap. 23). After its issuance in 1928, the common stock received successive stock dividends of 100 and 200%. The conversion price was accordingly first cut in half (from $118 to $59 per share) and then again reduced by two-thirds (to $19.66 per share).

A much less frequent provision merely reduces the conversion price to any lower figure at which new shares may be issued. This is, of course, more favorable to the holder of the convertible issue.[1]

Protection Against Dilution Not Complete. Although practically all convertibles now have antidilution provisions, there have been exceptions.[2] As a matter of course, a prospective buyer should make certain that such protection exists for the issue he is considering.

It should be borne in mind that the effect of these provisions is to preserve only the principal or par value of the privileged issue against dilution. If a convertible is selling considerably above par, the *premium* will still be subject to impairment through additional stock issues or a special dividend. A simple illustration will make this clear.

A bond is convertible into stock, par for par. The usual antidilution clauses are present. Both bond and stock are selling at 200.

Stockholders are given the right to buy new stock, share for share, at par ($100). These rights will be worth $50 per share, and the new stock (or the old stock "ex-rights") will be worth 150. No change will be made in the conversion basis, because the new stock is not issued below the old conversion price. However, the effect of offering these rights must be to compel immediate conversion of the bonds, since otherwise they would lose 25% of their value. As the stock will be worth only 150 "ex-rights," instead of 200, the value of the unconverted bonds would drop proportionately.

The foregoing discussion indicates that, when a large premium or market profit is created for a privileged issue, the situation is vulnerable to sudden change. Although prompt action will always prevent loss through such changes, their effect is always to terminate the effective

---

[1] See Appendix Note 37 for an example (Consolidated Textile Corporation 7s, due 1923).

[2] See Appendix Note 38 for an example (American Telephone and Telegraph Company Convertible $4^{1}/2$s, due 1933).

life of the privilege.[3] The same result will follow, of course, from the calling of a privileged issue for redemption at a price below its then conversion value.

Where the number of shares is *reduced* through recapitalization, it is customary to *increase* the conversion price proportionately. Such recapitalization measures include increases in par value, "reverse split-ups" (*e.g.*, issuance of 1 no-par share in place of, say, 5 old shares), and exchanges of the old stock for fewer new shares through consolidation with another company.[4]

Sliding Scales Designed to Accelerate Conversion. The provisions just discussed are intended to maintain equitably the original basis of conversion in the event of subsequent capitalization changes. On the other hand, a "sliding-scale" arrangement is intended definitely to reduce the value of the privilege as time goes on. The underlying purpose is to accelerate conversion, in other words, to curtail the effective duration and hence the real value of the option. Obviously, any diminution of the worth of the privilege to its recipients must correspondingly benefit the donors of the privilege, who are the company's common shareholders.

The more usual terms of a sliding scale prescribe a series of increases in the conversion price in successive periods of time. A more recent variation makes the conversion price increase as soon as a certain portion of the issue has been exchanged.

Examples: American Telephone and Telegraph Company Ten-year Debenture 4¹/2s, due 1939, issued in 1929, were made convertible into common at $180 per share during 1930, at $190 per share during 1931 and 1932, and at $200 per share during 1933 to 1937, inclusive. These prices were later reduced through the issuance of additional stock at $100, in accordance with the standard antidilution provision.

---

[3] To guard against this form of dilution, holders of convertible issues are sometimes given the right to subscribe to any new offerings of common stock on the same basis as if they owned the amount of common shares into which their holdings are convertible. See the indentures securing New York, New Haven and Hartford Railroad Company, Convertible Debenture 6s, due 1948, and Commercial Investment Trust Corporation Convertible Debenture 5¹/2s, due 1949.

[4] See Appendix Note 39 for an example of Dodge Brothers, Inc., Convertible Debenture 6s, due 1940.

Anaconda Copper Mining Company Debenture 7s, due 1938, were issued in the amount of $50,000,000. The first $10,000,000 presented were convertible into common stock at $53 per share; the second $10,000,000 were convertible at $56; the third at $59; the fourth at $62, and the final lot at $65. An $8,000,000 issue of Hiram Walker-Goderham and Worts 4^{1}/4s, due 1945, was convertible as follows: at $40 per share for the first $2,000,000 block of bonds; at $45 per share for the next block of $2,000,000; the third block at $55; and the final block at $60 per share.

Sliding Scale Based on Time Intervals. The former type of sliding scale, based on time intervals, is a readily understandable method of reducing the liberality of a conversion privilege. Its effect can be shown in the case of Porto Rican-American Tobacco Company 6s, due 1942. These were convertible into pledged Congress Cigar Company, Inc., stock at $80 per share prior to January 2, 1929, at $85 during the next three years and at $90 thereafter. During 1928 the highest price reached by Congress Cigar was 87^{1}/4, which was only a moderate premium above the conversion price. Nevertheless a number of holders were induced to convert before the year-end, because of the impending rise in the conversion basis. These conversions proved very ill-advised, since the price of the common fell to 43 in 1929, against a low of 89 for the bonds. In this instance, the adverse change in the conversion basis not only meant a smaller potential profit for those who delayed conversion until after 1928 but also involved a risk of serious loss through inducing conversion at the wrong time.

Sliding Scale Based on Extent Privilege Is Exercised. The second method, however, based on the quantities converted, is not so simple in its implications. Since it gives the first lot of bonds converted an advantage over the next, it evidently provides a *competitive* stimulus to early conversion. By so doing it creates a conflict in the minds of the holder between the desire to retain his senior position and the fear of losing the more favorable basis of conversion through prior action by other bondholders. This fear of being forestalled will ordinarily result in large-scale conversions as soon as the stock advances moderately above the initial conversion price, *i.e.*, as soon as the bond is worth slightly more than the original cost. Accordingly, the price of the senior issue should oscillate over a relatively narrow range while the common stock is advancing and while successive blocks of bonds are being converted.

Example: The sequence of events normally to be expected is shown fairly well by the market action of Hiram Walker-Goderham and Worts Convertible 4¹/4s described on the previous page. The bonds, issued in 1936 at par, ranged in price between 100 and 111¹/4 during 1936–1939. In the same period the stock ranged between 26¹/8 and 54. If the initial conversion price of 40 for the stock had prevailed throughout the period, the bonds should have sold for at least 135 when the stock sold at 54. But meanwhile, as the price of the stock rose, successive blocks of the bonds were converted (partly under the impetus supplied by successive calls for redemption of parts of the issue), thus tipping off higher conversion prices until the $55 bracket was reached in 1937. In consequence the bonds did not appreciate commensurately with the rise in the price of the stock.[5]

When the last block under such a sliding scale is reached, the *competitive* element disappears, and the bond or preferred stock is then in the position of an ordinary convertible, free to advance indefinitely with the stock.

It should be pointed out that issues with such a sliding-scale provision do not always follow this theoretical behavior pattern. The Anaconda Copper Company Convertible 7s, for example, actually sold at a high premium (30%) in 1928, before the first block was exhausted. This seems to have been one of the anomalous incidents of the highly speculative atmosphere at the time.[6] From the standpoint of critical analysis, a convertible of this type must be considered as having very limited possibilities of enhancement until the common stock approaches the last and highest conversion price.[7]

The sliding-scale privilege on a "block" basis belongs to the objectionable category of devices that tend to mislead the holder of securities as

---

[5] See pp. 266–267 of the 1934 edition of this work for a more detailed exhibit of a similar record in Engineers Public Service Company $5 Convertible Preferred in 1928–1929.

[6] The size of the premium was due in part to the high coupon rate. The bonds were, however, callable at 110, a point that the market ignored.

[7] In some cases (*e.g.*, Porto Rican-American 6s, already mentioned, and International Paper and Power Company First Preferred) the conversion privilege ceases entirely after a certain fraction of the issue has been converted. This maintains the competitive factor throughout the life of the privilege and in theory should prevent it from ever having any substantial value.

to the real nature and value of what he owns. The competitive pressure to take advantage of a limited opportunity introduces an element of compulsion into the exercise of the conversion right which is directly opposed to that freedom of choice for a reasonable time which is the essential merit of such a privilege. There seems no reason why investment bankers should inject so confusing and contradictory a feature into a security issue. Sound practice would dictate its complete abandonment or in any event the avoidance of such issues by intelligent investors.

Issues Convertible into Preferred Stock. Many bond issues were formerly made convertible into preferred stock. Ordinarily some increase in income was offered to make the provision appear attractive. (For examples, see Missouri-Kansas-Texas Railroad Company Adjustment 5s, due 1967, convertible prior to January 1, 1932 into $7 preferred stock; Central States Electric Corporation Debenture 5s, due 1948, convertible into $6 preferred stock; G. R. Kinney Company Secured 7$1/2$s, due 1936, convertible into $8 preferred stock; American Electric Power Corporation 6s, due 1957, convertible into $7 preferred stock.)

There have been instances in which a fair-sized profit has been realized through such a conversion right, but the upper limitation on the market value of the ordinary preferred stock is likely to keep down the maximum benefits from such a privilege to a modest figure. Moreover, since developments in recent years have made preferred stocks in general appear far less desirable than formerly, the right to convert, say, from a 4% bond into a 5% preferred is likely to constitute more of a danger to the unwary than an inducement to the alert investor. If the latter is looking for convertibles, he should canvass the market thoroughly and endeavor to find a suitably secured issue convertible into common stock. In a few cases where bonds are convertible into preferred stock, the latter is in turn convertible into common or participates therewith, and this double arrangement may be equivalent to convertibility of the bond into common stock. For example, International Hydro-Electric System 6s, due 1944, are convertible into Class A stock, which is in reality a participating second preferred.

There are also bond issues convertible into either preferred or common or into a combination of certain amounts of each.[8] Although any individual issue of this sort may turn out well, in general it may be said that complicated provisions of this sort should be avoided (both by issuing companies and by security buyers) because they tend to create confusion.

Bonds Convertible at the Option of the Company. The unending flood of variations in the terms of conversion and other privileges that developed during the 1920s made it difficult for the untrained investor to distinguish between the attractive, the merely harmless, and the positively harmful. Hence he proved an easy victim to unsound financing practices which in former times might have stood out as questionable because of their departure from the standard. As an example of this sort we cite the various Associated Gas and Electric Company "Convertible Obligations" which were made convertible by their terms into preferred or Class *A* stock *at the option of the company*. Such a contraption was nothing more than a preferred stock masquerading as a bond. If the purchasers were entirely aware of this fact and were willing to invest in the preferred stock, they would presumably have no cause to complain. But it goes without saying that an artifice of this kind lends itself far too readily to concealment and possible misrepresentation.[9]

---

[8] See, for example, the Chicago, Milwaukee, St. Paul and Pacific Railroad Company Convertible Adjustment Mortgage 5s, Series *A*, due Jan. 1, 2000, which are convertible into 5 shares of the preferred and 5 shares of common. For other examples see p. 623 in the Appendix of the 1934 edition of this work.

[9] These anomalous securities were variously entitled "investment certificates," "convertible debenture certificates," "interest-bearing allotment certificates," and "convertible obligations." In 1932 the company compelled the conversion of the large majority of them, but the holder was given an option (in addition to those already granted by the terms of the issues) of converting into equally anomalous "Convertible Obligations, Series *A* and *B*, due 2022," which are likewise convertible into stock at the option of the company. The company was deterred from compelling the conversion of some $17,000,000 "5$1/2$% Investment Certificates" after Nov. 15, 1933, by a provision in the indenture for that issue prohibiting the exercise of the company's option in case dividends on the $5.50 Dividend Series Preferred were in arrears (no dividends having been paid thereon since June 15, 1932).

It is interesting to note that the Pennsylvania Securities Commission prohibited the sale of these "Convertible Obligations" in December 1932 because of their objectionable provisions. The company resisted the Commission's order in the Federal District Court of

Bonds Convertible into Other Bonds. Some bonds are convertible into other bonds. The usual case is that of a short-term issue, the holder of which is given the right to exchange into a long-term bond of the same company. Frequently the long-term bond is deposited as collateral security for the note. (For example, Interborough Rapid Transit Company 7s, due 1932, were secured by deposit of $1,736 of the same company's First and Refunding 5s, due 1966, for each $1,000 note, and they were also convertible into the deposited collateral, the final rate being $1,000 of 5s for $900 of 7% notes.) The holder thus has an option either to demand repayment at an early date or to make a long-term commitment in the enterprise. In practice, this amounts merely to the chance of a moderate profit at or before maturity, in the event that the company prospers, or interest rates fall, or both.

Unlike the case of a bond convertible into a preferred stock, there is usually a *reduction* in the coupon rate when a short-term note is converted into a long-term bond. The reason is that short-term notes are ordinarily issued when interest rates, either in general or for the specific company, are regarded as abnormally high, so that the company is unwilling to incur so steep a rate for a long-term bond. It is thus expected that, when normal conditions return, long-term bonds can be floated at a much lower rate; and hence the right to exchange the note for a long-term bond, even on a basis involving some reduction in income, may prove to be valuable.[10]

Convertible Bonds with an Original Market Value in Excess of Par. One of the extraordinary developments of the 1928–1929 financial pyrotech-

---

Philadelphia but later dropped its suit (see 135 *Chronicle* 4383, 4559; 136 *Chronicle* 326, 1011).

[10] See the following issues taken from the 1920–1921 period: Shawinigan Water and Power Company 7 1/2% Gold Notes, issued in 1920 and due in 1926, convertible into First and Refunding 6s, Series B, due 1950, which were pledged as security; San Joaquin Light and Power Corporation Convertible Collateral Trust 8s, issued in 1920 and due in 1935, convertible into the pledged Series C First and Refunding 6s, due 1950; Great Western Power Company of California Convertible Gold 8s, issued in 1920 and due in 1930, convertible into pledged First and Refunding 7s, Series B, due in 1950.

Another type of bond-for-bond conversion is represented by Dawson Railway and Coal 5s, due 1951, which are convertible into El Paso and Southwestern Railroad Company First 5s, due 1965 (the parent company, which in turn is a subsidiary of the Southern Pacific). Such examples are rare and do not invite generalization.

nics was the offering of convertible issues with an original market value greatly in excess of par. This is illustrated by Atchison, Topeka and Santa Fe Railway Company Convertible 4¹/₂s, due 1948, and by American Telephone and Telegraph Company Convertible 4¹/₂s, due 1939. Initial trading in the former on the New York Curb Market (on a "when issued" basis) in November 1928 was around 125, and initial trading in the latter on the New York Stock Exchange (on a "when issued" basis) on May 1, 1929, was at 142. Obviously investment in the bonds at these levels represented primarily a commitment in the common stock, since they were immediately subject to the danger of a substantial loss of principal value if the stock declined. Furthermore the income return was entirely too low to come under our definition of investment. Although it may be thought that the stockholders were acquiring a normal investment through the exercise of their subscription right to purchase the issues at par, the essential nature of their commitment was determined by the initial market value of the security to which they were subscribing. For this reason we think such financing should be condemned, because under the guise of an attractive investment it created a basically speculative form of security.

A Technical Feature of Some Convertible Issues. A technical feature of the American Telephone and Telegraph convertible issue deserves mention. The bonds were made convertible at 180, but, instead of presenting $180 of bonds to obtain a share of stock, the holder might present $100 of bonds and $80 in cash. The effect of such an option is to make the bond more valuable whenever the stock sells above 180 (*i.e.*, whenever the conversion value of the bond exceeds 100). This is illustrated as follows:

If the stock sells at 360, a straight conversion basis of 180 would make the bond worth 200. But by the provision accepting $80 per share in cash, the value of the bond becomes $360 - 80 = 280$.

This arrangement may be characterized as a combination of a conversion privilege at 180 with a stock purchase right at 100.

Delayed Conversion Privilege. The privilege of converting is sometimes not operative immediately upon issuance of the obligation.

Examples: This was true, for example, of Brooklyn Union Gas Company Convertible 5¹/₂s, discussed in Appendix Note 38. Although they were issued in December 1925, the right to convert did not accrue until January 1, 1929. Similarly, New York, New Haven, and Hartford Railroad Company Convertible Debenture 6s, due in 1948, although issued in 1907, were not convertible until January 15, 1923; Chesapeake Corporation Convertible 5s, due 1947, were issued in 1927 but did not become convertible until May 15, 1932.

More commonly the suspension of the conversion privilege does not last so long as these examples indicate, but in any event this practice introduces an additional factor of uncertainty and tends to render the privilege less valuable than it would be otherwise. This feature may account in part for the spread, indicated in Appendix Note 38, which existed during 1926, 1927, and the early part of 1928 between the Brooklyn Union Gas Company 5¹/₂s and the related common stock.

See Chapter 25, "Senior Securities with Warrants. Participating Issues. Switching and Hedging" online at www.mhprofessional.com/ SecurityAnalysis7.

CHAPTER 26

Senior Securities of Questionable Safety

AT THE LOW POINT of the 1932 securities market the safety of at least 80% of all corporate bonds and preferred stocks was open to some appreciable degree of doubt.[1] Even prior to the 1929 crash the number of speculative senior securities was very large, and it must inevitably be still larger for some years to come. The financial world is faced, therefore, with the unpleasant fact that a considerable proportion of American securities belong to what may be called a misfit category. A low-grade bond or preferred stock constitutes a relatively unpopular form of commitment. The investor must not buy them, and the speculator generally prefers to devote his attention to common stocks. There seems to be much logic to the view that if one decides to speculate he should choose a thoroughly speculative medium and not subject himself to the upper limitations of market value and income return, or to the possibility of confusion between speculation and investment, which attach to the lower priced bonds and preferred stocks.

Limitation of Profit on Low-Priced Bonds Not a Real Drawback. But however impressive may be the objection to these nondescript securities, the fact remains that they exist in enormous quantities, that they are owned by innumerable security holders, and that hence they must be taken seriously into account in any survey of security analysis. It is reasonable to conclude that the large supply of such issues, coupled with the lack of a natural demand for them, will make for a level of prices below their intrinsic value. Even if an inherent unattractiveness in the *form* of such securities be admitted, this may be more than offset by the attractive *price* at which they may be purchased. Furthermore, the limitations of

---

[1] See Appendix Note 42 for data on bond prices in 1931–1934 and 1939.

301

principal profit in the case of a low-priced bond, as compared with a common stock, may be of only minor practical importance, because the profit
actually *realized* by the common-stock buyer is ordinarily no greater than
that obtainable from a speculative senior security. If, for example, we are
considering a 4% bond selling at 35, its maximum possible price appreciation is about 70 points, or 200%. The average common-stock purchase
at 35 cannot be held for a greater profit than this without a dangerous
surrender to "bull-market psychology."

Two Viewpoints with Respect to Speculative Bonds. There are two
directly opposite angles from which a speculative bond may be viewed.
It may be considered in its relation to investment standards and yields,
in which case the leading question is whether or not the low price and
higher income return will compensate for the concession made in the
safety factor. Or it may be thought of in terms of a common-stock commitment, in which event the contrary question arises; *viz.*, "Does the
smaller risk of loss involved in this low-priced bond, as compared with
a common stock, compensate for the smaller possibilities of profit?" The
nearer a bond comes to meeting investment requirements—and the
closer it sells to an investment price—the more likely are those interested
to regard it from the investment viewpoint. The opposite approach is evidently suggested in the case of a bond in default or selling at an extremely
low price. We are faced here with the familiar difficulty of classification
arising from the absence of definite lines of demarcation. Some issues
can always be found reflecting any conceivable status in the gamut
between complete worthlessness and absolute safety.

Common-Stock Approach Preferable. We believe, however, that the
sounder and more fruitful approach to the field of speculative senior
securities lies from the direction of common stocks. This will carry with
it a more thorough appreciation of the risk involved and therefore a
greater insistence upon either reasonable assurance of safety or especially
attractive possibilities of profit or both. It induces also—among intelligent security buyers at least—a more intensive examination of the corporate picture than would ordinarily be made in viewing a security from
the investment angle.

Such an approach would be distinctly unfavorable to the purchase of
slightly substandard bonds selling at moderate discounts from par.
These, together with high-coupon bonds of second grade, belong in the

category of "business men's investments" which we considered and decided against in Chap. 7. It may be objected that a general adoption of this attitude would result in wide and sudden fluctuations in the price of many issues. Assuming that a 4% bond deserves to sell at par as long as it meets strict investment standards, then as soon as it falls slightly below these standards its price would suffer a precipitous decline, say, to 70; and, conversely, a slight improvement in its exhibit would warrant its jumping suddenly back to par. Apparently there would be no justification for intermediate quotations between 70 and 100.

The real situation is not so simple as this, however. Differences of opinion may properly exist in the minds of investors as to whether or not a given issue is adequately secured, particularly since the standards are qualitative and personal as well as arithmetical and objective. The range between 70 and 100 may therefore logically reflect a greater or lesser agreement concerning the safety of the issue. This would mean that an investor would be justified in buying such a bond, say, at 85, if his own considered judgment regarded it as sound, although he would recognize that there was doubt on this score in the minds of other investors that would account for its appreciable discount from a prime investment price. According to this view, the levels between 70 and 100, approximately, may be designated as the range of "subjective variations" in the status of the issue.

The field of speculative values proper would therefore commence somewhere near the 70 level (for bonds with a coupon rate of 4% or larger) and would offer maximum possibilities of appreciation of at least 50% of the cost. (In the case of other senior issues, 70% of *normal value* might be taken as the dividing line.) In making such commitments, it is recommended that the same general attitude be taken as in the careful purchase of a common stock; in other words, that the income account and the balance sheet be submitted to the same intensive analysis and that the same effort be made to evaluate future possibilities—favorable and unfavorable.

Important Distinctions Between Common Stocks and Speculative Senior Issues. We shall not seek, therefore, to set up standards of selection for speculative senior issues in any sense corresponding to the quantitative tests applicable to fixed-value securities. On the other hand, although they should preferably be considered in their relationship to the common-stock approach and technique, it is necessary to appreciate certain rather important points of difference that exist between common stocks as a class and speculative senior issues.

Low-Priced Bonds Associated with Corporate Weakness. The limitation on the profit possibilities of senior securities has already been referred to. Its significance varies with the individual case, but in general we do not consider it a controlling disadvantage. A more emphatic objection is made against low-priced bonds and preferred stocks on the ground that they are associated with corporate weakness, retrogression, or depression. Obviously the enterprise behind such a security is not highly successful, and furthermore, it must have been following a downward course, since the issue originally sold at a much higher level. In 1928 and 1929 this consideration was enough to condemn all such issues absolutely in the eyes of the general public. Businesses were divided into two groups: those which were successful and progressing, and those which were on the downgrade or making no headway. The common shares of the first group were desirable no matter how high the price; but no security belonging to the second group was attractive, irrespective of how low it sold.

This concept of permanently strong and permanently weak corporations has been pretty well dissipated by the subsequent depression, and we are back to the older realization that time brings unpredictable changes in the fortunes of business undertakings.[2] The fact that the low price of a bond or preferred stock results from a decline in earnings need not signify that the company's outlook is hopeless and that there is nothing ahead but still poorer results. Many of the companies that fared very badly in 1931–1933 regained a good part of their former earning power, and their senior securities recovered from exceedingly low prices to investment levels. It turned out, therefore, that there was just as much reason to expect substantial recoveries in the quotations of depressed senior securities as in the price of common stocks generally.

Many Undervalued in Relation to Their Status and Contractual Position. We have already mentioned that the unpopularity of speculative senior securities tends to make them sell at lower prices than common stocks, in relation to their intrinsic value. From the standpoint of the intelligent buyer this must be considered a point in their favor. With

---

[2] But see later references to *The Ebb and Flow of Investment Value*, by Mead and Grodinski, published in 1939, which strongly espouses the thesis stated in the previous paragraph (Chap. 28 and Appendix Note 71.

respect to their intrinsic position, speculative bonds—and, to a lesser degree, preferred stocks—derive important advantages from their contractual rights. The fixed obligation to pay bond interest will usually result in the continuation of such payments as long as they are in any way possible. If we assume that a fairly large proportion of a group of carefully selected low-priced bonds will escape default, the income received on the group as a whole over a period of time will undoubtedly far exceed the dividend return on similarly priced common stocks.

Preferred shares occupy an immeasurably weaker position in this regard, but even here the provisions transferring voting control to the senior shares in the event of suspension of dividends will be found in some cases to impel their continuance. Where the cash resources are ample, the desire to maintain an unbroken record and to avoid accumulations will frequently result in paying preferred dividends even though poor earnings have depressed the market price.

Examples: Century Ribbon Mills, Inc., failed to earn its 7% preferred dividend in eight out of the thirteen years from 1926 to 1938, inclusive, and the price repeatedly declined to about 50. Yet the preferred dividend was continued without interruption during this entire period, while the common received a total of but 50 cents. Similarly, a purchaser of Universal Pictures Company First Preferred at about 30 in 1929 would have received the 8% dividend during three years of depression before the payment was finally suspended.

Contrasting Importance of Contractual Terms in Speculation and Investment. The reader should appreciate the distinction between the *investment* and the *speculative* qualities of preferred stocks in this matter of dividend continuance. From the investment standpoint, *i.e.*, the *dependability* of the dividend, the absence of an enforceable claim is a disadvantage as compared with bonds. From the speculative standpoint, *i.e.*, the possibility of dividends' being continued under unfavorable conditions, preferred stocks have certain semicontractual claims to consideration by the directors that undoubtedly give them an advantage over common stocks.

Bearing of Working-Capital and Sinking-Fund Factors on Safety of Speculative Senior Issues.

A large working capital, which has been characteristic of even nonprosperous industrials for some years past, is much more directly advantageous to the senior securities than to the common stock. Not only does it make possible the continuance of interest or preferred-dividend payments, but it has an important bearing also on the retirement of the principal, either at maturity or by sinking-fund operations or by voluntary repurchase. Sinking-fund provisions, for bonds as well as preferred stocks, contribute to the improvement of both the market quotation and the intrinsic position of the issue. This advantage is not found in the case of common stocks.

Examples: Francis H. Leggett Company, manufacturers and wholesalers of food products, issued $2,000,000 of 7% preferred stock carrying a sinking-fund provision which retired 3% of the issue annually. By June 30, 1932, the amount outstanding had been reduced to $608,500, and, because of the small balance remaining, the issue was called for redemption at 110, *in the depth of the depression.* Similarly, Century Ribbon Mills Preferred was reduced from $2,000,000 to $544,000 between 1922 and 1938; and Lawrence Portland Cement Company Debenture 5^1/$_2$s were reduced from $2,000,000 to $650,000 on December 31, 1938, the balance being called for redemption on April 1, 1939.

Importance of Large Net-Current-Asset Coverage. Where a low-priced bond is covered several times over by net current assets, it presents a special type of opportunity, because experience shows that the chances of repayment are good, even though the earnings may be poor or irregular.

Examples: Electric Refrigeration Corporation (Kelvinator) 6s, due 1936, sold at 66 in November 1929 when the net current assets of the company according to its latest statement amounted to $6,008,900 for the $2,528,500 of bonds outstanding. It is true that the company had operated at a deficit in 1927 and 1928, but fixed charges were earned nearly nine times in the year ended September 30, 1929, and the net current assets were nearly four times the market value of the bond issue. The bonds recovered to a price close to par in 1930 and were redeemed at 105 in 1931. Similarly, Electric Refrigeration Building Corporation First 6s, due 1936, which were in effect guaranteed by Kelvinator Corporation under a lease, sold at 70 in July 1932 when the net current assets of the parent company amounted to about six times the $1,073,000 of bonds outstanding and over eight times the total market value of the issue. The bonds were called at 101^1/$_2$ in 1933.

Other examples that may be cited in this connection are Murray Corporation First 6^1/$_2$s, due 1934, which sold at 68 in 1932 (because of current operating deficits) although the company had net current assets of over $2^{1}/_{2}$ times the par value of the issue and nearly four times their market value at that price; Sidney Blumenthal and Company 7% Notes, due 1936, which sold at 70 in 1926 when the company had net current assets of twice the par value of the issue and nearly three times the total market value thereof (they were called at 103 in 1930); Belding, Heminway Company 6s, due 1936, which sold at 67 in 1930 when the company had net current assets of nearly three times the par value of the issue and over four times its market value. In the latter case drastic liquidation of inventories occurred in 1930 and 1931, proceeds from which were used to retire about 80% of the bond issue through purchases in the market. The balance of the issue was called for payment at 101 early in 1934.

In the typical case of this kind the chance of profit will exceed the chance of loss, and the probable amount of profit will exceed the probable amount of loss. It may well be that the risk involved in each individual case is still so considerable as to preclude us from applying the term "investment" to such a commitment. Nevertheless, we suggest that if the insurance principle of diversification of risk be followed by making a number of such commitments at the same time, the net result should be sufficiently dependable to warrant our calling the group purchase an *investment operation.* This was one of the possibilities envisaged in our broadened definition of investment as given in Chap. 4.

Limitations upon Importance of Current-Asset Position. It is clear that considerable weight attaches to the working-capital exhibit in selecting speculative bonds. This importance must not be exaggerated, however, to the point of assuming that, whenever a bond is fully covered by net current assets, its safety is thereby assured. The current assets shown in any balance sheet may be greatly reduced by subsequent operating losses; more important still, the stated values frequently prove entirely undependable in the event of insolvency.[3]

Of the many examples of this point which can be given, we shall mention R. Hoe and Company 7% Notes and Ajax Rubber Company First 8s. Although these obligations were covered by net working capital in 1929, they subsequently sold as low as 2 cents on the dollar. (See also our

---

[3] The comparative reliability of the various components in the current-assets figure (cash assets, receivables, inventories) will receive detailed treatment in a discussion of balance-sheet analysis in Part VI.

discussion of Willys-Overland Company First 6^1/$_2$s and Berkey and Gay Furniture Company First 6s in Appendix Note 34.[4])

Examples of Low-Priced Industrial Bonds Covered by Net Current Assets, 1932*

Name of issue	Due	Low price 1932	Date of balance sheet	Net current assets†	Funded debt at part†	Normal interest coverage	
						Period	Times earned‡
American Seating 6s	1936	17	Sept. 1932	$ 3,826	$ 3,056	1924–1930	5.2
Crucible Steel 5s	1940	39	June 1932	16,163	13,250	1924–1930	9.4
McKesson & Robbins 5^1/$_2$s	1950	25	June 1932	42,885	20,848	1925–1930	4.1
Marion Steam Shovel 6s	1947	21	June 1932	4,598	2,417	1922–1930	3.9
National Acme 6s	1942	54	Dec. 1931	4,327	1,963	1922–1930	5.5

* See Appendix Note 43 for a brief discussion of the sequel to these examples first given in the 1934 edition of this work.
† 000 omitted.
‡ Coverage for 1931 charges, adjusted where necessary.

We must distinguish, therefore, between the mere fact that the working capital, as reported, covers the funded debt and the more significant fact that it exceeds the bond issue *many times over*. The former statement is always interesting, but by no means conclusive. If added to other favorable factors, such as a good earnings coverage in normal years and a generally satisfactory qualitative showing, it might make the issue quite attractive but preferably as part of a group-purchase in the field.

Speculative Preferred Stocks. *Stages in Their Price History.* Speculative preferred stocks are more subject than speculative bonds to irrational activity, so that from time to time such preferred shares are overvalued in the market in the same way as common stocks. We thus have three possible stages in the price history of a preferred issue, in each of which the market quotation tends to be out of line with the value:

1. The first stage is that of original issuance, when investors are persuaded to buy the offering at a full investment price not justified by its intrinsic merit.

---

[4] Perhaps it should be added that three of the four issues mentioned in this paragraph had spectacular recoveries from the low prices of the depression (*e.g.*, the new Hoe 7s, which were exchanged for the old 7s, sold at 100 in 1937).

2. In the second stage the lack of investment merit has become manifest, and the price drops to a speculative level. During this period the decline is likely to be overdone, for reasons previously discussed.

3. A third stage sometimes appears in which the issue advances speculatively in the same fashion as common stocks. On such occasions certain factors of questionable importance—such as the amount of dividend accumulations—are overemphasized.

An example of this third or irrational stage will be given a little later.

The Rule of "Maximum Valuation for Senior Issues." Both as a safeguard against being led astray by the propaganda that is characteristic of the third stage and also as a general guide in dealing with speculative senior issues, the following principle of security analysis is presented, which we shall call "the rule of maximum valuation for senior issues."

> *A senior issue cannot be worth, intrinsically, any more than a common stock would be worth if it occupied the position of that senior issue, with no junior securities outstanding.*

This statement may be understood more readily by means of an example.

Company *X* and Company *Y* have the same value. Company *X* has 80,000 shares of preferred and 200,000 shares of common. Company *Y* has only 80,000 shares of common and no preferred. Then our principle states that a share of Company *X* preferred cannot be worth more than a share of Company *Y* common. This is true because Company *Y* common represents the same value that lies behind *both* the preferred and common of Company *X*.

Instead of comparing two equivalent companies such as *X* and *Y*, we may assume that Company *X* is recapitalized so that the old common is eliminated and the preferred becomes the sole stock issue, *i.e.*, the new common stock. (To coin a term, we may call such an assumed change the "communizing" of a preferred stock.) Then our principle merely states the obvious fact that the value of such a hypothetical common stock cannot be *less* than the value of the preferred stock it replaces, because it is equivalent to the preferred *plus* the old common. The same idea may be applied to a speculative bond, followed either by common stock only or by both preferred and common. If the bond is "communized," *i.e.*, if it is assumed to be turned into a common stock, with the old stock issues eliminated, then the value of the new common stock thus created cannot be less than the present value of the bond.

This relationship must hold true regardless of how high the coupon or dividend rate, the par value or the redemption price of the senior issue may be and, particularly, regardless of what amount of unpaid interest or dividends may have accumulated. For if we had a preferred stock with accumulations of $1,000 per share, the value of the issue could be no greater than if it were a common stock (without dividend accumulations) representing complete ownership of the business. The unpaid dividends cannot create any additional value for the company's securities in the aggregate; they merely affect the division of the total value between the preferred and the common.

Excessive Emphasis Placed on Amount of Accrued Dividends. Although a very small amount of analysis will show the above statements to be almost self-evident truths, the public fails to observe the simplest rules of logic when once it is in a gambling mood. Hence preferred shares with large dividend accruals have lent themselves readily to market manipulation in which the accumulations are made the basis for a large advance in the price of both the preferred and common. An excellent example of such a performance was provided by American Zinc, Lead, and Smelting Company shares in 1928.

American Zinc preferred stock was created in 1916 as a stock dividend on the common, the transaction thus amounting to a split-up of old common into preferred and new common. The preferred was given a stated par of $25 but had all the attributes of a $100-par stock ($6 cumulative dividends, redemption and liquidating value of $100). This arrangement was evidently a device to permit carrying the preferred issue in the balance sheet as a much smaller liability than it actually represented. Between 1920 and 1927 the company reported continuous deficits (except for a negligible profit in 1922); preferred dividends were suspended in 1921, and by 1928 about $40 per share had accumulated.

In 1928 the company benefited moderately from the prevailing prosperity and barely earned $6 per share on the preferred. However, the company's issues were subjected to manipulation that advanced the price of the preferred from 35 in 1927 to 118 in 1928, while the common rose even more spectacularly from 6 to 57. These advances were accompanied by rumors of a plan to pay off the accumulated dividends—

exactly how, not being stated. Naturally enough, this development failed to materialize.[5]

The irrationality of the gambling spirit is well shown here by the absurd acceptance of unpaid preferred dividends *as a source of value for both the preferred and the common.* The speculative argument in behalf of the common stock ran as follows: "The accumulated preferred dividends are going to be paid off. This will be good for the common. Therefore let us buy the common." According to this topsy-turvy reasoning, if there were no unpaid preferred dividends ahead of the common it would be less attractive (even at the same price), because there would then be in prospect no wonderful plan for clearing up the accumulations.

We may use the American Zinc example to demonstrate the practical application of our "rule of maximum valuation for senior issues." Was American Zinc Preferred too high at 118 in 1928? Assuming the preferred stockholders owned the company completely, this would then mean a price of 118 for a *common* stock earning $6 per share in 1928 after eight years of deficits. Even in the hectic days of 1928 speculators would not have been at all attracted to such a common stock at that price, so that the application of our rule should have prevented the purchase of the preferred stock at its inflated value.

The quotation of 57 reached by American Zinc common was evidently the height of absurdity, since it represented the following valuation for the company:

Preferred stock, 80,000 sh. @ 118	$ 9,440,000
Common stock, 200,000 sh. @ 57	11,400,000
Total valuation	$20,840,000
Earnings, 1928	481,000
Average earnings, 1920–1927	*188,000(d)*

In order to equal the above valuation for the American Zinc Company the hypothetical common stock (80,000 shares basis) would have had to sell at $260 *per share,* earning a bare $6 and paying no divi-

---

[5] But years later, in 1936, accumulated preferred dividends were taken care of by a recapitalization plan which gave the preferred stockholders the bulk of the enlarged common issue.

dend. This figure indicates the extent to which the heedless public was led astray in this case by the exploitation of unpaid dividends.

American Hide and Leather Company offers another, but less striking, example of this point. In no year between 1922 and 1928, inclusive, did the company earn more than $4.41 on the preferred, and the average profits were very small. Yet in each of these seven years, the preferred stock sold as high as 66 or higher. This recurring strength was based largely on the speculative appeal of the enormous accumulated preferred dividends which grew from about $120 to $175 per share during this period.

Applying our rule, we may consider American Hide and Leather Preferred as representing complete ownership of the business, which to all intents and purposes it did. We should then have a common stock which had paid no dividends for many years and with average earnings at best (using the 1922–1927 period) of barely $2 per share. Evidently a price of above 65 for such a common stock would be far too high. Consequently this price was excessive for American Hide and Leather Preferred, nor could the existence of accumulated dividends, however large, affect this conclusion in the slightest.

Variation in Capital Structure Affects Total Market Value of Securities.
From the foregoing discussion it might be inferred that the value of a single capital-stock issue must always be equivalent to the combined values of any preferred and common stock issues into which it might be split. In a theoretical sense this is entirely true, but in practice it may not be true at all, because a division of capitalization into senior securities and common stock may have a real advantage over a single common-stock issue. This subject will receive extended treatment under the heading of "Capitalization Structure" in Chap. 40.

The distinction between the idea just suggested and our "rule of maximum valuation" may be clarified as follows:

1. Assume Company X = Company Y

2. Company X has preferred (P) and common (C); Company Y has common only (C')

3. Then it *would appear* that

$$\text{Value of } P + \text{value of } C = \text{value of } C'$$

since each side of the equation represents equal things, namely the total value of each company.

But this apparent relationship may not hold good in practice because the preferred-and-common capitalization method may have real advantages over a single common-stock issue.

On the other hand, our "rule of maximum valuation" merely states that the value of P *alone* cannot exceed value of C'. This should hold true in practice as well as in theory, except in so far as manipulative or heedlessly speculative activity brushes aside all rational considerations.

Our rule is stated in negative form and is therefore essentially negative in its application. It is most useful in detecting instances where preferred stocks or bonds are *not worth* their market price. To apply it positively it would be necessary, first, to arrive at a value for the preferred on a "communized" basis (*i.e.*, representing complete ownership of the business) and then to determine what deduction from this value should be made to reflect the part of the ownership fairly ascribable to the existing common stock. At times this approach will be found useful in establishing the fact that a given senior issue is worth more than its market price. But such a procedure brings us far outside the range of mathematical formulas and into the difficult and indefinite field of common-stock valuation, with which we have next to deal.

PART IV

Theory of Common-Stock Investment. The Dividend Factor

Finding Value in Common Stocks

by Todd Combs

Some nine decades after Graham and Dodd's *Security Analysis* was first published, many if not most of the principles it laid out still hold true. Certainly, the need to perform thorough analysis of potential investments and the importance of downside protection resonate as much with me now as when I read *Security Analysis* the first time many years ago. Given the authors were writing only a few years removed from the 1929 crash and in the middle of the Great Depression, their approach to investing was completely understandable. Investing, according to Graham and Dodd, could be considered a "negative art," focused more on downside protection than on the pursuit of upside.

When done well, investing involves learning how to process information in order to determine when the odds are in your favor; the goal is to make educated bets based on facts and not stories. In investing, and in life for that matter, you can't choose outcomes, but you can choose the decisions that may get you the outcomes you want. With timeless wisdom like this, *Security Analysis* retains its relevance and, indeed, has been an invaluable pillar of my career.

Security Analysis was published during the latter stages of the industrial revolution, a time when the great businesses of the day were massively capital-intensive endeavors. Maintaining plant and equipment required significant capital spending, and growing a business necessitated still more, the end result being low returns on invested capital compared to today's largest enterprises.

The world of business and investment has changed significantly over the past century, and many of today's largest companies have only a limited amount invested in tangible assets, yet extraordinary cash-generation capability. In many cases, their primary assets are people, intellectual property, and brands; there are no assembly lines or blast furnaces, no locomotives or steam shovels. Profit margins for such businesses are far above those of the typical asset-heavy firms from generations past. The value of a contemporary company is consequently less bound up with the value of its physical assets. This may require us to tilt the prism of analysis to adjust to today's reality, but the original concepts put forward by Graham and Dodd remain the same: (1) that imprecise but reasonably accurate intrinsic values can be determined through careful assessment and analysis of earnings power, and (2) there are investment opportunities to be had in purchasing shares of a company at a price below these intrinsic values.

But what does it take these days to determine a company's intrinsic value? We will work our way to the answer.

LESSONS LEARNED

Investing in equities has been described as simple but not easy. Concepts such as "don't overpay," "identify good management teams," "avoid speculation," "be patient," "verify the accuracy of financial statements," "the market is a voting machine and not a weighing machine," and "focus on qualitative, as well as quantitative aspects of a business" are all bandied about, but they are easier to invoke in principle than in practice.

In attempting to value companies over my career, I've come to appreciate that the difference between a good analyst and a great one lies in the ability to keep things simple and determine what matters most.

People misinterpret this to mean that investors should keep things at the surface level. In fact, it paradoxically takes a great deal of depth to stay simple. The analyst's job is to tear apart an investment in order to understand its essential elements. A great security analyst is willing to rip a company down to its studs and understand each part before they reassemble it. In the massive sea of information that an analyst is continuously ingesting, there is always one piece that matters more than the others. Finding that morsel is what keeping it simple means.

An example that stands out most in my mind dates back to 2002. I was a young analyst attending a "payments" conference, and I was looking at Mastercard for the first time. Although it was still a private company, management was nevertheless presenting on the company, which intrigued me. Perhaps because it was private and therefore not offering a clear way to invest in or profit from researching it, only a few of us were on hand for the presentation. I continued to follow the company closely and felt I understood it well by the time it came public in the spring of 2006. The company was being brought public to fund a large legal settlement. The Wall Street narrative at the time of Mastercard's IPO was that the company did not have pricing power. Surely bank consolidation was destined to squeeze its margins. But we saw things differently.

There were several key qualitative considerations in my Mastercard analysis. For example, as banks benefited from higher interchange revenues, their incentives were actually aligned with Mastercard's, and long-term pricing power was likely to remain strong. We believed growth would continue for a long time as credit cards continued to replace cash. And having publicly traded shares (rather than being owned by banks) facilitated creation of an incentive structure for management (just as in many past demutualizations of insurance companies and other customer-owned companies) to run a tight ship. Also, many of the apparent risks seemed overstated.

Banking industry consolidation was far from certain to continue unabated. Also, legal risks facing the company seemed likely to be resolved without significant impairment.

Investors must always remember that a spreadsheet, no matter how good, is not business reality. The numbers laid out in a spreadsheet tell a precise story, but sometimes it's not the right story. For example, overemphasis of the quantitative can lead to missing the qualitative, and vice versa. In the end, assessing both can be very valuable. Because finding simplicity can be complicated, I break down my process into three buckets—find a good business, with good management, at a good valuation. You don't need or expect to find all three of these to the same degree in every investment; there can be a sliding scale with puts and takes. Nonetheless, all three must be present. Think of it as a multiplicative series where a zero in any of the cells will yield a zero overall regardless of how high the other elements may rate.

KEEPING IT SIMPLE PRINCIPLE 1: FINDING A GOOD BUSINESS

The question I'm asked most often is what exactly constitutes a good business? The short answer begins with having a competitive advantage, or what Warren Buffett calls a "moat." The wider the moat the better. Add on characteristics like low capital intensity, pricing power, recurring revenues, staying power, and the likelihood of long-term growth, and you have a great business. In determining if a business is great, I like to start on the quantitative side: I focus on the balance sheet, accounting practices, and unit economics, and then turn to cash flow generation. Meanwhile, the qualitative side involves reference calls to assess the quality of management and channel checks to reveal how a company's products are selling in real time.

Balance Sheet and Accounting

While much of the analytical focus will be on the income statement, proper and thorough analysis of the balance sheet and a company's accounting are like having a solid foundation in a construction project. They are easy for a casual observer to overlook or take for granted and may matter only once in a while. But when they matter, it's like access to oxygen—it's all that matters.

In seeking to determine intrinsic values, I like to start with the concept of working inside out versus outside in. Start with facts and not opinions. If you start with opinions, it's very easy to become wedded to them even when the facts run counter to the popular narrative. Start with SEC filings, annual reports, and trade magazine articles—not with management or colleagues' narratives or sell-side reports. The biggest mistake an analyst can make in the initial stage of their research is to start their assessment by looking at earnings (or even worse, management's presentation of adjusted earnings). When you look at these reported numbers, keep in mind that you're not looking at completely objective facts so much as a management team's perception of them. The income statement is a snapshot of what has recently transpired, and this snapshot may well have been photoshopped. I want to focus on process rather than outcomes, so starting with the income statement is putting the cart before the horse.

When we start with cash flow and the balance sheet, we focus on the process and understand the flow of the resources required to run the business. I like to think of the business not only in broad terms but also in terms of its unit economics. Think in terms of a dollar of revenue that flows into a business and runs through the cash flow statement, then the balance sheet, and last the income statement. This is ultimately how we derive a company's return on invested capital, which is usually a reliable shorthand for the quality of the business. Financial snapshots from various points in time are necessary but not sufficient. I like to review the last 10 years and examine the changes in retained earnings, debt, and overall capital intensity as compared to the top-line growth of the business itself. I will often summarize this over 10 years in a DuPont analysis, a framework for analyzing fundamental performance popularized by the DuPont Corporation. This technique is used to decompose the different drivers of return on equity (ROE), with profit margin, asset turns, and return on assets broken out by year.

It is through this kind of analysis that one can see changes in earning power over time. When companies or industries earn excess returns, it invites competition. The response to that competition can often be seen in a company's balance sheet. If a company generated $10 billion of earnings over a trailing 10-year period, but its retained earnings remained flat while debt increased significantly, earnings may have grown, but the growing leverage on the balance sheet indicates that the company may need to run harder merely to stand still.

Balance sheets are also incredibly useful in identifying both funding sources and quality of earnings. We may find, for example, that a company has short-term variable-rate funding rather than longer-term fixed-rate liabilities. In such a situation, the income statement may report earnings that are artificially inflated because of a risky financing decision, making the company extremely vulnerable to rising rates. A risky balance sheet together with aggressive accounting practices can be a recipe for disaster. I find it interesting to take two very similar companies and align their accounting practices. When I compare such factors as their expensing versus capitalizing of expenses, gain on sale accounting versus long-term holding of mortgage securities, acquisition accounting practices, and balance sheet variances, I'm often flabbergasted at the difference. The point is that earnings are a by-product of many assumptions and choices made by management. The treatment of reserves, choice of a discount rate on contingent valuations, assumed pension returns, and method of funding lead to a result that can be either significantly overrated or underrated.

The number of games that can be played here is almost limitless. These aggressive measures continue to infect the quality of earnings at American firms and are often undetected even by smart investors. Take nothing for granted; if it seems too good to be true, it probably is. Aggressive balance sheets and accounting are typically not associated with conservative management teams or those planting seeds for future generations. They are typically associated with borrowing from the future. Verifying and exploring this is the basis from which our qualitative analysis flows.

Unit Economics

Acquiring a thorough understanding of the balance sheet mechanics will allow us to then identify the key items on the balance sheet and drill down into them at a micro level, in order to understand attributes like the unit economics of a business. Just as you can drop a dollar of revenue or cost through the cash flow statement and balance sheet, you can do the same in replicating unit economics of the company. For example, looking at the earnings for Costco is one thing, examining the balance sheet another, but understanding the unit economics of an individual store is far more powerful than either of those. While the company doesn't overtly disclose store-by-store unit economics, in the case of Costco we can use company disclosures to triangulate into the average cost to build a store. Then by estimating the approximate time to get to run rate revenues and margins, we can approximate the individual store ROI.

This calculation should reveal much about the overall business economics but often does not, typically for one of two reasons. One, management teams often present the best possible narrative, for example, by including only variable costs and understating maintenance capital expenditures. Project or unit economic IRRs are almost always overstated for investors when they exclude important fixed costs and overstate growth capital expenditures to make the business appear better than it is. This is directly akin to relying on the undemanding metric EBITDA compared to Graham's focus on "owner earnings."

The second reason is that the accounting often reflects front-loaded expenses while failing to match the duration required to get to a normalized state. This was the case with the cell tower industry, some "razor-razor blade" businesses, and certain retail and software businesses. American Tower was a breakeven business when it had an average of two tenants per cellphone tower, but adding a third tenant led to extremely attractive unit economics per tower and a compelling overall ROI. Similarly, Walmart did not generate earnings or cash flow for over a decade while they were growing, but a look at the store unit economics led to the true story and foreshadowed what the picture would look like in the future.

The goal is to get past management discussion or analyst reports and drill down into the business as if you were the owner. Then, and only then, can you begin connecting the dots.

KEEPING IT SIMPLE PRINCIPLE 2: FIND GOOD MANAGEMENT TEAMS

The importance of good management is almost universally underestimated, yet it is one of the most crucial determinants of a company's intrinsic value. As Graham and Dodd said, "You cannot make a quantitative deduction to allow for an unscrupulous management; the only way to deal with such situations is to avoid them." (Chap. 33) We must recognize that businesses are composed of individuals whose decisions and judgments set the metabolism for the entire enterprise. Many analysts seem inclined to assess the quality of management based on conventional marketplace narratives about a business. One must go deeper.

The way to assess management's track record is to examine their incentives, learn how they spend their time, and perform scuttlebutt research. Notice that I did not mention listening to investor day presentations or meeting with management. Examining a management team's track record requires a holistic, detailed, and nuanced perspective. Businesses can take a long time to either turn around or to decay. Decisions made 3, 5, and even 10 years ago are likely still impacting the bottom-line today. A manager who appears to be doing a great job may, in fact, be benefiting from seeds planted many years before. Meanwhile, the economic environment in which a company operates often changes, sometimes dramatically. Just as a rising market can make any investment professional seem smarter than he or she is, persistent tailwinds can also make a corporate management team seem smarter than they are. A strength today can be a weakness tomorrow, either through ingrained fragility or simply because the competitive dynamic has shifted. Outsourcing, for example, can fatten a company's profit margins for decades until it becomes evident that it's been taken too far, and the company's basic competencies have been hollowed out. Good capital allocation is crucial; a wonderful business and a talented CEO is not enough to offset poor capital allocation. Too many companies repurchase shares above intrinsic value, pursue value destructive mergers and acquisitions, or fail to adapt their capital allocation in response to changing conditions or emergent opportunities. Capital allocation is one of the most important parts of the track record that must be examined by prospective investors.

Examine Incentives

It has been said that seeing the incentives will explain the outcome. While we know that a long-term perspective is crucial in running a business, there are often unfortunate incentives to become overly short-term oriented. The private owner of a great business isn't worried about quarterly earnings, meeting market expectations, stuffing sales channels, pursuing aggressive accounting treatments, or withholding long-term investments to improve reported short-term results. To better understand management's incentives, I start with the proxy statement and look for changes year to year. Is the basis for management compensation and stock option awards sensible? Are they being measured for enduring accomplishments or instead for favorable short-term share price fluctuations that could be purely the result of luck or even manipulation? Do they reward actual returns on capital or simply profitless growth? Do they create asymmetric upside for the CEO for taking outsized risks? Is the CEO regularly selling his or her shares for "personal reasons," or are they acting like a true owner and fiduciary? If the company were private, how different would the structure of the CEO's compensation and incentives be?

Market pundits can focus excessively on the absolute level of management compensation rather than the context of what was required to achieve that compensation. High absolute compensation can be warranted when it rewards the achievement of demanding goals and the delivery of exceptional results.

Learn How CEOs Spend Their Time

Time management is also important. I have never met a CEO who is on the road for hundreds of days a year, meeting investors and promoting themselves or their stock—who is fully steeped in the details of their company. Ask yourself, if this were your family business, wouldn't you want your CEO single-mindedly focused on running the business? I want to back CEOs who are focused on substance, not collecting style points.

Perform Scuttlebutt Research on CEOs

Finally, I like to speak to current and former executives who have either reported to the CEO under consideration or have had that individual report to them. This provides a good way to triangulate information. I want to go deeply into personalities in order to gain context. For example, an intense executive with an emphasis on hyperefficiency may at some point become culturally toxic, leaving employees afraid, the company fragile, the team less than candid, and the business unable to respond to change. Intellectual honesty is also crucial in a management team. As American theoretical physicist Richard Feynman said, "You must not fool yourself, and you are the easiest person to fool."[1]

KEEPING IT SIMPLE PRINCIPLE 3: FINDING THE "RIGHT" PRICE

About pricing, legendary investor and author Philip A. Fisher said, "The only true test of whether a stock is 'cheap' or 'high' is not its current price in relation to some former price, no matter how accustomed we may have become to that former price, but whether the company's fundamentals are significantly more or less favorable than the current financial-community appraisal of that stock."[2] Investors must deeply understand the companies behind the stock prices.

The Research Process

Scuttlebutt research (also mentioned earlier in the chapter) is a term used by Philip A. Fisher that suggests the investor play the role of an investigative journalist, trying to get as close to the truth as possible. I've seen many investors who start their work on a potential holding by hearing a story, calling some friends to vet the story, listening to some conference calls, reading some research reports, and starting to form an opinion. The danger of this process is that it often leads to the

---

[1] Richard P. Feynman, "Cargo Cult Science," *Caltech Magazine*, California Institute of Technology, June 1, 1974, http://calteches.library.caltech.edu/3043/.

[2] Philip A. Fisher, *Common Stocks and Uncommon Profits and Other Writings*, Wiley, 1957.

formation of an opinion based on someone else's perception and analysis, rather than your own.

Instead, I start with the company's annual letters, annual reports, 10Ks and 10Qs, and other SEC filings, as well as trade magazine articles and press releases for the last 10 years. Has the company underpromised and overdelivered or vice versa? Then I work my way to earnings calls, again painting a picture of whether the company does what they say they are going to do. Once I have this picture based on facts instead of a story, then like an investigative reporter, I start to develop a picture of reality. But questions remain to be answered, and it's time to do channel checks.

Assessing Moats

How does one go about actually assessing the depth and breadth of a business moat? Precisely what is a company's competitive advantage, and how unassailable is it? Certainly, a long track record of high returns on invested capital seems like a quick and easy way to determine this. But the graveyards of capitalism are littered with companies that did, in fact, earn high ROICs for prolonged periods of time only to ultimately succumb to competition, either directly from a more astute rival or from a changing economic landscape. An investor must get down in the weeds and conduct scuttlebutt research to ascertain whether moats around a business are strong or porous.

Channel Checks

Channel checks are the proverbial equivalent of gumshoe research. They entail speaking to customers, suppliers, and former employees. I always ask myself, if I were considering putting 100% of my net worth in this business, what would I want to know? Has management been laying the groundwork for the future or borrowing from it? What kind of pricing power does the business have, and has the company taken steps to maximize it, or is there slack in the system that indicates further upside? Business moats are not static and come with different characteristics—brands, low costs, convenience, and network effects all constitute real but very different moats.

This deep and detailed inside-out research serves multiple purposes. For one, it helps us gain a deep understanding of how the business actually works, as well as the quality of the moat. Two, it helps us understand the trend of the business through the primary levers, which can help us understand whether the moat is shrinking or growing. Three, it facilitates developing a dispassionate analysis based on a foundation of facts versus opinions. This helps eliminate emotions, which are the enemy of rational decision-making. After such extensive analysis, if our security falls in price following our purchase, we will likely feel more comfortable owning more of it. Four, it helps us understand the fragility or "*anti-fragile*" nature of the business, a term coined by author Nassim Nicholas Taleb, to mean one that gets stronger under circumstances where others' fragility breaks them. The best businesses are anti-fragile; that is, they continue to thrive and even deepen their moats in times of adversity and volatility, such as when competitors get in trouble and their best customers and employees may be up for grabs. Five, it helps us create a base layer of understanding across many businesses and industries, which allows us to triangulate and compound our knowledge over time. This work can create mile markers of expectations and progress that we can compare and as necessary adjust over time. Six, there is great power to a broad-gauged approach in developing perspectives. Coming at this research with outside knowledge and perspective, combined with industry knowledge via these checks, can be a force multiplier.

Performing this detailed research via filings and channel checks enables you to gain comfort in your understanding of the business. Doing thorough work enables an investor to confidently answer some really important questions: Does the business have a sustainable and/or expanding moat? What are the weakest links over the next five years? Are there hidden path dependencies? Does the business have pricing power, and how has it been exercised? How (anti) fragile is the business, and will it thrive in the next downturn? What would it take to replicate this business? Will the business be in a better position with an even wider moat five years from now?

If you can answer these questions with confidence, you will have clarity on the things that truly matter and be well on your way to accurately assessing intrinsic value. Remember that simple is usually better; in investing, there is no extra credit for degree of difficulty. You can find straightforward businesses with strong, sustainable moats and franchises while avoiding the axiom, "when a strong management team meets a bad business, the business wins." None of this guarantees a good result, but it certainly helps.

Determining Intrinsic Value

As Warren Buffett wrote in his 1989 letter to the Berkshire Hathaway shareholders, "It's far better to buy a wonderful company at a fair price than a fair company at a wonderful price."

A business is worth the sum of its discounted cash flows in perpetuity. This concept sounds simple enough, but there are a few key variables involved in this calculation: the discount rate to be used and one's assessment of those cash flows in perpetuity. Estimating future cash flows entails a determination of a company's capital intensity, its growth rate, and management's allocation objectives. A couple of examples may demonstrate the power of these estimates.

Assuming a constant 10% discount rate, a business that will grow at 15% a year without requiring any additional capital is worth ≈26x its current earnings, whereas the same business growing at 15% but needing to reinvest much or all of its earnings to achieve that growth would be worth only ≈16x. A business that grows at 5% and doesn't need any capital would be worth ≈14x its current earnings, and the same business needing all of its earnings reinvested would be worth ≈7x. A return of 15% compounded over 30 years is worth over 87x the initial stake, whereas 5% compounded over the same period is worth just under 4.5x. In this example, a threefold increase in the compound rate (from 5% to 15%) leads to an almost twentyfold increase in return (87x vs 4.5x).

This example illustrates the power of finding capital light businesses that can grow for prolonged periods of time. Conversely, the worst business is actually one that grows and consumes increasing amounts of capital at returns that fail to exceed its cost of capital. There are, of course, businesses that require capital to grow, like a railroad, a financial institution, or retailers like Walmart or Amazon, where the returns on the newly deployed capital are perfectly acceptable; this growth capital will over time produce economic value. But price is paramount in determining returns. This was the great insight of Graham and Dodd. Great businesses can be terrible investments at the wrong price, and an average business can be a great investment at the right price. Fast-growing businesses can be attractive, but only at the right price. In recent years, during long periods of low interest rates, many investors flocked to growth at all costs under the simple and flawed formula of earnings yield plus growth rate. Because price is key, one must additionally adjust the growth rate by comparing today's price relative to a company's intrinsic value. The value of the growth is diminished because you've paid a significant price for it up front.

The market has historically traded around a 15x earnings multiple which equates to a 6.7% earnings yield. If you can find a better than average business with better than average management for less than this earnings multiple, it is likely a good start. Graham and Dodd called this a margin of safety.

There are two other considerations. One is to be sure to consider owner earnings and not EBITDA or even the more pernicious adjusted EBITDA (owner earnings is defined as unadjusted reported earnings plus depreciation, amortization, and certain other noncash charges less average annual maintenance capex required to fully maintain its competitive position). The other is the need to look at the entire corporate capital structure. Companies that are overlevered can experience large changes in their equity valuations with only the slightest change to owner earnings. Investors who look at a stock without incorporating the complete capitalization picture can miss a key component, because equity values are contingent, while debt is forever.

THE FINAL PRODUCT: WHAT MATTERS

Human beings constantly process complex information about the world and simplify it to make sense of it and put it into context. This allows us to make decisions. I go outside in the morning and look at my car, an intricate and complex network of metal parts and functions, but I simply process it as a thing called "car" and drive off to my job. Easy, right? But for whatever reason, investors tend to complexify a concept. In my own case, I am convinced following the process I've described allows me to get closest to the reality of what's in front of me, and the realities of intrinsic values and margins of safety are critical in investing. For example, I ask myself, what business is the company really in? What are the key drivers that will determine its success?

I'm now in a unique position of serving in two roles: as both the CEO of GEICO, and in my responsibility investing a substantial portfolio pool of capital at Berkshire Hathaway. Each of these roles impacts the other. My CEO role makes me more aware of the key challenges facing a CEO, the constant balancing act between short-term exigencies and long-term imperatives. As a CEO, I'm intensely aware of the dangerous oversimplification inherent in a spreadsheet.

But being an investor maintains my focus on both risk and on return. A CEO can be lost in the daily minutiae; wearing an investment hat places a consistent emphasis on the bottom line.

Warren Buffett has famously stated, "I am a better investor because I am a businessman, and a better businessman because I am an investor." Investors attempt to look behind the curtain of a company's operations, but they often realize how little they actually know. From this vantage point, one can appreciate that even extensive research will uncover only a small fraction of what one can possibly know about a business. Investors must find a way to navigate through uncertainty and randomness. There are decisions being made every day, and sometimes made decades earlier, that are still affecting outcomes today in every business and industry. There are intricate path dependencies that are often too complex even for very skilled upper management to fully understand the trade-offs involved. Perfect information does not exist; there are only confidence intervals. This is, of course, at the heart of why a margin of safety matters so greatly in investing. If you start with the premise that there is only so much one can know, of course you need a margin for error. The less you know, the greater the margin needed.

CHAPTER 27

The Theory of Common-Stock Investment

IN OUR INTRODUCTORY discussion we set forth the difficulties inherent in efforts to apply the analytical technique to speculative situations. Since the speculative factors bulk particularly large in common stocks, it follows that analysis of such issues is likely to prove inconclusive and unsatisfactory; and even where it appears to be conclusive, there is danger that it may be misleading. At this point it is necessary to consider the function of common-stock analysis in greater detail. We must begin with three realistic premises. The first is that common stocks are of basic importance in our financial scheme and of fascinating interest to many people; the second is that owners and buyers of common stocks are generally anxious to arrive at an intelligent idea of their value; the third is that, even when the underlying motive of purchase is mere speculative greed, human nature desires to conceal this unlovely impulse behind a screen of apparent logic and good sense. To adapt the aphorism of Voltaire, it may be said that if there were no such thing as common-stock analysis, it would be necessary to counterfeit it.

Broad Merits of Common-Stock Analysis. We are thus led to the question: "To what extent is common-stock analysis a valid and truly valuable exercise, and to what extent is it an empty but indispensable ceremony attending the wagering of money on the future of business and of the stock market?" We shall ultimately find the answer to run somewhat as follows: "As far as the *typical* common stock is concerned—an issue picked at random from the list—an analysis, however elaborate, is unlikely to yield a dependable conclusion as to its attractiveness or its real value. But in individual cases, the exhibit may be such as to permit reasonably confident conclusions to be drawn from the processes of analysis." It would follow that analysis is of positive or scientific value only in the case of the exceptional common stock, and that for common stocks in general it must be regarded either as a somewhat questionable aid to speculative judgment or as a highly illusory method of aiming at values that defy calculation and that must somehow be calculated none the less.

Perhaps the most effective way of clarifying the subject is through the historical approach. Such a survey will throw light not only upon the changing status of common-stock analysis but also upon a closely related subject of major importance, *viz.*, the theory of common-stock investment. We shall encounter at first a set of old established and seemingly logical principles for common-stock investment. Through the advent of new conditions, we shall find the validity of these principles impaired. Their insufficiency will give rise to an entirely different concept of common-stock selection, the so-called "new-era theory," which beneath its superficial plausibility will hold possibilities of untold mischief in store. With the prewar theory obsolete and the new-era theory exploded, we must finally make the attempt to establish a new set of logically sound and reasonably dependable principles of common-stock investment.

History of Common-Stock Analysis. Turning first to the history of common-stock *analysis*, we shall find that two conflicting factors have been at work during the past 30 years. On the one hand there has been an increase in the *investment prestige* of common stocks as a class, due chiefly to the enlarged number that have shown substantial earnings, continued dividends, and a strong financial condition. Accompanying this progress was a considerable advance in the frequency and adequacy of corporate statements, thus supplying the public and the securities analyst with a wealth of statistical data. Finally, an impressive theory was constructed asserting the preeminence of common stocks as long-term investments. But at the time that the interest in common stocks reached its height, in the period between 1927 and 1929, the *basis of valuation* employed by the stock-buying public departed more and more from the factual approach and technique of security analysis and concerned itself increasingly with the elements of potentiality and prophecy. Moreover, the heightened instability in the affairs of industrial companies and groups of enterprises, which has undermined the investment quality of bonds in general, has of course been still more hostile to the maintenance of true investment quality in common stocks.

Analysis Vitiated by Two Types of Instability. The extent to which common-stock analysis has been vitiated by these two developments, (1) the instability of tangibles and (2) the dominant importance of intangibles, may be better realized by a contrast of specific common stocks prior to 1920 and in more recent times. Let us consider four typical examples: Pennsylvania Railroad; Atchison, Topeka, and Santa Fe Railway; National Biscuit; and American Can.

Pennsylvania Railroad Company

Year	Range for stock	Earned per share	Paid per share
1904	70–56	$4.63	$3.00
1905	74–66	4.98	3.00
1906	74–61	5.83	3.25
1907	71–52	5.32	3.50
1908	68–52	4.46	3.00
1909	76–63	4.37	3.00
1910	69–61	4.60	3.00
1911	65–59	4.14	3.00
1912	63–60	4.64	3.00
1913	62–53	4.20	3.00
1923	48–41	5.16	3.00
1924	50–42	3.82	3.00
1925	55–43	6.23	3.00
1926	57–49	6.77	3.125
1927	68–57	6.83	3.50
1928	77–62	7.34	3.50
1929	110–73	8.82	3.875
1930	87–53	5.28	4.00
1931	64–16	1.48	3.25
1932	23–7	1.03	0.50
1933	42–14	1.46	0.50
1934	38–20	1.43	1.00
1935	33–27	1.81	0.50
1936	45–28	2.94	2.00
1937	50–20	2.07	1.25
1938	25–14	0.84	0.50

Atchison, Topeka, and Santa Fe Railway Company

Year	Range of stock	Earned per share	Paid per share
1904	89–64	$ 9.47*	$ 4.00
1905	93–78	5.92*	4.00
1906	111–85	12.31*	4.50
1907	108–66	15.02*	6.00
1908	101–66	7.74*	5.00
1909	125–98	12.10*	5.50
1910	124–91	8.89*	6.00
1911	117–100	9.30*	6.00
1912	112–103	8.19*	6.00
1913	106–90	8.62*	6.00
1923	105–94	15.48	6.00
1924	121–97	15.47	6.00
1925	141–116	17.19	7.00
1926	172–122	23.42	7.00
1927	200–162	18.74	10.00
1928	204–183	18.09	10.00
1929	299–195	22.69	10.00
1930	243–168	12.86	10.00
1931	203–79	6.96	10.00
1932	94–18	0.55	2.50
1933	80–35	*1.03(d)*	Nil
1934	74–45	0.33	2.00
1935	60–36	1.38	2.00
1936	89–59	1.56	2.00
1937	95–33	0.60	2.00
1938	45–22	0.83	Nil

* Fiscal years ended June 30.

American Can was a typical example of a prewar speculative stock. It was speculative for three good and sufficient reasons: (1) It paid no dividend; (2) its earnings were small and irregular; (3) the issue was "watered," *i.e.*, a substantial part of its stated value represented no actual investment in the business. By contrast, Pennsylvania, Atchison, and National Biscuit were regarded as investment common stocks—also for three good and sufficient reasons: (1) They showed a satisfactory record of continued dividends; (2) the earnings were reasonably stable and averaged substantially in excess of the dividends paid; and (3) each dollar of stock was backed by a dollar or more of actual investment in the business.

National Biscuit Company

Year	Range for stock	Earned per share	Paid per share
1909	120–97	$ 7.67*	$ 5.75
1910	120–100	9.86*	6.00
1911	144–117	10.05*	8.75
1912	161–114	9.59*	7.00
1913	130–104	11.73*	7.00
1914	139–120	9.52*	7.00
1915	132–116	8.20*	7.00
1916	131–118	9.72*	7.00
1917	123–80	9.87†	7.00
1918	111–90	11.63	7.00
	(old basis)‡	(old basis)‡	(old basis)‡
1923	370–266	$35.42	$21.00
1924	541–352	38.15	28.00
1925	553–455	40.53	28.00
1926	714–518	44.24	35.00
1927	1,309–663	49.77	42.00
1928	1,367–1,117	51.17	49.00
1929	1,657–980	57.40	52.50
1930	1,628–1,148	59.68	56.00
1931	1,466–637	50.05	49.00
1932	820–354	42.70	49.00
1933	1,061–569	36.93	49.00
1934	866–453	27.48	42.00
1935	637–389	22.93	31.50
1936	678–503	30.28	35.00
1937	584–298	28.35	28.00
1938	490–271	30.80	28.00

* Earnings for the year ended Jan. 31 of the following year.
† Eleven months ending Dec. 31, 1917.
‡ Stock was split 4 for 1 in 1922, followed by a 75% stock dividend. In 1930 it was again split 2¹/₂ for 1. Published figures applicable to new stock were one-seventh of those given above for 1923–1929. Likewise the foregoing figures for 1930–1938 are 17¹/₂ times the published figures for those years.

If we study the range of market price of these issues during the decade preceding the World War (or the 1909–1918 period for National Biscuit), we note that American Can fluctuated widely from year to year in the fashion regularly associated with speculative media but that Pennsylvania, Atchison, and National Biscuit showed much narrower variations and evidently tended to oscillate about a base price (*i.e.*, 97 for Atchison, 64 for Pennsylvania, and 120 for National Biscuit) that seemed to represent a well-defined view of their investment or intrinsic value.

American Can Company

Year	Range for stock	Earned per share	Paid per share
1904	....	$ 0.51*	0
1905	....	*1.39(d)*†	0
1906	....	*1.30(d)*‡	0
1907	8–3	*0.57(d)*	0
1908	10–4	*0.44(d)*	0
1909	15–8	*0.32(d)*	0
1910	14–7	*0.15(d)*	0
1911	13–9	0.07	0
1912	47–11	8.86	0
1913	47–21	5.21	0
1923	108–74	19.64	$ 5.00
1924	164–96	20.51	6.00
1925	297–158	32.75	7.00
	(old basis)§	(old basis)§	(old basis)§
1926	379–233	26.34	13.25
1927	466–262	24.66	12.00
1928	705–423	41.16	12.00
1929	1,107–516	48.12	30.00
1930	940–628	48.48	30.00
1931	779–349	30.66	30.00
1932	443–178	19.56	24.00
1933	603–297	30.24	24.00
1934	689–542	50.32	24.00
1935	898–660	34.98	30.00
1936	825–660	34.80	36.00
1937	726–414	36.48	24.00
1938	631–425	26.10	24.00

* Fiscal year ended Mar. 31, 1905.
† Nine months ended Dec. 31, 1905.
‡ Excluding fire losses of 58 cents a share.
§ Stock was split 6 for 1 in 1926. Published figures applicable to new stock were one-sixth of those given for 1926–1938.

Prewar Conception of Investment in Common Stocks. Hence the prewar relationship between analysis and investment on the one hand and price changes and speculation on the other may be set forth as follows: Investment in common stocks was confined to those showing stable dividends and fairly stable earnings; and such issues in turn were expected to maintain a fairly stable market level. The function of analysis was primarily to search for elements of *weakness* in the picture. If the earnings were not properly stated; if the balance sheet revealed a poor current position, or the funded debt was growing too rapidly; if the physical plant was not properly maintained; if dangerous new competition was threatening, or if the company was losing ground in the industry; if the management was deteriorating or was likely to change for the worse; if there was reason to fear for the future of the industry as a whole—any of these defects or some other one might be sufficient to condemn the issue from the standpoint of the cautious investor.

On the positive side, analysis was concerned with finding those issues which met all the requirements of investment and *in addition* offered the best chance for future enhancement. The process was largely a matter of comparing similar issues in the investment class, *e.g.*, the group of dividend-paying Northwestern railroads. Chief emphasis would be laid upon the relative showing for past years, in particular the average earnings in relation to price and the stability and the trend of earnings. To a lesser extent, the analyst sought to look into the future and to select the industries or the individual companies that were likely to show the most rapid growth.

Speculation Characterized by Emphasis on Future Prospects. In the prewar period it was the well-considered view that when *prime emphasis* was laid upon what was expected of the future, instead of what had been accomplished in the past, a speculative attitude was thereby taken. Speculation, in its etymology, meant looking forward; investment was allied to "vested interests"—to property rights and values taking root in the *past*. The future was uncertain, therefore speculative; the past was known, therefore the source of safety. Let us consider a buyer of American Can common in 1910. He may have bought it believing that its price was going to advance or be "put up" or that its earnings were going to increase or that it was soon going to pay a dividend or possibly that it was destined to develop into one of the country's strongest industrials. From the prewar standpoint, although one of these reasons may have been more intelligent or creditable than another, each of them constituted a *speculative* motive for the purchase.

Technique of Investing in Common Stocks Resembled That for Bonds. Evidently there was a close similarity between the technique of investing in common stocks and that of investing in bonds. The common-stock investor, also, wanted a stable business and one showing an adequate margin of earnings over dividend requirements. Naturally he had to content himself with a smaller margin of safety than he would demand of a bond, a disadvantage that was offset by a larger income return (6% was standard on a good common stock compared with $4^{1}/_{2}$% on a high-grade bond), by the chance of an increased dividend if the business continued to prosper, and—generally of least importance in his eyes—by the possibility of a profit. A common-stock investor was likely to consider himself as in no very different position from that of a purchaser of second-grade bonds; essentially his venture amounted to sacrificing a certain *degree* of safety in return for larger income. The Pennsylvania and Atchison examples during the 1904–1913 decade will supply specific confirmation of the foregoing description.

Buying Common Stocks Viewed as Taking a Share in a Business. Another useful approach to the attitude of the prewar common-stock investor is from the standpoint of taking an interest in a private business. The typical common-stock investor was a business man, and it seemed sensible to him to value any corporate enterprise in much the same manner as he would value his own business. This meant that he gave at least as much attention to the asset values behind the shares as he did to their earnings records. It is essential to bear in mind the fact that a private business has always been valued primarily on the basis of the "net worth" as shown by its statement. A man contemplating the purchase of a partnership or stock interest in a private undertaking will always start with the value of that interest as shown "on the books," *i.e.,* the balance sheet, and will then consider whether or not the record and prospects are good enough to make such a commitment attractive. An interest in a private business may of course be sold for more or less than its proportionate asset value; but the book value is still invariably the starting point of the calculation, and the deal is finally made and viewed in terms of the premium or discount from book value involved.

Broadly speaking, the same attitude was formerly taken in an investment purchase of a marketable common stock. The first point of departure was the par value, presumably representing the amount of cash or property originally paid into the business; the second basal figure was the book value, representing the par value plus a ratable interest in the accumulated surplus. Hence in considering a common stock, investors asked themselves: "Is this issue a desirable purchase at the premium above book value, or the discount below book value, represented by the market price?" "Watered stock" was repeatedly inveighed against as a deception practiced upon the stock-buying public, who were misled by a fictitious statement of the asset values existing behind the shares. Hence one of the protective functions of security analysis was to discover whether or not the value of the fixed assets, as stated on the balance sheet of a company, fairly represented the actual cost or reasonable worth of the properties.

Investment in Common Stocks Based on Threefold Concept. We thus see that investment in common stocks was formerly based upon the threefold concept of: (1) a suitable and established dividend return, (2) a stable and adequate earnings record, and (3) a satisfactory backing of tangible assets. Each of these three elements could be made the subject of careful analytical study, viewing the issue both by itself and in comparison with others of its class. Common-stock commitments motivated by any other viewpoint were characterized as speculative, and it was not expected that they should be justified by a serious analysis.

THE NEW-ERA THEORY

During the postwar period, and particularly during the latter stage of the bull market culminating in 1929, the public acquired a completely different attitude towards the investment merits of common stocks. Two of the three elements above stated lost nearly all their significance, and the third, the earnings record, took on an entirely novel complexion. The new theory or principle may be summed up in the sentence: "The value of a common stock depends entirely upon what it will earn in the future."

From this dictum the following corollaries were drawn:

1. That the dividend rate should have slight bearing upon the value.

2. That since no relationship apparently existed between assets and earning power, the asset value was entirely devoid of importance.

3. That past earnings were significant only to the extent that they indicated what *changes* in the earnings were likely to take place in the future. This complete revolution in the philosophy of common-stock investment took place virtually without realization by the stock-buying public and with only the most superficial recognition by financial observers. An effort must be made to reach a thorough comprehension of what this changed viewpoint really signifies. To do so we must consider it from three angles: its causes, its consequences and its logical validity.

Causes for This Changed Viewpoint. Why did the *investing* public turn its attention from dividends, from asset values, and from average earnings to transfer it almost exclusively to the earnings *trend, i.e.,* to the *changes* in earnings expected in the future? The answer was, first, that the records of the past were proving an undependable guide to investment; and, second, that the rewards offered by the future had become irresistibly alluring.

The new-era concepts had their root first of all in the obsolescence of the old-established standards. During the last generation the tempo of economic change has been speeded up to such a degree that the fact of being *long established* has ceased to be, as once it was, a warranty of *stability*. Corporations enjoying decade-long prosperity have been precipitated into insolvency within a few years. Other enterprises, which had been small or unsuccessful or in doubtful repute, have just as quickly acquired dominant size, impressive earnings, and the highest rating. The major group upon which investment interest was chiefly concentrated, *viz.,* the railroads, failed signally to participate in the expansion of national wealth and income and showed repeated signs of definite retrogression. The street railways, another important medium of investment prior to 1914, rapidly lost the greater portion of their value as the result of the development of new transportation agencies. The electric and gas companies followed an irregular course during this period, since they were harmed rather than helped by the war and postwar inflation, and their impressive growth was a relatively recent phenomenon. The history of industrial companies was a hodge-podge of violent changes, in which the benefits of prosperity were so unequally and so impermanently distributed as to bring about the most unexpected failures alongside of the most dazzling successes.

In the face of all this instability it was inevitable that the threefold basis of common-stock investment should prove totally inadequate. Past earnings and dividends could no longer be considered, in themselves, an index of future earnings and dividends. Furthermore, these future earnings showed no tendency whatever to be controlled by the amount of the actual investment in the business—the asset values—but instead depended entirely upon a favorable industrial position and upon capable or fortunate managerial policies. In numerous cases of receivership, the current assets dwindled, and the fixed assets proved almost worthless. Because of this absence of any connection between both assets and earnings and between assets and realizable values in bankruptcy, less and less attention came to be paid either by financial writers or by the general public to the formerly important question of "net worth," or "book value"; and it may be said that by 1929 book value had practically disappeared as an element in determining the attractiveness of a security issue. It is a significant confirmation of this point that "watered stock," once so burning an issue, is now a forgotten phrase.

Attention Shifted to the Trend of Earnings. Thus the prewar approach to investment, based upon past records and tangible facts, became outworn and was discarded. Could anything be put in its place? A new conception was given central importance—that of *trend of earnings*. The past was important only in so far as it showed the direction in which the future could be expected to move. A continuous increase in profits proved that the company was on the upgrade and promised still better results in the future than had been accomplished to date. Conversely, if the earnings had declined or even remained stationary during a prosperous period, the future must be thought unpromising, and the issue was certainly to be avoided.

The Common-Stocks-as-Long-Term-Investments Doctrine. Along with this idea as to what constituted the basis for common-stock selection emerged a companion theory that common stocks represented the most profitable and therefore the most desirable media for long-term investment. This gospel was based upon a certain amount of research, showing that diversified lists of common stocks had regularly increased in value over stated intervals of time for many years past. The figures indicated that such diversified common-stock holdings yielded both a higher income return and a greater principal profit than purchases of standard bonds.

The combination of these two ideas supplied the "investment theory" upon which the 1927–1929 stock market proceeded. Amplifying the principle stated found in "The New-Era Theory" earlier, the theory ran as follows:

1. "The value of a common stock depends on what it can earn in the future."
2. "Good common stocks are those which have shown a rising trend of earnings."
3. "Good common stocks will prove sound and profitable investments."

These statements sound innocent and plausible. Yet they concealed two theoretical weaknesses that could and did result in untold mischief. The first of these defects was that they abolished the fundamental distinctions between investment and speculation. The second was that they ignored the *price* of a stock in determining whether or not it was a desirable purchase.

New-Era Investment Equivalent to Prewar Speculation. A moment's thought will show that "new-era investment," as practiced by the public and the investment trusts, was almost identical with speculation as popularly defined in preboom days. Such "investment" meant buying common stocks instead of bonds, emphasizing enhancement of principal instead of income, and stressing the changes of the future instead of the facts of the established past. It would not be inaccurate to state that new-era investment was simply old-style speculation confined to common stocks with a satisfactory trend of earnings. The impressive new concept underlying the greatest stock-market boom in history appears to be no more than a thinly disguised version of the old cynical epigram: "Investment is successful speculation."

Stocks Regarded as Attractive Irrespective of Their Prices. The notion that the desirability of a common stock was entirely independent of its price seems incredibly absurd. Yet the new-era theory led directly to this thesis. If a public-utility stock was selling at 35 times its *maximum* recorded earnings, instead of 10 times its *average* earnings, which was the preboom standard, the conclusion to be drawn was not that the stock was now too high but merely that the standard of value had been raised. Instead of judging the market price by established standards of value, the new era based its standards of value upon the market price. Hence all upper limits disappeared, not only upon the price at which a stock *could* sell but even upon the price at which it would *deserve* to sell. This fantastic reasoning actually led to the purchase at $100 per share of common stocks earning $2.50 per share. The identical reasoning would support the purchase of these same shares at $200, at $1,000, or at any conceivable price.

An alluring corollary of this principle was that making money in the stock market was now the easiest thing in the world. It was only necessary to buy "good" stocks, regardless of price, and then to let nature take her upward course. The results of such a doctrine could not fail to be tragic. Countless people asked themselves, "Why work for a living when a fortune can be made in Wall Street without working?" The ensuing migration from business into the financial district resembled the famous gold rush to the Klondike, except that gold was brought to Wall Street instead of taken from it.

Investment Trusts Adopted This New Doctrine. An ironical sidelight is thrown on this 1928–1929 theory by the practice of the investment trusts. These were formed for the purpose of giving the untrained public the benefit of expert administration of its funds—a plausible idea and one that had been working reasonably well in England. The earliest American investment trusts laid considerable emphasis upon certain time-tried principles of successful investment, which they were much better qualified to follow than the typical individual. The most important of these principles were:

1. To buy in times of depression and low prices and to sell out in times of prosperity and high prices.
2. To diversify holdings in many fields and probably in many countries.
3. To discover and acquire undervalued individual securities as the result of comprehensive and expert statistical investigations.

The rapidity and completeness with which these traditional principles disappeared from investment-trust technique is one of the many marvels of the period. The idea of buying in times of depression was obviously inapplicable. It suffered from the fatal weakness that investment trusts could be organized only in good times, so that they were virtually compelled to make their initial commitments in bull markets. The idea of world-wide geographical distribution had never exerted a powerful appeal upon the provincially minded Americans (who possibly were right in this respect), and with things going so much better here than abroad this principle was dropped by common consent.

Analysis Abandoned by Investment Trusts. But most paradoxical was the early abandonment of research and analysis in guiding investment-trust policies. However, since these financial institutions owed their existence to the new-era philosophy, it was natural and perhaps only just that they should adhere closely to it. Under its canons investment had now become so beautifully simple that research was unnecessary and elaborate statistical data a mere incumbrance. The investment process consisted merely of finding prominent companies with a rising trend of earnings and then buying their shares regardless of price. Hence the sound policy was to buy only what every one else was buying—a select list of highly popular and exceedingly expensive issues, appropriately known as the "blue chips." The original idea of searching for the undervalued and neglected issues dropped completely out of sight. Investment trusts actually boasted that their portfolios consisted exclusively of the active and standard (*i.e.*, the most popular and highest priced) common stocks. With but slight exaggeration, it might be asserted that under this convenient technique of investment, the affairs of a ten-million-dollar investment trust could be administered by the intelligence, the training and the actual labors of a single thirty-dollar-a-week clerk.

The man in the street, having been urged to entrust his funds to the superior skill of investment experts—for substantial compensation—was soon reassuringly told that the trusts would be careful to buy nothing except what the man in the street was buying himself.

The Justification Offered. Irrationality could go no further; yet it is important to note that mass speculation can flourish only in such an atmosphere of illogic and unreality. The self-deception of the mass speculator must, however, have its element of justification. This is usually some generalized statement, sound enough within its proper field, but twisted to fit the speculative mania. In real estate booms, the "reasoning" is usually based upon the inherent permanence and growth of land values. In the new-era bull market, the "rational" basis was the record of long-term improvement shown by diversified common-stock holdings.

A Sound Premise Used to Support an Unsound Conclusion. There was, however, a radical fallacy involved in the new-era application of this historical fact. This should be apparent from even a superficial examination of the data contained in the small and rather sketchy volume from which the new-era theory may be said to have sprung. The book is entitled *Common Stocks as Long Term Investments*, by Edgar Lawrence Smith, published in 1924.[1] Common stocks were shown to have a tendency to increase in value with the years, for the simple reason that they earned more than they paid out in dividends and thus the reinvested earnings added to their worth. In a representative case, the company would earn an average of 9%, pay 6% in dividends, and add 3% to surplus. With good management and reasonable luck the fair value of the stock would increase with its book value, at the annual rate of 3% *compounded*. This was, of course, a theoretical rather than a standard pattern, but the numerous instances of results poorer than "normal" might be offset by examples of more rapid growth.

The attractiveness of common stocks for the long pull thus lay essentially in the fact that they earned more than the bond-interest rate upon their cost. This would be true, typically, of a stock earning $10 and selling at 100. But as soon as the price was advanced to a much higher price in relation to earnings, this advantage disappeared, *and with it disappeared the entire theoretical basis for investment purchases of common stocks.* When in 1929 investors paid $200 per share for a stock earning $8, they were buying an earning power no greater than the bond-interest rate, without the extra protection afforded by a prior claim. Hence in using the past performances of common stocks as the reason for paying prices 20 to 40 times their earnings, the new-era exponents were starting with a sound premise and twisting it into a woefully unsound conclusion.

In fact their rush to take advantage of the inherent attractiveness of common stocks itself produced conditions entirely different from those which had given rise to this attractiveness and upon which it basically depended, *viz.*, the fact that earnings had averaged some 10% on market price. As we have seen, Edgar Lawrence Smith plausibly explained the growth of common-stock values as arising from the building up of asset values through the reinvestment of surplus earnings. Paradoxically enough, the new-era theory that exploited this finding refused to accord the slightest importance to the asset values behind the stocks it favored. Furthermore, the validity of Mr. Smith's conclusions rested necessarily upon the assumption that common stocks could be counted on to behave

---

[1] The reader is referred to Chelcie C. Bosland, *The Common Stock Theory of Investment, Its Development and Significance*, New York, 1937, for a survey of the literature on the common-stock theory. *Common Stock Indexes* by Alfred Cowles 3d and associates, Bloomington, Ind., 1939, is a significant work on this subject which has appeared since publication of Professor Bosland's book.

in the future about as they had in the past. Yet the new-era theory threw out of account the past earnings of corporations except in so far as they were regarded as pointing to a *trend* for the future.

Examples Showing Emphasis on Trend of Earnings. Take three companies with the following exhibits:

Earnings per Share

Year	Company *A* (Electric Power & Light)	Company *B* (Bangor & Aroostook R. R.)	Company *C* (Chicago Yellow Cab)
1925	$1.01	$6.22	$5.52
1926	1.45	8.69	5.60
1927	2.09	8.41	4.54
1928	2.37	6.94	4.58
1929	2.98	8.30	4.47
5-year average	$1.98	$7.71	$4.94
High price, 1929	86⅝	90⅜	35

The 1929 high prices for these three companies show that the new-era attitude was enthusiastically favorable to Company *A*, unimpressed by Company *B*, and definitely hostile to Company *C*. The market considered Company *A* shares worth more than twice as much as Company *C* shares, although the latter earned 50% more per share than Company *A* in 1929 and its average earnings were 150% greater.[2]

Average vs. Trend of Earnings. These relationships between price and earnings in 1929 show definitely that the past exhibit was no longer a measure of normal earning power but merely a weathervane to show which way the winds of profit were blowing. That the *average earnings* had ceased to be a dependable measure of future earnings must indeed be admitted, because of the greater instability of the typical business to which we have previously alluded. But it did not follow at all that the *trend of earnings* must therefore be a more dependable guide than the *average;* and even if it were more dependable, it would not necessarily provide a safe basis, entirely by itself, for investment.

---

[2] See Appendix Note 44 for a discussion of the subsequent performance of these three companies.

The accepted assumption that because earnings have moved in a certain direction for some years past they will continue to move in that direction is fundamentally no different from the discarded assumption that because earnings averaged a certain amount in the past they will continue to average about that amount in the future. It may well be that the earnings trend offers a more dependable clue to the future than does the earnings average. But at best such an indication of future results is far from certain, and, more important still, there is no method of establishing a logical relationship between trend and price.[3] This means that the value placed upon a satisfactory trend must be wholly arbitrary, and hence speculative, and hence inevitably subject to exaggeration and later collapse.

Danger in Projecting Trends into the Future. There are several reasons why we cannot be sure that a trend of profits shown in the past will continue in the future. In the broad economic sense, there is the law of diminishing returns and of increasing competition which must finally flatten out any sharply upward curve of growth. There is also the flow and ebb of the business cycle, from which the particular danger arises that the earnings curve will look most impressive on the very eve of a serious setback. Considering the 1927–1929 period we observe that since the trend-of-earnings theory was at bottom only a pretext to excuse rank speculation under the guise of "investment," the profit-mad public was quite willing to accept the flimsiest evidence of the existence of a favorable trend. Rising earnings for a period of five, or four, or even three years only, were regarded as an assurance of uninterrupted future growth and a warrant for projecting the curve of profits indefinitely upward.

---

[3] The new-era investment theory was conspicuously reticent on the mathematical side. The relationship between price and earnings, or price and trend of earnings was anything that the market pleased to make it (note the price of Electric Power and Light compared with its earnings record given on in the table on the previous page). If an attempt were to be made to give a mathematical expression to the underlying idea of valuation, it might be said that it was based on the *derivative* of the earnings, stated in terms of time. In recent years more serious efforts have been made to establish a mathematical basis for discounting expected future earnings or dividends. See Gabriel Preinreich, *The Theory of Dividends*, New York, 1935; and J. B. Williams, *The Theory of Investment Value*, Cambridge, Mass., 1938. The latter work is built on the premise that the value of a common stock is equal to the present value of all future dividends. This principle gives rise to an elaborate series of mathematical equations designed to calculate exactly what a common stock is worth, *assuming* certain vital facts about future earnings, distribution policy and interest rates.

Example: The prevalent heedlessness on this score was most evident in connection with the numerous common-stock flotations during this period. The craze for a showing of rising profits resulted in the promotion of many industrial enterprises that had been favored by temporary good fortune and were just approaching, or had already reached, the peak of their prosperity. A typical example of this practice is found in the offering of preferred and common stock of Schletter and Zander, Inc., a manufacturer of hosiery (name changed later to Signature Hosiery Company). The company was organized in 1929, to succeed a company organized in 1922, and the financing was effected by the sale of 44,810 shares of $3.50 convertible preferred shares at $50 per share and 261,349 voting-trust certificates for common stock at $26 per share. The offering circular presented the following exhibit of earnings from the constituent properties:

Year	Net after federal taxes	Per share of preferred	Per share of common
1925	$ 172,058	$ 3.84	$0.06
1926	339,920	7.58	0.70
1927	563,856	12.58	1.56
1928	1,021,308	22.79	3.31

The subsequent record was as follows:

1929	812,136	18.13	2.51
1930	179,875(d)	4.01(d)	1.81(d)

In 1931 liquidation of the company's assets was begun, and a total of $17 per share in liquidating dividends on the preferred had been paid up to the end of 1933. (Assets then remaining for liquidation were negligible.) The common was wiped out.

This example illustrates one of the paradoxes of financial history, *viz.*, that at the very period when the increasing instability of individual companies had made the purchase of common stocks far more precarious than before, the gospel of common stocks as safe and satisfactory investments was preached to and avidly accepted by the American public.

CHAPTER 28

Newer Canons of Common-Stock Investment

OUR EXTENDED DISCUSSION of the theory of common-stock investment has thus far led only to negative conclusions. The older approach, centering upon the conception of a stable average earning power, appears to have been vitiated by the increasing instability of the typical business. As for the new-era view, which turned upon the earnings trend as the sole criterion of value, whatever truth may lurk in this generalization, its blind adoption as a basis for common-stock purchases, without calculation or restraint, was certain to end in an appalling debacle. Is there anything at all left, then, of the idea of sound investment in common stocks?

A careful review of the preceding criticism will show that it need not be so destructive to the notion of investment in common stocks as a first impression would suggest. The instability of individual companies may conceivably be offset by means of thoroughgoing diversification. Moreover, the trend of earnings, although most dangerous as a *sole* basis for selection, may prove a useful *indication* of investment merit. If this approach is a sound one, there may be formulated an acceptable canon of common-stock investment, containing the following elements:

1. Investment is conceived as a *group* operation, in which diversification of risk is depended upon to yield a favorable average result.

2. The individual issues are selected by means of qualitative and quantitative tests corresponding to those employed in the choice of fixed-value investments.

3. A greater effort is made, than in the case of bond selection, to determine the future outlook of the issues considered.

Whether or not a policy of common-stock acquisition based upon the foregoing principles deserves the title of investment is undoubtedly open to debate. The importance of the question, and the lack of well-defined and authoritative views thereon, compel us to weigh here the leading arguments for and against this proposition.

THREE GENERAL APPROACHES

Secular Expansion as Basis. May the ownership of a carefully selected, diversified group of common stocks, purchased at reasonable prices, be characterized as a sound investment policy? An affirmative answer may be developed from any one of three different kinds of assumptions relating to the future of American business and the policy of selection that is followed. The first will posit that certain basic and long-established elements in this country's economic experience may still be counted upon. These are (1) that our national wealth and earning power will increase, (2) that such increase will reflect itself in the increased resources and profits of our important corporations, and (3) that such increases will in the main take place through the normal process of investment of new capital and reinvestment of undistributed earnings. The third part of this assumption signifies that a broad causal connection exists between accumulating surplus and future earning power, so that common-stock selection is not a matter purely of chance or guesswork but should be governed by an analysis of past records in relation to current market prices.

If these fundamental conditions still obtain, then common stocks with suitable exhibits should on the whole present the same favorable opportunities in the future as they have for generations past. The cardinal defect of instability may not be regarded, therefore, as menacing the long-range development of common stocks as a whole. It does indeed exert a powerful temporary effect upon all business through the variations of the economic cycle, and it has permanently adverse effects upon individual enterprises and single industries. But of these two dangers, the latter may be offset in part by careful selection and chiefly by wide diversification; the former may be guarded against by unvarying insistence upon the reasonableness of the price paid for each purchase.

They would be rash authors who would express themselves unequivocably for or against this basic assumption that American business will develop in the future pretty much as in the past. In our Introduction we point out that the experience of the last fifteen years weighs against this proposition. Without seeking to prophesy the future, may it not suffice to declare that the *investor* cannot safely rely upon a *general* growth of earnings to provide both safety and profit over the long pull? In this respect it would seem that we are back to the investor's attitude in 1913— with the difference that his caution *then* seemed needlessly blind to the powerful evidences of secular growth inherent in our economy. Our caution today would appear, at least, to be based on bitter experience and on the recognition of some newer and less promising factors in the whole business picture.

Individual Growth as Basis of Selection. Those who would reject the suggestion that common-stock investment may be founded securely on a *general* secular expansion may be attracted to a second approach. This stresses the element of selectivity and is based on the premise that *certain favored companies* may be relied on to grow steadily. Hence such companies, when located, can be bought with confidence as long-term investments. This philosophy of investment is set forth at some length in the 1938 report of National Investors Corporation, an investment trust, from which we quote as follows:

> The studies by this organization, directed specifically toward improved procedure in selection, afford evidence that the common stocks of growth companies—that is, companies whose earnings move forward from cycle to cycle, and are only temporarily interrupted by periodic business depressions—offer the most effective medium of investment in the field of common stocks, either in terms of dividend return or longer term capital appreciation. We believe that this general conclusion can be demonstrated statistically and is supported by economic analysis and practical reasoning.

In considering this statement critically, we must start with the emphatic but rather obvious assertion that the investor who can successfully identify such "growth companies" *when their shares are available at reasonable prices* is certain to do superlatively well with his capital. Nor can it be denied that there have been investors capable of making such selections with a high degree of accuracy and that they have benefited hugely from their foresight and good judgment. But the real question is whether or not *all* careful and intelligent investors can follow this policy with fair success.

Three Aspects of the Problem. Actually the problem falls into three parts: First, what is meant by a "growth company"? Second, can the investor identify such concerns with reasonable accuracy? Third, to what extent does the price paid for such stocks affect the success of the program?

1. *What Are Growth Companies?* The National Investors Corporation discussion defined growth companies as those "whose earnings move forward from cycle to cycle." How many cycles are needed to meet this definition? The fact of the matter seems to be that prior to 1930 a large proportion of *all* publicly owned American businesses grew from cycle to cycle. The distinguishing characteristic of growth companies, as now understood, developed only in the period between 1929 and 1936–1937. In this *one* cycle we find that most companies failed to regain their full depression losses. The minority that did so stand out from the rest, and it is these which are now given the complimentary title of "growth companies." But since this distinction is in reality based on performance during a single cycle, how sure can the investor be that it will be maintained over the longer future?

It is true, from what we have previously said, that many of the companies that expanded from 1929 to 1937 had participated in the general record of growth prior to 1929, so that they combine the advantages of a long period of upbuilding and an *exceptional* ability to expand in the last decade. The following are examples of large and well-known companies of this class:

Air Reduction	Monsanto Chemical
Allis Chalmers	Owens-Illinois Glass
Coca-Cola	J. C. Penney
Commercial Credit	Procter & Gamble
Dow Chemical	Sherwin-Williams Paint
Du Pont	Standard Oil of New Jersey
International Business Machines	Scott Paper
International Nickel	Union Carbide and Carbon
Libbey-Owens-Ford	

2. *Can the Investor Identify Them?* But our natural enthusiasm for such excellent records is tempered somewhat by a sobering consideration. This is the fact that, viewed historically, most successful companies

of the past are found to have pursued a well-defined life cycle, consisting first of a series of struggles and setbacks; second, of a halcyon period of prosperity and persistent growth; which in turn passes over into a final phase of supermaturity—characterized by a slackening of expansion and perhaps an actual loss of leadership or even profitability.[1] It follows that a business that has enjoyed a very long period of increasing earnings may *ipso facto* be nearing its own "saturation point." Hence the seeker for growth stocks really faces a dilemma; for if he chooses newer companies with a short record of expansion, he runs the risk of being deceived by a temporary prosperity; and if he chooses enterprises that have advanced through several business cycles, he may find this apparent strength to be the harbinger of coming weakness.

We see, therefore, that the identification of a growth company is not so simple a matter as it may at first appear. It cannot be accomplished solely by an examination of the statistics and records but requires a considerable supplement of special investigation and of business judgment. Proponents of the growth-company principle of investment are wont currently to lay great emphasis on the element of industrial research. In the absence of *general* business expansion, exceptional gains are likely to be made by companies supplying new products or processes. These in turn are likely to emerge from research laboratories. The profits realized from cellophane, ethyl gas and various plastics, and from advances in the arts of radio, photography, refrigeration, aeronautics, etc., have created a natural enthusiasm for research as a business asset and a natural tendency to consider the possession of research facilities as the *sine qua non* of industrial progress.

Still here, too, caution is needed. If the mere ownership of a research laboratory could guarantee a successful future, every company in the land would have one. Hence, the investor must pay heed to the kind of facilities owned, the abilities of the researchers and the potentialities of the field under investigation. It is not impossible to study these points successfully, but the task is not easy, and the chance of error is great.

3. *Does the Price Discount Potential Growth?* The third source of difficulty is perhaps the greatest. Assuming a fair degree of confidence on

---

[1] This characteristic pattern of successful enterprise is discussed at length in the 1938 report of National Investors Corporation, pp. 4–6.

the part of the investor that the company will expand in the future, what *price* is he justified in paying for this attractive element? Obviously, if he can get a good future for *nothing, i.e.,* if the price reflects only the past record, he is making a sound investment. But this is not the case, of course, *if the market itself is counting on future growth.* Characteristically, stocks thought to have good prospects sell at relatively high prices. How can the investor tell whether or not the price is *too* high? We think that there is no good answer to this question—in fact we are inclined to think that even if one knew for a certainty just what a company is fated to earn over a long period of years, it would still be impossible to tell what is a fair price to pay for it today. It follows that *once the investor pays a substantial amount for the growth factor,* he is inevitably assuming certain kinds of risk; *viz.,* that the growth will be less than he anticipates, that over the long pull he will have paid too much for what he gets, that for a considerable period the market will value the stock less optimistically than he does.

On the other hand, assume that the investor strives to avoid paying a high premium for future prospects by choosing companies about which he is personally optimistic, although they are not favorites of the stock market. No doubt this is the type of judgment that, if sound, will prove most remunerative. But, by the very nature of the case, it must represent the activity of strong-minded and daring individuals rather than investment in accordance with accepted rules and standards.[2]

May Such Purchases Be Described as Investment Commitments? This has been a longish discussion because the subject is important and not too well comprehended in Wall Street. Our emphasis has been laid more on the pitfalls of investing for future growth than on its advantages. But we repeat that this method may be followed successfully if it is pursued with skill, intelligence and diligent study. If so, is it appropriate to call such purchases by the name of "investment"? Our answer is "yes," provided that two factors are present: the first, already mentioned, that the elements affecting the future are examined with real care and a wholesome scepticism, rather than

---

[2] The "expanding-industry" criterion of common-stock investment is vigorously championed in an arresting book *The Ebb and Flow of Investment Values*, New York, 1939, by Edward S. Mead and J. Grodinsky. For a consideration of their views in some detail see Appendix Note 71.

accepted quickly via some easy generalization; the second, that the price paid be not substantially different from what a prudent business man would be willing to pay for a similar opportunity presented to him to invest in a private undertaking over which he could exercise control.

We believe that the second criterion will supply a useful touchstone to determine whether the buyer is making a well-considered and legitimate commitment in an enterprise with an attractive future, or instead, under the guise of "investment," he is really taking a flier in a popular stock or else letting his private enthusiasm run away with his judgment.

It will be argued, perhaps, that common-stock investments such as we have been discussing may properly be made at a considerably higher price than would be justified in the case of a private business, first, because of the great advantage of marketability that attaches to listed stocks and, second, because the large size and financial power of publicly owned companies make them inherently more attractive than any private enterprise could be. As to the second point, the price to be paid should suitably reflect any advantages accruing by reason of size and financial strength, but this criterion does not really depend on whether the company is publicly or privately owned. On the first point, there is room for some difference of opinion whether or not the ability to *control* a private business affords a full counterweight (in value analysis) to the advantage of marketability enjoyed by a listed stock. To those who believe marketability is more valuable than control, we might suggest that in any event the premium to be paid for this advantage cannot well be placed above, say, 20% of the value otherwise justified without danger of introducing a definitely speculative element into the picture.

Selection Based on Margin-of-Safety Principle. The third approach to common-stock investment is based on the margin-of-safety principle. If the analyst is convinced that a stock is *worth more* than he pays for it, and if he is *reasonably optimistic* as to the company's future, he would regard the issue as a suitable component of a group investment in common stocks. This attack on the problem lends itself to two possible techniques. One is to buy *at times when the general market is low*, measured by quantitative standards of value. Presumably the purchases would then be confined to representative and fairly active issues. The other technique would be employed to discover undervalued *individual* common stocks, which presumably are available even when the general market is not particularly low. In either case the "margin of safety" resides in the discount at which the stock is selling below its minimum intrinsic value, as measured by the analyst. But with respect to the hazards and the psychological factors involved, the two approaches differ considerably. Let us discuss them in their order.

Factors Complicating Efforts to Exploit General Market Swings. A glance at Chart A in "Introduction to the Second Edition," shows the fluctuations of common-stock prices since 1900, would suggest that prices are recurrently too high and too low and that consequently there should be repeated opportunities to buy stocks at less than their value and to sell them out later at fair value or higher. A crude method of doing this—but one apparently encouraged by the chart itself—would consist simply of drawing a straight line through the approximate midpoints of past market swings and then planning to buy somewhere below this line and to sell somewhere above it.

Perhaps such a "system" would be as practical as any, but the analyst is likely to insist on a more scientific approach. One possible refinement would operate as follows:

1. Select a diversified list of leading industrial common stocks.

2. Determine a base or "normal" value for the group by capitalizing their average earnings at some suitable figure, related to the going long-term interest rate.

3. Determine a buying point at some percentage below this normal value and a selling point above it. (Or buying and selling may be done "on a scale down" and "on a scale up.")

A method of this kind has plausible logic to recommend it, and it is favored also by an age-old tradition that success in the stock market is gained by buying at depressed levels and selling out when the public is optimistic. But the reader will suspect at once that there is a catch to it somewhere. What are its drawbacks?

As we see it, the difficulties attending this idea are threefold: First, although the *general* pattern of the market's behavior may be properly anticipated, the specific buying and selling points may turn out to have been badly chosen, and the operator may miss his opportunity at one extreme or the other. Second, there is always a chance that the character of the market's behavior may change significantly, so that a scheme of operation that would have worked well in the past will cease to be practicable. Third, the method itself requires a considerable amount of human fortitude. It generally involves buying and selling when the prevalent psychology favors the opposite course, watching one's shares go lower after purchase and higher after sale and often staying out of the market for long periods (*e.g.*, 1927–1930) when most people are actively interested in stocks. But despite these disadvantages, which we do not minimize, it is our view that this method has a good deal to commend it to those temperamentally qualified to follow it.

The Undervalued-Individual-Issue Approach. The other application of the principle of investing in undervalued common stocks is directed at individual issues, which upon analysis appear to be worth substantially more than they are selling for. It is rare that a common stock will appear satisfactory *from every qualitative angle* and at the same time will be found to be selling at a low price by such quantitative standards as earnings, dividends, and assets. Issues of this type would undoubtedly be eligible for a group purchase that would fulfill our supplementary criterion of "investment" given in Chap. 4. ("An investment operation is one that can be justified on both qualitative and quantitative grounds.")

Of more practical importance is the question whether or not investment can be successfully carried on in common stocks that appear cheap from the quantitative angle and that—upon study—seem to have *average* prospects for the future. Securities of this type can be found in reasonable abundance, as a result of the stock market's obsession with companies considered to have *unusually good prospects of growth*. Because of this emphasis on the growth factor, quite a number of enterprises that are long established, well financed, important in their industries and presumably destined to stay in business and make profits indefinitely in the future, but that have no speculative or growth appeal, tend to be discriminated against by the stock market—especially in years of subnormal profits— and to sell *for considerably less than the business would be worth to a private owner.*[3]

---

[3] Note that we have applied the touchstone of "value to a private investor" to justify *two* different types of *investment* in common stocks: (1) purchase of issues thought to have exceptional prospects at no higher price than would be paid for a corresponding interest in a private business, and (2) purchase of issues with good records and *average* prospects at a much *lower* price than the business is worth to a private owner. See Appendix Note 45 for the exhibit of an issue of the latter type (Swift and Company).

We incline strongly to the belief that this last criterion—a price far less than value to a private owner—will constitute a sound touchstone for the discovery of true investment opportunities in common stocks. This view runs counter to the convictions and practice of most people seeking to invest in equities, including practically all the investment trusts. Their emphasis is mainly on long-term growth, prospects for the next year, or the indicated trend of the stock market itself. Undoubtedly any of these three viewpoints may be followed successfully by those especially well equipped by experience and native ability to exploit them. But we are not so sure that any of these approaches can be developed into a system or technique that can be confidently followed by everyone of sound intelligence who has studied it with care. Hence we must raise our solitary voice against the use of the term *investment* to characterize these methods of operating in common stocks, however profitable they may be to the truly skillful. Trading in the market, forecasting next year's results for various businesses, selecting the best media for long-term expansion—all these have a useful place in Wall Street. But we think that the interests of investors and of Wall Street as an institution would be better served if operations based primarily on these factors were called by some other name than investment.

Whether or not our own concept of common-stock investment is a valid one may be more intelligently considered after we have given extended treatment to the chief factors that enter into a statistical analysis of a stock issue. The need for such analysis is quite independent of our investment philosophy. After all, common stocks exist and are actively dealt in by the public. Those who buy and sell will properly seek to arm themselves with an adequate knowledge of financial practice and with the tools and technique necessary for an intelligent analysis of corporate statements.

Such information and equipment for the common-stock investor form the subject matter of the following chapters.

CHAPTER 29

The Dividend Factor
in Common-Stock Analysis

A NATURAL classification of the elements entering into the valuation of a
common stock would be under the three headings:

1. The dividend rate and record.
2. Income-account factors (earning power).
3. Balance-sheet factors (asset value).

The dividend rate is a simple fact and requires no analysis, but its exact
significance is exceedingly difficult to appraise. From one point of view
the dividend rate is all-important, but from another and equally valid
standpoint it must be considered an accidental and minor factor. A basic
confusion has grown up in the minds of managements and stockholders
alike as to what constitutes a proper dividend policy. The result has been
to create a definite conflict between two aspects of common-stock ownership: one being the possession of a marketable security, and the other
being the assumption of a partnership interest in a business. Let us
consider the matter in detail from this twofold approach.

Dividend Return as a Factor in Common-Stock Investment. Until recent
years the dividend return was the overshadowing factor in common-
stock investment. This point of view was based on simple logic. The
prime purpose of a business corporation is to pay dividends to its owners.
A successful company is one that can pay dividends regularly and presumably increase the rate as time goes on. Since the idea of investment
is closely bound up with that of dependable income, it follows that investment in common stocks would ordinarily be confined to those with a
well-established dividend. It would follow also that the *price* paid for an
investment common stock would be determined chiefly by the amount
of the dividend.

We have seen that the traditional common-stock investor sought to place himself as nearly as possible in the position of an investor in a bond or a preferred stock. He aimed primarily at a steady income return, which in general would be both somewhat larger and somewhat less certain than that provided by good senior securities. Excellent illustrations of the effect of this attitude upon the price of common stocks are afforded by the records of the earnings, dividends and annual price variations of American Sugar Refining between 1907 and 1913 and of Atchison, Topeka, and Santa Fe Railway between 1916 and 1925 presented herewith.

American Sugar Refining Company

Year	Range for stock	Earned per share	Paid per share
1907	138–93	$10.22	$7.00
1908	138–99	7.45	7.00
1909	136–115	14.20	7.00
1910	128–112	5.38	7.00
1911	123–113	18.92	7.00
1912	134–114	5.34	7.00
1913	118–100	*0.02(d)*	7.00

Atchison, Topeka, and Santa Fe Railway Company

Year	Range for stock	Earned per share	Paid per share
1916	109–100	$14.74	$6
1917	108–75	14.50	6
1918	100–81	10.59*	6
1919	104–81	15.41*	6
1920	90–76	12.54*	6
1921	94–76	14.69†	6
1922	109–92	12.41	6
1923	105–94	15.48	6
1924	121–97	15.47	6
1925	141–116	17.19	7

* Results for these years based on actual operations. Results of federal operation were: 1918—$9.98; 1919—$16.55; 1920—$13.98.
† Includes nonrecurrent income. Excluding the latter the figure for 1921 would have been $11.29.

The market range of both issues is surprisingly narrow, considering the continuous gyrations of the stock market generally during those periods. The most striking feature of the exhibit is the slight influence exercised both by the irregular earnings of American Sugar and by the exceptionally well-maintained and increasing earning power on the part of Atchison. It is clear that the price of American Sugar was dominated throughout by its $7 rate and that of Atchison by its $6 rate, even though the earnings records would apparently have justified an entirely different range of relative market values.

Established Principle of Withholding Dividends. We have, therefore, on the one hand an ingrained and powerfully motivated tradition which centers investment interest upon the present and past dividend rate. But on the other hand we have an equally authoritative and well-established principle of *corporate management* which subordinates the current dividend to the future welfare of the company and its shareholders. It is considered proper managerial policy to withhold current earnings from stockholders, for the sake of any of the following advantages:

1. To strengthen the financial (working-capital) position.
2. To increase productive capacity.
3. To eliminate an original overcapitalization.

When a management withholds and reinvests profits, thus building up an accumulated surplus, it claims confidently to be acting for the best interests of the shareholders. For by this policy the continuance of the established dividend rate is undoubtedly better assured, and furthermore a gradual but continuous increase in the regular payment is thereby made possible. The rank and file of stockholders will give such policies their support, either because they are individually convinced that this procedure redounds to their advantage or because they accept uncritically the authority of the managements and bankers who recommend it.

But this approval by stockholders of what is called a "conservative dividend policy" has about it a peculiar element of the perfunctory and even the reluctant. The typical investor would most certainly prefer to have his dividend today and let tomorrow take care of itself. No instances are on record in which the withholding of dividends for the sake of future profits has been hailed with such enthusiasm as to advance the price of the stock. The direct opposite has invariably been true. *Given two companies in the same general position and with the same earning power, the one paying the larger dividend will always sell at the higher price.*

Policy of Withholding Dividends Questionable. This is an arresting fact, and it should serve to call into question the traditional theory of corporate finance that the smaller the percentage of earnings paid out in dividends the better for the company and its stockholders. Although investors have been taught to pay lip service to this theory, their instincts—and perhaps their better judgment—are in revolt against it. If we try to bring a fresh and critical viewpoint to bear upon this subject, we shall find that weighty objections may be leveled against the accepted dividend policy of American corporations.

Examining this policy more closely, we see that it rests upon two quite distinct assumptions. The first is that it is advantageous to the stockholders to leave a substantial part of the annual earnings in the business; the second is that it is desirable to maintain a steady dividend rate in the face of fluctuations in profits. As to the second point, there would be no question at all, provided the dividend *stability* is achieved without too great sacrifice in the *amount* of the dividend. Assume that the earnings vary between $5 and $15 annually over a period of years, averaging $10. No doubt the stockholder's advantage would be best served by maintaining a stable dividend rate of $8, sometimes drawing upon the surplus to maintain it, but on the average increasing the surplus at the rate of $2 per share annually.

This would be an ideal arrangement. But in practice it is rarely followed. We find that stability of dividends is usually accomplished by the simple expedient of paying out a *small part* of the average earnings. By a *reductio ad absurdum* it is clear that any company that earned $10 per share on the average could readily stabilize its dividend at $1. The question arises very properly if the shareholders might not prefer a much larger aggregate dividend, even with some irregularity. This point is well illustrated in the case of Atchison.

The Case of Atchison. Atchison maintained its dividend at the annual rate of $6 for the 15 years between 1910 and 1924. During this time the average earnings were in excess of $12 per share, so that the stability was attained by withholding over half the earnings from the stockholders. Eventually this policy bore fruit in an advance of the dividend to $10, which rate was paid between 1927 and 1931, and was accompanied by a rise in the market price to nearly $300 per share in 1929. Within six months after the last payment at the $10 rate (in December 1931) the dividend was omitted entirely. Viewed critically, the stability of the Atchison dividend between 1910 and 1924 must be considered as of dubious benefit to the stockholders. During its continuance they received an unduly small return in relation to the earnings; when the rate was finally advanced, the importance attached to such a move promoted excessive speculation in the shares; finally, the reinvestment of the enormous sums out of earnings failed to protect the shareholders from a complete loss of income in 1932. Allowance must be made, of course, for the unprecedented character of the depression in 1932. But the fact remains that the actual operating losses in dollars per share up to the passing of the dividend were entirely insignificant in comparison with the surplus accumulated out of the profits of previous years.

United States Steel, Another Example. The Atchison case illustrates the two major objections to what is characterized and generally approved of as a "conservative dividend policy." The first objection is that stockholders receive *both currently and ultimately* too low a return in relation to the earnings of their property; the second is that the "saving up of profits for a rainy day" often fails to safeguard even the moderate dividend rate when the rainy day actually arrives. A similarly striking example of the ineffectiveness of a large accumulated surplus is shown by that leading industrial enterprise, United States Steel.

The following figures tell a remarkable story:

Profits available for the common stock, 1901–1930 ....$2,344,000,000
   Dividends paid:
      Cash .... .891,000,000
      Stock .... .203,000,000
   Undistributed earnings 1,250,000,000
   Loss after preferred dividends Jan. 1, 1931–June 30, 1932 ...... .59,000,000
   Common dividend passed June 30, 1932.

A year and a half of declining business was sufficient to outweigh the beneficial influence of 30 years of practically continuous reinvestment of profits.

The Merits of "Plowing-Back" Earnings. These examples serve to direct our critical attention to the other assumption on which American dividend policies are based, *viz.*, that it is advantageous to the stockholders if a large portion of the annual earnings are retained in the business. This may well be true, but in determining its truth a number of factors must be considered that are usually left out of account. The customary reasoning on this point may be stated in the form of a syllogism, as follows:

> Major premise—Whatever benefits the company benefits the stockholders.
> Minor premise—A company is benefited if its earnings are retained rather than paid out in dividends.
> Conclusion—Stockholders are benefited by the withholding of corporate earnings.

The weakness of the foregoing reasoning rests of course in the major premise. Whatever benefits a business benefits its owners, *provided* the benefit is not conferred upon the corporation at the *expense* of the stockholders. Taking money away from the stockholders and presenting it to the company will undoubtedly strengthen the enterprise, but whether or not it is to the owners' advantage is an entirely different question. It is customary to commend managements for "plowing earnings back into the property"; but, in measuring the benefits from such a policy, the time element is usually left out of account. It stands to reason that, if a business paid out only a small part of its earnings in dividends, the value of the stock should increase over a period of years, but it is by no means so certain that this increase will compensate the stockholders for the dividends withheld from them, *particularly if interest on these amounts is compounded.*

An inductive study would undoubtedly show that the earning power of corporations does not in general expand proportionately with increases in accumulated surplus. *Assuming that the reported earnings were actually available for distribution*, then stockholders in general would certainly fare better in dollars and cents if they drew out practically all of these earnings in dividends. An unconscious realization of this fact has much to do with the tendency of common stocks paying liberal dividends to sell higher than others with the same earning power but paying out only a small part thereof.

Dividend Policies Arbitrary and Sometimes Selfishly Determined. One of the obstacles in the way of an intelligent understanding by stockholders of the dividend question is the accepted notion that the determination of dividend policies is entirely a managerial function, in the same way as the general running of the business. This is legally true, and the courts will not interfere with the dividend action or inaction except upon an exceedingly convincing showing of unfairness. But if stockholders' opinions were properly informed, it would insist upon curtailing the despotic powers given the directorate over the dividend policy. Experience shows that these unrestricted powers are likely to be abused for various reasons. Boards of directors usually consist largely of executive officers and their friends. The officers are naturally desirous of retaining as much cash as possible in the treasury, in order to simplify their financial problems; they are also inclined to expand the business persistently for the sake of personal aggrandizement and to secure higher salaries. This is a leading cause of the unwise increase of manufacturing facilities which has proved recurrently one of the chief unsettling factors in our economic situation.

The discretionary power over the dividend policy may also be abused in more sinister fashion, sometimes to permit the acquisition of shares at an unduly low price, at other times to facilitate unloading at a high quotation. The heavy surtaxes imposed upon large incomes frequently make it undesirable from the standpoint of the large stockholders that earnings be paid out in dividends. Hence dividend policies may be determined at times from the standpoint of the taxable status of the large stockholders who control the directorate. This is particularly true in cases where these dominant stockholders receive substantial salaries as executives. In such cases they are perfectly willing to leave their share of the earnings in the corporate treasury, since the latter is under their control and since by so doing they retain control over the earnings accruing to the other stockholders as well.

Arbitrary Control of Dividend Policy Complicates Analysis of Common Stocks. Viewing American corporate dividend policies as a whole, it cannot be said that the virtually unlimited power given the management on this score has redounded to the benefit of the stockholders. In entirely too many cases the right to pay out or withhold earnings at will is exercised in an unintelligent or inequitable manner. Dividend policies are often so arbitrarily managed as to introduce an additional uncertainty in the analysis of a common stock. Besides the difficulty of judging the earning power, there is the second difficulty of predicting what part of the earnings the directors will see fit to disburse in dividends.

It is important to note that this feature is peculiar to American corporate finance and has no close counterpart in the other important countries. The typical English, French, or German company pays out practically all the earnings of each year, except those carried to reserves.[1] Hence they do not build up large profit-and-loss surpluses, such as are common in the United States. Capital for expansion purposes is provided abroad not out of undistributed earnings but through the sale of additional stock. To some extent, perhaps, the reserve accounts shown in foreign balance sheets will serve the same purpose as an American surplus account, but these reserve accounts rarely attain a comparable magnitude.

Plowing Back Due to Watered Stock. The American theory of "plowing back" earnings appears to have grown out of the stock-watering practices of prewar days. Many of our large industrial companies made their initial appearance with no tangible assets behind their common shares and with inadequate protection for their preferred issues. Hence it was natural that the management should seek to make good these deficiencies out of subsequent earnings. This was particularly true because additional stock could not be sold at its par value, and it was difficult therefore to obtain new capital for expansion except through undistributed profits.[2]

Examples: Concrete examples of the relation between overcapitalization and dividend policies are afforded by the outstanding cases of Woolworth and United States Steel Corporation.

In the original sale of F. W. Woolworth Company shares to the public, made in 1911, the company issued preferred stock to represent all the tangible assets and common stock to represent the good-will. The balance sheet accordingly carried a good-will item of $50,000,000 among the assets, offsetting a corresponding liability for 500,000 shares of common, par $100.[3] As Woolworth prospered, a large surplus was built up out of

---

[1] See Appendix Note 46 for discussion and examples.

[2] The no-par-value device is largely a post-1918 development.

[3] This was for many years a standard scheme for financing of industrial companies. It was followed by Sears Roebuck, Cluett Peabody, National Cloak and Suit, and others.

earnings, and amounts were charged against this surplus to reduce the good-will account, until finally it was written down to $1.[4]

In the case of United States Steel Corporation, the original capitalization exceeded tangible assets by no less than $768,000,000, representing all the common and more than half the preferred stock. This "water" in the balance sheet was not shown as a good-will item, as in the case of Woolworth, but was concealed by an overvaluation of the fixed assets (*i.e.*, of the "Property Investment Accounts"). Through various accounting methods, however, the management applied earnings from operations to the writing off of these intangible or fictitious assets. By the end of 1929 a total of $508,000,000—equal to the entire original common-stock issue—had been taken from earnings or surplus and deducted from the property account. The balance of $260,000,000 was set up separately as an intangible asset in the 1937 report and then written off entirely in 1938 by means of a reduction in the stated value of the common stock.

Some of the accounting policies above referred to will be discussed again, with respect to their influence on investment values, in our chapters on Analysis of the Income Account and Balance-sheet Analysis. From the dividend standpoint it is clear that in both of these examples the decision to retain large amounts of earnings, instead of paying them out to the stockholders, was due in part to the desire to eliminate intangible items from the asset accounts.

Conclusions from the Foregoing. From the foregoing discussion certain conclusions may be drawn. These bear, first on the very practical question of what significance should be accorded the dividend rate as compared with the reported earnings and, secondly, upon the more theoretical but exceedingly important question of what dividend policies should be considered as most desirable from the standpoint of the stockholders' interest.

Experience would confirm the established verdict of the stock market that a dollar of earnings is worth more to the stockholder if paid him in dividends than when carried to surplus. The common-stock investor should ordinarily require both an adequate earning power and an adequate

---

[4] It should be noted that when the good-will of Woolworth was originally listed in the balance sheet at $50,000,000, its actual value (as measured by the market price of the shares) was only some $20,000,000. But when the good-will was written down to $1, in 1925, its real value was apparently many times $50,000,000.

dividend. If the dividend is disproportionately small, an investment purchase will be justified only on an exceptionally impressive showing of earnings (or by a very special situation with respect to liquid assets). On the other hand, of course, an extra-liberal dividend policy cannot compensate for inadequate earnings, since with such a showing the dividend rate must necessarily be undependable.

To aid in developing these ideas quantitatively, we submit the following definitions:

> The *dividend rate* is the amount of annual dividends paid per share, expressed either in dollars or as a percentage of a $100 par value. (If the par value is less than $100, it is inadvisable to refer to the dividend rate as a percentage figure since this may lead to confusion.)
>
> The *earnings rate* is the amount of annual earnings per share, expressed either in dollars or as a percentage of a $100 par value.
>
> The *dividend ratio*, *dividend return* or *dividend yield*, is the ratio of the dividend paid to the market price (*e.g.*, a stock paying $6 annually and selling at 120 has a dividend ratio of 5%).
>
> The *earnings ratio*, *earnings return* or *earnings yield*, is the ratio of the annual earnings to the market price (*e.g.*, a stock earning $6 and selling at 50 shows an earnings yield of 12%).[5]

Let us assume that a common stock *A*, with average prospects, earning $7 and paying $5 should sell at 100. This is a 7% earnings ratio and 5% dividend return. Then a similar common stock, *B*, earning $7 but paying only $4, should sell lower than 100. Its price evidently should be somewhere between 80 (representing a 5% dividend yield) and 100 (representing a 7% earnings yield). In general the price should tend to be established nearer to the lower limit than to the upper limit. A fair approximation of the proper relative price would be about 90, at which level the dividend yield is 4.44%, and the earnings ratio is 7.78%. If the investor makes a small concession in dividend yield below the standard, he is entitled to demand a more than corresponding increase in the earning power above standard.

In the opposite case a similar stock, *C*, may earn $7 but pay $6. Here the investor is justified in paying some premium above 100 because of

---

[5] The term *earnings basis* has the same meaning as *earnings ratio*. However, the term *dividend basis* is ambiguous, since it is used sometimes to denote the rate and sometimes the ratio.

the larger dividend. The upper limit, of course, would be 120 at which price the dividend ratio would be the standard 5%, but the earnings ratio would be only 5.83%. Here again the proper price should be closer to the lower than to the upper limit, say, 108, at which figure the dividend yield would be 5.56% and the earnings ratio 6.48%.

Suggested Principle for Dividend Payments. Although these figures are arbitrarily taken, they correspond fairly well with the actualities of investment values under what seem now to be reasonably normal conditions in the stock market. The dividend *rate* is seen to be important, apart from the earnings, not only because the investor naturally wants cash income from his capital but also because the earnings that are *not* paid out in dividends have a tendency to lose part of their effective value for the stockholder. Because of this fact American shareholders would do well to adopt a different attitude than hitherto with respect to corporate dividend policies. We should suggest the following principle as a desirable modification of the traditional viewpoint:

Principle: Stockholders are entitled to receive the earnings on their capital except to the extent they decide to reinvest them in the business. The management should retain or reinvest earnings only with the specific approval of the stockholders. Such "earnings" as must be retained to protect the company's position are not true earnings at all. They should not be reported as profits but should be deducted in the income statement as necessary reserves, with an adequate explanation thereof. *A compulsory surplus is an imaginary surplus.*[6]

Were this principle to be generally accepted, the withholding of earnings would not be taken as a matter of course and of arbitrary determination by the management, but it would require justification corresponding to that now expected in the case of changes in capitalization and of the sale of additional stock. The result would be to subject dividend policies to greater scrutiny and more intelligent criticism than they now receive, thus imposing a salutary check upon the tendency of managements to expand unwisely and to accumulate excessive working capital.[7]

---

[6] We refer here to a surplus which *had to be accumulated* in order to *maintain* the company's status, and not to a surplus accumulated as a part of good management.

[7] The suggested procedure under the British Companies Act of 1929 requires that dividend payments be approved by the shareholders at their annual meeting but prohibits the

If it should become the standard policy to disburse the major portion of each year's earnings (as is done abroad), then the rate of dividend will vary with business conditions. This would apparently introduce an added factor of instability into stock values. But the objection to the present practice is that it *fails* to produce the stable dividend rate which is its avowed purpose and the justification for the sacrifice it imposes. Hence instead of a dependable dividend that mitigates the uncertainty of earnings we have a frequently arbitrary and unaccountable dividend policy that aggravates the earnings hazard. The sensible remedy would be to transfer to the stockholder the task of averaging out his own annual income return. Since the common-stock investor must form some fairly satisfactory opinion of average earning power, which transcends the annual fluctuations, he may as readily accustom himself to forming a similar idea of average *income*. As in fact the two ideas are substantially identical, dividend fluctuations *of this kind* would not make matters more difficult for the common-stock investor. In the end such fluctuations will work out more to his advantage than the present method of attempting, usually unsuccessfully, to stabilize the dividend by large additions to the surplus account.[8] On the former basis, the stockholder's average income would probably be considerably larger.

A Paradox. Although we have concluded that the payment of a liberal portion of the earnings in dividends adds definitely to the attractiveness of a common stock, it must be recognized that this conclusion involves a curious paradox. Value is increased by taking away value. The more the stockholder subtracts in dividends from the capital and surplus fund the larger value he places upon what is left. It is like the famous legend of the Sibylline Books, except that here the price of the remainder is *increased* because part has been taken away.

---

approval of a rate greater than that recommended by the directors. Despite the latter proviso, the mere fact that the dividend policy is submitted to the stockholders for their specific approval or criticism carries an exceedingly valuable reminder to the management of its responsibilities, and to the owners of their rights, on this important question.

Although this procedure is not required by the Companies Act in all cases, it is generally followed in England. See Companies Act of 1929, Sections 6–10; Table A to the Companies Act of 1929, pars. 89–93; *Palmer's Company Law*, pp. 222–224, 13th ed., 1929.

[8] For a comprehensive study of the effects of withholding earnings on the regularity of dividend payments, see O. J. Curry, *Utilization of Corporate Profits in Prosperity and Depression*, Ann Arbor, 1941.

This point is well illustrated by a comparison of Atchison and Union Pacific—two railroads of similar standing—over the ten-year period between January 1, 1915, and December 31, 1924.

	Per share of common	
Item	Union Pacific	Atchison
Earned, 10 years 1915–1924	$142.00	$137
Net adjustments in surplus account	dr. 1.50*	cr. 13
Total available for stockholders	$140.50	$150
Dividends paid	$97.50	$60
Increase in market price	33.00	25
Total realizable by stockholders	$130.50	$85
Increase in earnings, 1924 over 1914	9%†	109%†
Increase in book value, 1924 over 1914	25%	70%
Increase in dividend rate, 1924 over 1914	25%	none
Increase in market price, 1924 over 1914	28%	27%
Market price, Dec. 31, 1914	116	93
Market price, Dec. 31, 1924	149	118
Earnings, year ended June 30, 1914	$13.10	$7.40
Earnings, calendar year 1924	14.30	15.45

* Excluding about $7 per share transferred from reserves to surplus.
† Calendar year 1924 compared with year ended June 30, 1914.

It is to be noted that because Atchison failed to increase its dividend the market price of the shares failed to reflect adequately the large increase both in earning power and in book value. The more liberal dividend policy of Union Pacific produced the opposite result.

This anomaly of the stock market is explained in good part by the underlying conflict of the two prevailing ideas regarding dividends which we have discussed in this chapter. In the following brief summary of the situation we endeavor to indicate the relation between the theoretical and the practical aspects of the dividend question.

Summary

1. In some cases the stockholders derive positive benefits from an ultraconservative dividend policy, *i.e.*, through much larger eventual earnings and dividends. In such instances the market's judgment proves to be wrong in penalizing the shares because of their small dividend. The price of these shares should be higher rather than lower on account of the fact that profits have been added to surplus instead of having been paid out in dividends.

2. Far more frequently, however, the stockholders derive much greater benefits from dividend payments than from additions to surplus. This happens because either: (*a*) the reinvested profits fail to add proportionately to the earning power or (*b*) they are not true "profits" at all but reserves that *had* to be retained merely to protect the business. In this majority of cases the market's disposition to emphasize the dividend and to ignore the additions to surplus turns out to be sound.

3. The confusion of thought arises from the fact that the stockholder votes in accordance with the first premise and invests on the basis of the second. If the stockholders asserted themselves intelligently, this paradox would tend to disappear. For in that case the withholding of a large percentage of the earnings would become an exceptional practice, subject to close scrutiny by the stockholders and presumably approved by them from a considered conviction that such retention would be beneficial to the owners of the shares. Such a ceremonious endorsement of a low dividend rate would probably and properly dispel the stock market's scepticism on this point and permit the price to reflect the earnings that are accumulating as well as those which were paid out.

The foregoing discussion may appear to conflict with the suggestion, advanced in the previous chapter, that long-term increases in common-stock values are often due to the reinvestment of undistributed profits. We must distinguish here between the two lines of argument. Taking our standard case of a company earning $10 per share and paying dividends of $7, we have pointed out that the repeated annual additions of $3 per share to surplus should serve to increase the value of the stock over a period of years. This may very well be true, and at the same time the rate of increase in value may be substantially less than $3 per annum compounded. If we take the reverse case, *viz.*, $3 paid in dividends and $7 added to surplus, the distinction is clearer. Undoubtedly the large addition to surplus will expand the value of the stock, but quite probably also this value will fail to increase at the annual rate of $7 compounded. Hence the argument against reinvesting large proportions of the yearly earnings would remain perfectly valid. Our criticism is advanced against the latter type of policy, *e.g.*, the retention of 70% of the earnings, and not against the normal reinvestment of some 30% of the profits.

Dividend Policies Since 1934. If the dividend practice of American corporations were to be judged solely by the record during 1934–1939, the criticism expressed in this chapter would have to be softened considerably. In these recent years there has been a definite tendency towards greater liberality in dividend payments, particularly by companies that do not have clearly defined opportunities for profitable expansion. Retention of earnings by rapidly growing enterprises, *e.g.*, airplane manufacturers, is hardly open to objection. Since the end of 1932, on the other hand, General Motors Corporation has disbursed about 80% of earnings to common-stock holders, with no wide deviation in any year through 1939. In 1939 the Treasury Department announced that it would use 70% as a rough or preliminary test to decide whether or not a company is subject to the penalty taxes for improper accumulation of surplus.

As far as stock prices are concerned, it can hardly be said that they have been unduly influenced by arbitrary dividend policies in these recent years. For not only have the policies themselves been far less arbitrary than in former times, but there has been a definite tendency in the stock market to subordinate the dividend factor to the reported and prospective earnings.

The Undistributed-Profits Tax. The more liberal dividends of recent years have been due in part to the highly controversial tax on undistributed profits. This was imposed by Congress in 1936, on a graduated scale running from 7 to 27%. Following violent criticism, the tax was reduced to a vestigial $2^1/2$% in 1938 and repealed entirely the following year. Its main object was to compel companies to distribute their earnings, so that they might be subject to personal income taxes levied against the stockholders. A secondary objective appears to have been to restrict the accumulation of corporate surpluses, which were thought by some to be injurious, either because they withheld purchasing power from individuals or because they were conducive to unwise expansion. But the tax was widely and violently condemned, chiefly on the ground that it prevented the creation of surplus or reserve funds essential to meet future losses or emergencies or expansion needs. It was said to lay a heavy penalty on corporate thrift and prudence and to bear with particular severity on small or new corporations which must rely largely on retained profits for their growth.

Law Objectionable but Criticized on Wrong Grounds. In our own opinion the law was a very bad one, but it has been criticized largely on the wrong grounds. Its objective, as first announced, was to tax corporations exactly as if they were partnerships and hence to equalize the taxation basis of corporate and unincorporated businesses. Much could be said in favor of this aim. But as the bill was finally passed it effectively superposed partnership taxation on top of corporate taxation, thus heavily discriminating against the corporate form and especially against small stockholders. Nor was it a practicable tax as far as wealthy holders were concerned, because the extremely high personal tax rates, combined with the corporation taxes (state and federal), created an over-all burden undoubtedly hostile to individual initiative. Fully as bad were the technical details of the tax law, which compelled distributions in excess of actual accounting profits, disregarded very real capital losses and allowed no flexibility in the treatment of inventory values.

Despite the almost universal opinion to the contrary, we do not believe that the undistributed profits tax really prevented the reinvestment of earnings, except to the extent that these were diminished by personal income taxes—as they would be in an unincorporated business. Corporations had available a number of methods for retaining or recovering these earnings, without subjecting them to the penalty tax. These devices included (1) declaration of taxable stock dividends (*e.g.*, in preferred stock); (2) payment of "optional" dividends, so contrived as to impel the stockholders to take stock rather than cash; (3) offering of additional stock on attractive terms at the time of payment of cash dividends. Critics of the tax have asserted that these methods are inconvenient or impracticable. Our own observation is that they were quite practicable and were resorted to by a fair number of corporations in 1936 and 1937,[9]

---

[9] See Rolbein, David L., "Noncash Dividends and Stock Rights as Methods for Avoidance of the Undistributed Profits Tax," XII *The Journal of Business of the University of Chicago* 221–264,

but that they were avoided by the majority, either from unfamiliarity or from a desire to throw as harsh a light as possible upon the law.

Proper Dividend Policy. In view of the scepticism that we have expressed as to whether or not stockholders are really benefited by dividend-withholding policies, we may be thought sympathetic to the idea of preventing reinvestment of profits by imposing penalty taxes thereon. This is far from true. Dividend and reinvestment policies should be controlled not by law but by the intelligent decision of stockholders. Individual cases may well justify retention of earnings to an extent far greater than is ordinarily desirable. The practice should vary with the circumstances; the policy should be determined and proposed in the first instance by the management; but it should be subject to independent consideration and appraisal by stockholders in their own interest, as distinguished from that of the corporation as a separate entity or the management as a special group.

July, 1939. For more comprehensive surveys of this tax see Alfred G. Buehler, *The Undistributed Profits Tax*, New York, 1937 (an adverse appraisal), and Graham, Benjamin, "The Undistributed Profits Tax and the Investor," LXVI *Yale Law Journal* 1–18, November, 1936, elaborating the views expressed above.

See Chapter 30, "Stock Dividends" online at
www.mhprofessional.com/SecurityAnalysis7.

PART V

Analysis of the Income Account. The Earnings Factor in Common-Stock Valuation

The Evolution of a Value Investor

by Steven Romick

E arning a Bachelor of Science degree in education from Northwestern University is not the most traditional path to a career in finance. Nonetheless, a manager of a successful investment partnership hired me out of college in 1985 as an experiment. He said that he was tired of "unlearning" MBAs of their erroneous theories. It helped that he was friends with my father.

At the time I received that job offer, I had already been accepted to a top law school and had intended to get both JD and MBA degrees, but I thought that a career in investing could be exciting. I lugged home a few dozen prospectuses after my first day on the job, since I didn't have a clue as to what makes something a good investment or a good business, and I had no understanding of how to read a financial statement. Hopefully, the law school that saw fit to accept me once would do so again if this experiment didn't work out. In the meantime, I committed myself to learning as much as I could about investing. Someone directed me to Benjamin Graham's *The Intelligent Investor*, which in turn led me to Graham and David Dodd's *Security Analysis*. And that, along with night classes in accounting at UCLA, became the basis for my education as an investor.

Graham and Dodd introduced me to the foundations of value investing. I learned that if you were to buy a stake in a business with enough of a margin of safety, it would be hard to lose money. If the gap between the price paid and intrinsic value narrowed, then money would be made. If that business were to grow beyond expectations, you'd likely make even more.

What I learned from Graham and Dodd has served me well, but I came to realize that I had remained anchored for longer than I should have to their tight focus on the importance of balance sheets, book value, and current cash flow or earnings. While my evolution as a value investor began with Graham and Dodd, my continuing education in the real world fostered a more nuanced understanding of value. For example, as my career progressed, it became clear to me that many of the better businesses in the world hardly ever trade at a discount to book value, let alone below net working capital, and many of these businesses never seemed to sell at a low multiple of current cash flow. While Graham and Dodd got me to focus on the price paid in comparison to balance sheet metrics as the essential arbiter of downside protection, I've come to appreciate that the substance of a business—things like its competitive position, its profit margins, and its growth rate—has greater importance.

I also came to realize two other things: (1) an assessment of a business's value that includes both its current and estimated future earnings could also provide a valuable margin of safety for the investor, and (2) a seemingly inexpensive business with significant current earnings and apparent balance sheet protection could nonetheless prove to be an unattractive investment if its basic business model is disrupted.

Many investors tend to think of value investing as the practice of owning the shares of humdrum established businesses, often those in cyclical industries, that are not experiencing much growth. Conversely, they consider growth stocks to be those businesses that can grow at a vigorous rate for years while experiencing limited economic cyclicality. But I've come to appreciate that there is not a bright line that divides growth and value. Value can be found in rapidly growing businesses, and growth can be found in what appear to be more traditional value investments.

PHILOSOPHY

Rather than relying on labels, investors need to have their own philosophical paradigm to help frame opportunities and make more productive the quotidian work that occurs day-to-day. Otherwise, as to paraphrase Lewis Carroll's Cheshire Cat in *Alice's Adventures in Wonderland*, "If you don't know where you are going, any road will get you there." I call myself a value investor, but that label does not offer a clear-cut definition. The growth investor presumably believes the companies they own are a "value" as much as a value investor does. My approach is to commit capital to an opportunity when the risk of losing money is limited, while at the same time, there is asymmetric upside potential. I am philosophically aligned with those investors genetically predisposed to not losing money. The whole point of having a margin of safety is that even if everything doesn't go according to plan, investors may still come out close to whole.

My firm's approach is to seek out good quality businesses at a reasonable price. We assess quality in terms of such attributes as a business's return on capital, the defensibility of its market position, its pricing power, the caliber of management, and its growth potential. Holding a concentrated portfolio of shares in good, growing businesses for longer periods is likely to be more beneficial than holding superficially "cheap" securities in inferior businesses and trading them frequently. Indeed, a benefit of owning a high-quality business with favorable growth prospects is that the shares can be held for many years and the business does the work of compounding investors' capital. For taxable investors, this approach is a particularly tax-efficient one.

Investors are best off when they can maintain a longer-term time horizon. I consider time horizons of five to seven years to be a typical market cycle. This can help investors avoid the poor trading decisions that become commonplace in periods of high volatility. A short-term orientation, generally rooted in what I regard as an illusory belief in being able to time a market, can distort thinking and distract from long-range investment goals.

Longer-term success requires accepting periods of under-performance. An investor must maintain the resolve and staying power to avoid market fads and bubbles. There are no shortages of these: recent examples include the whimsical valuations found in the tech-stock/internet bubble of 1997–2000, the housing bubble and associated subprime lending that reached its zenith in 2005–2007, the overreaction to Covid-19's impact in 2020, and the casino mentality that drove many new technology companies to unjustifiable heights that same year.

Great patience is a necessary ingredient in investing, and that patience can be sorely tested. Operational changes at a company might take longer than expected to have an impact. A weak economy might create unexpected challenges to even the best corporate strategies. General market malaise, volatility, or discordant news can vex an investor. While shares in a high quality, growing business purchased at a reasonable price should perform well over time, that doesn't mean they will perform well all of the time.

Investment success is usually not linear; it comes in bursts and is often followed by setbacks. Investors should focus on the destination while bracing themselves for the journey. Even the most successful long-term investments have prolonged periods of underperformance.

Case Study: Microsoft

I find that tracking exceptional businesses over time—those that have compounded investor capital at robust rates for a number of years—helps in identifying attractive entry points for investors. Let's consider Microsoft as a case study.

While its fastest growth might have been behind it by 2010, I believed this great business franchise would deliver reasonable growth.

The market had legitimate fears about recent developments, like the transition from desktop PCs to tablets, real operating system competition for Windows from Apple's iOS, and the potential for Google Chrome to take word-processing market share from Office. Moreover, the Microsoft management team had not been covering itself in glory.

While the stock market was pricing the company as one whose prospects had dimmed, we felt that Microsoft was underappreciated. For example, Salesforce.com, a leading cloud player with $2 billion in revenues, was valued at more than 100x forward earnings. Microsoft was also a leading cloud player, as measured by number of users and revenue, yet the market awarded it just one-twelfth the P/E of Salesforce. To bolster its place in the cloud, in 2010 Microsoft said it would spend 90% of the company's annual $9.6 billion R&D budget on its cloud strategy (a sum more than 4x Salesforce.com total revenues). With Microsoft's R&D staff of 40,000 and a portfolio of product offerings that touches almost every organization in one way or another, we were confident the company would remain relevant in the burgeoning world of corporate cloud computing

While Microsoft's earnings grew at an annualized rate of 17.4% from 1999 to 2009, its stock price declined at an annualized 5.3%. Applying the principles of Graham and Dodd, we determined that Microsoft's intrinsic value was well in excess of its market value and moreover, it had good growth prospects. We bought the stock in 2010 at 12x trailing earnings net of cash (13.4x reported), a 20% discount to the S&P 500 that traded at a P/E of around 15x at that time.

From 2010 to 2020, the company's earnings per share grew at a 10.8% annual rate, aided by repurchasing almost 13% of its shares. Its price earnings multiple expanded to 38.3x trailing earnings, which drove a 25.9% annualized total return over the decade, inclusive of dividends.

Was Microsoft a growth stock or a value stock? It was both! While the company delivered sound earnings growth, the price at which we were able to acquire the shares made it a good value. Purchasing shares in a durable, good quality business that is growing faster than the market but trades at a discount should be a recipe for making money over time.

Finding opportunities with asymmetric risk/reward ratios and better than a 50/50 likelihood of a favorable outcome should improve one's slugging percentage. We believed that was the case with Microsoft, where we felt the odds of success had been miscalculated. The downside would have been limited even if earnings had fallen below our estimates, providing a margin of safety, while the potential for upside was sizable. We also believed the prospects for corporate success improved further once new leadership was put in place in 2014.

Nonetheless, there will always be mistakes while abiding by this process. There's an old Yiddish adage, *Mann tracht, un Gott lacht*—"Man plans, and God laughs." New competitors emerge and disrupt. Venerable competitors raise their game. Management makes mistakes. The macroeconomic environment unleashes a surprise. Since the world is in a constant state of flux, it is imperative to regularly revisit an investment thesis and actively seek reconfirmation.

I have made my share of mistakes. Investments in Circuit City, Semi-Tech Global, and Conseco were all sold at a loss. I failed to properly weigh such crucial elements as changing competition, weak management, and poor underwriting.

Being good at investing doesn't mean batting 1,000; even Major League Baseball's All-Stars get on base only 30% of the time. One of my former partners, Bob Rodriguez, managed the FPA Capital Fund and delivered the best performance of any diversified mutual fund over the quarter century between 1984 and 2010, yet he also had two positions that went to zero. Accepting that you will make some big mistakes is part of investing.

Since we believe investors cannot successfully "time" the market, we believe cash should be the residual component of the investment process. When there are no compelling opportunities at hand, we choose to wait. Sitting on your hands can be difficult when you see the portfolios of others increase in value, but we believe this is better than owning positions you don't find attractive. In their fiscal year 2000 Annual Letter to Shareholders, Leucadia National Corporation's former chairman, Ian Cumming, and former president, Joseph Steinberg, spoke to this dynamic, likening themselves to groundhogs: "We pop out of our holes each and every morning and look around the marketplace for investment opportunities.[1] The first question we ask is, 'Do we see anything that can earn more than the risk-free rate, adjusted for risk?' When the markets are as high as they have been in the last many years, we saw very little of interest and went back down our holes. . . . Patience is required for this process, but it is not complicated." Unfortunately, most investors prefer to see stock prices appreciating before they invest, and they usually sell when they get scared, which is often after experiencing a measurable decline in the value of their portfolio. As a result, the average investor underperforms stock indexes and their own goals, missing many large market moves to the upside, while still participating in the downside.

If you can ultimately match the return of the market while truncating the worst periods of market downside, you're delivering considerable value to your clients. A broad, unfettered mandate has allowed us to accomplish this, using a diverse tool kit to invest in a broad range of markets and instruments. We have allocated capital across a company's capital structure. We have put money into public and private credit, as well as in a variety of market capitalizations, industries, geographies, and asset classes. We have even had short positions from time to time.

I believe it is foolish to give a money manager an overly narrow mandate. The marketing conversations may be easier, but the

---

[1] Leucadia National is now part of Jefferies Financial Group.

investment outcomes are likely to be poorer. I'm confident our clients benefit from our broad mandate. Consider the real estate market; the decision to buy a 10-story, 30-story, or 70-story office building is analogous to buying a small, medium, or large-cap company. The factors are the same in determining the value of these commercial buildings and include examining comparable in-market sales, capitalization rates, replacement costs, and local occupancy levels. A value investor should invest in the building that has the best relationship of price to value, regardless of size. If none of the buildings offer a favorable opportunity, then an investment should not be made.

But what if the 70-story building wasn't priced at a level where you would want to own it, or you can't buy it because it isn't available for sale? What if its first mortgage can be purchased at such a discount that if the building owner were to default, you could foreclose and take control of the building at a price that would make it very hard to lose money? That's what happened to Rockefeller Center in 1995 when Mitsubishi Estate Company, its former majority owner, filed for bankruptcy protection. The debt of Rockefeller Center Properties Inc., the real estate investment trust that held its mortgage, traded at a discount to par, allowing for a double-digit rate of return in a worst-case scenario. In the event of a foreclosure, we had good downside protection: we would have taken control of Rockefeller Center at a discount to replacement cost.

RECOGNIZING OPPORTUNITY

While investors need to be open to opportunities, they also need to be aware of limitations. As we've noted, we seek opportunity across a broad range of countries, markets, securities, and strategies. But simply because we can invest with such breadth does not mean we always should. Instead, we only invest where we believe there is an excellent prospect for return combined with a margin of safety. This applies to a number of asset classes.

Equity

When we make an equity investment in a business, we go beyond balance sheet analyses and the search for a margin of safety to seek out growing businesses with defensible niches, good returns on capital, and reasonable valuations. Such businesses should also be involved in expanding industries in countries where the rule of law is strongly enforced. We shy away from those businesses and industries where the potential range of outcomes is particularly wide and avoid entirely those where our skill set limits our ability to either evaluate the business or handicap the likelihood of a particular outcome. Over the years, we have found our better investments have been those with more than one way to win and with substantial upside potential so that a lot of money can be made if things turn out favorably.

CVS Health, one of the nation's two largest pharmacy retailers, had many of the characteristics we like to see, including inexpensive multiples of cash flow and earnings, industry growth, and good management. Besides its ubiquitous drugstores, it owned Caremark, a pharmacy benefit management (PBM) business. To assess the value of its shares, we separated the business into its two primary parts. In 2010, the company as a whole traded at about 11.5x estimated one-year forward earnings; however, if we applied the same valuations to CVS's PBM that were applied to its peers, then the valuation of the remaining business (primarily CVS pharmacy and retail) was just 9.4x one-year forward earnings—that is, it was inexpensive and there was a margin of safety.

The pharmacy segment was well-positioned to benefit from several industry macro trends, including an aging U.S. population that would be needing more prescription medicines, Federal healthcare reform that would dramatically increase the number of insured and therefore the number of prescription buyers, and improved profit margins from the continuing shift to generic drugs. CVS's private brands represented 17% of total sales. By contrast, Kroger, which operated grocery stores that included drugstores, had 28% private brand penetration. That, in turn, paled next to UK-based Tesco's 50%. This left CVS with a lot of runway for margin expansion. We expected the retail segment to continue to benefit from a greater volume of private label products that would offer a roughly 10 percentage point increase in gross margin.

Meanwhile, CVS had historic growth through acquisitions, and its management was beginning to focus its attention on the substantial potential for operational improvements. At one point, the retail and pharmacy division operated with seven inventory management systems, while Caremark had five different claims platforms. By 2013, their goal was to be down to one platform each, which should allow them to reduce retail store inventories by $2 billion, representing about $1.50 per CVS share, or 4.2% of the share price at that time. Moreover, we believed that CVS's Caremark PBM could improve its contribution to CVS EPS and potentially add an additional $3–$4 per share in value over three years.

We also liked that CVS's skilled management acted with the mentality of an owner/operator. They had substantial financial stakes in the company, which was likely to ensure they pursued what was in the best interests of shareholders.

We believed CVS's pharmacy and retail business had a larger moat than its PBM segment and offered a clear road map for sales growth and operational improvement. Given that there were publicly traded PBM peers like Medco Containment and Express Scripts, we believed we gained exposure to a business at a lower valuation by shorting these more highly valued companies in rough proportion to our conservative view of the intrinsic value of CVS's own PBM.

Company	Price (FPA Cost)	EV/Ebitda		Price/Earnings	
	2010	2011E	2012E	2011E	2012E
CVS	$31.83	6.6x	6.1x	11.5x	10.1x
CVS (net of hedge)		5.2x	4.8x	9.4x	8.6x
Medco Containment	$62.60	9.4x	8.0x	15.4x	12.3x
Express Scripts	$57.42	11.1x	9.6x	17.8x	14.7x

In short, we felt whatever risks CVS faced were outweighed by a low valuation that provided both a likelihood of investment success and a margin of safety. However, successful investing requires not only getting in at a good time but exiting at a good time as well. We accumulated our CVS position in 2010, and about five years later, we concluded that we had received the full benefits of management's solid execution of its business plan, as well as the favorable macro trends we had expected. Going forward, we also felt the changing competitive landscape meant CVS would face more online retailers offering more convenience, often at better prices, and that would put pressure on the sales of its general merchandise in the front of the store.

With the price no longer compelling, we decided to sell our position in CVS in 2015. By then CVS's earnings growth and P/E multiple expansion translated into a stock price that tripled from 2010 to 2015. Meanwhile, we achieved a roughly breakeven result on the short sales.[2]

---

[2] CVS epilogue: Management went on to purchase Aetna in 2018, and despite their claims that this would create a more integrated solution that they could offer their customers, we felt the acquisition was defensive. Our inability to underwrite the likelihood of its success validated our earlier decision to liquidate the position.

Credit

Similar principles have informed our investing in fixed income. There
are three types of credit instruments in which we generally traffic:
performing bonds, distressed debt, and private credits. In buying a
performing bond, we strive to ensure not only that we will be repaid
on a timely basis, but also that we can obtain a yield-to-maturity that
is "equity-like," generally 9% to 11%. Given the greater risks associated
with distressed credits, we have generally set the target yield at a mid-
teens or higher yield to maturity. Our experience is that private credit
markets can be particularly inefficient, thereby offering excess returns
for the risk involved.

The financial markets can be an emotional pendulum that swings
from exuberance to fear. Financial stocks were greatly overvalued in
the euphoric conditions that preceded 2008's Great Financial Crisis,
for example, and then they swung too far in the other direction. But
that mispricing created opportunities in the corporate debt of
financials and distressed mortgages. We knew that subprime
mortgages were particularly hated, so we investigated whether investor
fears might be overblown.

By the end of 2009, the housing market has declined
approximately 29.5% in the largest 20 metro markets. We identified a
basket of distressed mortgages (Alt-A) that we purchased at a 66%
discount to the original appraised home value and a 37% discount to
the 2009 year-end depressed home value. We concluded that the
underlying group of homes would have to decline an additional 30%
before we would be at risk of losing money. With this margin of
safety, we were likely to earn an attractive fixed-income return on our
position with a minimal potential for loss.

Distressed Mortgage Pool #1

Number of loans	246
Original appraised value	$71.4mm
Unpaid principal balance	$58.8mm
2009 estimated home value	$38.6mm
Purchase price	$24.3mm
Discount to original appraised value	66.0%
Discount to current home value	37.0%

At our purchase price, we effectively owned the homes underlying these mortgages at an average value of approximately $99,000 per home. This home value provided us an additional margin of safety because these homes were competitive with apartment rentals at this price.

By midyear 2010, we saw that the performance of this mortgage pool, including interest, had returned more than 30% of our initial capital investment. Looking just at the properties unwound, they generated a total return on our investment of more than 24%. In addition, we earned a better than 8% current yield on our remaining basis in the portfolio.

Since the early returns validated our initial thesis, we continued to buy additional pools, aggregating thousands of mostly nonperforming mortgages. While the early results were better than we would have expected, it was too soon to declare victory. The difficult tail end of the portfolio (deferred maintenance, property damage, and litigious situations) remained. Fortunately, the tail played out within the range of expectations, and the weighted average return of these distressed mortgages turned out to be 12.5%.

Charlie Munger once explained, "Part of the reason we have a decent record is we pick things that are easy. Other people think they're so smart that they can take on things that are really difficult. That

proves to be more dangerous. You have to be shrewd and you have to
be patient."[3] He added, "For an ordinary person, can you imagine just
sitting there for five years doing nothing? It's so contrary to human
nature. You don't feel active. You don't feel useful, so you do
something stupid." A big part of investing is indeed waiting patiently
for a "fat pitch" right over home plate and then swinging aggressively.

DUE DILIGENCE/PROCESS

As value investors, we focus on what is out of favor or misunderstood.
We begin our process of determining which asset classes, industries,
or regions might offer the best opportunities to reach our established
longer-range goal of equity-like returns with less than market risk and
allocate our time accordingly. We spend a lot of time asking a lot of
questions about both the problems and prospects of a potential
investment: What are the forces that will shape its fate? What's the
downside? What if . . . ? We regularly seek a contrary view to avoid
the positive reinforcement of an echo chamber, and we invert our
thesis to see the investment from a different lens, where things may
not look as rosy. These efforts have helped us identify areas of
opportunity, like in early 2009 when distressed debt was priced for a
depression scenario, while avoiding others like financials for much of
the early to mid 2000s when prices failed to reflect the risk of
subprime debt proliferation and the interrelated housing bubble.

We speak to relatively few "investment professionals" outside our
firm. We prefer to spend less time on Wall Street and more time with
people on Main Street—customers, competitors, company executives,
and industry experts—because we believe this interaction improves
our understanding of businesses and industries. We read a lot,
everything from SEC filings and conference call transcripts, to

---

[3] Charlie Munger, Daily Journal Corporation Annual Meeting, September 10, 2014.

pertinent periodicals and industry studies. We work to gain a knowledge edge—a level of understanding of a business or industry that may not be universal. Of course, some companies are followed so extensively that we can't differentiate ourselves in this fashion.

When analyzing businesses, sometimes financial statements tell the story; in those cases, we favor investments that typically appear "cheap" based on reported financial results. But in other situations, information not in the financial statements might be most relevant, such as data regarding a company's position on the industry cost curve, characteristics of its total addressable market, its customer acquisition costs and lifetime value, and real assets marked-to-market. In these situations, our holding might appear "expensive" based on reported financial results, but when you look deeper into these other factors, you can discern why we think such companies are undervalued.

Since we operate with imperfect knowledge, we prefer to establish a potential range of outcomes. We build financial models that look out a few years with low, base, and high cases. A good investment is one where an acceptable return can be had in the base case, and where the high case scenario should be more likely than that of the low case. As we seek to find a good business and understand it, one thing we pay close attention to is its free cash flow—rather than net income, a metric that does not, among other things, take into account capital spending and working capital.

In our view, all sensible fundamental investing is value investing, by which we mean buying a business or asset for less than what it is worth under reasonable scenarios. Buying growing businesses with an adequate margin of safety is just as much value investing as buying, for example, a financial firm at a discount to tangible book value or a holding company at a discount to readily ascertainable net asset value.

Conversely, while growth stock investing is often characterized by high valuations, that doesn't mean the prices are unwarranted. A company trading at 50x earnings that grows 30% annually over the next five years could still deliver a 17.4% return even if its P/E falls to 30x at the end of that span. However, there is a perishability to such high valuations on the front end. If that company grows at a respectable 15% but its P/E shrinks to 20x, then the stock price would be lower by almost 20%, a negative 4.3% IRR in those five years. And that's only if you were right about the earnings over that five-year period.

PSYCHOLOGY/RISK

Thoroughly understanding a business and the competitive landscape of its industry is necessary but not sufficient. This process is significantly enhanced by an ability to work through corporate financial statements (including the footnotes).

There's another crucial skill in successful investing—understanding investor psychology, both your own and that of others. Are you likely to act without a good thesis and proper due diligence, just because you heard a good story? Or are you more apt to not act at all, because you are fearful of losing money? Can you recognize a mistake and sell a stock, or are you more likely to hold on, hoping for a higher price, believing you haven't really experienced a loss until you actually sell the holding? In the last few decades, the study of investor psychology called behavioral finance has taken on a growing role in the field. While we will not rid ourselves of emotions, which make us human, we should recognize the psychological factors—the fear and greed, the inertia as well as hyperactive trading—that can weigh on investors. These are necessarily bound up with the due diligence and rational decision-making that shape investment decisions. Investors need to recognize their own behavioral settings and biases, and compensate for them as warranted.

Attitudes toward risk are always at the core of investing. We cannot eliminate risk, but we can seek to identify it, understand it, minimize it, and be adequately compensated for it. We recognize that mispriced risk can create a buying opportunity. The risks we consider in our investing include credit, currency, business obsolescence, fraud, sovereign, interest rate, inflation, litigation, expropriation, customer concentration, vendor disruption, competition, economic, balance sheet, and political. We believe the ultimate investment risk is a permanent loss of capital.

Some confuse risk and volatility, but what happens as a result of short-term market volatility should be entirely irrelevant. If your portfolio is traded at $1,000 today, and it drops to $750 next year, but you ultimately sell it for $2,000 five years from now, you've compounded your capital at almost 15%. If, on the other hand, the 25% drop to $750 leads you to sell, then you've unfortunately let price, rather than value, be your guide. In this case, volatility has become your enemy. If you have good reason to trust your investment thesis, better to make volatility your friend and buy more at $750, and thereby achieve a 28% return on your incremental investment for the next four years.

While the stock market functions as a voting machine from day to day, it's effectively a weighing machine over the long term, as Graham and Dodd famously observed. Just as a thermometer gives you a temperature reading today but says nothing about tomorrow, a stock price or its movement over shorter time frames say nothing about how much that business might be worth in the future. Like Graham and Dodd before us, the irrational behavior of others has allowed us to both buy at a discount and sell at a premium.

Foolish investing behavior exists broadly. Investors in mutual funds, for example, have a tendency to deify those managers after a great run—the worst possible time. Morningstar developed an illuminating report that held up one particular mutual fund as an unambiguous example of this behavior:[4] "Assets flowing into a certain fund peaked in 2007, following an 80% commodity-fueled return that

---

[4] I've hidden the fund name as the inappropriate timing of purchases and sales was the fault of the fund's investors rather than its portfolio manager.

year, just in time for the fund to shed half its value in 2008. Not only have most investors not pocketed any of the fund's 18% gain during the past decade, but the typical investor in the fund has lost nearly 14% per year—a stunning 32-percentage-point investor return/total return gap." This fund had LIFO investors, last-in first-out, and they came and went at precisely the wrong times.

Just as it's easy to be too active, it's also easy to allow complacency to lead you to do the same things tomorrow that you did yesterday. That's true with investment processes, as well as with the choice of individual investments. Inertia could have kept me in my balance-sheet centric value investing box, but I recognized the need to change. I recognized that the world of business was changing around me at a more accelerated rate than at any point in history, and if I didn't change with it, then I would likely suffer long-term underperformance and irrelevancy. This is particularly true with regard to technological change. While there are a host of social, political, and economic forces buffeting markets, day-by-day technological innovation continues to impair the economics of many businesses and render others obsolete.

The recent accelerated pace of technological innovation has created a multitude of new businesses, while long-established businesses are eroding at an accelerating rate. I could have appreciated more quickly that historic technological advances were adversely impacting the businesses of our more traditional value investments. I was more entrenched philosophically than one of my partners who exhibited greater flexibility and helped move our portfolio, to the benefit of our investors, further in the direction of reasonably priced, higher quality, growing companies characterized by unquestionable competitive strength, solid balance sheets, and shareholder-centric management. An important component of investing includes surrounding yourself with smart people, considering diverse points of view, and being willing to admit when you are wrong.

While businesses face the daily choice of how fast to reinvent themselves, the same can be said of investors, who must not only psychologically condition themselves to question the status quo (including their own) but to gird for the surprises that will inevitably occur that will impact positions in their portfolio. As the Roman philosopher Pliny the Elder noted two thousand years ago, "The only certainty is that nothing is certain," or as has been attributed to that modern-day philosopher Mike Tyson: "Everyone has a plan till they get punched in the mouth."[5] Knowing there will be surprises takes some of the emotional sting out of them when they occur, allowing for a more clinical approach to investing. It keeps us from getting scared out of investments as much as it keeps us from getting scared into them. Knowing in advance that we will periodically be out of favor helps us act rationally when we are. You can't control broad investor behavior but you can control your own.

CONCLUSION

At the end of the day, I am a value investor because it makes sense to me and fits my risk-averse personality. While much has changed since Graham and Dodd wrote their masterwork, investing in companies at a price that offers a margin of safety continues to serve investors well. I believe that value investing is, for me, the best means to preserve capital and generate attractive returns over the long term. The most relevant financial variables and indicators may change, but the principles remain sound.

---

[5] Mike Tyson, "Everyone Has a Plan till They Get Punched in the Mouth. #Miketyson #Vintagetyson Pic.twitter.com/Yjghgqxrkk," Twitter, October 17, 2018, https://twitter.com/MikeTyson/status/1052665864401633299.

Investing with Owner-Operators
The Importance of Alignment

by Benjamin Stein and Zachary Sternberg

The two of us have been very fortunate beneficiaries of the tradition of intellectual generosity and mentorship among value investors, a tradition whose roots date back to Benjamin Graham and David Dodd's publication of *Security Analysis*. In the summer of 2004, as a 17-year-old on the beach, one of us worked through the 1940 edition, underlining the following two sections of this timeless classic.

We must recognize, however, that intrinsic value is an elusive concept . . . The essential point is that security analysis does not seek to determine exactly what is the intrinsic value of a given security. It needs only to establish either that the value is *adequate* to protect a bond or to justify a stock purchase—or else that the value is considerably higher or considerably lower than the market price.

It will be evident from the chart that the influence of what we call analytical factors over the market price is both *partial* and *indirect*—partial, because it frequently competes with purely speculative factors which influence the price in the opposite direction; and indirect because it acts through the intermediary of people's sentiments and decisions. In other words, the market is not a *weighing machine*, on which the value of each issue is recorded by an exact and impersonal mechanism, in accordance with its specific qualities. Rather should we say that the market is a *voting machine*, whereon countless individuals register choices which are the product partly of reason and partly emotion.

(Survey and Approach, pp. 20–22, 27, 1940 edition)

Reading these lines today, they ring as true as ever. They clearly lay out the goal of the security analyst and offer a framework for applying its simplest message: buy companies for less than they are worth, and understand that doing so is an art and not a science. The chart previously referenced sets out the elements that Graham and Dodd considered "intrinsic value factors." These include earnings, dividends, assets, capital structure, terms of the issue, and others. And then there are "future value factors," including management and reputation, competitive conditions and prospects, and possible and probable changes in volume, price, and costs. Future value factors straddle the labels "speculation" and "investment," but since the value of every asset is the present value of its future cash flows, we focus our efforts on the quantitative and qualitative inputs that in our judgment will affect future cash flows.

It was the Berkshire Hathaway annual shareholder letters, written by Graham's best-known student, Warren Buffett, that initially inspired us to go down the value investing path. The basic premise of owning equity in businesses that can grow and increase in value for long periods of time made sense to us immediately. When you invest in a business that is growing, time is your friend; for a stagnant business, it decidedly is not. The idea of long-term business partnership with great managers, such as Warren Buffett has done with Berkshire Hathaway, resonated most with us and felt in sync with our personalities; betting on the movement of share prices, by contrast, felt short-term oriented and unnecessarily transactional.

The two of us met in 2004 during our freshman year at the University of Pennsylvania, and we became friends living in the Spruce House dormitory. At age 20, we ran the math and realized that $1 compounded in value at 20% per year would turn into $9,100 by the time we were 70. Even at 15%, each dollar would be worth $1,084. We quickly came to the conclusion that we should get started immediately.

Time really was our friend, and so long as we remained disciplined and focused, we would have a chance to begin to achieve our goals.

We realized that each day was a fresh opportunity to study a publicly owned business and perhaps reach the conclusion that its shares were worth owning. We knew that we could pull up the annual letters and financial statements of any company in a matter of seconds. It was an exciting idea then (and still is today) that almost every day we could decide to own a small piece of almost any business, in any industry, in any part of the world. So we put some of our own capital together, opened an E*TRADE account, and a year later went around hat in hand to try and gather support from friends and family.

We loved investing from our dorm rooms and love it even more years later. Our original mindset and culture remain part of our value system today. Spruce House is not a hedge fund, but a friends-and-family investment partnership, with only a handful of large institutional partners, and a concentrated portfolio composed of holdings in a group of public and private companies run exclusively by founders. We have no investor relations function or capital raising effort, and we hope to have the same group of partners around the table for decades to come. From the beginning, the idea was to have only a few reliable and long-term oriented partners for whom we could have a material beneficial impact over a very long period of time.

Today, 17 years after we started investing together, we continue to manage the capital entrusted to us as if the two of us would be lifelong partners and the capital were all our own. This is because our sole mission has always been to create an environment that allows us to compound our capital at the highest rate possible, not to build an asset management business.

Over the years we have invested in many different types of businesses, and while we have always had a sharp pencil on price, our most successful investments have all been the result of being right on two essential factors: figuring out *which* businesses we wanted our net worths invested in, and even more important, *whom* we wanted our net worths invested alongside. We call this having the right cards in the right hands.

In Berkshire Hathaway's 1987 annual report, Warren Buffett pointed out "the lack of skill that many CEOs have at capital allocation is no small matter: after ten years on the job, a CEO whose company annually retains earnings equal to 10% of net worth will have been responsible for the deployment of more than 60% of all the capital at work in the business." This simple truth has major consequences for a long-term owner of equity: over time, the returns on capital of the entire business will converge with the returns from these additional capital commitments. Either management thinks rationally about reinvesting capital at satisfactory returns across their four options—to reinvest in the business, acquire other businesses, repurchase shares, or pay dividends—or they don't.

Graham was skeptical on this subject. In the section on the Theory of Common-Stock Investment entitled "The Merits of 'Plowing-back' Earnings," Graham points out the weakness in the assumptions many make regarding managements retaining earnings: "Whatever benefits a business benefits its owners, provided the benefit is not conferred upon the corporation at the expense of the shareholders." That exception is no small matter. Alignment of interests is essential in investing capital, whether in markets or in businesses. If you are going to own interests in companies for the long term, you effectively own the sum of all the decisions made in the organization each day, so understanding managements and how they think seemed very important to us.

We developed the view that founders who live and breathe their businesses 24/7 make the best business partners. They are able to clearly articulate a true-north goal within their organizations, which increases the likelihood that business decisions are made with that goal in mind.

By contrast, a CEO hired to run a company may have multiple objectives as well as a shorter-term orientation. A long-term oriented and focused founder is more likely to be an excellent allocator of capital than committees of board members who do not own much stock in the company. (We jokingly call these "asterisk boards" because the proxy statement lists director ownership of less than 1% as an *.)

One question we always ask public company founders is which decisions they would make differently if they owned 100% of the equity themselves and the company were private. Ideally, they say there are few, if any, differences from what they are already doing. It is crucial that they avoid the short-term orientation that afflicts so many CEOs and boards of publicly traded companies. These founders know that the truth about a company's value resides not in its ephemeral share price but in its prospects for longer-term cash flow generation.

For example, several years ago, Spruce House was one of the largest shareholders of XPO Logistics, one of the largest logistics companies in the United States, run by Brad Jacobs. In December 2018, Jacobs, a meticulous acquirer of businesses, was about to close the largest acquisition in XPO's history. However, XPO's share price dropped 42% in a matter of days, and instead of chasing the deal, Jacobs pivoted virtually overnight and repurchased $1 billion of XPO shares instead, ultimately buying back 24% of the company. As Jacobs explained to us at the time, he looks at each decision through the lens of return on capital and return on time, and both pointed to a large share repurchase instead of the acquisition. He could not beat the return on time achieved by calling his broker and owning a lot more of a business he already knew intimately at a discounted price. This compared very favorably to the effort involved in negotiating, financing, and integrating an acquisition he inherently knew less about than his own business. We find this type of clarity and agility to be rare, and it certainly does not reside in the collective consciousness of most boards. It is not a coincidence that since Jacobs took control of XPO in September of 2011, the compound annual return through year-end 2021 was 36%.

The main qualities we are looking for in founders are rational thinking and intellectual honesty. We get particularly interested when clarity of mind is accompanied by leadership and operating skills and a clear framework for allocating capital to build business value as measured by cash flow per share.

During our summers at Penn, we worked for the noted value investor Bob Robotti, who would come to be both a mentor and a friend. We are eternally grateful and indebted to Bob. He gave us an office, spent as much time teaching us as we could absorb, and always set an example of extraordinary integrity. We also had so much fun traveling around the world with him visiting companies. Bob has hosted many investment partnerships in his office over the years; each of them had a slightly different strategy, but all were heavily influenced by the intellectual roots laid down in *Security Analysis*. Naturally, we studied many of the companies that Bob had owned for years. He knew virtually limitless details on how these businesses worked and the economics of the eco-systems in which they operated, which gave him a nuanced understanding of how the competitive dynamics of an industry were likely to evolve and affect future returns.

Robotti's approach led us to study and invest in many different types of businesses early on. Like so many influenced by Graham and Dodd, we began by focusing on buying companies with balance sheets trading at a discount, with downside protection supported by hard asset value. We owned shares in companies operating in offshore oil drilling, oil and gas services, insurance, and shipping, as well as a housing distribution businesses coming out of the other side of the 2008 financial crisis post their restructuring. These businesses often relied on large amounts of financing, had cyclical end markets, and had customers with substantial bargaining power. While we could mathematically assess the limited downside, the reality was that realizing a return over a long-term holding period would be based largely on management's reinvestment decisions. In some cases, the reinvestment opportunities for such companies were primarily in capital-intensive, cyclical assets, which could be a daunting prospect. Although we experienced some success in such businesses, this tended to be a result of us buying into and then selling them well. We did not think we could count on that continuing into the future. We felt more comfortable trying to identify businesses we might be able to own for a decade or more with excellent-owner operator CEOs at the helm.

One example dates back to 2011, when we began buying shares in FirstService Corporation, which had a market capitalization of just over $1 billion and owned several businesses, including the commercial real estate services brokerage Colliers International; FirstService Residential, the largest manager of housing units in the United States; and several well-known housing-related franchise businesses, such as California Closets. But most important, FirstService Corporation had Jay Hennick, who had compounded the share price since the company went public in 1995 at 20% per year. Hennick is a natural entrepreneur. His first job as a lifeguard in high school sparked the idea of starting a pool-cleaning business, which opened his mind to the opportunities available in selling a broad array of real estate services. Hennick has taken the approach of "creating value one step at a time." By 2015, FirstService and Colliers had become separate public companies, with a combined market capitalization of over $10 billion, and Colliers has since developed a real estate fund management business with $88 billion of assets under management, another real estate services business, which did not exist when we purchased our first shares; good things happen when you invest with good people with the right priorities. (The opposite is also true—unfortunately, we have learned this lesson the hard way.)

We are attracted to investments in which we have both a margin of safety and multiple ways to win. Jay Hennick's disciplined deployment of capital into attractively priced acquisitions, with contractual terms structured to protect the downside, has led to extensive, low-risk growth. The company had one built-in opportunity to expand—as the best and only liquid buyer of Colliers' local market affiliates. This allowed us to project the future by evaluating the company's current operations and past success acquiring franchisees. From time to time we were able to purchase Colliers shares at significant discounts to our conservative estimate of the future cash flows of its various businesses, and even at multiples of our original cost, because of the growth runway that continually seemed to grow longer as Hennick figured out the next strategic move. Today, one of us serves on the Colliers board of directors, and we are as excited about the future of Colliers today as we were 10 years ago.

A number of the companies we have invested in follow an organic-growth-plus-acquisitions model. They may not be in the most exciting industries, but are leaders in areas such as real estate services, flooring, insulation, and logistics. Each enjoys large end markets, provides a basic and necessary product or service, experiences high levels of industry fragmentation, and can capture economies of scale. However, without an owner-operator on a mission to compound capital at high rates, these would not be particularly exciting investments. We think it is important to recognize that the founders did not fall into these businesses, but rather hand-picked these industries for their specific attributes, which would enable large-scale wealth creation through consolidation and continually improving their customer value proposition relative to competitors.

As we spent more and more time with founder CEOs and continued to calibrate how we wanted our net worths invested, we started thinking harder about the future and handicapping what it could look like. For example, we have been long-term shareholders in

Wayfair and Carvana, which we see as logistics networks that are very difficult to build and which enable a consumer offering that is hard to compete with and improves (for both the consumer and for shareholders) with scale. Both of these founder-run businesses are investing heavily in providing consumers the largest selection and fastest delivery of two very basic products, home goods and used cars, which simply cannot be replicated by competitors outsourcing key functions to third parties. We learned to disaggregate and re-create income statements in order to unmask quantifiable growth investments. The goal was to understand underlying unit economics and figure out at what price and what growth rates we would be willing to purchase shares, while also understanding the sources of downside protection in the long term. Because the growth prospects had not yet turned into current cash flows, Ben Graham would call this speculation. We were (and still are) willing to bet that the winner-takes-most dynamics of shifts in the economy, such as those from large, fragmented, offline markets to online markets, will provide more than a commensurate return. This is particularly true for businesses that have a proven ability to operate profitably and are clearly choosing to reinvest current cash flows to meet customer demand.

In many ways, parts of our approach continue to evolve to reflect our own interpretation of Graham, such as when he writes that "investment is most intelligent when it is most businesslike." Over the years, some of the people we look up to most have told us being a businessperson has made them a better investor, and being an investor has made them a better businessperson. We have really taken that to heart and tried to apply it to Graham's observation.

In recent years, a number of wild cards have made investing more challenging, namely the Covid-19 pandemic and the government's monetary and fiscal response, the war in Ukraine, and then the ensuing inflation and central bank tightening. It has become more difficult for

CEOs to forecast and operate their businesses amid such conditions, and we are keenly aware that other unknown challenges certainly lie ahead. As we write, in 2022, many of the businesses we own and follow are available at what appear to be deep bargain levels while management teams adjust operating expenses in the light of shortfalls in forecasted revenues. Meanwhile, short interest has often risen to extraordinary levels across many of these companies, temporarily depressing share prices further. While we have great humility when short sellers take a position in one of our investments and always challenge ourselves to understand where we could be wrong, it is also important to remember Graham and Dodd's sage observation that market prices are there to serve you, not to inform you.

Graham started his partnership when he was 31 years old, and three years later he managed it through the crash of 1929, followed by the Great Depression and then World War II. It's difficult to imagine how much of a challenge it was investing in those times. In the preface to the first edition of *Security Analysis* in May of 1934, Graham and Dodd wrote, "While we were writing, we had to combat a wide-spread conviction that financial debacle was to be the permanent order . . . ." When headlines and casual business conversations cannot help but turn to fear of the macroeconomic environment, we are reminded of Warren Buffett's comment in Berkshire Hathaway's 1994 annual report:[1]

> We will continue to ignore political and economic forecasts, which are an expensive distraction for many investors and businessmen. Thirty years ago, no one could have foreseen the huge expansion of the Vietnam War, wage and price controls, two oil shocks, the resignation of a president, the dissolution of the Soviet Union, a one day drop in the Dow of 508 points (22.6%), or treasury bill yields fluctuating between 2.8% and 17.4% But, surprise—none of these blockbuster

---

Buffett, Warren. "Chairman's Letter." Berkshire Hathaway Inc., March 7, 1995. https://www.berkshirehathaway.com/letters/1994.html.

events made the slightest dent in Ben Graham's investment principles. Nor did they render unsound the negotiated purchases of fine businesses at sensible prices. Imagine the cost to us, then, if we had let a fear of unknowns cause us to defer or alter the deployment of capital. Indeed, we have usually made our best purchases when apprehensions about some macro event were at a peak. Fear is the foe of the faddist, but the friend of the fundamentalist.

We would note, however, that these macro shocks can be particularly painful for higher-growth businesses, because a steep and sudden reduction in demand can have larger implications for their balance sheets than just a few years earlier. All of their revenue and expense line items have so many more dollars running through them than when the firms were smaller. As a result, we have been encouraging faster-growing companies to build in an extra margin of safety in their balance sheets, especially at times when capital is readily available to them and there seems to be no immediate need for it. While we are acutely aware of the costs of dilution from maintaining a stronger balance sheet, we believe managements should always prioritize investing in technology, systems, and talent. Failure to do so can erode a company's competitive advantage and if funded with debt, can limit the company's future flexibility to invest in new, potentially high-returning ideas. In high-growth businesses, which are likely to produce growing sums of free cash flow in the not-too-distant future, ensuring the operating financial strength and depth of talent must be paramount. Maintaining all of the flexibility that comes with being in a position of strength has allowed several of the businesses we own to make acquisitions, repurchase shares at very attractive prices, and continue to build up future earnings power through difficult economic periods. It's powerful if you can work on the numerator and the denominator at the same time.

Investing is hard and often humbling. We are regularly reminded that we must remain intellectually open, constantly learning, and focused on calibrating a multitude of potential opportunities to ensure that each dollar entrusted to us is hard at work. As we have slowly grown our client base over time, we think about how any new partner might behave in difficult times. We seek only those partners who truly have a multidecade view. If you own a very concentrated portfolio of companies as we do, and don't short or hedge, you are guaranteed to have significant volatility in your returns; there is no way around it. Warren Buffett has famously written about having his net worth cut in half three times in his life; Ben Graham reportedly nearly went broke twice. As we write, in the fall of 2022, we are going through one of these very painful drawdowns. A truly long-term view is the only way we know of to look past near-term business performance and short-term share price volatility and to make actionable estimates of value five years from now. Investing with a deep fundamental understanding of each business, a tightly aligned group of partners, and not using leverage are the key ingredients needed to get through these periods. It's crucial to remember that no business grows in a straight line. What might look like obvious rewards from owning successful businesses today were nonetheless tested more than once with periods of anxiety, uncertainty, and stress along the way. The investors we admire most have an even temperament that means not getting too excited in the good times, or too downtrodden and emotional in the tough times. They have the patience and discipline to swing only at pitches they are comfortable with, they have done the work to ride out often unpopular views, and perhaps most important, they all possess a deep sense of optimism that each day the next great investment is out there waiting to be discovered.

CHAPTER 31

Analysis of the
Income Account

IN OUR HISTORICAL DISCUSSION of the theory of investment in common stocks we traced the transfer of emphasis from the net worth of an enterprise to its capitalized earning power. Although there are sound and compelling reasons behind this development, it is none the less one that has removed much of the firm ground that formerly lay—or seemed to lie—beneath investment analysis and has subjected it to a multiplicity of added hazards. When an investor was able to take very much the same attitude in valuing shares of stock as in valuing his own business, he was dealing with concepts familiar to his individual experience and matured judgment. Given sufficient information, he was not likely to go far astray, except perhaps in his estimate of future earning power. The interrelations of balance sheet and income statement gave him a double check on intrinsic values, which corresponded to the formulas of banks or credit agencies in appraising the eligibility of the enterprise for credit.

Disadvantages of Sole Emphasis on Earning Power. Now that common-stock values have come to depend exclusively upon the earnings exhibit, a gulf has been created between the concepts of private business and the guiding rules of investment. When the business man lays down his own statement and picks up the report of a large corporation, he apparently enters a new and entirely different world of values. For certainly he does not appraise his own business solely on the basis of its recent operating results without reference to its financial resources. When in his capacity as investor or speculator the business man elects to pay no attention whatever to corporate balance sheets, he is placing himself at a serious disadvantage in several different respects: In the first place, he is embracing a *new* set of ideas that are alien to his everyday business experience. In the second place, instead of the twofold test of value afforded by both earnings and assets, he is relying upon a *single* and therefore less dependable criterion. In the third place, these earnings statements on which he relies exclusively are subject to more rapid and radical *changes* than those which occur in balance sheets. Hence an exaggerated degree of instability is introduced into his concept of stock values. In the fourth place, the earnings statements are far more subject to *misleading* presentation and mistaken inferences than is the typical balance sheet when scrutinized by an investor of experience.

Warning Against Sole Reliance upon Earnings Exhibit. In approaching the analysis of earnings statements we must, therefore, utter an emphatic warning against exclusive preoccupation with this factor in dealing with investment values. With due recognition of the greatly restricted importance of the asset picture, it must nevertheless be asserted that a company's resources still have some significance and require some attention. This is particularly true, as will be seen later on, because the meaning of any income statement cannot properly be understood except with reference to the balance sheet at the beginning and the end of the period.

Simplified Statement of Wall Street's Method of Appraising Common Stocks. Viewing the subject from another angle, we may say that the Wall-Street method of appraising common stocks has been simplified to the following standard formula:

1. Find out what the stock is earning. (This usually means the earnings per share as shown in the last report.)

2. Multiply these per-share earnings by some suitable "coefficient of quality" which will reflect:

    a. The dividend rate and record.

    b. The standing of the company—its size, reputation, financial position, and prospects.

    c. The type of business (*e.g.,* a cigarette manufacturer will sell at a higher multiple of earnings than a cigar company).

    d. The temper of the general market. (Bull-market multipliers are larger than those used in bear markets.)

The foregoing may be summarized in the following formula:

Price = current earnings per share × quality coefficient.[1]

The result of this procedure is that in most cases the "earnings per share" have attained a weight in determining value that is equivalent to the *weight of all the other factors taken together.* The truth of this is evident if it be remembered that the "quality coefficient" is itself largely determined by the *earnings trend,* which in turn is taken from the stated earnings over a period.

Earnings Not Only Fluctuate but Are Subject to Arbitrary Determination. But these earnings per share, on which the entire edifice of value has come to be built, are not only highly fluctuating but are subject also in extraordinary degree to arbitrary determination and manipulation. It will be illuminating if we summarize at this point the various devices, legitimate and otherwise, by which the per-share earnings may *at the choice of those in control* be made to appear either larger or smaller.

1. By allocating items to surplus instead of to income, or *vice versa.*

2. By over-or understating amortization and other reserve charges.

3. By varying the capital structure, as between senior securities and common stock. (Such moves are decided upon by managements and ratified by the stockholders as a matter of course.)

4. By the use made of large capital funds not employed in the conduct of the business.

Significance of the Foregoing to the Analyst. These intricacies of corporate accounting and financial policies undoubtedly provide a broad field for the activities of the securities analyst. There are unbounded opportunities for shrewd detective work, for critical comparisons, for discovering and pointing out a state of affairs quite different from that indicated by the publicized "per-share earnings."

---

[1] Where there are no earnings or where the amount is recognized as being far below "normal," Wall Street is reluctantly compelled to apply what is at bottom a more rational method of valuation, *i.e.,* one ascribing greater weight to *average* earning power, working capital, etc. But this is the *exceptional* procedure.

That this work may be of exceeding value cannot be denied. In a number of cases it will lead to a convincing conclusion that the market price is far out of line with intrinsic or comparative worth and hence to profitable action based upon this sound foundation. But it is necessary to caution the analyst against overconfidence in the practical utility of his findings. It is always good to know the truth, but it may not always be wise to act upon it, particularly in Wall Street. And it must always be remembered that the truth that the analyst uncovers is first of all not the *whole* truth and, secondly, not the *immutable* truth. The result of his study is only a *more nearly correct version of the past.* His information may have lost its relevance by the time he acquires it, or in any event by the time the market place is finally ready to respond to it.

With full allowance for these pitfalls, it goes without saying, none the less, that security analysis must devote thoroughgoing study to corporate income accounts. It will aid our exposition if we classify this study under three headings, *viz.*:

1. The accounting aspect. Leading question: What are the true earnings for the period studied?

2. The business aspect. Leading question: What indications does the earnings record carry as to the *future* earning power of the company?

3. The aspect of investment finance. Leading question: What elements in the earnings exhibit must be taken into account, and what standards followed, in endeavoring to arrive at a reasonable *valuation* of the shares?

CRITICISM AND RESTATEMENT
OF THE INCOME ACCOUNT

If an income statement is to be informing in any true sense, it must at least present a fair and undistorted picture of the year's operating results. Direct misstatement of the figures in the case of publicly owned companies is a rare occurrence. The Ivar Kreuger frauds, revealed in 1932, partook of this character, but these were quite unique in the baldness as well as in the extent of the deception. The statements of most important companies are audited by independent public accountants, and their reports are reasonably dependable within the rather limited sphere of accounting accuracy.[2] But from the standpoint of common-stock analysis these

---

[2] In recent years several instances of gross overstatements of earnings and current assets in audited statements have come to light—notably the case of McKesson and Robbins

audited statements may require critical interpretation and adjustment, especially with respect to three important elements:

1. Nonrecurrent profits and losses.
2. Operations of subsidiaries or affiliates.
3. Reserves.

General Observations on the Income Account. Accounting procedure allows considerable leeway to the management in the method of treating nonrecurrent items. It is a standard and proper rule that transactions applicable to past years should be excluded from current income and entered as a charge or credit direct to the surplus account. Yet there are many kinds of entries that may technically be considered part of the current year's results but that are none the less of a special and nonrecurrent nature. Accounting rules permit the management to decide whether to show these operations as part of the *income* or to report them as adjustments of *surplus*. Following are a number of examples of entries of this type:

1. Profit or loss on sale of fixed assets.
2. Profit or loss on sale of marketable securities.
3. Discount or premium on retirement of capital obligations.
4. Proceeds of life insurance policies.
5. Tax refunds and interest thereon.
6. Gain or loss as result of litigation.
7. Extraordinary write-downs of inventory.
8. Extraordinary write-downs of receivables.
9. Cost of maintaining nonoperating properties.

Wide variations will be found in corporate practice respecting items such as the foregoing. Under each heading examples may be given of either inclusion in or exclusion from the income account. Which is the better accounting procedure in some of these cases may be a rather controversial question, but, as far as the analyst is concerned, his object requires that all these items be segregated from the *ordinary operating results* of the year. For what the investor chiefly wants to learn from an annual report is the *indicated earning power* under the given set of

---

Company in 1938. (Interstate Hosiery Mills and Illinois Zinc Corporation are other examples also uncovered in 1938.) Despite the sensational impression caused by the McKesson and Robbins scandal, it must be recognized that over a long period of years only an infinitesimal percentage of publicly owned companies have been involved in frauds of this character.

conditions, *i.e.*, what the company might be expected to earn year after year if the business conditions prevailing during the period were to continue unchanged. (On the other hand, as we shall point out later, all these extraordinary items enter properly into the calculation of earning power as actually shown over a *period of years* in the past.)

The analyst must endeavor also to adjust the reported earnings so as to reflect as accurately as possible the company's interest in results of controlled or affiliated companies. In most cases consolidated reports are made, so that such adjustments are unnecessary. But numerous instances have occurred in which the statements are incomplete or misleading because either: (1) they fail to reflect any part of the profits or losses of important subsidiaries or (2) they include as income dividends from subsidiaries that are substantially less or greater than the current earnings of the controlled enterprises.

The third aspect of the income account to which the analyst must give critical attention is the matter of reserves for depreciation and other amortization, and reserves for future losses and other contingencies. These reserves are subject in good part to arbitrary determination by the management. Hence they may readily be overstated or understated, in which case the final figure of reported earnings will be correspondingly distorted. With respect to amortization charges, another and more subtle element enters which may at times be of considerable importance, and that is the fact that the deductions from income, as calculated by the management based on the book cost of the property, may not properly reflect the amortization that the *individual investor* should charge against his own commitment in the enterprise.

Nonrecurrent Items: Profits or Losses from Sale of Fixed Assets. We shall proceed to a more detailed discussion of these three types of adjustment of the reported income account, beginning with the subject of nonrecurrent items.[3] Profits or losses from the sale of fixed assets belong quite obviously to this category, and they should be excluded from the

---

[3] The Securities Act of 1933 and the Securities Exchange Act of 1934 specifically empower the Commission to prescribe the methods to be followed in differentiating between recurrent and nonrecurrent items in the reports of registered companies which must be filed with the S.E.C. and with the exchanges [Sec. 19(a) of the 1933 act and Sec. 13(b) of the 1934 act]. The initial registration forms (A-1, A-2 and 10) and the annual report form (10-K) require separation of nonrecurrent profit-and-loss items within the income account.

year's result in order to gain an idea of the "indicated earning power" based on the assumed continuance of the business conditions existing then. Approved accounting practice recommends that profit on sales of capital assets be shown only as a credit to the surplus account. In numerous instances, however, such profits are reported by the company as part of its current net income, creating a distorted picture of the earnings for the period.

Examples: A glaring example of this practice is presented by the report of the Manhattan Electrical Supply Company for 1926. This showed earnings of $882,000, or $10.25 per share, which was regarded as a very favorable exhibit. But a subsequent application to list additional shares on the New York Stock Exchange revealed that out of this $882,000 reported as earned, no less than $586,700 had been realized through the sale of the company's battery business. Hence the earnings from ordinary operations were only $295,300, or about $3.40 per share. The inclusion of this special profit in income was particularly objectionable because in the very same year the company had charged to surplus extraordinary *losses* amounting to $544,000. Obviously the special losses belonged to the same category as the special profits, and the two items should have been grouped together. The effect of including the one in income and charging the other to surplus was misleading in the highest degree. Still more discreditable was the failure to make any clear reference to the profit from the battery sale either in the income account itself or in the extended remarks that accompanied it in the annual report.[4]

During 1931 the United States Steel Corporation reported "special income" of some $19,300,000, the greater part of which was due to "profit on sale of fixed property"—understood to be certain public-utility holdings in Gary, Indiana. This item was included in the year's earnings and resulted in a final "net income" of $13,000,000. But since this credit was definitely of a nonrecurring nature, the analyst would be compelled to eliminate it from his consideration of the 1931 operating results, which would accordingly register a *loss* of $6,300,000 before preferred dividends. United States Steel's accounting method in 1931 is at variance with its previous

---

[4] The president's remarks contained only the following in respect to this transaction: "After several years of unprofitable experience in the battery business the directors arranged a sale of same on satisfactory terms." In 1930 a scandal developed by reason of the president's manipulation of this company's shares on the New York Stock Exchange.

policy, as shown by its treatment of the large sums received in the form of income-tax refunds in the three preceding years. These receipts were not reported as current income but were credited directly to surplus.

Profits from Sale of Marketable Securities. Profits realized by a business corporation from the sale of marketable securities are also of a special character and must be separated from the ordinary operating results.

Examples: The report of National Transit Company, a former Standard Oil subsidiary, for the year 1928 illustrates the distorting effect due to the inclusion in the income account of profits from this source. The method of presenting the story to the stockholders is also open to serious criticism. The consolidated income account for 1927 and 1928 was stated in approximately the following terms:

Item	1927	1928
Operating revenues	$3,432,000	$3,419,000
Dividends, interest, and miscellaneous income	463,000	370,000
Total revenues	$3,895,000	$3,789,000
"Operating expenses, including depreciation and profit and loss direct items" (in 1928 "including profits from sale of securities")	3,264,000	2,599,000
Net income	$631,000	$1,190,000
(Earned per share)	($1.24)	($2.34)

The increase in the earnings per share appeared quite impressive. But a study of the detailed figures of the parent company alone, as submitted to the Interstate Commerce Commission, would have revealed that $560,000 of the 1928 income was due to its profits from the sale of securities. This happens to be almost exactly equal to the increase in consolidated net earnings over the previous year. Allowing on the one hand for income tax and other offsets against these special profits but on the other hand for probable additional profits from the sale of securities by the manufacturing subsidiary, it seems likely that all or nearly all of the apparent improvement in earnings for 1928 was due to nonoperating items. Such gains must clearly be eliminated from any comparison or calculation of *earning power*. The form of statement resorted to by National Transit, in which such profits are applied to *reduce operating expenses,* is bizarre to say the least.

The sale by the New York, Chicago, and St. Louis Railroad Company, through a subsidiary, of its holdings of Pere Marquette stock in 1929 gave rise later to an even more extraordinary form of bookkeeping manipulation. We shall describe these transactions in connection with our treatment of items involving nonconsolidated subsidiaries. During 1931 F.W. Woolworth Company included in its income a profit of nearly $10,000,000 on the sale of a part interest in its British subsidiary. The effect of this inclusion was to make the per-share earnings appear larger than any previous year, when in fact they had experienced a recession. It is somewhat surprising to note that in the same year the company charged against *surplus* an additional tax accrual of $2,000,000 which seemed to be closely related to the special profit included in *income.*

Reduction in the market value of securities should be considered as a nonrecurring item in the same way as losses from the sale of such securities. The same would be true of shrinkage in the value of foreign exchange. In most cases corporations charge such write-downs, when made, against surplus. The General Motors report for 1931 included both such adjustments, totaling $20,575,000 as deductions from *income,* but was careful to designate them as "extraordinary and nonrecurring losses."

Methods Used by Investment Trusts in Reporting Sale of Marketable Securities. Investment-trust statements raise special questions with respect to the treatment of profits or losses realized from the sale of securities and changes in security values. Prior to 1930 most of these companies reported profits from the sale of securities as part of their regular income, but they showed the appreciation on *unsold* securities in the form of a memorandum or footnote to the balance sheet. But when large losses were taken in 1930 and subsequently, they were shown in most cases not in the income account but as charges against capital, surplus, or reserves. The *unrealized* depreciation was still recorded by most companies in the form of an explanatory comment on the balance sheet, which continued to carry the securities owned at original cost. A minority of investment trusts reduced the carrying price of their portfolio to the market by means of charges against capital and surplus.

It may logically be contended that, since dealing in securities is an integral part of the investment-trust business, the results from sales and even the changes in portfolio values should be regarded as ordinary rather than extraordinary elements in the year's report. Certainly a study confined to the interest and dividend receipts less expenses would prove of negligible value. If *any* useful results can be expected from an analysis of investment-trust exhibits, such analysis must clearly be based on the three items: investment income, profits or losses on the sale of securities and changes in market values. It is equally obvious that the gain or shrinkage, so computed, in any one year is no indication whatever of *earning power* in the recurrent sense. Nor can an average taken over several years have any significance for the future unless the results are first compared with some appropriate measure of general market performance. Assuming that an investment trust has done substantially better than the relevant "average," this is of course a *prima facie* indication of capable management. But even here it would be difficult to distinguish confidently between superior ability and luckier guesses on the market.

The gist of this critique is twofold: (1) the over-all change in principal value is the only available measure of investment-trust performance, but (2) this measure cannot be regarded as an index of "normal earning power" in any sense analogous to the recorded earnings of a well-entrenched industrial business.[5]

Similar Problem in the Case of Banks and Insurance Companies. A like problem is involved in analyzing the results shown by insurance companies and by banks. Public interest in insurance securities is concentrated largely upon the shares of fire insurance companies. These enterprises represent a combination of the insurance business and the investment-trust business. They have available for investment their capital funds plus substantial amounts received as premiums paid in advance. Generally speaking, only a small portion of these funds is subject to legal restrictions as regards investment, and the balance is handled in much the same way as the resources of the investment trusts. The underwriting business as such has rarely proved highly profitable. Frequently it shows a deficit, which is offset, however, by interest and dividend income. The profits or losses shown on security operations, including changes in their market value, exert a predominant influence upon the public's attitude toward

---

[5] See Appendix Note 47 for a summary of the findings of the S.E.C. in its investigation of management investment-trust performance and for further comment by the authors concerning the record and practices of management investment trusts.

fire-insurance-company stocks. The same has been true of bank stocks to a smaller, but none the less significant, degree. The tremendous overspeculation in these issues during the late 1920s was stimulated largely by the participation of the banks, directly or through affiliates, in the fabulous profits made in the securities markets.

Since 1933 banks have been required to divorce themselves from their affiliates, and their operations in securities other than government issues have been more carefully supervised and restricted. But in view of the large portion of their resources invested in bonds, substantial changes in bond prices are still likely to exert a pronounced effect upon their reported earnings.

The fact that the operations of financial institutions generally—such as investment trusts, banks and insurance companies—must necessarily reflect changes in security values makes their shares a dangerous medium for widespread public dealings. Since in these enterprises an increase in security values may be held to be part of the year's profits, there is an inevitable tendency to regard the gains made in good times as part of the "earning power" and to value the shares accordingly. This results of course in an absurd overvaluation, to be followed by collapse and a correspondingly excessive depreciation. Such violent fluctuations are particularly harmful in the case of financial institutions because they may affect public confidence. It is true also that rampant speculation (called "investment") in bank and insurance-company stocks leads to the ill-advised launching of new enterprises, to the unwise expansion of old ones and to a general relaxation of established standards of conservatism and even of probity.

The securities analyst, in discharging his function of investment counsellor, should do his best to discourage the purchase of stocks of banking and insurance institutions by the ordinary small investor. Prior to the boom of the 1920s such securities were owned almost exclusively by those having or commanding large financial experience and matured judgment. These qualities are needed to avoid the special danger of misjudging values in this field by reason of the dependence of their reported earnings upon fluctuations in security prices.

Herein lies also a paradoxical difficulty of the investment-trust movement. Given a proper technique of management, these organizations may well prove a logical vehicle for the placing of small investor's funds. But considered as a marketable security dealt in by small investors, the investment-trust stock itself is a dangerously volatile instrument. Apparently this troublesome factor can be held in check only be educating or by effectively cautioning the general public on the interpretation of investment-trust reports. The prospects of accomplishing this are none too bright.

Profits Through Repurchase of Senior Securities at a Discount. At times a substantial profit is realized by corporations through the repurchase of their own senior securities at less than par value. The inclusion of such gains in current income is certainly a misleading practice, first, because they are obviously nonrecurring and, second, because this is at best a questionable sort of profit, since it is made at the expense of the company's own security holders.

Example: A peculiar example of this accounting practice was furnished as long ago as 1915 by Utah Securities Corporation, a holding company controlling Utah Power and Light Company. The following income account illustrates this point:

Year Ended March 31, 1915

Earnings of Utah Securities Corporation	
including surplus of subsidiaries accruing to it	$ 771,299
Expenses and taxes	30,288
Net earnings	$ 741,011
Profit on redemption of 6% notes.	1,309,657
Income from all sources accruing to Utah	
Securities Corporation	$ 2,050,668
Deduct interest charges on 6% notes	1,063,009
Combined net income for the year.	$ 987,659

The foregoing income account shows that the chief "earnings" of Utah Securities were derived from the repurchase of its own obligations at a discount. Had it not been for this extraordinary item the company would have failed to cover its interest charges.

The widespread repurchases of senior securities at a substantial discount constituted one of the unique features of the 1931–1933 depression years. It was made possible by the disproportion that existed between the strong cash positions and the poor earnings of many enterprises. Because of the latter influence the senior securities sold at low prices, and because of the former the issuing companies were able to buy them back in large amounts. This practice was most in evidence among the investment trusts.

Examples: The International Securities Corporation of America, to use an outstanding example, repurchased in the fiscal year ending November 30, 1932, no less than $12,684,000 of its 5% bonds, representing nearly half of the issue. The average price paid was about 55, and the operation showed a profit of about $6,000,000, which served to offset the shrinkage in the value of the investment portfolio.

In the industrial field we note the report of Armour and Company for 1932. This showed net earnings of $1,633,000 but only after including in income a profit of $5,520,000 on bonds bought in at a heavy discount. Similarly, more than all of the 1933 net of Goodrich Rubber, United Drug, Bush Terminal Building Company and others was ascribable to this nonrecurring source. A like condition was disclosed in the report of United Cigar-Whelan Stores for the first half of 1938.[6] (Observe, on the other hand, that some companies, *e.g.,* Gulf States Steel Corporation in 1933, have followed the better practice of crediting this profit direct to surplus.)

A contrary result appears when senior securities are retired at a cost exceeding the face or stated value. When this premium involves a large amount, it is always charged against surplus and not against current income.

Examples: As prominent illustrations of this practice, we cite the charge of $40,600,000 against surplus made by United States Steel Corporation in 1929, in connection with the retirement at 110 of $307,000,000 of its own and subsidiaries' bonds, also the charge of $9,600,000 made against surplus in 1927 by Goodyear Tire and Rubber Company, growing out of the retirement at a premium of various bond and preferred-stock issues and their replacement by new securities bearing lower coupon and dividend rates. From the analyst's standpoint, either profit or expense in such special transactions involving the company's own securities should be regarded as nonrecurring and excluded from the operating results in studying a single year's performance.

A Comprehensive Example. American Machine and Metals, Inc. (successor to Manhattan Electrical Supply Company mentioned earlier in this chapter), included in its current *income* for 1932 a profit realized from the repurchase of its own bonds at a discount. Because the reports for 1931 and 1932 illustrate to an unusual degree the arbitrary nature of

---

[6] The report for the full year 1938 credited this profit to *surplus.*

Report of American Machine and Metals, Inc., for 1931 and 1932

Item	1932	1931
Income account:		
Net before depreciation and interest	Loss $ 136,885	Profit $101,534
Add profit on bonds repurchased	174,278	270,701
Profit, including bonds repurchased	37,393	372,236
Depreciation	87,918	184,562
Bond interest	119,273	140,658
Final net profit or loss	Loss 169,798	Profit 47,015
Charges against capital, capital surplus and earned surplus:		
Deferred moving expense and mine development	111,014	
Provision for losses on:		
Doubtful notes, interest thereon, and claims	600,000	
Inventories	385,000	
Investments	54,999	
Liquidation of subsidiary	39,298	
Depletion of ore reserves	28,406	32,515
Write-down of fixed assets (net)	557,578	
Reduction of ore reserves and mineral rights	681,742	
Federal tax refund, etc.	cr. 7,198	cr. 12,269
Total charges not shown in income account	$2,450,839	$20,246
Result shown in income account	dr. 169,798	cr. 47,015
Received from sale of additional stock	cr. 44,000	
Combined change in capital and surplus	dr. $2,576,637	cr. $26,769

much corporate accounting, we reproduce herewith in full the income account and the appended capital and surplus adjustments.

We find again in 1932, as in 1926, the highly objectionable practice of including extraordinary profits in income while charging special losses to surplus. It does not make much difference that in the later year the nature of the special profit—gain through repurchase of bonds at less than par—is disclosed in the report. Stockholders and stock buyers for the most part pay attention only to the final figure of earnings per share, as presented by the company; nor are they likely to inquire carefully into the manner in which it is determined. The significance of some of the charges made by this company against surplus in 1932 will be taken up later under the appropriate headings.

Other Nonrecurrent Items. The remaining group of nonrecurrent profit items is not important enough to merit detailed discussion. In most cases it is of minor consequence whether they appear as part of the year's earnings or are credited to surplus where they properly belong.

Examples: Gimbel Brothers included the sum of $167,660, proceeds of life insurance policies, in income for 1938, designating it as a "nontrading item." On the other hand, United Merchants and Manufacturers, receiving a similar payment of $1,579,000 in its 1938 fiscal year, more soundly credited it to surplus—although it had sustained a large loss from operations.

Bendix Aviation Corporation reported as income for the year 1929 the sum of $901,282 received in settlement of a patent suit, and again in 1931 it included in current earnings an amount $242,656 paid to it as back royalties collected through litigation. The 1932 earnings of Gulf Oil Corporation included the sum of $5,512,000 representing the value of oil previously in litigation. By means of this item, designated as nonrecurrent, it was able to turn a loss of $2,768,000 into a profit of $2,743,000. Although tax refunds are regularly shown as credits to surplus only, the accumulated interest received thereon sometimes appears as part of the income account, *e.g.*, $2,000,000 reported by E. I. du Pont de Nemours and Company in 1926 and an unstated but apparently much larger sum included in the earnings of United States Steel for 1930.

CHAPTER 32

Extraordinary Losses and Other Special Items in the Income Account

THE QUESTION OF NONRECURRENT LOSSES is likely to create peculiar difficulties in the analysis of income accounts. To what extent should writedowns of inventories and receivables be regarded as extraordinary deductions not fairly chargeable against the year's operating results? In the disastrous year 1932 such charge-offs were made by nearly every business. The accounting methods used showed wide divergences, but the majority of companies spared their income accounts as much as possible and subtracted these losses from surplus. On the other hand the milder inventory losses of the 1937–1938 recession were almost universally charged into the earnings statement.

Inventory losses are directly related to the conduct of the business and are, therefore, by no means extraordinary in their general character. The collapse of inventory values in 1931–1932 might be considered extraordinary in its *extent*, in the same way as the business results as a whole were exceptional. It follows from this reasoning that if the 1931–1932 results are taken into account at all, *e.g.*, in computing a long-term average, all losses on inventories and receivables must be considered part of the operating deficit of those years even though charged to surplus. In Chap. 37 we shall consider the role of extraordinary years in determining the average earning power.

Manufactured Earnings. An examination of the wholesale charges made against surplus in 1932 by American Machine and Metals, detailed in Chap. 31, suggests the possibility that *excessive* provision for losses may have been made in that year with the intention of benefiting future income accounts. If the receivables and inventories were written down to an unduly low figure on December 31, 1932, this artificially low "cost price" would give rise to a correspondingly inflated profit in the following years. This point may be made clear by the use of hypothetical figures as follows:

Assume fair value of inventory and receivables on
    Dec. 31, 1932 to be $2,000,000
Assume profit for 1933 based on such fair value   200,000
But assume that, by special and excessive charges to surplus,
    the inventory and receivables had been written down to   1,600,000
Then the amounts realized therefrom will show a
    correspondingly greater profit for 1933, which might
    mean *reported* earnings for 1933 of   600,000
This would be three times the proper figure.

The foregoing example illustrates a whole set of practices that constitute perhaps the most vicious type of accounting manipulation. They consist, in brief, of taking sums out of surplus (or even capital) and then reporting these same sums as income. The charge to surplus goes unnoticed; the credit to income may have a determining influence upon the market price of the securities of the company.[1] We shall later point out that the "conservative" writing down of the property account has precisely this result, in that it permits a decreased depreciation charge and hence an increase in the apparent earnings. The dangers inherent in accounting methods of this sort are the more serious because they are so little realized by the public, so difficult to detect even by the expert analyst and so impervious to legislative or stock-exchange correction.

The basing of common-stock values on reported per-share earnings has made it much easier for managements to exercise an arbitrary and

---

[1] The United States Industrial Alcohol Company reports for 1932 and subsequent years reflect a situation somewhat similar to that here suggested. This company departed from its usual practice in 1932 by setting up a reserve for $1,500,000 out of surplus to reduce molasses inventory to estimated current market value. (Previously this item had regularly been carried at cost.) Later reports state that earnings for 1933, 1934 and 1935 had benefited by this reserve to the extent of $772,000, $677,000 and $51,000 respectively. Significantly, income tax for 1934 was based on $677,000 less than the reported profit. (See pp. 626–627 in the sixth edition for a broad summary of the effect of this company's accounting methods on its reported per-share earnings for the years 1929–1938.)

unwholesome control over the price level of their shares. Whereas it should be emphasized that the overwhelming majority of managements are honest, it must be emphasized also that loose or "purposive" accounting is a highly contagious disease.

Reserves for Inventory Losses. The accounting for inventory losses is frequently complicated by the use of reserves set up before the loss is actually realized. These reserves are usually created by a charge to surplus, on the theory that it is a function of the surplus account to act as a sort of contingency reserve to absorb unusual future losses. If later the inventory shrinkage actually takes place, it is naturally charged against the reserve already created to meet it. The result is that in *no year* does the income account reflect the inventory loss, although it is just as much a hazard of operations as a decline in selling prices. When a company charges inventory losses to surplus—whether directly or through the intermediary of a reserve device—the analyst must take this practice carefully into account, especially in comparing the published results with those of other companies. A good illustration of this rule is afforded by a comparison of the reports submitted by United States Rubber Company and by Goodyear Tire and Rubber Company for the years 1925–1927, during which time rubber prices were subject to wide fluctuations.

In these three years Goodyear charged against *earnings* a total of $11,500,000 as reserves against decline of raw-material prices. Of this amount one-half was used to absorb actual losses sustained and the other half was carried forward into 1928 (and eventually used up in 1930).

United States Rubber during this period charged a total of $20,446,000 for inventory reserves and write-downs, all of which was absorbed by actual losses taken. But the form of annual statement, as submitted to the stockholders, excluded these deductions from income and made them appear as special adjustments of surplus. (In 1927, moreover, the inventory loss of $8,910,000 was apparently offset by a special credit of $8,000,000 from the transfer of *past* earnings of the crude-rubber producing subsidiary.)

The result of these divergent bases of reporting annual income was that the per-share earnings of the two companies, as compiled by the statistical manuals, made an entirely misleading comparative exhibit. The following per-share earnings are taken from *Poor's Manual* for 1928:

Year	U.S. Rubber	Goodyear
1925	$14.92	$9.45
1926	10.54	3.79
1927	1.26	9.02
3-year average	$ 8.91	$7.42

For proper comparative purposes the statements must manifestly be considered on an identical basis, or as close thereto as possible. Such a comparison might be made by three possible methods, *viz.:*

1. As reported by United States Rubber, *i.e.*, excluding inventory reserves and losses from the current income account.

2. As reported by Goodyear, *i.e.*, reducing the earnings of the period of high prices for crude rubber by a reserve for future losses and using this reserve to absorb the later shrinkage.

3. Eliminating such reserves, as an arbitrary effort of the management to level out the earnings. On this basis the inventory losses would be deducted from the results of the year in which they were actually sustained. (The Standard Statistics Company's analysis of Goodyear includes a revision of the reported earnings in conformity with this approach.)

We have then, for comparative purposes, three statements of the per-share earnings for the period:

Year	1. Omitting adjustments of inventory		2. Allowing for inventory adjustments, as made by the companies		3. Excluding *reserves* and charging losses to the year in which decline occurred	
	U.S. Rubber	Goodyear	U.S. Rubber	Goodyear	U.S. Rubber	Goodyear
1925	$14.92	$18.48	$11.21	$9.45	$14.92	$18.48
1926	10.54	3.79	0.00	3.79	14.71(d)	2.53(d)
1927	1.26*	13.24	9.73(d)*	9.02	1.26*	13.24
3-year average	$8.91	$12.17	$0.49	$7.42	$0.49	$9.73

* Excluding credit for profits made prior to 1926 by United States Rubber Plantations, Inc.

The range of market prices for the two common issues during this period suggests that the accounting methods followed by United States

Rubber served rather effectively to obscure the unsatisfactory nature of its results for these years.

Year	U.S. Rubber common		Goodyear common	
	High	Low	High	Low
1925	97	33	50	25
1926	88	50	40	27
1927	67	37	69	29
Average of highs and lows	62		40	

More recently United States Rubber has followed the Goodyear practice of taking out of the earnings of prosperous years a reserve for future inventory shrinkage. As a result of this policy, the company somewhat understated its earnings for 1935 and 1936 but overstated them for 1937.

A More Recent Contrast. The packing industry supplies us with a more extreme divergence in the method used by two companies to handle the matter of probable future inventory losses.

Wilson and Company set up a reserve of $750,000 prior to the beginning of its 1934 fiscal year, for "Fluctuation in Inventory Valuation." This was taken partly from surplus and partly from income. In 1934 it reduced its opening inventory by this reserve, thus increasing the year's reported profit by $750,000. The S.E.C., however, required it to amend its registration statement so as to credit this amount to surplus and not to income.

On the other hand, Swift and Company reduced its reported earnings in the fiscal years 1933–1935 by $16,767,000, which was set up as a reserve for future inventory decline. In 1938 the expected decline occurred; but instead of drawing on this reserve to spare the income account, the company charged the full loss against the year's operations and then transferred $11,000,000 of the reserve directly to surplus. In this exceptional case the net income for the six-year period 1933–1938 was *understated*, since amounts were actually taken out of income and turned over to surplus.[2]

Other Elements in Inventory Accounting. The student of corporate reports must familiarize himself with two permissible variations from the

---

[2] Standard Statistics has restated the Swift annual reports by listing the 1933–1935 deductions for inventory declines as charges to *surplus*.

usual accounting practice in handling inventories. As is well known, the standard procedure consists of taking inventory at the close of the year at the lower of cost or market. The "cost of goods sold" is then found by adding purchases to the opening inventory and subtracting the closing inventory, valued as described.

Last-In, First-Out. The first variation from this method consists of taking as the cost of goods sold the actual amount paid for the *most recently acquired* lots. The theory behind this method is that a merchant's selling price is related mainly to the current replacement price or the recent cost of the article sold. The point is of importance only when there are substantial changes in unit values from year to year; it cannot affect the aggregate reported profits over a long period but only the division of results from one year to another; it may be useful in reducing income tax by avoiding alternations of loss and profit due to inventory fluctuations.[3]

The Normal-Stock or Basic-Stock Inventory Method. A more radical method of minimizing fluctuations due to inventory values has been followed by a considerable number of companies for some years past. This method is based on the theory that the company must regularly carry a certain physical stock of materials and that there is no more reason to vary the value of this "normal stock" from year to year—because of market changes—than there would be to vary the value of the manufacturing plant as the price index rises or falls and to reflect this change in the year's operations. In order to permit the base inventory to be carried at an unchanging figure, the practice is to mark it down to a very low unit price level—so low that it should never be necessary to reduce it further to get it down to current market.

As long ago as 1913 National Lead Company applied this method to the three principal constituents of its inventory, *viz.*, lead, tin and antimony. The method was subsequently adopted also by American Smelting and Refining Company and American Metals Company. Some of the New England cotton mills had followed a like policy, prior to the collapse in the cotton market in 1930, by carrying their raw cotton and work in process at very low base prices. In 1936 the Plymouth Cordage Company

---

[3] Corporations were first permitted to use this so-called "last-in, first-out" method by the terms of the Revenue Acts of 1938 and 1939, applying to 1939 and subsequent years. A hypothetical example to illustrate the difference between the two inventory methods is given in Appendix Note 48.

adopted the normal-stock inventory method, after following a somewhat similar policy in 1933–1935; and for purpose of concrete illustration we supply the relevant data for this company, covering the years 1930–1939, in Appendix Note 49.

Idle-Plant Expense. The cost of carrying nonoperating properties is almost always charged against income. Many statements for 1932 earmarked substantial deductions under this heading.

Examples: Youngstown Sheet and Tube Company reported a charge of $2,759,000 for "Maintenance Expense, Insurance and Taxes of Plants, Mines, and Other Properties that were Idle." Stewart Warner Corporation followed the exceptional policy of charging against *surplus* in 1932, instead of income, the sum of $309,000 for "Depreciation of Plant Facilities not used in current year's production." The 1938 report of Botany Worsted Mills contained a charge against income of $166,732, picturesquely termed "cost of idleness."

The analyst may properly consider idle-plant expense as belonging to a somewhat different category from ordinary charges against income. In theory, at least, these expenses should be of a temporary and therefore nonrecurring type. Presumably the management can terminate these losses at any time by disposing of or abandoning the property. If, for the time being, the company elects to spend money to carry these assets along in the expectation that future value will justify the outlay, it does not seem logical to consider these assets as equivalent to a permanent liability, *i.e.*, as a permanent drag upon the company's earning power, which makes the stock worth considerably less than it would be if these "assets" did not exist.

Example: The practical implications of this point are illustrated by the case of New York Transit Company, a carrier of oil by pipe line. In 1926, owing to new competitive conditions, it lost all the business formerly carried by its principal line, which thereupon became "idle plant." The depreciation, taxes and other expenses of this property were so heavy as to absorb the earnings of the company's other profitable assets (consisting of a smaller pipe line and high-grade-bond investments). This created an apparent net loss and caused the dividend to be passed. The price of the stock accordingly declined to a figure far less than the company's holdings of cash and marketable securities alone. In this uncritical appraisal by the stock market, the idle asset was considered equivalent to a serious and permanent liability.

In 1928, however, the directors determined to put an end to these heavy carrying charges and succeeded in selling the unused pipe line for a substantial sum of money. Thereafter, the stockholders received special cash distributions aggregating $72 per share (nearly twice the average market price for 1926 and 1927), and they still retained ownership of a profitable business which resumed regular dividends. Even if no money had been realized from the idle property, its mere abandonment would have led to a considerable increase in the value of the shares.

This is an impressive, if somewhat extreme, example of the practical utility of security analysis in detecting discrepancies between intrinsic value and market price. It is customary to refer with great respect to the "bloodless verdict of the market place," as though it represented invariably the composite judgment of countless shrewd, informed and calculating minds. Very frequently, however, these appraisals are based on mob psychology, on faulty reasoning, and on the most superficial examination of inadequate information. The analyst, on his side, is usually unable to apply his technique effectively to correcting or taking advantage of these popular errors, for the reason that surrounding conditions change so rapidly that his own conclusions may become inapplicable before he can profit by them. But in the exceptional case, as illustrated by our last example, the facts and the logic of the case may be sharply enough defined to warrant a high degree of confidence in the practical value of his analysis.

Deferred Charges. A business sometimes incurs expenses that may fairly be considered as applicable to a number of years following rather than to the single 12-month period in which the outlay was made. Under this heading might be included the following:

> Organization expense (legal fees, etc.).
> Moving expenses.
> Development expenses (for new products or processes, also for opening up a mine, etc.).
> Discount on obligations sold.

Under approved accounting methods such costs are spread over an appropriate period of years. The amount involved is entered upon the balance sheet as a Deferred Charge, which is written off by annual charges against earnings. In the case of bond-discount the period is fixed by the life of the issue; mine development expenses are similarly prorated on the basis of the tonnage mined. For most other items the number of years must be arbitrarily taken, five years being a customary figure.

In order to relieve the reported earnings of these annual deductions it has become common practice to write off such expense applicable to future years by a single charge against surplus. In theory this practice is improper, because it results in the understatement of operating expenses for a succeeding period of years and hence in the exaggeration of the net income. If, to take a simple example, the president's salary were paid for ten years in advance and the entire outlay charged against surplus as a "special expense," it is clear that the profits of the ensuing period would thereby be overstated.[4] There is the danger also that expenses of a character frequently repeated, e.g., advertising campaigns, or cost of developing new automobile models, might be omitted from the income account by designating them as deferred charges and then writing them off against surplus.[5]

Ordinarily the amounts involved in such accounting transactions are not large enough to warrant the analyst's making an issue of them. Security analysis is a severely practical activity, and it must not linger over matters that are not likely to affect the ultimate judgment. At times however, these items may assume appreciable importance.

Examples: The Kraft Cheese Company for example, during some years prior to 1927 carried a substantial part of its advertising outlays as a deferred charge to be absorbed in the operations of subsequent years. In 1926 it spent about $1,000,000 for advertising and charged only one-half of this amount against current income. But in the same year the balance of this expenditure was deducted from surplus, and furthermore an additional $480,000 was similarly written off against surplus to cancel the balance carried forward from prior years as a deferred charge. By this means the company was able to report to its stockholders the sum of $1,071,000 as earned for 1926. But when in the following year it applied to list additional shares, it found it necessary to adopt a less questionable

---

[4] See Appendix Note 50 for details of accounting methods followed by Interstate Department Stores in 1934–1936, which resembled somewhat the hypothetical case given above.

[5] A similar objection lies against the practice of charging against surplus the loss incurred in closing chain-store units. *Example:* The charge of $326,000 made by F. G. Shattuck Company for this purpose in 1935. This would seem to be a recurrent expense of chain-store enterprises, which frequently add and close down units.

basis of reporting its income to the New York Stock Exchange, so that its profit for 1926 was restated to read $461,296, instead of $1,071,000.

The 1932 report of International Telephone and Telegraph Company showed various charges *against surplus* aggregating $35,817,000, which included the following: "Write-off of certain deferred charges that have today no tangible value although originally set up to be amortized over a period of years in accordance with accepted accounting principles, $4,655,696."

Hudson Motor Car Company charged against surplus instead of income the following items (among others) during 1930–1931.

1930	Special adjustment of tools and materials due to development of new models	$2,266,000
1931	Reserve for special tools	2,000,000
	Rearrangement of plant equipment	633,000
	Special advertising	1,400,000

In 1933 Hecker Products (then called Gold Dust Corporation) appropriated out of surplus the sum of $2,000,000 as a reserve for the "net cost of introduction and exploitation of new products." About three-quarters of this amount was expended in years 1933–1936, and the balance then transferred to "General and Contingency Reserves."

The effect of these accounting practices is to relieve the reported earnings of expenditures that most companies charge currently thereagainst, and that in any event should be charged against earnings in installments over a short period of years.

Amortization of Bond Discount. Bonds are usually floated by corporations at a price to net the treasury less than par. The discount suffered is part of the cost of borrowing the money, *i.e.*, part of the interest burden, and it should be amortized over the life of the bond issue by an annual charge against earnings, included with the statement of interest paid. It was formerly considered "conservative" to write off such bond discounts by a single charge against surplus, in order not to show so intangible an item among the assets on the balance sheet. More recently these write-offs against surplus have become popular for the opposite reason, *viz.*, to eliminate future annual deductions from earnings and in that way to make the shares more "valuable."

Example: Associated Gas and Electric Company charged against surplus in 1932 the sum of $5,892,000 for "debt discount and expense" written off.

This practice has aroused considerable criticism in recent years both from the New York Stock Exchange and from the S.E.C. As a result of these objections a number of companies have reversed their previous charge to surplus and are again charging amortization of bond discounts annually against earnings.[6]

---

[6] See the changed accounting practice of Northern States Power Company (Minnesota) following a controversy over this point in connection with the registration of a bond issue in 1984. (The total amount involved here was over $8,000,000.) It is noteworthy, also, that *even on called bonds* companies have been required to carry forward the unamortized discount to be written off by an annual charge against earnings during the life of the refunding issue. (See the report of Columbia Gas and Electric Company for 1936, p. 17.)

Some of the bond refundings in recent years seem to have involved a surprisingly small net saving of interest when the premium paid to retire the old issue is taken into account. Perhaps an explanation of some of these operations lies in the fact that (1) the company has been able to charge both the premium paid and the balance of the original discount against surplus, thus relieving future earnings of this very real burden; and (2) both these items have been chargeable to profits subject to *income tax*, thus reducing this tax substantially and increasing the *apparent* profits for the year.

CHAPTER 33

Misleading Artifices in the Income Account. Earnings of Subsidiaries

Flagrant Example of Padded Income Account. On comparatively rare occasions, managements resort to padding their income account by including items in earnings that have no real existence. Perhaps the most flagrant instance of this kind that has come to our knowledge occurred in the 1929–1930 reports of Park and Tilford, Inc., an enterprise with shares listed on the New York Stock Exchange. For these years the company reported net income as follows:

> 1929—$1,001,130 = $4.72 per share.
> 1930—   124,563 = 0.57 per share.

An examination of the balance sheets discloses that during these two years the item of Good-will and Trade-marks was written up successively from $1,000,000 to $1,600,000 and then to $2,000,000, and these increases *deducted* from the expenses for the period. The extraordinary character of the bookkeeping employed will be apparent from a study of the condensed balance sheets as of three dates, shown on the next page.

These figures show a reduction of $1,600,000 in net current assets in 15 months, or $1,000,000 more than the cash dividends paid. This shrinkage was concealed by a $1,000,000 write-up of Good-will and Trademarks. No statement relating to these amazing entries was vouchsafed to the stockholders in the annual reports or to the New York Stock Exchange in subsequent listing applications. In answer to an individual inquiry, however, the company stated that these additions to Good-will and Trademarks represented expenditures for advertising and other sales efforts to develop the business of Tintex Company, Inc., a subsidiary.[1]

---

[1] In the 1930 report the wording in the balance sheet was changed from "Good-will and Trade-marks" to "Tintex Good-will and Trade-marks." In 1939 the Good-will item was written off, and the $1,000,000 write-up of 1929–1930 deducted from earned surplus.

439

Park and Tilford, Inc.

Balance sheet	Sept. 30, 1929	Dec. 31, 1929	Dec. 31, 1930
Assets:			
Fixed assets	$1,250,000	$1,250,000	$1,250,000
Deferred charges	132,000	163,000	32,000
Goodwill and Trademarks	1,000,000	1,600,000	2,000,000
Net current assets	4,797,000	4,080,000	3,154,000
Liabilities:			
Bonds and mortgages	2,195,000	2,195,000	2,095,000
Capital and surplus	4,984,000	4,898,000	4,341,000
Total of assets and liabilities	$7,179,000	$7,093,000	$6,436,000

Adjusted earnings	First 9 months, 1929	Last 3 months, 1929	Year, 1929	Year, 1930
Earnings for stock as reported	$929,000	$ 72,000	$1,001,000	$125,000
Cash dividends paid	463,000	158,000	621,000	453,000
Charges against surplus				229,000
Added to capital and surplus	466,000	decrease 86,000	380,000	decrease 557,000
Earnings for stock as corrected (excluding increase in intangibles and deducting charges to surplus)	929,000	528,000(*d*)	401,000	504,000(*d*)

The charging of current advertising expense to the good-will account is inadmissible under all canons of sound accounting. To do so without any disclosure to the stockholders is still more discreditable. It is difficult to believe, moreover, that the sum of $600,000 could have been expended for this purpose by Park and Tilford in the *three months* between September 30 and December 31, 1929. The entry appears therefore to have included a recrediting to *current* income of expenditures made in a *previous period*, and to that extent the results for the fourth quarter of 1929 may have been flagrantly distorted. Needless to say, no accountants' certificate accompanied the annual statements of this enterprise.

Balance-Sheet and Income-Tax Checks upon the Published Earnings Statements. The Park and Tilford case illustrates the necessity of relating an analysis of income accounts to an examination of the appurtenant balance sheets. This is a point that cannot be stressed too strongly, in view of Wall Street's naïve acceptance of reported income and reported earnings per share. Our example suggests also a further check upon the reliability of the published earnings statements, *viz.*, by the amount of the federal income tax accrued. The taxable profit can be calculated fairly readily from the income-tax accrual, and this profit compared in turn with the earnings reported to stockholders. The two figures should not necessarily be the same, since the intricacies of the tax laws may give rise to a number of divergences.[2] We do not suggest that any effort be made to reconcile the amounts absolutely but only that very wide differences be noted and made the subject of further inquiry.

The Park and Tilford figures analyzed from this viewpoint supply the suggestive results as shown in the table on the following page.

The close correspondence of the tax accrual with the reported income during the earlier period makes the later discrepancy appear the more striking. These figures eloquently cast suspicion upon the truthfulness of the reports made to the stockholders during 1927–1929, at which time considerable manipulation was apparently going on in the shares.

This and other examples discussed herein point strongly to the need for independent audits of corporate statements by certified public accountants. It may be suggested also that annual reports should include a detailed reconcilement of the net earnings reported to the shareholders

---

[2] See Appendix Note 51 for a brief résumé of these divergences.

with the net income upon which the federal tax is paid. In our opinion a good deal of the information relative to minor matters that appears in registration statements and prospectuses might be dispensed with to general advantage; but if, in lieu thereof, the S.E.C. were to require such a reconcilement, the cause of security analysis would be greatly advanced.

Period	Federal income tax accrued	Rate of tax, per cent	Net income before federal tax	
			A. As indicated by the tax accrued	B. As reported to the stockholders
5 mo. to Dec. 1925	$36,881	13	$283,000	$ 297,000
1926	66,624	13^1/$_2$	493,000	533,000
1927	51,319	13^1/$_2$	380,000	792,000
1928	79,852	12	665,000	1,315,000
1929	81,623*	11	744,000	1,076,000

* Including $6,623 additional paid in 1931.

Another Extraordinary Case of Manipulated Accounting. An accounting vagary fully as extraordinary as that of Park and Tilford, though exercising a smaller influence on the reported earnings, was indulged in by United Cigar Stores Company of America, from 1924–1927. The "theory" behind the entries was explained by the company for the first time in May 1927 in a listing application that contained the following paragraphs:[3]

> The Company owns several hundred long-term leaseholds on business buildings in the principal cities of the United States, which up until May, 1924, were not set up on the books. Accordingly, at that time they were appraised by the Company and Messrs. F. W. Lafrentz and Company, certified public accountants of New York City, in excess of $20,000,000.
>
> The Board of Directors have, since that time, authorized every three months the setting up among the assets of the Company a portion of this valuation and the capitalization thereof, in the form of dividends, payable in Common Stock at par on the Common Stock on the quarterly basis of 1^1/$_4$% on the Common Stock issued and outstanding.

[3] See application to list 6% Cumulative Preferred Stock of United Cigar Stores Company of America on the New York Stock Exchange, dated May 18, 1927 (Application #A-7552).

The entire capital surplus created in this manner has been absorbed by the issuance of Common Stock at par for an equal amount and accordingly is not a part of the existing surplus of the Company. No cash dividends have been declared out of such capital surplus so created.

The present estimated value of such leaseholds, using the same basis of appraisal as in 1924, is more than twice the present value shown on the books of the Company.

The effect of the inclusion of "Appreciation of Leaseholds" in earnings is shown herewith:

Year	Net earnings as reported	Earned per share of common ($25-par basis)	Market range ($25-par basis)	Amount of "Leasehold Appreciation" included in earnings	Earned per share of common excluding lease appreciation
1924	$6,697,000	$4.69	64–43	$1,248,000	$3.77
1925	8,813,000	5.95	116–60	1,295,000*	5.05
1926	9,855,000	5.02	110–83	2,302,000	3.81
1927	9,952,000†	4.63	100–81	2,437,000	3.43

* The 5% stock dividend paid in 1925 amounted to $1,737,770. There is an unexplained difference between the two figures, which in the other years are identical.
† Excluding refund of federal taxes of $229,017 applicable to prior years.

In passing judgment on the inclusion of leasehold appreciation in the current earnings of United Cigar Stores, a number of considerations might well be borne in mind.

1. Leaseholds are essentially as much a liability as they are an asset. They are an obligation to pay rent for premises occupied. Ironically enough, these very leaseholds of United Cigar Stores eventually plunged it into bankruptcy.

2. Assuming leaseholds may acquire a capital value to the occupant, such value is highly intangible, and it is contrary to accounting principles to mark up above actual cost the value of such intangibles in a balance sheet.

3. If the value of any capital asset is to be marked up, such enhancement must be credited to Capital Surplus. By no stretch of the imagination can it be considered as *income*.

4. The $20,000,000 appreciation of the United Cigar Stores leases took place prior to May 1924, but it was *treated as income in subsequent years*. There was thus no connection between the $2,437,000 appreciation included in the profits of 1927 and the operations or developments of that year.

5. If the leaseholds had really increased in value, the effect should be visible in *larger earnings* realized from these favorable locations. Any other recognition given this enhancement would mean counting the same value twice. In fact, however, allowing for extensions of the business financed by additional capitalization, the per-share earnings of United Cigar Stores showed no advancing trend.

6. Whatever value is given to leaseholds must be amortized over the life of the lease. If the United Cigar Stores investors were paying a high price for the shares because of earnings produced by these valuable leases, then they should *deduct* from earnings an allowance to write off this capital value by the time it disappears through the expiration of the leases.[4] The United Cigar Stores Company continued to amortize its leaseholds on the basis of *original cost*, which apparently was practically nothing.

The surprising truth of the matter, therefore, is that the effect of the appreciation of leasehold values—if it had occurred—should have been to *reduce* the subsequent operating profits by an increased amortization charge.

7. The padding of the United Cigar Stores income for 1924–1927 was made the more reprehensible by the failure to reveal the facts clearly in the annual reports to shareholders.[5] Disclosure of the essential facts to the New York Stock Exchange was made nearly three years after the practice was initiated. It may have been compelled by legal considerations growing out of the sale to the public at that time of a new issue of preferred stock, underwritten by large financial institutions. The following year the policy of including leasehold appreciation in earnings was discontinued.

These accounting maneuvers of United Cigar Stores may be fairly described, therefore, as the *unexplained* inclusion in current earnings of

---

[4] This subject is treated fully in a succeeding chapter.

[5] The reports stated the "Net Profit for the year, including Enhancement of Leasehold Values" (giving amount of the latter), but no indication was afforded that this enhancement was arbitrarily computed and had taken place in previous years.

an *imaginary* appreciation of an *intangible* asset—the asset being in reality a *liability*, the enhancement being related to a *previous* period and the proper effect of the appreciation, if it had occurred, being to *reduce* the subsequent realized earnings by virtue of higher amortization charges.

The federal-income-tax check, described in the Park and Tilford example, will also give interesting results if applied to United Cigar Stores as shown in the table below.

Moral Drawn from Foregoing Examples. A moral of considerable practical utility may be drawn from the United Cigar Stores example. When an enterprise pursues questionable accounting policies, *all* its securities must be shunned by the investor, no matter how safe or attractive some of them may appear. This is well illustrated by United Cigar Stores Preferred, which made an exceedingly impressive statistical showing for many successive years but later narrowly escaped complete extinction. Investors confronted with the strange bookkeeping detailed above might have reasoned that the issue was still perfectly sound, because, when the overstatement of earnings was corrected, the margin of safety remained more than ample. Such reasoning is fallacious. You cannot make a quantitative deduction to allow for an unscrupulous management; the only way to deal with such situations is to avoid them.

Year	Federal tax reserve	Income before tax		
		A. Indicated by tax reserve	B. Reported to stockholders	C. Reported to stockholders less leasehold appreciation
1924	$700,000	$5,600,000	$7,397,000	$6,149,000
1925	825,000	6,346,000	9,638,000	8,343,000
1926	900,000	6,667,000	10,755,000	8,453,000
1927	900,000	6,667,000	10,852,000*	8,415,000*
1928	700,000	5,833,000	9,053,000	9,053,000
1929	13,000	118,000	3,132,000†	3,132,000†
1930	none	none	1,552,000	1,552,000

* Eliminating tax refund of $229,000 evidently applicable to prior years.
† This is also reported as $2,947,000, after an adjustment.

Fictitious Value Placed on Stock Dividends Received. From 1922 on most of the United Cigar Stores common shares were held by Tobacco Products Corporation, an enterprise controlled by the same interests. This was an important company, the market value of its shares averaging more than $100,000,000 in 1926 and 1927. The accounting practice of Tobacco Products introduced still another way of padding the income account, *viz.*, by placing a fictitious valuation upon stock dividends received.

For the year 1926 the company's earnings statement read as follows:

Net income	$10,790,000
Income tax	400,000
Class *A* dividend	3,136,000
Balance for common stock	7,254,000
Earned per share	11
Market range for common	117–95

Detailed information regarding the company's affairs during that period has never been published (the New York Stock Exchange having been unaccountably willing to list new shares on submission of an extremely sketchy exhibit). Sufficient information is available, however, to indicate that the net income was made up substantially as follows:

Rental received from lease of assets to American Tobacco Co.	$ 2,500,000
Cash dividends on United Cigar Stores common (80% of total paid) ..	2,950,000
Stock dividends on United Cigar Stores common	
(par value $1,840,000), less expenses	5,340,000
	$10,790,000

It is to be noted that Tobacco Products must have valued the stock dividends received from United Cigar Stores at about three times their face value, *i.e.*, at three times the value at which United Cigar charged them against surplus. Presumably the basis of this valuation by Tobacco Products was the market price of United Cigar Stores shares, which price was easily manipulated due to the small amount of stock not owned by Tobacco Products.

When a holding company takes into its income account stock dividends received at a higher value than that assigned them by the subsidiary that pays them, we have a particularly dangerous form of pyramiding of earnings. The New York Stock Exchange, beginning in 1929, has made stringent regulations forbidding this practice. (The point was discussed in Chap. 30.) In the case of Tobacco Products the device was especially objectionable because the stock dividend was issued in the first instance to represent a fictitious element of earnings, *i.e.*, the appreciation of leasehold values. By unscrupulous exploitation of the holding-company mechanism these imaginary profits were effectively multiplied by three.

On a consolidated earnings basis, the report of Tobacco Products for 1926 would read as follows:

American Tobacco Co. lease income, less income tax, etc.	$2,100,000
80% of earnings on United Cigar Stores common	6,828,000*
	$8,928,000
Class A dividend	3,136,000
Balance for common	$5,792,000
Earned per share	$7.27

* Excluding leasehold appreciation.

The reported earnings for Tobacco Products common given as $11 per share are seen to have been overstated by about 50%.

It may be stated as a Wall-Street maxim that where manipulation of accounts is found, stock juggling will be found also in some form or other. Familiarity with the methods of questionable finance should assist the analyst and perhaps even the public, in detecting such practices when they are perpetrated.[6]

SUBSIDIARY COMPANIES AND CONSOLIDATED REPORTS

This title introduces our second general type of adjustment of reported earnings. When an enterprise controls one or more important subsidiaries, a *consolidated* income account is necessary to supply a true

---

[6] To avoid an implication of inconsistency, because of our favorable comments on Tobacco Products Corporation $6\frac{1}{2}$s, due 2022, in a previous chapter, we must point out that a complete change of management took place in this situation during 1930. There have also been two complete changes in the management of United Cigar Stores and its successor.

picture of the year's operations. Figures showing the parent company's results only are incomplete and may be quite misleading. As previously remarked, they may either understate the earnings by not showing all the current profits made by the subsidiaries, or they may overstate the earnings by failure to deduct subsidiaries' losses or by including dividends from subsidiaries in excess of their actual income for the year.

Former and Current Practices. In earlier years disclosure of subsidiaries' results was a matter of arbitrary election by management, and in many cases important data of this kind were kept secret.[7] For some time prior to 1933 the New York Stock Exchange had insisted in connection with *new* listings that the results of subsidiaries be presented either in a consolidated statement or separately. But since passage of the 1934 act, all registered companies are required to supply this information in their annual reports to the Commission, and therefore practically all follow the same procedure in their statements to stockholders.

Degree of Consolidation. Even in so-called "consolidated statements" the degree of consolidation varies considerably. Woolworth consolidates its domestic and Canadian subsidiaries but not its foreign affiliates. American Tobacco consolidates only its wholly owned domestic subsidiaries. Most utilities now issue consolidated reports including all companies controlled by them (by ownership of a majority of the voting stock) and deduct the portion of the earnings applicable to others under the heading of "minority interest."[8] In the railroad field results are rarely consolidated unless the subsidiary is both 100% owned and also operated as an integral part of the system. Hence, Atlantic Coast Line does not reflect its share of the results after dividends of Louisville and Nashville, which is 51% owned but separately operated. The same is true with respect to the 53% voting control of Wheeling and Lake Erie held by the Nickel Plate (New York, Chicago, and St. Louis Railroad Company).

---

[7] For a discussion of the misleading effect of such policies in former years, see references to Reading Company, Consolidated Gas Company (now Consolidated Edison Company), and Warren Brothers Company, on pp. 380–381 of the first edition of this work. Prior to the S.E.C. legislation, most railroad companies failed to supply any information regarding the earnings of their nontransportation subsidiaries, some of which were of substantial importance. *Examples:* Northern Pacific, Atchison.

[8] North American Company has been somewhat exceptional in that it consolidates only subsidiaries at least 75% owned and thus excludes two important companies in which its interest in 1939 was 73.5 and 51%, respectively.

Allowance for Nonconsolidated Profits and Losses. It is now frequent procedure for industrial companies to indicate either in the income account or in a footnote thereto their equity in the profits or losses of nonconsolidated subsidiaries after allowance for dividends.

Examples: The 1938 report of American Tobacco Company showed by way of footnote that dividends received from nonconsolidated subsidiaries exceeded their earnings by $427,000. Hercules Powder reported a similar figure of $257,514 for that year, in footnote form, whereas prior to 1937 it had included its share of the undistributed earnings of such affiliates under the heading "Other Income." Railroad companies handle this matter differently. The Atchison, for example, now supplies full balance sheet and income account data of affiliates in an Appendix to its own report, which continues to reflect only the dividends received from these companies.

The analyst should adjust the reported earnings for the results of nonconsolidated affiliates, if this has not already been done in the income account and if the amounts involved are significant. The criterion here is not the technical question of control but the *importance* of the holdings.

Examples: On the one hand it is not customary, nor does it seem worth while, to make such calculations with respect to the holdings of Union Pacific in Illinois Central and other railroads. These holdings, although substantial, do not bulk large enough to affect the Union Pacific common stock materially. On the other hand, the adjustment is clearly indicated in the case of the ownership of Chicago, Burlington, and Quincy stock by Northern Pacific and Great Northern, each holding less than a controlling interest (48.6%).

Year	Du Pont earnings per share	Adjustments to reflect Du Pont's interest in operating results of General Motors	Earnings per share of Du Pont as adjusted
1929	$6.99	+$2.07	$9.06
1930	4.52	+ 0.04	4.56
1931	4.30	− 0.51	3.79
1932	1.81	− 1.35	0.46
1933	2.93	+ 0.43	3.36
1934	3.63	+ 0.44	4.07
1935	5.02	+ 1.30	6.32
1936	7.53	+ 0.77	8.30
1937	7.25	+ 0.57	7.82
1938	3.74	+ 0.61	4.35

Similarly, the interest of Du Pont in General Motors, representing about 23% of the total issue, is undoubtedly significant enough in its effect on the owning company to warrant adjustment of its earnings to reflect the results of General Motors. This is actually done by Du Pont each year in the form of an adjustment of *surplus* to reflect the previous year's change in the book value of its General Motors holdings. The analyst would prefer, however, to make the adjustment concurrently and to include it in the calculated earnings of Du Pont. The effect of such adjustments on the earnings of Du Pont for 1929–1938 is shown in the previous table.

The report of General Motors Corporation for 1931 is worthy of appreciative attention because it includes a supplementary calculation of the kind suggested in this and the previous chapter *i.e.*, exclusive of special and nonrecurring profits or losses and inclusive of General Motors' interest in the results of nonconsolidated subsidiaries. The report contains the following statement of per-share earnings for 1931 and 1930:

Earnings per Share, Including the Equity in Undivided Profits or Losses of Nonconsolidated Subsidiaries

Year	Including nonrecurrent items	Excluding nonrecurrent items
1931	$2.01	$2.43
1930	3.25	3.04

Suggested Procedure for Statistical Agencies. Although this procedure may seem to complicate a report, it is in fact a salutary antidote against the oversimplification of common-stock analysis which resulted from exclusive preoccupation with the single figure of per-share earnings. The statistical manuals and agencies have naturally come to feature the per-share earnings in their analyses of corporations. They might, however, perform a more useful service if they omitted a calculation of the per-share earnings in all cases where the company's reports appear to contain irregularities or complications in any of the following directions and where a satisfactory correction is not practicable:

1. By reason of nonrecurrent items included in income or because of charges to surplus that might properly belong in the income account.

2. Because current results of subsidiaries are not accurately reflected in the parent company's statements.

3. Because the depreciation and other amortization charges are irregularly computed.[9]

Special Dividends Paid by Subsidiaries. When earnings of nonconsolidated subsidiaries are allowed to accumulate in their surplus accounts, they may be used later to bolster up the results of a poor year by means of a large special dividend paid over to the parent company.

Examples: Such dividends, amounting to $11,000,000, were taken by the Erie Railroad Company in 1922 from the Pennsylvania Coal Company and Hillside Coal and Iron Company. The Northern Pacific Railway Company similarly eked out its depleted earnings in 1930 and 1931 by means of large sums taken as special dividends from the Chicago, Burlington, and Quincy Railroad Company, the Northern Express Company, and the Northwestern Improvement Company, the last being a real-estate, coal and iron-ore subsidiary. The 1931 earnings of the New York, Chicago, and St. Louis Railroad Company included a back dividend of some $1,600,000 on its holdings of Wheeling and Lake Erie Railway Company Prior Preferred Stock, only a part of which was earned in that year by the Wheeling road.

This device of concealing a subsidiary's profits in good years and drawing upon them in bad ones may seem quite praise-worthy as a method of stabilizing the reported earning power. But such benevolent deceptions are frowned upon by enlightened opinion, as illustrated by the more recent regulations of the New York Stock Exchange which insist upon full disclosure of subsidiaries' earnings. It is the duty of management to disclose the truth and the whole truth about the results of each period; it is the function of the stockholders to deduce the "normal earning power" of their company by averaging out the earnings of prosperity and depression. Manipulation of the reported earnings by the management even for the desirable purpose of maintaining them on an even keel is objectionable none the less because it may too readily lead to manipulation for more sinister reasons.

Distorted Earnings Through Parent-Subsidiary Relationships. Examples are available of the use of the parent-subsidiary relationship to produce astonishing distortions in the reported income. We shall give two illustrations taken from the railroad field. These instances are the more impressive because the stringent accounting regulations of the Interstate

---

[9] Standard Statistics does not calculate per-share earnings if depreciation has not been deducted.

Commerce Commission might be expected to prevent any misrepresentation of earnings.

Examples: In 1925 Western Pacific Railroad *Corporation* paid dividends of $7.56 upon its preferred stock and $5 upon its common stock. Its income account showed earnings slightly exceeding the dividends paid. These earnings consisted almost entirely of dividends aggregating $4,450,000 received from its operating subsidiary, the Western Pacific Railroad *Company.* The year's earnings of the railroad, itself, however, were only $2,450,000. Furthermore its accumulated surplus was insufficient to permit the larger dividend that the parent company desired to report as its income for the year. To achieve this end, the parent company went to the extraordinary lengths of *donating* the sum of $1,500,000 to the operating company, and it immediately took the same money back as a *dividend* from its subsidiary. The donation it charged against its *surplus;* the receipt of the same money as dividends it reported as *earnings.* In this devious fashion it was able to report $5 "earned" upon its common stock, when in fact the applicable earnings were only about $2 per share.

In support of our previous statement that bad accounting practices are contagious, we may point out that the Western Pacific example of 1925 was followed by the New York, Chicago, and St. Louis Railroad Company ("Nickel Plate") in 1930 and 1931. The details are briefly as follows:

In 1929 Nickel Plate sold, through a subsidiary, its holdings of Pere Marquette stock to Chesapeake and Ohio, which was under the same control. A profit of $10,665,000 was realized on this sale, which gain was properly credited to surplus. In 1930 Nickel Plate needed to increase its income; whereupon it took the $10,665,000 profit out of its surplus, returned it to the subsidiary's treasury and then took $3,000,000 thereof in the form of a "dividend" from this subsidiary, which it included in its 1930 *income.* A similar dividend of $2,100,000 was included in the income account for 1931.

These extraordinary devices may have been resorted to for what was considered the necessary purpose of establishing a net income large enough to keep the company's bonds legal for trust-fund investments.[10]

---

[10] For an extreme example of this kind see the annual reports of Wabash Railway Company and Ann Arbor Railroad Company for 1930 and the comment thereon at p. 1022 of *Moody's*

The result, however, was the same as that from all other misleading accounting practices, *viz.*, to lead the public astray and to give those "on the inside" an unfair advantage.

Broader Significance of Subsidiaries' Losses. We have suggested in this chapter that security analysis must make full allowance for the results of subsidiaries, whether they be profits or losses. But the question may well be raised: Is the loss of a subsidiary necessarily a direct offset against the parent company's earnings? Why should a company be worth *less* because it owns something—in this case, an unprofitable interest? Could it not at any time put an end to the loss by selling, liquidating or even abandoning the subsidiary? Hence, if good management is assumed, must we not also assume that the subsidiary losses are at most temporary and therefore to be regarded as nonrecurring items rather than as deductions from normal earnings?

This point is similar to that discussed in the previous chapter relative to idle-plant expense and similar also to the matter of unprofitable *divisions* of a business, to be touched upon later. There is no one, simple answer to the questions that we have raised. Actually, if the subsidiary could be wound up *without an adverse effect upon the rest of the business*, it would be logical to view such losses as temporary—since good sense would dictate that in a short time the subsidiary must either become profitable or be disposed of. But if there are important business relations between the parent company and the subsidiary, *e.g.*, if the latter affords an outlet for goods or supplies cheap materials or absorbs an important share of the overhead, then the termination of its losses is not so simple a matter. It may turn out, upon further analysis, that all or a good part of the subsidiary's loss is a necessary factor in the parent company's profit. It is not an easy task to determine just what business relationships

---

Manual of Investments (Steam Railroads), 1931. The Wabash owned 99% of both the preferred and the common stock of the Ann Arbor. In December 1930 the Ann Arbor directors declared a $5 dividend per share on the preferred and a $27 dividend per share on the common. This action was taken in the face of a working-capital deficit and net earnings available of little over 10% of the dividends thus declared. Neither dividend was ever paid. This maneuver, however, enabled the Wabash to credit its share of the dividends declared to its income account as "dividend income" to the extent of $1,073,455, which was sufficient to raise the fixed-charge coverage of the Wabash from about 1.3 times to a figure slightly in excess of 1.5 times.

are involved in each instance. Like so many other elements in analysis, this point usually requires an investigation going well beyond the reported figures. The following examples will illustrate the type of situation and analysis with which we have been dealing.

Example A: Purity Bakeries Corporation. This large maker of bread and cake operates through a number of subsidiaries, of which one of the largest is Cushman's Sons, Inc., of New York. Cushman's has outstanding $7 and $8 cumulative preferred stock, not guaranteed by Purity. The annual reports of Purity are on a consolidated basis and show earnings after deduction of full dividends on those Cushman's preferred shares not owned by Purity, whether earned or paid. The separate reports of Cushman's reveal that between 1934 and 1937 its operations resulted in a considerable loss to Purity, on its accounting basis, *viz.*:

(000 omitted)

Year	Purity net income as reported	Loss of Cushman's after full preferred dividends	Purity earnings excluding Cushman's operations
1937	$463	$426	$889
1936	690	620	1,310
1935	225 (d.)	930	678
1934	209	173	382
Average 4 years	278	537	815
Per share of Purity	0.36	0.71	1.06

The earnings are thus seen to be three times as large excluding Cushman's as they were including Cushman's. Could the analyst have reasoned that the former provides the truer measure of Purity's earning power, since the company can be expected either again to earn money from that subsidiary (as it had earned it in the past up to 1934) or to drop it? The question of inter-corporate relationships would have to be considered. A note in the 1937 report of Cushman's indicated that Purity was making a fairly large service charge in connection with its subsidiaries' operations, which suggests that Cushman's might be of some extra value in absorbing overhead. This matter would call for a careful inquiry.

But the report for the next year, 1938, showed, first, that Cushman's had earned the preferred dividend deduction, and secondly, that two unprofitable retail plants (in Philadelphia and Chicago) had been closed. Subject to further investigation, therefore, the analyst might well infer that the subsidiary's losses were nonpermanent in nature and that the reported results for 1934–1937 are to be viewed with this point in mind.

Example B: Lehigh Coal and Navigation Company. This enterprise has derived its income from various sources, chief of which has been the lease of its railroad property to the Central Railroad of New Jersey for an annual rental of $2,268,000. Its next largest holding consists of anthracite coal mines, which since 1930 have been operated at a loss. In 1937 this loss was equivalent to about 90 cents per share of Lehigh stock. As a result the company reported a *consolidated* net loss of $306,000 for the year, as contrasted with a profit on a parent-company basis only of $1,125,000, or 64 cents per share.

But in this case the analyst could not safely make the assumption that the Lehigh stock was not worth *less* by reason of its ownership of the mining properties than it would be worth without them. Operation of the mines supplied an important tonnage to the railroad division. If the mines were shut down, the ability of the Jersey Central to pay the annual rental might have been critically impaired, especially since the lessee road had been doing poorly for some years past. (In fact the claim was later made by the Jersey Central that the Lehigh Coal and Navigation was obligated in connection with the lease to supply a certain tonnage from its coal properties). Hence, in this rather complicated set-up the investor could not safely go behind the consolidated results, including the losses of the anthracite subsidiary.

Example C: Barnsdall Oil Company. We have here a situation opposite from the other two. Barnsdall Oil owned both refining and producing properties, the latter profitable, the former unprofitable. In 1935 it segregated the refineries (and marketing units) in a separate company, of which it distributed the common stock to its own stockholders, retaining, however, the preferred stock and substantial claims against the new company. In 1936–1938 the refineries and stations continued to lose; Barnsdall Oil advanced considerable sums to cover these losses and wrote them off by charges first against capital surplus and then against earned surplus. On the other hand, its *income account*, freed from the burden of these refining losses, showed profits from producing operations at a steady rate from June 1, 1933, to the end of 1938.

In 1939, however, the New York Stock Exchange called upon the company to correct its statements to stockholders by advising them of the effect upon the reported profits of charging there-against the write-downs of the investment in the refining company. These losses would have reduced the indicated profits by more than one-third.

It is clear, from the standpoint of proper accounting, *that as long as a company continues to control an unprofitable division*, its losses must be shown as deductions from its other earnings. The analyst must decide what the chances are of terminating the losses in the future, and view the current price of the stock accordingly. The method followed by the Barnsdall Oil Company appears therefore clearly open to criticism, since it served merely to terminate the *reporting* of its refining losses without really terminating the losses themselves. (At the end of 1939 the company set steps into motion for an apparent complete divorcement and sale of the refining and marketing divisions.)

Summary. To avoid leaving this point in confusion, we shall summarize our treatment by suggesting:

1. In the first instance, subsidiary losses are to be deducted in every analysis.

2. If the amount involved is significant, the analyst should investigate whether or not the losses may be subject to early termination.

3. If the result of this examination is favorable, the analyst may consider all or part of the subsidiary's loss as the equivalent of a nonrecurring item.

CHAPTER 34

The Relation of Depreciation and Similar Charges to Earning Power

A CRITICAL ANALYSIS of an income account must pay particular attention to the amounts deducted for depreciation and kindred charges. These items differ from ordinary operating expenses in that they do not signify a current and corresponding outlay of cash. They represent the estimated shrinkage in the value of the fixed or capital assets, due to wearing out, to using up or to their approaching extinction for whatever cause. The important charges of this character may be classified as follows:

1. Depreciation (and obsolescence), replacements, renewals or retirements.
2. Depletion or exhaustion.
3. Amortization of leaseholds, leasehold improvements, licenses, etc.
4. Amortization of patents.

All these items may properly be embraced under the title "amortization," but we shall sometimes refer to them generically as "depreciation items," or simply as "depreciation," because the latter is a more familiar term.

Leading Questions Relative to Depreciation. The accounting theory that governs depreciation charges is simple enough. If a capital asset has a limited life, provision must be made to write off the cost of that asset by charges against earnings distributed over the period of its life. But behind this innocent statement lie complications of a threefold character. First we find that accounting rules themselves may permit a value other than cost as the base for the amortization charge. Second, we find many ways in which companies fail to follow accepted accounting practice in stating their depreciation deduction in the income account. Third, there are occasions when an allowance that may be justified from an accounting standpoint will fail to meet the situation properly from an investment standpoint. These problems will engage our attention in this and the next two chapters. Our discussion will be directed first towards industrial companies generally, following which we shall consider special aspects having to do with oil companies, mining companies and public utilities.[1]

THE DEPRECIATION BASE

Depreciation Base Other than Cost. There is support in accounting circles for the theory that the function of the depreciation allowance is to provide for the *replacement* of the asset at the end of its life rather than merely to write off its *cost*. If this idea were actually followed, the current or expected future replacement cost would be the basis for the depreciation charge, and it would vary not only with the value of the identical asset but also with changes in the character of the item that is expected to replace the one worn out.

Whatever may be said for or against this theory,[2] it is virtually never followed in the form stated. But we do meet in practice with a variant of the idea, *viz.*, the substitution of the replacement value of all the fixed assets *as of a given date* in place of cost on the balance sheet, followed usually by annual depreciation charges based on the new value.

Since 1914 there have been two waves of such revaluations. The first, taking place in the 1920's, marked up prewar costs to the higher values currently prevailing. The second, appearing in 1931–1933, marked down property accounts to the much lower valuations associated with the depression.[3]

Examples: In 1926 American Ice Company wrote up its fixed assets by $7,868,000, and in 1935 it wrote them down correspondingly to restore the valuations to a cost basis. The 1926 write-up resulted in larger depreciation charges thereafter against income, and the 1935 reduction resulted in lower depreciation charges. In 1933 American Locomotive Company

---

[1] With a very few exceptions the *railroads* charge depreciation only on their equipment (including this item in the maintenance charges). For the year 1937 Class I railroads charged a total of $191,798,000 for depreciation of equipment and only $5,236,000 for depreciation of way and structures.

[2] In our view it is at once simpler and more logical to base depreciation on original cost. Replacement cost should affect the accounts *after* replacement takes place (which may never happen) rather than before.

[3] See Fabricant, Solomon, "Revaluations of Fixed Assets, 1925–1934" (*National Bureau of Economic Research Bulletin* 62, 1936), and *Capital Consumption and Adjustment*, National Bureau of Economic Research, Chap. XII, 1938.

reduced the stated value of its stock from $50 to $5 a share and utilized most of the capital surplus thus created to write down fixed properties by nearly $26,000,000 and its investment in General Steel Castings Corporation by about $6,200,000. The net effect on the income account was to reduce depreciation charges to about 40% of their former level.

There is some criticism in accounting circles of the propriety of such sporadic changes in the depreciation base from original cost. In our opinion they are not objectionable *provided:*

1. The new values are set up in the *bona fide* conviction that they represent existing realities more fairly than the old values.
2. Proper depreciation against these new values is charged in the income account.

In many cases, however, we find that companies revaluing their fixed assets fail to observe one or the other of these conditions.

Mark-Downs to Reduce Depreciation Charges. Perhaps the most striking phenomenon in the field of depreciation accounting is the recent marking down of the fixed assets, not in the interests of conservatism but with the precisely opposite intent of making a better earnings exhibit and thereby *increasing* the apparent value of the shares.

We believe that it will be more convenient for the reader if we defer consideration of the significance to security analysis of these devices until our chapter devoted to "Amortization Charges from the Investor's Standpoint." At this time, since we are dealing with accounting methods, we shall merely remark that in our opinion excessive write-downs of fixed assets, for the avowed or obvious purpose of decreasing depreciation and increasing reported earnings, constitute an inexcusable subterfuge and should not be condoned by the accounting profession. Registration statements submitted to the S.E.C. include a statement of how much lower the earnings would have been if the former plant values had been retained. We think that such information should also appear as a footnote to the income account in the annual reports to stockholders, but it would be better practice still if accountants refused to certify a report containing such mark-downs and insisted on restoration of the proper figures to the company's accounts.

Balance Sheet–Income Account Discrepancies. Many corporations that have marked up their fixed assets fail to increase correspondingly their depreciation charges against the income account. They are in effect attempting to get the benefit of the higher valuation in their balance sheet without accepting the burden of consequently higher depreciation charges against earnings. This practice has been especially prevalent in the case of mining and oil companies. Two examples drawn from the general industrial field are given here:

Examples: Hall Printing Company wrote up its property account by $6,222,000 in 1926 and 1931, crediting this "appraisal increment" to capital surplus. Depreciation on this appreciated value was then charged to capital surplus, instead of to income; *e.g.,* typically, in the year ended March 1938 the company charged $406,000 for such depreciation against surplus and $864,000 for "regular" depreciation against income. In April 1938 the balance of the appraisal increment was eliminated by writing down both property account and capital surplus; and the special depreciation charge was then discontinued.

Borg Warner has been charging about $102,000 per annum since 1935 (and various amounts in prior years) to "Appreciation Surplus," instead of to income, to amortize a write-up of fixed assets made in 1927.

It should be obvious that no company should use one set of values for its balance sheet and another for its income account. The more recent tendency is to correct these disparities by eliminating the previous write-up from the balance sheet, thus returning to original cost.

THE RATE OF DEPRECIATION. STANDARD AND NONSTANDARD PRACTICE

1. As Shown by Listing Statements. The vast majority of industrial companies follow the standard policy of charging an appropriate depreciation rate against each class of depreciable asset. The analyst can readily check this fact by reference to New York Stock Exchange listing applications or to a prospectus or registration statement.

Examples: If standard methods are followed, they are likely to be announced in somewhat the following manner:

(From listing application of Electric Storage Battery Company, dated December 17, 1928.)

> The policy of this Company in regard to depreciation . . . is as follows: On buildings the term of life is twenty to thirty-three years, depending upon the character of construction. Machinery, tools and fixtures are written off at the rate of one to ten years, depending upon the character of the equipment.

Office furniture and fixtures are written off in ten years. On all depreciable properties rates are determined by actual experience and engineers' estimates as to the productive life of the equipment. In respect to depreciation of current assets, a reserve is set aside to cover probable loss from bad debts.

(From the listing application of Midland Steel Products Company, dated February 11, 1930.)

The following are the rates of depreciation used:

	Rate of depreciation per year, %
Buildings	2
Grounds, driveways and walks	2
Machinery	7
Furniture and fixtures	10
Railroad sidings	2
Automobiles and trucks	.25

Tools and dies—amortized over life of job when number of units required can be determined, otherwise written off at close of each fiscal year.

These rates have been used by the Company for several years, being standard practice in the industry.

The rates are based upon the estimated life of the respective property involved. Thus, with respect to buildings, the cost is depreciated, over 50 years; grounds, driveways, and walks, over 50 years; machinery over 14 years; furniture and fixtures, over 10 years; railroad sidings, over 50 years. No residual value at the expiration of said periods is considered in determining the rates used.

In contrast with this standard policy, now all but universally followed, we may point to the questionable practice on this important point formerly resorted to by such important companies as American Car and Foundry, American Sugar Refining and Baldwin Locomotive Works.

The American Sugar Refining Company's listing application, dated December 6, 1923, contained the following statement:

The Company maintains a very liberal policy as to depreciation as shown by the annual profit and loss statement of past years. The value of its properties is at all times fully maintained by the making of all needful and proper repairs thereto and renewals and replacements thereof.

This declaration sounds reassuring, but it is far too indefinite to satisfy the analyst. The actual depreciation charges, as shown in the following record, disclose an unusually arbitrary and erratic policy.

Annual Charges by American Sugar Refining Company for Depreciation

Year	Charged to income	Charged to surplus
1916–1920	$2,000,000	None
1921	None	None
1922–1923	1,000,000	None
1924	None	None
1925	1,000,000	None
1926	1,000,000	$2,000,000
1927	1,000,000	1,000,000
1928	1,250,000	500,000
1929	1,000,000	500,000
1930	1,000,000	542,631
1931	1,000,000	None
1932	1,000,000	None

The additional charges to surplus made in the years 1926–1930, inclusive, appear to strengthen our contention that American Sugar's depreciation allowances have been both arbitrary and inadequate.

The American Car and Foundry's application, dated April 2, 1925, contains the following:

> The Company has no depreciation account as such. However, its equivalent is found in the policy and the practice of the Company to maintain at all times its plants and properties in first class physical condition and in a high state of efficiency by repairing, renewing and replacing equipment and buildings as their physical conditions may require, and by replacing facilities with those of more modern type, when such action results in more economical production. This procedure amply covers depreciation and obsolescence and the cost is charged to Operating Expenses.

Here again a sceptical attitude on the part of the analyst is "amply" warranted. The same is true in respect of American Can which managed—inexplicably—to avoid all reference to its depreciation policy in its listing application dated February 26, 1926, although it did mention that the company had spent approximately $50,000,000 on extensions and improvement of properties since February 1907 and that "during this period properties have been depreciated by at least $20,000,000."

Baldwin Locomotive Works, in its listing application dated October 3, 1929, makes the following rather astonishing statement on depreciation:

The amount of the depreciation upon plant and equipment as determined by the Federal Government for the five years 1924 to 1928 inclusive has totaled $5,112,258.09 which has been deducted either from income or surplus as follows:

Year	From income	From surplus	Total depreciation
1924	$600,000	None	$600,000.00
1925	None	None	None
1926	None	None	None
1927	1,000,000	$2,637,881.01	3,637,881.01
1928	600,000	274,377.08	874,377.08
	$2,200,000	$2,912,258.09	$5,112,258.09

It is expected that in future years the amount of depreciation based upon the estimated useful life of depreciable properties as determined by the Federal Government, allowed by the Commissioner of Taxes as a proper deduction from income and agreed to by our engineers, will govern the amount to be used by the Works in its calculation of depreciation.

Evidently the income statements of Baldwin for this period were anything but accurate. The average annual earnings per share of common stock for 1924–1928, as reported to the stockholders, were strikingly higher than the correct figure, as shown at the top of the next page.

2. As Shown by Comparisons of Two Companies. When the analyst knows that a company's depreciation policy differs from the standard, there is special reason to check the adequacy of the allowance. Comparison with a single company in the same field may yield significant results, as is shown by the table in the middle of the next page respecting American Sugar and American Car and Foundry.

Earnings per Share of Common

Year	As reported	As corrected for annual depreciation charge of $1,022,000
1924	$0.40(d)	$2.51(d)
1925	6.02(d)	11.13(d)
1926	22.42	17.31
1927	5.21	5.10
1928	5.34(d)	7.45(d)
5-year average	$3.33	$0.06

Company	Average property account (net) 1928–1932	Average depreciation charge 1928–1932	% of depreciation charge to property account
American Sugar Refining	$60,665,000	$1,050,000*	1.73†
National Sugar Refining	19,250,000‡	922,000‡	4.79‡
American Car and Foundry	72,000,000	1,186,000§	1.65
American Steel Foundries	31,000,000	1,136,000	3.66

* Exclusive of depreciation charged to surplus. Including the latter, this figure would be $1,358,500.
† Including depreciation charged to surplus this figure would be 2.24%.
‡ Based on the four years 1929–1932, inclusive. Figure for 1928 unavailable.
§ Estimated at one-half of the expenditures for renewals and repairs. In the case of United States Steel for the period 1901–1933, the charge for depreciation averaged about 40% of the total allowances for both maintenance and depreciation.

Both comparatively and absolutely the depreciation allowances made by American Sugar and American Car and Foundry appear to have been inadequate.[4]

---

[4] For examples of insufficient charges and charges less than income tax deductions by industrial companies see: Harbison-Walker Refractories Company charge of $296,000 in 1936, termed "grossly inadequate" by new management and revised to $472,000; McKeesport Tin Plate Corporation report for 1937 stating that the charge on the income tax return was $803,000 vs. $425,000 in statement to stockholders. Similarly, National Enameling and Stamping Company for each year 1935–1937 charged about $185,000 in its income account as contrasted with about $280,000 on its tax return. In 1938 insufficient depreciation for 1933–1937 was cured by a charge of $443,000 to surplus. The auditors for the Cudahy Packing Company stated in the certificate accompanying the 1939 report that in their opinion the reserves for depreciation set up by the company in years prior to Oct. 29, 1938, were inadequate.

Depreciation Charges Often an Issue in Mergers. Comparative depreciation charges at times become quite an issue in determining the fairness of proposed terms of consolidation.

Example: In 1924 a merger plan was announced embracing the Chesapeake and Ohio, Hocking Valley, Pere Marquette, "Nickel Plate," and Erie railroads. Some Chesapeake and Ohio stockholders dissented, and they convinced the Interstate Commerce Commission that the terms of the consolidation were highly unfair to their road. Among other matters they pointed out that the earnings of Chesapeake and Ohio in the preceding three years had in reality been much higher than stated, due to the unusually heavy charges made against them for depreciation and retirement of equipment.[5] A similar objection was made in connection with the projected merger of Bethlehem Steel and Youngstown Sheet and Tube in 1929, which plan was also defeated. Some figures on these two steel producers are given as shown in the following table.

Concealed Depreciation. That nothing can be taken for granted in security analysis is shown by the strange case of American Can, which until 1937 had failed to reveal details of its depreciation policy to its shareholders. During the years 1922–1936 it deducted annually a flat $2,000,000 for this purpose. A comparison with Continental Can— which charged about the same amount against a much smaller plant investment—would have suggested that American Can's earning power had been overstated. But the annual report for 1934 disclosed to stockholders for the first time that the company had also been charging sums to operating expenses for "replacements," without giving the amount. The fact (but not the amounts) that such charges had been made in 1935 and 1936 was also revealed in those years. Meanwhile Form 10-K for 1935, filed with the S.E.C., revealed that the amount of these extra

---

Conversely, for cases of excessive depreciation, note: Depreciation charges of Acme Steel for 1932–1935 were found by the federal government to have been $555,000 too high. This amount, less income tax thereon of $104,000, was credited to surplus in 1936. (This is almost the exact opposite of the National Enameling case.) Chicago Yellow Cab Company in 1938 credited to surplus $483,000 for excess depreciation in former years.

[5] Large expenditures made by Chesapeake and Ohio upon its equipment in 1926–1928 and charged to operating expense were later claimed by the Interstate Commerce Commission to represent *capital* outlays. In 1933 this controversy was taken into the courts, and the Interstate Commerce Commission was sustained.

charges was about $2,400,000. Finally the annual report for 1937 advised the stockholders that the corresponding extra charge-off amounted to approximately $3,275,000 for the year 1936. Beginning with 1937 the company made "regular" depreciation charges, amounting to $5,702,000 in that year and to $6,085,000 in 1938. Thus, by easy stages, the owners of the business were told the facts of life bearing on their property.

1928	Bethlehem Steel	Youngstown Sheet & Tube
Property account, Dec. 31, 1927	$673,000,000	$204,000,000
Sales	295,000,000	141,000,00
Depreciation, depletion, and obsolescence	13,658,000	8,321,000
Ratio: depreciation to property account	2.03%	4.08%
Ratio: depreciation to sales	4.63%	5.90%

In the light of this later disclosure, the earlier inference[6] that American Can had understated its depreciation charges must give way to the remark that the company had failed to reveal the facts.

A Case of Excessive Depreciation Charges Concealed by Accounting Methods. The American Can example suggests comparison with the earlier practice of National Biscuit Company, an enterprise controlled largely by the same interests. For many years prior to 1922 the company was constantly adding to the number of its factories, but its property account failed to show any appreciable increase, except in the single year 1920. The reports to stockholders were supremely ambiguous on the matter of depreciation charges,[7] but according to the financial manuals the company's policy was as follows: "Depreciation is $300,000 per annum, and all items of replacement and building alterations are charged direct to operating expense."

It is difficult to avoid the conclusion, however, that the capital investments in additional plants were actually being charged against the profits

---

[6] Drawn in the 1934 edition of this book.

[7] Prior to 1919, the company's balance sheet each year stated its fixed assets "Less Depreciation Account—$300,000." Evidently this was the deduction for the current year and not the amount accumulated.

National Biscuit Company

Year ended	Earnings for common stock	Net plant account at end of year
Jan. 31, 1911	$2,883,000	$53,159,000
1912	2,937,000	53,464,000
1913	2,803,000	53,740,000
1914	3,432,000	54,777,000
1915	2,784,000	54,886,000
1916	2,393,000	55,207,000
1917	2,843,000	55,484,000
Dec. 31, 1917	2,886,000 (11 mo.)	53,231,000
1918	3,400,000	52,678,000
1919	3,614,000	53,955,000
1920	3,807,000	57,788,000
1921	3,941,000	57,925,000
1922	9,289,000	61,700,000
1923	10,357,000	64,400,000
1924	11,145,000	67,292,000
1925	11,845,000	69,745,000

and that the real earnings were in all probability much larger than those reported to the public. Coincident with the issuance of seven shares of stock for one and the tripling of the cash-dividend rate in 1922, this policy of understating earnings was terminated. The result was a sudden doubling of the apparent earning power, accompanied by an equally sudden expansion in the plant account. The contrast between the two periods is shown forcibly in the table on this page.

Failure to State Depreciation Charges. Prior to the S.E.C. regulation some of the important companies reported earnings after depreciation but failed to state the amount deducted for this purpose. Fortunately, this information must now be supplied in the case of every registered company.[8]

---

[8] Allied Chemical and Dye Corporation endeavored to have this and other data held confidential, but after considerable delay it was made public (in 1938). This company, like a few others, still excludes its sales and depreciation figures from its reports to stockholders, but this important information is available in the annual reports to the S.E.C. (Form 10-K).

AMORTIZATION CHARGES OF
OIL AND MINING COMPANIES

These important sectors of the industrial field are subject to special factors bearing on amortization. In addition to depreciation in the ordinary sense—which they usually calculate in the same way as do other companies[9] they must allow for depletion of their ore or oil reserves. In the case of mining concerns there is also the factor of development expense. Oil producers, on the other hand, have additional charges for intangible drilling costs and for unproductive leases. These items are important in their bearing on the true profits, and they are troublesome because of the varying methods that are followed by different enterprises.

Depletion Charges of Mining Companies. Depletion represents the using up of capital assets by turning them into products for sale. It applies to companies producing metals, oil and gas, sulphur, timber, etc. As the holdings, or reserves, of these products are exhausted, their value must gradually be written off through charges against earnings. In the case of the older mining companies (including particularly the copper and sulphur producers) the depletion charges are determined by certain technical requirements of the federal income tax law, which rest upon the amount and value of the reserves as they were supposed to exist on March 1, 1913, or by applying certain percentages to the value of the product. Because of the artificial base used in these computations, many companies have omitted the depletion charge from their reports to stockholders.

Independent Calculation by Investor Necessary. As we shall show later, the investor in a mining concern must ordinarily compute his own depletion allowance, based upon the *amount that he has paid* for his share of the mining property. Consequently a depletion charge based either on the company's original book cost or on the special figure set up for income-tax purposes would be confusing rather than helpful. The omission of the depletion charge of mining companies is not to be criticized, therefore; but the stockholder in such enterprises must be well aware of the fact in studying their reports. Furthermore, in any comparison of

---

[9] However, the cost of equipment and materials on *oil-producing properties* is often written off through the depletion charge (which is based on the barrels produced) instead of the depreciation account (which is based on the *time* elapsing).

mining companies a proper distinction must be drawn between those which do and those which do not deduct their depletion charges in reporting their earnings. Following are some examples of companies that pursue one or the other policy:

Companies That Report Earnings without Deduction for Depletion:	Companies That Report Earnings after Deduction for Depletion:
Alaska Juneau Gold Mining Co.	Cerro de Pasco Copper Corp.
Anaconda Copper Mining Co.	Granby Consolidated Mining, etc., Co. (copper)
Dome Mines, Ltd. (gold)	Homestake Mining Co. (gold)
Kennecott Copper Corp.	International Nickel Co. of Canada, Ltd.
Noranda Mines, Ltd. (copper and gold)	Patino Mines, etc. (tin)
Texas Gulf Sulphur Co.	Phelps Dodge Corp. (copper)
	St. Joseph Lead Co.

Depletion and Similar Charges in the Oil Industry. In the oil industry depletion charges are more closely related to the actual cost of doing business than in the case of mining enterprises. The latter ordinarily invest in a single property or group of properties, the cost of which is then written off over a fairly long period of years. But the typical large oil producer normally spends substantial sums each year on new leases and new wells. These additional holdings are needed to make up for the shrinkage of reserves through production. The depletion charge corresponds in some measure, therefore, to a current cash outlay for the purpose of maintaining reserves and production. New wells may yield as high as 80% of their total output during the first year. Hence nearly all the cost of such "flush production" must be written off in a single fiscal period, and most of the "earnings" from this source are in reality a return of the capital expended thereon. If the investment is not written off rapidly through depletion and other charges, the profit and the value of the property account will both be grossly overstated. In the case of an oil company actively engaged in development work, the various headings under which write-offs must be made include the following:

1. *Depreciation* of tangible assets.
2. *Depletion* of oil and gas reserves, based upon the cost of the leases.
3. *Unprofitable leases* written off. Part of the acquisitions and exploration will always prove totally valueless and must be charged against the revenue from the productive leases.

4. *Intangible drilling costs.* These are either written off at one time, as equivalent to an operating expense, or amortized over the life of the well.

Example: The case of Marland Oil in 1926 illustrates the extent to which reported earnings of oil companies are dependent upon the accounting policies with respect to amortization. This company spent large sums annually on new leases and wells to maintain its rate of production. Prior to 1926 it charged the so-called "intangible drilling costs" to capital account and then wrote them off against earnings through an annual amortization charge. In 1926 Marland adopted the more conservative policy of charging off all these "intangible costs" currently against earnings. The effect on profits is shown in the following table.

Marland Oil Company

Item	1925	1926	1927
Gross earnings and miscellaneous income	$73,231,000	$87,360,000	$58,980,000
Net before reserves	24,495,000	30,303,000	9,808,000
Amortization charges	9,696,000	18,612,000	17,499,000
Balance for stock	14,799,000	11,691,000	*7,691,000(d)*

In the past ten years significant changes have occurred in the policies followed by the important oil companies. Prior to the depression the general tendency was towards charging the "intangible drilling costs" to earnings—as shown in the change made by Marland in 1926. But since the depression many of the large companies have switched over to the less conservative basis of capitalizing these costs, subject to annual amortization.[10] This change seems justified in good part by the wide adoption of state proration laws, which effectively spread out the total production of a new well over many years instead of concentrating it within a relatively few months. This makes an oil well a fairly long-term capital asset, so that charging off a good part of its cost (now often running to very high figures) against a single year's profits would be unduly severe.

The companies have also aided their earnings by large write-downs of fixed assets, with corresponding reductions in the annual amortization

---

[10] Companies making this change since 1930 include Standard Oil of Indiana and New Jersey, Gulf Oil, Tidewater Associated, Consolidated Oil.

charges against them. This practice has perhaps been more widespread among oil companies than in any other industrial group. Some producers have also switched their charges for property *retirements* from earnings to the depreciation reserve. Finally, we have examples of a reduction in amortization charge being brought about by adoption of an "over-all" basis" instead of a lease basis for depletion. By this means, oil produced from high-cost leases is written off not at its actual cost but at the average cost of all the oil reserves owned.

The significance of these changes in accounting policy is illustrated by the following:[11]

Examples: Gulf Oil Corporation increased its 1932 earnings by $3,621,000, by capitalizing intangible drilling costs instead of charging them off, as formerly.

Socony-Vacuum increased its 1932 earnings by $6,095,000 (and subsequent earnings correspondingly) as a result of a write-down of fixed assets with consequent reduction in depreciation charges. In 1935 its profits were increased $1,376,000 by charging this sum—representing losses on certain retired property—to depreciation reserve instead of to income, as theretofore. In 1936 it began to capitalize intangible drilling costs, adding about $8,850,000 to profits in that year through this change. In 1937 the company made a further revision in its depreciation policy (apparently intended to place it on the standard basis), which added some $2,500,000 to that year's profits.

Pure Oil Company reduced its 1934 depletion charges and increased its earnings by $1,698,000 through adoption of the "over-all" basis.

The Meaning of These Variations to the Analyst and the Investor. These differences of accounting methods are highly confusing and may arouse some resentment in the investor. We must recognize, however, that most of them are technically admissible, in that they represent choices between the ordinary and the more conservative basis of amortizing the fixed assets. What is called for, in consequence, is not so much censure as sound interpretation.

Suggested Standards. The analyst should seek to apply a uniform and reasonably conservative rate of amortization to a property base that

---

[11] These examples are drawn largely from Alfred Braunthal, "Are Oil Earnings Reports Fictitious?" *Barron's,* Mar. 8, 1937.

reflects the realities of the proposed investment. We suggest the following standards, in so far as it may be feasible to apply them:

1. *Depreciation on Tangible Assets.* This should always be taken at the well-established rates, applied to cost—or to a figure substantially less than cost only if the facts clearly justify the write-down.

2. *Intangible Drilling Costs.* We believe that capitalizing these costs, and then writing them off as oil is produced—although less "conserva-tive"—is the preferable basis both for comparative purposes and to sup-ply a fair reflection of current earnings. In comparing companies that use one and the other method, the analyst must make the best allowance he can for the understatement of earnings by the companies that charge off 100% the first year.

Example: The difficulty of making this adjustment in practice may be shown by comparing the 1938 reports of Continental Oil Company and Ohio Oil Company. These two concerns are roughly similar in their set-up. Both produced about 20 million barrels in 1938; Continental Oil refined about two-thirds, and Ohio Oil about one-third its output. Continental charges all its intangible drilling costs direct to income, while Ohio capitalizes these costs and writes them off over the life of the wells.

It might be expected that the total amortization charges of Continental, including drilling expense on the 100% basis, would be relatively higher than those of Ohio. Yet in 1938 Ohio charged off $11,602,000, or 21½% of its $54 million sales; while Continental charged off $14,038,000, or 17.6% of its $80 million gross. Apparently no adjustment would be needed by the analyst to equalize the two accounting methods. The reasons may be found in several circumstances; *e.g.*, (*a*) after a number of years the gradual write-off method approximates the 100% method, since amortization of old drilling expense becomes continuously greater. (*b*) In the case of Continental, this concern wrote down its property account in 1932 by some $45,000,000 and thus reduced its normal depreciation and depletion charges considerably in succeeding years.

3. *Property Retirement and Abandoned Leases.* We think that loss on property retired (in excess of depreciation already accrued) should be charged against the year's earnings, rather than against surplus as is done by most companies in other fields. The reason is that property retire-ments are likely to be a normal and recurrent factor in the business of a

large, integrated oil company, instead of happening only sporadically as in other lines. Abandoned leases come under this general heading, and the loss thereon should be charged to earnings.

4. *Depletion of Oil Reserves.* The proper *theoretical* principle here is that the analyst should allow for depletion on the basis at which the oil reserves are valued in the market. This point, as applied to amortization generally, will be discussed in the next chapter. It implies, as we shall see, that what may be the correct *accounting* basis for computing depletion may not be the most suitable basis for the analysis of investment values.

Unfortunately, business practice in the oil industry has been such as to make the sound application of this principle exceedingly difficult. The oil-producing part of the industry has apparently accounted for most of the profits; the refining and marketing divisions have earned little, if anything, on their investment. If *earnings* were the criterion of value here, most of the market price of a typical oil stock would be ascribable to the producing division, and on this basis a comparatively high depletion charge against each barrel taken out would be called for. On the other hand, if the division were made in proportion to *book values*, the refining and marketing sections would loom large, the oil reserves would have a much smaller value, and the depletion charge would be proportionately smaller.

We do not see any really satisfactory answer to the dilemma that we have posed—for it seems to us that the partition of earning power in the industry between production and the other branches is an essentially artificial one and cannot be viewed as permanent. We therefore are led to suggest the following *practical compromise* with the problem:

1. In the case of *integrated* oil companies, accept the company's depletion figure as the best available. (This includes acceptance of the "over-all" basis, if used, since this method would seem to reflect the facts fairly.) However, any charges for depletion made against an "appreciation" account in the balance sheet should be deducted from income.

2. In the case of companies that are solely oil producers, or virtually so, the analyst can compute *what the market is paying* for the total developed oil reserves (if an estimate of these is published). Hence he can make his own depletion calculation, for the particular purpose of his analysis, in such an instance in the same manner as in the case of a mining proposition. (For a calculation of this kind applied to Texas Gulf Producing Company see Chap. 36.)

OTHER TYPES OF AMORTIZATION OF CAPITAL ASSETS

Leaseholds and Leasehold Improvements. The ordinary lease involves no capital investment by the lessee, who merely undertakes to pay rent in return for the use of property. But if the rental payments are considerably less than the use of the property is worth, and if the arrangement has a considerable period to run, the leasehold—as it is called—may have a substantial value. Oil lands are leased on a standard basis for a royalty amounting usually to one-eighth of the production. Leaseholds on which a substantial output is developed or assured are worth a large bonus above the rental payments involved, and they are bought and sold in the same way as the fee ownership of the property. Similar bonuses are paid—in boom times usually—for long-term leases on urban real estate.

If a company has paid money for a leasehold, the cost is regarded as a capital investment that should be written off during the life of the lease. (In the case of an oil lease the write-off is made against each barrel produced, rather than on a time basis, since the output declines rapidly from the initial flush figure.) These charges are in reality part of the rent paid for the property and must obviously be included in current operating expense.

When structures are built on leased property or alterations made or fixtures installed, they are designated as "leasehold improvements." Hence their cost must be written down to nothing during the life of the lease, since they belong to the landlord when the lease expires. The annual charge-off for this purpose is called "amortization of leasehold improvements." It partakes to some extent of the nature of a depreciation charge. Chain-store enterprises frequently invest considerable sums in such leasehold improvements, and consequently the annual write-offs thereof may be of appreciable importance in their income accounts.

Example: The December 31, 1938, balance sheet of F.W. Woolworth Company carried "Buildings Owned and Improvements on Leased Premises to be amortized over periods of leases" at a net valuation of $46,717,000. The charge against 1938 earnings for amortization of these buildings and leasehold improvements amounted to $3,925,283.

Since these items belong to the amortization group, they lend themselves to the same kind of arbitrary treatment as do the others. By making the annual charge against surplus instead of income or by writing down the entire capital investment to $1 and thus eliminating the annual charge entirely, a corporation can exclude these items of operating cost from its reported per-share earnings and thus make the latter appear deceptively large.

Amortization of Patents. In theory, a patent should be dealt with in exactly the same way as a mining property; *i.e.*, its cost to the investor should be written off against earnings during its remaining life. It is obvious, therefore, that charges made against earnings by the company—which are based on the *book value* of the patent—have ordinarily little relevance to the real situation. Consideration of this question belongs chiefly to a later chapter on amortization from the investor's standpoint, and to avoid dividing our treatment we shall postpone to the same place our brief discussion of the accounting methods relative to patents encountered in corporate reports.

Amortization of Goodwill. This is a matter of very minor importance. A few companies have followed the rather extraordinary policy of charging off their goodwill account against earnings in a number of annual installments.

Examples: Radio Corporation of America charged $310,000 a year for this purpose between 1934 and 1937. This was applicable to the goodwill account of its subsidiary National Broadcasting Company and was discontinued in 1938, although $1,876,000 remained unamortized.

Obviously, this practice has no factual basis, since goodwill has no duration of life apart from that of the business as a whole. Where the item is of any size, the analyst should adjust the earnings by canceling the charge.

See Chapter 35, "Public-Utility Depreciation Policies," and Chapter 36, "Amortization Charges from the Investor's Standpoint" online at www.mhprofessional.com/SecurityAnalysis7.

CHAPTER 37

Significance of the Earnings Record

IN THE LAST SIX CHAPTERS our attention was devoted to a critical examination of the income account for the purpose of arriving at a fair and informing statement of the results for the period covered. The second main question confronting the analyst is concerned with the utility of this past record as an indicator of future earnings. This is at once the most important and the least satisfactory aspect of security analysis. It is the most important because the sole practical value of our laborious study of the past lies in the clue it may offer to the future; it is the least satisfactory because this clue is never thoroughly reliable and it frequently turns out to be quite valueless. These shortcomings detract seriously from the value of the analyst's work, but they do not destroy it. The past exhibit remains a sufficiently dependable guide, in a sufficient proportion of cases, to warrant its continued use as the chief point of departure in the valuation and selection of securities.

The Concept of Earning Power. The concept of *earning power* has a definite and important place in investment theory. It combines a statement of actual earnings, shown over a period of years, with a reasonable expectation that these will be approximated in the future, unless extraordinary conditions supervene. The record must cover a number of years, first because a continued or repeated performance is always more impressive than a single occurrence and secondly because the average of a fairly long period will tend to absorb and equalize the distorting influences of the business cycle.

A distinction must be drawn, however, between an average that is the mere arithmetical resultant of an assortment of disconnected figures and an average that is "normal" or "modal," in the sense that the annual results show a definite tendency to approximate the average. The contrast between one type of earning power and the other may be clearer from the following examples:

Adjusted Earnings per Share 1923–1932

Year	S. H. Kress	Hudson Motors
1932	$2.80	$3.54(d)
1931	4.19	1.25(d)
1930	4.49	0.20
1929	5.92	7.26
1928	5.76	8.43
1927	5.26	9.04
1926	4.65	3.37
1925	4.12	13.39
1924	3.06	5.09
1923	3.39	5.56
10-year average	$4.36	$ 4.75

The average earnings of about $4.50 per share shown by S. H. Kress and Company can truly be called its "indicated earning power," for the reason that the figures of each separate year show only moderate variations from this norm. On the other hand the Hudson Motors average of $4.75 per share is merely an abstraction from ten widely varying figures, and there was no convincing reason to believe that the earnings from 1933 onward would bear a recognizable relationship to this average. A similar conclusion was drawn from our discussion of the exhibit of J. I. Case Company in Chap. 1.

These conclusions, reached in 1933, are supported by the results of the six years following:

Earnings per Share

Year	S. H. Kress[1]	Hudson Motors	J. I. Case
1933	$4.23	$2.87(d)	$14.66(d)
1934	4.76	2.10(d)	7.38(d)
1935	4.63	0.38	5.70
1936	4.62	2.14	12.37
1937	4.62	0.42	19.20
1938	2.76	2.94(d)	8.89
1939	3.86	0.86(d)	1.87(d)

[1] Stated on basis of old capitalization, before 2-for-1 split-up in 1936.

Quantitative Analysis Should Be Supplemented by Qualitative Considerations. In studying earnings records an important principle of security analysis must be borne in mind:

Quantitative data are useful only to the extent that they are supported by a qualitative survey of the enterprise.

In order for a company's business to be regarded as reasonably stable, it does not suffice that the past record should show stability. The nature of the undertaking, considered apart from any figures, must be such as to indicate an inherent permanence of earning power. The importance of this additional criterion was well illustrated by the case of the Studebaker Corporation which was used as an example in our discussion of qualitative factors in analysis Chap. 2. It is possible, on the other hand, that there may be considerable variation in yearly earnings, but there is a reasonable basis nevertheless for taking the average as a rough index at least of future performance. In 1934 we cited United States Steel Corporation as a leading case in point. The text of our discussion was as follows:

The annual earnings for 1923–1932 are given below.

United States Steel Corporation, 1923–1932

Year	Earnings per share of common*	Output of finished steel, tons	% of total output of country	Net per ton before deprec.
1932	$11.08(d)	3,591,000	34.4	$3.54(d)
1931	1.40(d)	7,196,000	37.5	5.71
1930	9.12	11,609,000	39.3	13.10
1929	21.19	15,303,000	37.3	16.90
1928	12.50	13,972,000	37.1	13.83
1927	8.81	12,979,000	39.5	12.66
1926	12.85	14,334,000	40.4	13.89
1925	9.19	13,271,000	39.7	12.49
1924	8.41	11,723,000	41.7	13.05
1923	11.73	14,721,000	44.2	12.20
10-year average	$ 8.13	11,870,000	39.1	11.03

* Adjusted for changes in capitalization.

If compared with those of Studebaker for 1920–1929, the foregoing earnings show much greater instability. Yet the average of about $8 per share for the ten-year period has far more significance as a guide to the future than had Studebaker's indicated earning power of about $6.75 per share. This greater dependability arises from the entrenched position of United States Steel in its industry; and also from the relatively narrow fluctuations in both the annual output and the profit per ton over most of this period. These two elements may be used as a basis for calculating approximate "normal earnings" of U. S. Steel, somewhat as follows:

Normal or usual annual production of finished goods	13,000,000 tons
Gross receipts per ton of finished products	$100.00
Net earnings per ton before depreciation	$12.50
Net earnings on 13,000,000 tons	$160,000,000.00
Depreciation, bond interest, and preferred dividends	90,000,000.00
Balance for 8,700,000 shares of common	70,000,000.00
Normal earnings per share	$8.00

The average earnings for the 1923–1932 decade are thus seen to approximate a theoretical figure based upon a fairly well-defined "normal" output and profit margin. (The increase in number of shares outstanding prevents this normal figure from exceeding the ten-year average.) Although a substantial margin of error must be allowed for in such a computation, it at least supplies a starting point for an intelligent estimate of future probabilities.

Examining this analysis six years later, we may draw some conflicting conclusions as to its value. United States Steel's earnings did recover to $7.88 per share in 1937 ($8.31 before the surtax on undistributed profits). The price advanced from the 1933 average of 45½ to a high of 126 in March 1937. Hence our implication that the company had a better earning power than the 1932 results and stock prices reflected would seem to have been amply justified by the event.

But actually the average earnings for 1934–1939 have been quite disappointing (amounting to no more than 14 cents per share). If these results have as much validity for the steel industry as they have for most lines of business, we should have to admit that the analysis based on 1923–1932 was not really useful, because the underlying conditions in steel have changed for the worse. (The change consists chiefly in much higher unit costs and a lower average output, selling prices on the whole having been well maintained.[1])

Current Earnings Should Not Be the Primary Basis of Appraisal. The *market level* of common stocks is governed more by their current earnings than by their long-term average. This fact accounts in good part for the wide fluctuations in common-stock prices, which largely (though by no means invariably) parallel the changes in their earnings between good years and bad. Obviously the stock market is quite irrational in thus varying its valuation of a company proportionately with the temporary changes in its reported profits.[2] A private business might easily earn twice as much in a boom year as in poor times, but its owner would never think of correspondingly marking up or down the value of his capital investment.

This is one of the most important lines of cleavage between Wall Street practice and the canons of ordinary business. Because the speculative public is clearly wrong in its attitude on this point, it would seem that its errors should afford profitable opportunities to the more logically minded to buy common stocks at the low prices occasioned by temporarily reduced earnings and to sell them at inflated levels created by abnormal prosperity.

The Classical Formula for "Beating the Stock Market." We have here the long-accepted and classical formula for "beating the stock market." Obviously it requires strength of character in order to think and to act in opposite fashion from the crowd and also patience to wait for opportunities that may be spaced years apart. But there are still other considerations that greatly complicate this apparently simple rule for successful

---

[1] It may be interesting to note that our 1933 conclusions as to the earning power of United States Steel are quite similar to those reached by J. B. Williams in his elaborate study of this company contained in his book *The Theory of Investment Value,* pp. 409–462. But note also, as against the foregoing indication of normal earning power, the rather pessimistic implications of the longer range study of United States Steel's position on pp. 607–611 below. The company's failure to reestablish this earning power in 1934–1939 might suggest that the latter analysis deserved the greater weight.

[2] The rise of United States Steel to 126 in March 1937, already mentioned, is a striking example of this folly of the stock market. It was based on a single good year, following six bad or mediocre ones. Within twelve months the price had declined to 42—a loss of two-thirds of its quotation, and over $730,000,000 in aggregate market value for this single issue. The range of Youngstown Sheet and Tube and Jones and Laughlin Steel in that period was even wider.

operations in stocks. In actual practice the selection of suitable buying and selling levels becomes a difficult matter. Taking the long market cycle of 1921–1933, an investor might well have sold out at the end of 1925 and remained out of the market in 1926–1930 and bought again in the depression year 1931. The first of these moves would later have seemed a bad mistake of judgment, and the last would have had most disturbing consequences. In other market cycles of lesser amplitude such serious miscalculations are not so likely to occur, but there is always a good deal of doubt with regard to the correct time for applying the simple principle of "buy low and sell high."

It is true also that underlying values may change substantially from one market cycle to another, more so, of course, in the case of individual issues than for the market as a whole. Hence if a common stock is sold at what seems to be a generous price in relation to the average of past earnings, it may later so improve its position as to justify a still higher quotation even in the next depression. The converse may occur in the purchase of securities at subnormal prices. If such permanent changes did not frequently develop, it is doubtful if the market would respond so vigorously to current variations in the business picture. The mistake of the market lies in its assumption that *in every case* changes of this sort are likely to go farther, or at least to persist, whereas experience shows that such developments are exceptional and that the *probabilities* favor a swing of the pendulum in the opposite direction.

The analyst cannot follow the stock market in its indiscriminate tendency to value issues on the basis of current earnings. He may on occasion attach predominant weight to the recent figures rather than to the average, but only when persuasive evidence is at hand pointing to the continuance of these current results.

Average vs. Trend of Earnings. In addition to emphasizing strongly the current showing of a company, the stock market attaches great weight to the indicated *trend of earnings*. In Chap. 27 we pointed out the twofold danger inhering in this magnification of the trend—the first being that the supposed trend might prove deceptive, and the second being that valuations based upon trend obey no arithmetical rules and therefore may too easily be exaggerated. There is indeed a fundamental conflict between the concepts of the *average* and of the *trend*, as applied to an earnings record. This may be illustrated by the following simplified example:

Company	Earned per share in successive years						7th (current)	Average of 7 years	Trend
	1st	2nd	3d	4th	5th	6th			
A	$1	$2	$3	$4	$5	$6	$7	$4	Excellent
B	7	7	7	7	7	7	7	7	Neutral
C	13	12	11	10	9	8	7	10	Bad

On the basis of these figures the better the trend, when compared with the same current earnings (in this case $7 per share), the poorer the average and the higher the average the poorer the trend. They suggest an important question respecting the theoretical and practical interpretation of earnings records: Is not the trend at least as significant for the future as the average? Concretely, in judging the probable performance of Companies A and C over the next five years, would not there be more reason to think in terms of a sequence of $8, $9, $10, $11, and $12 for A and a sequence of $7, $6, $5, $4, and $3 for C rather than in terms of the past average of $4 for A and $10 for C?

The answer to this problem derives from common sense rather than from formal or *a priori* logic. The favorable trend of Company A's results must certainly be taken into account, but not by a mere automatic projection of the line of growth into the distant future. On the contrary, it must be remembered that the automatic or normal economic forces militate *against* the indefinite continuance of a given trend.[3] Competition, regulation, the law of diminishing returns, etc., are powerful foes to unlimited expansion, and in smaller degree opposite elements may operate to check a continued decline. Hence instead of taking the maintenance of a favorable trend for granted—as the stock market is wont to do—the analyst must approach the matter with caution, seeking to determine the causes of the superior showing and to weigh the specific elements of strength in the company's position against the general obstacles in the way of continued growth.

Attitude of Analyst Where Trend Is Upward. If such a *qualitative* study leads to a favorable verdict—as frequently it should—the analyst's philosophy must still impel him to base his investment valuation on an assumed earning power no larger than the company has already achieved

---

[3] See our discussion of the Schletter and Zander example in Chap. 27.

in a period of normal business. This is suggested because, in our opinion, investment values can be related only to demonstrated performance; so that neither expected increases nor even past results under conditions of abnormal business activity may be taken as a basis. As we shall point out in the next chapter, this assumed earning power may properly be capitalized more liberally when the prospects appear excellent than in the ordinary case, but we shall also suggest that the maximum multiplier be held to a conservative figure (say, 20, under the conditions of 1940) if the valuation reached is to be kept within strictly *investment* limits. On this basis, assuming that general business conditions in the current year are not unusually good, the earning power of Company *A* might be taken at $7 per share, and its investment value might be set as high as 140.[4] The divergence in method between the stock market and the analyst—as we define his viewpoint—would mean in general that the price levels ruling for the so-called "good stocks" under normal market conditions are likely to appear overgenerous to the conservative student. This does not mean that the analyst is convinced that the market valuation is wrong but rather that he is not convinced that its valuation is right. He would call a substantial part of the price a "speculative component," in the sense that it is paid not for *demonstrated* but for expected results. (This subject is discussed further in Chap. 39.)

Attitude of Analyst Where Trend Is Downward. Where the trend has been definitely downward, as that of Company *C*, the analyst will assign great weight to this unfavorable factor. He will not assume that the downcurve *must* presently turn upward, nor can he accept the past average—which is much higher than the current figure—as a normal index of future earnings. But he will be equally chary about any hasty conclusions to the effect that the company's outlook is hopeless, that its earnings are certain to disappear entirely and that the stock is therefore without merit or value. Here again a qualitative study of the company's situation and prospects is essential to forming an opinion whether *at some price*, relatively low, of course, the issue may not be a bargain, despite its declining earnings trend. Once more we identify the viewpoint of the analyst with that of a sensible business man looking into the pros and cons of some privately owned enterprise.

---

[4] See Appendix Note 53 for a reference to the more conservative viewpoint on this matter expressed by us in the 1934 edition of this work and the reasons for the change.

To illustrate this reasoning, we append the record of net earnings for 1925–1933 of Continental Baking Corporation and American Laundry Machinery Company.

Year	Continental Baking	American Laundry Machinery
1933	$2,788,000	$1,187,000(d)
1932	2,759,000	986,000(d)
1931	4,243,000	772,000
1930	6,114,000	1,849,000
1929	6,671,000	3,542,000
1928	5,273,000	4,128,000
1927	5,570,000	4,221,000
1926	6,547,000	4,807,000
1925	8,794,000	5,101,000

The profits of American Laundry Machinery reveal an uninterrupted decline, and the trend shown by Continental Baking is almost as bad. It will be noted that in 1929—the peak of prosperity for most companies—the profits of these concerns were substantially less than they were four years earlier.

Wall Street reasoning would be prone to conclude from this exhibit that both enterprises are definitely on the downward path. But such extreme pessimism would be far from logical. A study of these two businesses from the qualitative standpoint would indicate first that the respective industries are permanent and reasonably stable and secondly that each company occupies a leading position in its industry and is well fortified financially. The inference would properly follow that the unfavorable tendency shown during 1925–1932 was probably due to accidental or nonpermanent conditions and that in gaging the future earning power more enlightenment will be derived from the substantial *average* than from the seemingly disastrous trend.[5]

Deficits a Qualitative, Not a Quantitative Factor. When a company reports a deficit for the year, it is customary to calculate the amount in dollars per share or in relation to interest requirements. The statistical

---

[5] The results since 1933 would tend to bear out this earlier conclusion, at least in part.

manuals will state, for example, that in 1932 United States Steel Corporation earned its bond-interest "deficit 12.40 times" and that it showed a deficit of $11.08 per share on its common stock. It should be recognized that such figures, when taken by themselves, *have no quantitative significance* and that their value in forming an *average* may often be open to serious question.

Let us assume that Company A lost $5 per share of common in the last year and Company B lost $7 per share. Both issues sell at 25. Is this an indication of any sort that Company A stock is preferable to Company B stock? Obviously not; for assuming it were so, it would mean that the more shares there were outstanding the more valuable each share would be. If Company B issues 2 shares for 1, the loss would be reduced to $3.50 per share, and on the assumption just made, each new share would then be worth more than an old one. The same reasoning applies to bond interest. Suppose that Company A and Company B each lost $1,000,000 in 1932. Company A has $4,000,000 of 5% bonds and Company B has $10,000,000 of 5% bonds. Company A would then show interest earned "deficit 5 times" and Company B would earn its interest "deficit 2 times." These figures should not be construed as an indication of any kind that Company A's bonds are less secure than Company B's bonds. For, if so, it would mean that the smaller the bond issue the poorer its position—a manifest absurdity.

When an *average* is taken over a period that includes a number of deficits, some question must arise as to whether or not the resultant figure is really indicative of the *earning power*. For the wide variation in the individual figures must detract from the representative character of the average. This point is of considerable importance in view of the prevalence of deficits during the depression of the 1930s. In the case of most companies the average of the years since 1933 may now be thought more representative of indicated earning power than, say, a ten-year average 1930–1939.[6]

Intuition Not a Part of the Analyst's Stock in Trade. In the absence of indications to the contrary we accept the past record as a basis for judging the future. But the analyst must be on the lookout for any such indica-

---

[6] It is an open question whether or not either the ten-year period 1930–1939 or the six years 1934–1939 fairly reflect the future earning power of companies in the heavy industries, *e.g.*, United States Steel, Bethlehem Steel, American Locomotive.

tions to the contrary. Here we must distinguish between vision or intuition on the one hand, and ordinary sound reasoning on the other. The ability to see what is coming is of inestimable value, but it cannot be expected to be part of the analyst's stock in trade. (If he had it, he could dispense with analysis.) He can be asked to show only that moderate degree of foresight which springs from logic and from experience intelligently pondered. It was not to be demanded of the securities statistician, for example, that he foretell the enormous increase in cigarette consumption since 1915 or the decline in the cigar business or the astonishing stability of the snuff industry; nor could he have predicted—to use another example—that the two large can companies would be permitted to enjoy the full benefits from the increasing demand for their product, without the intrusion of that demoralizing competition which ruined the profits of even faster growing industries, e.g., radio.

Analysis of the Future Should Be Penetrating Rather than Prophetic. Analytical reasoning with regard to the future is of a somewhat different character, being penetrating rather than prophetic.[7]

Example: Let us take the situation presented by Intertype Corporation in March-July 1939, when the stock was selling at $8 per share. This old, established company was one of the leaders in a relatively small industry (line-casting machines, etc., for the printing trade). Its recent earnings had not been favorable, nor did there seem to be any particular reason for optimistic expectations as to the near-term outlook. The analyst, however, could not fail to be impressed by the balance sheet, which showed net current assets available for the stock amounting to close to $20 per share. The ten-year earnings, dividend and price record of the common stock was as shown in the following table.

Certainly there is nothing attractive in this record, marked as it is by irregularity and the absence of a favorable trend. But although these facts would undoubtedly condemn the issue in the eyes of the speculator, the reasoning of the analyst might conceivably run along different lines.

The essential question for him would be whether or not the company can be counted on to remain in business and to participate about as before in good times and bad. On this point consideration of the indus-

---

[7] See Appendix Note 54 for an example (Mack Trucks, Inc.) used in the first edition of this work, together with its sequel.

Year	Earned per share	Dividend paid	Price range
1938	$0.57	0.45	$12^3/4$–8
1937	1.41	0.80	$26^1/2$–9
1936	1.42	0.75	$22^3/4$–15
1935	0.75	0.40	16–$6^1/8$
1934	0.21		10–$5^5/8$
1933	0.77(d)		$11^1/4$–$1^7/8$
1932	1.82(d)		7–$2^1/2$
1931	0.56	1.00	$18^1/2$–$4^5/8$
1930	1.46	2.00	32–12
1929	3.05	1.75	$38^7/8$–17
Average 1934–1938	0.87		
Average 1929–1938	0.68		

try, the company's prominent position in it and the strong financial set-up would clearly suggest an affirmative answer. If this were granted, the analyst would then point out that the shares could be bought at 8 with very small chance of ultimate loss and with every indication that under the next set of favorable conditions the value of the stock would double. Note that in 3 years out of the past 5 and in 6 out of the past 10, the stock sold between 2 and 4 times the July 1939 price.

This type of reasoning, it will be noted, lays emphasis not upon an accurate prediction of future trends but rather on reaching the general conclusion that the company will continue to do business pretty much as before.

Wall Street is inclined to doubt that any such presumption may be applied to companies with an irregular trend, and to consider that it is just as difficult and hazardous to reach a conclusion of this kind as to determine that a "growing company" will continue to grow. But in our view the Intertype form of reasoning has two definite advantages over the customary attitude, *e.g.*, that which would prefer a company such as Coca-Cola, at 22 times recent earnings and 35 times its asset value, because of the virtually uninterrupted expansion of its profits for more than 15 years.

The first advantage is that, after all, private business is conducted and investments made therein on the same kind of assumptions that we have made with respect to Intertype. The second is that reasoning of this kind can be *conservative* in that it allows for a liberal margin of safety in case of error or disappointment. It runs considerably less risk of confusion between "confidence in the future" and mere speculative enthusiasm.

Large Profits Frequently Transitory. More frequently we have the opposite type of situation from that just discussed. Here the analyst finds reason to question the indefinite continuance of past prosperity.

Examples: Consider a company like J. W. Watson ("Stabilator") Company, engaged chiefly in the manufacture of a single type of automotive accessory. The success of such a "gadget" is normally short-lived; competition and changes in the art are an ever present threat to the stability of earning power. Hence in such a case the student could have pointed out that the market price, bearing the usual ratio to current and average earnings, reflected a quite unwarranted confidence in the permanence of profits that by their nature were likely to be transitory. Some of the pertinent data relative to this judgment are given in the table below, with respect to this company.[8]

The J. W. Watson Company

Year	Net for common	Per share	Price range for common	Dividend
1932	$214,026(d)	$1.07(d)	$3/8$–$1/8$	None
1931	240,149(d)	1.20(d)	2–$1/8$	None
1930	264,269(d)	1.32(d)	6–1	None
1929	323,137(d)	1.61(d)	$14^7/8$–$1^5/8$	None
1928	348,930(d)	1.74(d)	20–$5^1/4$	50 cents
1927	503,725	2.16	$25^3/4$–$18^7/8$	50 cents
1926	577,450*	2.88*	(Issue not quoted prior to 1927)	
1925	502,593*	2.51*		
1924	29,285*	0.15*		
1923	173,907*	0.86*		
1922	142,701*	0.71*		

* Earnings are for predecessor companies, applied to 1932 capitalization.

---

[8] The common stock of the company was originally offered in September 1927 at $24.50 per share, a price 17.3 times the average earnings of the predecessor companies during the preceding five years. This relatively high price was accounted for in part by the apparently

A similar consideration would apply to the exhibit of Coty, Inc., in 1928. Here was a company with an excellent earnings record, but the earnings were derived from the popularity of a trade-marked line of cosmetics. This was a field in which the variable tastes of femininity could readily destroy profits as well as build them up. The inference that rapidly rising profits in previous years meant much larger profits in the future was thus especially fallacious in this case, because *by the nature of the business* a peak of popularity was likely to be reached at some not distant point, after which a substantial falling off would be, if not inevitable, at least highly probable. Some of the data appearing on the Coty exhibit are as follows:

Year	Net income	Earned per share (adjusted)
1923	$1,070,000	$0.86
1924	2,046,000	1.66
1925	2,505,000	2.02
1926	2,943,000	2.38
1927	3,341,000	2.70
1928	4,047,000	3.09
1929	4,058,000	2.73

At the high price of 82 in 1929, Coty, Inc., was selling in the market for about $120,000,000, or thirty times its *maximum* earnings. The actual investment in the business (capital and surplus) amounted to about $14,000,000.

Subsequent earnings were as shown in the following table.

Coty, Inc.

Year	Net income	Earned per share
1930	$1,318,000	$0.86
1931	991,000	0.65
1932	521,000	0.34 (low price in 1932–1^1/2)

---

favorable "trend" of earnings, in part by the high recent and current earnings and in part by the reckless standards of appraisal beginning to prevail at the time.

See pp. 438–440 of the 1934 edition of this work for a companion case—The Gabriel Company.

A third variety of this kind of reasoning could be applied to the brewery-stock flotations in 1933. These issues showed substantial current or prospective earnings based upon capacity operations and the indicated profit per barrel. Without claiming the gift of second sight, an analyst could confidently predict that the flood of capital being poured into this new industry would ultimately result in overcapacity and keen competition.

Hence a continued large return on the actual cash investment was scarcely probable; it was likely, moreover, that many of the individual companies would prove financial failures, and most of the others would be unable to earn enough to justify the optimistic price quotations engendered by their initial success.[9]

---

[9] See Appendix Note 55 for brief comments on the subsequent performance of the brewery issues of 1933.

CHAPTER 38

Specific Reasons for Questioning or Rejecting the Past Record

IN ANALYZING AN INDIVIDUAL company, each of the governing elements in the operating results must be scrutinized for signs of possible unfavorable changes in the future. This procedure may be illustrated by various examples drawn from the mining field. The four governing elements in such situations would be: (1) life of the mine, (2) annual output, (3) production costs and (4) selling price. The significance of the first factor has already been discussed in connection with charges against earnings for depletion. Both the output and the costs may be affected adversely if the ore to be mined in the future differs from that previously mined in location, character or grade.[1]

Rate of Output and Operating Costs. *Examples: Calumet and Hecla Consolidated Copper Company.* The reports of this copper producer for 1936 and previous years illustrate various questions with respect to ore reserves. The income account for 1936 may be summarized as follows:

Copper produced	78,500,000 lb.
Copper sold	95,200,000 lb. @ 9.80 cents
Profit before depreciation and depletion	$3,855,000
Depreciation	1,276,000
Depletion	1,726,000
Earned per share after depreciation but before depletion on 2,006,000 shares	$1.29

---

[1] When ore reserves are stated only as so many tons, or so many years of life, these data may be misleading in the absence of assurance regarding the *quality* of ore remaining. *Example:* The depletion charges of Alaska Juneau Gold Mining Company suggested a remaining life of some 85 years from 1934. The registration statement however, claimed only some 25 years of life from 1934. The implication (confirmed upon inquiry) is that the longer "life" included much low-grade ore of noncommercial character.

Early in 1937 the stock sold at $20 per share, a valuation of $40,000,000 for the company, or $30,000,000 for the mining properties plus $10,000,000 for the working capital.

A detailed analysis of the make-up of the 1936 earnings would have shown them to be derived from four separate sources, approximately as follows:

Source of copper	Number of pounds, millions	Profit before depreciation and depletion	
		Cents per pound (approximate)	Total (approximate)
Copper previously produced	17.3	4.5	$ 775,000
Conglomerate mine	36.3	3.6	1,305,000
Ahmeek mine	23.0	3.3	760,000
Reclamation plants	19.2	5.3	1,015,000
	95.8	4.0	$3,855,000

Of these four sources of profit, all but the smallest were definitely limited in life. The sale of copper produced in prior years was obviously nonrecurring. The mainstay of the company's production for 70 years—the Conglomerate Branch—was facing exhaustion "in the course of 12 or 14 months." The reclamation-plant copper, recovered by reworking old tailings and providing the cheapest metal, was limited to a life of 5 to 7 years. There remained as the only more permanent source of future output the Ahmeek Mine, which was the highest cost operation and which had therefore been shut down from April 1932 through 1935. (There were also certain other high-cost properties that were still shut down in 1936.)

Analysis would indicate, therefore, that probably not more than a total of some 7 to 8 millions in profit could be expected in the future from the Conglomerate and the reclamation operations. Hence, aside from new developments of a speculative character, the greater part of the 40 millions of valuation for the company would have to be supported by earnings from higher cost properties *which had contributed only a minor part of the 1936 results.*[2]

---

[2] In the 1934 edition of this book we discussed a similar situation existing in this company in 1927, at which time the largest part of the profits were being contributed by the reclamation-plant operations, which were known to have a limited life.

Freeport Sulphur Company. The exhibit of the then Freeport Texas Company in 1933 supplies the same type of problem for the analyst, and it also raises the question of the propriety of the use, under such circumstances, of the past earnings record to support the sale of new securities. An issue of $2,500,000 of 6% cumulative convertible preferred stock was sold at $100 per share in January 1933 in order to raise funds to equip a new sulphur property leased from certain other companies.

The offering circular stated among other things:

1. That the sulphur reserves had an estimated life of at least 25 years based upon the average annual sales for 1928–1932;
2. That the earnings for the period 1928–1932 averaged $2,952,500, or 19.6 times the preferred-dividend requirement.

The implication of these statements would be that, assuming no change in the price received for sulphur, the company could confidently be expected to earn over the next 25 years approximately the amounts earned in the past.

The facts in the case, however, did not warrant any such deduction. The company's past earnings were derived from the operation of two properties, at Bryanmound and at Hoskins Mound, respectively. The Bryanmound area was owned by the company and had contributed the bulk of the profits. But by 1933 its life was "definitely limited" (in the words of the listing application); *in fact the reserves were not likely to last more than about three years.* The Hoskins Mound was leased from the Texas Company. After paying $1.06 per ton fixed royalty, no less than 70% of the remaining profits were payable to Texas Company as rental.[3] One half of Freeport's sales were required to be made from sulphur produced at Hoskins. The new property at Grande Ecaille, La., now to be developed, would require royalty payments amounting to some 40% of the net earnings.

When these facts are studied, it will be seen that the earnings of Freeport Texas for 1928–1932 had no direct bearing on the results to be expected from future operations. The sulphur reserves, stated to be good for 25 years, represented mineral located in an entirely different place and

---

[3] The rate had been 50% until Freeport recouped its capital expenditures on the property. Illustrative of the general theme of this chapter is the break in Freeport's price from 109$^{1}/_{4}$ to 65$^{5}/_{8}$ in January–February 1928 coincident with the change in the royalty rate. The student may examine a similar development in the case of Texas Gulf Sulphur, occurring in 1934–1935.

to be extracted under entirely different conditions from those obtaining in the past. A large profit-sharing royalty would be payable on the sulphur produced from the new project, whereas the old Bryanmound was owned outright by Freeport and hence its profits accrued 100% to the company.

In addition to this known element of higher cost, great stress must be laid also upon the fact that the major future profits of Freeport were now expected from a *new project*. The Grande Ecaille property was not yet equipped and in operation, and hence it was subject to the many hazards that attach to enterprises in the development stage. The cost of production at the new mine might conceivably be much higher, or much lower, than at Bryanmound. From the standpoint of security analysis the important point is that, where two quite different properties are involved, you have two virtually separate enterprises. Hence the 1928–1932 record of Freeport Texas was hardly more relevant to its future history than were the figures of some entirely different sulphur company, *e.g.*, Texas Gulf Sulphur.

Returning once more to the business man's viewpoint on security values, the Freeport Texas exhibit suggests the following interesting line of reasoning. In June 1933 this enterprise was selling in the market for about $32,000,000 (25,000 shares of preferred at 125 and 730,000 shares of common at 40). The major portion of its future profits were expected to be derived from an investment of $3,000,000 to equip a new property leased from three large oil companies. Presumably these oil companies drove as good a bargain for themselves as possible in the terms of the lease. The market was in effect placing a valuation of some $20,000,000, or more, upon a new enterprise in which only $3,000,000 was to be invested. It was possible, of course, that this enterprise would prove to be worth much more than six times the money put into it. But from the standpoint of ordinary business procedure the payment of such an enormous premium for anticipated future results would appear imprudent in the extreme.[4]

Evidently the stock market—like the heart, in the French proverb— has reasons all its own. In the writers' view, where these reasons depart

---

[4] Since the Freeport Texas preferred issue was relatively small, representing less than one-tenth of the total market value of the company, this analysis would not call into question the safety of the senior issue, but reflects only upon the soundness of the valuation accorded the common stock—judged by investment standards. After 1933 the company did in fact encounter serious problems of production, which held down the earnings and depressed the market price, but these problems were later solved. Yet the maximum earnings attained by 1940—$3.30 per share in 1937—could scarcely justify the price of 49 paid by speculators in 1933.

violently from sound sense and business experience, common-stock buyers must inevitably lose money in the end, even though large speculative gains may temporarily accrue, and even though certain fortunate purchases may turn out to be permanently profitable.

The Future Price of the Product. The three preceding examples related to the future continuance of the rate of output and the operating costs upon which the past record of earnings was predicted. We must also consider such indications as may be available in regard to the *future selling price* of the product. Here we must ordinarily enter into the field of surmise or of prophecy. The analyst can truthfully say very little about future prices, except that they fall outside the realm of sound prediction. Now and then a more illuminating statement may be justified by the facts. Adhering to the mining field for our examples, we may mention the enormous profits made by zinc producers during the Great War, because of the high price of spelter. Butte and Superior Mining Company earned no less than $64 per share before depreciation and depletion in the two years 1915–1916, as the result of obtaining about 13 cents per pound for its output of zinc, against a prewar average of about $5^1/4$ cents. Obviously the future earning power of this company was almost certain to shrink far below the war-time figures, nor could these properly be taken together with the results of any other years in order to arrive at the average or supposedly "normal" earnings.[5]

Change in Status of Low-Cost Producers. The copper-mining industry offers an example of wider significance. An analysis of companies in this field must take into account the fact that since 1914 a substantial number of new low-cost producers have been developed and that other companies have succeeded in reducing extraction costs through metallurgical improvements. This means that there has been a definite lowering of the "center of gravity" of production costs for the entire industry. Other things being equal, this would make for a lower selling price in the future than obtained in the past. (Such a development is more strikingly illustrated by the crude-rubber industry.) Differently stated, mines that formerly rated as low-cost producers, *i.e.,* as having costs well below the average, may have lost this advantage, unless they have also greatly improved their technique of pro-

---

[5] The same type of reasoning clearly applies to the *volume of business* due to war conditions, as well illustrated by the exhibits of airplane companies in 1939–1940.

duction. The analyst would have to allow for these developments in his calculations, by taking a cautious view of future copper prices—at least as compared with the prewar or the predepression average.[6]

Anomalous Prices and Price Relationships in the History of the I.R.T. System. The checkered history of the Interborough Rapid Transit System in New York City has presented a great variety of divergences between market prices and the real or relative values ascertainable by analysis. Two of these discrepancies turn upon the fact that *for specific reasons* the then current and past earnings should not have been accepted as indicative of future earning power. In abbreviated form the details of these two situations are as follows:

For a number of years prior to 1918 the Interborough Rapid Transit Company was very prosperous. In the 12 months ended June 30, 1917, it earned $26 per share on its capital stock and paid dividends of $20 per share. Nearly all of this stock was owned by Interborough Consolidated Corporation, a holding concern (previously called Interborough-Metropolitan Corporation) which in turn had outstanding collateral trust bonds, 6% preferred stock and common stock. Including its share of the undistributed earnings of the operating company it earned about $11.50 per share on its preferred stock and about $2.50 on the common. The preferred sold in the market at 60, and the common at 10. These issues were actively traded in, and they were highly recommended to the public by various financial agencies which stressed the phenomenal growth of the subway traffic.

A modicum of analysis would have shown that the real picture was entirely different from what appeared on the surface. New rapid transit facilities were being constructed under contract between the City of New York and the Interborough (as well as others under contract between the City and the Brooklyn Rapid Transit Company). As soon as the new lines were placed in operation, which was to be the following year, the earnings available for Interborough were to be limited under this contract to the figure prevailing in 1911–1913, *which was far less than the current profits.*

---

[6] On the other hand, the rise in the price of gold in 1933 invalidated *for statistical purposes* previous earnings of gold producers based on $20.67 gold. Whether or not the future price of gold will remain at $35 is anyone's guess, but there seems no reason to make any calculations based on the old value.

The City would then be entitled to receive a high return on its enormous investment in the new lines. If and after all such payments were made in full, including back accruals, the City and the Interborough would then share equally in surplus profits. However, the preferential payments due the City would be so heavy that experts had testified that under the most favorable conditions it would be *more than 30 years* before there could be any surplus income to divide with the company.

The subjoined brief table shows the significance of these facts.

Interborough Rapid Transit System

Item	Actual earnings 1917	*Maximum* earnings when contract with City became operative
Balance for I.R.T. stock	$9,100,000	$5,200,000
Share applicable to Interborough Consolidated Corp.	8,800,000	5,000,000
Interest on Inter. Consol. bonds	3,520,000	3,520,000
Balance for Inter. Consol. pfd.	5,280,000	1,480,000
Preferred dividend requirements	2,740,000	2,740,000
Balance for Inter. Consol. common	2,540,000	*1,260,000(d)*
Earned per share, Inter. Consol. pfd.	$11.50	$3.25
Earned per share, Inter. Consol. common	2.50	nil

The underlying facts proved beyond question, therefore, that instead of a brilliant future being in store for Interborough, it was destined to suffer a severe loss of earning power within a year's time. It would then be quite impossible to maintain the $6 dividend on the holding company's preferred stock, and no earnings at all would be available for the common for a generation or more. On this showing it was mathematically certain that both Interborough Consolidated stock issues were worth far less than their current selling prices.[7]

---

[7] Indications pointed strongly to manipulative efforts by insiders in 1916–1917 to foist these shares upon the public at high prices before the period of lower earnings began. The payment of full dividends on the preferred stock, during an interlude of large earnings known to be temporary, was inexcusable from the standpoint of corporate policy but understandable as a

The sequel not only bore out this criticism, which it was bound to do, but demonstrated also that where an *upper limit* of earnings or value is fixed, there is usually danger that the actual figure will be less than the maximum. The opening of the new subway lines coincided with a large increase in operating costs, due to war-time inflation; and also, as was to be expected, it diminished the profits of the older routes. Interborough Rapid Transit Company was promptly compelled to reduce its dividend, and it was omitted entirely in 1919. In consequence the holding company, Interborough Consolidated, suspended its preferred dividends in 1918. The next year it defaulted the interest on its bonds, became bankrupt and disappeared from the scene, *with the complete extinction of both its preferred and common stock*. Two years later Interborough Rapid Transit Company, recently so prosperous, barely escaped an imminent receivership by means of a "voluntary" reorganization which extended a maturing note issue. When this extended issue matured in 1932, the company was again unable to pay, and this time receivers took over the property.

During the ten-year period between the two receivership applications another earnings situation developed, somewhat similar to that of 1917.[8] In 1928 the Interborough reported earnings of $3,000,000, or $8.50 per share for its common stock, and the shares sold as high as 62. But these earnings included $4,000,000 of "back preferential" from the subway division. The latter represented a limited amount due the Interborough Rapid Transit out of subway earnings to make good a deficiency in the profits of the early years of operating the new lines. On June 30, 1928 the amount of back preferential remaining to be paid the company was only

---

device to aid in unloading stock. These dividend distributions were not only unfair to the $4^{1}/_{2}\%$ bondholders, but, because of certain prior developments, they were probably illegal as well. (Reference to this aspect of the case was made in Chap. 20.)

[8] See Appendix Note 56 for a concise discussion of the numerous anomalies in price between various Interborough System securities, *viz.*:

1. Between Interborough Metropolitan $4^{1}/_{2}$s and Interborough Consolidated Preferred in 1919.
2. Between I.R.T. 5s and I.R.T. 7s in 1920.
3. Between I.R.T. stock and Manhattan "Modified" stock in 1929.
4. Between I.R.T. 5s and I.R.T. 7s in 1933.
5. Between Manhattan "Modified" and Manhattan "Unmodified" stock in 1933.

$1,413,000. *Hence all the profits available for Interborough stock were due to a special source of revenue that could continue for only a few months longer.* Heedless speculators, however, were capitalizing as permanent an earning power of Interborough stock which analysis would show was of entirely nonrecurrent and temporary character.

CHAPTER 39

Price-Earnings Ratios for Common Stocks. Adjustments for Changes in Capitalization

IN PREVIOUS CHAPTERS various references have been made to Wall Street's ideas on the relation of earnings to values. A given common stock is generally considered to be worth a certain number of times its current earnings. This number of times, or multiplier, depends partly on the prevailing psychology and partly on the nature and record of the enterprise. Prior to the 1927–1929 bull market ten times earnings was the accepted standard of measurement. More accurately speaking, it was the common point of departure for valuing common stocks, so that an issue would have to be considered exceptionally desirable to justify a higher ratio, and conversely.

Beginning about 1927 the ten-times-earnings standard was superseded by a rather confusing set of new yardsticks. On the one hand, there was a tendency to value common stocks in general more liberally than before. This was summarized in a famous dictum of a financial leader implying that good stocks were worth fifteen times their earnings.[1] There was also the tendency to make more sweeping distinctions in the valuations of different kinds of common stocks. Companies in especially favored groups, *e.g.*, public utilities and chain stores, in 1928–1929, sold at a very high multiple of current earnings, say, twenty-five to forty times. This was true also of the "blue chip" issues, which comprised leading units in miscellaneous fields. As pointed out before, these generous valuations were based upon the assumed continuance of the upward trend

---

[1] The wording of this statement, as quoted in the *Wall Street Journal* of March 26, 1928, was as follows: " 'General Motors shares, according to the Dow, Jones & Co. averages,' Mr. Raskob remarked, 'should sell at fifteen times earning power, or in the neighborhood of $225 per share, whereas at the present level of $180 they sell at approximately only twelve times current earnings.' "

shown over a longer or shorter period in the past. Subsequent to 1932 there developed a tendency for prices to rule higher in relation to earnings because of the sharp drop in long-term interest rates.

Exact Appraisal Impossible. Security analysis cannot presume to lay down general rules as to the "proper value" of any given common stock. Practically speaking, there is no such thing. The bases of value are too shifting to admit of any formulation that could claim to be even reasonably accurate. The whole idea of basing the value upon current earnings seems inherently absurd, since we know that the current earnings are constantly changing. And whether the multiplier should be ten or fifteen or thirty would seem at bottom a matter of purely arbitrary choice.

But the stock market itself has no time for such scientific scruples. It must make its values first and find its reasons afterwards. Its position is much like that of a jury in a breach-of-promise suit; there is no sound way of measuring the values involved, and yet they must be measured somehow and a verdict rendered. Hence the prices of common stocks are not carefully thought out computations but the resultants of a welter of human reactions. The stock market is a voting machine rather than a weighing machine. It responds to factual data not directly but only as they affect the decisions of buyers and sellers.

Limited Functions of the Analyst in Field of Appraisal of Stock Prices. Confronted by this mixture of changing facts and fluctuating human fancies, the securities analyst is clearly incapable of passing judgment on common-stock prices generally. There are, however, some concrete, if limited, functions that he may carry on in this field, of which the following are representative:

1. He may set up a basis for *conservative* or *investment* valuation of common stocks, as distinguished from speculative valuations.
2. He may point out the significance of: (*a*) the capitalization structure; and (*b*) the source of income, as bearing upon the valuation of a given stock issue.
3. He may find unusual elements in the balance sheet which affect the implications of the earnings picture.

A Suggested Basis of Maximum Appraisal for Investment. The investor in common stocks, equally with the speculator, is dependent on future rather than past earnings. His fundamental basis of appraisal must be an intelligent and conservative estimate of the future earning power. But his *measure* of future earnings can be conservative only if it is limited by actual performance over a period of time. We have suggested, however, that the profits of the most recent year, taken singly, might be accepted as the gage of future earnings, *if* (1) general business conditions in that year were not exceptionally good, (2) the company has shown an upward trend of earnings for some years past and (3) the investor's study of the industry gives him confidence in its continued growth. In a very exceptional case, the investor may be justified in counting on higher earnings in the future than at any time in the past. This might follow from developments involving a patent or the discovery of new ore in a mine or some similar specific and significant occurrence. But in most instances he will derive the investment value of a common stock from the average earnings of a period between five and ten years. This does not mean that all common stocks with the same average earnings should have the same value. The common-stock investor (*i.e.*, the *conservative* buyer) will properly accord a more liberal valuation to those issues which have current earnings above the average or which may reasonably be considered to possess better than average prospects or an inherently stable earning power. But it is the essence of our viewpoint that some moderate upper limit must *in every case* be placed on the multiplier in order to stay within the bounds of conservative valuation. We would suggest that *about 20 times average earnings* is as high a price as can be paid in an *investment* purchase of a common stock.

Although this rule is of necessity arbitrary in its nature, it is not entirely so. Investment presupposes demonstrable value, and the typical common stock's value can be demonstrated only by means of an established, *i.e.*, an average, earning power. But it is difficult to see how average earnings of *less than* 5% upon the market price could ever be considered as vindicating that price. Clearly such a price-earnings ratio could not provide that *margin of safety* which we have associated with the investor's position. It might be accepted by a purchaser in the expectation that future earnings will be larger than in the past. But in the original and most useful sense of the term such a basis of valuation is *speculative*.[2] It falls outside the purview of common-stock investment.

---

[2] See Appendix Note 57 for a discussion of the relationship between bond-interest rates and the "multiplier" for common stocks.

Higher Prices May Prevail for Speculative Commitments. The intent of this distinction must be clearly understood. We do not imply that it is a mistake to pay more than 20 times average earnings for any common stock. We do suggest that such a price would be speculative. The purchase may easily turn out to be highly profitable, but in that case it will have proved a wise or fortunate speculation. It is proper to remark, moreover, that very few people are consistently wise or fortunate in their speculative operations. Hence we may submit, as a corollary of no small practical importance, *that people who habitually purchase common stocks at more than about 20 times their average earnings are likely to lose considerable money in the long run.* This is the more probable because, in the absence of such a mechanical check, they are prone to succumb recurrently to the lure of bull markets, which always find some specious argument to justify paying extravagant prices for common stocks.

Other Requisites for Common Stocks of Investment Grade and a Corollary Therefrom. It should be pointed out that if 20 times average earnings is taken as the *upper limit* of price for an investment purchase, then ordinarily the price paid should be substantially less than this maximum. This suggests that about 12 or 12^1/$_2$ times average earnings may be suitable for the typical case of a company with neutral prospects. We must emphasize also that a reasonable ratio of market price to average earnings is not the only requisite for a common-stock investment. It is a necessary but not a sufficient condition. The company must be satisfactory also in its financial set-up and management, and not unsatisfactory in its prospects.

From this principle there follows another important corollary, *viz.:* *An attractive common-stock investment is an attractive speculation.* This is true because, if a common stock can meet the demand of a conservative investor that he get full value for his money *plus* not unsatisfactory future prospects, then such an issue must also have a fair chance of appreciating in market value.

Examples of Speculative and Investment Common Stocks. Our definition of an investment basis for common-stock purchases is at variance with the Wall Street practice in respect to common stocks of high rating. For such issues a price of considerably more than 20 times average earnings is held to be warranted, and furthermore these stocks are designated as "investment issues" regardless of the price at which they sell. According to our view, the high prices paid for "the best common stocks" make these purchases essentially speculative, because they require future growth to justify them. Hence common-stock investment operations, as we define them, will occupy a middle ground in the market, lying between low-price issues that are speculative because of doubtful quality and well-entrenched issues that are speculative, none the less, because of their high price.

Group A: Common Stocks Speculative in December 1938
Because of Their High Price (Figures adjusted to reflect changes in capitalization)

Item	Group A		
	General Electric	Coca-Cola	Johns-Manville
Amount Earned per Share of Common:			
1938	$0.96	$5.95	$1.09
1937	2.20	5.73	5.80
1936	1.52	4.66	5.13
1935	0.97	3.48	2.17
1934	0.59	3.12	0.22
1933	0.38	2.20	0.64(d)
1932	0.41	2.17	4.47(d)
1931	1.33	2.96	0.45
1930	1.90	2.79	3.66
1929	2.24	2.56	8.09
10-yr. average	$1.25	$3.56	$2.15
5-yr. average (1934–1938)	$1.25	$4.59	$2.88
Bonds	None	None	None
Pfd. Stock	None	600,000 sh. @ 60	75,000 sh. @ 130
		$36,000,000	$9,750,000
Common Stock	28,784,000 sh. @ 43$\frac{1}{2}$	3,992,000 sh. @ 132$\frac{1}{4}$	850,000 sh. @ 105
	$1,250,000,000	$529,500,000	$89,300,000
Total capitalization	$1,250,000,000	$565,500,000	$99,050,000
Net tangible assets, 12/31/38	$335,182,000	$43,486,000	$48,001,000
Net current assets, 12/31/38	$155,023,000	$25,094,000	$17,418,000
Average earnings on common-stock price, 1929–1938	2.9%	2.7%	2.0%
Maximum earnings on common-stock price, 1929–1938	5.1%	4.5%	7.7%
Minimum earnings on common-stock price, 1929–1938	0.9%	1.6%	(d)
Average earnings on common-stock price, 1934–1938	2.9%	3.5%	2.7%

These distinctions are illustrated by[3] the accompanying nine examples, taken as of December 31, 1938.
Comments on the Various Groups. The companies listed in Group *A* are representative of the so-called "first-grade" or "blue chip" industrials,

Group B: Common Stocks Speculative in December 1938
Because of Their Irregular Record

	Group B		
Item	Goodyear Tire and Rubber	Simmons	Youngstown Sheet and Tube
Amount earned per share of common:			
1938	$1.34	$1.42	$0.89(d)
1937	1.95	2.88	6.79
1936	3.90	3.53	7.03
1935	0.12	1.14	0.64
1934	0.66(d)	0.84(d)	2.95(d)
1933	0.79(d)	0.04	7.76(d)
1932	4.24(d)	2.57(d)	11.75(d)
1931	0.04	0.79(d)	6.55(d)
1930	0.37(d)	1.05(d)	5.17
1929	10.23	4.15	17.28
10-yr. average	$1.15	$0.79	$0.70
5-yr. average (1934–1938)	$ 1.35	$1.63	$2.12
Bonds	$50,235,000	$10,000,000	$87,000,000
Pfd. stock	650,000 sh. @ 108	None	150,000 sh. @ 81
	70,250,000		12,165,000
Common stock	2,059,000 sh. @ 37⅝	1,158,000 sh. @ 32	1,675,000 sh. @ 54¼
	$77,500,000	$37,050,000	$90,900,000
Total capitalization	$197,985,000	$47,050,000	$190,065,000
Net tangible assets, 12/31/38	$170,322,000	$28,446,000	$224,678,000
Net current assets, 12/31/38	$96,979,000	$14,788,000	$83,375,000
Average earnings on common- stock price, 1929–1938	3.1%	2.5%	1.3%
Maximum earnings on common- stock price, 1929–1938	27.2%	13.0%	31.8%
Minimum earnings on common- stock price, 1929–1938	(d)	(d)	(d)
Average earnings on common- stock price, 1934–1938	3.6%	5.1%	3.9%

---

[3] See Appendix Note 58 for the examples given in the 1934 edition, and their later performance.

which were particularly favored in the great speculation of 1928–1929 and in the markets of ensuing years. They are characterized by a strong financial position, by presumably excellent prospects and in most cases by relatively stable or growing earnings in the past. *The market price* of the shares, however, was higher than would be justified by their average earnings. In fact the profits of the *best* year in the 1929–1938 decade were less than 8% of the

Group C: Common Stocks Meeting Investment Tests in December 1938 from the Quantitative Standpoint

| Item | Group C | | |
	Adams-Millis	American Safety Razor	J. J. Newberry
Amount earned per share of common:			
1938	$3.21	$1.48	$4.05
1937	2.77	2.47	5.27
1936	2.55	2.70	6.03
1935	2.93	2.42	4.94
1934	3.41	2.03	5.38
1933	2.63	1.40	3.06
1932	1.03	1.14	1.07
1931	4.72	1.58	1.73
1930	4.83	2.50	2.27
1929	4.83	2.57	3.15
10-yr. average	$3.29	$2.03	$3.70
5-yr. average (1934–1938)	$2.97	$2.22	$5.13
Bonds	None	None	$5,587,000
Pfd. stock	None	None	51,000 sh. @ 106
			$5,405,000
Common stock	156,000 sh. @ 21	524,000 sh. @ 14$7/8$	380,000 sh. @ 34$1/2$
	$3,280,000	$7,800,000	$13,110,000
Total capitalization	$3,280,000	$7,800,000	$24,102,000
Net tangible assets, 12/31/38	$3,320,000	$6,484,000	$25,551,000
Net current assets, 12/31/38	$926,000	$3,649,000	$8,745,000
Average earnings on common-stock price, 1929–1938	15.7%	13.7%	10.7%
Maximum earnings on common-stock price, 1929–1938	23.0%	18.2%	17.5%
Minimum earnings on common-stock price, 1929–1938	4.9%	7.7%	3.1%
Average earnings on common-stock price, 1934–1938	14.1%	14.9%	14.9%

December 1938 market price. It is also characteristic of such issues that they sell for enormous premiums above the actual capital invested.

The companies analyzed in Group *B* are obviously speculative, because of the great instability of their earnings records. They show varying relationships of market price to average earnings, maximum earnings, and asset values.

The common stocks shown in Group *C* are examples of those which meet specific and quantitative tests of investment quality. These tests include the following:

1. The earnings have been reasonably stable, allowing for the tremendous fluctuations in business conditions during the ten-year period.
2. The average earnings bear a satisfactory ratio to market price.[4]
3. The financial set-up is sufficiently conservative, and the working-capital position is strong.

Although we do not suggest that a common stock bought for investment be *required* to show asset values equal to the price paid, it is none the less characteristic of issues in Group *C* that, as a whole, they will not sell for a huge premium above the companies' actual resources.

Common-stock *investment*, as we envisage it, will confine itself to issues making exhibits of the kind illustrated by Group *C*. But the actual purchase of any such issues must require *also* that the purchaser be satisfied in his own mind that the prospects of the enterprise are at least reasonably favorable.

ALLOWANCES FOR CHANGES IN CAPITALIZATION

In dealing with the past record of earnings, when given on a per-share basis, it is elementary that the figures must be adjusted to reflect any important changes in the capitalization which have taken place during the period. In the simplest case these will involve a change only in the number of shares of common stock due to stock dividends, split-ups, etc. All that is necessary then is to restate the capitalization throughout the period on the basis of the current number of shares. (Such recalculations are made by some of the statistical services but not by others.)

---

[4] Note that the *average* earnings of the three companies in Group *C* were nearly two and one-half times as large relative to market price as the *maximum* earnings of the companies in Group *A*.

When the change in capitalization has been due to the sale of additional stock at a comparatively low price (usually through the exercise of subscription rights or warrants) or to the conversion of senior securities, the adjustment is more difficult. In such cases the earnings available for the common during the earlier period must be increased by whatever gain would have followed from the issuance of the additional shares. When bonds or preferred stocks have been converted into common, the charges formerly paid thereon are to be added back to the earnings and the new figure then applied to the larger number of shares. If stock has been sold at a relatively low price, a proper adjustment would allow earnings of, say, 5 to 8% on the proceeds of the sale. (Such recalculations need not be made unless the changes indicated thereby are substantial.)

A corresponding adjustment of the per-share earnings must be made at times to reflect the possible *future* increase in the number of shares outstanding as a result of conversions or exercise of option warrants. When other security holders have a choice of any kind, sound analysis must allow for the possible adverse effect upon the per-share earnings of the common stock that would follow from the exercise of the option.

Examples: This type of adjustment must be made in analyzing the reported earnings of American Airlines, Inc., for the 12 months ended September 30, 1939.

Earnings as reported......................	$1,128,000
Per share on about 300,000 shares outstanding..	$3.76

(Price December 1939 about 37)

But there were outstanding $2,600,000 of $4^{1}/_{2}$% debentures, convertible into common stock at $12.50 per share. The analyst must *assume* conversion of the bonds, giving the following adjusted result:

Earnings, adding back $117,000 interest	$1,245,000
Per share on 508,000 shares	$2.45

More than one-third of the reported earnings per share are lost when the necessary adjustment is made.

American Water Works and Electric Company can be used to illustrate both types of adjustment. (See the next page.)

Adjustment *A* reflects the payment of stock dividends in 1928, 1929 and 1930.

Adjustment B assumes conversion of the $15,000,000 of convertible 5s, issued in 1934, thus increasing the earnings by the amount of the interest charges but also increasing the common-stock issue by 750,000 shares. (The foregoing adjustments are independent of any possible modifications in the reported earnings arising from the questioning of the depreciation charges, etc., as previously discussed.)

Year	Earnings* for common as reported			Adjustment A			Adjustment B	
	Amount of shares	Number	Per share	Number of shares	Earned per share	Amount	Number of shares	Earned per share
1933	$2,392	1,751	$1.37	1,751	$1.37	$3,140	2,501	$1.26
1932	2,491	1,751	1.42	1,751	1.42	3,240	2,501	1.30
1931	4,904	1,751	2.80	1,751	2.80	5,650	2,501	2.26
1930	5,424	1,751	3.10	1,751	3.10	6,170	2,501	2.47
1929	6,621	1,657	4.00	1,741	3.80	7,370	2,491	2.95
1928	5,009	1,432	3.49	1,739	2.88	5,760	2,489	2.30
1927	3,660	1,361	2.69	1,737	2.11	4,410	2,487	1.76
7-year average			$2.70		$2.50			$2.04

* Number of shares and earnings in thousands.

Corresponding adjustments in book values or current-asset values per share of common stock should be made in analyzing the balance sheet. This technique is followed in our discussion of the Baldwin Locomotive Works exhibit in Appendix Note 70 in which outstanding warrants are allowed for.

ALLOWANCES FOR PARTICIPATING INTERESTS

In calculating the earnings available for the common, full recognition must be given to the rights of holders of participating issues, whether or not the amounts involved are actually being paid thereon. Similar allowances must be made for the effect of management contracts providing for a substantial percentage of the profits as compensation, as in the case of investment trusts. Unusual cases sometimes arise involving "restricted shares," dividends on which are contingent upon earnings or other considerations.

Example: Trico Products Corporation, a large manufacturer of automobile accessories, is capitalized at 675,000 shares of common stock, of which 450,000 shares (owned by the president) were originally "restricted" as to dividends. The unrestricted stock is first entitled to dividends of $2.50 per share, after which both classes share equally in further dividends. In addition, successive blocks of the restricted stock were to be released from the restriction according as the earnings for 1925 and successive years reached certain stipulated figures. (To the end of 1938, a total of 239,951 shares had been thus released.)

Adjusted Earnings: Trico Products Corporation[1]

Year	Earnings for common	Earned per share on unrestricted stock		
		A. Ignoring restricted shares	B. Maximum distribution on unrestricted shares	C. Allowing for release of restricted shares (*i.e.*, on total capitalization)
1929	$2,250,000	$6.67	$4.58	$3.33
1930	1,908,000	5.09	3.94	2.83
1931	1,763,000	4.70	3.72	2.61
1932	965,000	2.57	2.54	1.44
1933	1,418,000	3.78	3.21	2.10
1934	1,772,000	4.72	3.74	2.62
1935	3,567,000	9.84	6.52	5.38
1936	4,185,000	9.75	7.25	6.39
1937	3,792,000	8.97	6.82	5.99
1938	2,320,000	5.56	4.53	3.70
10-year average	$3,394,000	$6.17	$4.69	$3.64

[1] The calculations for the years 1935–1938 have been affected by repurchases of unrestricted shares by the corporation.

In the above table Column *C* supplies the soundest measure of the earning power shown for the unrestricted shares. Column *A* is irrelevant.

A situation similar to that in Trico Products Corporation obtained in the case of Montana Power Company stock prior to June 1921.

General Rule. The material in the last few pages may be summarized in the following general rule:

> The intrinsic value of a common stock preceded by convertible securities, or subject to dilution through the exercise of stock options or through participating privileges enjoyed by other security holders, cannot reasonably be appraised at a higher figure than would be justified if all such privileges were exercised in full.

CHAPTER 40

Capitalization Structure

THE DIVISION of a company's total capitalization between senior securities and common stock has an important bearing upon the significance of the earning power per share. A set of hypothetical examples will help make this point clear. For this purpose we shall postulate three industrial companies, *A, B* and *C*, each with an earning power (*i.e.*, with average and recent earnings) of $1,000,000. They are identical in all respects save capitalization structure. Company *A* is capitalized solely at 100,000 shares of common stock. Company *B* has outstanding $6,000,000 of 4% bonds and 100,000 shares of common stock. Company *C* has outstanding $12,000,000 of 4% bonds and 100,000 shares of common stock.

We shall assume that the bonds are worth par and that the common stocks are worth about 12 times their per-share earnings. Then the value of the three companies will work out as follows:

Company	Earnings for common stock	Value of common stock	Value of bonds	Total value of company
A	$1,000,000	$12,000,000		$12,000,000
B	760,000	9,000,000	$6,000,000	15,000,000
C	520,000	6,000,000	12,000,000	18,000,000

These results challenge attention. Companies with identical earning power appear to have widely differing values, due solely to the arrangement of their capitalization. But the capitalization structure is itself a matter of voluntary determination by those in control. Does this mean that the fair value of an enterprise can be arbitrarily increased or decreased by changing around the relative proportions of senior securities and common stock?

Can the Value of an Enterprise Be Altered Through Arbitrary Variations in Capital Structure? To answer this question properly we must scrutinize our examples with greater care. In working out the value of the three companies we assumed that the bonds would be worth par and that the stocks would be worth twelve times their earnings. Are these assumptions tenable? Let us consider first the case of Company B. If there are no unfavorable elements in the picture, the bonds might well sell at about 100, since the interest is earned four times. Nor would the presence of this funded debt ordinarily prevent the common stock from selling at 12 times its established earning power.

It will be urged however, that, if Company B shares are worth 12 times their earnings, Company A shares should be worth more than this multiple because they have no debt ahead of them. The risk is therefore smaller, and they are less vulnerable to the effect of a shrinkage in earnings than is the stock of Company B. This is obviously true, and yet it is equally true that Company B shares will be more responsive to an *increase* in earnings. The following figures bring this point out clearly:

	Earned per share		Change in earnings per share from base	
Assumed earnings	Co. A	Co. B	Co. A	Co. B
$1,000,000	$10.00	$ 7.60	(Base)	(Base)
750,000	7.50	5.10	−25%	−33%
1,250,000	12.50	10.10	+25%	+33%

Would it not be fair to assume that the greater sensitivity of Company B to a possible decline in profits is offset by its greater sensitivity to a possible increase? Furthermore, if the investor expects higher earnings in the future—and presumably he selects his common stocks with this in mind—would he not be justified in selecting the issue that will benefit more from a given degree of improvement? We are thus led back to the original conclusions that Company B may be worth $3,000,000, or 25% more than Company A due solely to its distribution of capitalization between bonds and stock.

Principle of Optimum Capitalization Structure. Paradoxical as this conclusion may seem, it is supported by the actual behavior of common stocks in the market. If we subject this contradiction to closer analysis, we shall find that it arises from what may be called an *oversimplification* of Company *A*'s capital structure. Company *A*'s common stock evidently contains the two elements represented by the bonds and stock of Company *B*. Part of Company *A*'s stock is at bottom equivalent to Company *B*'s bonds and should *in theory* be valued on the same basis, *i.e.*, 4%. The remainder of Company *A*'s stock should then be valued at 12 times earnings. This theoretical reasoning would give us a combined value of $15,000,000, *i.e.*, an average 6²/₃% basis, for the two components of Company *A* stock, which, of course, is the same as that of Company *B* bonds and stock taken together.

But this $15,000,000 value for Company *A* stock would not ordinarily be realized *in practice*. The obvious reason is that the common-stock buyer will rarely recognize the existence of a "bond component" in a common-stock issue, and in any event, not wanting such a bond component, he is unwilling to pay extra for it.[1] This fact leads us to an important principle, both for the security buyer and for corporate management, *viz*.:

The optimum capitalization structure for any enterprise includes senior securities to the extent that they may safely be issued and bought for investment.

Concretely this means that the capitalization arrangement of Company *B* is preferable to that of Company *A* from the stockholder's standpoint, assuming that in both cases the $6,000,000 bond issue would constitute a sound investment. (This might require, among other things, that the companies show a net working capital of not less than $6,000,000 in accordance with the stringent tests for sound industrial issues recommended in Chap. 13.) Under such conditions the contribution of the entire capital by the common stockholders may be called an *over*conservative set-up, as it tends generally to make the stockholder's dollar less productive to him than if a reasonable part of the capital were borrowed. An analogous situation holds true in most private businesses, where it is

---

[1] See our discussion of American Laundry Machinery Company on pp. 505–507 of the 1934 edition of this work for an illustration of the possible effect of a change of capital structure from an all-stock to a stock-and-bond combination. Actual changes of this kind were made by American Zinc (through a dividend in preferred stock in 1916) and by Maytag Company through similar distributions in 1928. The usual method of introducing a speculative capitalization structure into a company with a conservative set-up is through formation of a holding company that issues its own senior securities and common stock against acquisition of the operating company's common. *Examples:* Chesapeake Corporation in 1927, Kaufmann Department Stores Securities Corporation in 1925.

recognized as profitable and proper policy to use a conservative amount of banking accommodation for seasonal needs rather than to finance operations entirely by owners' capital.

Corporate Practices Resulting in Shortage of Sound Industrial Bonds.
Furthermore, just as it is desirable from the bank's standpoint that sound businesses borrow seasonally, it is also desirable from the standpoint of investors generally that strong industrial corporations raise an appropriate part of their capital through the sale of bonds. Such a policy would increase the number of high-grade bond issues on the market, giving the bond investor a wider range of choice and making it deservedly difficult to sell unsound bonds. Unfortunately the practice of industrial corporations in recent years has tended to produce a shortage of good industrial bond issues. Strong enterprises have in general refrained from floating new bonds and in many cases have retired old ones. But this avoidance of bonded debt by the strongest industrial companies has in fact produced results demoralizing to investors and investment policies in a number of ways. The following observations on this point, written in 1934, are still applicable in good part:

1. It has tended to restrict new industrial-bond financing to companies of weaker standing. The relative scarcity of good bonds impelled investment houses to sell and investors to buy inferior issues, with inevitably disastrous results.

2. The shortage of good bonds also tended to drive investors into the preferred-stock field. For reasons previously detailed (in Chap. XIV) straight preferred stocks are unsound in theory, and they are therefore likely to prove unsatisfactory investment media as a class.

3. The elimination (or virtual elimination) of senior securities in the set-up of many large corporations has, of course, added somewhat to the investment quality of their common stocks, but it has added even more to the investor's demand for these common stocks. This in turn has resulted in a good deal of common-stock buying by people whose circumstances required that they purchase sound bonds. Furthermore it has supplied a superficial justification for the creation of excessive prices for these common stocks; and finally it contributed powerfully to that confusion between investment motives and speculative motives which during 1927–1929 served to debauch so large a proportion of the country's erstwhile careful investors.

Appraisal of Earnings Where Capital Structure Is Top-Heavy. In order to carry this theory of capitalization structure a step further, let us examine the case of Company C. We arrived at a valuation of $18,000,000 for this enterprise by assuming that its $12,000,000 bond issue would sell at par and the stock would sell for 12 times its earnings of $5.20 per share. But this assumption as to the price of the bonds is clearly fallacious. Earnings of twice interest charges are not sufficient protection for an industrial bond, and hence investors would be unwise to purchase such an issue at par. In fact this very example supplies a useful demonstration of our contention that a coverage of two times interest is inadequate. If it were ample—as some investors seem to believe—the owners of any reasonably prosperous business, earning 8% on the money invested, could get back their entire capital by selling a 4% bond issue, and they would still have control of the business together with one-half of its earnings. Such an arrangement would be exceedingly attractive for the proprietors but idiotic from the standpoint of those who buy the bonds.

Our Company C example also sheds some light on the effect of the rate of interest on the apparent safety of the senior security. If the $12,000,000 bond issue had carried a 6% coupon, the interest charges of $720,000 would then be earned less than $1\frac{1}{2}$ times. Let us assume that Company D had such a bond issue. An unwary investor, looking at the two exhibits, might reject Company D's 6% bonds as unsafe because their interest coverage was only 1.39 but yet accept the Company C bonds at par because he was satisfied with earnings of twice fixed charges. Such discrimination would be scarcely intelligent. Our investor would be rejecting a bond *merely because* it pays him a generous coupon rate, and he would be accepting another bond *merely because* it pays him a low interest rate. The real point, however, is that the minimum margin of safety behind bond issues must be set high enough to avoid the possibility that safety may even *appear* to be achieved by a mere lowering of the interest rate. The same reasoning would apply of course to the dividend rate on preferred stocks.

Since Company C bonds are not safe, because of the excessive size of the issue, they are likely to sell at a considerable discount from par. We cannot suggest the proper price level for such an issue, but we have indicated in Chap. 26 that a bond speculative because of inadequate safety should not ordinarily be purchased above 70. It is also quite possible that the presence of this excessive bond issue might prevent the stock from selling at 12 times its earnings, because conservative stock buyers would avoid Company C as subject to too great hazard of financial difficulties in the event of untoward developments. The result may well be that, instead of being worth $18,000,000 in the market as originally assumed, the combined bond and stock issues of Company C will sell for less than $15,000,000 (the Company B valuation), or even for less than $12,000,000 (the value of Company A).

As a matter of cold fact, it should be recognized that this unfavorable result may not necessarily follow. If investors are sufficiently careless and if speculators are sufficiently enthusiastic, the securities of Company C may conceivably sell in the market for $18,000,000 or even more. But such a situation would be unwarranted and unsound.[2] Our theory of capitalization structure could not admit a Company C arrangement as in any sense standard or suitable. This indicates that there are definite limits upon the advantages to be gained by the use of senior securities. We have already expressed this fact in our principle of the optimum capitalization structure, for senior securities cease to be an advantage at the point where their amount becomes larger than can safely be issued or bought for investment.

We have characterized the Company A type of capitalization arrangement as "overconservative"; the Company C type may be termed "speculative," whereas that of Company B may well be called "suitable" or "appropriate."

The Factor of Leverage in Speculative Capitalization Structure. Although a speculative capitalization structure throws all the company's securities outside the pale of investment, it may give the common stock a definite speculative advantage. A 25% increase in the earnings of Company C (from $1,000,000 to $1,250,000) will mean about a 50% increase in the earnings per share of common (from $5.20 to $7.70). Because of this fact there is some tendency for speculatively capitalized

---

[2] In 1925 Dodge Brothers (motor) securities were sold to the public on the basis of $160,000,000 principal value of bonds and preferred stock and about $50,000,000 market value of common. Net tangible assets were only $80,000,000, and average earnings about $16,000,000. This obviously top-heavy capitalization structure did not militate against the security values at first, but a severe decline in earnings in 1927 soon revealed the unsoundness of the financial setup. (In 1928 the company was taken over by Chrysler.)

enterprises to sell at relatively high values in the aggregate during good times or good markets. Conversely, of course, they may be subject to a greater degree of undervaluation in depression. There is, however, a real advantage in the fact that such issues, when selling on a deflated basis, can advance much further than they can decline.

American Water Works and Electric Company

Item	1921	1923	1924	1929	Ratio of 1929 figures to 1921 figures
Gross earnings*	$20,574	$36,380	$38,356	$54,119	2.63 :1
Net for charges*	6,692	12,684	13,770	22,776	3.44 :1
Fixed charges and preferred dividends*	6,353	11,315	12,780	16,154	2.54 :1
Balance for common*	339	1,369	990	6,622	19.53 :1
1921 basis:†					
Number of shares of common	92,000	100,000	100,000	130,000	1.41 :1
Earned per share	$3.68	$13.69	$9.90	$51.00	13.86 :1
High price of common	6¹/₂	44³/₄	209	about 2500	385.00 :1
% earned on high price of common	56.6%	30.6%	4.7%	2.04%	0.037 :1
As reported:					
Number of shares of common	92,000	100,000	500,000	1,657,000	
Earned per share	$3.68	$13.69	$1.98	$4.00	
High price of common	6¹/₂	44³/₄	41⁷/₈	199	

* In thousands.
† Number of shares and price adjusted to eliminate effect of stock dividends and split-ups.

The record of American Water Works and Electric Company common stock between 1921 and 1929 presents an almost fabulous picture of enhancement in value, a great part of which was due to the influence of a highly speculative capitalization structure. Four annual exhibits during this period are summarized in the table above.

The purchaser of 1 share of American Water Works common stock at the high price of 6¹/₂ in 1921, if he retained the distributions made in stock, would have owned about 12¹/₂ shares when the common sold at its high price of 199 in 1929. His $6.50 would have grown to about $2,500. While the market value of the common shares was thus increasing some 400-fold, the gross earnings had expanded to only 2.6 times the earlier figure. The tremendously disproportionate rise in the common-stock value was due to the following elements, in order of importance:

1. A much higher valuation placed upon the per-share earnings of this issue. In 1921 the company's capitalization was recognized as top-heavy; its bonds sold at a low price, and the earnings per share of common were not taken seriously, especially since no dividends were being paid on the second preferred. In 1929 the general enthusiasm for public-utility shares resulted in a price for the common issue of nearly 50 times its highest recorded earnings.

2. The speculative capitalization structure allowed the common stock to gain an enormous advantage from the expansion of the company's properties and earnings. Nearly all the additional funds needed were raised by the sale of senior securities. It will be observed that whereas the gross revenues increased about 160% from 1921 to 1929, the balance per share of old common stock grew 14-fold during the same period.

3. The margin of profit improved during these years, as shown by the higher ratio of net to gross. The speculative capital structure greatly accentuated the benefit to the common stock from the additional net profits so derived.[3]

Other Examples: The behavior of speculatively capitalized enterprises *under varying business conditions* is well illustrated by the appended analysis of A. E. Staley Manufacturing Company, manufacturers of corn products. For comparison there is given also a corresponding analysis of American Maize Products Company, a conservatively capitalized enterprise in the same field.

The most striking aspect of the Staley exhibit is the extraordinary fluctuation in the yearly earnings per share of common stock. The business itself is evidently subject to wide variations in net profit, and the effect of

---

[3] See Appendix Note 59 for data illustrating the reverse process applied to American Water Works from 1929 through 1938; also for a similar speculative opportunity in United Light and Power Company Preferred Stock in 1935.

these variations on the common stock is immensely magnified by reason of the small amount of common stock in comparison with the senior securities.[4] The large depreciation allowance acts also as the equivalent of a heavy fixed charge. Hence a decline in net before depreciation from $3,266,000 in 1929 to $1,540,000 the next year, somewhat over 50%, resulted in a drop in earnings *per share of common* from $84 to only $3.74. The net profits of American Maize Products were fully as variable, but the small amount of prior charges made the fluctuations in common-stock earnings far less spectacular.

A. E. Staley

Year	Net before depreciation*	Depreciation*	Fixed charges and pfd. dividends*	Balance for common*	Earned per share
1933	$2,563	$743	$652	$1,168	$55.63
1932	1,546	753	678	114	5.43
1931	892	696	692	496(d)	23.60(d)
1930	1,540	753	708	79	3.74
1929	3,266	743	757	1,766	84.09
1928	1,491	641	696	154	7.35
1927	1,303	531	541	231	11.01
1926	2,433	495	430	1,507	71.77
1925	792	452	358	18(d)	0.87(d)
1924	1,339	419	439	481	22.89

---

[4] In 1934 the company declared a 100% stock dividend, thus doubling the number of shares of common, and in 1937 split the stock 10 for 1 and changed the par value from $100 to $10. These two developments multiplied the outstanding shares by 20. Persistence of the variable factor in the earnings for the common stock is shown by the following per-share figures, based on the 1933 capitalization:

1934	$28.46
1935	2.76(d)
1936	52.88
1937	18.40(d)
1938	38.80
1939	68.00

American Maize Products

Year	Net before depreciation*	Depreciation*	Fixed charges and pfd. dividends*	Balance for common*	Earned per share
1933	$1,022	$301		$721	$2.40
1932	687	299		388	1.29
1931	460	299		161	0.54
1930	1,246	306	22	918	3.06
1929	1,835	312	80	1,443	4.81
1928	906	317	105	484	1.61
1927	400	318	105	23(d)	0.08(d)

* 000 omitted.

Capitalization (as of January 1933)

Item	A. E. Staley	American Maize Products
6% bonds	($4,000,000* @ 75) $3,000,000	
$7 pfd. stock	(50,000 sh. @ 44) 2,200,000	
Common stock	(21,000 sh. @ 45) 950,000	(300,000 sh. @ 20) $6,000,000
Total capitalization	$6,150,000	$6,000,000
Average earnings, 1927–1932, about	900,000	615,000
% of these earning on 1933 capitalization	14.6%	10.3%†
Average earnings per sh. of common	$14.76	$1.87
% earned on price of common	32.8%	9.4%†
Working capital, Dec. 31, 1932	$3,664,000	$2,843,000
Net assets, Dec. 31, 1932	$15,000,000	$4,827,000

* Deducting estimated amount of bonds in treasury.
† The difference between these two figures is due to the varying treatment of the preferred stock outstanding during 1927–1930. A very small amount of preferred stock remaining in 1931–1933 is ignored in the above calculations.

Speculative Capitalization May Cause Valuation of Total Enterprise at an Unduly Low Figure.

The market situation of the Staley securities in January 1933 presents a practical confirmation of our theoretical analysis of Company C above. The top-heavy capitalization structure resulted in a low price for the bonds and the preferred stock, the latter being affected particularly by the temporary suspension of its dividend in 1931. The result was that, instead of showing an increased total value by reason of the presence of senior securities, the company sold in the market at a much lower relative price than the conservatively capitalized American Maize Products. (The latter company showed a normal relationship between average earnings and market value. It should not properly be termed *overconservatively* capitalized because the variations in its annual earnings would constitute a good reason for avoiding any substantial amount of senior securities. A bond or preferred stock issue of very small size, on the other hand, would be of no particular advantage or disadvantage.)

The indication that the A. E. Staley Company was undervalued in January 1933 in comparison with American Maize Products is strengthened by reference to the relative current-asset positions and total resources. Per dollar of net asset values the Staley company was selling only one-third as high as American Maize.

The overdeflation of a speculative issue like Staley common in unfavorable markets creates the possibility of an amazing price advance when conditions improve, because the earnings per share then show so violent an increase. Note that at the beginning of 1927 Staley common was quoted at about 75, and a year later it sold close to 300. Similarly the shares advanced from a low of 33 in 1932 to the equivalent of 320 in 1939.

A Corresponding Example. A more spectacular instance of tremendous price changes for the same reason is supplied by Mohawk Rubber. In 1927 the common sold at 15, representing a valuation of only $300,000 for the junior issue, which followed $1,960,000 of preferred. The company had lost $610,000 in 1926 on $6,400,000 of sales. In 1927 sales dropped to $5,700,000, but there was a net profit of $630,000. This amounted to over $23 per share on the small amount of common stock. The price consequently advanced from its low of 15 in 1927 to a high of 251 in 1928. In 1930 the company again lost $669,000, and the next year the price declined to the equivalent of only $4.

In a speculatively capitalized enterprise, the common stockholders benefit—or have the possibility of benefiting—at the expense of the senior security holders. The common stockholder is operating with a little of his own money and with a great deal of the senior security holder's money; as between him and them it is a case of "Heads I win, tails you lose." This strategic position of the common stockholder with relatively small commitment is an extreme form of what is called "trading on the equity." Using another expression, he may be said to have a "cheap call" on the future profits of the enterprise.

Speculative Attractiveness of "Shoe-String" Common Stocks Considered. Our discussion of fixed-value investment has emphasized as strongly as possible the disadvantage (amounting to unfairness) that attaches to the senior security holder's position where the junior capital is proportionately slight. The question would logically arise if there are not corresponding *advantages* to the common stock in such an arrangement, from which it gains a very high degree of speculative attractiveness. This inquiry would obviously take us entirely outside the field of common-stock *investment* but would represent an expedition into the realm of intelligent or even scientific speculation.

We have already seen from our A. E. Staley example that in bad times a speculative capitalization structure may react adversely on the market price of both the senior securities and the common stock. During such a period, then, the common stockholders do not derive a present benefit at the expense of the bondholder. This fact clearly detracts from the speculative advantage inherent in such common stocks. It is easy to suggest that these issues be purchased only when they are selling at abnormally low levels due to temporarily unfavorable conditions. But this is really begging the question, because it assumes that the intelligent speculator can consistently detect and wait for these abnormal and temporary conditions. If this were so, he could make a great deal of money regardless of what type of common stock he buys, and under such conditions he might be better advised to select high-grade common stocks at bargain prices rather than these more speculative issues.

Practical Aspects of the Foregoing. To view the matter in a practical light, the purchase of speculatively capitalized common stocks must be considered under general or market conditions that are supposedly normal, *i.e.*, under those which are not obviously inflated or deflated. Assuming (1) diversification, and (2) reasonably good judgment in selecting companies with satisfactory prospects, it would seem that the speculator should be able to profit rather substantially in the long run from commitments of this kind. In making such purchases, partiality should evidently be shown to those companies in which most of the senior capital is in the form of preferred stock rather than bonds. Such an arrangement removes or minimizes the danger of extinction of the junior equity through default in bad times and thus permits the shoe-string common stockholder to maintain his position until prosperity returns. (But just because the preferred-stock contract benefits the common shareholder in this way, it is clearly disadvantageous to the preferred stockholder himself.)

We must not forget, however, the peculiar practical difficulty in the way of realizing the full amount of prospective gain in any one of the purchases. As we pointed out in the analogous case of convertible bonds, as soon as a substantial profit appears the holder is in a dilemma, because he can hold for a further gain only by risking that already accrued. Just as a convertible bond loses its distinctive advantages when the price rises to a point that carries it clearly outside of the straight investment class, so a shoe-string common-stock commitment is transformed into a more and more substantial commitment as the price continues to rise. In our Mohawk Rubber example the intelligent purchaser at 15 could not have expected to hold it beyond 100—even though its quotation did reach 250—because at 100, or before, the shares had lost the distinctive characteristics of a speculatively capitalized junior issue.

CHAPTER 41

Low-Priced Common Stocks. Analysis of the Source of Income

LOW-PRICED STOCKS

The characteristics discussed in the preceding chapter are generally thought of by the public in connection with *low-priced stocks*. The majority of issues of the speculatively capitalized type do sell within the low-priced range. The definition of "low-priced" must, of course, be somewhat arbitrary. Prices below $10 per share belong to this category beyond question; those above $20 are ordinarily excluded; so that the dividing line would be set somewhere between $10 and $20.

Arithmetical Advantage of Low-Priced Issues. Low-priced common stocks appear to possess an inherent arithmetical advantage arising from the fact they can advance so much more than they can decline. It is a commonplace of the securities market that an issue will rise more readily from 10 to 40 than from 100 to 400. This fact is due in part to the preferences of the speculative public, which generally is much more partial to issues in the 10-to-40 range than to those selling above 100. But it is also true that in many cases low-price common stocks give the owner the advantage of an interest in, or "call" upon, a relatively large enterprise at relatively small expense.

A statistical study of the relative price behavior of industrial stocks in various price groups was presented in the April 1936 issue of *The Journal of Business of the University of Chicago*.[1] The study was devoted to the period 1926–1935[2] and revealed a continuous superiority of diversified,

---

[1] Fritzemeier, Louis H., "Relative Price Fluctuations of Industrial Stocks in Different Price Groups," *loc. cit.*, pp. 133–154.

[2] See pp. 473–474 of the 1934 edition of this work for reference to an earlier study devoted to the relative behavior of low-priced and high-priced issues when purchased at or near the

low-priced issues over diversified, high-priced issues as speculative media. The following quotation from the study summarizes the results and conclusions reached by the author:

> Unless there are serious uncompensated errors in the statistical work here presented, this investigation would seem to establish the existence of certain relationships between price level and price fluctuations which have hitherto gone unreported by students of stock-market phenomena. These relationships may be briefly stated as follows:
>
> 1. Low-price stocks tend to fluctuate relatively more than high-price stocks.
>
> 2. In a "bull" market the low-price stocks tend to go up relatively more than high-price stocks, and they do not lose these superior gains in the recessions which follow. In other words, the downward movement of low-price stocks is less than proportional to their upward movement, when compared with the upward and downward movement of high-price stocks.
>
> • • •
>
> Assuming (1) that the future behavior of the various price groups will be similar to their past behavior and (2) that the selection of stocks on the basis of the activity for the current year does not account completely, if at all, for the superior performance of the stocks in the low-price groups, it seems logical to conclude the following:
>
> 1. Low-price industrial stocks offer greater opportunities for speculative profits than high-price industrial stocks.
>
> 2. In case two or more issues of industrial stocks seem to offer equal prospective profits, the speculator should purchase the shares selling at the lowest price.

Some Reasons Why Most Buyers of Low-Priced Issues Lose Money. The pronounced liking of the public for "cheap stocks" would therefore seem to have a sound basis in logic. Yet it is undoubtedly true that most people who buy low-priced stocks lose money on their purchases. Why is this so? The underlying reason is that the public buys issues that are *sold* to it, and the sales effort is put forward to benefit the seller and not the buyer. In consequence the bulk of the low-priced purchases made by the public are of the wrong kind; *i.e.*, they do not provide the real advantages of this

bottoms of depressions in 1897, 1907, 1914 and 1921. Within its more limited scope this study, published in 1931 by J. H. Holmes and Company, led to conclusions similar to those of Fritzemeier.

security type. The reason may be either because the companies are in bad financial condition or because the common stock is low-priced in appearance only and actually represents a full or excessive commitment in relation to the size of the enterprise. The latter is preponderantly true of *new* security offerings in the low-priced range. In such cases, a *pseudo*-low price is accomplished by the simple artifice of creating so large a number of shares that even at a few dollars per share the total value of the common issue is excessive. This has been true of mining-stock flotations from of old and was encountered again in the liquor-stock offerings of 1933 and in the airplane issues in 1938–1939.

A *genuinely* low-priced common stock will show an aggregate value for the issue which is small in relation to the company's assets, sales and past or prospective profits. The examples shown herewith will illustrate the difference between a "genuine" and "pseudo-low" price.

Item	Wright-Hargreaves Mines, Ltd. (gold mining)	Barker Bros. Corp. (retail store)
July 1933:		
Price of common stock	7	5
Number of shares outstanding	5,500,000	148,500
Total value of common	$38,500,000	$ 743,000
Preferred stock at par		2,815,000
Preferred stock at market		500,000
Year 1932:		
Sales	$ 3,983,000	$ 8,154,000
Net earnings	2,001,000*	703,000(d)
Period 1924–1932:		
Maximum sales	$ 3,983,000	$16,261,000
Maximum net earnings	2,001,000*	1,100,000
Maximum earnings per share of common	$0.36*	$7.59
Working capital, Dec. 1932	$ 1,930,000	$ 5,010,000
Net tangible assets, Dec. 1932	4,544,000	7,200,000

* Before depletion.

The Wright-Hargreaves issue was low-priced in appearance only, for in fact the price registered a very high valuation for the company as compared with all parts of its financial exhibit. The opposite was true of Barker Brothers because here the $743,000 valuation represented by the common stock was exceedingly small in relation to the size of the enterprise. (Note also that the same statement could be applied to Barker Brothers Preferred, which at its quotation of 18 partook of the qualities of a low-priced common stock.)[3]

Observation of the stock market will show that the stocks of companies facing receivership are likely to be more active than those which are very low in price merely because of poor current earnings. This phenomenon is caused by the desire of insiders to dispose of their holdings before the receivership wipes them out, thus accounting for a large supply of these shares at a low level and also sometimes for unscrupulous efforts to persuade the unwary public to buy them. But where a low-priced stock fulfills our conditions of speculative attractiveness, there is apt to be no pressure to sell and no effort to create buying. Hence the issue is inactive and attracts little public attention. This analysis may explain why the public almost always buys the wrong low-priced issues and ignores the really promising opportunities in this field.

Low Price Coupled with Speculative Capitalization. Speculatively capitalized enterprises, according to our definition, are marked by a relatively large amount of senior securities and a comparatively small issue of common stock. Although in most cases the common stock will sell at a low price per share, it need not necessarily do so if the number of shares is small. In the Staley case, for example (referred to in Chap. 40) even at $50 per share for the common in 1933 the capitalization structure would still have been speculative, since the bonds and preferred at par would represent over 90% of the total. It is also true that even where there are no senior securities the common stock may have possibilities equivalent to those in a speculatively capitalized enterprise. These possibilities will occur wherever the market value of the common issue-represents a small

---

[3] See Appendix Note 60 for the sequel to these examples. For a more recent contrast along the same lines the student is invited to compare the showing of Continental Motors Corporation and Gilchrist Company when both were selling at $5 near the close of 1939. Beyond our basic distinction, founded on the relationship between the valuation of the company and its assets and sales, there is here a striking contrast in the earnings record and working-capital position.

amount of money in relation to the size of the business, regardless of how it is capitalized.

To illustrate this point we append a condensed analysis of Mandel Brothers, Inc., and Gimbel Brothers, Inc., two department-store enterprises, as of September 1939.

Item	Gimbel Bros.	Mandel Bros.
September 1939:		
Bonds at par	$26,753,000	
Preferred stock	197,000 sh. @ 50	
	$9,850,000	
Common stock	977,000 sh. @ 8	297,000 sh. @ 5
	$7,816,000	$1,485,000
Total capitalization	$44,419,000	$1,485,000
Results for 12 months to July 31, 1939:		
Sales	$87,963,000	$17,883,000
Net before interest	1,073	155,000
Balance for common	1,105(d)	155,000
Earned per share	1.13(d)	0.52
Period 1934–1938*:		
Maximum sales (1937)	$100,081,000	$19,378,000
Maximum net earnings (1937) for common	2,032,000	414,000
Maximum earnings per share of common (1937)	2.08	1.33
High price of common	29³/₈ (1937)	18 (1936)
Average earnings per share of common	0.23	0.46
Jan. 31, 1939:		
Net current assets	$22,916,000	$ 4,043,000
Net tangible assets	75,614,000	6,001,000
Rents paid 1937	1,401,000	867,000

* Based on report for succeeding Jan. 31.

Gimbel Brothers presents a typical picture of a speculatively capitalized enterprise. On the other hand Mandel Brothers has no senior securities ahead of the common, but despite this fact the relatively small market value of the entire issue imparts to the shares the same sort of speculative possibilities (though in somewhat lesser degree) as are found in the Gimbel Brothers set-up. Note, however, that the rental payments of Mandel Brothers are proportionately much higher than those of Gimbel Brothers and that these rental charges are equivalent in good part to senior securities.

Large Volume and High Production Cost Equivalent to Speculative Capital Structure. This example should lead us to widen our conception of a speculatively situated common stock. The speculative or *marginal* position may arise from any cause that reduces the percentage of gross available for the common to a subnormal figure and that therefore serves to create a subnormal value for the common stock in relation to the volume of business. Unusually high operating or production costs have the identical effect as excessive senior charges in cutting down the percentage of gross available for common. The following hypothetical examples of three copper producers will make this point more intelligible and also lead to some conclusions on the subject of large output versus low operating costs.

Item	Company A	Company B	Company C
Capitalization:			
6% Bonds		$50,000,000	
Common stock	1,000,000 sh.	1,000,000 sh.	1,000,000 sh.
Output	100,000,000 lb.	150,000,000 lb.	150,000,000 lb.
Cost of production (before interest)	7¢	7¢	9¢
Interest charge per pound		2¢	
Total cost per pound	7¢	9¢	9¢
A			
Assumed price of copper	10¢	10¢	
Profit per pound	3¢	1¢	
Output per share	100 lb.	150 lb.	
Profit per share	$3	$1.50	
Value of stock at 10 times earnings	$30	$15	
Output per $1 of market value of stock	3$^1/_3$ lb.	10 lb.	
B			
Assumed price of copper	13¢	13¢	
Profit per pound	6¢	4¢	
Profit per share	$6	$6	
Value per share at ten times earnings	$60	$60	
Output per $1 of market price of stock	1$^2/_3$ lb.	2$^1/_2$ lb.	

It is scarcely necessary to point out that the higher production cost of Company *C* will have exactly the same effect as the bond-interest require-ment of Company *B* (assuming output and production costs to continue as stated).

General Principle Derived. The foregoing table is perhaps more useful in showing concretely the inverse relationship that usually exists between profit per unit and output per dollar of stock value.

The general principle may be stated that the lower the unit cost the lower the production per dollar of market value of stock and *vice versa.* Since Company *A* has a 7-cent cost, its stock naturally sells at a higher price *per pound of output* than Company *C* with its 9-cent cost. Conversely, Company *C* produces more pounds per dollar of stock value than Company *A.* This fact is not without significance from the stand-point of speculative technique. When a rise in the price of the commodity occurs, there will ordinarily be a larger advance, percentagewise, in the shares of high-cost producers than in the shares of low-cost producers. The foregoing table indicates that a rise in the price of copper from 10 to 13 cents would increase the value of Company *A* shares by 100% and the value of Company *B* and *C* shares by 300%. Contrary to the general impression in Wall Street, the stocks of high-cost producers are more logical commitments than those of the low-cost producers when the buyer is convinced that a rise in the price of the product is imminent and he wishes to exploit this conviction to the utmost.[4] Exactly the same advantage attaches to the purchase of speculatively capitalized common stocks when a pronounced improvement in sales and profits is confi-dently anticipated.

THE SOURCES OF INCOME

The "source of income" will ordinarily be thought of as meaning the same thing as the "type of business." This consideration enters very largely into the basis on which the public will value the earnings per share shown by a given common stock. Different "multipliers" are used for different sorts of enterprise, but we must point out that these distinctions are themselves

---

[4] The action of the market in advancing Company *B* shares from 15 to 60 because copper rises from 10 to 13 cents is in itself extremely illogical, for there is ordinarily no warrant for suppos-ing that the higher metal price will be *permanent.* However, since the market does in fact behave in this irrational fashion, the speculator must recognize this behavior in his calculation.

subject to change with the changing times.[5] Prior to the World War the railroad stocks were valued most generously of all, because of their supposed stability. In 1927–1929 the public-utility group sold at the highest ratio to earnings, because of their record of steady growth. Between 1933 and 1939 adverse legislation and, in particular, the fear of government competition greatly reduced the relative popularity of the utility stocks. The most liberal valuations have recently been accorded to the large and well-entrenched industrial enterprises which were able to maintain substantial earnings during the depression and are considered to possess favorable long-term prospects. Because of these repeated variations in relative behavior and popularity, security analysis must hesitate to prescribe any definitive rules for valuing one type of business as against another. It is a truism to say that the more impressive the record and the more promising the prospects of stability and growth the more liberally the per-share earnings should be valued, subject always to our principle that a multiplier higher than about 20 (*i.e.*, an "earnings basis" of less than 5%) will carry the issue out of the *investment* price range.

A Special Phase: Three Examples. A more fruitful field for the technique of analysis is found in those cases where the source of income must be studied in relation to specific assets owned by the company, instead of in relation merely to the general nature of the business. This point may be quite important when a substantial portion of the income accrues from investment holdings or from some other fixed and dependable source. Three examples will be used to illuminate this rather subtle aspect of common-stock analysis.

1. *Northern Pipe Line Company.* For the years 1923–1925 the Northern Pipe Line Company reported earnings and dividends as follows:

Year	Net earnings	Earned per share*	Dividend paid
1923	$308,000	$7.70	$10, plus $15 extra
1924	214,000	5.35	8
1925	311,000	7.77	6

* Capitalization, 40,000 shares of common stock.

---

[5] See Cowles, Alfred, 3d, and associates (*Common Stock Indexes*, 1871–1937), pp. 43–46, 404–418, Bloomington, Ind., 1938, for a study of earnings-price ratios for different industrial groups in successive years from 1871 through 1937. Ratios for 1934–1938 and for 1936–1938 are supplied in our analysis of the New York Stock Exchange industrial list in Appendix Note 61.

In 1924 the shares sold as low as 72, in 1925 as low as 67¹/₂ and in 1926 as low as 64. These prices were on the whole somewhat less than ten times the reported earnings and reflected a lack of enthusiasm for the shares, due to a pronounced decline in profits from the figures of preceding years and also to the reductions in the dividend.

Analysis of the income account however, would have revealed the following division of the *sources of income:*[6]

Income	1923		1924		1925	
	Total	Per share	Total	Per share	Total	Per share
Earned from:						
Pipe-line operations	$179,000	$4.48	$ 69,000	$1.71	$103,000	$2.57
Interest and rents	164,000	4.10	159,000	3.99	170,000	4.25
Nonrecurrent items	dr. 35,000	dr. 0.88	dr. 14,000	0.35	cr. 38,000	cr. 0.95
	$308,000	$7.70	$214,000	$5.35	$311,000	$7.77

This income account is exceptional in that the greater part of the profits were derived from sources other than the pipe-line business itself. About $4 per share were regularly received in interest on investments and rentals. The balance sheet showed holdings of nearly $3,200,000 (or $80 per share) in Liberty Bonds and other gilt-edged marketable securities, on which the interest income was about 4%.

This fact meant that a special basis of valuation must be applied to the per-share earnings, inasmuch as the usual "ten-times-earnings" basis would result in a nonsensical conclusion. Gilt-edged investments of $80 per share would yield an income of $3.20 per share, and at ten times earnings this $80 would be "worth" only $32 per share, a *reductio ad absurdum.* Obviously, that part of the Northern Pipe Line income that was derived from its bond holdings should logically be valued at a higher basis than the portion derived from the fluctuating pipe-line business. A sound valuation of Northern Pipe Line stock would therefore have to proceed along the lines suggested below. The pipe-line earnings would have to be valued at a low basis because of their unsatisfactory trend. The interest

---

[6] Although the company's reports to its stockholders contained very little information, complete financial and operating data were on file with the Interstate Commerce Commission and open to public inspection.

and rental income must presumably be valued on a basis corresponding with the actual value of the assets producing the income. This analysis indicated clearly that, at the price of 64 in 1926, Northern Pipe Line stock was selling considerably below its intrinsic value.[7]

Average 1923–1925*		Valuation basis	Value per share
Earned per share from pipe line.	$2.92	15% (6²/₃ times earnings)	$ 20
Earned per share from interest and rentals	4.10	5% (20 times earnings)	80
Total	$7.02		$100

* The nonrecurrent profits and losses are not taken into account.

2. *Lackawanna Securities Company.* This company was organized to hold a large block of Glen Alden Coal Company 4% bonds formerly owned by the Delaware, Lackawanna and Western Railroad Company, and its shares were distributed pro rata to the Delaware, Lackawanna and Western stockholders. The Securities Company had outstanding 844,000 shares of common stock. On December 31, 1931 its sole asset—other than about $1 per share in cash—consisted of $51,000,000 face value of Glen Alden 4% first mortgage bonds. For the year 1931, the income account was as follows:

Interest received on Glen Alden bonds $2,084,000
Less:
    Expenses 17,000
    Federal taxes 250,000
Balance for stock 1,817,000
Earned per share $2.15

Superficially, the price of 23 in 1932 for a stock earning $2.15 did not appear out of line. But these earnings were derived, not from ordinary commercial or manufacturing operations, but from the holding of a bond

---

[7] A parallel situation existed in the case of Davis Coal and Coke Company prior to the distribution of $50 per share to stockholders out of its large holdings of government bonds in 1937–1938. Shortly prior to this action the stock had sold at 35. The student can see from the annual reports that the average earnings of $2.06 per share and average dividends of $2.56 in 1934–1937 came entirely from sources other than the coal business.

issue which presumably constituted a high-grade investment. (In 1931 the Glen Alden Coal Company earned $9,550,000 available for interest charges of $2,151,000, thus covering the bond requirements $4^{1}/_{2}$ times.) By valuing this interest income on about a 10% basis the market was in fact valuing the Glen Alden bonds at only 37 cents on the dollar. (The price of 23 for a share of Lackawanna Securities was equivalent to $60 face value of Glen Alden bonds at 37, plus $1 in cash)

Here again, as in the Northern Pipe Line example, analysis would show convincingly that the customary ten-times-earnings basis resulted in a glaring undervaluation of this specially situated issue.

Tobacco Products Corporation

Item	Price: December 1931	Market value
Capitalization		
2,240,000 shares of 7% Class A (par $20)	$6	$13,440,000
3,300,000 shares common	$2^{1}/_{4}$	7,425,000
Total		$20,825,000
Net income for the year 1931		about $2,200,000
Earned per share of Class A		about $1
Earned for common after Class A dividends		nil
Dividend paid on Class A		$0.80

3. *Tobacco Products Corporation of Virginia.* In this example, as in the other two, the company was selling in the market for about ten times the latest reported earnings. But the 1931 earnings of Tobacco Products were derived entirely from a lease of certain of its assets to American Tobacco Company, which provided for an annual rental of $2,500,000 for 99 years from 1923. Since the American Tobacco Company was able to meet its obligation without question, this annual rental income was equivalent to interest on a high-grade investment. Its value was therefore much more than ten times the income therefrom. This meant that the market valuation of the Tobacco Products stock issues in December 1931 was far less than was justified by the actual position of the company. (The value of the lease was in fact calculated to be about $35,600,000 on an amortized basis. The company also owned a large amount of United

Cigar Stores' stock, which later proved to be practically worthless, but these additional holdings did not, of course, detract from the value of its American Tobacco lease.)

Relative Importance of Situations of This Kind. The field of study represented by the foregoing examples is not important quantitatively, because, after all, only a very small percentage of the companies examined will fall within this group. Situations of this kind arise with sufficient frequency, however, to give this discussion practical value. It should be useful also in illustrating again the wide technical difference between the critical approach of security analysis and the highly superficial reactions and valuations of the stock market.

Two Lines of Conduct Suggested. When it can be shown that certain conditions, such as those last discussed, tend to give rise to undervaluations in the market, two different lines of conduct are thereby suggested. We have first an opportunity for the securities analyst to detect these undervaluations and eventually to profit from them. But there is also the indication that the financial set-up that causes this undervaluation is erroneous and that the stockholders' interests require the correction of this error. The very fact that a company constituted like Northern Pipe Line or Lackawanna Securities tends to sell in the market far below its true value proves as strongly as possible that the whole arrangement is wrong from the stand-point of the owners of the business.

At the bottom of these cases there is a basic principle of consistency involved. It is inconsistent for most of the capital of a pipe-line enterprise actually to be employed in the ownership of gilt-edged bonds. The whole set-up of Lackawanna Securities was also inconsistent, because it replaced a presumably high-grade bond issue, which investors might be willing to buy at a fair price, by a nondescript stock issue which no one would purchase except at an exceptionally low price. (In addition a heavy and needless burden of corporate income tax was involved, as was true in the Tobacco Products case.)

Illogical arrangements of this kind should be recognized by the real parties in interest, *i.e.*, the stockholders, and they should insist that the anomaly be rectified. This was finally done in the three examples just given. In the case of Northern Pipe Line the capital not needed in the pipe-line business was returned to the stockholders by means of special distributions aggregating $70 per share. The Lackawanna Securities Company was entirely dissolved and the Glen Alden bonds in its treasury distributed pro rata to the stockholders in lieu of their stock. Finally, the Tobacco Products Corporation was recapitalized on a basis by which 6^1/$_2$% bonds were issued against the American Tobacco lease, so that this asset of fixed value was represented by a fixed-value security (which later were redeemed at par) instead of by shares of stock in a corporation subject to highly speculative influences. By means of these corporate rearrangements the real values were speedily established in the market price.[8]

The situations that we have just analyzed required a transfer of attention from the income account figures to certain related features revealed in the balance sheet. Hence the foregoing topic—Sources of Income—carries us over into our next field of inquiry: The Balance Sheet.

---

[8] The student is invited to consider two further examples illustrating this point in 1939, *viz.*

1. Westmoreland Coal Company, selling at 8 although the company held some $18 per share in cash assets alone. This case is broadly similar to our Davis Coal and Coke example, although there were some differences. See discussion of this company on pp. 588–589.

2. American Cigarette and Cigar. In this case there is also a long-term lease to American Tobacco Company (as in the Tobacco Products example), but the situation is complicated by the company's own operations, which have produced losses, and by ownership of other assets.

Attention is drawn also to our discussion of Lehigh Coal and Navigation Company in Chap. 33, in which we suggested that the mining losses were perhaps inseparable from the large income from lease of the railroad.

PART VI

Balance-Sheet Analysis. Implications of Asset Values

The Evolving Utility of Balance Sheet Analysis

by Seth A. Klarman

E arly in my career, I took Graham and Dodd quite literally. When they advised close scrutiny of a company's balance sheet to assess value, I regarded that as a mandate. Find companies whose stocks were, for whatever reason, trading for less than the conservatively estimated liquidation value of those firm's underlying assets. Buy them, and then wait for the market to correct the mispricing. This seemed like a no-brainer. But over time, it became increasingly clear to me that this approach was overly simplistic and most of the time unactionable, a null or nearly null set. I realized that Graham himself had expressed the limitations of balance sheet analysis such as when he said, "The value of a company's assets as carried in its balance sheet has lost practically all its significance . . . bearing no relationship to the figure at which they would be sold or the figure which would be justified by the earnings." (Chap. 42)

A lot had changed since Graham's day—management practices, shareholder activism, the rate of technological innovation, the volume of corporate merger and acquisition activity—rendering a balance-sheet-oriented approach to valuation and downside protection much less useful. It is important to examine those changes—but to also see the valuable role that book value still plays in analyzing companies in certain industries and the utility of a balance sheet in understanding the underlying drivers of a business.

Security Analysis was written in the depths of the Great Depression, at a time when global economic activity had collapsed, and the U.S. stock market had plunged more than 80% in only three years. This market disarray left enormous carnage in its wake. In a period when not only the future prospects but even the immediate viability of many businesses seemed dim, identifying stocks trading below the liquidation value of the underlying companies was a fruitful filter. A great many securities were available on the bargain counter. Investing amid plunging prices and significant economic uncertainty, when others were fearing there was worse to come, might have seemed risky but actually conferred a favorable ratio of reward to risk for those intrepid enough to buy in.

However, most of the time, the economy is not in depression and relatively few securities meet the strict Graham and Dodd criteria. An investor focusing solely on buying what they called "net nets"— companies trading for less than the value of their working capital net of all liabilities—would be ignoring a vast universe of potential (and likely more attractive) opportunities—in higher quality businesses with better growth prospects. As with anyone following an overly narrow approach, investors must have an answer to the question, "What do you do when there's nothing to do?"

Investment approaches should be built not just to navigate one moment in time but to be relevant all the time. We must consider the opportunity to buy common stocks for less than the liquidation value of the underlying companies to be a rare aberration, one to be found only sporadically and at a small number of companies. Even if such valuations were found, we would need to be circumspect about whether the approach would bear fruit. The companies such a screen might reveal are likely to be those with significant problems and uncertain long-term viability. In today's economy, they are less likely to be hidden gems than deeply troubled enterprises.

Meanwhile, the ideas and tools for analyzing companies have been dramatically expanded. Investors—whether individuals or institutions—no longer depend on a slide rule or rudimentary calculator; they can rely on powerful Bloomberg terminals and desktop computers. Analyzing a company solely by its published financial statements confers no evident edge. To invest successfully amid deep-pocketed and technologically enabled competitors, investors must have an approach involving some sort of differentiated view or unique sourcing capability, and analyzing corporate balance sheets is unlikely to provide unique insights. Similarly, running a screen to identify companies trading below apparent liquidation value confers no apparent edge, because everyone can do that, and as a result, stocks don't often become and stay egregiously mispriced the way they may have many decades ago.

WHERE BALANCE SHEET ANALYSIS FALLS SHORT

A company is much more than the numbers on its financial statements. These days, the volume of public information and the analytical tools available to assess that information are truly extraordinary. Legions of Wall Street analysts focus intensely on the quality of businesses. They have developed sophisticated, albeit far from perfect, models for projecting near-term growth, profit margins, and cash flows. Managements are no longer inaccessible, nor can they speak only to favored shareholders. Indeed, most CEOs and CFOs of publicly traded companies hold quarterly earnings calls with shareholders, provide forecasts, and offer in-depth investor days. They also go on road shows to meet with investors in advance of large secondary offerings, spin-offs, and IPOs. Meanwhile, investment analysts use "expert networks" to gain insights into a company, its competitors, and its industry. Every investor is able to instantaneously call up financial statements for thousands of companies; Wall Street research reports on thousands of publicly traded firms are also readily available. Widely disseminated information confers no particular edge unless it is analyzed in differentiated ways; unique sources of information are hard to come by in a highly competitive world.

The intensified competition for investment insights makes it crucial for investors to consistently exhibit deep humility. The irony of the information age is that you can know more than you ever did before, and perhaps more than anyone ever did before, yet that wealth of information is less useful now, because it confers upon you no particular edge. Everybody knows what you know. Indeed, a naive approach based solely on using company financials to screen for opportunity could well be a sucker bet. Warren Buffett often notes that investing can be like playing poker, in one important sense. At a poker table, if you look to your left and to your right and you can't identify the patsy, the mark, the rube who has been invited to the game by the more experienced players, then it's probably you. Every investor should be worried by that thought and should work assiduously to never find themselves in that position.

Even if you could find shares in overlooked companies available below likely liquidation value, benefiting from their mispricing has become far from a sure thing, because liquidation value has become increasingly murky. Companies are not easily or frequently liquidated; all liabilities, including off–balance sheet and contingent ones, must be extinguished before liquidation proceeds are distributed to shareholders, whose interests are subordinated. Rent must be paid under leases that may extend well into the future. Employees may have been promised deferred compensation or termination benefits. Products may have extended warranties. Underfunded pension plans must be funded. Also, many companies that seem potentially discounted based on balance sheet analysis have a cash burn rate until the time that they achieve a future profitability. This especially applies to many of the smaller technology companies and biotech start-ups that may have prematurely come public in the euphoric environment of 2020–2021. For such companies, cash on hand today may not be available for shareholders tomorrow if it is spent on research and development, customer acquisition, new facilities, or acquisitions.

Another pitfall for investors overly focused on book value is that financial accounting standards are far from perfect. At best, they are an approximation that, like an Impressionist painting, can give a sense of reality without being reality. Accounting is a bit like throwing a dart from the far side of a room. You almost certainly won't hit the bull's-eye, and you may not even hit the target. Hopefully, you'll be close enough, but sometimes you won't be.

One of the many difficulties associated with accounting principles is that they provide a snapshot of a company's finances at a fixed point in time. But things change: companies may have inventories that are subject to rapid obsolescence, receivables that have become uncollectable, and plant and equipment that have become increasingly inefficient, outmoded, or obsolete. Some firms may have large off–balance sheet liabilities, resulting from environmental damage, product defects, or ongoing litigation. On the other side of the ledger, some companies hold "hidden assets," such as real estate that has appreciated far above amortized cost, ownership interest in an increasingly valuable fast-growing subsidiary, or a significantly overfunded pension plan.

The effects of sustained inflation over time have also wreaked havoc with the accuracy of assets accounted for using historic cost accounting. Consequently, two companies owning identical assets could report very different book values. Accounting is, of course, still very useful in the big picture. An approximation is obviously better than no information at all. Also, in some countries, accounting standards are less than rigorous, and investors would be wise to be even more skeptical than usual about the reported numbers. It pays to verify that the auditor is highly credible. The job of investors is not to simply accept the GAAP numbers, but rather to question and continuously refine them to achieve greater and greater accuracy.

Another accounting challenge investors face in using book value as a means of estimating business value is the impact of share buybacks over time. Accounting standards adjust shareholder's equity down for the cost of stock repurchases, meaning that a very profitable company that regularly buys back shares with free cash flow may have a low or even negative stated book value. Accounting principles for companies that execute large share repurchases over time can easily yield a misleading result.

The whole point of forming a company is to build an enterprise that is worth much more than the sum of its parts. The goal is to grow value to a level far above book value, significantly eclipsing the cost of the physical assets held by the business. The present value of the cash flows generated by a successful business will significantly exceed the cost of forming and building it, ideally by a very substantial margin. Value is, of course, created when a business offers a reliable product or service at a reasonable price that meets the needs and aspirations of its customers. The value of a business above the balance sheet value of its hard assets can be thought of as goodwill. (Not the financial statement goodwill sometimes booked in a takeover, but the general, conversational definition of goodwill, that is, the positive feelings, or "goodwill" that a company has engendered among its customers, suppliers, and other stakeholders as expressed through loyalty, trust, and symbiotic relationships.)

Another problem with focusing on book value is that it is often embodied by an industrial model that has been significantly disrupted by technology. The book value of large manufacturing companies is of necessity substantial, a measure of the resources necessary to be in such businesses. But some of the best businesses in the world have been formed since the advent of the internet, and many are "asset light." They outsource manufacturing and other activities; they rent rather than own assets. Their products are intellectual property such as computer software. For such businesses, book value is essentially irrelevant; their business value is considerably greater than the hard assets they own. Some companies are able to build increasingly wide moats around their businesses as a result of accumulating more and more data from their customers, creating a valuable network effect whereby today's commercial success leads to tomorrow's even greater competitive advantage.

Today, when a company loses its edge and comes under increased competitive threat, often because of technological disruption, the downside comes suddenly and relentlessly. With so many stocks trading at a hefty premium to book value (many for good reason), there is a long way to fall before the value of hard assets cushions the downside. These days, the small number of businesses trading at very depressed levels, levels at which the book value or liquidation value exceeds the share price, are likely to be those with commensurately less upside potential and inferior business models. Thus book value is no longer a screen for attractive opportunity, but instead for its opposite. The book value of a company that cannot generate cash flow is necessarily suspect, as are its component parts—inventory, receivables, and plant and equipment.

But wait: for certain businesses, it should be noted, book value does remain quite relevant. Regulated businesses such as utilities are entitled to a statutory return on capital, and most utilities trade in a reasonably narrow valuation range as a result. Banks and insurance companies are required by regulators to have a certain ratio of shareholder capital at risk compared to the size of the business. While some have created more enduring business moats than others, book value is a more relevant metric for financial institutions than for most other businesses if (and this is a big if) the assets on the balance sheet of those firms are worth at least their reported carrying value.

THE MOST USEFUL ASPECTS
OF BALANCE SHEET ANALYSIS

While book value has become considerably less relevant than in the past, nonetheless balance sheet analysis remains a highly valuable and necessary practice for all investors. A company's balance sheet can be an indicator of its financial health and even prosperity. Companies with limited debt are said to have a "clean" balance sheet and usually significant borrowing capacity in reserve, which confers operating and strategic flexibility. On the other hand, a highly leveraged balance sheet offers less flexibility, while raising the prospect of looming debt maturities that must be met. A heavily indebted company runs into trouble quickly when the economy turns down and its operating performance stumbles. That may launch a spiral in which maturing debt must be refinanced at increasingly higher cost, causing interest expense to gobble up a growing portion of corporate cash flow.

Balance sheet analysis will always be a useful tool to an investor in financially distressed or bankrupt companies. It remains an essential element in understanding the hierarchy of claims on the company's assets and determining the value of a business. Equity investors bear the risk that a downturn in business results could drive the need for dilutive share issuance at discounted prices.

Corporate managements regularly seek to optimize their balance sheets. Holding too much cash and other liquid assets lowers the return on invested capital. On the other hand, holding insufficient liquidity could cause a business to be vulnerable to sudden economic or market shocks. A company with a clean balance sheet has more degrees of freedom than a highly leveraged one.

Finally, a balance sheet can provide clues to a company's underlying business performance. It's important to be able to identify red flags. Are the reported earnings consistent with the free cash flow generated by a company? Are the days it takes to collect on receivables or the number of days that inventory is held longer than in the past? Are liabilities growing faster than the business is? Investors will want to conduct such analyses before taking a position.

Graham and Dodd's emphasis on book value may have been supplanted by newer metrics, but their focus on balance sheet analysis remains valid. Balance sheet scrutiny is a necessary though not sufficient step in analyzing investments. A successful investor should always delve into the smallest balance sheet details in order to ferret out clues as to the true merits of a business and the challenges facing it. No matter how robust an investor's models and algorithms may be, it always pays to read the footnotes.

CHAPTER 42

Balance-Sheet Analysis. Significance of Book Value

On numerous occasions prior to this point we have expressed our conviction that the balance sheet deserves more attention than Wall Street has been willing to accord it for many years past. By way of introduction to this section of our work, let us list five types of information and guidance that the investor may derive from a study of the balance sheet:

1. It shows how much capital is invested in the business.
2. It reveals the ease or stringency of the company's financial condition, *i.e.*, the working-capital position.
3. It contains the details of the capitalization structure.
4. It provides an important check upon the validity of the reported earnings.
5. It supplies the basis for analyzing the sources of income.

In dealing with the first of these functions of the balance sheet, we shall begin by presenting certain definitions. The *book value* of a stock is the value of the assets applicable thereto as shown in the balance sheet. It is customary to restrict this value to the tangible assets, *i.e.*, to eliminate from the calculation such items as good-will, trade names, patents, franchises, leaseholds. The book value is also referred to as the "asset value," and sometimes as the "tangible-asset value," to make clear that intangibles are not included. In the case of common stocks, it is also frequently termed the "equity."

Computation of Book Value. The *book value per share* of a common stock is found by adding up all the tangible assets, subtracting all liabilities and stock issues ahead of the common and then dividing by the number of shares.

In many cases the following formula will be found to furnish a short cut to the answer:

Book Value per share of common

$$= \frac{\text{Common Stock} + \text{Surplus Items} - \text{Intangibles}}{\text{Number of shares outstanding}}$$

By Surplus Items are meant not only items clearly marked as surplus but also premiums on capital stock and such reserves as are really part of the surplus. This would include, for example, reserves for preferred-stock retirement, for plant improvement, and for contingencies (unless known to be actually needed). Reserves of this character may be termed "Voluntary Reserves."

Calculation of Book Value of United States Steel Common on December 31, 1938
Condensed Balance Sheet December 31, 1938 (In millions)

Assets		Liabilities	
1. Property Investment Account		7. Common Stock	$653
(less depreciation)	$1,166	8. Preferred Stock	360
2. Mining Royalties	9	9. Subsidiary Stocks Publicly Held	5
3. Deferred Charges*	4	10. Bonded Debt............	232
4. Miscellaneous Investments ..	19	11. Mining Royalty Notes	12
5. Miscellaneous Other Assets ..	3	12. Current Liabilities	79
6. Current Assets	510	13. Contingency and Other Reserves	39
		14. Insurance Reserves	46
		15. Capital Surplus	38
		16. Earned Surplus	247
	$1,711		$1,711

Tangible assets $1,711,000,000

Less: All liabilities ahead of common (Sum of items 8–12) ... 688,000,000

Net assets for common stock $1,023,000,000

Book value per share (on 8,700,000 shares)................ $117.59

* Considerable argument could be staged over the question whether Deferred Charges are intangible or tangible assets, but as the amount involved is almost always small, the matter has no practical importance. It is more convenient, of course, to include the Deferred Charges with the other assets.

The alternative method of computation, which is usually shorter than the foregoing, is as follows:

Common stock $653,000,000

Surplus and voluntary reserves (Sum of items 13–16)   370,000,000

Net assets for common stock $1,023,000,000

Treatment of Preferred Stock When Calculating Book Value of Common.

In calculating the assets available for the common stock, care must be taken to subtract preferred stock at its proper valuation. Ordinarily, this will be the par or stated value of the preferred stock as it appears in the balance sheet. But there is a growing number of cases in which preferred stock is carried in the balance sheet at arbitrary values far lower than the real liability attaching thereto.

Island Creek Coal Company has a preferred stock of $1 par, which is entitled to annual dividends of $6 and to $120 per share in the event of dissolution. In 1939 the price of this issue ruled about 120. In the calculation of the asset value of Island Creek Coal Common the preferred stock should be deducted not at $1 per share but at $100 per share, its "true" or "effective" par, or else at 120. Capital Administration Company, Ltd., an investment trust, has outstanding preferred stock entitled to $3 cumulative dividends and to $50 or $55 in liquidation, but its par value is $10. It has also a Class *A* stock entitled to $20 in liquidation plus 70% of the assets remaining and to 70% of the earnings paid out after preferred dividends, but the par value of this issue is $1. Finally it has Class *B* stock, par 1 cent, entitled to the residue of earnings and assets. Obviously a balance sheet set up on the basis of par value is worse than meaningless in this case, and it must be corrected by the analyst somewhat as follows:

Balance Sheet December 31, 1938

As published		As revised	
Total assets (at cost)	$5,335,300	(at mkt.)	$5,862,500
Payables and accruals	1,661,200		1,661,200
Preferred stock (at par $10)	434,000	(at 55*)	2,387,000
Class *A* stock (at par $1)	143,400	(at 20*)	2,868,000
Common stock (at par 1 cent)	2,400		*1,043,600(d)*
Surplus and reserves	3,094,300		
Total liabilities	$5,335,300		$5,862,600

* These approximate the effective par values of the issues.

Coca-Cola Company has outstanding a no-par Class A stock entitled to preferential dividends of $3 per share, cumulative, and redeemable at 55. The company carries this issue as a liability at its "stated value" of $5 per share. But the true par value is clearly $50.[1]

In all instances such as the above an "effective par value" must be set up for the preferred stock that will correspond properly to its dividend rate. A strong argument may be advanced in favor of valuing all preferred stocks on a uniform dividend basis, say 5%, unless callable at a lower figure. This would mean that a $1,000,000 five per cent issue would be valued at $1,000,000, a $1,000,000 four per cent issue would be given an effective value of $800,000 and a $1,000,000 seven per cent noncallable issue would be given an effective value of $1,400,000. But it is more convenient, of course, to use the par value, and in most cases the result will be sufficiently accurate.[2] A simpler method, which would work well for most practical purposes, is to value preferred issues at par (plus back dividends) or market, whichever is higher.

Calculation of Book Value of Preferred Stocks. In calculating the book value of a preferred stock issue it is treated as a common stock and the issues junior to it are left out of consideration. The following computations from the December 31, 1932, balance sheet of Tubize Chatillon Corporation will illustrate the principles involved.

---

[1] Amusingly enough, in 1929 the company carried *as an asset* 194,000 repurchased shares of Class A stock at their cost of $9,434,000, although the entire issue of 1,000,000 shares appeared as a liability of only $5,000,000. For a similar accounting absurdity applied to common stocks, see the June 1939 balance sheet of Hecker Products—on which its net stated liability for its capital stock works out as a *minus* figure.

[2] Standard Statistics Company, Inc., follows the practice of deducting preferred stock at its value *in case of involuntary liquidation*, when computing the book value of the common. This is scarcely logical, because dissolution or liquidation is almost always a remote contingency and would take place under conditions quite different from those obtaining at the time of analysis. The Standard Statistics Company method results in placing a "value" of $115 per share on Procter and Gamble Company $5 Second Preferred and a value of only $100 per share on the same company's $8 First Preferred. The real or practical value of the preferred stockholder's claims in this case would be much nearer in the proportion of 160 for the First Preferred against 100 for the Second Preferred, a 5% dividend yield basis for both. In the case of investment-trust issues, liquidation values of preferred issues are more relevant and should generally be used.

Tubize Chatillon Corporation Balance Sheet, December 31, 1932

Assets		Liabilities	
Property and		7% First Preferred Stock	
Equipment............	$19,009,000	(par $100)	$ 2,500,000
Patents, Processes, etc	802,000	$7 Second Preferred Stock	
Miscellaneous Assets	478,000	(par $1)	136,000
Current Assets...........	4,258,000	Common Stock (par $1) ...	294,000
		Bonded Debt	2,000,000
		Current Liabilities	613,000
		Reserve for Deprecia-	
		tion, etc	11,456,000
		Surplus	7,548,000
Total Assets	$24,547,000	Total Liabilities	$24,547,000

The book value of the First Preferred is computed as follows:

Total Assets		$24,547,000
Less: Intangible Assets.............................	802,000	
Reserve for Depreciation, etc	11,456,000	
Bonds	2,000,000	
Current Liabilities	613,000	14,871,000
Net assets for First Preferred		$ 9,676,000
Book value per share		$387

Alternative method:

Capital Stock at par................................	$2,930,000
Surplus	7,548,000
	$10,478,000
Less Intangible Assets...............................	802,000
Net assets for First Preferred........................	$9,676,000

The Reserve for Depreciation and Miscellaneous Purposes was very large and might have included arbitrary allowances belonging in Surplus. But in the absence of details a reserve of this kind must be deducted from the assets. (It later transpired that a substantial part of the reserve was needed to absorb a write-off of plant abandoned owing to obsolescence.)

The book value of the Second Preferred stock is readily computed from the foregoing, as follows:

Net assets for First Preferred	$9,676,000
Less: First Preferred at par	2,500,000
Net assets for Second Preferred	$7,176,000
Book value per share	$52.75

In computing the book value of the common it would be an obvious error to deduct the Second Preferred at its nonrepresentative par value of $1. The "effective par" should be taken at not less than $100 per share, in view of the $7 dividend. Hence there are no assets available for the common stock, and its book value is nil.

Current-Asset Value and Cash-Asset Value. In addition to the well-known concept of book value, we wish to suggest two others of similar character, *viz.*, current-asset value and cash-asset value.

The current-asset value of a stock consists of the current assets alone, minus all liabilities and claims ahead of the issue. It excludes not only the intangible assets but the fixed and miscellaneous assets as well.

The cash-asset value of a stock consists of the cash assets alone, minus all liabilities and claims ahead of the issue.[3] Cash assets, other than cash itself, are defined as those directly equivalent to and held in place of cash. They include certificates of deposit, call loans, marketable securities at market value and cash-surrender value of insurance policies.

The following is an example of the computation of the three categories of asset value:

Otis Company (Cotton Goods) Balance Sheet, June 29, 1929

Assets		Liabilities	
1. Cash	$532,000	8. Accounts Payable	$79,000
2. Call Loans	1,200,000	9. Accrued Items, etc.	291,000
3. Accounts Receivable		10. Reserve for	
(less reserve)	1,090,000	Equipment, etc	210,000
4. Inventory (less reserve of		11. Preferred Stock	400,000
$425,000)*	1,648,000	12. Common Stock	4,079,000
5. Prepaid Items	108,000	13. Earned Surplus	1,944,000
6. Investments	15,000	14. Paid-in Surplus	1,154,000
7. Plant (less Depreciation)	3,564,000		
	$8,157,000		$8,157,000

* Inventories before reserves are valued at cost or market, whichever is lower.

[3] Cash assets per share of common are sometimes calculated without deduction of any liabilities. In our opinion this is a useful concept only when the other *current* assets exceed all liabilities ahead of the common.

A. Calculation of book value of common stock:

Total assets......................................		$8,157,000
Less: Payables................................	$ 79,000	
Accrued items............................	291,000	
Preferred stock...........................	400,000	770,000
		$7,387,000
Add voluntary reserve of $425,000 subtracted from inventory......................		425,000
Net assets for common stock		$7,812,000
Book value per share (on 40,790 shares).............		$191

B. Calculation of current-asset value of the common stock:

Total current assets (items 1,2,3, and 4)..............	$4,470,000
Add voluntary reserve against inventory	425,000
	$4,895,000
Less liabilities ahead of common (items 8, 9, and 11) .	770,000
Current assets available for common	$4,125,000
Current-asset value per share.....................	$101

C. Calculation of cash-asset value of the common stock:

Total cash assets (items 1 and 2)	$1,732,000
Less liabilities ahead of common (items 8, 9, and 11) .	770,000
Cash assets available for common..................	$ 962,000
Cash-asset value per share........................	$23.50

In these calculations it will be noted, first, that the inventory is increased by restoring the reserve of $425,000 subtracted therefrom in the balance sheet. This is done because the deduction taken by the company is clearly a reserve for contingent decline in value that has not yet taken place. As such it is entirely arbitrary or voluntary, and consistency of method would require the analyst to regard it as a surplus item. The same is true of the $210,000 "Reserve for Equipment and Other Expenses," which, as far as can be seen, represents neither an actual liability nor a necessary deduction from the value of any specific asset.

In June 1929 Otis Company common stock was selling at 35. The reader will observe an extraordinary divergence between this market price and the current-asset value of the shares. Its significance will engage our attention later.

Practical Significance of Book Value. The book value of a common stock was originally the most important element in its financial exhibit. It was supposed to show "the value" of the shares in the same way as a merchant's balance sheet shows him the value of his business. This idea has almost completely disappeared from the financial horizon. The value of a company's assets as carried in its balance sheet has lost practically all its significance. This change arose from the fact, first, that the value of the fixed assets, as stated, frequently bore no relationship to the actual cost and, secondly, that in an even larger proportion of cases these values bore no relationship to the figure at which they would be sold or the figure which would be justified by the earnings. The practice of inflating the book value of the fixed property is giving way to the opposite artifice of cutting it down to nothing in order to avoid depreciation charges, but both have the same consequence of depriving the book-value figures of any real significance. It is a bit strange, like a quaint survival from the past, that the leading statistical services still maintain the old procedure of calculating the book value per share of common stock from many, perhaps most, balance sheets that they publish.

Before we discard completely this time-honored conception of book value, let us ask if it may ever have practical significance for the analyst. In the ordinary case, probably not. But what of the extraordinary or extreme case? Let us consider the four exhibits shown on the following page, as representative of extreme relationships between book value and market price.

No thoughtful observer could fail to be impressed by the disparities revealed in the examples given. In the case of General Electric and Commercial Solvents the figures proclaim more than the bare fact that the market was valuing the shares at many times their book value. The stock ticker seems here to register an aggregate valuation for these enterprises that is totally unrelated to their standing as ordinary business enterprises. In other words, these are in no sense *business valuations;* they are products of Wall Street's legerdemain, or possibly of its clairvoyance.

Financial Reasoning vs. Business Reasoning. We have here the point that brings home more strikingly perhaps than any other the widened rift between financial thought and ordinary business thought. It is an almost unbelievable fact that Wall Street never asks, "How much is the business selling for?" Yet this should be the first question in considering a stock purchase. If a business man were offered a 5% interest in some concern for $10,000, his first mental process would be to multiply the asked price by 20 and thus establish a proposed value of $200,000 for the entire undertaking. The rest of his calculation would turn about the question whether or not the business was a "good buy" at $200,000.

Item	General Electric	Pepperell Manufacturing
Price	(1930) 95	(1932) 18
Number of shares	28,850,000	97,600
Market value of common	$2,740,000,000	$ 1,760,000
Balance sheet	(Dec. 1929)	(June 1932)
Fixed assets (less depreciation)	$ 52,000,000	$ 7,830,000
Miscellaneous assets	183,000,000	230,000
Net current assets	206,000,000	9,120,000
Total net assets	$ 441,000,000	$17,180,000
Less bonds and preferred	45,000,000	
Book value of common	$ 396,000,000	$17,180,000
Book value per share	$13.75	$176

Item	Commercial Solvents	Pennsylvania Coal and Coke
Price	(July 1933) 57	(July 1933) 3
Number of shares	2,493,000	165,000
Market value of common	$142,000,000	$ 495,000
Balance sheet	(Dec. 1932)	(Dec. 1932)
Fixed assets (less depreciation)		6,500,000
Miscellaneous assets	2,600,000	990,000
Net current assets	6,000,000	740,000
Total assets for common	$ 8,600,000	$8,230,000
Book value per share	$3.50	$50

This elementary and indispensable approach has been practically abandoned by those who purchase stocks. Of the thousands who "invested" in General Electric in 1929–1930 probably only an infinitesimal number had any idea that they were paying on the basis of about $2\frac{1}{2}$ billions of dollars for the company, of which over two billions represented a premium above the money actually invested in the business. The price of 57 established for Commercial Solvents in July 1933 was more of a gambling phenomenon, induced by the expected repeal of prohibition. But the gamblers in this instance were acting no differently from those who call themselves investors, in their blithe disregard of the fact that they were paying 140 millions for an enterprise with about 10 millions of resources. (The fixed assets of Commercial Solvents, written down to nothing in the balance sheet, had real value, of course, but not in excess of a few millions.)

The contrast in the other direction shown by our examples is almost as impressive. A going but unsuccessful concern like Pennsylvania Coal and Coke can be valued in the market at about one-sixteenth of its stated resources almost on the same day as a speculatively attractive issue is bid for at sixteen times its net worth. The Pepperell example is perhaps more striking still, because of the unquestioned reality of the figures of book value and also because of the high reputation, large earnings, and liberal dividends of the enterprise covering a long stretch of years. Yet part owners of this business—under the stress of depression, it is true—were willing to sell out their interest at one-tenth of the value that a single private owner would have unhesitatingly placed upon it.

Recommendation. These examples, extreme as they are, suggest rather forcibly that the book value deserves at least a fleeting glance by the public before it buys or sells shares in a business undertaking. In any particular case the message that the book value conveys may well prove to be inconsequential and unworthy of attention. But this testimony should be examined before it is rejected. Let the stock buyer, if he lays any claim to intelligence, at least be able to tell himself, first, what value he is actually setting on the business and, second, what he is actually getting for his money in terms of tangible resources.

There are indeed certain presumptions in favor of purchases made far below asset value and against those made at a high premium above it. (It is assumed that in the ordinary case the book figures may be accepted as roughly indicative of the actual cash invested in the enterprise.) A business that sells at a premium does so because it earns a large return upon its capital; this large return attracts competition, and, generally speaking, it is not likely to continue indefinitely. Conversely in the case of a business selling at a large discount because of abnormally low earnings. The absence of new competition, the withdrawal of old competition from the field, and other natural economic forces may tend eventually to improve the situation and restore a normal rate of profit on the investment.

Although this is orthodox economic theory, and undoubtedly valid in a broad sense, we doubt if it applies with sufficient certainty and celerity to make it useful as a governing factor in common-stock selection. It may be pointed out that under modern conditions the so-called "intangibles," *e.g.*, good-will or even a highly efficient organization, are every whit as real from a dollars-and-cents standpoint as are buildings and machinery.[4] Earnings based on these intangibles may be even less vulnerable to competition than those which require only a cash investment in productive facilities. Furthermore, when conditions are favorable the enterprise with the relatively small capital investment is likely to show a more rapid rate of growth. Ordinarily it can expand its sales and profits at slight expense and therefore more rapidly and profitably for its stockholders than a business requiring a large plant investment per dollar of sales.

We do not think, therefore, that any rules may reasonably be laid down on the subject of book value in relation to market price, except the strong recommendation already made that the purchaser know what he is doing on this score and be satisfied in his own mind that he is acting sensibly.

---

[4] Judicial valuations of intangible assets (in the case of close corporations) still seem to adhere to the old concept that they are less "real" than tangible assets and thus need larger earnings, relatively, to support them. The divergence between the stock market's bases of valuation and those of business men and the courts, as applied to private enterprises, would provide excellent material for a critical study.

For a quantitative study leading to the conclusion that "good-will" has, on the whole, proved more profitable than tangible assets, see Lawrence N. Bloomberg, *The Investment Value of Goodwill*, Baltimore, 1938.

CHAPTER 43

Significance of the Current-Asset Value

THE CURRENT-ASSET VALUE of a common stock is more likely to be an important figure than the book value, which includes the fixed assets. Our discussion of this point will develop the following theses:

1. The current-asset value is generally a rough index of the *liquidating value*.

2. A large number of common stocks sell for less than their current-asset value and therefore sell below the amount realizable in liquidation.

3. The phenomenon of many stocks selling persistently below their liquidating value is fundamentally illogical. It means that a serious error is being committed, either: (*a*) in the judgment of the stock market, (*b*) in the policies of the company's management, or (*c*) in the attitude of the stockholders toward their property.

Liquidating Value. By the liquidating value of an enterprise we mean the money that the owners could get out of it if they wanted to give it up. They might sell all or part of it to some one else, on a going-concern basis. Or else they might turn the various kinds of assets into cash, in piecemeal fashion, taking whatever time is needed to obtain the best realization from each. Such liquidations are of everyday occurrence in the field of private business. By contrast, however, they are very rare indeed in the field of publicly owned corporations. It is true that one company often sells out to another, usually at a price well above liquidating value, also that insolvency will at times result in the piecemeal sale of the assets; but the voluntary withdrawal from an unprofitable business, accompanied by the careful liquidation of the assets, is an infinitely more frequent happening among private than among publicly owned concerns. This divergence is not without its cause and meaning, as we shall show later.

Realizable Value of Assets Varies with Their Character. A company's balance sheet does not convey exact information as to its value in liquidation, but it does supply clues or hints which may prove useful. The first rule in calculating liquidating value is that the liabilities are real but the value of the assets must be questioned. This means that all true liabilities shown on the books must be deducted at their face amount. The value to be ascribed to the assets, however, will vary according to their character. The following schedule indicates fairly well the relative dependability of various types of assets in liquidation.

	% of liquidating value to book value	
Type of asset	Normal range	Rough average
Current assets:		
Cash assets (including securities at market)	100	100
Receivables (less usual reserves)*	75–90	80
Inventories (at lower of cost or market)	50–75	66²/₃
Fixed and miscellaneous assets:		
(Real estate, buildings, machinery, equipment,		
nonmarketable investments, intangibles, etc.)	1–50	15 (approx.)

* Note: Retail installment accounts must be valued for liquidation at a lower rate. Range about 30 to 60%. Average about 50%.

Calculation Illustrated. The calculation of approximate liquidating value in a specific case is illustrated as follows:

Example: White Motor Company. (See next page.)

Object of This Calculation. In studying this computation it must be borne in mind that our object is not to determine the exact liquidating value of White Motor but merely to form a rough idea of this liquidating value *in order to ascertain whether or not the shares are selling for less than the stockholders could actually take out of the business.* The latter question is answered very definitely in the affirmative. With full allowance for possible error, there was no doubt at all (in 1931) that White Motor would liquidate for a great deal more than $8 per share, or $5,200,000 for the company. The striking fact that the cash assets alone considerably exceed this figure, *after deducting all liabilities,* completely clinched the argument on this score.

Current-Asset Value a Rough Measure of Liquidating Value. The estimated values in liquidation as given for White Motor are somewhat lower in respect of inventories and somewhat higher as regards the fixed and miscellaneous assets than one might be inclined to adopt in other examples. We are allowing for the fact that motor-truck inventories are likely to be less salable than the average. On the other hand some of the assets listed as noncurrent, in particular the investment in White Motor Securities Corporation,

White Motor Company

Capitalization: 650,000 shares of common stock.

Price in December 1931: $8 per share.

Total market value of the company: $5,200,000.

Balance Sheet, December 31, 1931 (000 omitted)

Item	Book value	Estimated liquidating value % of book value	Amount
Cash	$ 4,057 ⎫	100	
U.S. Govt. and New York City bonds	4,573 ⎭		$ 8,600
Receivables (less reserves)	5,611	80	4,500
Inventory (lower of cost or market)	9,219	50	4,600
Total current assets	$23,460		$17,700
Less current liabilities	1,353		1,400
Net current assets	$22,107		$16,300
Plant account	16,036 ⎫		
Less depreciation	7,491 ⎪		
Plant account, net	$ 8,545 ⎪	20	4,000
Investments in subsidiaries, etc.	4,996 ⎬		
Deferred charges	388 ⎪		
Good-will	5,389 ⎭		
Total net assets for common stock	$41,425		$20,300

Estimated liquidating value per share	$31
Book value per share	55
Current-asset value per share	34
Cash-asset value per share	$11
Market price per share	8

would be likely to yield a larger proportion of their book values than the ordinary property account. It will be seen that White Motor's estimated liquidating value (about $31 per share) was not far from the current-asset value ($34 per share). In the typical case it may be said that the noncurrent assets are likely to realize enough to make up most of the shrinkage suffered in the liquidation of the current assets. Hence our first thesis, *viz.*, that the current-asset value affords a rough measure of the liquidating value.

Prevalence of Stocks Selling Below Liquidating Value. Our second point is that for some years past a considerable number of common stocks have been selling in the market well below their liquidating value. Naturally the percentage was largest during the depression. But even in the bull market of 1926–1929 instances of this kind were by no means rare. It will be noted that the striking case of Otis Company, presented in the last chapter, occurred during June 1929, at the very height of the boom. The Northern Pipe Line example, given in Chap. 41, dates from 1926. On the other hand, our Pepperell and White Motor illustrations were phenomena of the 1931–1933 collapse.

It seems to us that the most distinctive feature of the stock market of those three years was the large proportion of issues which sold below their liquidating value. Our computations indicate that over 40% of all the industrial companies listed on the New York Stock Exchange were quoted at some time in 1932 at less than their net current assets. A considerable number actually sold for less than their cash-asset value, as in the case of White Motor.[1] On reflection this must appear to be an extraordinary state of affairs. The typical American corporation was apparently worth more dead than alive. The owners of these great businesses could get more for their interest by shutting up shop than by selling out on a going-concern basis.

In the recession of 1937–1938 this situation was repeated on a smaller scale. Available data indicate that 20.5% of the industrial companies listed on the New York Stock Exchange sold in early 1938 at less than their net-current-asset value. (At the close of 1938, when the general price level was by no means abnormally low, a total of 54 companies out of 648 industrials studied sold for less than their net current assets.[2])

---

[1] See Appendix Note 62 for a representative list of issues selling for less than liquidating value in 1932.

[2] See Appendix Note 61 for other details on this point.

It is important to observe that these widespread discrepancies between price and current-asset value are a comparatively recent development. In the severe market depression of 1921 the proportion of industrial stocks in this class was quite small. Evidently the phenomena of 1932 (and 1938) were the direct out-growth of the new-era doctrine which transferred *all* the tests of value to the income account and completely ignored the balance-sheet picture. In consequence, a company without current earnings was regarded as having very little real value, and it was likely to sell in the market for the merest fraction of its realizable resources. Most of the sellers were not aware that they were disposing of their interest at far less than its scrap value. Many, however, who might have known the fact would have justified the low price on the ground that the liquidating value was of no practical importance, since the company had no intention of liquidating.

Logical Significance of This Phenomenon. This brings us to the third point, *viz.*, the logical significance of this "subliquidating-value" phenomenon from the standpoint of the market, of the managements and of the stockholders. The whole issue may be summarized in the form of a basic principle, *viz.*:

When a common stock sells persistently below its liquidating value, then either the price is too low or the company should be liquidated.

Two corollaries may be deduced from this principle:

Corollary I. Such a price should impel the stockholders to raise the question whether or not it is in their interest to continue the business.

Corollary II. Such a price should impel the management to take all proper steps to correct the obvious disparity between market quotation and intrinsic value, including a reconsideration of its own policies and a frank justification to the stockholders of its decision to continue the business.

The truth of the principle above stated should be self-evident. There can be no *sound* economic reason for a stock's selling continuously below its liquidation value. If the company is not worth more as a going concern than in liquidation, it should be liquidated. If it is worth more as a going concern, then the stock should sell for more than its liquidating value. Hence, on either premise, a price below liquidating value is unjustifiable.

Twofold Application of Foregoing Principle. Stated in the form of a logical alternative, our principle invites a twofold application. Stocks selling below liquidation value are in many cases too cheap and so offer an attractive medium for purchase. We have thus a profitable field here for the technique of security analysis. But in many cases also the fact that an issue sells below liquidating value is a signal that mistaken policies are being followed and that therefore the management should take corrective action—if not voluntarily, then under pressure from the stockholders. Let us consider these two lines of inquiry in order.

ATTRACTIVENESS OF SUCH ISSUES AS COMMITMENTS

Common stocks in this category practically always have an unsatisfactory trend of earnings. If the profits had been increasing steadily, it is obvious that the shares would not sell at so low a price. The objection to buying these issues lies in the probability, or at least the possibility, that earnings will decline or losses continue and that the resources will be dissipated and the intrinsic value ultimately become less than the price paid. It may not be denied that this does actually happen in individual cases. On the other hand, there is a much wider range of potential developments which may result in establishing a higher market price. These include the following:

1. The creation of an earning power commensurate with the company's assets. This may result from:
   a. General improvement in the industry.
   b. Favorable change in the company's operating policies, with or without a change in management. These changes include more efficient methods, new products, abandonment of unprofitable lines, etc.
2. A sale or merger, because some other concern is able to utilize the resources to better advantage and hence can pay at least liquidating value for the assets.
3. Complete or partial liquidation.

Examples of Effect of Favorable Developments on Such Issues. *General Improvement in the Industry.* Examples already given, and certain others, will illustrate the operation of these various kinds of favorable developments. In the case of Pepperell the low price of $17^1/_2$ coincided with a large loss for the year ended June 30, 1932. In the following year conditions in the textile industry improved; Pepperell earned over $9 per share and resumed dividends; consequently the price of the stock advanced to 100 in January 1934 and to $149^3/_4$ in 1936.

Changes in Operating Policies. Hamilton Woolen Company, another example in the textile field, is a case of individual rather than of general improvement. For several years prior to 1928 the company had operated at substantial losses, which amounted to nearly $20 and $12 per share in 1926 and 1927, respectively. Late in 1927 the common stock sold at $13 per share, although the company had net current assets of $38.50 per share at that time. In 1928 and 1929 changes in management and in managerial policies were made, new lines of product and direct sales methods were introduced, and certain phases of production were reorganized. This resulted in greatly improved earnings which averaged about $5.50 per share during the succeeding four years, and within a single year the stock had risen to a price of about $40.[3]

Sale or Merger. The White Motor instance is typical of the genesis and immediate effect of a sale or merger, as applied to an issue selling for less than liquidating value. (The later developments, however, were quite unusual.) The heavy losses of White Motor in 1930–1932 impelled the management to seek a new alignment. Studebaker Corporation believed it could combine its own operations with those of White to mutual advantage, and it was greatly attracted by White's large holdings of cash. Hence in September 1932 Studebaker offered to purchase all White Motor's stock, paying for each share as follows:

> $5 in cash.
> $25 in 10-year 6% notes of Studebaker Corporation.
> 1 share of Studebaker common, selling for about $10.

It will be seen that these terms of purchase were based not on the recent market price of White—below $7 per share—but primarily upon the current-asset value. White Motor shares promptly advanced to 27 and later sold at the equivalent of 31^1/2.[4]

An interesting example of the same kind, but of more recent date, is afforded by Standard Oil Company of Nebraska. The facts may be outlined as follows:

---

[3] For the later history of Hamilton Woolen Company, see Chap. 44.

[4] An extraordinary sequel of this transaction was the receivership of Studebaker Corporation in April 1933, ostensibly caused by the opposition of minority stockholders of White Motor to a merger of the two companies. But this development is quite unrelated to our point of discussion, which turns upon the fact that in a sale or merger full recognition should always be, and is ordinarily, given to liquidating value, even though the current market price may be much lower.

Early in 1939 the stock was selling at about $6, representing a total valuation of $1,000,000 for 161,000 shares comprising the entire capitalization. The December 31, 1938, balance sheet is summarized in the appended table.

Assets		Liabilities	
Fixed and miscellaneous assets (net)	$2,794,000	Current liabilities	$176,000
Cash assets	1,155,000	Capital stock and surplus	4,734,000
Other current assets	961,000		$4,910,000
	$4,910,000		
(Net) Cash assets per share	$6.07		
Net current assets per share	12.05		
Net tangible assets per share	29.33		

The company was engaged in the distribution of petroleum products in Nebraska. It was carrying on an annual business of some $5,000,000 without appreciable profit. For the years 1935–1938 the reported earnings before depreciation averaged $0.69 per share; after "expended depreciation" there was an average profit of $0.39 per share; and after depreciation as taken by the company there was an average loss of $0.39 per share.

Here was a company clearly selling for much less than liquidating value, the reason being its unsatisfactory earnings record. There was good reason to believe, however, that the company was really worth more than bare liquidating value, because the outlet it provided for gasoline, etc., would make its numerous retail and bulk stations a desirable acquisition for some large refining company.

In April 1939 private interests offered to pay $12 per share for 66²/₃% of the outstanding stock. This bid failed of acceptance by a sufficient majority, but it was followed immediately by an offer to pay $17.50 per share, made by Standard Oil Company of Indiana, the refiner that had been supplying Standard Oil Company of Nebraska with its gasoline and that evidently was loath to lose this important outlet. The deal was promptly ratified; hence the stock of Standard Oil Company of Nebraska nearly tripled in value during a four-month's period in which the general market had suffered a decline.[5]

---

[5] See I. Benesch and Sons, and United Shipyards "A" in the table in Chap. 44 for other examples of a rise in price due to sale of properties.

Complete Liquidation. Mohawk Mining Company supplies an excellent example of a cash profit equivalent to a large advance in market value caused by the actual liquidation of the enterprise.

In December 1931 the stock sold at $11 per share, representing a total valuation of $1,230,000 for the 112,000 shares outstanding. The balance sheet at the end of 1931 showed the following:

Cash and marketable securities at market	$1,381,000
Receivables	9,000
Copper at market value, about	1,800,000
Supplies	71,000
	$3,261,000
Less current liabilities	68,000
Net current assets	$3,193,000
Fixed assets, less depreciation and depletion	2,460,000
Miscellaneous assets	168,000
Total assets for common stock	$5,821,000
Book value per share*	$52
Current-asset value per share*	28.50
Cash-asset value per share*	11.75
Market price per share	11

* After reducing securities and copper inventory to market value.

Shortly thereafter the management decided to liquidate the property. Within the years 1932–1934 regular and liquidating dividends were paid, aggregating $28.50 per share. It will be noted that the amount actually received in liquidation proved identical with the current-asset value just before the liquidation began, and it was $2^1/2$ times the ruling market price at that time.

Partial Liquidation. Northern Pipe Line Company and Otis Company, already discussed, are examples of the establishment of a higher market value through partial liquidation. The two companies made the exhibits as shown in the table following.

In September 1929 Otis Company paid a special dividend of $4 per share, and in 1930 it made a distribution of $20 in partial liquidation, reducing the par value from $100 to $80. In April 1931 the shares sold at 45 and in April 1932 at 41. These prices were higher than the quotation in June 1929, despite the distributions of $24 per share made in the interim, and despite the fact also that the *general* market level had changed from fantastic inflation to equally fantastic deflation. Later the company went out of business altogether and paid its stockholders an additional $74 per share in liquidation—making the total received by them $102 per share since June 1929 (inclusive of other dividends in 1929–1934 amounting to $4 per share).[6]

Item	Northern Pipe Line	Otis Company
Date	1926	June 1929
Market price	$64	$35
Cash-asset value per share	79	$23^1/_2$
Current-asset value per share	82	101
Book value per share	116	191

Northern Pipe Line Company distributed $50 per share to its stockholders in 1928, as a return of capital, *i.e.*, partial liquidation. This development resulted in an approximate doubling of the market price between 1926 and 1928. Later a second distribution of $20 per share was made, so that the stockholders received more in cash than in the low market price of 1925 and 1926, and they also retained their full interest in the pipe-line business. Similar liberal distributions were made by most of the pipe-line companies of the so-called Standard Oil group. (Note also the partial liquidation of Davis Coal and Coke Company, described in Chap. 44 Note 5.)

Discrimination Required in Selecting Such Issues. There is scarcely any doubt that common stocks selling well below liquidating value represent on the whole a class of undervalued securities. They have declined in price more severely than the actual conditions justify. This must mean that *on the whole* these stocks afford profitable opportunities for purchase. Nevertheless, the securities analyst should exercise as much discrimination as possible in the choice of issues falling within this category. He will lean toward those for which he sees a fairly imminent prospect of some one of the favorable developments listed above. Or else he will be partial to such as reveal other attractive statistical features besides their

---

[6] For other examples of liquidation bringing stockholders more than the previous market price see the table in Chap. 44.

liquid-asset position, *e.g.*, satisfactory current earnings and dividends or a high average earning power in the past. The analyst will avoid issues that have been losing their current assets at a rapid rate and show no definite signs of ceasing to do so.

Examples: This latter point will be illustrated by the following comparison of two companies, the shares of which sold well below liquidating value early in 1933.

Item	Manhattan Shirt Company		Hupp Motor Car Corporation	
Price, January 1933	6		2¹/₂	
Total market value of Company	$1,476,000		$3,323,000	
Balance sheet	Nov. 30, 1932	Nov. 30, 1929	Dec. 31, 1932	Dec. 31, 1929
Preferred stock at par		$ 300,000		
Number of shares of common	246,000	281,000	1,329,000	1,475,000
Cash assets	$1,961,000	$ 885,000	$ 4,615,000	$10,156,000
Receivables	771,000	2,621,000	226,000	1,246,000
Inventories	1,289,000	4,330,000	2,115,000	8,481,000
Total current assets	$4,021,000	$7,836,000	$ 6,956,000	$19,883,000
Current liabilities	100,000	2,574,000	1,181,000	2,541,000
Net current assets	$3,921,000	$5,262,000	$ 5,775,000	$17,342,000
Other tangible assets	1,124,000	2,066,000	9,757,000	17,870,000
Total assets for common (and preferred)	$5,045,000	$7,328,000	$15,532,000	$35,212,000
Cash-asset value per share	$ 7.50	Nil	$2.625	$ 5.125
Current-asset value per share	16.00	$17.50	4.375	11.75

Both of these companies disclose an interesting relationship of current assets to market price at the close of 1932. But a comparison with the balance-sheet situation of three years previously will yield much more satisfactory indications for Manhattan Shirt than for Hupp Motors. The latter concern had lost more than half of its cash assets and more than 60% of its net current assets during the depression period. On the other hand, the current-asset value of Manhattan Shirt common was reduced by only 10% during these difficult times, and furthermore, its cash-asset position was greatly improved. The latter result was obtained through the liquidation of receivables and inventories, the proceeds of which paid off the 1929 bank loans and largely increased the cash resources.

From the viewpoint of past indications, therefore, the two companies must be placed in different categories. In the Hupp Motors case, we should have to take into account the possibility that the remaining excess of current assets over market price might soon be dissipated. This is not true so far as Manhattan Shirt is concerned, and in fact the achievement of the company in strengthening its cash position during the depression must be given favorable consideration. We shall recur later to this phase of security analysis, *viz.*, the comparison of balance sheets over a period in order to determine the true progress of an enterprise. The former point—that attention should be paid also to the past earnings record—may be brought home by a brief comparison of two companies in early 1939.

Item	Ely & Walker Dry Goods Co.		Pacific Mills	
Price, January, 1939	17		14	
Per share:	Dec. 31, 1932	Dec. 31, 1938	Dec. 31, 1932	Dec. 31, 1938
Net current assets	$30.00	$39.50	$26.95	$24.50
Net tangible assets	37.73	46.42	90.85	79.50
Average earnings, 1933–1938		1.82		2.41(d)
Average dividend, 1933–1938		1.25		0.50

The losses of Pacific Mills did not have a serious effect upon the balance-sheet position because they have come mainly out of the balance sheet via the depreciation allowance. But unless there were special reasons to expect a reversal of the operating results, the analyst would obviously prefer Ely & Walker as an investment purchase.

Bargains of This Type. Common stocks that (1) are selling below their liquid-asset value, (2) are apparently in no danger of dissipating these assets, and (3) have formerly shown a large earning power on the market price, may be said truthfully to constitute a class of *investment bargains*. They are indubitably *worth* considerably more than they are selling for, and there is a reasonably good chance that this greater worth will sooner or later reflect itself in the market price. At their low price these bargain stocks actually enjoy a high degree of safety, meaning by safety a relatively small risk of loss of principal.

It may be pointed out, however, that investment in such bargain issues needs to be carried on with some regard to general market conditions at the time. Strangely enough, this is a type of operation that fares best, relatively speaking, when price levels are neither extremely high nor extremely low. The purchase of "cheap stocks" when the market as a whole seems much higher than it should be, *e.g.*, in 1929 or early 1937, will not work out well, because the ensuing decline is likely to bear almost as severely on these neglected or unappreciated issues as on the general list. On the other hand, when all stocks are very cheap—as in 1932—there would seem to be fully as much reason to buy undervalued leading issues as to pick out less popular stocks, even though these may be selling at even lower prices by comparison.

A Common Stock Representing the Entire Business Cannot Be Less Safe than a Bond Having a Claim to Only a Part Thereof. In considering these issues it will be helpful to apply the converse of the proposition developed earlier in this book with reference to senior securities. We pointed out (Chap. 26) that a bond or preferred stock could not be worth more than its value would be if it represented full ownership of the company, *i.e.*, if it were a common stock without senior claims ahead of it. The converse is also true. A common stock cannot be *less safe* than it would be if it were a bond, *i.e.*, if instead of representing full ownership of the company it were given a fixed and limited claim, with some new common stock created to own what was left. This idea, which may appear somewhat abstract at first, may be clarified by a concrete comparison between a common stock and a bond issue of the types just described. Two companies in the investment-trust field are particularly well suited to illustrate our point, because they were both organized by the same banking interests, and they have identical officers.

The following table should make clear that Shawmut Association *stock* cannot be less safe intrinsically than the Investment Trust *senior debentures* at 85. For, with the same management behind them, the stock investment has behind it 180% in assets, whereas the bonds are protected by only 122% (of their market price) in assets. In addition to having this greater protection the Association stock represents the entire ownership of the company's assets, whereas the interest of the Investment Trust bonds is limited to their principal amount, the balance of the equity belonging to the junior holders. (In fact this junior equity can be fairly substantial, as measured by market price, even when the bonds are selling at a considerable discount.)

As of December 1939	Shawmut Association	Shawmut Bank Investment Trust
Bonds	None	$3,040,000 Senior Debenture
		$4^{1}/_{2}$s and 5s @ 85 (average)
		= $2,585,000
		$950,000 Junior Debenture
		6s @ 50 (est) = $480,000
Stock	390,000 sh. @ $10^{1}/_{4}$ $4,000,000	75,000 sh. @ $3^{1}/_{2}$ 260,000
Total capitalization	$4,000,000	$3,325,000
Net asset value (September 1939)	7,201,000	(November 1939) 3,153,000
Ratio: Senior bonds at market to net assets		82%
Ratio: Total capitalization at market to net assets	55%	107%
12 months' investment income*	(To September 30) 198,000	(To November 30) 114,000
Per cent earned on capitalization at market	5.0	3.5

* Excluding gain or loss on security sales.

That the Shawmut *Association* stock is more attractive than the *Investment Trust* debentures at the prices quoted is scarcely open to challenge. Undoubtedly, also, the investor who would consider the bond issue to be "safer" than the Association shares is being misled by the *form* into overlooking the *essence*. Yet something remains to be said of the effect of these diverse forms upon the experience of the investor and consequently upon his attitude. The Investment Trust bonds do carry a certain assurance of continued income, because interest must be paid regularly or else the company faces insolvency. It is true for the same reason that special efforts will be made to pay them off at or before maturity in 1942 and 1952. Therefore we find that the company has a special inducement to buy in bonds at a discount—since they must ultimately be paid at par—and thus one-third of the issue has been reacquired. This policy has served to maintain the market price to an important extent and to improve the position of the remaining bonds.

None of this is true with respect to the Shawmut Association shares. They have in fact received continuous dividends since 1929, averaging 65 cents, or $6^{1}/_{2}$% on the current price. But the rate has been variable, and the average stockholder feels that he is at the mercy of the management's decisions. (This is not entirely so in fact, since the penalty clauses in the Revenue Act virtually compel disbursement of the net income realized by investment trusts.) Nor has the market price been maintained by company repurchases at a reasonable discount from break-up value, so that the investor has been unable to look to the management to save him from the hard necessity of sacrificing his shares at as much as 50% below their intrinsic worth.

In the 1934 edition we illustrated this same point by considering American Laundry Machinery stock at its price of 7 in January 1933, which was equivalent to $4,300,000 for the entire company—as compared with over $4,000,000 in cash, $21,000,000 in net current assets, $27,000,000 in net tangible assets and 10-year average earnings of over $3,000,000 (including, however, a loss of $1,000,000 in 1932). The last two paragraphs of the chapter were as follows:

> Wall Street would have considered American Laundry Machinery stock "unsafe" at 7, but it would unquestionably have accepted a $4,500,000 bond issue of the same company. Its "reasoning" would have run that the interest on the bond was sure to be continued but that the 40-cent dividend then being paid on the stock was very insecure. In one case the directors had no choice but to pay interest and therefore would surely do so; in the other case the directors could pay or not as they saw fit and therefore would very likely suspend the dividend. But Wall Street is here confusing the temporary continuance of income with the more fundamental question of safety of principal. Dividends paid to common-stock holders do not in themselves make the stock any safer. The directors are merely turning over to the stockholders part of their own property; if the money were left in the treasury, it would still be the stockholder's property. There must therefore be an underlying fallacy in assuming that if the stockholders were given the power to compel payment of income—*i.e.*, if they were made bondholders in whole or in part—their position would thus be made intrinsically sounder. It is little short of idiocy to assume that the stockholders would be better off if they surrendered their complete ownership of the company in exchange for a limited claim against the same property at the rate of 5 or 6% on the investment. This is exactly what the public would do if it were willing to buy a $4,500,000 bond issue of American Laundry Machinery but would reject as "unsafe" the present common stock at $7 per share.

Nevertheless, Wall Street persists in thinking in these irrational terms, and it does so in part with practical justification. Somehow or other, common-stock ownership does not seem to give the public the same powers and possibilities—the same *values*, in short—as are vested in the private owners of a business. This brings us to the second line of reasoning on the subjects of stocks selling below liquidating value.

CHAPTER 44

Implications of Liquidating Value. Stockholder-Management Relationships

WALL STREET HOLDS that liquidating value is of slight importance because the typical company has no intention of liquidating. This view is logical, as far as it goes. When applied to a stock selling below break-up value, the Wall Street view may be amplified into the following: "Although this stock would liquidate for more than its market price, it is not worth buying because (1) the company cannot earn a satisfactory profit, and (2) it is not going to liquidate. In the previous chapter we suggested that the first assumption is likely to be wrong in a number of instances, for, although past earnings may have been disappointing, there is always a chance that through external or internal changes the concern may again earn a reasonable amount on its capital. But in a considerable proportion of cases the pessimism of the market will at least *appear* to be justified. We are led, therefore, to ask the question: "Why is it that no matter how poor a corporation's prospects may seem, its owners permit it to remain in business until its resources are exhausted?"

The answer to this question takes us into the heart of one of the strangest phenomena of American finance—the relations of stockholders to the businesses that they own. The subject transcends in its scope the narrow field of security analysis, but we shall discuss it here briefly because there is a distinct relationship between the value of securities and the intelligence and alertness of those who own them. The choice of a common stock is a single act; its ownership is a continuing process. Certainly there is just as much reason to exercise care and judgment in *being* as in *becoming* a stockholder.

Typical Stockholder Apathetic and Docile. It is a notorious fact, however, that the typical American stockholder is the most docile and apathetic animal in captivity. He does what the board of directors tell him to do and rarely thinks of asserting his individual rights as owner of the business and employer of its paid officers. The result is that the effective control of many, perhaps most, large American corporations is exercised not by those who together own a majority of the stock but by a small group known as "the management." This situation has been effectively described by Berle and Means in their significant work *The Modern Corporation and Private Property*. In Chap. I of Book IV the authors say:

> It is traditional that a corporation should be run for the benefit of its owners, the stockholders, and that to them should go any profits which are distributed. We now know, however, that a controlling group may hold the power to divert profits into their own pockets. There is no longer any certainty that a corporation will in fact be run primarily in the interests of the stockholders. The extensive separation of ownership and control, and the strengthening of the powers of control, raise a new situation calling for a decision whether social and legal pressure should be applied in an effort to insure corporate operation primarily in the interests of the owners or whether such pressure shall be applied in the interests of some other or wider group.

Again (in Chap. 26) the authors restate this view in their concluding chapter as follows:

> ... A third possibility exists, however. On the one hand, the owners of passive property, by surrendering control and responsibility over the active property, have surrendered the right that the corporation should be operated in their sole interest—they have released the community from the obligation to protect them to the full extent implied in the doctrine of strict property rights. At the same time, the controlling groups, by means of the extension of corporate powers, have in their own interest broken the bars of tradition which require that the corporation be operated solely for the benefit of the owners of passive property. Eliminating the sole interest of the passive owner, however, does not necessarily lay a basis for the alternative claim that the new powers should be used in the interest of the controlling groups. The latter have not presented, in acts or words, any acceptable defense of the proposition that these powers should be so used. No tradition supports that proposition. The control groups have, rather, cleared the way for the claims of a group far wider than either the owners or the control. They have placed the community in a position to demand that the modern corporation serve not alone the owners or the control but all society.

Plausible but Partly Fallacious Assumptions by Stockholders. Alert stockholders—if there are any such—are not likely to agree fully with the conclusion of Messrs. Berle and Means that they definitely have "surrendered the right that the corporation should be operated in their sole interest." After all, the American stockholder has abdicated not intentionally but by default. He can reassert the rights of control that inhere in ownership. Quite probably he would do so if he were properly informed and guided. In good part his docility and seeming apathy are results of certain traditional but unsound viewpoints which he seems to absorb by inheritance or by contagion. These cherished notions include the following:

1. The management knows more about the business than the stockholders do, and therefore its judgment on all matters of policy is to be accepted.

2. The management has no interest in or responsibility for the prices at which the company's securities sell.

3. If a stockholder disapproves of any major policy of the management, his proper move is to sell his stock.

Assumed Wisdom and Efficiency of Management Not Always Justified. These statements sound plausible, but they are in fact only half truths— the more dangerous because they are not wholly false. It is nearly always true that the management is in the best position to judge which policies are most expedient. But it does not follow that it will always either recognize or adopt the course most beneficial to the shareholders. It may err grievously through incompetence. Stockholders of any given company appear to take it for granted that their management is capable. Yet the art of selecting stocks is said to turn largely on choosing the well-managed enterprise and rejecting others. This must imply that many companies are poorly directed. Should not this mean also that the stockholders of any company should be open-minded on the question whether its management is efficient or the reverse?

Interests of Stockholders and Officers Conflict at Certain Points. But a second reason for not always accepting implicitly the decisions of the management is that *on certain points* the interests of the officers and the stockholders may be in conflict. This field includes the following:

1. Compensation to officers—Comprising salaries, bonuses, options to buy stock.

2. Expansion of the business—Involving the right to larger salaries and the acquisition of more power and prestige by the officers.

3. Payment of dividends—Should the money earned remain under the control of the management or pass into the hands of the stockholders?

4. Continuance of the stockholders' investment in the company— Should the business continue as before, although unprofitable, or should part of the capital be withdrawn, or should it be wound up completely?

5. Information to stockholders—Should those in control be able to benefit through having information not given to stockholders generally?

On all of these questions the decisions of the management are *interested* decisions, and for that reason they require scrutiny by the stockholders. We do not imply that corporate managements are not to be trusted. On the contrary, the officers of our large corporations constitute a group of men above the average in probity as well as in ability. But this does not mean that they should be given *carte blanche* in all matters affecting their own interests. A private employer hires only men he can trust, but he does not let these men fix their own salaries or decide how much capital he should place or leave in the business.

Directors Not Always Free from Self-interest in Connection with These Matters. In publicly owned corporations these matters are passed on by the board of directors, whom the stockholders elect and to whom the officials are responsible. Theoretically, the directors will represent the stockholders' interests, when need be, as against the opposing interests of the officers. But this cannot be counted upon in practice. In many companies a majority, and in most companies a substantial part, of the board is composed of paid officials. The directors who are not officers are frequently joined by many close ties to the chief executives. It may be said in fact that the officers choose the directors more often than the directors choose the officers. Hence the necessity remains for the stockholders to exercise critical and independent judgments on all matters where the personal advantage of the officers may conceivably be opposed to their own. In other words, in this field the usual presumption of superior knowledge and judgment on the part of the management should not obtain, and any criticism offered in good faith deserves careful consideration by the stockholders.

Abuse of Managerial Compensation. Numerous cases have come to light in which the actions of the management in the matter of its own compensation have been open to serious question. Most of these relate to the years before 1933. In the case of Bethlehem Steel Corporation, cash bonuses clearly excessive in amount were paid. In the case of American Tobacco Company, rights to buy stock below the market price, of an enormous aggregate value, were allotted to the officers. These privileges to buy stock are readily subject to abuse. In the case of Electric Bond and Share Company, the management permitted itself to buy many shares of stock at far below market price. When later the price of the stock collapsed to a figure less than the subscription price, the obligation to pay for the shares was cancelled, and the sums already paid were returned to the officers. A similar procedure was followed in the case of White Motor Company, which will be more fully discussed later in this chapter.

Some of these transactions are explained, and partly justified, by the extraordinary conditions of 1928–1932. Others are inexcusable from any point of view. Nevertheless, human nature being what it is, such developments are not in the least surprising. They do not really reflect upon the character of corporate managements but rather on the patent unwisdom of leaving such matters within the virtually uncontrolled discretion of those who are to benefit by their own decisions.

The new regulations have done much to dispel the mist of secrecy that formerly shrouded the emoluments and stockholdings of corporate officials. Information on salaries, bonuses and stock options must be filed in connection with new security offerings, with the registration of issues on a national exchange, with the subsequent annual reports to the Commission and with the solicitation of proxies.[1] Although these data are not complete, they are sufficient for the practical purpose of advising the stockholders as to the cost of their management. Similarly, stockholdings of officers, directors and those owning 10% of a stock issue must be revealed monthly.

Since this information is not too readily accessible to the individual stockholder, the statistical agencies could further improve their already excellent service by subjoining the salary and stockholding data to their annual lists of officers and directors.

---

[1] Also, under provisions of the Revenue Act of 1936 the Treasury published the names and compensation of all corporate officers receiving over $15,000 in that year. The Revenue Act of 1938 requires these data for salaries of $75,000 or more, beginning with 1938.

In recent years the question of excessive compensation to management has excited considerable attention, and the public understands fairly well that here is a field where the officers' views do not necessarily represent the highest wisdom. It is not so clearly realized that to a considerable extent the same limitations apply in matters affecting the use of the stockholders' capital and surplus. We have alluded to certain aspects of this subject in our discussion of dividend policies (Chap. 29). It should be evident also that the matter of raising *new capital* for expansion is affected by the same reasoning as applies to the withholding of dividends for this purpose.

Wisdom of Continuing the Business Should Be Considered. A third question, *viz.*, that of retaining the stockholder's capital in the business, involves considerations that are basically identical. Managements are naturally loath to return any part of the capital to its owners, even though this capital may be far more useful—and therefore valuable—outside of the business than in it. Returning *a portion* of the capital (*e.g.*, excess cash holdings) means curtailing the resources of the enterprise, perhaps creating financial problems later on and certainly reducing somewhat the prestige of the officers. Complete liquidation means the loss of the job itself. It is scarcely to be expected, therefore, that the paid officers will consider the question of continuing or winding up the business from the standpoint solely of what is in the best interests of the owners. We must emphasize again that the directors are often so closely allied with the officers—who are themselves members of the board—that they too cannot be counted upon to consider such problems purely from the stockholders' point of view.

Thus it appears that the question whether or not a business should be continued is one that at times may deserve independent thought by its proprietors, the stockholders. (It should be pointed out also that this is, by its formal or legal nature, an *ownership problem* and not a *management problem*.) And a logical reason for devoting thought to this question would arise precisely from the fact that the stock has long been selling considerably below its liquidating value. After all, this situation *must* mean that either the market is wrong in its valuation or the management is wrong in keeping the enterprise alive. It is altogether proper that the stockholders should seek to determine which of these is wrong. In this determination the views and explanations of the management deserve the most appreciative attention, but the whole proceeding would be stultified if the management's opinion on this subject were to be accepted as final *per se.*

It is an unhappy fact that in many cases where a management's policies are attacked the critic has some personal axe to grind. This too is perhaps inevitable. There is very little altruism in finance. Wars against corporate managements take time, energy and money. It is hardly to be expected that individuals will expend all these merely to see the right thing done. In such matters the most impressive and creditable moves are those made by a group of substantial stockholders, having an important stake of their own to protect and impelled thereby to act in the interests of the share-holders generally. Representations from such a source, *in any matter where the interest of the officers and the owners may conceivably be opposed,* should gain a more respectful hearing from the rank and file of stockholders than has hitherto been accorded them in most cases.[2]

Broadcast criticisms initiated by stockholders, proxy battles, and various kinds of legal proceedings are exceedingly vexatious to managements, and in many cases they are unwisely or improperly motivated. Yet these should be regarded as one of the drawbacks of being a corporate official and as part of the price of a vigilant stock ownership. The public must learn to judge such controversies on their merits, as developed by statements of fact and by reasoned argument. It must not allow itself to be swayed by mere accusation or by irrelevant personalities.

The subject of liquidation must not be left without some reference to the employees' vital interest therein. It seems heartless in the extreme to discuss such a decision solely from the standpoint of what will be best for the stockholder's pocketbook. Yet nothing is to be gained by confusing the issue. If the reason for continuing the business is primarily to keep the workers employed, and if this means a real sacrifice by the owners, they are entitled to know and to face the fact. They should not be told that it would be unwise for them to liquidate, when in truth it would be profitable but inhumane. It is fair to point out that under our present economic system the owners of a business are not expected to dissipate their capital for the sake of continuing employment. In privately owned enterprises such

---

[2] The proxy regulations of the S.E.C. seek to facilitate the presentation of viewpoints opposed to the management by requiring the company to send out requests for proxies (and covering letters) supplied by individual stockholders, postage to be paid by the latter.

philanthropy is rare. Whether or not a sacrifice of capital for this purpose is conducive to the economic welfare of the country as a whole is a moot point also, but it is not within our province to discuss it here. Our object has been to clarify the issue and to stress the fact that a market price below liquidating value has special significance to the stockholders and should lead them to ask their management some searching questions.

Management May Properly Take Some Interest in Market Price for Shares. Managements have succeeded very well in avoiding these questions with the aid of the time-honored principle that market prices are no concern or responsibility of theirs. It is true, of course, that a company's officers are not responsible for fluctuations in the price of its securities. But this is very far from saying that market prices should *never* be a matter of concern to the management. This idea is not only basically wrong, but it has the added vice of being thoroughly hypocritical. It is wrong because the marketability of securities is one of the chief qualities considered in their purchase. But marketability must presuppose not only a place where they can be sold but also an opportunity to sell them at a *fair price*. It is at least as important to the stockholders that they be able to obtain a fair price for their shares as it is that the dividends, earnings and assets be conserved and increased. It follows that the responsibility of managements to act in the interest of their shareholders includes the obligation to prevent—in so far as they are able—the establishment of either absurdly high or unduly low prices for their securities.

It is difficult not to lose patience with the sanctimonious attitude of many corporate executives who profess not even to know the market price of their securities. In many cases they have a vital personal interest in these very market prices, and at times they use their inside knowledge to take advantage in the market of the outside public and of their own stockholders.[3] Not as a startling innovation but as a common-sense

---

[3] This reached such scandalous proportions "in the good old days" that the Securities Exchange Act of 1934 made "insiders" accountable to the corporation for profits realized on purchases and sales, or *vice versa*, completed within a six months' period. Enforcement must be through a stockholder's suit. This provision has been bitterly criticized in Wall Street as preventing legitimate activities of officers and directors, including support of the market price at critical times. Our own view is that, on balance, both logic and practicality are against the provision as it now stands. Publicity of operations—perhaps immediate rather than monthly—should supply a sufficient safeguard against fraud and a check upon questionable conduct.

recognition of things as they are, we recommend that directors be held to the duty of observing the market price of their securities and of using all proper efforts to correct patent discrepancies, in the same way as they would endeavor to remedy any other corporate condition inimical to the stockholders' interest.

Various Possible Moves for Correcting Market Prices for Shares. The forms that these proper efforts might take are various. In the first place the stockholders' attention may be called officially to the fact that the liquidating, and therefore the minimum, value of the shares is substantially higher than the market price. If, as will usually be the case, the directors are convinced that continuance is preferable to liquidation, the reasons leading to this conclusion should at the same time be supplied. A second line of action is in the direction of dividends. A special endeavor should be made to establish a dividend rate proportionate at least to the liquidating value, in order that the stockholders should not suffer a loss of income through keeping the business alive. This may be done even if current earnings are insufficient, provided there are accumulated profits and provided also the cash position is strong enough to permit such payments.

A third procedure consists of returning to the stockholders such cash capital as is not needed for the conduct of the business. This may be done through a pro rata distribution, accompanied usually by a reduction in par value or through an offer to purchase a certain number of shares pro rata at a fair price. Finally, a careful consideration by the directors of the discrepancy between earning power and liquidating value may lead them to conclude that a sale or winding up of the enterprise is the most sensible corrective step—in which case they should act accordingly.

Examples: Otis Company, 1929–1939. The course of action followed by the Otis Company management in 1929–1930 combined a number of these remedial moves. In July 1929 the president circularized the shareholders, presenting an intermediate balance sheet as of June 30 and emphasizing the disparity between the current bid price and the liquidating value. In September of that year—although earnings were no larger than before—dividend payments were resumed, a step permitted by the company's large cash holdings and substantial surplus. In 1930 a good part of the cash, apparently not needed in the business, was returned to the stockholders through the redemption of the small preferred issue and the repayment of $20 per share of common stock on account of capital.[4]

Subsequently the company embarked on a policy of piecemeal liquidation which resulted in a series of payments on capital account. From September 1929 to the final distribution in 1940 there was paid a total of $94 per share as return of capital, as well as $8 in the form of dividends. As we pointed out in our last chapter, these steps were highly effective in improving the status of the Otis stockholders during a period when most other issues were suffering a shrinkage in value, and ultimately gave them a far larger return than they were likely to receive through the continuance of the business.

Hamilton Woolen Company. The history of this enterprise since 1926 is even more interesting in this connection because it suggests a model technique for the handling by directors of problems affecting the stockholders' investment. In 1927 continued operating losses had resulted in a market price well below liquidating value. There was danger that the losses might continue and wipe out the capital. On the other hand, there was a possibility of much better results in the future, especially if new policies were adopted. A statement of the arguments for and against liquidation was forwarded to the stockholders, and they were asked to vote on the question. They voted to continue the business, with a new operating head; and the decision proved a wise one, since good earnings were realized, and the price advanced above liquidating value.

In 1934, however, the company again showed a large loss, occasioned in good part by serious labor difficulties. The management again submitted the question of liquidation to the stockholders, and this time a winding up of the business was voted. A sale of the business was promptly arranged, and the stockholders received somewhat more than the November 1934 current-asset value.

Particularly noteworthy were the details of the 1927 proceedings. The ultimate decision—to continue or to quit—was put up to the stockholders in whose province it lay; the management supplied information,

---

[4] Other examples of partial return of capital by companies continuing in business include: Cuban Atlantic Sugar Company (1938–1939), Great Southern Lumber Company (1927–1937), Keystone Watch Case Corporation (1932–1933) as well as Davis Coal and Coke Company and the several Standard Oil pipe line companies previously referred to (Chaps. 41 and 43).

expressed its own opinion and permitted an adequate statement of the other side of the case.

Other Examples of Voluntary Liquidation. The subjoined partial list will demonstrate an obvious but fundamental fact, *viz.*, that the liquidation (or sale) of an unprofitable company holding substantial assets (particularly current) is almost certain to realize for the stockholders considerably more than the previously existing market price. The reason is, of course, that the market price is governed chiefly by the earnings, whereas the proceeds of liquidation depend upon the assets.

Company	Year liquidation or sale voted	Price shortly before vote to liquidate or sell	Amount realized for stock
American Glue	1930	$53	$139.00+
I. Benesch & Sons	1939	2¹/₄	6.63
Federal Knitting Mills	1937	20	34.20
Lyman Mills	1927	112	220.25
Mohawk Mining	1933	11	28.50
Signature Hosiery Pfd	1931	3¹/₈	17.00
Standard Oil of Nebraska	1939	6	17.50
United Shipyards A	1938	2¹/₄	11.10*

* To Dec. 31, 1939.

Repurchase of Shares Pro Rata from Shareholders. The Hamilton Woolen management is also to be commended for its action during 1932 and 1933 in employing excess cash capital to repurchase pro rata a substantial number of shares at a reasonable price. This reversed the procedure followed in 1929 when additional shares were offered for subscription to the stockholders. The contraction in business that accompanied the depression made this additional capital no longer necessary, and it was therefore a logical move to give most of it back to the stockholders, to whom it was of greater benefit when in their own pockets than in the treasury of the corporation.[5]

---

[5] Hamilton Woolen sold 13,000 shares pro rata to stockholders at $50 per share in 1929. It repurchased, pro rata, 6,500 shares at $65 in 1932 and 1,200 shares at $50 in 1933. Faultless Rubber Company followed a similar procedure in 1934. Simms Petroleum Company reacquired stock both directly from the shareholders on a pro rata basis and in the open market. Its repurchases by both means between 1930 and 1933 aggregated nearly 45% of the shares outstanding at the end of 1929. Julian and Kokenge (Shoe) Company made pro rata repurchases of common stock in 1932, 1934 and 1939.

Abuse of Shareholders Through Open-Market Purchase of Shares. During the 1930–1933 depression repurchases of their own shares were made by many industrial companies out of their surplus cash assets,[6] but the procedure generally followed was open to grave objection. The stock was bought in the open market without notice to the shareholders. This method introduced a number of unwholesome elements into the situation. It was thought to be "in the interest of the corporation" to acquire the stock at the lowest possible price. The consequence of this idea is that those stockholders who sell their shares back to the company are made to suffer as large a loss as possible, for the presumable benefit of those who hold on. Although this is a proper viewpoint to follow in purchasing other kinds of assets for the business, there is no warrant in logic or in ethics for applying it to the acquisition of shares of stock from the company's own stockholders. The management is the more obligated to act fairly toward the sellers because the company is itself on the buying side.

But, in fact, the desire to buy back shares cheaply may lead to a determination to reduce or pass the dividend, especially in times of general uncertainty. Such conduct would be injurious to nearly all the stockholders, whether they sell or not, and it is for that reason that we spoke of the repurchase of shares at an unconscionably low price as only *presumably* to the advantage of those who retained their interest.

Example: White Motor Company. In the previous chapter attention was called to the extraordinary discrepancy between the market level of White Motor's stock in 1931–1932 and the minimum liquidating value of the shares. It will be instructive to see how the policies followed by the management contributed mightily to the creation of a state of affairs so unfortunate for the stockholders.

White Motor Company paid dividends of $4 per share (8%) practically from its incorporation in 1916 through 1926. This period included the depression year 1921, in which the company reported a loss of nearly $5,000,000. It drew, however, upon its accumulated surplus to maintain the full dividend, a policy that prevented the price of the shares from declining below 29. With the return of prosperity the quotation advanced

---

[6] Figures published by the New York Stock Exchange in February 1934 revealed that 259 corporations with shares listed thereon had reacquired portions of their own stock.

to 72$^1/_2$ in 1924 and 104$^1/_2$ in 1925. In 1926 the stockholders were offered 200,000 shares at par ($50), increasing the company's capital by $10,000,000. A stock dividend of 20% was paid at the same time.

Hardly had the owners of the business paid in this additional cash, when the earnings began to shrink, and the dividend was reduced. In 1928 about $3 were earned (consolidated basis), but only $1 was disbursed. In the 12 months ending June 30, 1931 the company lost about $2,500,000. The next dividend payment was omitted entirely, and the price of the stock collapsed to 7$^1/_2$.

The contrast between 1931 and 1921 is striking. In the earlier year the losses were larger, the profit-and-loss surplus was smaller and the cash holdings far lower than in 1931. But in 1921 the dividend was maintained, and the price thereby supported. A decade later, despite redundant holdings of cash and the presence of substantial undistributed profits, a single year's operating losses sufficed to persuade the management to suspend the dividend and permit the establishment of a grotesquely low market price for the shares.

During the period before and after the omission of the dividend the company was active in buying its own shares in the open market. These purchases began in 1929 under a plan adopted for the benefit of "those filling certain managerial positions." By June 1931 about 100,000 shares had been bought in at a cost of $2,800,000. With the passing of the dividend, the officers and employees were relieved of whatever obligations they had assumed to pay for these shares, and the plan was dropped. In the next six months, aided by the collapse in the market price, the company acquired 50,000 additional shares in the market at an average cost of about $11 per share. The total holdings of 150,000 shares were then retired and cancelled.

These facts, thus briefly stated, illustrate the vicious possibilities inherent in permitting managements to exercise discretionary powers to purchase shares with the company's funds. We note first the painful contrast between the treatment accorded to the White Motor managerial employees and to its stockholders. An extraordinarily large amount of stock was bought for the benefit of these employees at what seemed to be an attractive price. All the money to carry these shares was supplied by the stockholders. If the business had improved, the value of the stock would have advanced greatly, and all the benefits would have gone to the employees.

When things became worse, "those in managerial positions" were relieved of any loss, and the entire burden fell upon the stockholders.[7]

In its transactions *directly with its stockholders*, we see White Motor soliciting $10,000,000 in new capital in 1926. We see some of this additional capital (not needed to finance sales) employed to buy back many of these very shares at one-fifth of the subscription price. The passing of the dividend was a major factor in making possible these repurchases at such low quotations. The facts just related without further evidence might well raise a suspicion in the mind of a stockholder that the omission of the dividend was in some way related to a desire to depress the price of the shares. If the reason for the passing of the dividend was a desire to preserve cash, then it is not easy to see why, since there was money available to buy in stock, there was not money available to continue a dividend previously paid without interruption for 15 years.

The spectacle of a company overrich in cash passing its dividend, in order to impel desperate stockholders to sell out at a ruinous price, is not pleasant to contemplate.

Westmoreland Coal Company: Another Example. A more recent illustration of the dubious advantage accruing to stockholders from a policy of open-market repurchases of common stock is supplied by the case of Westmoreland Coal. In the ten years 1929–1938 this company reported a net loss in the aggregate amounting to $309,000, or $1.70 per share. However, these losses resulted after deduction of depreciation and depletion allowances totaling $2,658,000, which was largely in excess of new capital expenditures. Thus the company's cash position actually improved considerably during this period, despite payment of very irregular dividends aggregating $4.10 per share.

In 1935, according to its annual reports, the company began to repurchase its own stock in the open market. By the end of 1938 it had thus acquired 44,634 shares, which were more than 22% of the entire issue. The average price paid for this stock was $8.67 per share. Note here the extraordinary fact that this average price paid *was less than one-half the cash-asset holdings alone* per share, without counting the very large other

---

[7] In the sale to Studebaker in 1933 the directors set aside 15,000 shares of treasury stock as a donation to key men in the organization. Some White stockholders brought suit to set aside this donation, and the suit was settled by payment of 31 cents per share on White stock not acquired by Studebaker.

tangible assets. Note also that at no time between 1930 and 1939 did the stock sell so high as its cash assets alone. (At the end of 1938 the company reported cash and marketable securities totaling $2,772,000, while the entire stock issue was selling for $1,400,000.)

If this situation is analyzed, the following facts appear clear:

1. The low market price of the stock was due to the absence of earnings and the irregular dividend. Under such conditions the quoted price would not reflect the very large cash holding theoretically available for the shares. Stocks sell on earnings and dividends and not on cash-asset values—unless distribution of these cash assets is in prospect.

2. The true obligation of managements is to recognize the realities of such a situation and to do all in their power to protect every stockholder against unwarranted depreciation of his investment, and particularly against unnecessary sacrifice of a large part of the true value of his shares. Such sacrifices are likely to be widespread under conditions of this kind, because many stockholders will be moved by necessity or the desire for steady income or by a discouraged view of the coal industry to sell their shares for what they can get.

3. The anomaly presented by exceptionally large cash holdings and an absurdly low market price was obviously preventable. That the company had more cash than it needed is confessed by the fact that it had money available to buy in cheap stock—even if it were not evident from a study of the unusual relationship between cash holdings and annual business done.

4. All cash that could possibly be spared should have been returned to the stockholders on a pro rata basis. The use of some of it to buy in shares as cheaply as possible is unjust to the many stockholders induced by need or ignorance to sell. It favors those strong enough to hold their shares indefinitely. It particularly advantages those in control of the company, for *in their case* the company's cash applicable to their stock is readily available to them if they should need it (since they could then bring about a distribution). Just because this situation is distinctly not true of the rank and file of the stockholders, the market discounts so cruelly the value of their cash when held by the company instead of themselves.[8]

---

[8] Two additional factors in this situation deserve brief mention. The company had a rental obligation of 10 cents per ton, but not less than $189,000 annually, for mining coal from leased lands. This liability was an additional consideration, besides the ordinary ones, which argued

Summary and Conclusion. The relationship between stockholders and their managements, after undergoing many unsound developments during the hectic years from 1928 to 1933, have since been subjected to salutary controls—emanating both from S.E.C. regulation and from a more critical viewpoint generally. Certain elementary facts, once well-nigh forgotten, might well be emphasized here: Corporations are in law the mere creatures and property of the stockholders who own them; the officers are only the paid employees of the stockholders; the directors, however chosen, are virtually trustees, whose legal duty it is to act solely in behalf of the owners of the business.[9]

To make these general truths more effective in practice, it is necessary that the stock-owning public be educated to a clearer idea of what are the true interests of the stockholders in such matters as dividend policies, expansion policies, the use of corporate cash to repurchase shares, the various methods of compensating management, and the fundamental question of whether the owners' capital shall remain in the business or be taken out by them in whole or in part.

---

for maintenance of a comfortable cash position, but it could not justify the immobilizing of far more cash than the whole company appeared to be worth at any time between 1930 and 1939.

In October 1939 the company made application to the S.E.C. to terminate trading in its shares on the Philadelphia Stock Exchange and the New York Curb Exchange, intimating that the infrequency of transactions might be responsible for their unduly low price. The reader may judge whether or not, in the circumstances, the plight of the stockholders would be relieved in any wise by destroying the established market for their shares. (The application was later withdrawn.)

[9] The management of American Telephone and Telegraph Company has repeatedly asserted that it considers itself a trustee for the interests of stockholders, employees and the public, in equal measure. A policy of this kind, if frankly announced and sincerely followed, can scarcely be criticized in the case of a quasi-civic enterprise. But given the ordinary business company, the issue is more likely to be whether the management is acting as trustees for the stockholders or as trustees for the management.

CHAPTER 45

Balance-Sheet
Analysis (*Concluded*)

OUR DISCUSSION in the preceding chapters has related chiefly to situations in which the balance-sheet exhibit apparently justified a higher price than prevailed in the market. But the more usual purpose of balance-sheet analysis is to detect the opposite state of affairs, *viz.*, the presence of financial weaknesses that may detract from the investment or speculative merits of an issue. Careful buyers of securities scrutinize the balance sheet to see if the cash is adequate, if the current assets bear a suitable ratio to the current liabilities, and if there is any indebtedness of near maturity that may threaten to develop into a refinancing problem.

WORKING-CAPITAL POSITION
AND DEBT MATURITIES

Basic Rules Concerning Working Capital. Nothing useful may be said here on the subject of how much cash a corporation should hold. The investor must form his own opinion as to what is needed in any particular case and also as to how seriously an apparent deficiency of cash should be regarded. On the subject of the *working-capital ratio*, a minimum of $2 of current assets for $1 of current liabilities was formerly regarded as a standard for industrial companies.

But since the late 1920's a tendency towards a stronger current position developed in most industries, and we find that the great majority of industrial corporations show a ratio well in excess of 2 to 1.[1] There is some tendency now to hold that a company falling below the average of its

---

[1] See Appendix Note 61 for comprehensive data with reference to industrial corporations listed on the New York Stock Exchanges at the end of 1938. See also the annual compilations in *Moody's Manual of Industrials*.

group should be viewed with suspicion.[2] This idea seems to us to contain something of a logical fallacy, since it necessarily penalizes the lower half of any group, regardless of how satisfactory the showing may be, considered by itself. We are unable to suggest a better figure than the old 2-to-1 criterion to use as a *definite quantitative test* of a sufficiently comfortable financial position. Naturally the investor would favor companies that well exceed this minimum requirement, but the problem is whether or not a higher ratio *must* be exacted as a condition for purchase, so that an issue otherwise satisfactory would necessarily be rejected if the current assets are only twice current liabilities. We hesitate to suggest such a rule, nor do we know what new figure to prescribe.

A second measure of financial strength is the so-called "acid test," which requires that current assets *exclusive of inventories* be at least equal to current liabilities. Ordinarily the investor might well expect of a company that it meet *both* the 2-to-1 test and the acid test. If *neither* of these criteria is met it would in most cases reflect strongly upon the investment standing of a common-stock issue—as it would in the case of a bond or preferred stock—and it would supply an argument against the security from the speculative standpoint as well.

Archer-Daniels-Midland Company

Item	June 30, 1933	June 30, 1932
Cash assets	$ 1,392,000	$3,230,000
Receivables	4,391,000	2,279,000
Inventories	12,184,000	4,081,000
Total current assets	$17,967,000	$9,590,000
Current liabilities	8,387,000	778,000
Working capital	$ 9,580,000	$8,812,000
Working capital excluding inventories	−2,604,000	+4,731,000

Exceptions and Examples. As in all arbitrary rules of this kind, exceptions must be allowed if justified by special circumstances. Consider, for example, the current position of Archer-Daniels-Midland Company on June 30, 1933, as compared with the previous year's figures.

---

[2] See Roy A. Foulke, *Signs of the Times*, pp. 17–19, 25 *et seq.*, New York 1938; and Alexander Wall, *How to Evaluate Financial Statements*, pp. 82–97, New York, 1936. Note, however, Wall's criticism of mere arithmetical averages as bases for comparison.

The position of this company on June 30, 1933, was evidently much less comfortable than a year before, and, judged by the usual standards, it might appear somewhat overextended. But in this case the increase in payables represented a return to the normal practice in the vegetable-oil industry, under which fairly large seasonal borrowings are regularly incurred to carry grain and flaxseed supplies. Upon investigation, therefore, the analyst would not consider the financial condition shown in the 1933 balance sheet as in any sense disturbing.

Contrasting examples on this point are supplied by Douglas Aircraft Company and Stokely Brothers and Company in 1936–1938.

A Working-Capital Comparison (000 omitted)

Item	Stokely Brothers and Company			Douglas Aircraft Company		
	May 31, 1936	May 31 1937	May 31, 1938	Nov. 30, 1936	Nov. 30, 1937	Nov. 30, 1938
Current assets:						
Cash and receivables	$2,274	$2,176	$1,827	$2,885	$ 2,559	$4,673
Inventories	5,282	7,323	6,034	6,392	12,240	4,084
Total	$7,556	$9,499	$8,861	$9,277	$14,749	$8,757
Current liabilities:						
Notes payable	$2,000	$2,000	$2,500	$1,390	$ 5,230	
Other	1,527	1,286	1,320	1,179	3,183	2,129
Total	$3,527	$3,286	$3,820	$2,569	$ 8,413	$2,129
Bank loans due 1–3 years		3,000	3,000			
Total current liabilities plus 1–3 year notes	3,527	6,286	6,820	2,569	8,413	2,129
Net earnings for year	1,382	353(d)	713(d)	976	1,082	2,147

The situation in Douglas Aircraft in 1937 was not a seasonal matter, as in the case of Archer-Daniels-Midland, but grew out of the receipt of certain types of orders requiring considerable working capital. Upon inquiry the investor could have satisfied himself that the need for bank accommodation was likely to be temporary and that, in any event, the new business was sufficiently profitable to make any necessary financing an easy affair. The Stokely picture was quite different, since the large current debt had developed out of expanding inventories in an unprofitable market. Hence the May 1937 balance sheet of Stokely carried a serious warning for the preferred and common stockholder, as the table shows.

A year later Douglas Aircraft had paid off its bank loans and showed a current ratio of 4 to 1. Stokely suspended preferred dividends in October 1938, and in that year the price of the issue fell from 21 (par $25) to 10.

As we pointed out in our discussion of bond selection (Chap. 13), no standard requirements such as we have been discussing are recognized as applicable to railroads and public utilities. It must not be inferred therefrom that the working-capital exhibit of these companies is entirely unimportant—the contrary will soon be shown to be true—but only that it is not to be tested by any cut-and-dried formulas.

Large Bank Debt Frequently a Sign of Weakness. Financial difficulties are almost always heralded by the presence of bank loans or of other debt due in a short time. In other words, it is rare for a weak financial position to be created solely by ordinary trade accounts payable. This does not mean that bank debt is a bad sign in itself; the use of a reasonable amount of bank credit—particularly for seasonal needs—is not only legitimate but even desirable. But, whenever the statement shows Notes or Bills Payable, the analyst will subject the financial picture to a somewhat closer scrutiny than in cases where there is a "clean" balance sheet.

The postwar boom in 1919 was marked by an enormous expansion of industrial inventories carried at high prices and financed largely by bank loans. The 1920–1921 collapse of commodity prices made these industrial bank loans a major problem. But the depression of the 1930s had different characteristics. Industrial borrowings in 1929 had been remarkably small, due first to the absence of commodity or inventory speculation and secondly to the huge sales of stock to provide additional working capital. (Naturally there were exceptions, such as, notably, Anaconda Copper Mining Company which owed $35,000,000 to banks at the end of 1929, increased to $70,500,000 three years later.) The large bank borrowings were shown more frequently by the railroads and public utilities. These were contracted to pay for property additions or to meet maturing debt or—in the case of some railways—to carry unearned fixed charges. The expectation in all these cases was that the bank loans would be refunded by permanent financing; but in many instances such refinancing proved impossible, and receivership resulted. The collapse of the Insull system of public-utility holding companies was precipitated in this way.

Examples: It is difficult to say exactly how apprehensively the investor or speculator should have viewed the presence of $68,000,000 of bank loans in the New York Central balance sheet at the end of 1932 or the bills payable of $69,000,000 owned by Cities Service Company on December 31, 1931. But certainly this adverse sign should not have been ignored. The more conservatively minded would have taken it as a strong argument against any and all securities of companies in such a position, except possibly issues selling at so low a price as to constitute an admitted but attractive gamble. An improvement in conditions will, of course, permit such bank loans to be refunded, but logic requires us to recognize that the improvement is prospective whereas the bank loans themselves are very real and very menacing.[3]

When a company's earnings are substantial, it rarely becomes insolvent because of bank loans. But if refinancing is impracticable—as frequently it was in the 1931–1933 period—the lenders may require suspension of dividends in order to make all the profits available to reduce the debt. It is for this reason that the dividend on Brooklyn-Manhattan Transit Corporation common was passed in 1932 and the preferred dividend of New York Water Service Corporation was passed in 1931, although both companies were reporting earnings about as large as in previous years.

The 1937–1938 recession did not create corporate financial problems comparable with those arising out of the two previous depressions. In this respect there is a significant contrast between the stock markets of 1919–1921 and 1937–1938. For the decline in stock prices was actually greater—both in dollars and percentagewise—in the recent period than in the postwar collapse, although intrinsically the 1937–1938 downturn was of much smaller importance, since it had relatively slight effect upon the position of American corporations generally.[4] This may be taken as a rather disquieting sign that stock prices have been growing more irrationally sensitive to temporary fluctuations in business—a fact that we

---

[3] Improvement in general business, plus easy money rates (plus in the case of railroads a misguided optimism on the part of investors) enabled many companies to fund bank loans that looked dangerous in 1931–1933.

[4] The Stokely case is an exception to this statement, but there were surprisingly few of the kind.

are inclined to ascribe to the disappearance of the old-line distinctions between stock investors and stock speculators.

Intercorporate Indebtedness. Current debt to a parent or to an affiliated company is theoretically as serious as any other short-term liability, but in practice it is rarely made the basis of an embarrassing claim for payment.

Example: United Gas Corporation has owed $26,000,000 on open account to its parent Electric Bond and Share Company since 1930—so that it constantly reports a large excess of current liabilities over current assets. Yet this debt has not prevented it from paying first preferred dividends in 1936–1939. In 1932, however, with somewhat larger earnings than in 1939, it had been compelled to suspend the senior dividend because it had large bank loans in addition to its intercompany debt. The conservative buyer would naturally prefer to see the obligations to affiliates in some form other than a current liability.

The Danger of Early Maturing Funded Debt. A large bond issue coming due in a short time constitutes a critical financial problem when operating results are unfavorable. Investors and speculators should both give serious thought to such a situation when revealed by a balance sheet. Maturing funded debt is a frequent cause of insolvency.

Examples: Fisk Rubber Company was thrown into receivership by its inability to pay off an $8,000,000 note issue at the end of 1930. The insolvency of Colorado Fuel and Iron Company and of the Chicago, Rock Island and Pacific Railway Company in 1933 were both closely related to the fact that large bond issues fell due in 1934. The heedlessness of speculators is well shown by the price of $54 established for Colorado Fuel and Iron Preferred in June 1933, when its short-term bond issue (Colorado Industrial Company 5s, due 1934, guaranteed by the parent company) was selling at 45, *an indicated yield of well over* 100% *per annum.* This price for the bonds was an almost certain sign of trouble ahead. Failure to meet the maturity would in all likelihood mean insolvency (for a voluntary extension could by no means be counted upon) and the danger of complete extinction of the stock issues. It was typical of the speculator to ignore so obvious a hazard and typical also that he suffered a large loss for his carelessness. (Two months later, on announcement of the receivership, the price of the preferred stock dropped to 17^{1}/$_{4}$.)

New York, Chicago, and St. Louis Railroad Company has been faced
with a continuous financial problem growing out of the sale of a three-
year note issue in 1929. Since the first maturity in 1932 it was repeatedly
extended under threat of receivership as an alternative. Typical of speculative disregard of financial problems was the advance of this company's
preferred stock from 18$^1/2$ to 45$^3/4$ in 1939, against a low price that year
of only 50 for the notes due in 1941.

Even when the maturing debt can probably be taken care of in some
way, the possible cost of the refinancing must be taken into account.

Examples: This point is well illustrated by the $14,000,000 issue of
American Rolling Mill Company 4$^1/2$% Notes, due November 1, 1933. In
June 1933 the notes were selling at 80, which meant an annual yield basis
of about 75%. At the same time the common stock had advanced from
3 to 24 and then represented a total valuation for the common stock of
over $40,000,000. Speculators buying the stock because of improvement
in the steel industry failed to consider the fact that, in order to refund the
notes in the poor market than existing for new capital issues, a very
attractive conversion privilege would have to be offered. This would necessarily react against the profit possibilities of the common stock. As it
happened, a new 5% note issue, convertible into stock at 25, was offered
in exchange for the 4$^1/2$% notes. The result was the establishment of a
price of 101 for the notes in August 1933 against a coincident price of 21
for the common stock; and a price of 15 for the stock on November 1,
1933, when the notes were taken care of at par.

The impending maturity of a bond issue is of importance to the holders of all the company's securities, including mortgage debt ranking ahead
of the maturing issue. For even the prior bonds will in all likelihood be
seriously affected if the company is unable to take care of the junior issue.
This point is illustrated in striking fashion by the Fisk Rubber Company
First Mortgage 8s, due 1941. Although they were deemed to be superior
in their position to the 5$^1/2$% unsecured notes, their holders suffered grievously from the receivership occasioned by the maturity of the 5$^1/2$s. The
price of the 8s declined from 115 in 1929 to 16 in 1932.[5]

Bank Loans of Intermediate Maturity. The combination of very low interest
rates and the drying up of ordinary commercial bank loans has produced a

---

[5] See other references to the two Fisk bond issues in Chaps. 6, 18, and 50.

new phenomenon in recent years—the loaning of money to corporations by banks, repayable over a period of several years. Most of this money has been borrowed for the purpose of retiring bond issues (*e.g.*, Commercial Investment Trust Corporation in November 1939) and even preferred stock (*e.g.*, Archer-Daniels-Midland Company in 1939). In some cases such loans have been made for additional working capital (*e.g.*, Western Auto Supply Company in 1937) or to replace ordinary short-term bank credit (*e.g.*, American Commercial Alcohol, Stokely Brothers). In most cases it is stipulated or expected that the loans will be retired in annual installments.

From the standpoint of security analysis this bank credit resembles the short-term notes that used to be sold to the public as a familiar part of corporate financing. It must be considered partly equivalent to current liabilities and partly to early maturing debt. It is not dangerous if either the current-asset position is so strong that the loans could readily be taken care of as current liabilities or the earning power is so large and dependable as to make refinancing a simple problem. But if neither of these conditions is present (as in the Stokely example earlier), the analyst must view the presence of a substantial amount of intermediate bank debt as a potential threat to dividends or even to solvency.

It should not be necessary to dilate further upon the prime necessity of examining the balance sheet for any possible adverse features in the nature of bank loans or other short-term debt.

COMPARISON OF BALANCE SHEETS
OVER A PERIOD OF TIME

This important part of security analysis may be considered under three aspects, *viz.:*

1. As a check-up on the reported earnings per share.
2. To determine the effect of losses (or profits) on the financial position of the company.
3. To trace the relationship between the company's resources and its earning power over a long period.

Check-up on Reported Earnings per Share, via the Balance Sheet. Some of this technique has already been used in connection with related phases of security analysis. In Chap. 36, for instance, we gave an example of the first aspect, in checking the reported earnings of American Commercial

Alcohol Corporation for 1931 and 1932. As an example covering a larger stretch of years we submit the following contrast between the average earnings of United States Industrial Alcohol Company for the ten years 1929–1938, as shown by the reported per-share figures and as indicated by the changes in its net worth in the balance sheet.

U. S. Industrial Alcohol Company, 1929–1938
1. Net earnings as reported

1929	$4,721,000	*per share: $12.63
1930	1,105,000	2.95
1931	*1,834,000(d)*	*4.90(d)*
1932	176,000	0.47
1933	1,393,000	3.56
1934	1,580,000	4.03
1935	844,000	2.15
1936	78,000	0.20
1937	*456,000(d)*	*1.17(d)*
1938	*668,000(d)*	*1.71(d)*
Total for 10 years	$6,782,000	$18.21

* As stated in the company's annual reports.

2. Discrepancy between earnings as above and changes in the surplus account

Net earnings 1929–1938, as reported.........................	$ 6,782,000
Less dividends paid..	5,959,000
(A) Indicated balance to surplus...............................	823,000
Earned surplus Dec. 31, 1928................................	14,214,000
Less charge @ write-down of plant account to $1 in 1933..........	455,000
Earned surplus Dec. 31, 1928, as adjusted......................	13,759,000
Earned surplus and contingency reserve, Dec. 31, 1938...........	5,736,000
(B) Decrease in surplus on balance sheet........................	8,023,000
Discrepancy between earnings shown in income accounts and those indicated by balance sheets........................	$ 8,846,000

3. Explanation of Discrepancy

Charges made to surplus and not deducted in income account from which earnings per share were computed by company:

Mark-down of inventory	$4,500,000
Charge-off and write-down of various assets	3,969,000
Miscellaneous adjustments, net................................	377,000
	$8,846,000

In addition to the foregoing the company wrote down its fixed assets to $1 in 1933 by a charge of $19,301,000, of which $18,846,000 was taken out of capital account and the balance out of surplus. To the extent that depreciation charges since 1932 may have been insufficient because of this write-down (Chap. 36), the reported earnings for the period were further overstated.

4. Restatement of Earnings for 1929–1938

Earnings per income account	$6,782,000
Less charges made to surplus	8,846,000
Earnings for period as corrected	$2,064,000(d)

5. Working Capital Comparison: 1938 vs. 1928

Net working capital Dec. 31,1928	$11,336,000
Net working capital Dec. 31, 1938	8,144,000
Decrease for ten years	3,192,000
Add proceeds of sales of capital stock	6,582,000
Real shrinkage in working capital for period	$9,774,000

The foregoing analysis does not require extended discussion, since most of the points involved were covered in Chaps. 31 to 36. Virtually all the charges made to surplus between 1929 and 1938 (except for the write-down of the plant account to $1) represented a real diminution of the reported earning power of United States Industrial Alcohol during this ten-year period. It seems likely, also, that the surplus would have shrunk considerably farther if the plant account had been carried at a proper fig-ure and appropriate depreciation charged against it since 1932. The fact that the company's working capital decreased by $3,192,000, despite receipt of $6,582,000 from the sale of additional stock, is further evidence that, instead of there being a surplus above dividends as reported, the company actually lost money before dividends during these ten years.[6]

Checking the Effect of Losses or Profits on the Financial Position of the Company. An example of the second aspect was given in Chap. 43, in

---

[6] An analysis of the exhibit of Stewart Warner Corporation for 1925–1932, leading to simi-lar conclusions, appeared at this point in our 1934 edition. *Cf.* W. A. Hosmer, "The Effect of Direct Charges to Surplus on the Measurement of Income," *Business and Modern Society*, ed. by M.P. McNair and H. T. Lewis. pp. 113–151, Harvard University Press, 1938.

the comparison of the 1929–1932 balance sheets of Manhattan Shirt Company and Hupp Motor Car Corporation respectively. A similar comparison is shown below, covering the exhibit of Plymouth Cordage Company and H. R. Mallinson and Company during the same period, 1929–1932.

Examples:

Item	Plymouth Cordage Co.	H. R. Mallinson & Co.
Earnings reported:		
1930	$ 288,000	*$1,457,000(d)*
1931	25,000	*561,000(d)*
1932	*233,000(d)*	*200,000(d)*
Total (3 years) profit	$ 80,000	*$2,218,000(d)*
Dividends	1,348,000	66,000
Charges to surplus and reserves	2,733,000	116,000
Decrease in surplus and reserve for 3 years	$4,001,000	$2,400,000

Comparative Balance Sheets (000 omitted)

	Plymouth Cordage		H. R. Mallinson	
Item	Sept. 30, 1929	Sept. 30, 1932	Dec. 31, 1929	Dec. 31, 1932
Fixed and miscellaneous assets (net)	$ 7,211	$ 5,157	$2,539	$2,224
Cash assets	1,721	3,784	526	20
Receivables	1,156	668	1,177	170
Inventories	8,059	3,150	3,060	621
Total assets	$18,147	$12,759	$7,302	$3,035
Current liabilities	$ 982	$ 309	$2,292	$ 486*
Preferred stock			1,342	1,281
Common stock	8,108	7,394	500	500
Surplus and miscellaneous reserves	9,057	5,056	3,168	768
Total liabilities	$18,147	$12,759	$7,302	$3,035
Net current assets	$ 9,954	$ 7,298	$2,471	$ 357
Net current assets excluding inventory	1,895	4,143	*589(d)*	*264(d)*

* Including $32,000 of "deferred liabilities."

Despite the large reduction in the surplus of Plymouth Cordage during these years, its financial position was even stronger at the end of the period than at the beginning, and the liquidating value per share (as distinct from book value) was probably somewhat higher. On the other hand, the losses of Mallinson almost denuded it of working capital and thereby created an extremely serious obstacle to a restoration of its former earning power.

Taking Losses on Inventories May Strengthen Financial Position. It is obvious that losses that are represented solely by a decline in the inventory account are not so serious as those which must be financed by an increase in current liabilities. If the shrinkage in the inventory exceeds the losses, so that there is an actual increase in cash or reduction in payables, it may then be proper to say—somewhat paradoxically—that the company's financial position has been strengthened even though it has been suffering losses. This reasoning has a concrete application in analyzing issues selling at less than liquidating value. It will be recalled that, in estimating break-up value, inventories are ordinarily taken at about 50 to 75% of the balance sheet figure, even though the latter is based on the lower of cost or market.

Manhattan Shirt Company (000 omitted)

Item	Balance sheet, Nov. 30, 1929		Balance sheet, Nov. 30, 1932	
	Book value	Estimated liquidating value	Book value	Estimated liquidating value
Cash and bonds at market	$ 885	$ 885	$1,961	$1,961
Receivables	2,621	2,100	771	620
Inventories	4,330	2,900	1,289	850
Fixed and other assets	2,065*	500	1,124	300
Total assets	$9,901	$6,385	$5,145	$3,731
Current liabilities	2,574	2,574	100	100
Preferred stock	299	299		
Balance for common	$7,028	$3,513	$5,045	$3,631
Number of shares	281,000	281,000	246,000	246,000
Value per share	$25.00	$12.50	$20.50	$14.75

* Excluding good-will.

(*Continues*)

Income account 1930–1932

Balance after preferred dividends:

1930	*318,000(d)*
1931	93,000
1932	*139,000(d)*
3 years	*364,000(d)*
Charges to surplus	505,000*
Common dividends paid	723,000
	$1,592,000
Less discount on common stock bought	481,000
Decrease in surplus for period	$1,111,000*

* Eliminating transfer of $100,000 to Contingency Reserve.

The result is that what appears as an operating loss in the company's statement may have the actual effect of a profit from the standpoint of the investor who has valued the inventory in his own mind at considerably less than the book figure. This idea is concretely illustrated in the Manhattan Shirt Company example in the previous table.

If we consider only the company's figures there was evidently a loss for the period, with a consequent shrinkage in the value of the common stock. But if an investor had bought the stock, say, at $8 per share in 1930 (the low price in that year was 6$^{1}/_{8}$), he would more logically have appraised the stock in his own mind on the basis of its liquidating value rather than its book value. From his point of view, therefore, the intrinsic value of his holdings would have *increased* during the depression period from $12.50 to $14.75 per share, even after deducting the substantial dividends paid. What really happened was that Manhattan Shirt turned the larger portion of its assets into cash during these three years and sustained a much smaller loss in so doing than a conservative buyer of the stock would have anticipated. This accomplishment can be summarized in the following table.

We have here a direct contrast between the superficial indications of the income account and the truer story told by the successive balance sheets. Situations of this kind justify our repeated assertion that income-account analysis must be supplemented and confirmed by balance-sheet analysis.[7]

---

[7] The student will note a similar development in Manhattan Shirt, though on a smaller scale, between December 1937 and December 1938.

Assets turned into cash and application of proceeds	Amount	"Expected loss" thereon and application of difference
Reduction in inventory	$3,000,000	$1,000,000
Reduction in receivables	1,800,000	350,000
Reduction in plant, etc.	1,000,000	750,000
	$5,800,000	$2,100,000
Actual loss sustained	800,000	800,000
Net amount realized	$5,000,000	"Gain" on basis of
		liquidation values $1,300,000
Applied as follows:		Applied as follows:
To common dividends	$ 700,000	To common dividends $700,000
To payment of liabilities	2,500,000	To increase liquidating
		value $600,000
To redemption of preferred	300,000	
To retirement of common	500,000	
To increase in cash assets	1,000,000	
	$5,000,000	

Is Shrinkage in Value of Normal Inventory an Operating Loss? A further question may be raised with respect to changes in the inventory account, *i.e.*, whether or not a mere reduction in the *carrying price* should be regarded as creating an operating loss. In the case of Plymouth Cordage we note the following comparative figures:

Inventory Sept. 30, 1929 . . . . $8,059,000
Inventory Sept. 30, 1932 3,150,000
Decrease 60%

In the meantime the price of fibers had declined more than 50%, and there was good reason to believe that the actual number of pounds of fiber, rope and twine contained in the company's inventory was not very much smaller in 1932 than in 1929. At least half of the decline in the inventory account was therefore due solely to the fall in unit prices. Did this portion of the shrinkage in inventory values constitute an operating loss? Could it not be argued that its fixed assets had suffered a similar reduction in their appraisal value and that there was as much reason to charge this shrinkage against earnings as to charge the shrinkage in the carrying price of a certain physical amount of inventory?

We have already discussed this point in our exposition of the "normal-stock" basis of inventory valuation (in Chap. 32), a method adopted by Plymouth Cordage itself after 1932. In theory the analyst might attempt to put all companies on a normal-stock basis for the purpose of calculating their earning power exclusive of inventory fluctuations and for uniform comparisons. Actually, he has not the data necessary for such calculations. Hence he is reduced—here, as in many fields of analysis—to the necessity of making general rather than exact allowance for the distorting effect of inventory price changes.

Profits from Inventory Inflation. That the importance of inventory price changes is not confined to a depression period is emphatically shown by the events of 1919 and 1920. In 1919 the profits of industrial companies were very large; in 1920 the reported earnings were irregular but in the aggregate quite substantial. Yet the gains shown in these two years were in many cases the result of an *inventory inflation, i.e.,* a huge and speculative advance in commodity prices. Not only was the authenticity of these profits thereby made open to question, but the situation was replete with danger because of the large bank loans contracted to finance these overvalued inventories.

Examples: The following tabulation, which covers a number of the leading industrial companies, will bring out the significant contrast between the apparently satisfactory earnings developments and the

Twelve Industrial Companies (Aggregate Figures)

	Year 1919	Year 1920	Years 1919–1920
Earned for common stock	$100,000,000	$ 48,000,000	$148,000,000
Dividends paid	35,000,000	68,000,000	103,000,000
Charges to surplus	5,000,000	10,000,000	15,000,000
Added to surplus	60,000,000	*30,000,000* (decr.)	30,000,000
Inventories increased	57,000,000	84,000,000	141,000,000
Change in other net current assets	+30,000,000	*131,000,000* (decr.)	*101,000,000* (decr.)
Plant, etc. increased	33,000,000	169,000,000	202,000,000
Capitalization increased	69,000,000	141,000,000	210,000,000
Reserve increased		12,000,000	12,000,000

undoubtedly disquieting balance-sheet developments between the end of 1918 and the end of 1920.

The companies included in the foregoing computation were American Can, American Smelting and Refining, American Woolen, Baldwin Locomotive Works, Central Leather, Corn Products Refining, General Electric, B. F. Goodrich, Lackawanna Steel, Republic Iron and Steel, Studebaker, United States Rubber.

We append also the individual figures for United States Rubber, in order to add concreteness to our illustration:

U. S. Rubber (1919–1920)

Earned for common stock:

1919	$12,670,000	Per share: $17.60
1920	16,002,000	19.76
Total	$28,672,000	$37.36
Cash dividends paid	8,580,000	
Stock dividend paid	9,000,000	
Transferred to contingency reserve	6,000,000	
Adjustments of surplus and reserves	cr. 2,210,000	
Net increase in surplus and miscellaneous reserves		$7,300,000

Balance Sheet (000 omitted)

Item	Dec. 31, 1918	Dec. 31, 1920	Increase
Plant and miscellaneous assets (net)	$131,000	$185,500	$54,500
Inventories	70,700	123,500	52,800
Cash and receivables	49,500	63,600	14,100
Total assets	$251,200	$372,600	$121,400
Current liabilities	$ 26,500	$ 74,300	$ 47,800
Bonds	68,600	87,000	18,400
Preferred and common stock	98,400	146,300	49,900
Surplus and miscellaneous reserves	57,700	65,000	7,300
Total liabilities	$251,200	$372,600	$121,400
Working capital	93,700	112,800	19,100
Working capital excluding inventory	23,000	10,700(d)	33,700(d)

The United States Rubber figures for 1919–1920 present the complete reverse of Manhattan Shirt's exhibit for 1930–1932. In the Rubber example we have large earnings but a coincident deterioration of the financial position due to heavy expenditures on plant and a dangerous expansion of inventory. The stock buyer would have been led astray completely had he confined his attention solely to United States Rubber's reported earnings of nearly $20 per share in 1920; and, conversely, the securities markets were equally mistaken in considering only the losses reported during 1930–1932, without reference to the favorable changes occurring at the same time in the balance-sheet position of many companies.

It will be noted from our discussion here and in Chap. 32 that the matter of inventory profits or losses belongs almost equally in the field of income account and of balance-sheet analysis.

Long-Range Study of Earning Power and Resources. The third aspect of the comparison of successive balance sheets is of restricted interest because it comes into play only in an exhaustive study of a company's record and inherent characteristics. The purpose of this kind of analysis may best be conveyed by means of the following applications to the long-term exhibits of United States Steel Corporation and Corn Products Refining Company.

I. UNITED STATES STEEL CORPORATION: ANALYSIS OF OPERATING
RESULTS AND FINANCIAL CHANGES BY DECADES, 1903–1932
(ANALYSIS WAS MADE IN 1933)

The balance sheets are adjusted to exclude an intangible item ("water"), amounting to $508,000,000, originally added to the Fixed Property Account. This was subsequently written off between 1902 and 1929 by means of an annual sinking-fund charge (aggregating $182,000,000) and by special appropriations from surplus. The sinking-fund charges in question are also eliminated from the income account.

A. Operating Results (In millions)

Item	First decade 1903–1912	Second decade 1913–1922	Third decade 1923–1932	Total for 30 years
Finished goods produced	93.4 tons	123.3 tons	118.7 tons	335.4 tons
Gross sales (excluding inter-company items)	$4,583	$9,200	$9,185	$22,968
Net earnings*	979	1,674	1,096	3,749
Bond interest	303	301	184	788
Preferred dividends	257	252	252	761
Common dividends	140	356	609†	1,105†
Balance to surplus and "voluntary reserves"	279	765	51	1,095

* After depreciation, but eliminating parent company sinking-fund charges.
† Including $204,000,000 paid in stock.

B. Relation of Earnings to Average Capital (All dollar figures in millions)

Item	First decade	Second decade	Third decade	Total for 30 years
Capital at beginning	$ 987	$1,416	$2,072	$ 987
Capital at end	1,416	2,072	2,112	2,112
Average capital about	1,200	1,750	2,100	1,700
% earned on average capital, per year	8.1%	9.6%	5.2%	7.4%
% paid per year in interest and dividends on average capital	5.8%	5.2%	4.0%*	5.2%*
Average common stock equity (common stock, surplus, and reserves)	$237	$620	$1,389	$816
% earned on common stock equity	17.7%	18.3%	4.8%	9.0%
% paid on common stock equity	5.9%	5.7%	2.9%*	3.7%*
Depreciation per year	$24	$34	$46	$35
Average fixed property account	1,000	1,320	1,600	1,300
Ratio of depreciation to fixed property	2.4%	2.6%	2.9%	2.7%

* Excluding stock dividend.

C. Balance-Sheet Changes (All figures in millions)

Item	Dec. 31, 1902	Dec. 31, 1912	Changes in first decade	Dec. 31, 1922	Changes in second decade	Dec. 31, 1932	Changes in third decade	Changes in 30 years
Assets:								
Fixed (less deprec.) and misc.*	$820	$1,160	+$340	$1,466	+$306	$1,741	+$275	+ $921
Net current assets	167	256	+ 89	606	+ 350	371	− 235	+ 204
Total	$987	$1,416	+$429	$2,072	+$656	$2,112	+$40	+$1,125
Liabilities:								
Bonds	$380	$680	+$300	$571	−$109	$116	−$455	− $264
Preferred stock	510	360	− 150	360		360		− 150
Preferred dividends accrued						5	+ 5	+ 5
Common stock	508	508		508		952†	+ 444	+ 444
Surplus and "voluntary" reserves*	411(d)	132(d)	+ 279	633	+ 765	679	+ 46	+ 1,090
Total	$987	$1,416	+$429	$2,072	+$656	$2,112	+ $40	+$1,125

* Eliminating initial mark-up of $508,000,000, later written off.
† Including premiums of $81,000,000 and stock dividend of $204,000,000.

610

The Significance of the Foregoing Figures. The three decades had, superficially at least, a somewhat equal distribution of good years and bad. In the first decade 1904 and 1908 were depression years, while 1911 and 1912 were subnormal. The second period had three bad years, *viz.*, 1914, 1921 and 1922—the last due to high costs rather than to small volume. The third decade was made up of eight years of prosperity followed by two of unprecedented depression.

The figures show that the war period, which occurred in the middle decade, was a windfall for United States Steel and added more than 300 millions to profits, as compared with the rate established in the first ten years. On the other hand, the last ten years were marked by a drastic falling off in the rate of earnings on the invested capital. The difference between the 5.2% actually earned and the 8% that might be regarded as a satisfactory annual average amounted to close to 600 million dollars for the ten-year period.

Viewing the picture from another angle, we note that in the thirty years the actual investment in United States Steel Corporation was more than doubled and its productive capacity was increased threefold. Yet the average annual production was only 27% higher, and the average annual earnings before interest charges were only 12% higher, in 1923–1932 than in 1903–1912. This analysis would serve to raise the question: (1) if, since the end of the war, steel production has been transformed from a reasonably prosperous into a relatively unprofitable industry and (2) if this transformation is due in good part to excessive reinvestment of earnings in additional plant, thus creating a condition of overcapacity with resultant reduction in the margin of profit.

Postscript. The soundness of the foregoing analysis, made in 1933, may be judged by developments since then. It should be pointed out that both the plant account figures and the annual earnings should be adjusted downward in the light of the later disclosures, *viz.*: (1) segregation from plant account in 1937 of $269,000,000 (and write-off of this amount in 1938), representing intangible assets at organization in addition to the $508,000,000 written off to 1929; (2) a charge to surplus of $270,000,000 in 1935 for additional amortization of fixed assets, presumably applicable to the entire preceding period. These later revisions, however, do not affect in any essential degree the conclusions drawn above.

The showing of United States Steel in the years since 1932 would appear to bear out the pessimistic implications of the 1933 study. During the six years 1934–1939, which is most instances supply a fair test period for judging normal earning power, "Steel" common earned an average of but 14¢ per share. New developments in products, processes or other factors—including war profits—may change the picture for the better, but this has become a matter for speculative anticipation of future improvement rather than a reasonable expectation based on past performance.

II. Similar Analysis of Corn Products Refining Company
February 28, 1906 to Dec. 31, 1935

A. Average Annual Income Account
(000 omitted from dollar figures)

	1906–1915	1916–1925	1926–1935
Earned before depreciation	$3,798	$12,770	$14,220
Depreciation	811	2,538	2,557
Balance for interest and dividends	2,987	10,232	11,663
Bond interest	516	264	88
Preferred dividends (paid or accrued)	2,042	1,879	1,738
Balance for common	429	8,089	9,837
Common dividends		2,751	8,421
Balance to surplus	429	5,338	1,416
Balance to surplus for period	4,290	53,384	14,159
Adjustment of common stock, surplus and reserves	cr. 1,282	cr. 6,026	dr. 5,986
Increase in common stock, surplus and reserves	5,572	59,410	7,173

B. Balance Sheets

	Feb. 28, 1906	Dec. 31, 1915	Dec. 31, 1925	Dec. 31, 1935
Plant (less depreciation) and miscellaneous assets	$49,000	$51,840	$ 47,865	$ 34,532
Investment in affiliates	2,000	4,706	16,203	33,141
Net current assets	1,000	11,091	42,528	43,192
Total	$52,000	$67,637	$106,596	$110,865
Bonds	9,571	12,763	2,474	
Preferred stock	28,293	29,873	25,004	24,574
Common stock, surplus and miscellaneous reserves	14,136	19,708	79,118	86,291
Preferred dividend accrued		5,293		
Total	$52,000	$67,637	$106,596	$110,865

C. Percentage Earned[1] and Paid on Total Capitalization
and on Common-stock Equity

Item	1906–1915	1916–1925	1926–1935	29⁵/₆ years
Average capitalization	$59,818	$87,116	$108,730	$81,432
Earned thereon	5.0%	11.8%	10.7%	10.2%
Paid thereon	4.2%	5.6%	9.4%	7.3%
Average common equity	$16,922	$49,413	$82,704	$50,213
Earned thereon	2.5%	16.4%	11.9%	12.2%
Paid thereon	nil	5.6%	10.2%	7.8%

[1] Adjustments to Surplus and Reserves are excluded from earnings.

Notes on Foregoing Computation

1. The plant account and common-stock equity are corrected throughout to reflect a write-down of $36,000,000 made in 1922 and 1923.

2. Bonds outstanding are increased in 1906 and 1912 to reflect liability for issues of subsidiaries. Plant, etc., is increased in the same amounts.

3. Estimates considered to be sufficiently accurate are used in the initial balance sheet.

4. Deductions for bond interest are partly estimated for the first two periods.

5. The adjustments of Common Stock, Surplus, and Reserves represent chiefly changes in Miscellaneous Reserves and shrinkage of marketable securities.

Comment on the Corn Products Refining Company Exhibit. The early period was one of subnormal earnings, which would have been still poorer if more nearly adequate depreciation charges had been made. As in the case of United States Steel, the war period brought enormous earnings to Corn Products. The decade 1916–1925 was marked as a whole by a great increase in working capital and a substantial reduction in funded debt and preferred stock. Depreciation charges exceeded expenditures on new plant.

In the 1926–1935 period we note a striking divergence from the exhibit of United States Steel for 1923–1932. Despite inclusion of the depression years Corn Products was almost able to increase its earning power proportionately with its enlarged capital investment. Its annual profits (both before and after depreciation) were about four times as large in this decade as in the period ending in 1915. (If we use the same years for comparison, we shall find that United States Steel actually earned less in 1926–1935 than in 1906–1915.) The balance-sheet changes were marked by a further substantial shrinkage in the property account (due to the liberal depreciation charged) but by a larger increase in the investment in affiliated companies—indicating a broad expansion of the company's activities.

It is clear that the record of Corn Products Refining Company does not suggest the same questions or doubts as arise from an examination of the United States Steel Corporation's exhibit.

PART VII

Additional Aspects of Security Analysis. Discrepancies Between Price and Value

The Market Is Still Not Efficient

by Nancy Zimmerman

D iving again into this classic work by Benjamin Graham and David Dodd brings me back in time, to my adolescent encounter with Graham and Dodd's other major work, *The Intelligent Investor*. That book was my first exposure to the idea that investing begins with fundamental analysis. Somewhat later, I picked up *Security Analysis* and started to realize that investing might be something one could do professionally. Seth Klarman's invitation to join this 88-year-old book club prompts fond memories of those early impressions of Graham and Dodd.

Rereading the clear prose and fine examples of Part VII of *Security Analysis* reminds me of those moments when I first understood that the hard work of analysis, coupled with a patient and disciplined approach, could lead to an intellectually challenging and rewarding career. It also reminds me of the scores of investments I have made where Graham and Dodd's analytical precepts have continued to ring true. I share Benjamin Graham's view that good investing starts with a meticulous analysis of the security that you are proposing to go long or short. Sound investment analysis is forward-looking and involves both hard work and humility. Many decades after the publication of *Security Analysis*, the market still offers opportunities where the potential excess returns warrant the risks to which an investor's capital is exposed—what this book poetically terms a "margin of safety."

In the 1980s, during the summer after my sophomore year of college, I was offered a wonderful opportunity to learn more about markets and investing at O'Connor and Associates, an options trading firm in Chicago. An astute partner believed that mathematically inclined and curious students would make good colleagues and good market makers. The firm emphasized avoiding what Graham and Dodd would call *market analysis* and had a strong focus on a bottom-up effort to use mathematical techniques to price derivatives on single stocks, indices, bonds, and foreign exchange. O'Connor principals readily acknowledged that they did not know "where the market was going." Rather, they felt that O'Connor could earn an attractive return on capital by making prices on the options of many stocks and indexes, while laying off risk by trading options against each other, "locking in" pricing disparities. The market makers were encouraged to avoid any directional bets on individual stocks. The group responsible for assessing individual stock risk was a cerebral bunch who believed in reading as much as in mathematical modeling. At the top of their list, next to *Security Analysis*, was a biography of Jesse Livermore, a cautionary tale about speculation and leverage.

When I was introduced to options markets at O'Connor that summer, a nascent though increasingly complex world of indexes, index options, currency options, and U.S. Treasury bond options was beginning to take off. I developed an abiding conviction that there was no way to generate excess returns simply by doing market analysis, that is, placing trades based on particular market patterns. It was at that time I read what Graham and Dodd had written so many years earlier about technical analysis; rereading these words again recently reinforced the folly of using historical prices to predict future prices. Nevertheless, these backward-looking approaches continue to generate substantial interest in the financial media as well as on Wall Street as each new crop of market participants arrives eager to beat the market.

Graham and Dodd emphasized that outperformance is best
pursued by looking on a bottom-up basis for individual securities that
have a margin of safety relative to the risks entailed by the investment.
One of the key observations of my career has been that this margin is
most recognizable when comparing substantially similar securities.
The enduring wisdom of Part VII of *Security Analysis* is clear: markets
are not efficient, and the assiduous analyst can find opportunities,
particularly in situations where very similar securities trade at different
prices for the same risk, violating the financial theorem—known as
"the law of one price"—that identical securities (or baskets of
securities) should have the same price across different markets.

When I plowed through *Security Analysis* after my second summer at
O'Connor, I was seized by the granular examples from an era gone by. I
was worried that I had simply been born just a little too late: while
Graham and Dodd had been able to make profitable discoveries by
looking bottom-up at companies, surely such opportunities did not
persist in the modern world of finance. I was lucky to be wrong about
this. In the next few decades, moving to Wall Street to understand the
buyside, and then founding and running a firm focused on fixed-income
relative value opportunities, I would find that Graham and Dodd's
taxonomy of the factors that create discrepancies between price and value
is one of the world's greatest shopping lists. It offers many places to look
for opportunities even in large, liquid, seemingly overfished markets.
However, it often requires substantially more math and modeling work
to understand when and how the same kinds of inefficiencies present
themselves in our current, supposedly more sophisticated world.

In Chap. 50, "Discrepancies Between Price and Value" and Chap.
51, "Discrepancies Between Price and Value (*Continued*)," Graham and
Dodd review opportunities to profit from various aberrations in the
securities market. Markets in the 1930s were certainly rife with price
discrepancies, both those that were accessible to a professional investor

with the ability to transact globally, and those more obviously wrong but completely unhedgeable. Graham and Dodd describe some historical reasons for these discrepancies, including both asynchronous reporting of financial results and opaque dissemination of contractual details. Many decades have passed since their writing, yet amazingly, each category of price disparities remains alive and well today. Along the way we have learned how to think about these discrepancies more systematically. One of the most fascinating developments in the last several decades is the integration of Graham and Dodd's ideas with modern finance. The themes that they sounded and the illustrations they provided have clear counterparts in today's financial economics and well as in the practice of financial management and arbitrage.

Graham and Dodd bring several broad ideas to life. First, the "law of one price" is often violated in financial markets. Identical, or very similar, assets trade at different prices in different markets, whether defined by currencies, exchanges, instruments used, or other domains of differentiation.

Second, the sources of these deviations vary. Sometimes they occur because one market is dominated by a set of investors who are less involved in other markets. In fixed-income markets, the reasons for the deviations from the law of one price often have to do with professional investment manager mandates and tendencies to track a benchmark. Some securities are included in indexes, for example, and as such become overpriced relative to very similar securities that are not part of those indexes. Some standardized securities are preferred by institutional investors, relative to other more complicated instruments. Today, portfolios of securities can increasingly be replicated (with better prospective returns) by using portfolios of other securities and instruments that trade at a lower valuation for what are effectively the same expected returns.

Third, in thinking about which securities are identical (or very similar) to each other, live data feeds, enormous computational power, and more sophisticated modeling of contingent claims have taken us much further than Graham and Dodd could have imagined. In their writing, they focused on the most likely scenarios, but now we have ways to imagine and model many scenarios beyond just the most likely ones. The forward march of technology has allowed us to build sophisticated models that were not available in the slide rule era. It has allowed us to aggregate these securities in portfolios and look at the cash flows alone or in combinations. It also allows us to stress-test individual securities, capital structures, and even entire portfolios of securities. We can compare the distribution of outcomes implied by one security to those of another security. Moreover, we can price options using any distribution we can define.

Fourth, we know that while prices of identical or nearly identical securities often eventually converge, they may take a long time to do so, and in fact they may further diverge before they correct. Arbitrage, even of identical securities, is not riskless in the short run. It is wise to diversify one's holdings. The problem deepens when financial crises and other dislocations create unexpected and artificial correlations in the movements of unrelated securities. Leverage, including through the use of derivatives, can both magnify the problem or allow the manager to implement useful hedging arrangements. Even with perfect arbitrage, one can only make money on average, not always.

Finally, at a somewhat broader level, Graham and Dodd's strategies point to the value of arbitrage strategies of the sort they envisioned for a long-term investor. That's because, at least in the medium term, the returns on these strategies are uncorrelated with those on other parts of the portfolio. As Graham and Dodd taught us, you cannot predict the movements of the market. For a sophisticated investor, this points to the benefit of having at least some part of the portfolio untethered from these movements.

SOME EXAMPLES FROM MODERN TIMES

Relative price dislocations between specific securities are the stuff that fixed-income relative value strategies are made of. We have seen our share of them in recent decades. The art, as Graham and Dodd preach, is to keep looking for opportunities while not being hesitant to pass and await something more attractive. As their prominent disciple Warren Buffett said, "The trick in investing is just to sit there and watch pitch after pitch go by and wait for the one right in your sweet spot. And if people are yelling, 'Swing, you bum!,' ignore them."[1]

An example of what Graham and Dodd discuss in the section titled "Comparison of Definitely Related Issues" occurred in late 2018, when investment grade bonds denominated in euros traded systematically tight relative to dollar-denominated investment grade bonds. This mispricing across currencies was largely caused by technical aspects of supply and demand, and secondarily by differences in the currency. The European Central Bank (ECB) exacerbated the cross-currency differential particularly on securities from European issuers that were part of a major ECB corporate sector buyback program intended to provide monetary policy accommodation and generally boost the euro-area economy. As Graham and Dodd discuss in "Discrepancies Due to Special Supply and Demand Factors" (Chap. 51), a large buyer can create significant dislocations between two *pari passu* bonds. Corporate bond market investors willing to look across both EUR and USD markets could be rewarded by taking advantage of significant discrepancies in the trading levels of bonds issued by the same company. For example, General Electric, which has had a global

---

[1] Peter Kunhardt, *Becoming Warren Buffett*, Kunhardt Films, Home Box Office (HBO), 2017.

footprint through wide-ranging businesses for many years, is ultimately a U.S. issuer. Though bonds issued by GE (even those denominated in euros) were not included in the ECB buyback program, they were still swept tighter along with other euro-denominated bonds. GE senior notes denominated in USD traded at a spread 100 basis points wider than GE senior notes denominated in EUR (after accounting for the underlying currency and interest rate risk). Furthermore, the USD-denominated issue was priced about 6 points lower. An alert investor would readily conclude that these GE bonds were "definitely related," presenting the opportunity to invest in the undervalued USD bond and sell the EUR bond. Indeed, after only two months, the spread differential converged to 50 basis points and the price to within 1 point.

The law of one price is continually disrupted. In the summer of 2022, for example, a 10-year vanilla USD interest rate swap with identical terms traded at different rates in Chicago and in London. One of the trades from my earliest days in the markets that remains a source of opportunity is U.S. Treasury cash versus futures arbitrage. This type of basis trading involves a basket of U.S. Treasury bonds on a certain part of the curve hedged with a futures contract into which those bonds are deliverable. At any given time, one bond in the basket will be the cheapest to deliver into the futures contract, but relative price changes within the basket driven by changes in the shape of the yield curve or other idiosyncratic factors might make another bond the cheapest. When the futures contract is rich to the deliverable bond, a position that is short the futures contract and long the deliverable bond is poised to capture not only the pricing discrepancy, but also potential further gains should a different bond become cheapest to deliver. This trade also offers the optionality that it could be unwound before the delivery date if the relationship normalizes. It is particularly nice to put on a profitable trade with a definite expiration date, offering a clear catalyst on one side of the trade with the optionality of a more favorable outcome a distinct possibility.

The business of the arbitrageur, or assiduous analyst in Graham and Dodd parlance, is to find which opportunities are genuine and which are illusory traps. Capital structures that are designed to last forever, like closed-end mutual funds, often divorce the economic interests of investors from control of decision-making; as a result, these can often be a trap, seemingly mispriced but with a discount that may never close. Graham and Dodd provide an excellent introduction to the costs and risks of investing through various investment structures. Chapter 47 discusses "investment trust financing" and lays out how cash fees, preferred stock, conversion privileges, and warrants create differing economics and incentives for deal promoters versus the investing public. As Graham and Dodd recount by carefully calculating the "cost of management" in these vehicles (Chap. 47), such permanent fee-paying arrangements that burden capital might look a lot like arbitrages when they trade at discounts to the value of the assets trapped in the structure, but they may turn out to be value traps. An example of this is the Grayscale Bitcoin Trust (GBTC), a passive trust that has allowed investors, for a 2% annual fee, to gain exposure to Bitcoin in the form of a security, avoiding the difficulties associated with buying and storing Bitcoin directly. GBTC remained a modest product for several years after launching in 2013, but as the price of Bitcoin and other cryptocurrencies soared in 2020, GBTC harnessed the greed of the crypto universe using a marketing pitch that the trust would durably trade at a premium to Bitcoin for economic reasons. Crypto investors were encouraged to buy Bitcoin, deposit it in the trust, and receive locked-up shares of GBTC that would become marketable in six months to "harvest the premium." Once deposited, the assets became subject to a 2% annual fee in perpetuity. While this was appealing to some speculators in the heady days of Bitcoin, the value proposition was obviously not enduring, and as soon as the glow came off, the trust came under urgent selling pressure. By the summer of 2022, GBTC traded at a 30% discount to its net asset value. If one wished to try and capture this discount, there were very straightforward ways to get short Bitcoin with a creditworthy counterpart, most notably the future traded at the Chicago Mercantile Exchange. Would this be an opportunity? There might not be any near-term catalyst that forces a convergence, although optimists might focus on Grayscale's persistent campaign to persuade the U.S. Securities and Exchange Commission (SEC) to permit conversion of the trust into an ETF. In the absence of a catalyst such as maturity or the ability to access the underlying Bitcoin and realize its value, this looks less like an opportunity for profit and more like a curiosity. Graham and Dodd would also point to the risk of "possession of control by those who have no real capital investment." (Chap. 48)

Thinking about which securities are nearly identical (or very similar) with the benefit of modern finance and its probability state analysis has turbocharged the ideas behind Graham and Dodd. In their writing, Graham and Dodd tend to focus on the most likely scenarios and then build in a margin of safety. Now we have ways to imagine and model many scenarios, not just the most likely ones. We have a much more sophisticated way of thinking about risks than was possible when Graham and Dodd presented their ideas, because we have both the models and the requisite computational power. We can even compare the various "margins of safety" or excess return per unit of risk.

During the early days of my firm's efforts to extract market neutral returns from fixed-income securities and derivative markets, there was a great deal of turmoil in the U.S. interest rate market. Short rates coming out of the very weak economic period of 1993 were less than 3%, and five-year yields were around 5.2%. As the economy improved, more and more rate hikes were anticipated by the interest rate curve. In December

1994, the changes in the shape of the yield curve caused a serious disruption among overleveraged market participants, including Mexico, Orange County, and many small banks. The de-risking of balance sheets and the unwinding of portfolios put pressure on rates. Interestingly, a steady stream of long volatility positions were also being unwound at the same time. This selling pressure left interest rate options trading at levels that implied that volatility would be well below where it had been historically. These depressed levels for options provided a ready hedge for any short volatility securities (*e.g.*, mortgages) or a way to create an asymmetric profile of returns by taking a position against the extreme scenario priced into the market that the Fed would hike 200 basis points between Christmas and Easter, in the middle of a meltdown. Modern analytical tools enabled both identification of the pricing discrepancy and the ability to calculate with greater certainty the possibility that the aberrational pricing would normalize.

Graham and Dodd do a fine job of categorizing and analyzing the price dislocations between two similar assets in "Comparison of Definitely Related Issues" (Chap. 51). An interesting and useful contemporary example of an arbitrage using related instruments involves trading corporate bonds versus credit default swaps (CDS) referencing the bond issuer, a common relative value strategy known as CDS basis trading.

To pursue such a strategy, an investor can buy a cash bond together with insurance on that cash bond through a CDS contract with a creditworthy counterparty. Depending on the specific nature of the mispricing in question, one might expect their "margin of safety" or alpha to come from one or more types of cheapness: the spread over riskless rates on the bond exceeding the spread on the CDS; the bond trading at a lower price than the implied price of the CDS, which would be realized in an event of default; or perhaps from the cheapest to deliver option arising from the provision that any *pari passu* bond can be delivered in the event of default.

Because of the tightness of the arbitrage and the inherent optionality, in the years from the dawn of the CDS market in the 1990s until the early market unraveling of 2007—which grew into the Great Financial Crisis—we rarely observed basis packages of matched maturity bonds and CDS trading more than a few basis points cheap. The term of art for this cheapness is "negative basis." But in the years leading up to and following the Great Financial Crisis of 2008, we saw dramatic examples of how basis trades were impacted by the pressures on and behavior of many market participants. First, the negative basis exploded for a variety of reasons, attributable to holders of both the long cash instruments and the holders of negative basis packages. Then when these participants became distressed, selling was conducted without regard for the economic status of the underlying company or asset, and there was insufficient arbitrage capital willing to take the other side of the trade to keep it tethered to value.

The golden age of structured finance before the financial crisis created a seemingly endless supply of synthetic collateralized debt obligations (CDOs). The magic of structuring, or less charitably the gaming of rating agencies, allowed CDO managers to sell highly rated tranches of CDS portfolios at spreads well below their component parts, generating selling pressure on CDS. This drove CDS spreads to extremely low levels, both on an absolute basis and compared to cash bonds. This was also an era of cheap financing. Some banks in Europe, as well as proprietary trading desks of U.S. banks, found an irresistible combination: negative basis opportunities with positive carry (higher bond coupon received than CDS running spread paid) and seemingly infinite funding at LIBOR flat (i.e., without any spread over LIBOR) or better. Banks and proprietary trading desks put on negative basis trades in vast sizes, largely indiscriminately across corporate names, anytime their yield bogey was met. These trades also boosted the earnings of more than a few financial institutions because their

accountants let them recognize the present value of this annuity over
the lifetime of the package. They had found a money machine!

But starting in late 2007, cheap financing disappeared, and banks, let
alone proprietary trading desks, could not rely on LIBOR flat financing
or infinite balance sheets. This funding pressure alone would likely have
caused cash bonds to underperform CDS, but the forced unwinding of
large positions by highly levered institutions caused even more pressure
and pushed the relationship even more negative. A number of
institutions, unwilling to take the financing risk or the mark-to-market
volatility on what had been a low-value, positive carry trade, simply
closed out of their positions. Particularly painful were the basis packages
where the underlying cash security lost its investment grade rating and
holders had to "de-book" the profits at a particularly poor moment.

The Great Financial Crisis dramatically underscored the risk that
banks and other financial participants take on when they pile
substantial leverage on top of a small mispricing, one good idea
coupled with an incredibly bad one. It also highlighted the importance
of establishing sustainable financing arrangements, and not being
overly reliant on any financing that is not clearly contractually agreed
at the outset of the trade. While the extreme negative basis spreads of
2008 and their immediate aftermath have not been revisited, the
"zero-ish bound" has been relegated to the trash can, and negative
basis packages with hundreds of basis points or even double-digit
points continue to be seen in the wild.

THE FOLLY OF TECHNICAL ANALYSIS

I was particularly pleased to reread Graham and Dodd's thoughts in
Chapter 52 about technical analysis. Their wisdom about the futility of
using past price movements to predict future market movements is a
searing rebuttal to all backward-looking techniques that rely on the
assumption that the future is easily gleaned by scrutinizing past price

data. This extends from technical analysis to excessive reliance on historical regressions. Anyone considering handing their financial future over to any strategy based on "the general idea that a study confined to past price movements can be availed of profitably to foretell the movements of the future" (Chap. 52) should examine whether they can rebut Graham and Dodd's basic objections. The strategies they call into question include VAR-based risk modeling, which implicitly promises that the market will move a predictable amount and exhibit stable correlations in the future. Consider Graham and Dodd's third conclusion on this topic in Chap. 52:

> The theoretical basis of chart reading runs somewhat as follows:
>
> a. The action of the market (or of a particular stock) reflects the activities and the attitude of those interested in it.
>
> b. Therefore, by studying the record of market action, we can tell what is going to happen next in the market.

Graham and Dodd caution us that "[t]he premise may well be true, but the conclusion does not necessarily follow." Before going blindly into strategies that rely on historical patterns, one must have clear answers to the question of how might "the technical position of any stock or position tell me anything more than about the behavior of the investors in that instrument?" How is the behavior of the investors relevant to the instant situation? It is essential to tether this technical information to the fundamental properties of the issuer's business and the contractual relationships of the securities in question.

WHERE DO DISCREPANCIES COME FROM

Identifying and exploiting discrepancies between price and value and striving to isolate whether there is a "margin of safety" that can deliver alpha is the central activity of market-neutral investing. Which disparities are worth pursuing, and which are best left to be merely observed and learned from? It is helpful to follow Graham and Dodd's path and trace the forces causing the discrepancy between price and value.

Perhaps the most significant of these factors over time has proven to be indexation. According to Bloomberg Intelligence,[2] the market share of passive equity strategies overtook that of active strategies around August 2018 and was nearly 55% by 2021, driven largely by the growth of funds tracking the S&P 500 and other broad U.S. indexes. This shift has been accelerated by a variety of forces, including the advent of robo-advisers, the rising adoption of model portfolios by advisers, and the growth in advisers' use of passive ETFs and funds. Active managers still dominate in fixed income, although passive's share rose to 34% from 31% in the third quarter of 2021 following the worst bond returns in decades amid rising rates and capital outflows. Given the significant amount of "closet indexing" in fixed-income markets, those percentages likely understate the true impact of index inclusion or exclusion on the universe of likely buyers (or forced sellers) for a given bond. When demand for a security is created by its mere inclusion on a list, without regard to its fundamental value, the price will change in ways that are not related to fundamental developments.

This brings us to the rating agencies—the organizations to whom passive market participants have outsourced the work that Graham and Dodd implore the assiduous analyst to undertake. The agencies have proven time and again to be backward looking, belatedly downgrading in response to past performance. Their ratings also demonstrate positive serial correlation, so we know they do not move their ratings enough each time to get to a place where the new rating reflects all available information at that moment. This reality makes it clear that spreads should and do move much faster than ratings and invite

---

[2] Bloomberg Intelligence, "Passive Likely Overtakes Active by 2026, Earlier if Bear Market" March 11, 2021, https://www.bloomberg.com/professional/blog/passive-likely-overtakes-active-by-2026-earlier-if-bear-market/.

participants to game downgrades in order to "pick up spreads," creating additional inefficiencies. Many fixed-income indexes rely on ratings as an inclusion factor, and several types of institutional investors are required, by mandate or regulation, to restrict themselves to bonds over a certain ratings threshold. Putting all these factors together, there is forced selling on downgrades by passive vehicles on the date of an index exclusion. This puts pressure on the price of the assets even when the information driving the downgrade has been fully processed. These well-documented inefficiencies lead to another set of dislocations where institutional investors try to predict behavior that is noneconomic, and the participant is worse off on a net present value basis.

Another frequent culprit is the presence of noneconomic or constrained economic agents in a market. Often this takes the form of some sort of official sector intervention program with strictly defined criteria for inclusion. The ECB has employed many such programs, including the previously mentioned corporate sector buyback program and others targeting an array of asset types. The assets that are included frequently become displaced relative to otherwise similar assets outside the scope of such a program. Other times it is a matter of habitat preference for certain investors. There are investors who either must for regulatory reasons, or merely prefer to for ease of operations, own bonds that are denominated in their own currency, traded in their home market, or issued in their own legal jurisdiction. Such investors will care little if bonds of the same issuer in other currencies trade significantly rich or cheap, relative to the bonds they own. In times of market stress, many of these factors act in concert to amplify these dislocations.

In the modern financial world, all of these kinds of forces are being exerted across many time zones and regulatory regimes, and there are obvious short circuits that can sever the market prices of instruments reflecting the same underlying risk. One might be able to observe the risk of a given company through its debt, its CDS, the cash and derivative indexes in which it is included, and tranches on those indexes. One might see different levels of implied risk for a country in its native interest rates, currency forwards, local debt, and external debt.

An important part of modern security analysis is trying to figure out which of these factors are transitory and which are permanent. Are there catalysts that will cause the price to converge? How long will it take? How much capital will it use up? How does this dislocation compare to others happening at the same time? How is it correlated with those dislocations?

FINAL THOUGHTS

Graham and Dodd's enduring insight is that all good investment practice is based on doing detailed bottoms-up work. Investing requires thoroughly understanding the contractual relationships that govern a security and the real-life factors that are involved in enforcing contractual obligations should the need arise. All investment finance turns on accurately modeling the cash flows, determining an appropriate discount rate, and assessing the likelihood that you get them! The stark reality that markets are not efficient—and highly unlikely ever to be so—instructs us to focus our time and allocate our capital to those situations where we see the greatest dislocation between price and value. At the same time, we need to keep a clear eye on the unexpected, the real-life vicissitudes that turn potential opportunities into traps. We need catalysts to force prices to converge to value; while we are waiting for those catalysts, the capabilities and character of management are very important. Whether you are thinking of investing in uncorrelated arbitrages or buying the cheapest security of a quality company, Graham and Dodd's work exhorts us to read the documents, understand the structures, model the cash flows with precision, and in a modern world, use our computational power to think probabilistically.

See Chapter 46, "Stock-Option Warrants" online at www.mhprofessional.com/SecurityAnalysis7.

CHAPTER 47

Cost of Financing
and Management

LET US CONSIDER in more detail the organization and financing of Petroleum Corporation of America, mentioned in the last chapter. This was a large investment company formed for the purpose of specializing in securities of enterprises in the oil industry. The public was offered 3,250,000 shares of capital stock at $34 per share. The company received therefore a net amount of $31 per share, or $100,750,000 in cash. It issued to unnamed recipients—presumably promoters, investment bankers and the management—warrants, good for five years, to buy 1,625,000 shares of additional stock, also at $34 per share.

This example is representative of the investment trust financing of the period. Moreover, as we shall see, the technique on this score that developed in boom years was carried over through the ensuing depression, and it threatened to be accepted as the standard practice for stock financing of all kinds of enterprises. But there is good reason to ask the real meaning of a set-up of this kind, first, with respect to what the buyer of the stock gets for his money, and second, with respect to the position occupied by the investment banking houses floating these issues.

Cost of Management; Three Items. A new investment trust—such as Petroleum Corporation in January 1929—starts with two assets: cash and management. Buyers of the stock at $34 per share were asked to pay for the management in three ways, *viz.:*

1. By the difference between what the stock cost them and the amount received by the corporation.

It is true that this difference of $3 per share was paid not to the management but to those underwriting and selling the shares. But from the standpoint of the stock buyer the only justification for paying more for the stock than the initial cash behind it would lie in his belief that the management was worth the difference.

2. By the value of the option warrants issued to the organizing interests.

These warrants in essence entitled the owners to receive one-third of whatever appreciation might take place in the value of the enterprise over the next five years. (From the 1929 view-point a five-year period gave ample opportunity to participate in the future success of the business.) This block of warrants had a real value, and that value in turn was taken out of the initial value of the common stock.

The price relationships usually obtaining between stock and warrants suggest that the 1,625,000 warrants would take about one-sixth of the value away from the common stock. On this basis, one-sixth of the $100,750,000 cash originally received by the company would be applicable to the warrants, and five-sixths to the stock.

3. By the salaries that the officers were to receive, and also by the extra taxes incurred through the use of the corporate form.

Summarizing the foregoing analysis, we find that buyers of Petroleum Corporation shares were paying the following price for the managerial skill to be applied to the investment of their money:

1. Cost of financing ($3 per share)	$9,750,000
2. Value of warrants (1/6th of remaining cash)	about 16,790,000
3. Future deductions for managerial salaries, etc	?
Total	$26,540,000+

The three items together may be said to absorb between 25 and 30% of the amount contributed by the public to the enterprise. By this we mean not merely a deduction of that percentage of future profits but an actual sacrifice of invested *principal* in return for management.

What Was Received for the Price Paid? Carrying the study a step farther, let us ask what kind of managerial skill this enterprise was to enjoy? The board of directors consisted of many men prominent in finance, and their judgment on investments was considered well worth having. But two serious limitations on the value of this judgment must here be noted. The first is that the directors were not obligated to devote themselves exclusively or even preponderantly to this enterprise. They were permitted, and seemingly intended, to multiply these activities indefinitely. Common sense would suggest that the value of their expert judgment to

Petroleum Corporation would be greatly diminished by the fact that so many other claims were being made upon it at the same time. A more obvious limitation appears from the Corporation's projected activities. It proposed to devote itself to investments in a single field—petroleum. The scope for judgment and analysis was thereby greatly circumscribed. As it turned out, the funds were largely concentrated, first in two related companies—Prairie Pipe Line Company and Prairie Oil and Gas Company—and then in a single successor enterprise (Consolidated Oil Corporation). Thus Petroleum Corporation took on the complexion of a holding company, in which the exercise of managerial skill appears to be reduced to a minimum once the original acquisitions are made.[1]

We are forced to conclude that financial schemes of the kind illustrated by Petroleum Corporation of America are unsatisfactory from the standpoint of the stock buyer. This is true not only because the total cost to him for management is excessive in relation to the value of the services rendered but also because the cost is not clearly disclosed, being concealed in good measure by the use of the warrant artifice.[2] (The foregoing reasoning does not rest in any way upon the fact that Petroleum Corporation's investments proved unprofitable.[3])

Position of Investment Banking Firms in This Connection. The second line of inquiry suggested by this example is also of major importance. What is the position occupied by the investment banking firms floating an issue such as Petroleum Corporation of America, and how does this

---

[1] The same logical objection to the payment of a large "managerial bonus," in the form of option warrants to those organizing a holding company, may be urged against the set-up of Alleghany Corporation and United Corporation.

[2] In a series of "Notes" on the history of United Corporation financing by Sanford L. Schamus, in *Columbia Law Review* of May, June and November, 1937, the proposal was advanced that prospectuses issued under S.E.C. legislation should carry a tabulation showing the effect of the exercise of warrants on earnings and asset values. See November 1937 issue, pp. 1173–1174.

[3] A review of the operations of Petroleum Corporation, published by the S.E.C. in May 1939, criticizes severely a number of deals in which the management was interested on the other side. After 1933 a unique turn was given to the status of Petroleum Corporation through acquisition of a large interest (39.8%) therein by Consolidated Oil. The two companies thus became the largest stockholders of each other, an extraordinary and highly objectionable situation. See Part 3, Chap. II (2d sec.), of the *Report of the S.E.C. on Investment Trusts and Investment Companies*.

compare with the practice of former years? Prior to the late 1920s, the sale of stock to the public by reputable houses of issue was governed by the following three important principles:

1. The enterprise must be well established and offer a record and financial exhibit adequate to justify the purchase of the shares at the issue price.

2. The investment banker must act primarily as the representative of the buyers of the stock, and he must deal at arm's-length with the company's management. His duty includes protecting his clients against the payment of excessive compensation to the officers or any other policies inimical to the stockholders' interest.

3. The compensation taken by the investment banker must be reasonable. It represents a fee paid by the corporation for the service of raising capital.

These rules of conduct afforded a clear line of demarcation between responsible and disreputable stock financing. It was an established Wall Street maxim that capital for a new enterprise must be raised from private sources.[4] These private interests would be in a position to make their own investigation, work out their own deal and keep in close touch with the enterprise, all of which safeguards (in addition to the chance to make a large profit) were considered necessary to justify a commitment in any new venture. Hence the public sale of securities in a *new enterprise* was confined almost exclusively to "blue sky" promoters and small houses of questionable standing. The great majority of such flotations were either downright swindles or closely equivalent thereto by reason of the unconscionable financing charges taken out of the price paid by the public.

Investment-trust financing, by its very nature, was compelled to contravene these three established criteria of reputable stock flotations. The investment trusts were *new* enterprises; their management and their bankers were generally *identical*; the compensation for financing and management had to be determined solely by the recipients, without accepted standards of reasonableness to control them. In the absence of such standards, and in the absence also of the invaluable arm's-length bar-

---

[4] An apparent exception might be made sometimes in a case such as Chile Copper Company where the demonstrated presence of huge bodies of ore was regarded as justifying public financing to bring the mine into production. The sale of stock of the Lincoln Motor Company in 1920 was one of the few real exceptions to the rule as here stated. In this instance an unusually high personal reputation was behind the enterprise, but it resulted in disastrous failure.

gaining between corporation and banker, it was scarcely to be hoped that the interests of the security buyer would be adequately protected. Allowance must be made besides for the generally distorted and egotistical views prevalent in the financial world during 1928 and 1929.

Developments Since 1929. For a time it appeared that the demoralizing influence of investment-trust financing was likely to spread to the entire field of common-stock flotations and that even the leading banking houses were prepared to sell shares of new or virtually new commercial enterprises, without past records and on the basis entirely of their expected future earnings. (There were definite signs of this tendency in the beer-and liquor-stock flotations of 1933.) Fortunately, a reversal of sentiment has since taken place, and we find that the relatively few common-stock issues sponsored by the first-line houses are now similar in character and arrangements to those of former days.[5]

However, there has been a fair amount of activity in the common-stock flotation field since 1933, carried on by houses of secondary size or standing. Most of these issues represent shares of new enterprises, which in turn tend to fall in whatever industrial group is easiest to exploit at the time. Thus in 1933 we had many gold-, liquor- and beer-stock flotations, and in 1938–1939 there was a deluge of airplane issues. The formation of new investment companies, on the other hand, appears to be a perennial industry. In surveying such common-stock flotations, the starting point must be the realization that the investment banker behind them is not acting primarily in behalf of his clients who buy the issue. For on the one side the new corporation is not an independent entity, which can negotiate at arm's-length with various bankers representing clients with money to invest, and on the other side, the banker is himself in part a promoter, in part a proprietor of the new business. In an important sense, he is raising funds from the public *for himself.*

New Role of Such Investment Bankers. More exactly stated, the investment banker who floats such issues is operating in a double guise. He makes a deal on his own behalf with the originators of the enterprise, and then he makes a separate deal with the public to raise from them the funds he has promised the business. He demands—and no doubt is enti-

---

[5] See, for example, the offerings of New Idea Company common in 1937, General Shoe Company common in 1938, Julius Garfinckel and Company in 1939.

tled to—a liberal reward for his pains. But the very size of his compensation introduces a significant change in his relationship to the public.
For it makes a very real difference whether a stock buyer can consider
the investment banker as essentially his agent and representative or must
view the issuing house as a promoter-proprietor-manager of a business,
endeavoring to raise funds to carry it on.

When investment banking becomes identified with the latter
approach, the interests of the general public are certain to suffer. The
Securities Act of 1933 aims to safeguard the security buyer by requiring
full disclosure of the pertinent facts and by extending the previously existing liability for concealment or misrepresentation. Although full disclosure is undoubtedly desirable, it may not be of much practical help except
to the skilled and shrewd investor or to the trained analyst. It is to be
feared that the typical stock buyer will neither read the long prospectus
carefully nor understand the implications of all it contains. Modern
financing methods are not far different from a magician's bag of tricks;
they can be executed in full view of the public without its being very much
the wiser. The use of stock options as part of the underwriter-promoter's
compensation is one of the newer and more deceptive tricks of the trade.

Two examples of new enterprise financing, in 1936 and 1939, will be
discussed in some detail, with the object of illustrating both the character
of these flotations and the technique of analysis required to appraise them.[6]

Example A: American Bantam Car Corporation, July 1936. This
offering consisted of 100,000 shares of 6% Cumulative Convertible
Preference stock, sold to the public at $10 per share, its par value. Each
share was convertible into 3 shares of common stock. The "underwriters"
received a gross commission of $2 per share, or 20% of the selling price;
however, this compensation was for selling effort only, without any guarantee to take or place the shares.

The new company had acquired the plant of the American Austin
Car Company, which had started out in 1929 with $3,692,000 in cash
capital and had ended in bankruptcy. The organizers of the Bantam

---

[6] In the 1934 edition we analyzed, at this point, the offering of stock in Mouquin, Inc.
(liquor importers) made in September 1933 at $6.75 per share. The facts showed that the
public was asked to place a valuation of $1,670,000 on an enterprise with physical assets of
$424,000 and no earnings record. The company passed out of existence in 1937, and the
public's investment was wiped out.

enterprise bought in the Austin assets, subject to various liabilities, for only $5,000. They then turned over their purchase, plus $500 in cash, to the new company for 300,000 shares of its common stock. In other words, the entire common issue cost the promoters $5,500 cash plus their time and effort.

The prospectus stated—what was an obvious fact—that the preference stock was "offered as a speculation." That speculation could work out successfully only if the conversion privilege proved valuable, since the mere 6% return on a preferred stock was scarcely an adequate reward for the risk involved. (The character of the risk was shown clearly enough in the enormous losses of the predecessor company.) But note that before the conversion privilege could be worth anything, the common stock would have to sell for more than $3$1/3$ per share—and *in that case the* $5,500 *investment of the organizers would be worth over* $1,000,000. In other words, before the public could make *any* profit, the organizers would have to multiply their stake 180 *times*.

Sequel. By June 30, 1939, the company had accumulated a deficit of $750,000; it was compelled to borrow money from the R.F.C., and the preferred-stock holder no longer had any equity in current assets. The price of the preference stock declined to 3, but at the same time the common was quoted at $3/4$ bid. This meant (if the quoted price could be trusted) that, although the public had lost 70% of its investment, the organizers' $5,500 contribution had still a nominal market value of $225,000.

Example B: Aeronautical Corporation of America, December 1939. This company offered to the public 60,000 shares of new common stock at $6.25 per share. The "underwriters," who made no firm commitment to take any shares, received on the sale of each share the following three kinds of compensation: (1) 90 cents in cash; (2) $1/20$ of a share of stock, ostensibly worth 31 cents, donated by the principal stockholders; (3) a warrant to buy $1/2$ share of stock at prices varying between $6.25 and $8.00 per share. If the common stock was fairly worth the $6.25 offering price, these warrants were undoubtedly worth at least $1 per share called for. This would mean an aggregate commission for selling effort of $2.34 per share, or more than one-third the amount paid over by the public.

The company had been in business since 1928 and had been manufacturing its light Aeronca planes since 1931. Its business had grown steadily from $124,000 sales in 1934 to about $850,000 sales in 1939.

However, the enterprise had been definitely unprofitable to the end of 1938, showing an aggregate deficit at that time of over $500,000 (including development expense written off). In $9^1/_2$ months to October 15, 1939, it had earned $50,000. Prior to this offering of new shares to the public there were outstanding 66,000 shares of stock, which had a net asset value of only $1.28 per share. In addition to the warrants for 30,000 shares to be given the underwriters, there were like warrants for 15,000 shares in the hands of the officers.

There seemed strong reason to believe that the company occupied a favorable position in a growing industry. But analysis would show that the participation of the public in any future increase in earnings was seriously diluted in three different ways: by the cash selling expense subtracted from the price to be paid for the new stock, by the small tangible assets contributed by the original owners for their stock interest and by the warrants which would siphon off part of any increased value. To show the effect of this dilution, let us assume that the company proves so successful that its fair value is twice its tangible assets after completion of this financing—say, about $1,000,000 as compared with $484,000 of tangible assets. What could then be the value of the stock for which the public paid $6.25? If there were no warrants outstanding, this value would be about $8 per share on 126,000 shares. But allowing for a value of say $2.00 per share for the warrants, the stock itself would be worth only $7.25 per share. Hence even a very substantial degree of success on the part of this enterprise would add a mere 16% to the value of the public's purchase. Should things go the other way, a very large part of the investment would soon be dissipated.

Should the Public Finance New Ventures? Fairly complete observation of new-enterprise financing registered with the S.E.C. since 1933 has given us a pessimistic opinion as to its soundness and its economic value to the nation. The venturing of capital into new businesses is essential to American progress, but no substantial contribution to the upbuilding of the country has ever been made by *new* ventures *publicly* financed. Wall Street has always realized that the capital for such undertakings should properly be supplied on a private and personal basis—by the organizers themselves or people close to them. Hence the sale of shares in new businesses has never been a truly reputable pursuit, and the leading banking houses will not engage in it. The less fastidious channels through which such financing is done exact so high an over-all selling cost—*to the public*—that the chance of success of the new enterprise, small enough at best, is thereby greatly diminished.

It is our considered view that the nation's interest would be served by amending the Securities Act so as to prohibit the public offering of securities of new and definitely unseasoned ventures. It would not be easy to define precisely the criteria of "seasoning,"—*e.g.*, size, number of years' operation without loss—and it may be necessary to vest some discretion on this score with the S.E.C. We think, however, that borderline and difficult cases will be relatively few in number (although our second example above belongs, perhaps, in this category). We should be glad to see the powers and duties of the S.E.C. diminished in many details of minor significance; but on this point of protecting a public incapable of protecting itself, our view leans strongly towards more drastic legislation.

Blue-Sky Promotions. In the "good old days" fraudulent stock promoters relied so largely upon high pressure salesmanship that they rarely bothered to give their proposition any semblance of serious merit. They could sell shares in a mine that was not even a "hole in the ground" or in an invention the chief recommendation for which was the enormous profit made by Henry Ford's early partners. The victim was in fact buying "blue sky" and nothing else. Any one with the slightest business sense could have detected the complete worthlessness of these ventures almost at a glance; in fact, the glossy paper used for the prospectus was in itself sufficient to identify the proposition as fraudulent.

The tightening of federal and state regulations against these swindles has led to a different type of security promotion. Instead of offering something entirely worthless, the promoter selects a real enterprise that he can sell at much more than its fair value. By this means the law can be obeyed and the public exploited just the same. Oil and mining ventures lend themselves best to such stock flotations, because it is easy to instill in the uninitiated an exaggerated notion of their true worth. The S.E.C. has been concerning itself more and more seriously with endeavors to defeat this type of semifraud. In theory a promoter may offer something worth $1 per share at $5, provided he discloses all the facts and adds no false representations. The Commission is not authorized to pass upon the soundness of new securities or the fairness of their price (except in the case of public-utility issues which come under the terms of the Public Utility Holding

Company Act of 1935). Actually, it appears to be doing its best, by various pressures, to discourage and even prevent the more grossly inequitable offerings. But it is essential that the public recognize that the Commission's powers in this respect are severely limited and that only a sceptical analysis by the intending buyer can assure him against exploitation.

Promotional activities are attracted especially to any new industry that is in the public eye. Profits made by those first in the field, or even currently by the enterprise floated, can be given a fictitious guise of permanence and of future enhancement. Hence gross overvaluations can be made plausible enough to sell. In the liquor flotations of 1933 the degree of overvaluation depended entirely upon the conscience of the sponsors. Accordingly, the list of stock offerings showed all gradations from the thoroughly legitimate down to the almost completely fraudulent.[7] A somewhat similar picture is presented by the aircraft flotations of 1938–1939. The public would do well to remember that whenever it becomes easy to raise capital for a particular industry, both the chances of unfair deals are magnified and the danger of overdevelopment of the industry itself becomes very real.

Repercussions of Unsound Investment Banking. The relaxation of investment bankers' standards in the late 1920s, and their use of ingenious means to enlarge their compensation, had unwholesome repercussions in the field of corporate management. Operating officials felt themselves entitled not only to handsome salaries but also to a substantial participation in the profits of the enterprise. In this respect the investment-trust arrangements, devised by the banking houses for their own benefit, set a stimulating example to the world of "big business."

Whether or not it is proper for executives of a large and prosperous concern to receive annual compensation running into hundreds of thousands or even millions of dollars is perhaps an open question. Its answer will depend upon the extent to which the corporation's success is due to their unique or surpassing ability, and this must be very difficult to determine with assurance. But it may not be denied that devious and questionable means were frequently employed to secure these large bonuses to the management without full disclosure of their extent to the stockholders. Stock-option warrants (or long-term subscription rights) to buy

---

[7] See Appendix Note 55 relative to investors' experience with brewery-stock flotations of 1933.

shares at low prices, proved an excellent instrument for this purpose—as we have already pointed out in our discussion of stockholder-management relationships. In this field complete and continued publicity is not only theoretically desirable but of practical utility as well. The legislation of 1933–1934 marks an undeniable forward step in this regard, since the major facts of managerial compensation must now be disclosed in registration statements and in annual supplements thereto (Form 10-K). With publicity given to this compensation, we believe that the self-interest of stockholders may be relied on fairly well to prevent it from passing all reasonable limits.

CHAPTER 48

Some Aspects of
Corporate Pyramiding

PYRAMIDING IN CORPORATE finance is the creation of a speculative capital structure by means of a holding company or a series of holding companies. Usually the predominating purpose of such an arrangement is to enable the organizers to control a large business with the investment of little or no capital and also to secure to themselves the major part of its surplus profits and increased going-concern value. The device is most often utilized by dominant interests to "cash in" speculative profits on their holdings and at the same time to retain control. With the funds so provided, these successful captains of finance generally endeavor to extend their control over additional operating enterprises. The technique of pyramiding is well illustrated by the successive maneuvers of O. P. and M. J. Van Sweringen, which started with purchase of control of the then relatively unimportant New York, Chicago, and St. Louis Railroad and rapidly developed into a far-flung railroad "empire."[1]

Example: The Van Sweringen Pyramid. The original transaction of the Van Sweringens in the railroad field took place in 1916. It consisted of the

---

[1] The complete story of how this pyramiding was effected is told in the *Hearings before the Committee on Banking and Currency, United States Senate*, 73d Congress, 1st Session, on Senate Resolution 84 of the 72d Congress and Senate Resolution 56 of the 73d Congress, Part 2, pp. 563–777, June 5 to 8, 1933—on "Stock Exchange Practices." The story is also set forth in greater detail and with graphic portrayal in *Regulation of Stock Ownership in Railroads, Part* 2, pp. 820–1173 (House Report No. 2789, 71st Congress, 3d Session), especially the inserts at p. 878 thereof. For graphic and other presentation of the effects of pyramiding in the public-utility field see Utility Corporations (Sen. Doc. 92, 70th Congress, 1st Session, pt. 72-A), pp. 154–166.

The most notorious pyramided structure of recent years was the Insull set-up. An interesting example of a different type is presented by the United States and Foreign Securities Corporation—United States and International Securities Corporation relationship. These two situations are briefly described in Appendix Note 64.

purchase from the New York Central Railroad Company, for the sum of $8,500,000, of common and preferred stock constituting control of the New York, Chicago, and St. Louis Railroad Company (known as the "Nickel Plate"). This purchase was financed by giving a note to the seller for $6,500,000 and by a cash payment of $2,000,000, which in turn was borrowed from a Cleveland bank. Subsequent acquisitions of control of many other companies were effected by various means, including the following:

1. The formation of a private corporation for the purpose (*e.g.*, Western Corporation to acquire control of Lake Erie and Western Railroad Company, and Clover Leaf Corporation to acquire control of Toledo, St. Louis and Western Railroad Company—both in 1922).

2. The use of the resources of one controlled railroad to acquire control of others (*e.g.*, the New York, Chicago and St. Louis Railroad Company purchased large amounts of stock of Chesapeake and Ohio Railway and Pere Marquette Railway Company during 1923–1925).

3. The formation of a holding company to control an individual road, with sale of the holding company's securities to the public (*e.g.*, Chesapeake Corporation, which took over control of Chesapeake and Ohio Railway Company and sold its own bonds and stock to the public, in 1927).

4. Formation of a general holding company (*e.g.*, Alleghany Corporation, chartered in 1929. This ambitious project took over control of many railroad, coal, and miscellaneous enterprises).

The report on the "Van Sweringen Holding Companies" made to the House of Representatives in 1930[2] includes an interesting chart showing the contrast between the control exercised by the Van Sweringens and their relatively small equity or financial interest in the capital of the enterprises controlled. In the following table, we append a summary of these data. The figures in Column *A* show the percentage of voting securities held or controlled by the Van Sweringens; the figures in Column *B* show the proportion of the "contributed capital" (bonds, stock, and surplus) actually owned directly or indirectly by them.

It is worth recalling that similar use of the holding company for pyramiding control of railroad properties had been made before the war—notably in the case of the Rock Island Company. This enterprise was organized in 1902. Through an intermediate subsidiary it acquired nearly

---

[2] House Report 2789, 71st Congress, 3d Session, Part 2, pp. 820–1173.

all the common stock of the Chicago, Rock Island and Pacific Railway Company and about 60% of the capital stock of the St. Louis and San Francisco Railway Company. Against these shares the two holding companies issued large amounts of collateral trust bonds, preferred stock and common stock. In 1909 the stock of the St. Louis and San Francisco was sold. In 1915 the Rock Island Company and its intermediate subsidiary both went into bankruptcy; the stock of the operating company was taken over by the collateral trust bondholders; and the holding company stock issues were wiped out completely.

Companies	A. Control, %	B. Equity, %
Holding companies:		
The Vaness Co.	80.0	27.7
General Securities Corp.	90.0	51.8
Geneva Corp.	100.0	27.7
Alleghany Corp.	41.8	8.6
The Chesapeake Corp.	71.0	4.1
The Pere Marquette Corp.	100.0	0.7
Virginia Transportation Corp.	100.0	0.8
The Pittston Co.	81.8	4.3
Railroad Companies:		
The New York, Chicago and St. Louis R.R. Co.	49.6	0.7
The Chesapeake and Ohio Railway Co.	54.4	1.0
Pere Marquette Railway Co.	48.3	0.6
Erie Railroad Co.	30.8	0.6
Missouri Pacific Railroad Co.	50.5	1.7
The Hocking Valley Railway Co.	81.0	0.2
The Wheeling and Lake Erie Railway Co.	53.3	0.3
Kansas City Southern Railway Co.	20.8	0.9

The ignominious collapse of this venture was accepted at the time as marking the end of "high finance" in the railroad field. Yet some ten years later the same unsound practices were introduced once again, but on a larger scale and with correspondingly severer losses to investors. It remains to add that the Congressional investigation of railroad holding companies instituted in 1930 had its counterpart in a similar inquiry into the finances of the Rock Island Company made by the

Interstate Commerce Commission in 1914. The memory of the financial community is proverbially and distressingly short.

Evils of Corporate Pyramiding. The pyramiding device is harmful to the security-buying public from several standpoints. It results in the creation and sale to investors of large amounts of unsound senior securities. It produces common stocks of holding companies which are subject to deceptively rapid increases in earning power in favorable years and which are invariably made the vehicle of wild and disastrous public speculation. The possession of control by those who have no real capital investment (or a relatively minor one) is inequitable[3] and makes for irresponsible and unsound managerial policies. Finally the holding company device permits of financial practices that exaggerate the indicated earnings, dividend return, or "book value," during boom times, and thus intensify speculative fervor and facilitate market manipulation. Of these four objections to corporate pyramiding, the first three are plainly evident, but the last one requires a certain amount of analytical treatment in order to present its various implications.

Overstatement of Earnings. Holding companies can overstate their apparent earning power by valuing at an unduly high price the stock dividends they receive from subsidiaries or by including in their income profits made from the sale of stock of subsidiary companies.

Examples: The chief asset of Central States Electric Corporation was a large block of North American Company common on which regular stock dividends were paid. Prior to the end of 1929, these stock dividends were reported as income by Central States at the market value then current. As explained in our chapter on stock dividends, such market prices averaged far in excess of the value at which North American charged the stock dividends against its surplus and also far in excess of the distributable earnings on North American common. Hence the income account of Central States Electric gave a misleading impression of the earnings accruing to the company.

A transaction of somewhat different character but of similar effect to the foregoing was disclosed by the report of American Founders Trust for 1927. In November 1927 American Founders offered its shareholders the privilege of buying about 88,400 shares of International Securities Corporation of

---

[3] See Appendix Note 65 for examples on this point.

America Class *B* Common at $16 per share. International Securities Corporation was a subsidiary of American Founders, and the latter had acquired the Class *B* stock of the former at a cash cost of $3.70 per share in 1926. American Founders reported net earnings for common stock in 1927 amounting to $1,316,488, most of which was created by its own stockholders through their purchase of shares of the subsidiary as indicated above.[4]

Distortion of Dividend Return. Just as a holding company's income may be exaggerated by reason of stock dividends received, so the dividend return on its shares may be distorted in the public's mind by payment of periodic stock dividends with a market value exceeding current earnings. People are readily persuaded also to regard the value of frequent subscription rights as equivalent to an income return on the common stock. Pyramided enterprises are prodigal with subscription rights, for they flow naturally from the succession of new acquisitions and new financing which both promote the ambitions of those in control and maintain speculative interest at fever heat—until the inevitable collapse.

The issuance of subscription rights sometimes gives the stock market an opportunity to indulge in that peculiar circular reasoning which is the joy of the manipulator and the despair of the analyst. Company *A*'s stock is apparently worth no more than 25. Speculation or pool activity has advanced it to 75. Rights are offered to buy additional shares at 25, and the rights have a market value of, say, $10 each. To the speculative fraternity these rights are practically equivalent to a special dividend of $10. It is a bonus that not only justifies the rise to 75 but warrants more optimism and a still higher price. To the analyst the whole proceeding is a delusion and a snare. Whatever value the rights command is manufactured solely out of speculators' misguided enthusiasm, yet this chimerical value is accepted as tangible income and as vindication of the enthusiasm that gave it birth. Thus, with the encouragement of the manipulator, the speculative public pulls itself up by its bootstraps to dizzier heights of irrationality.

---

[4] In the three years 1928–1930 the American Founders group reported total net investment profits of about $43,300,000; but all of this sum and more was derived from profits on intercompany transactions of the kind described above. See the S.E.C.'s Over-all Report on Investment Trusts, Part III, Chapter VI, Sections II and III, released February 12, 1940.

Example: Between August 1928 and February 1929 American and Foreign Power Company common stock advanced from 33 to 138⁷/₈, although paying no dividend. Rights were offered to the common stockholders (and other security holders) to buy second preferred stock with detached stock-purchase warrants. The offering of these rights, which had an initial market value of about $3 each, was construed by many as the equivalent of a dividend on the common stock.

Exaggeration of Book Value. The exaggeration of book value may be effected in cases where a holding company owns most of the shares of a subsidiary and where consequently an artificially high quotation may readily be established for the subsidiary issue by manipulating the small amount of stock remaining in the market. This high quotation is then taken as the basis of figuring the book value (sometimes called the "break-up value") of the share of the holding company. For an early example of these practices we may point to Tobacco Products Corporation (Va.) which owned about 80% of the common stock of United Cigar Stores Company of America. An unduly high market price seems to have been established in 1927 for the small amount of Cigar Stores stock available in the market, and this high price was used to make Tobacco Products shares appear attractive to the unwary buyer. The thoroughly objectionable accounting and stock dividend policies of United Cigar Stores, which we have previously discussed, were adjuncts to this manipulative campaign.

The most extraordinary example of such exaggeration of the book value is found, perhaps, in the case of Electric Bond and Share Company and was founded on its ownership of most of the American and Foreign Power Company warrants. The whole set-up seems to have been contrived to induce the public to pay absolutely fantastic prices without their complete absurdity being too apparent. A brief review of the various steps in this phantasmagoria of inflated values should be illuminating to the student of security analysis.

First, American and Foreign Power Company issued in all 1,600,000 shares of common and warrants to buy 7,100,000 more shares at $25. This permitted a price to be established for the common stock that generously capitalized its earnings and prospects but paid no attention to the existence of the warrants. The quotation of the common was aided by the issuance of rights, as explained above.

Second, the high price registered for the relatively small common-stock issue automatically created a correspondingly high value for the millions of warrants.

Third, Electric Bond and Share could apply these high values to its large holdings of American and Foreign Power common and its enormous block of warrants, thus setting up a correspondingly inflated value for its own common stock.

Exploitation of the Stock-Purchase-Warrant Device. The result of this process, at its farthest point in 1929, was almost incredible. The earnings available for American and Foreign Power common stock had shown the following rising trend (due in good part, however, to continuous new acquisitions):

Year	Earnings for common	Number of shares	Earned per share
1926	$216,000	1,243,988	0.17
1927	856,000	1,244,388	0.69
1928	1,528,000	1,248,930	1.22
1929	6,510,000	1,624,357	4.01

On the theory that a "good public-utility stock is worth up to 50 times its current earnings," a price of $199^1/4$ per share was recorded for American and Foreign Power common. This produced in turn a price of 174 for the warrants. Hence, by the insane magic of Wall Street, earnings of $6,500,000 were transmuted into a market value of $320,000,000 for the common shares and $1,240,000,000 for the warrants, a staggering total of $1,560,000,000.

Since over 80% of the warrants were owned by Electric Bond and Share Company, the effect of these absurd prices for American and Foreign Power junior securities was to establish a correspondingly absurd break-up value for Electric Bond and Share common. This break-up value was industriously exploited to justify higher and higher quotations for the latter issue. In March 1929 attention was called to the fact that the market value of this company's portfolio was equivalent to about $108 per share (of new stock), against a range of 91 to 97 for its own market quotation. The implication was that Electric Bond and Share stock was "undervalued." In September 1929 the price had advanced to $184^1/2$. It was then computed that the "break-up value" amounted to about 150, "allowing no value for the company's supervisory and construction business." The public did not stop to reflect that a considerable part of this "book value" was based upon an essentially fictitious market quotation for an asset that the company had received *for nothing* only a few years before (as a bonus with American and Foreign Power Second Preferred stock).

This exploitation of the warrants had a peculiar vitality which made itself felt even in the depth of the depression in 1932–1933. Time having brought its usual revenge, the once dazzling American and Foreign Power Company had trembled on the brink of receivership, as shown by a price of only $15^1/_4$ for its 5% bonds. Nevertheless, in November 1933 the highly unsubstantial warrants still commanded an aggregate market quotation of nearly $50,000,000, a figure that bore a ridiculous relationship to the exceedingly low values placed upon the senior securities. The following table shows how absurd this situation was, the more so since it existed in a time of deflated stock prices, when relative values are presumably subjected to more critical appraisal.

(000 omitted in market value)

Issue	Amount outstanding	Price Nov. 1933	Total market value, 1933	Price Dec. 31, 1938	Total market value, 1938
5% Debentures	$50,000	40	$20,000	53	26,500
$7 First Preferred shares	480	21	10,100	$19^7/_8$	9,300
$6 First Preferred shares	387	15	5,800	15	5,800
$7 Second Preferred shares	2,655	12	31,900	$9^1/_4$	24,900
Common shares	1,850	10	18,500	$3^1/_2$	6,500
Warrants shares	6,874	7	48,100	1	6,900

By the end of 1938, as the table indicates, a good part of the absurdity had been corrected.

Some Holding Companies Not Guilty of Excessive Pyramiding. To avoid creating a false impression, we must point out that, although pyramiding is usually effected by means of holding companies, it does not follow that all holding companies are created for this purpose and are therefore reprehensible. The holding company is often utilized for entirely legitimate purposes, *e.g.*, to permit unified and economical operations of separate units, to diversify investment and risk and to gain certain technical advantages of flexibility and convenience. Many sound and important enterprises are in holding company form.

Examples: United States Steel Corporation is entirely a holding company; although originally there was some element of pyramiding in its capital set-up, this defect disappeared in later years. American Telephone and Telegraph Company is preponderantly a holding company, but its financial structure has never been subject to serious criticism. General Motors Corporation is largely a holding company.

A holding-company exhibit must therefore be considered on its merits. American Light and Traction Company is a typical example of the holding company organized entirely for legitimate purposes. On the other hand the acquisition of control of this enterprise by United Light and Railways Company (Del.) must be regarded as a pyramiding move on the part of the United Light and Power interests.

Speculative Capital Structure May Be Created in Other Ways. It may be pointed out also that a speculative capital structure can be created without the use of a holding company.

Examples: The Maytag Company recapitalization, discussed in an earlier chapter, yielded results usually attained by the formation of a holding company and the sale of its senior securities. In the case of Continental Baking Corporation—to cite another example—the holding company form was not an essential part of the pyramided result there attained. The speculative structure was due entirely to the creation of large preferred issues by the parent company, and it would still have existed if Continental Baking had acquired all its properties directly, eliminating its subsidiaries. (As it happened, in 1938 this company took steps to acquire the assets of its chief subsidiaries, thus largely eliminating the holding-company form but retaining the speculative capital structure.)

Legislative Restraints on Pyramiding. So spectacular were the disastrous effects of the public-utility pyramiding of the 1920s that Congress was moved to drastic action. The Public Utility Holding Company Act of 1935 includes the so-called "death sentence" for many of the existing systems, requiring them ultimately to simplify their capital structures and to dispose of subsidiaries operating in noncontiguous territory. Formation of new pyramids is effectively blocked by requiring Commission approval for all acquisitions and all new financing. Similar steps are in prospect to regulate present railroad holding companies and to prevent creation of new ones.[5]

We may say with some confidence that the spectacle of the Van Sweringen debacle succeeding the Rock Island Company debacle is not likely to be duplicated in the future. The industrial field never offered the same romantic possibilities for high finance as were found among the rails and utilities, but it may well be that the ingenious talents of promoters and financial wizards will be directed towards the industrials in the future. The investor and the analyst should be on their guard against such new dazzlements.

---

[5] See Senate Resolution 71 of the 74th Congress and 21 volumes of hearings thereon which have appeared to date (December 1939). See also Senate Report No. 180, 75th Congress, 1st Session, and Senate Report No. 25, pts. 1, 4 and 5, 76th Congress, 1st Session.

CHAPTER 49

Comparative Analysis of Companies in the Same Field

STATISTICAL COMPARISONS of groups of concerns operating in a given industry are a more or less routine part of the analyst's work. Such tabulations permit each company's showing to be studied against a background of the industry as a whole. They frequently bring to light instances of undervaluation or overvaluation or lead to the conclusion that the securities of one enterprise should be replaced by those of another in the same field.

In this chapter we shall suggest standard forms for such comparative analyses, and we shall also discuss the significance of the various items included therein. Needless to say, these forms are called "standard" only in the sense that they can be used generally to good advantage; no claim of perfection is made for them, and the student is free to make any changes that he thinks will serve his particular purpose.

FORM I.   RAILROAD COMPARISON

A.   Capitalization:
1. Fixed charges.*
2. Effective debt (fixed charges* multiplied by 22).
3. Preferred stock at market (number of shares x market price).
4. Common stock at market (number of shares x market price).
5. Total capitalization.
6. Ratio of effective debt to total capitalization.
7. Ratio of preferred stock to total capitalization.
8. Ratio of common stock to total capitalization.

B.   Income Account:
9. Gross revenues.
10. Ratio of maintenance to gross.

11. Ratio of railway operating income (net after taxes) to gross.

12. Ratio of fixed charges* to gross.

13. Ratio of preferred dividends to gross.

14. Ratio of balance for common to gross.

C. Calculations:

15. Number of times fixed charges* earned.

15. I.P.† Number of times fixed charges* plus preferred
    dividends earned.

16. Earned on common stock, per share.

17. Earned on common stock, % of market price.

18. Ratio of gross to aggregate market value of common stock (9 ÷ 4).

16. S.P.‡ Earned on preferred stock, per share.

17. S.P. Earned on preferred stock, % of market price.

18. S.P. Ratio of gross to aggregate market value of preferred stock (9 ÷ 3).

19. Credit or debit to earnings for undistributed profit or loss of subsidiaries
    (if important).

D. Seven-year average figures:

20. Earned on common stock, per share.

21. Earned on common stock, % of current market price of common.

20. S.P. Earned on preferred stock, per share.

21. S.P. Earned on preferred stock, % of current market price of preferred.

22. Number of times net deductions earned.

23. Number of times fixed charges earned.

22. I.P. Number of times net deductions plus preferred
    dividends earned.

23. I.P. Number of times fixed charges plus preferred dividends earned.

E. Trend figure:

24 to 30. Earned per share on common stock each year for past seven years.
    (Where necessary, earnings should be adjusted to present capitalization.)

24. S.P. to 30. S.P. Same data for speculative preferred stock, if wanted.

F. Dividends:

31. Dividend rate on common.

32. Dividend yield on common.

31. P. Dividend rate on preferred.

32. P. Dividend yield on preferred.

* Or net deductions if larger.
† I.P. = for studying an investment preferred stock.
‡ S.P. = for studying a speculative preferred stock.

Observations on the Railroad Comparison.[1] It has formerly been the custom to base earnings studies on the figures for the previous calendar years, with certain references to later interim reports. But since complete figures are now available month by month, it is more logical and effective practice to ignore the calendar-year division and to use instead the results for the twelve months to the latest date available. The simplest way to arrive at such a twelve months' figure is to apply the *change* shown for the current year to date to the results of the previous calendar year.

Example:

Gross Earnings of Pennsylvania Railroad System for 12 Months Ended June, 1939

(1) 6 months to June 1939 (as reported)	$189,623,000
(2) 6 months to June 1938 (as reported)	167,524,000
(3) Difference	+22,099,000
(4) Calender year 1938	360,384,000
12 months to June 1939 (4 plus 3)	$382,483,000

Our table includes a few significant calculations based on the seven-year average. In an intensive study, average results should be scrutinized in more detail. To save time, it is suggested that additional average figures be computed only for those roads which the analyst selects for further investigation after he has studied the exhibits in the "standard form." Whether the period of averaging should cover seven years or a longer or shorter time is largely a matter for individual judgment. In theory it should be just long enough to cover a full cyclical fluctuation but not so long as to include factors or results that are totally out of date. The six years 1934–1939 might well be regarded as a somewhat better criterion, for example, than the longer period 1933–1939.

Figures relating to preferred stocks fall into two different classes, depending on whether the issue is considered for fixed-value investment or as a speculative commitment. (Usually the market price will indicate

---

[1] Reference is made to earlier chapters for explanation of the terminology and the critical tests referred to in this discussion.

clearly enough in which category a particular issue belongs.) The items marked "I.P." are to be used in studying an investment preferred stock, and those marked "S.P." in studying a speculative preferred. Where there are junior income bonds, the simplest and most satisfactory procedure will be to treat them in all respects as a preferred stock issue, with a footnote referring to their actual title. Such contingent bond interest will therefore be excluded from the net deductions or the fixed charges.

In this tabular comparison we follow the suggestion previously offered that the effective debt be computed by capitalizing the larger of net deductions or fixed charges. In using the table as an aid to the selection of senior issues for investment, chief attention will be paid to items 22 and 23 (or 22 "I.P." and 23 "I.P."), showing the average margin above interest (and preferred dividend) requirements. Consideration should be given also to items 6, 7 and 8, showing the division of total capitalization between senior securities and junior equity. (In dealing with bonds, the preferred stock is part of the junior equity; in considering a preferred stock for investment, it must be included with the effective debt.) Items 10 and 19 should also be examined to see if the earnings have been overstated by reason of inadequate maintenance or by the inclusion of unearned dividends from subsidiaries.

Speculative preferred stocks will ordinarily be analyzed in much the same way as common stocks, and the similarity becomes greater as the price of the preferred stock is lower. It should be remembered, however, that a preferred stock is always less attractive, logically considered, than a common stock making the same showing. For example, a $6 preferred earning $5 per share is intrinsically less desirable than a common stock earning $5 per share (and with the same prior charges), since the latter is entitled to all the present and future equity, whereas the preferred stock is strictly limited in its claim upon the future.

In comparing railroad common stocks (and preferred shares equivalent thereto), the point of departure is the percentage earned on the market price. This may be qualified, to an extent more or less important, by consideration of items 10 and 19. Items 12 and 18 will indicate at once whether the company is speculatively or conservatively capitalized, relatively speaking. A speculatively capitalized road will show a large ratio of net deductions to gross and (ordinarily) a small ratio of common stock at market value to gross. The converse will be true for a conservatively capitalized road.

Limitation upon Comparison of Speculatively and Conservatively Capitalized Companies in the Same Field. The analyst must beware of trying to draw conclusions as to the relative attractiveness of two railroad common stocks when one is speculatively and the other is conservatively capitalized. Two such issues will respond quite differently to changes for the better or the worse, so that an advantage possessed by one of them under current conditions may readily be lost if conditions should change.

Example: The example shown in Chap. 50 illustrates in a twofold fashion the fallacy of comparing a conservatively capitalized with a speculatively capitalized common stock. In 1922 the earnings of Union Pacific common were nearly four times as high in relation to market price as were those of Rock Island common. A conclusion that Union Pacific was "cheaper," based on these figures, would have been fallacious, because the relative capitalization structures were so different as to make the two companies noncomparable. This fact is shown graphically by the much larger expansion of the earnings and the market price of Rock Island common that accompanied the moderate rise in gross business during the five years following.

The situation in 1927 was substantially the opposite. At that time Rock Island common was earning proportionately more than Union Pacific common. But it would have been equally fallacious to conclude that Rock Island common was "intrinsically cheaper." The speculative capitalization structure of the latter road made it highly vulnerable to unfavorable development, so that it was unable to withstand the post-1929 depression.

Other Illustrations in Appendix. The practical approach to comparative analysis of railroad stocks (and bonds) may best be illustrated by the reproduction of several such comparisons made by one of the authors a number of years ago and published as part of the service rendered to clients by a New York Stock Exchange firm. These will be found in Appendix Note 66. It will be observed that the comparisons were made between roads in approximately the same class as regards capitalization structure, with the exception of the comparison between Atchison and New York Central, in which instance special reference was made to the greater sensitivity of New York Central to changes in either direction.

Comparison of Union Pacific and Rock Island Common Stocks

Item	Union Pacific R.R.	Chicago, Rock Island, & Pacific Ry.
A. Showing the effect of general improvement:		
Average price of common, 1922	140	40
Earned per share, 1922	$12.76	$0.96
% earned on market price, 1922	9.1%	2.4%
Fixed charges and preferred dividends earned, 1922	2.39 times	1.05 times
Ratio of gross to market value of common, 1922	62%	419%
Increase in gross, 1927 over 1922	5.7%	12.9%
Earned per share of common, 1927	$16.05	$12.08
Increase in earnings on common, 1927 over 1922	26%	1,158%
Average price of common, 1927	179	92
Increase in average price, 1927 over 1922	28%	130%
B. Showing the effect of a general decline in business:		
Earned on average price, 1927	9.0%	13.1%
Fixed charges and preferred dividends earned, 1927	2.64 times	1.58 times
Ratio of gross to market value of common, 1927	51%	204%
Decrease in gross, 1933 below 1927	46%	54%
Earned on common, 1933	$7.88	$20.40(d)
Decrease in earnings for common, 1933 below 1927	51%	269%
Average price of common, 1933	97	6
Decrease in average price, 1933 below 1927	46%	93%

Note: In June 1933 trustees in bankruptcy were appointed for the Rock Island.

FORM II.   PUBLIC-UTILITY COMPARISON

The public-utility comparison form is practically the same as that for railroads. The only changes are the following: Fixed charges (as mentioned in line 1 and elsewhere) should include subsidiary-preferred dividends. Line 2 should be called "Funded debt and subsidiary preferred stock," and these should be taken from the balance sheet. Items 22 and 22 I.P., relating to net deductions, are not needed. Item 10 becomes "ratio of depreciation to gross." An item, 10M, may be included to show "ratio of maintenance to gross" for the companies which publish this information.

Our observations regarding the use of the railroad comparison apply as well to the public-utility comparison. Variations in the depreciation rate are fully as important as variations in the railroad maintenance ratios. When a wide difference appears, it should not be taken for granted that one property is unduly conservative or the other not conservative enough, but a *presumption* to this effect does arise, and the question should be investigated as thoroughly as possible. A statistical indication that one utility stock is more attractive than another should not be acted upon until (among other qualitative matters) some study has been made of the rate situation and the relative prospects for favorable or unfavorable changes therein. In view of experience since 1933, careful attention should also be given to the dangers of municipal or federal competition.

FORM III.   INDUSTRIAL COMPARISON
(FOR COMPANIES IN THE SAME FIELD)

Since this form differs in numerous respects from the two preceding, it is given in full herewith:

   A. Capitalization:

      1. Bonds at par.
      2. Preferred stock at market value
         (number of shares x market price).
      3. Common stock at market value
         (number of shares x market price).
      4. Total capitalization.
      5. Ratio of bonds to capitalization.
      6. Ratio of aggregate market value of preferred to capitalization.
      7. Ratio of aggregate market value of common to capitalization.

B. Income Account (most recent year):

    8. Gross sales.

    9. Depreciation.

   10. Net available for bond interest.

   11. Bond interest.

   12. Preferred dividend requirements.

   13. Balance for common.

   14. Margin of profit (ratio of 10 to 8).

   15. % earned on total capitalization (ratio of 10 to 4).

C. Calculations:

   16. Number of times interest charges earned.

   16. I.P. Number of times interest charges plus preferred
       dividends earned.

   17. Earned on common, per share.

   18. Earned on common, % of market price.

   17. S.P. Earned on preferred, per share.

   18. S.P. Earned on preferred, % of market price.

   19. Ratio of gross to aggregate market value of common.

   19. S.P. Ratio of gross to aggregate market value of preferred.

D. Seven-year average:

   20. Number of times interest charges earned.

   21. Earned on common stock per share.

   22. Earned on common stock, % of current market price.
       (20 I.P., 21 S.P. and 22 S.P.—Same calculation for preferred
       stock if wanted.)

E. Trend figure:

   23. Earned per share of common stock each year for past seven years
       (adjustments in number of shares outstanding to be made where
       necessary).

   23. S.P. Same data for speculative preferred issues, if wanted.

F. Dividends:

   24. Dividend rate on common.

   25. Dividend yield on common.

24. P. Dividend rate on preferred.
25. P. Dividend yield on preferred.

G. Balance sheet:

26. Cash assets.
27. Receivables (less reserves).
28. Inventories (less proper reserves).
29. Total current assets.
30. Total current liabilities.
30. N. Notes Payable (Including "Bank Loans" and "Bills Payable").
31. Net current assets.
32. Ratio of current assets to current liabilities.
33. Ratio of inventory to sales.
34. Ratio of receivables to sales.
35. Net tangible assets available for total capitalization.
36. Cash-asset-value of common per share (deducting all prior obligations).
37. Net-current-asset-value of common per share (deducting all prior obligations).
38. Net-tangible-asset-value of common per share (deducting all prior obligations).

(36 S.P., 37 S.P., 38 S.P.—Same data for speculative preferred issues, if wanted.)

H. Supplementary data (when available):

1. Physical output:
   Number of units; receipts per unit; cost per unit; profit per unit; total capitalization per unit; common stock valuation per unit.
2. Miscellaneous:
   For example: number of stores operated; sales per store; profit per store; ore reserves; life of mine at current (or average) rate of production.

Observations on the Industrial Comparison. Some remarks regarding the use of this suggested form may be helpful. The net earnings figure must be corrected for any known distortions or omissions, including adjustments for undistributed earnings or losses of subsidiaries. If it appears to be misleading and cannot be adequately corrected, it should not be used as a basis of comparisons. (Inferences drawn from unreliable figures must themselves be unreliable.) No attempt should be made to subject the depreciation figures to exact comparisons; they are useful only in disclosing wide and obvious disparities in the rates used. The calculation of bond-interest-coverage is subject to the qualification discussed in Chap. 17, with respect to companies that may have important rental obligations equivalent to interest charges.

Whereas the percentage earned on the market price of the common (item 18) is a leading figure in all comparisons, almost equal attention must be given to item 15, showing the percentage earned on total capitalization. These figures, together with items 7 and 19 (ratio of aggregate market value of common stock to sales and to capitalization), will indicate the part played by conservative or speculative capitalization structures among the companies compared. (The theory of capitalization structure was considered in Chap. 40.)

As a matter of practical procedure it is not safe to rely upon the fact that the earnings ratio for the common stock (item 18) is higher than the average for the industry, unless the percentage earned on the total capitalization (item 15) is also higher. Furthermore, if the company with the poorer earnings exhibit shows much larger sales-per-dollar-of-common-stock (item 19), it may have better speculative possibilities in the event of general business improvement.

The balance-sheet computations do not have primary significance unless they indicate either definite financial weakness or a substantial excess of current-asset-value over the market price. The division of importance as between the current results, the seven-year average and the trend is something entirely for the analyst's judgment to decide. Naturally, he will have the more confidence in any suggested conclusion if it is confirmed on each of these counts.

Example of the Use of Standard Forms. An example of the use of the standard form to reach a conclusion concerning comparative values should be of interest. A survey of the common stocks of the listed steel producers in July 1938 indicated that Continental Steel had made a better exhibit than the average, whereas Granite City Steel had shown much smaller earning power. The two companies operated to some extent in the same branches of the steel industry; they were very similar in size, and the price of their common stocks was identical. In the tabulation presented in a following table we supply comparative figures for these two enterprises, omitting some of the items on our standard form as immaterial to this analysis.

Comments on the Comparison. The use of five-year average figures for each item, presented along with those of the most recent twelve months, is suggested here because the subnormal business conditions in the year ended June 30, 1938 made it inadvisable to lay too great emphasis on the results for this single period. Granite City reports on calendar-year basis, whereas Continental used both a June 30 and a December 31 fiscal year during 1934–1938. However, the availability of quarterly or semiannual figures makes it a simple matter for the analyst to construct his average and 12 months' figures to end in the middle of the year.

Analysis of the data reveals only one point of superiority for Granite City Steel—the smaller amount of senior securities. But even this is not necessarily an advantage, since the relatively fewer shares of Continental common make them more sensitive to favorable as well as unfavorable developments. The exhibit for the June 1938 year, and five-year average, show a statistical superiority for Continental on each of the following important points:

> Earnings on market price of common stock.
> Earnings on total capitalization.
> Ratio of gross to market value of common.
> Margin of profit.
> Depreciation in relation to plant account.
> Working-capital position.
> Tangible asset values.
> Dividend return.
> Trend of earnings.

If the comparison is carried back prior to 1934, Granite City is found to have enjoyed a marked advantage in the depression years from mid-1930 to mid-1933. During this time it earned and paid dividends while Continental Steel was reporting moderate losses. It is curious to observe that in the more recent recession the tables were exactly turned, and Continental Steel did very well while Granite City fared badly. Obviously the 1937–1938 results would command more attention than those in the longer past. Nevertheless, the thorough analyst would endeavor to learn as much as possible about the basic reasons underlying the change in the relative performance of the two companies.

Study of Qualitative Factors also Necessary. Our last observation leads to the more general remark that conclusions suggested by comparative tabulations of this sort should not be accepted until careful thought has been given to the qualitative factors. When one issue seems to be selling much too low on the basis of the exhibit in relation to that of another in the same field, there may be adequate reasons for this disparity that the statistics do not disclose. Among such valid reasons may be a definitely poorer outlook or a questionable management. A lower dividend return for a common stock should not ordinarily be considered as a strong offsetting factor, since the dividend is usually adjusted to the earning power within a reasonable time.

Although overconservative dividend policies are sometimes followed for a considerable period (a subject referred to in Chap. 29), there is a well-defined tendency even in these cases for the market price to reflect the earning power sooner or later.

Relative popularity and relative market activity are two elements not connected with intrinsic value that nevertheless exert a powerful and often a continuing effect upon the market quotation. The analyst must give these factors respectful heed, but his work would be stultified if he always favored the more active and the more popular issue.

The recommendation of an exchange of one security for another seems to involve a greater personal accountability on the part of the analyst than the selection of an issue for original purchase. The reason is that holders of securities for investment are loath to make changes, and thus they are particularly irritated if the subsequent market action makes the move appear to have been unwise. Speculative holders will naturally gage all advice by the test of market results—usually immediate results. Bearing these human-nature factors in mind, the analyst must avoid suggesting common-stock exchanges to speculators (except possibly if accompanied by an emphatic disclaimer of responsibility for subsequent market action), and he must hesitate to suggest such exchanges to holders for investment unless the statistical superiority of the issue recommended is quite impressive. As an arbitrary rule, we might say that there should be good reason to believe that by making the exchange the investor would be getting at least 50% more for his money.

Variations in Homogeneity Affect the Values of Comparative Analysis. The dependability of industrial comparisons will vary with the nature

Comparison of Continental Steel and Granite City Steel
(000 omitted, except those per share)

Item	Continental Steel	Granite City Steel
Market price of common, July 1938	17	17
1. Bonds at par	$1,202	$1,618
2. Preferred stock at market	2,450	
3. Common stock at market	3,410	6,494
4. Total capitalization	7,062	8,112
5. Ratio of common to total capitalization	48.3%	80.0%

	Average of 5 years ended 6/30/38	Year ended 6/30/38	Average of 5 years ended 6/30/38	Year ended 6/30/38
8. Gross sales	$15,049	$13,989	$8,715	$8,554
9. Depreciation	500	445	390	459
10. Net available for bond interest	704	559	336	287(d)
11. Bond interest	81	67	(Est.) 18	(Est.) 54
12. Preferred dividends	179	171		
13. Balance for common	444	321	318	341(d)
14. Margin of profit	4.7%	4.0%	3.9%	(def.)
15. % earned on total capitalization	10.0	7.9%	4.1%	(def.)
16. Interest charges earned	8.7 times	8.3 times	18.7 times	(def.)
17. Earned on common, per share	$2.29	$1.60	$1.20	$0.89(d)
18. Earned on common, % of market price	13.5	9.4	7.1	(d)
19. Ratio of gross to market value of common	441.5%	409.8%	134.3%	131.8%
Trend figures:				
23. Earned per share by years:				
Year ended June 30, 1938	$1.60		$0.89(d)	
Year ended June 30, 1937	3.83	1.31		
Year ended June 30, 1936	2.67		1.49	
Year ended June 30, 1935	1.69		1.45	
Year ended June 30, 1934	1.66		2.65	
Dividends:				
24. Dividend rate on common		$1.00		None
25. Dividend yield on common		5.9%		
Financial position (dates):		6/30/38		12/31/37
29. Total current assets		$6,467		$4,179
30. Total current liabilities		1,198		1,164
31. Net current assets		5,269		3,015
35. Net tangible assets for total capitalization		13,498		13,556

of the industry considered. The basic question, of course, is whether future developments are likely to affect all the companies in the group similarly or dissimilarly. If similarly, then substantial weight may be accorded to the relative performance in the past, as shown by the statistical exhibit. An industrial group of this type may be called "homogeneous." But, if the individual companies in the field are likely to respond quite variously to new conditions, then the relative showing must be regarded as a much less reliable guide. A group of this kind may be termed "heterogeneous."

With certain exceptions for traffic and geographical variations, *e.g.*, in particular, the Pocahontas soft-coal carriers, the railroads must be considered a highly homogeneous group. The same is true of the larger light, heat and power utilities. In the industrial field the best examples of homogeneous groups are afforded by the producers of raw materials and of other standardized products in which the trade name is a minor factor. These would include producers of sugar, coal, metals, steel products, cement, cotton print cloths, etc. The larger oil companies may be considered as fairly homogeneous; the smaller concerns are not well suited to comparison because they are subject to sudden important changes in production, reserves and relative price received. The larger baking, dairy and packing companies fall into fairly homogeneous groups. The same is true of the larger chain-store enterprises when compared with other units in the same subgroups, *e.g.*, grocery, five-and-ten-cent, restaurant, etc. Department stores are less homogeneous, but comparisons in this field are by no means far-fetched.

Makers of manufactured goods sold under advertised trade-marks must generally be regarded as belonging to heterogeneous groups. In these fields one concern frequently prospers at the expense of its competitors, so that the units in the industry do not improve or decline together. Among automobile manufactures, for example, there have been continuous and pronounced variations in relative standing. Producers of all the various classes of machinery and equipment are subject to somewhat the same conditions. This is true also of the proprietary drug manufacturers. Intermediate positions from this point of view are occupied by such groups as the larger makers of tires, of tobacco products, of shoes, wherein changes of relative position are not so frequent.[2]

---

[2] But significant changes do occur, of course. Note, for example, the phenomenal growth of Philip Morris, relative to its large competitors, the somewhat less spectacular development of

The analyst must be most cautious about drawing comparative conclusions from the statistical data when dealing with companies in a heterogeneous group. No doubt preference may properly be accorded in these fields to the companies making the best quantitative showing (if not offset by known qualitative factors)—for this basis of selection would seem sounder than any other—but the analyst and the investor should be fully aware that such superiority may prove evanescent. As a general rule, the less homogeneous the group the more attention must be paid to the qualitative factors in making comparisons.

More General Limitations on the Value of Comparative Analysis. It may be well once again to caution the student against being deluded by the mathematical exactitude of his comparative tables into believing that their indicated conclusions are equally exact. We have mentioned the need of considering qualitative factors and of allowing for lack of homogeneity. But beyond these points lie all the various obstacles to the success of the analyst that we presented in some detail in our first chapter. The technique of comparative analysis may lessen some of the hazards of his work, but it can never exempt him from the vicissitudes of the future or the stubborness of the stock market itself or the consequences of his own failure—often unavoidable—to learn all the important facts. He must expect to appear wrong often and to be wrong on occasion; but with intelligence and prudence his work should yield better over-all results than the guesses or the superficial judgments of the typical stock buyer.

General Shoe and the exceptional comparative showing of Lee Tire, in the three fields mentioned. All three of these were relatively small enterprises.

CHAPTER 50

Discrepancies Between Price and Value

OUR EXPOSITION of the technique of security analysis has included many different examples of overvaluation and undervaluation. Evidently the processes by which the securities market arrives at its appraisals are frequently illogical and erroneous. These processes, as we pointed out in our first chapter, are not automatic or mechanical but psychological, for they go on in the minds of people who buy or sell. The mistakes of the market are thus the mistakes of groups or masses of individuals. Most of them can be traced to one or more of three basic causes: exaggeration, oversimplification or neglect.

In this chapter and the next we shall attempt a concise review of the various aberrations of the securities market. We shall approach the subject from the standpoint of the practical activities of the analyst, seeking in each case to determine the extent to which it offers an opportunity for profitable action on his part. This inquiry will thus constitute an amplification of our early chapter on the scope and limitations of security analysis, drawing upon the material developed in the succeeding discussions, to which a number of references will be made.

General Procedure of the Analyst. Since we have emphasized that analysis will lead to a positive conclusion only in the exceptional case, it follows that many securities must be examined before one is found that has real possibilities for the analyst. By what practical means does he proceed to make his discoveries? Mainly by hard and systematic work. There are two broad methods that he may follow. The first consists of a series of comparative analyses by industrial groups along the lines described in the previous chapter. Such studies will give him a fair idea of the standard or usual characteristics of each group and also point out those companies which deviate widely from the modal exhibit. If, for example, he discovers that a certain steel common stock has been earning about twice as much on its market price as the industry as a whole, he has a clue to work on—or rather a suggestion to be pursued by dint of a thoroughgoing investigation of all the important qualitative and quantitative factors relating to the enterprise.

The same type of methodical inquiry may be applied to the field of bonds and preferred stocks. The wide area of receivership railroad bonds can best be explored by means of a comparative analysis of the showing of the bonds of roughly the same rank issued by, say, a dozen of the major carriers in trusteeship. Or a large number of public-utility preferred stocks could be listed according to: (1) their over-all dividend and interest coverage, (2) their stock-value ratio and (3) their price and yield. Such a simple grouping might indicate a few issues that either were well secured and returned more than the average or else were clearly selling too high in view of their inadequate statistical protection. And so on.

The second general method consists in scrutinizing corporate reports as they make their appearance and relating their showing to the market price of their bonds or stocks. These reports can be seen—in summary form, at least—in various daily papers; a more comprehensive presentation can be found in the daily corporation-report sheets of the financial services or weekly in the *Commercial and Financial Chronicle.* A quick glance at a hundred of such reports may reveal between five and ten that look interesting enough from the earnings or current-asset standpoint to warrant more intensive study.

Can Cyclical Swings of Prices Be Exploited? The best understood disparities between price and value are those which accompany the recurrent broad swings of the market through boom and depression. It is a mere truism that stocks sell too high in a bull market and too low in a bear market. For at bottom this is simply equivalent to saying that any upward or downward movement of prices must finally reach a limit, and since prices do not remain at such limits (or at any other level) permanently, it must turn out in retrospect that prices will have advanced or declined too far.

Can the analyst exploit successfully the repeated exaggerations of the general market? Experience suggests that a procedure somewhat like the following should turn out to be reasonably satisfactory:

1. Select a diversified list of leading common stocks, *e.g.*, those in the "Dow-Jones Industrial Average."

2. Determine an indicated "normal" value for this group by applying a suitable multiplier to average earnings. The multiplier might be equivalent to capitalizing the earnings at, say, twice the current interest rate on highest grade industrial bonds. The period for averaging earnings would ordinarily be seven to ten years, but exceptional conditions such as occurred in 1931–1933 might suggest a different method, e.g., basing the average on the period beginning in 1934, when operating in 1939 or later.

3. Make composite purchases of the list when the shares can be bought at a substantial discount from normal value, say, at 2/3 such value. Or purchases may be made on a scale downwards, beginning say, at 80% of normal value.

4. Sell out such purchases when a price is reached substantially above normal value, say, 1/3 higher, or from 20% to 50% higher on a scale basis.

This was the general scheme of operations developed by Roger Babson many years ago. It yielded quite satisfactory results prior to 1925. But—as we pointed out in Chap. 37—during the 1921–1933 cycle (measuring from low point to low point) it would have called for purchasing during 1921, selling out probably in 1926, thus requiring complete abstinence from the market during the great boom of 1927–1929, and repurchasing in 1931, to be followed by a severe shrinkage in market values. A program of this character would have made far too heavy demands upon human fortitude.

The behavior of the market since 1933 has offered difficulties of a different sort in applying these mechanical formulas—particularly in determining normal earnings from which to compute normal values. It is scarcely to be expected that an idea as basically simple as this one can be utilized with any high degree of accuracy in catching the broad market swings. But for those who realize its inherent limitations it may have considerable utility, for at least it is likely on the average to result in purchases at intrinsically attractive levels—which is more than half the battle in common-stock investment.

"Catching the Swings" on a Marginal Basis Impracticable. From the ordinary speculative standpoint, involving purchases on margin and short sales, this method of operation must be set down as impracticable. The outright owner can afford to buy too soon and to sell too soon. In fact he must expect to do both and to see the market decline farther after he buys and advance farther after he sells out. But the margin trader is necessarily concerned with immediate results; he swims with the tide, hoping to gage the exact moment when the tide will turn and to reverse his stroke the moment before. In this he rarely succeeds, so that his typical experience is temporary success ending in complete disaster. It is the essential character of the speculator that he buys because he thinks stocks are going up not because they are cheap, and conversely when he sells. Hence there is a fundamental cleavage of viewpoint between the speculator and the securities analyst, which militates strongly against any enduringly satisfactory association between them.

Bond prices tend undoubtedly to swing through cycles in somewhat the same way as stocks, and it is frequently suggested that bond investors follow the policy of selling their holdings near the top of these cycles and repurchasing them near the bottom. We are doubtful if this can be done with satisfactory results in the typical case. There are no well-defined standards as to when high-grade bond prices are cheap or dear corresponding to the earnings-ratio test for common stocks, and the operations have to be guided chiefly by a technique of gaging market moves that seems rather far removed from "investment." The loss of interest on funds between the time of sale and repurchase is a strong debit factor, and in our opinion the net advantage is not sufficient to warrant incurring the psychological dangers that inhere in any placing of emphasis by the investor upon market movements.

Opportunities in "Secondary" or Little-Known Issues. Returning to common stocks, although overvaluation or undervaluation of leading issues occurs only at certain points in the stock-market cycle, the large field of "nonrepresentative" or "secondary" issues is likely to yield instances of undervaluation at all times. When the market leaders are cheap, some of the less prominent common stocks are likely to be a good deal cheaper. During 1932–1933, for example, stocks such as Plymouth Cordage, Pepperell Manufacturing, American Laundry Machinery and many others, sold at unbelievably low prices in relation to their past records and current financial exhibits. It is probably a matter for individual preference whether the investor should purchase an outstanding issue like General Motors at about 50% of its conservative valuation or a less prominent stock like Pepperell at about 25% of such value.

The Impermanence of Leadership. The composition of the market-leader group has varied greatly from year to year, especially in view of the recent shift of attention from past performance to assumed prospects.

If we examine the list during the decline of 1937–1938, we shall find quite a number of once outstanding issues that sold at surprisingly low prices in relation to their statistical exhibits.

Example: A startling example of this sort is provided by Great Atlantic and Pacific Tea Company common, which in 1929 sold as high as 494 and in 1938 as low as 36. Salient data on this issue are as follows:

Year[1]	Sales (000 omitted)	Net (000 omitted)	Earned per share of common	Dividend paid on common	Price range of common
1938	$ 878,972	$15,834	$ 6.71	$4.00	72–36
1937	881,703	9,119	3.50	6.25	$117^1/_2$–$45^1/_4$
1936	907,371	17,085	7.31	7.00	$130^1/_2$–$110^1/_2$
1935	872,244	16,593	7.08	7.00	140 –121
1934	842,016	16,709	7.13	7.00	150–122
1933	819,617	20,478	8.94	7.00	$181^1/_2$–115
1932	863,048	22,733	10.02	7.00	168–$103^1/_2$
1931	1,008,325	29,793	13.40	6.50	260–130
1930	1,065,807	30,743	13.86	5.25	260–155
1929	1,053,693	26,220	11.77	4.50	494–162

[1] Year ended following Jan. 31, except price range.

The balance sheet of January 31, 1938, showed cash assets of 85 millions and net current assets of 134 millions. At the 1938 low prices, the preferred and common together were selling for 126 millions. Here, then, was a company whose spectacular growth was one of the great romances of American business, a company that was without doubt the largest retail enterprise in America and perhaps in the world, that had an uninterrupted record of earnings and dividends for many years—and yet was selling for less than its net current assets alone. Thus one of the outstanding businesses of the country was considered by Wall Street in 1938 to be worth less as a going concern than if it were liquidated. Why? First, because of chain-store tax threats; second, because of a recent decline in earnings; and, third, because the general market was depressed.

We doubt that a better illustration can be found of the real nature of the stock market, which does not aim to evaluate businesses with any exactitude but rather to express its likes and dislikes, its hopes and fears, in the form of daily changing quotations. There is indeed enough sound sense and selective judgment in the market's activities to create on most occasions some degree of correspondence between market price and ascertainable or intrinsic value. In particular, as was pointed out in Chap. 4, when we are dealing with something as elusive and nonmathematical as the evaluation of future prospects, we are generally led to accept the market's verdict as better than anything that the analyst can arrive at. But, on enough occasions to keep the analyst busy, the emotions of the stock market carry it in either direction beyond the limits of sound judgment.

Opportunities in Normal Markets. During the intermediate period, when average prices show no definite signs of being either too low or too high, common stocks may usually be found that seem definitely undervalued on a statistical basis. These generally fall into two classes: (1) Those showing high current and average earnings in relation to market price and (2) those making a reasonably satisfactory exhibit of earnings and selling at a low price in relation to net-current-asset value. Obviously, such companies will not be large and well known, or else the trend of

Group A. Common Stocks Selling at the End of 1938 or 1939 at Less than
7 Times Past Year's Earnings and also at Less than Net Current Asset Value

Company	Year taken	Price Dec. 31	Earnings for year per share	Average earnings 1934–1938 or 1934–1939 per share	Net current asset value per share	Net tangible asset value per share
J. D. Adams Mfg.	1938	8	$1.15	$1.20	$12.07	$14.38
American Seating	1939	10¹/₄	1.82	1.75	11.42	23.95
Bunte Bros.	1938	10	2.10	2.14	12.84	27.83
Grand Union	1939	10	1.80	1.25	13.60†	20.00†
International Silver	1939	26³/₄	4.98	*def* 0.10	39.67	97.50
I. B. Kleinert	1938	8¹/₂	1.27	0.80	11.04	16.90
New Idea	1939	12¹/₈	2.18	1.78	13.44	16.02
*N. Y. Merchandise	1939	7³/₄	1.44	1.44	11.66	14.05
*Pacific Commercial	1938	11¹/₂	2.31	2.77	24.18	27.74
Seton Leather	1938	6¹/₄	1.38	0.94	8.38	11.27

* These stocks belong also in Group *B*.
† Partly estimated.

earnings will not have been encouraging. In the appended table are given a number of companies falling in each group as of the end of 1938 or 1939, at which times the market level for industrial stocks did not appear to be especially high or especially low.

Group *B*. Common Stocks Selling at the End of 1938 or 1939 at Two-Thirds, or Less, of Net Current Asset Value and also at Less than 12 Times Either Past Year's or Average Earnings

Company	Year taken	Price Dec. 31	Earnings for year per share	Average earnings 1934–1938 or 1934–1939 per share	Net current asset value per share	Net tangible asset value per share
Butler Bros.	1939	7	$0.83	$0.27	$12.75	$19.59
Ely & Walker	1939	18	2.30	1.83	41.60	48.51
Gilchrist	1939	4³/₄	0.70*	0.85*	13.85	17.39
Hale Bros. Stores	1939	14	1.81	2.00	22.13	28.14
Intertype	1939	8³/₄	0.55	0.82	19.77	22.35
Lee & Cady	1939	6	0.77	0.73	11.35	12.61
H. D. Lee Mercantile	1938	14	0.87	1.35	25.00	31.56
Manhattan Shirt	1938	11¹/₂	0.73	1.06	19.36	23.62
Reliance Mfg.	1939	12	1.69	0.94	18.97	22.21
S. Stroock	1939	9¹/₄	1.21	1.39	14.90	26.61

* Years ended following Jan 31.

It is not difficult for the assiduous analyst to find interesting statistical exhibits such as those presented in our table. Much more difficult is the task of determining whether or not the qualitative factors will justify following the quantitative indications—in other words, whether or not the investor may have sufficient confidence in the company's future to consider its shares a real bargain at the apparently subnormal price.

On this question the weight of financial opinion appears inclined to a generally pessimistic conclusion. The investment trusts, with all their facilities for discovering opportunities of this type, have paid little attention to them—partly, it is true, because they are difficult to buy and sell in the large quantities that the trusts prefer, but also because of their conviction that however good the statistical exhibit of a secondary company may be it is not likely to prove a profitable purchase *unless there is specific ground for optimism regarding its future.*

The main drawback of a typical smaller sized company is its vulnerability to a sudden and perhaps permanent loss of its earning power. Undoubtedly such adverse developments occur in a larger proportion of cases in this group than among the larger enterprises. As an offset to this we have the fact that the successful small company can multiply its value far more impressively than those which are already of enormous size. For example, the growth of Philip Morris, Inc., in market value from 5 millions in 1934 to 90 millions in 1939, accompanying a 1,200% increase in net earnings, would have been quite inconceivable in the case of American Tobacco. Similarly, the growth of Pepsi-Cola has far outstripped in percentage that of Coca-Cola; the same is true of General Shoe vs. International Shoe; etc.

But most students will try to locate the potential Philip Morris opportunities, by gaging future possibilities with greater or less care, and will then buy their shares even at a fairly high price—rather than make their commitments in a diversified group of "bargain issues" with only ordinary prospects. Our own experience leads us to favor the latter technique, although we cannot guarantee brilliant results therefrom under present-day conditions. Yet judging from observations made over a number of years, it would seem that investment in apparently undervalued common stocks can be carried on with a very fair degree of over-all success, provided average alertness and good judgment are used in passing on the future-prospect question—and provided also that commitments are avoided at times when the general market is statistically much too high. Two older examples of this type of opportunity are given here, to afford the reader some notion of former stock markets.

Florence Stove Common		Firestone Tire & Rubber Common	
Price in Jan. 1935	.35	Price in Nov. 1925	120
Dividend	$2	Dividend	$6
Earned per share:		Earned per share year ended Oct.:	
1934	$7.93	1925	32.57*
1933	7.98	1924	16.92
1932	3.33	1923	14.06
1931	2.27	1922	17.08

* Earnings before contingency reserves were $40.95 per share.

In these cases the market price had failed to reflect adequately the indicated earning power.

Market Behavior of Standard and Nonstandard Issues. A close study of the market action of common stocks suggests the following further general observations:

1. Standard or leading issues almost always respond rapidly to changes in their reported profits—so much so that they tend regularly to exaggerate marketwise the significance of year-to-year fluctuations in earnings.

2. The action of the less familiar issues depends largely upon what attitude is taken towards them by professional market operators. If interest is lacking, the price may lag far behind the statistical showing. If interest is attracted to the issue, either manipulatively or more legitimately, the opposite result can readily be attained, and the price will respond in extreme fashion to changes in the company's exhibit.

Examples of Behavior of Nonstandard Issues. The following two examples will illustrate this diversity of behavior of nonrepresentative common stocks.

Butte and Superior Copper (Actually Zinc) Company Common

Period	Earnings per share	Dividend per share	Price range
Year, 1914	$ 5.21	$ 2.25	44–24
1st quarter, 1915	4.27	0.75	50–36
2d quarter, 1915	7.73	3.25	80–45
3d quarter, 1915	10.13	5.75	73–57
4th quarter, 1915	11.34	8.25	75–59
Year 1915	$33.47	$18.00	80–36
Year 1916	30.58	34.00	105–42

These were extraordinarily large earnings and dividends. Even allowing for the fact that they were due to wartime prices for zinc, the market price showed none the less a striking disregard of the company's spectacular exhibit. The reason was lack of general interest or of individual market sponsorship.

Contrast the foregoing with the appended showing of the common stock of Mullins Body (later Mullins Manufacturing) Corporation.

Between 1924 and 1926 we note the characteristic market swings of a low-priced "secondary" common-stock issue. At the beginning of 1927 the shares were undoubtedly attractive, speculatively, at about 10, for the price was low in relation to the earnings of the three years previously. A substantial, but by no means spectacular, rise in profits during 1927–1928 resulted in a typical stock-market exploitation. The price advanced from 10 in 1927 to 95 in 1928 and fell back again to 10 in 1929.

Year	Earned per share	Dividend	Price range
1924	$1.91	None	18–9
1925	2.47	None	22–13
1926	1.97	None	20–8
1927	5.13	None	79–10
1928	6.53	None	95–69
1929	2.67	None	82–10

A contrast of another kind is afforded by the behavior of the aircraft-manufacturing stocks in 1938–1939, as compared with that of war beneficiaries in 1915–1918. The two following examples will illustrate the relationship between market price in 1938 and 1939 and actual performance at the time.

	Boeing Airplane Co.	Glenn L. Martin Co.
Date	December 1938	November 1939
Market value of company	$25,270,000	$49,413,000
	(722,000 sh. @ 35)	(1,092,000 sh. @ 45$^{1}/_4$)
Sales 1938	2,006,000	12,417,000
Net 1938	555,000(d)	2,349,000
Sales, 9 months 1939	6,566,000	8,506,000
Net, 9 months 1939	2,606,000(d)	1,514,000
Tangible assets, Sept. 30, 1939	4,527,000	15,200,000

In these cases the market was evidently capitalizing the as yet unrealized profits from war orders as if they supplied a *permanent* basis of future earnings. The contrast between the Butte and Superior price-earnings ratio in 1915–1916 and that of these aircraft concerns in 1938–1939 is very striking.

Relationship of the Analyst to Such Situations. The analyst can deal intelligently and fairly successfully with situations such as Wright Aeronautical, Bangor and Aroostook, Firestone and Butte and Superior at the periods referred to. He could even have formed a worth-while opinion about Mullins early in 1927. But once this issue fell into market operators' hands it passed beyond the pale of analytical judgment. As far as Wall Street was concerned, Mullins had ceased to be a business and had become a symbol on the ticker tape. To buy it or to sell it was equally hazardous; the analyst could warn of the hazard, but he could have no idea of the limits of its rise or fall. (As it happened, however, the company issued a convertible preferred stock in 1928 which made possible a profitable hedging operation, consisting of the purchase of the preferred and the sale of the common.) Similarly with the airplane issues in 1939, the analyst could go no further than to indicate the obvious hazard that lay in treating as permanent a source of business that the whole world must necessarily hope was essentially temporary.

When the general market appears dangerously high to the analyst, he must be hesitant about recommending unfamiliar common stocks, even though they may seem to be of the bargain type. A severe decline in the general market will affect all stock prices adversely, and the less active issues may prove especially vulnerable to the effects of necessitous selling.

Market Exaggerations Due to Factors Other than Changes in Earnings: *Dividend Changes.* The inveterate tendency of the stock market to exaggerate extends to factors other than changes in earnings. Overemphasis is laid upon such matters as dividend changes, stock split-ups, mergers and segregations. An increase in the cash dividend is a favorable development, but it is absurd to add $20 to the price of a stock just because the dividend rate is advanced from $5 to $6 annually. The buyer at the higher price is paying out in advance all the additional dividends that he will receive at the new rate *over the next 20 years*. The excited responses often made to stock dividends are even more illogical, since they are in essence nothing more than pieces of paper. The same is true of split-ups, which create more shares but give the stockholder nothing he did not have before—except the minor advantage of a possibly broader market due to the lower price level.[1]

Mergers and Segregations. Wall Street becomes easily enthusiastic over mergers and just as ebullient over segregations, which are the exact opposite. Putting two and two together frequently produces five in the stock market, and this five may later be split up into three and three. Such inductive studies as have been made of the results following mergers seem to cast considerable doubt upon the efficacy of consolidation as an aid to earning power.[2] There is also reason to believe that the personal element in corporate management often stands in the way of really advantageous consolidations and that those which are consummated are due sometimes to knowledge by those in control of unfavorable conditions ahead.

The exaggerated response made by the stock market to developments that seem relatively unimportant in themselves is readily explained in terms of the psychology of the speculator. He wants "action," first of all; and he is willing to contribute to this action if he can be given any pretext for bullish excitement. (Whether through hypocrisy or self-deception, brokerage-house customers generally refuse to admit they are merely gambling with ticker quotations and insist upon some ostensible "reason" for their purchases.) Stock dividends and other "favorable developments" of this character supply the desired pretexts, and they have been exploited by the professional market operators, sometimes with the connivance of the corporate officials. The whole thing would be childish if it were not so vicious. The securities analyst should understand how these absurdities of Wall Street come into being, but he would do well to avoid any form of contact with them.

---

[1] In the Atlas Tack manipulation of 1933 an effort was made to attract public buying by promising a split-up of the stock, 3 shares for 1. Obviously, such a move could make no real difference of any kind in the case of an issue selling in the 30s. The circumstances surrounding the rise of Atlas Tack from $1^1/2$ to $34^3/4$ in 1933 and its precipitous fall to 10 are worth studying as a perfect example of the manipulative pattern. It is illuminating to compare the price-earnings and the price-assets relationships of the same stock prior to 1929.

[2] See, for example, Arthur S. Dewing, "A Statistical Test of the Success of Consolidations," published in *Quarterly Journal of Economics*, November 1921 and reprinted in his *Financial Policy of Corporations*, pp. 885–898, New York, 1926. But see Henry R. Seager and Charles A. Gullick, *Trust and Corporation Problems*, pp. 659–661, New York, 1929, and *Report of the Committee on Recent Economic Changes*, Vol. I, pp. 194 *ff.*, New York, 1929.

Litigation. The tendency of Wall Street to go to extremes is illustrated in the opposite direction by its tremendous dislike of litigation. A lawsuit of any significance casts a damper on the securities affected, and the extent of the decline may be out of all proportion to the merits of the case. Developments of this kind may offer real opportunities to the analyst, though of course they are of a specialized nature. The aspect of broadest importance is that of receivership. Since the undervaluations resulting therefrom are almost always confined to bond issues, we shall discuss this subject later in the chapter in connection with senior securities.

Example: A rather striking example of the effect of litigation on common-stock values is afforded by the Reading Company case. In 1913 the United States government brought suit to compel separation of the company's railroad and coal properties. The stock market, having its own ideas of consistency, considered this move as a dangerous attack on Reading, despite the fact that the segregation would in itself ordinarily be considered as "bullish." A plan was later agreed upon (in 1921) under which the coal subsidiary's stock was in effect to be distributed pro rata among the Reading Company's common and preferred shareholders. This was hailed in turn as a favorable development, although in fact it constituted a victory for the government against the company.

Some common stockholders, however, objected to the participation of the preferred stock in the coal company "rights." Suit was brought to restrict these rights to the common stock. Amusingly, but not surprisingly, the effect of this move was to depress the price of Reading common. In logic, the common should have advanced, since, if the suit were successful, there would be more value for the junior shares, and, if it failed (as it did), there would be no less value than before. But the stock market reasoned merely that here was some new litigation and hence Reading common should be "let alone."

Situations involving litigation frequently permit the analyst to pursue to advantage his quantitative approach in contrast with the qualitative attitude of security holders in general. Assume that the assets of a bankrupt concern have been turned into cash and there is available for distribution to its bondholders the sum of, say, 50% net. But there is a suit pending, brought by others, to collect a good part of this money. It may be that the action is so far-fetched as to be almost absurd; it may be that it has been defeated in the lower courts, and even on appeal, and that it has now but a microscopic chance to be heard by the United States Supreme Court. Nevertheless, the mere pendency of this litigation will severely reduce the market value of the bonds. Under the conditions named, they are likely to sell as low as 35 instead of 50 cents on the dollar. The anomaly here is that a remote claim, which the plaintiff can regard as having scarcely any real value to him, is made the equivalent in the market to a heavy liability on the part of the defendant. We thus have a mathematically demonstrable case of undervaluations, and, taking these as a class, they lend themselves exceedingly well to exploitation by the securities analyst.

Examples: Island Oil and Transport 8% Notes. In June 1933 these notes were selling at 18. The receiver held a cash fund equivalent to about 45% on the issue, from which were deductible certain fees and allowances, indicating a net distributable balance of about 30 for the notes. The distribution was being delayed by a suit for damages that had been repeatedly unsuccessful in its various legal stages and was now approaching final determination. This suit was exerting an adverse effect upon the market value of the notes out of all proportion to its merits, a statement that is demonstrable from the fact that the litigation could have been settled by payment of a relatively small amount. After the earlier decisions were finally sustained by the higher courts, the noteholders received a distribution of $290 per $1,000 in April 1934. A small additional distribution was indicated.[3]

A similar situation arose in the case of United Shipyards Corporation stock after ratification of the sale of its properties to Bethlehem Steel Company in 1938. Dissenting holders brought suit to set the sale aside on the ground that the price was grossly inadequate. The effect of this litigation was to hold down the price of the Class *B* common to $1^1/4$ in January 1939, as against a realizable value of between $2^1/2$ to 3 if the sale was upheld. Obviously, if the suit had any merit, the stock should have been worth more rather than less than $2^1/2$; alternatively, if it had no merit, as seemed clear, then the shares were clearly worth twice their sell-

---

[3] A very similar situation existed in 1938 in connection with the various bond issues of National Bondholders Corporation, which was engaged in liquidating various properties and claims. These securities were selling at considerably less than the amount realizable for them in liquidation, chiefly because of certain suits involving a substantial cash fund. As in the Island Oil example, this litigation was in the last stages of appeal, and the decisions theretofore had all been favorable to the bondholders. Following the final decision the value of a typical issue advanced from 26 bid in 1938 to the equivalent of 41 bid in 1939.

ing price. (A similar disparity existed in connection with the price of the Class *A* stock.)

Undervalued Investment Issues. Undervalued bonds and preferred stocks of investment caliber may be discovered in any period by means of assiduous search. In many cases the low price of a bond or preferred stock is due to a poor market, which in turn results from the small size of the issue, but this very small size may make for greater inherent security. The Electric Refrigeration Building Corporation 6s, due 1936, described in Chap. 26, are a good example of this paradox.

At times some specific development greatly strengthens the position of a senior issue, but the price is slow to reflect this improvement, and thus a bargain situation is created. These developments relate usually to the capitalization structure or to corporate relationships. Several examples will illustrate our point.

Examples: In 1923 Youngstown Sheet and Tube Company purchased the properties of Steel and Tube Company of America and assumed liability for the latter's General Mortgage 7s, due 1951. Youngstown sold a 6% debenture issue at 99 to supply funds for this purchase. The following price relationship obtained at the time:

Company	Price	Yield, %
Youngstown Sheet and Tube Debenture 6s	99	6.02
Steel and Tube General 7s	102	6.85

The market failed to realize the altered status of the Steel and Tube bonds, and thus they sold illogically at a higher yield than the unsecured issue of the same obligor company. This presented a clear-cut opportunity to the analyst to recommend a purchase or an exchange.

In 1922 the City of Detroit purchased the urban lines of Detroit United Railway Company and agreed to pay therefor sums sufficient to retire the Detroit United Railway First 4^1/2s, due 1932. Unusually strong protective provisions were inserted in the purchase contract which practically, if not technically, made the City of Detroit liable for the bonds. But, after the deal was consummated, the bonds sold at 82, yielding more than 7%. The bond market failed to recognize their true status as virtual obligations of the City of Detroit.

In 1924 Congoleum Company had outstanding $1,800,000 of 7% preferred stock junior to $2,890,000 of bonds and followed by 960,000 shares of common stock having an average market value of some $48,000,000. In October of that year the company issued 681,000 additional shares of common for the business of the Nairn Linoleum Company, a large unit in the same field, with $15,000,000 of tangible assets. The enormous equity thus created for the small senior issues made them safe beyond question, but the price of the preferred stock remained under par.

In 1927 Electric Refrigeration Corporation (now Kelvinator Corporation) sold 373,000 shares of common stock for $6,600,000, making a total of 1,000,000 shares of common stock, with average market value of about $21,000,000, coming behind only $2,880,000 of 6% notes, due in 1936. The notes sold at 74, however, to yield 11%. The low price was due to a large operating deficit incurred in 1927, but the market failed to take into account the fact that the receipt of a much greater amount of new cash from the sale of additional stock had established a very strong backing for the small note issue.

These four senior issues have all been paid off at par or higher. (The Congoleum-Nairn Preferred was called for payment at 107 in 1934.) Examples of this kind are convenient for the authors since they do not involve the risk of some later mischance casting doubt upon their judgment. To avoid loading the dice too heavily in our favor, we add another illustration which is current as this chapter is written.

A Current Example. Choctaw and Memphis Railroad Company First 5s, due 1949, were selling in 1939 at about 35, carrying more than 5 years' unpaid interest. They were a first lien on underlying mileage of the Chicago, Rock Island and Pacific System. The Rock Island had been reporting poor earnings since 1930, and all its obligations were in default. However, a segregation of the 1937 earnings by mortgage divisions showed that the Choctaw and Memphis mileage was very profitable and that its interest charges had been covered 2.6 times in that year even though the company had earned only $2,700,000 toward total interest of $14,080,000. Furthermore, the several reorganization plans presented up to 1939, including that of the I.C.C. examiner, had all provided for principal and back interest on this issue in full, although virtually the entire remaining bond structure was to be drastically cut down, and total interest charges were to be reduced to less than $2,500,000 annually.

Assuming, as seemed inevitable, that the company was to be reorganized along the lines proposed, it was clear that these Choctaw and Memphis bonds would enjoy a very strong position, whether they were to be left undisturbed with their lien on a valuable mileage and their back interest paid off, or were to be given par for par in a new, small first mortgage on the entire system. This conclusion would be inescapable unless it were true that a railroad with minimum gross earnings of 65 millions could not be counted on to meet charges of $2^{1}/_{2}$ millions annually—less than *one-fifth* its former burden.

Thus all the quantitative factors would seem to indicate strongly that the Choctaw and Memphis 5s were greatly undervalued at 35 and that *once the recapitalization was completed* the entrenched position of this issue should become manifest.[4]

Price-Value Discrepancies in Receiverships. In Chap. 18, dealing with reorganization procedure, we gave two diverse examples of disparities arising under a receivership: the Fisk Rubber case, in which the obligations sold at a ridiculously low price compared with the current assets available for them; and the Studebaker case, in which the price of the 6% notes was clearly out of line with that of the stock. A general statement may fairly be made that in cases where substantial values are ultimately realized out of a receivership, the senior securities will be found to have sold at much too low a price. This characteristic has a twofold consequence. It has previously led us to advise strongly against buying at investment levels *any* securities of a company that is likely to fall into financial difficulties; it now leads us to suggest that *after* these difficulties have arisen they may produce attractive analytical opportunities.

This will be true not only of issues so strongly entrenched as to come through reorganization unscathed (*e.g.*, Brooklyn Union Elevated 5s, as described in Chap. 2) but also of senior securities which are "scaled down" or otherwise affected in a readjustment plan. It seems to hold

---

[4] See Appendix Note 67 for text of the material in the 1934 edition relating to the Fox Film 6% Notes, due 1936, which in 1933 were selling at 75 to yield 20% to maturity.

Further Example: In 1938 Tung Sol Lamp Company 4% Notes, due 1941, were selling at 50. The very small size of this issue, in relation to the company's resources and earnings, made payment apparently certain. (In fact they were called in 1939 in advance of maturity.)

most consistently in cases where liquidation or a sale to outside interests results ultimately in a cash distribution or its equivalent.

Examples: Three typical examples of such a consummation are given herewith.

1. *Ontario Power Service Corporation First 5¹/2s, Due 1950.* This issue defaulted interest payment on July 1, 1932. About this time the bonds sold as low as 21. The Hydro-Electric Commission of Ontario purchased the property soon afterwards, on a basis that gave $900 of new debentures, fully guaranteed by the Province of Ontario, for each $1,000 Ontario Power Service bond. The new debentures were quoted at 90 in December 1933, equivalent to 81 for the old bonds. The small number of bondholders not making the exchange received 70% in cash.

2. *Amalgamated Laundries, Inc., 6¹/2s, Due 1936.* Receivers were appointed in February 1932. The bonds were quoted at 4 in April 1932. In June 1932 the properties were sold to outside interests, and liquidating dividends of 12¹/2% and 2% were paid in August 1932 and March 1933. In December 1933 the bonds were still quoted at 4, indicating expectation of at least that amount in further distributions.

3. *Fisk Rubber Company First 8s and Debenture 5¹/2s, Due 1941 and 1931.* Information regarding these issues was given in Chap. 18. Receivership was announced in January 1931. In 1932 the 8s and 5¹/2s sold as low as 16 and 10¹/2 respectively. In 1933 a reorganization was effected, which distributed 40% in cash on the 8s and 37% on the 5¹/2s, together with securities of two successor companies. The aggregate values of the cash and the new securities at the close of 1933 came close to 100% for the 8% bonds and 70% for the debenture 5¹/2s.

Price Patterns Produced by Insolvency. Certain price patterns are likely to be followed during receivership or bankruptcy proceedings, especially if they are protracted. In the first place, there is often a tendency for the stock issues to sell too high, not only in relation to the price of the bond issues but also absolutely, *i.e.*, in relation to their probable ultimate value. This is due to the incidence of speculative interest, which is attracted by a seemingly low price range. In the case of senior issues, popular interest steadily decreases, and the price tends to decline accordingly, as the proceedings wear on. Consequently, the lowest levels are likely to be reached a short time before a reorganization plan is ready to be announced.

A profitable field of analytical activity should be found therefore in keeping in close touch with such situations, endeavoring to discover securities that appear to be selling far under their intrinsic value and to determine approximately the best time for making a commitment in them. But in these, as in all analytical situations, we must warn against an endeavor to gage too nicely the proper time to buy. An essential characteristic of security analysis, as we understand it, is that the time factor is a subordinate consideration. Hence our use of the qualifying word "approximately," which is intended to allow a leeway of several months and sometimes even longer, in judging the "right time" to enter upon the operation.

Opportunities in Railroad Trusteeships. In the years following 1932 a large part of the country's railroad mileage went into the hands of trustees. At the close of 1938 a total of 111 railway companies operating 78,016 miles (31% of the total railway mileage in the United States) were in the hands of receivers or trustees. This is the greatest mileage ever in the hands of the courts at any one time. Reorganization in every case has been long delayed, owing on the one hand to the complicated capital structures to be dealt with and on the other to the uncertainty as to future normal earnings. As a result the price of a great many issues fell to extremely low levels—which would undoubtedly have presented excellent opportunities for the shrewd investor, had it not been that the earnings of the railroads as a whole continued for some years to make disappointing showings as compared with general business.

Viewing the situation about the end of 1939, it appeared that many of the first-mortgage liens on important mileage had fallen to lower levels than were warranted by anything but a most pessimistic view of the future of the carriers. Certainly, these issues were cheaper than the bonds and stocks of solvent roads, which sold for the most part at liberal prices in relation to their current exhibits and which in many cases would be in danger of insolvency if future conditions turned out as badly as the low price of trusteeships issues seemed to anticipate. The technique of analyzing issues of the latter group is covered in Chap. 12 and in Appendix Note 66.

CHAPTER 51

Discrepancies Between Price and Value *(Continued)*

THE PRACTICAL DISTINCTIONS drawn in our last chapter between leading and secondary common stocks have their counterpart in the field of senior securities as between seasoned and unseasoned issues. A seasoned issue may be defined as an issue of a company long and favorably known to the investment public. (The security itself may be of recent creation so long as the company has a high reputation among investors.) Seasoned and unseasoned issues tend at times to follow divergent patterns of conduct in the market, *viz.:*

1. The price of seasoned issues is often maintained despite a considerable weakening of their investment position.
2. Unseasoned issues are very sensitive to adverse developments of any nature. Hence they often fall to prices far lower than seem to be warranted by their statistical exhibit.

Price Inertia of Seasoned Issues. These opposite characteristics are due, in part at least, to the inertia and lack of penetration of the typical investor. He buys by reputation rather than by analysis and he holds tenaciously to what he has bought. Hence holders of long-established issues do not sell them readily, and even a small decline in price attracts buyers long familiar with the security.

Example: This trait of seasoned issues is well illustrated by the market history of the United States Rubber Company 8% Noncumulative Preferred. The issue received full dividends between 1905 and 1927. In each year of this period except 1924 there were investors who paid higher than par for this stock. Its popularity was based entirely upon its reputation and its dividend record, for the statistical exhibit of the company during most of the period was anything but impressive, even for an industrial bond, and hence ridiculously inadequate to justify the purchase of a noncumulative industrial preferred stock. Between the years 1922 and 1927, the following coverage was shown for interest charges and preferred dividends combined:

1922	1.20 times
1923	1.18 times
1924	1.32 times
1925	1.79 times
1926	1.00 times
1927	1.01 times

In 1928 the stock sold as high as 109. During that year the company sustained an enormous loss, and the preferred dividend was discontinued. Despite the miserable showing and the absence of any dividend, the issue actually sold at $92^1/_2$ in 1929. (In 1932 it sold at $3^1/_8$.)[1]

Vulnerability of Unseasoned Issues. Turning to unseasoned issues, we may point out that these belong almost entirely to the industrial field. The element of seasoning plays a very small part as between the various senior issues of the railroads; and in the public-utility group proper (*i.e.*, electric, manufactured gas, telephone and water companies) price variations will be found to follow the statistical showing fairly closely, without being strongly influenced by the factor of popularity or familiarity—except in the case of very small concerns.

Industrial financing has brought into the market a continuous stream of bond and preferred stock issues of companies new to the investment list. Investors have been persuaded to buy these offerings largely through the appeal of a yield moderately higher than the standard rate for seasoned securities of comparable grade. If the earning power is maintained uninterruptedly after issuance, the new security naturally proves a satisfactory commitment. But any adverse development will ordinarily induce a severe decline in the market price. This vulnerability of unseasoned issues gives rise to the practical conclusion that it is unwise to buy a *new* industrial bond or preferred stock for straight investment.

---

[1] A more recent example of the same kind is presented by Curtis Publishing 7% Preferred, which sold at 114 in 1936 and $109^1/_2$ in 1937, despite an exceedingly inadequate showing of earnings (and tangible assets). The high price of many railroad bonds in those years, notwithstanding their unsatisfactory earnings exhibit, illustrates this point more broadly.

Since such issues are unduly sensitive to unfavorable developments, it would seem that the price would often fall too low and in that case they would afford attractive opportunities to purchase. This is undoubtedly true, but there is great need of caution in endeavoring to take advantage of these disparities. In the first place, the disfavor accorded to unseasoned securities in the market is not merely a subjective matter, due to lack of knowledge. Seasoning is usually defined as an objective quality, arising from a demonstrated ability to weather business storms. Although this definition is not entirely accurate, there is enough truth in it to justify in good part the investor's preference for seasoned issues.

More important, perhaps, is the broad distinction of size and prominence that can be drawn between seasoned and unseasoned securities. The larger companies are generally the older companies, having senior issues long familiar to the public. Hence unseasoned bonds and preferred stocks are for the most part issues of concerns of secondary importance. But we have pointed out, in our discussion of industrial investments (Chap. 7), that in this field dominant size may reasonably be considered a most desirable trait. It follows, therefore, that in this respect unseasoned issues must suffer as a class from a not inconsiderable disadvantage.

Unseasoned Industrial Issues Rarely Deserve an Investment Rating. The logical and practical result is that unseasoned industrial issues can very rarely deserve an investment rating, and consequently they should only be bought on an admittedly speculative basis. This requires in turn that the market price be low enough to permit of a substantial rise; *e.g.*, the price must ordinarily be below 70.

It will be recalled that in our treatment of speculative senior issues (Chap. 26), we referred to the price sector of about 70 to 100 as the "range of subjective variation," in which an issue might properly sell because of a legitimate difference of opinion as to whether or not it was sound. It seems, however, that in the case of unseasoned industrial bonds or preferred stocks the analyst should not be attracted by a price level within this range, even though the quantitative showing be quite satisfactory. He should favor such issues only when they can be bought at a frankly speculative price.

Exception may be made to this rule when the statistical exhibit is extraordinarily strong, as perhaps in the case of the Fox Film 6% notes mentioned in the preceding chapter and described in Appendix Note 67. We doubt if such exceptions can prudently include any unseasoned industrial preferred stocks, because of the contractual weakness of such issues. (In the case of Congoleum preferred, described above, the company was of dominant size in its field, and the preferred stock was not so much "unseasoned" as it was inactive marketwise.)

Discrepancies in Comparative Prices. Comparisons may or may not be odious, but they hold a somewhat deceptive fascination for the analyst. It seems a much simpler process to decide that issue *A* is preferable to issue *B* than to determine that issue *A* is an attractive purchase in its own right. But in our chapter on comparative analysis we have alluded to the particular responsibility that attaches to the recommendation of security exchanges, and we have warned against an overready acceptance of a purely quantitative superiority. The future is often no respecter of statistical data. We may frame this caveat in another way by suggesting that the analyst should not urge a security exchange unless either (1) the issue to be bought is attractive, regarded by itself, or (2) there is a definite contractual relationship between the two issues in question. Let us illustrate consideration (1) by two examples of comparisons taken from our records.

Examples: I. Comparison Made in March 1932.

Item	Ward Baking First 6s, due 1937. Price 85$^{1}/_{4}$, yield 9.70%	Bethlehem Steel First & Ref. 5s, due 1942. Price 93, yield 5.90%
Total interest charges earned:		
1931	8.1 times	1.0 times
1930	8.2 times	4.3 times
1929	11.0 times	4.8 times
1928	11.2 times	2.7 times
1927	14.0 times	2.3 times
1926	14.5 times	2.6 times
1925	12.6 times	2.1 times
Seven-year average	11.4 times	2.8 times
Amount of bond issues	$ 4,546,000	$145,000,000*
Market value of stock issues (March '32 average)	12,200,000	116,000,000
Cash assets	3,438,000	50,300,000
Net working capital	3,494,000	116,300,000

* Including guaranteed stock.

In this comparison the Ward Baking issue made a far stronger statistical showing than the Bethlehem Steel bonds. Furthermore, it appeared sufficiently well protected to justify an investment rating, despite the high return. The qualitative factors, although not impressive, did not suggest any danger of collapse of the business. Hence the bonds could be recommended either as an original purchase or as an advantageous substitute for the Bethlehem Steel 5s.

II. Comparison Made in March 1929.

Item	Spear & Co. (Furniture Stores) 7% First Preferred. Price 77, yielding 9.09%	Republic Iron & Steel 7% Preferred. Price 112, yielding 6.25%
(Interest and) preferred dividends earned:		
1928	2.4 times	1.9 times
1927	4.0 times	1.5 times
1926	3.0 times	2.1 times
1925	2.5 times	1.7 times
1924	4.7 times	1.1 times
1923	6.5 times	2.5 times
1922	4.3 times	0.5 times
Seven-year average	3.9 times	1.6 times
Amount of bond issues	None	$32,700,000
Amount of (1st) preferred issue	$ 3,900,000	25,000,000
Market value of junior issues	3,200,000*	62,000,000
Net working capital	10,460,000	21,500,000

* Includes Second Preferred estimated at 50.

In this comparison the Spear and Company issue undoubtedly made a better statistical showing than Republic Iron and Steel Preferred. Taken by itself, however, its exhibit was not sufficiently impressive to carry conviction of investment merit, considering the type of business and the fact that we were dealing with a preferred stock. The price of the issue was not low enough to warrant recommendation on a fully speculative basis, *i.e.*, with prime emphasis on the opportunity for enhancement of principal. This meant in turn that it could not consistently be recommended in exchange for another issue, such as Republic Iron and Steel Preferred.

Comparison of Definitely Related Issues. When the issues examined are definitely related, a different situation obtains. An exchange can then be considered solely from the standpoint of the respective merits within the given situation; the responsibility for entering into or remaining in the situation need not be assumed by the analyst. In our previous chapters we have considered a number of cases in which relative prices were clearly out of line, permitting authoritative recommendations of exchange. These disparities arise from the frequent failure of the general market to recognize the effect of contractual provisions and often also from a tendency for speculative markets to concentrate attention on the common stocks and to neglect the senior securities. Examples of the first type were given in our discussion of price discrepancies involving guaranteed issues in Chap. 17. The price discrepancies between various Interborough Rapid Transit Company issues, discussed in Appendix Note 56, and between Brooklyn Union Elevated Railroad 5s and Brooklyn-Manhattan Transit Corporation 6s, referred to in Chap. 2, are other illustrations in this category.[2]

The illogical price relationships between a senior convertible issue and the common stock, discussed in Chap. 25, are examples of opportunities arising from the concentration of speculative interest on the more active junior shares. A different manifestation of the same general tendency is shown by the spread of 7 points existing in August 1933 between the price of American Water Works and Electric Company "free" common and the less active voting trust certificates for the same issue. Such phenomena invite not only direct exchanges but also hedging operations.

A similar comparison could be made in July 1933 between Southern Railway 5% Noncumulative Preferred, paying no dividend and selling at 49, and the Mobile and Ohio Stock Trust Certificates, which were an obligation of the same road, bearing a perpetual guaranty of a 4% dividend and selling concurrently at $39^3/4$. Even if the preferred dividend had been immediately resumed and continued without interruption, the yield

---

[2] The student is invited to consider the price relationships between Pierce Petroleum and Pierce Oil preferred and common in 1929; between Central States Electric Corporation $5^1/2$% bonds and North American Company common in 1934; between the common issues of Advance-Rumely Corporation and Allis-Chalmers Manufacturing Company in 1933; between Ventures, Ltd., and Falconbridge Nickel, and between Chesapeake Corporation and Chesapeake and Ohio Railway common stocks in 1939—as examples of disparities arising from ownership by one company of securities in another.

thereon would have been no higher than that obtainable from the senior fixed-interest obligation. (In 1939 Southern Railway Preferred, still paying no dividend, sold at 35 against a price of about 40 for the Mobile and Ohio 4% certificates. At these prices the advantage still appeared clearly on the side of the guaranteed issue.)

Other and Less Certain Discrepancies. In the foregoing examples the aberrations are mathematically demonstrable. There is a larger class of disparities between senior and junior securities that may not be proved quite so conclusively but are sufficiently certain for practical purposes. As an example of these, consider Colorado Industrial Company 5s, due August 1, 1934, guaranteed by Colorado Fuel and Iron Company, which in May 1933 sold at 43, while the Colorado Fuel and Iron 8% Preferred, paying no dividend, sold at 45. The bond issue had to be paid off in full within 14 months' time, or else the preferred stock was faced with the possibility of complete extinction through receivership. In order that the preferred stock might prove more valuable than the bonds bought at the same price, it would be necessary not only that the bonds be paid off at par in little over a year but that preferred dividends be resumed and back dividends discharged within that short time. This was almost, if not quite, inconceivable.

In comparing nonconvertible preferred stocks with common stocks of the same company, we find the same tendency for the latter to sell too high, relatively, when both issues are on a speculative basis. Comparisons of this kind can be safely drawn, however, only when the preferred stock bears cumulative dividends. (The reason for this restriction should be clear from our detailed discussion of the disabilities of noncumulative issues in Chap. 15.) A price of 10 for American and Foreign Power Company common when the $7 Cumulative Second Preferred was selling at 11 in April 1933 was clearly unwarranted. A similar remark may be made of the price of 21^1/$_2$ for Chicago Great Western Railroad Company common in February 1927, against 32^1/$_2$ for the 4% preferred stock on which dividends of $44 per share had accumulated.

It is true that if extraordinary prosperity should develop in situations of this kind, the common shares might eventually be worth substantially more than the preferred. But even if this should occur, the company is bound to pass through an intermediate period during which the improved situation permits it to resume preferred dividends and then to discharge the accumulations. Since such developments benefit the preferred stock directly, they are likely to establish (for a while at least) a market value for the senior issues far higher than that of the common stock. Hence, assuming any appreciable degree of improvement, a purchase of the preferred shares at the low levels should fare better than one made in the common stock.

Discrepancies Due to Special Supply and Demand Factors. The illogical relationships that we have been considering grow out of supply and demand conditions that are, in turn, the product of unthinking speculative purchases. Sometimes discrepancies are occasioned by special and temporary causes affecting either demand or supply.

Examples: In the illogical relationship between the prices of Interboro Rapid Transit Company 5s and 7s in 1933, the operations of a substantial sinking fund, which purchased the 5s and not the 7s, were undoubtedly instrumental in raising the price of the former disproportionately. An outstanding example of this kind is found in the market action of United States Liberty 4^1/$_4$s during the postwar readjustment of 1921–1922. Large amounts of these bonds had been bought during the war for patriotic reasons and financed by bank loans. A general desire to liquidate these loans later on induced a heavy volume of sales which drove the price down. This special selling pressure actually resulted in establishing a lower price basis for Liberty Bonds than for high-grade railroad issues, which were, of course, inferior in security and at a greater disadvantage also in the matter of taxation. Compare the following simultaneous prices in September 1920.

Issue	Price	Yield
United States Liberty Fourth 4^1/$_4$s, due 1938	84^1/$_2$	5.64%*
Union Pacific First 4s, due 1947	80	5.42%

* Not allowing for tax exemption.

This situation supplied an excellent opportunity for the securities analyst to advise exchanges from the old-line railroad issues into Liberty Bonds.

A less striking disparity appeared a little later between the price of these Liberty Bonds and of United States Victory 4^3/$_4$s, due 1923. This state of affairs is discussed in a circular, prepared by one of the authors and issued at that time, a copy of which is given in Appendix Note 68 as an additional example of "practical security analysis."

United States Savings Bonds Offer Similar Opportunity. For the investor of moderate means the disparity between United States government and corporate obligations has reappeared in recent years. The yield on United States Savings Bonds (available to any one individual to the extent of $10,000 principal amount each year) is 2.90% on the regular compound-interest basis of calculation and 3.33% on a simple-interest basis. This yield is definitely higher than that returned by best-rated public-utility and industrial issues.[3] In addition to their safety factor, which at present must clearly be set higher than that of any corporate issue, the United States Savings Bonds have the minor advantage of exemption from normal income tax and the major advantage of being redeemable *at the option of the holder* at any time, thus guaranteeing him against intermediate loss in market value.

---

[3] The average yields for such bonds for the first 3 months of 1940, carrying A1+ ratings of Standard Statistics Company, were only 2.62% and 2.44%, respectively.

CHAPTER 52

Market Analysis and Security Analysis

FORECASTING SECURITY PRICES is not properly a part of security analysis. However, the two activities are generally thought to be closely allied, and they are frequently carried on by the same individuals and organizations. Endeavors to predict the course of prices have a variety of objectives and a still greater variety of techniques. Most emphasis is laid in Wall Street upon the science, or art, or pastime, of prophesying the immediate action of the "general market," which is fairly represented by the various averages used in the financial press. Some of the services or experts confine their aim to predicting the longer term trend of the market, purporting to ignore day-to-day fluctuations and to consider the broader "swings" covering a period of, say, several months. A great deal of attention is given also to prophesying the market action of individual issues, as distinct from the market as a whole.

Market Analysis as a Substitute for or Adjunct to Security Analysis. Assuming that these activities are carried on with sufficient seriousness to represent more than mere guesses, we may refer to all or any of them by the designation of "market analysis." In this chapter we wish to consider the extent to which market analysis may seriously be considered as a substitute for or a supplement to security analysis. The question is important. If, as many believe, one can dependably foretell the movements of stock prices without any reference to the underlying values, then it would be sensible to confine security analysis to the selection of fixed-value investments only. For, when it comes to the common-stock type of issue, it would manifestly be more profitable to master the technique of determining when to buy or sell, or of selecting the issues that are going to have the greatest or quickest advance, than to devote painstaking efforts to forming conclusions about intrinsic value. Many other people believe that the best results can be obtained by an analysis of the market position of a stock in conjunction with an analysis of its intrinsic value. If this is so, the securities analyst who ventures outside the fixed-value field must qualify as a market analyst as well and be prepared to view each situation from both standpoints at the same time.

It is not within our province to attempt a detailed criticism of the theories and the technique underlying all the different methods of market analysis. We shall confine ourselves to considering the broader lines of reasoning that are involved in the major premises of price forecasting. Even with this sketchy treatment it should be possible to reach some useful conclusions on the perplexing question of the relationship between market analysis and security analysis.

Two Kinds of Market Analysis. A distinction may be made between two kinds of market analysis. The first finds the material for its predictions exclusively in the past action of the stock market. The second considers all sorts of economic factors, *e.g.*, business conditions, general and specific; money rates; the political outlook. (The market's behavior is itself only one of these numerous elements of study.) The underlying theory of the first approach may be summed up in the declaration that "the market is its own best forecaster." The behavior of the market is generally studied by means of charts on which are plotted the movements of individual stocks or of "averages." Those who devote themselves primarily to a study of these price movements are known as "chartists," and their procedure is often called "chart reading."

But it must be pointed out that much present-day market analysis represents a combination of the two kinds described, in the sense that the market's action alone constitutes the predominant but not the exclusive field of study. General economic indications play a subordinate but still significant role. Considerable latitude is therefore left for individual judgment, not only in interpreting the technical indications of the market's action but also in reconciling such indications with outside factors. The "Dow theory," however, which is the best known method of market analysis, limits itself essentially to a study of the market's behavior. Hence we feel justified in dealing separately with chart reading as applied exclusively to stock prices.

Implication of the First Type of Market Analysis. It must be recognized that the vogue of such "technical study" has increased immensely during the past fifteen years. Whereas security analysis suffered a distinct loss of prestige beginning about 1927—from which it has not entirely recovered—chart reading apparently increased the number of its followers even during the long depression and in the years thereafter. Many sceptics, it is true, are inclined to dismiss the whole procedure as akin to astrology or necromancy, but the sheer weight of its importance in Wall Street requires that its pretensions be examined with some degree of care. In order to confine our discussion within the framework of logical reasoning, we shall purposely omit even a condensed summary of the main tenets of chart reading.[1] We wish to consider only the implications of the general idea that a study confined to past price movements can be availed of profitably to foretell the movements of the future.

Such consideration, we believe, should lead to the following conclusions:

1. Chart reading cannot possibly be a science.
2. It has not proved itself in the past to be a dependable method of making profits in the stock market.
3. Its theoretical basis rests upon faulty logic or else upon mere assertion.
4. Its vogue is due to certain advantages it possesses over haphazard speculation, but these advantages tend to diminish as the number of chart students increases.

1. *Chart Reading Not a Science and Its Practice Cannot Be Continuously Successful.* That chart reading cannot be a science is clearly demonstrable. If it were a science, its conclusions would be as a rule dependable. In that case everybody could predict tomorrow's or next week's price changes, and hence everyone could make money continuously by buying and selling at the right time. This is patently impossible. A moment's thought will show that there can be no such thing as a scientific prediction of economic events under human control. The very "dependability" of such a prediction will cause human actions that will invalidate it. Hence thoughtful chartists admit that continued success is dependent upon keeping the successful method known to only a few people.

---

[1] For detailed statements concerning the theory and practice of chart reading the student is referred to: R. W. Shabacker, *Stock Market Profits*, B. C. Forbes, New York, 1934; Robert Rhea, "The Dow Theory," *passim, Barron's*, New York, 1932; H. M. Gartley, "Analyzing the Stock Market," a series of articles in *Barron's* beginning with the issue of Sept. 19, 1932 and ending with the issue of Dec. 5, 1932. See Appendix Note 69 for a brief statement of the main tenets of the Dow theory.

2. Because of this fact it follows that there is no generally known method of chart reading that has been continuously successful for a long period of time.[2] If it were known, it would be speedily adopted by numberless traders. This very following would bring its usefulness to an end.

3. *Theoretical Basis Open to Question.* The theoretical basis of chart reading runs somewhat as follows:

a. The action of the market (or of a particular stock) reflects the activities and the attitude of those interested in it.

b. Therefore, by studying the record of market action, we can tell what is going to happen next in the market.

The premise may well be true, but the conclusion does not necessarily follow. You may learn a great deal about the technical position of a stock by studying its chart, and yet you may not learn *enough* to permit you to operate profitably in the issue. A good analogy is provided by the "past performances" of race horses, which are so assiduously studied by the devotees of the race track. Undoubtedly these charts afford considerable information concerning the relative merits of the entries; they will often enable the student to pick the winner of a race; but the trouble is that they do not furnish that valuable information *often enough* to make betting on horse races a profitable diversion.

Coming nearer home, we have a similar situation in security analysis itself. The past earnings of a company supply a useful indication of its future earnings—useful, but not infallible. Security analysis and market analysis are alike, therefore, in the fact that they deal with data that are not conclusive as to the future. The difference, as we shall point out, is that the securities analyst can protect himself by a *margin of safety* that is denied to the market analyst.

Undoubtedly, there are times when the behavior of the market, as revealed on the charts, carries a definite and trustworthy meaning of particular value to those who are skilled in its interpretation. If reliance on chart indications were confined to those really convincing cases, a more positive argument could be made in favor of "technical study." But such

---

[2] Adherents of the Dow theory claim that it has been continuously successful for a great many years. We believe this statement to be open to much doubt—turning, in part, on certain disputed interpretations of what the theory indicated on various key occasions.

precise signals seem to occur only at wide intervals, and in the meantime human impatience plus the exigencies of the chart reader's profession impel him to draw more frequent conclusions from less convincing data.

4. *Other Theoretical and Practical Weaknesses.* The appeal of chart reading to the stock-market trader is something like that of a patent medicine to an incurable invalid. The stock speculator does suffer, in fact, from a well-nigh incurable ailment. The cure he seeks, however, is not abstinence from speculation but profits. Despite all experience, he persuades himself that these can be made and retained; he grasps greedily and uncritically at every plausible means to this end.

The plausibility of chart reading, in our opinion, derives largely from its insistence on the sound gambling maxim that losses should be cut short and profits allowed to run. This principle usually prevents sudden large losses, and at times it permits a large profit to be taken. The results are likely to be better, therefore, than those produced by the haphazard following of "market tips." Traders, noticing this advantage, are certain that by developing the technique of chart reading farther they will so increase its reliability as to assure themselves continued profits.

But in this conclusion there lurks a double fallacy. Many players at roulette follow a similar system, which limits their losses at any one session and permits them at times to realize a substantial gain. But in the end they always find that the aggregate of small losses exceeds the few large profits. (This must be so, since the mathematical odds against them are inexorable over a period of time.) The same is true of the stock trader, who will find that the expense of trading weights the dice heavily against him. A second difficulty is that, as the methods of chart reading gain in popularity, the amount of the loss taken in unprofitable trades tends to increase and the profits also tend to diminish. For as more and more people, following the same system, receive the signal to buy at about the same time, the result of this competitive buying must be that a higher average price is paid by the group. Conversely, when this larger group decides to sell out at the same time, either to cut short a loss or to protect a profit, the effect must again be that a lower average price is received. (The growth in the use of "stop-loss orders," formerly a helpful technical device of the trader, had this very effect of detracting greatly from their value as a protective measure.)

The more intelligent chart students recognize these theoretical weaknesses, we believe, and take the view that market forecasting is an *art* that requires talent, judgment, intuition and other personal qualities. They admit that no rules of procedure can be laid down, the automatic following of which will insure success. Hence the widespread tendency in Wall Street circles towards a composite or eclectic approach, in which a very thorough study of the market's performance is projected against the general economic background, and the whole is subjected to the appraisal of experienced judgment.

The Second Type of Mechanical Forecasting. Before considering the significance of this injection of the judgment factor, let us pass on to the other type of mechanical forecasting, which is based upon factors outside of the market itself. As far as the general market is concerned, the usual procedure is to construct indices representing various economic factors, e.g., money rates, carloadings, steel production, and to deduce impending changes in the market from an observation of a recent change in these indices.[3] One of the earliest methods of the kind, and a very simple one, was based upon the percentage of blast furnaces in operation.

This theory was developed by Col. Leonard P. Ayres of the Cleveland Trust Company and ran to the effect that security prices usually reached a bottom when blast furnaces in operation declined through 60% of the total and that conversely they usually reached a top when blast furnaces in operation passed through the 60% mark on the upswing in use thereof.[4] A companion theory of Colonel Ayres was that the high point in bond prices is reached about 14 months subsequent to the low point in pig-iron production and that the peak in stock prices is reached about two years following the low point for pig-iron production.[5]

This simple method is representative of all mechanical forecasting systems, in that (1) it sounds vaguely *plausible* on the basis of *a priori*

---

[3] These indices may also be plotted on charts, in which case the forecasting takes on the aspect of chart reading. *Examples:* The *A, B,* and *C* lines of the *Harvard Economic Service* which were published in weekly letters from Jan. 3, 1922, to Dec. 26, 1931 (since continued through 1939 at less frequent intervals in *The Review of Economic Statistics*); also the single composite Index Line in the "Investment Timing Service" offered by Independence Fund of North America, Inc., in 1939.

[4] See *Bulletin of the Cleveland Trust Company,* July 15, 1924, cited by David F. Jordan, in *Practical Business Forecasting,* p. 203n, New York, 1927.

[5] See *Business Recovery Following Depression,* a pamphlet published by the Cleveland Trust Company in 1922. The conclusions of Colonel Ayres are summarized on p. 31 of the pamphlet.

reasoning and (2) it relies for its *convincingness* on the fact that it has "worked" for a number of years past. The necessary weakness of all these systems lies in the time element. It is easy and safe to prophesy, for example, that a period of high interest rates will lead to a sharp decline in the market. The question is, "How soon?" There is no scientific way of answering this question. Many of the forecasting services are therefore driven to a sort of pseudo-science, in which they take it for granted that certain time lags or certain coincidences that happened to occur several times in the past (or have been worked out laboriously by a process of trial and error), can be counted upon to occur in much the same way in the future.

Broadly speaking, therefore, the endeavor to forecast security-price changes by reference to mechanical indices is open to the same objections as the methods of the chart readers. They are not truly scientific, because there is no convincing reasoning to support them and because, furthermore, really scientific (*i.e.*, entirely dependable) forecasting in the economic field is a logical impossibility.

Disadvantages of Market Analysis as Compared with Security Analysis. We return in consequence to our earlier conclusion that market analysis is an art for which special talent is needed in order to pursue it successfully. Security analysis is also an art; and it, too, will not yield satisfactory results unless the analyst has ability as well as knowledge. We think, however, that security analysis has several advantages over market analysis, which are likely to make the former a more successful field of activity for those with training and intelligence. In security analysis the prime stress is laid upon protection against untoward events. We obtain this protection by insisting upon margins of safety, or values well in excess of the price paid. The underlying idea is that even if the security turns out to be less attractive than it appeared, the commitment might still prove a satisfactory one. In market analysis there are no margins of safety; you are either right or wrong, and, if you are wrong, you lose money.[6]

---

[6] Viewing the two activities as possible professions, we are inclined to draw an analogous comparison between the law and the concert stage. A talented lawyer should be able to make a respectable living; a talented, *i.e.*, a "merely talented," musician faces heartbreaking obstacles to a successful concert career. Thus, as we see it, a thoroughly competent securities analyst should be able to obtain satisfactory results from his work, whereas permanent success as a market analyst requires unusual qualities—or unusual luck.

The cardinal rule of the market analyst that losses should be cut short and profits safeguarded (by selling when a decline commences) leads in the direction of active trading. This means in turn that the cost of buying and selling becomes a heavily adverse factor in aggregate results. Operations based on security analysis are ordinarily of the investment type and do not involve active trading.

A third disadvantage of market analysis is that it involves essentially a battle of wits. Profits made by trading in the market are for the most part realized at the expense of others who are trying to do the same thing. The trader necessarily favors the more active issues, and the price changes in these are the resultant of the activities of numerous operators of his own type. The market analyst can be hopeful of success only upon the assumption that he will be more clever or perhaps luckier than his competitors.

The work of the securities analyst, on the other hand, is in no similar sense competitive with that of his fellow analysts. In the typical case the issue that he elects to buy is not sold by some one who has made an equally painstaking analysis of its value. We must emphasize the point that the security analyst examines a far larger list of securities than does the market analyst. Out of this large list, he selects the exceptional cases in which the market price falls far short of reflecting intrinsic value, either through neglect or because of undue emphasis laid upon unfavorable factors that are probably temporary.

Market analysis seems easier than security analysis, and its rewards may be realized much more quickly. For these very reasons, it is likely to prove more disappointing in the long run. There are no dependable ways of making money easily and quickly, either in Wall Street or anywhere else.

Prophesies Based on Near-Term Prospects. A good part of the analysis and advice supplied in the financial district rests upon the near-term business prospects of the company considered. It is assumed that, if the outlook favors increased earnings, the issue should be bought in the expectation of a higher price when the larger profits are actually reported. In this reasoning, security analysis and market analysis are made to coincide. The market prospect is thought to be identical with the business prospect.

But to our mind the theory of buying stocks chiefly upon the basis of their immediate outlook makes the selection of speculative securities entirely too simple a matter. Its weakness lies in the fact that the current market price already takes into account the consensus of opinion as to future prospects. And in many cases the prospects will have been given *more* than their just need of recognition. When a stock is recommended for the reason that next year's earnings are expected to show improvement, a twofold hazard is involved. First, the forecast of next year's results may prove incorrect; second, even if correct, it may have been discounted or even overdiscounted in the current price.

If markets generally reflected only this year's earnings, then a good estimate of next year's results would be of inestimable value. But the premise is not correct. Our table that follows shows on the one hand the annual earnings per share of United States Steel Corporation common and on the other hand the price range of that issue for the years 1902–1939. Excluding the 1928–1933 period (in which business changes were so extreme as necessarily to induce corresponding changes in stock prices), it is difficult to establish any definite correlation between fluctuations in earnings and fluctuations in market quotations.

In Appendix Note 70, we reproduce significant parts of the analysis and recommendation concerning two common stocks made by an important statistical and advisory service in the latter part of 1933. The recommendations are seen to be based largely upon the apparent outlook for 1934. There is no indication of any endeavor to ascertain the fair value of the business and to compare this value with the current price. A thorough-going statistical analysis would point to the conclusion that the issue of which the sale is advised was selling below its intrinsic value, just because of the unfavorable immediate prospects, and that the opposite was true of the common stock recommended as worth holding because of its satisfactory outlook.

We are sceptical of the ability of the analyst to forecast with a fair degree of success the market behavior of individual issues over the near-term future—whether he base his predictions upon the technical position of the market or upon the general outlook for business or upon the specific outlook for the individual companies. More satisfactory results are to be obtained, in our opinion, by confining the positive conclusions of the analyst to the following fields of endeavor:

1. The selection of standard senior issues that meet exacting tests of safety.
2. The discovery of senior issues that merit an investment rating but that also have opportunities of an appreciable enhancement in value.

3. The discovery of common stocks, or speculative senior issues, that appear to be selling at far less than their intrinsic value.

4. The determination of definite price discrepancies existing between related securities, which situations may justify making exchanges or initiating hedging or arbitrage operations.

A SUMMARY OF OUR VIEWS ON INVESTMENT POLICIES

If we transfer our attention, finally, from the analyst to the owner of securities, we may briefly express our views on what he may soundly do and not do. The following résumé makes some allowance for different categories of investors.

A. The Investor of Small Means. *1. Investment for Income. In his case the only sensible investment for safety and accumulated income, under present conditions, is found in United States Savings Bonds.* Other good investments yield little if any more, and they have not equal protection against both ultimate and intermediate loss. Straight bonds and preferred stocks ostensibly offering a higher return are almost certain to involve an appreciable risk factor. The various types of "savings plans" and similar securities offered by salesmen are full of pitfalls; the investor persuaded by their promise of liberal income to prefer them to United States Savings Bonds is very, very likely to regret his choice.

2. Investment for Profit. Four approaches are open to both the small and the large investor:

a. Purchase of representative common stocks when the market level is clearly low as judged by objective, long-term standards. This policy requires patience and courage and is by no means free from the possibility of grave miscalculation. Over a long period we believe that it will show good results.

b. Purchase of individual issues with special growth possibilities, when these can be obtained at reasonable prices in relation to actual accomplishment.

Where growth is *generally* expected, the price is rarely reasonable. If the basis of purchase is a confidence in future growth not held by the public, the operation may prove sound and profitable; it may also prove ill-founded and costly.

c. Purchase of well-secured privileged senior issues. A combination of really adequate security with a promising conversion or similar right

United States Steel Common, 1901–1939

Year	Earned per share	Range of market price		
		High	Low	Average
1901	$ 9.1	55	24	40
1902	10.7	47	30	39
1903	4.9	40	10	25
1904	1.0	34	8	21
1905	8.5	43	25	34
1906	14.3	50	33	42
1907	15.6	50	22	36
1908	4.1	59	26	48
1909	10.6	95	41	68
1910	12.2	91	61	76
1911	5.9	82	50	66
1912	5.7	81	58	70
1913	11.0	69	50	60
1914	0.3(d)	67	48	58
1915	10.0	90	38	64
1916	48.5	130	80	105
1917	39.2	137	80	109
1918	22.1	117	87	102
1919	10.1	116	88	102
1920	16.6	109	76	93
1921	2.2	87	70	79
1922	2.8	112	82	97
1923	16.4	110	86	98
1924	11.8	121	94	108
1925	12.9	139	112	126
1926	18.0	161	117	139
1927*	12.3	246	155	201
1927†	8.8	176	111	144
1928	12.5	173	132	153
1929	21.2	262	150	206
1930	9.1	199	134	167
1931	1.4(d)	152	36	99
1932	11.1(d)	53	21	37
1933	7.1(d)	68	23	46
1934	5.4(d)	60	29	45
1935	2.8(d)	51	28	40
1936	2.9	80	46	63
1937	8.0	127	49	88
1938	3.8(d)	71	38	55
1939	1.84	83	41	62

* Before allowing for 40% stock dividend.
† After allowing for 40% stock dividend.

is a rare but by no means unknown phenomenon. A policy of careful selection in this field should bring good results, provided the investor has the patience and persistence needed to find his opportunities.

d. Purchase of securities selling well below intrinsic value. Intrinsic value takes into account not only past earnings and liquid asset values but also future earning power, conservatively estimated—in other words, qualitative as well as quantitative elements. We think that since a large percentage of *all* issues nowadays are relatively unpopular, there must be many cases in which the market goes clearly and crassly astray, thus creating real opportunities for the discriminating student. These may be found in bonds, preferred stocks and common stocks.

In our view, the search for and the recognition of security values of the types just discussed are not beyond the competence of the small investor who wishes to practice security analysis in a nonprofessional capacity, although he will undoubtedly need better than average intelligence and training. But we think it should be a necessary rule that the nonprofessional investor submit his ideas to the criticism of a professional analyst, such as the statistician of a New York Stock Exchange firm. Surely modesty is not incompatible with self-confidence; and there is logic in the thought that unless a man is qualified to advise others professionally, he should not, unaided, prescribe for himself.

3. *Speculation.* The investor of small means is privileged, of course, to step out of his role and become a speculator. (He is also privileged to regret his action afterwards.) There are various types of speculation, and they offer varying chances of success:

a. Buying stock in new or virtually new ventures. This we can condemn unhesitatingly and with emphasis. The odds are so strongly against the man who buys into these new flotations that he might as well throw three-quarters of the money out of the window and keep the rest in the bank.

b. Trading in the market. It is fortunate for Wall Street as an institution that a small minority of people can trade successfully and that many others think they can. The accepted view holds that stock trading is like anything else; *i.e.*, with intelligence and application, or with good professional guidance, profits can be realized. Our own opinion is sceptical, perhaps jaundiced. We think that, regardless of preparation and method, success in trading is either accidental and impermanent or else due to a highly uncommon talent. Hence the vast majority of stock traders are inevitably doomed to failure. We do not expect this conclusion to have much effect on the public. (Note our basic distinction between purchasing stocks at objectively low levels and selling them at high levels—which we term investment—and the popular practice of buying only when the market is "expected" to advance and selling when it is "due" to decline—which we call speculation.)

c. Purchase of "growth stocks" at generous prices. In calling this "speculation," we contravene most authoritative views. For reasons previously expressed, we consider this popular approach to be inherently dangerous and increasingly so as it becomes more popular. But the chances of individual success are much brighter here than in the other forms of speculation, and there is a better field for the exercise of foresight, judgment and moderation.

B. The Individual Investor of Large Means. Although he has obvious technical advantages over the small investor, he suffers from three special handicaps:

1. He cannot solve his straight investment problem simply by buying nothing but United States Savings Bonds, since the amount that any individual may purchase is limited. Hence he must, perforce, consider the broader field of fixed-value investment. We believe that strict application of quantitative tests, plus reasonably good judgment in the qualitative area, should afford a satisfactory end result.

2. However, the extraneous problem of possible inflation is more serious to him than to the small investor. Since 1932 there has been a strong common-sense argument for *some* common-stock holdings as a defensive measure. In addition, a substantial holding of common stocks corresponds with the traditional attitude and practice of the wealthy individual.

3. The size of his investment unit is more likely to induce the large investor to concentrate on the popular and active issues. To some extent, therefore, he is handicapped in the application of the undervalued-security technique. However, we imagine that a more serious obstacle thereto will be found in his preferences and prejudices.

C. Investment by Business Corporations. We believe that United States government bonds, carrying exemption from corporate income taxes, are almost the only logical medium for such business funds as may properly

be invested for a term of years. (Under 1940 conditions short-time investment involves as much trouble as income.) It seems fairly evident, on the
whole, that other types of investments by business enterprises—whether
in bonds or in stocks—can offer an appreciably higher return only at risk
of loss and of criticism.

D. Institutional Investment. We shall not presume to suggest policies
for financial institutions whose business it is to be versed in the theory
and practice of investment. The same might be said for philanthropic
and educational institutions, since these generally have the benefit of
experienced financiers in shaping their financial policies. But in order
not to dodge completely a very difficult issue, we venture the following
final observation: An institution that can manage to get along on the low
income provided by high-grade fixed-value issues should, in our opinion,
confine its holdings to this field. We doubt if the better performance of
common-stock indexes over past periods will, in itself, warrant the heavy
responsibilities and the recurring uncertainties that are inseparable from
a common-stock investment program. This conclusion may perhaps be
modified either if there is substantial unanimity of view that inflation
must be guarded against or if the insufficiency of income compels search
for a higher return. In such case those in charge may be warranted in setting aside a portion of the institution's funds for administration in other
than fixed-value fields, in accordance with the canons and technique of
security analysis.[7]

---

[7] Yale University now follows a policy of investing part of its funds in "equities"—defined as
common stocks and nonpaying senior issues. The percentage varies in accordance with a
fixed formula, somewhat as follows: The initial proportion is 30% of the total fund.
Whenever a rise in the market level advances this figure to 40%, one-eighth of each stock
holding is switched into bonds. Conversely, whenever a decline in the market reduces the
proportion to 15%, bonds are sold and one-third additional of each stock is bought. See
address of Laurence G. Tighe, Associate Treasurer of Yale University entitled "Present Day
Investment Problems of Endowed Institutions," delivered on February 14, 1940 before the
Trust Division of the American Bankers Association. It was summarized in the *New York
Sun* of February 20, 1940.

PART VIII

Contemporary Concepts in Value Investing

International Investing

by Bill Duhamel, Ashish Pant, and Jason Moment

Benjamin Graham and David Dodd did not discuss international investments in any of the first four editions of *Security Analysis*. When they were writing the first edition in 1934, not only was investing in markets outside the United States difficult and costly, but there were few international markets of any size beyond Great Britain, France, and Japan.[1] However, the world today has become more interconnected and economic activity much more global. For instance, today semiconductors are often designed in California, fabricated in Taiwan, packaged and tested in Malaysia or Vietnam, and assembled into smartphones and PCs in China, before being sold globally by U.S., Korean, and Chinese multinationals. Exports have risen from just 5% of global GDP in the 1930s to 25% today.[2] Companies in the S&P 500 Index generate over 30% of their revenues from foreign markets, and many companies in such sectors as technology, materials, and consumer staples generate over half of

---

[1] Elroy Dimson, Paul Marsh, and Mike Staunton, "Credit Suisse Global Investment Returns Yearbook 2022 Summary Edition," Credit Suisse Research Institute, February 2022, http://www.cepii.fr/pdf_pub/wp/2016/wp2016-14.pdf.

[2] Michel Fouquin and Jules Hugot, "Two Centuries of Bilateral Trade and Gravity Data: 1827–2014," CEPII Working Paper, Centre d'Etudes Prospectives et d'Informations Internationales, May 2016, p.14, https://ourworldindata.org/grapher/merchandise-exports-gdp-cepii?country=OWID_WRL.

their revenues and profits abroad.[3] Meanwhile, companies around the world do a great deal of business in the United States, so any analysis of an American company is incomplete without considering its international suppliers, competitors, and customers. In short, American investors must consider "foreign" companies to be part of their purview and the global economy an essential component of many "American" businesses.

The rapid growth in global trade and investment has also ushered in the globalization of financial markets. Markets outside the United States have become larger and more accessible, and many countries have adopted uniform IFRS global accounting standards and securities regulations akin to those of the United States. In addition, the emergence of global custodians, reduced settlement costs, and access to electronic trading have reduced the costs and hassles of cross-border investing. The growth of international markets has resulted in the U.S. share of global market capitalization falling from 70% in 1970 to 40% today. When you include international investments, the investment opportunity set for U.S. investors has almost doubled since the days of Graham and Dodd.

Were Graham and Dodd writing *Security Analysis* today, a discussion on international investing would surely figure prominently in their book. While the task of updating the original edition to include a section on international investing is daunting, it is nonetheless essential for the text to be made contemporary. Though this chapter has been written by U.S.-based global investors, the perspective it offers should be applicable to any international investor.

---

[3] Emmanual L. Bacani, "S&P 500 Companies' Non-US Revenue Share Hits 10-Year Low—Goldman Sachs," S&P Global Market Intelligence, June 18, 2020, https://www.spglobal.com/marketintelligence/en/news-insights/latest-news-headlines/s-p-500-companies-non-us-revenue-share-hits-10-year-low-8211-goldman-sachs-59094991.

WHY INVEST INTERNATIONALLY?

Despite the increased globalization of financial markets, it is still reasonable to ask why U.S. investors should bother looking beyond their home market. After all, the United States offers a vast array of financial investments in an immense marketplace characterized by substantial liquidity and low transaction costs. There is an enormous range of research and analysis, substantial disclosure requirements, and detailed and enforceable regulations. The U.S. economy has fared well over the years, its political and social framework has been stable, and it has a well-established body of business law and a predictable legal system. Indeed, the United States has long been the "safe haven" to which investors retreat in any "flight to quality" during times of uncertainty.

There are two compelling reasons for U.S. investors today to consider investments abroad. The first is the possibility of earning higher risk-adjusted returns than are available in the United States. In *Security Analysis*, Graham and Dodd pointed out that irrational selling and the associated reduction of equity capital in a market produces bargains for value investors. (Chap. 4) These factors are exacerbated in many international markets due to limited domestic risk capital, and this makes stock prices in these markets more volatile than in the United States. This can present opportunities for patient long-term value investors to acquire shares in great businesses at very attractive prices.

The second reason is that an international portfolio provides diversification that reduces overall volatility while enhancing returns. There is a saying that when the United States sneezes, the world catches cold; in reality, many foreign economies have business cycles— and market cycles—that are not always aligned with those in the United States. International investments provide an opportunity to zig when the United States zags. Although the United States has been the top-performing market over the past decade, this certainly will not always be the case. Indeed, for most of the decades since 1950, the U.S. market has underperformed an equal-weighted global basket of developed market stocks.[4]

INTRINSIC VALUE IN INTERNATIONAL MARKETS

Those who accept the case for investing in international markets must then grapple with the analytical challenges this presents. Assessing the intrinsic value of a security in international markets can be more difficult than in the United States. In *Security Analysis*, Graham and Dodd identify three obstacles in assessing intrinsic value. (Chap. 1) The first, inadequate or incorrect data, is an obstacle that they found to be the least important for the U.S. market, concluding that "deliberate falsification of data is rare" due to "the result of regulations." While this may not be entirely accurate for the U.S. market, the availability of adequate and correct data is certainly a bigger challenge in many international markets. More lenient accounting practices and regulatory enforcement provide managements more leeway to manipulate or falsify financial results abroad, such as in the cases of prominent frauds like Wirecard (2020)[5] or Steinhoff (2017).[6] Analysts must take care when analyzing the books and records of international companies, looking for telltale signs of questionable practices, ranging from unusual recurring charges or other related party transactions, suspicious patterns of litigation, and large and frequent insider share transactions. In addition, high inflation, currency devaluations, and currency

---

[4] Sean Duffin, "Benefits of Global Diversification," Cambridge Associates, April 27, 2020, https://www.cambridgeassociates.com/insight/benefits-of-global-diversification/.

[5] Dan McCrum, *Money Men: A Hot Start-Up, a Billion Dollar Fraud, a Fight for the Truth*, Bantam Press, 2022.

[6] Tiisetso Motsoeneng and Emma Rumney, "Pwc Investigation Finds $7.4 Billion Accounting Fraud at Steinhoff, Company Says," Reuters, March 15, 2019, https://www.reuters.com/article/us-steinhoff-intln-accounts/pwc-investigation-finds-7-4-billion-accounting-fraud-at-steinhoff-company-says-idUSKCN1QW2C2.

mismatches between assets and liabilities make international balance
sheets less useful for determining intrinsic and liquidation values.

Graham and Dodd name "uncertainties of the future" as the
second challenge in determining intrinsic value. Volatile economies,
substantial currency risks, and unexpected changes in regulations and
politics make predicting the future more challenging in many
countries outside the United States.

The third challenge Graham and Dodd identify is the risk that
should "the irrational behavior of the market" persist long enough, then
a security's intrinsic value could decline due to changes in a company's
fundamentals in the interim. This risk is enhanced in international
and especially developing markets, not only because of added
macroeconomic and financial risks, but also due to potential actions by
a controlling shareholder that can harm minority shareholders.

In short, it is evident that investment risks are greater in
international markets, which makes the determination of intrinsic
value more difficult and its persistence more vulnerable. While
investing in high quality companies with strong management is an
important mitigant to these elevated risks, a prudent investor must
demand a larger discount to intrinsic value—a greater margin of
safety—when investing in a foreign security.

Another reason to seek greater margin of safety in international
markets is the greater volatility caused by thin liquidity and more
fickle capital flows. This volatility is not limited to emerging markets.
The small markets of Amsterdam, Brussels, and the Nordic countries
are dominated by a few major companies; the other listed companies
in these markets attract only limited investor interest. These factors
can drive market prices to deeper discounts to intrinsic value than is
typical in the United States. As Figure 1 indicates, emerging markets
traded at price-earnings multiples that were at a 50% to 60% discount
to the U.S. market during 1998–1999 and 2001–2002. Conversely,

during 1995–1996 and around 2013, emerging markets traded at parity or even a premium to the U.S. markets. As we write this, the current discount is 40% to 50%. These swings between undervalued and overvalued is a source of opportunity for disciplined investors who can handle the volatility.

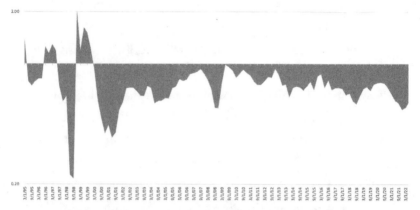

FIGURE 1   Valuation of Emerging Markets Relative to the S&P
Source: Bloomberg Data: relative P/E ratio of S&P 500 (SPX) to MSCI Emerging Markets Index (MXEF), month end 12/1995 to 6/2022.

Before proceeding further, it is important to highlight the distinction between developed international markets and developing markets, because these two types of markets can present distinct risks. The larger developed financial markets, particularly Canada, the United Kingdom, and Australia, closely resemble the U.S. market in terms of reporting standards, securities regulation, market liquidity, and corporate governance. The analytical principles laid out by Graham and Dodd to uncover undervalued securities can be applied in these developed international markets with one additional consideration—that of foreign exchange risk, whereby a significant change in the exchange rate could overwhelm the importance of a company's fundamentals. While we would still require higher potential returns than comparable U.S. investments to invest in developed international markets, we would not seek a substantially higher premium to do so.

Developing international markets such as Indonesia, Argentina, and Nigeria are a different story. In these markets, investors must take substantial additional risks into account when assessing the intrinsic value of a security, and as a result must demand much higher prospective returns, or a much larger margin of safety, than they require in developed markets. Periods of economic or political uncertainty are more common in these less mature and more illiquid markets, which can be rich hunting grounds for investors amid such turmoil. Economic crisis leading to investment bargains is not a preserve of developing markets alone: in the summer of 2012, Greece threatened to default on its debt, and in turn the other Europeans threatened to kick it out of the euro, resulting in chaotic selling and very attractive investment opportunities for value investors. Similarly, the March 2011 Fukushima earthquake and the ensuing nuclear disaster resulted in a significant sell-off of the Tokyo market and near bankruptcy of Japan's largest utility.

DEVELOPING A LOCAL NETWORK

Each international market has its own unique set of rules and regulations, challenges and opportunities, and scoundrels and heroes. Jumping into a new market without adequate preparation is akin to sitting down at an unfamiliar poker table without first learning who the sharks and patsies are. Our first step in looking at a new market is to develop a network of relationships in the country. This network is much broader than just investment analysts and stockbrokers. It includes local journalists, former government officials, retired corporate executives, former diplomats, and economists from institutions such as the local central bank or the IMF. We meet with the customers, competitors, and regulators of the companies we are analyzing.

Constructing this network requires time and involves multiple trips to a country. It is often easiest to build a network when an entire country is distressed. During such times, not only companies but even government officials are keen to meet new potential investors to attract capital into their country. In July 2001, when we went on a scouting trip to India, it was possible to meet with almost any CEO, and they would take the time to patiently explain their businesses to us. Conversely, in July 2006, when the Indian market was booming, it was hard to even get a meeting with a company's investor relations manager. On our research trips to Vietnam in 2011, even though we had full schedules, our broker would receive unsolicited calls from businesses looking for capital while we were traveling from one meeting to the next.

We are uncomfortable considering investments in a foreign market without building such a network, which takes significant time and effort. Helpfully, we have found that after the network has been built, it can be useful again and again, so long as we work to maintain and update it. In this way, we are able to get up to speed more quickly on subsequent opportunities. For this reason, we find ourselves coming back again and again to the same markets.

This network also helps us understand the local culture. When we assess culture, we are referring to the nuances of communication and language in a country, as well as adherence to the rule of law. When a management in the United States provides financial targets to investors and analysts, for example, these come with a degree of commitment to meeting those targets. This is not the case in every country; in some places, financial targets are aspirations rather than commitments. Culture also encompasses the shared values and motivations of the key political and business leaders of a country. What are these leaders seeking to accomplish, and are we as minority investors aligned with their goals?

Our network also permits us to investigate the reputations of local businesspeople. Before investing in a company, we want to have at least a dozen good reference checks on a management that we do not already know well. A question we often ask locals is, "If you had to invest your family's money in five companies for the next decade, and valuation was not a consideration, in which companies would you invest?" Instead of pitching stocks they think would work best in the short term, locals' answer to this question tends to be focused on the quality and integrity of the management.

We spend weeks, months, or longer in a country before we first commit any capital there. We would rather miss an opportunity than make a major mistake. In the case of Vietnam, we visited the country seven times before we invested. We made six trips to Greece over a two-month period to find investments, while also spending time in Germany meeting policy makers and politicians to underwrite the risk of a Greek default. One of our partners lived in Korea for a month in the early 2000s and spent another month in Thailand following its 2006 military coup. We continue to visit countries such as Great Britain, Germany, India, and Brazil at least twice per year, even when we are not active, to maintain our contacts and to search out new opportunities.

WHY NOW?

As we focus on finding pockets of undervaluation, we always stop to ask ourselves why a security has become undervalued. What caused a reasonable shareholder to sell the security, and why should we be buying instead? We never start with the assumption that the sellers are wrong; instead, we want to understand their rationale. We also attempt to translate macroeconomic developments into our bottom-up company analysis. In an economic crisis, for example, when a currency is weak and interest rates are high, we want to examine how these forces will impact the specific securities and companies we are analyzing, and we want to understand how resilient these companies and their managements are against these forces.

We have seen many examples of country or regional crises creating opportunities for investors. In 2004 the incumbent reformist Bharatiya Janata Party (BJP) suffered a surprise electoral defeat in Indian elections. Since no party received a majority of seats in the Parliament, the prospect of an unstable and indecisive coalition government drove the Indian stock index down more than 15% on May 17, 2004. Although the prospect of a coalition government raised myriad uncertainties, we saw little to no risk that it would impair the continued success of the private banks, and so this sell-off provided an opportunity to acquire great banking franchises at attractive prices. A 2010 banking crisis in Vietnam impaired the values of property companies, and in this case the resulting problem loans made most local banks unanalyzable, but this was an opportunity to purchase shares of excellently managed consumer businesses that were unaffected. Every crisis presents its own set of problems and opportunities.

Indeed, crises often provide countries and companies with an opportunity to fix structural problems and end up having a beneficial longer-term impact for those who can survive the relentless headlines and volatility. The 1991 Indian balance of payments crisis catalyzed the liberalization of the economy, including reduction of import tariffs, promotion of a private banking sector, and opening the Indian stock market to foreign institutional investors. These actions laid the foundation for the subsequent 30 years of growth for the Indian economy and its capital markets.

INTERNATIONAL INDICES VERSUS SINGLE STOCK SELECTION

While there has been dramatic growth in the use of passive index funds in the United States, internationally we have found that buying specific stocks is superior to owning an index. In many international markets, stock market indices are overweighted to large but poorly managed state-owned or family-controlled enterprises, undercapitalized banks, and overregulated utilities. They often include volatile commodity producers as well as low-return property companies. Abroad, innovation and growth are often concentrated within a subset of privately controlled entrepreneurial companies that are often only small constituents of local indexes, if included at all.

BUSINESS QUALITY IS THE BEST PROTECTION FROM MACROECONOMIC SHOCKS

Along with a bargain purchase price, business quality can also insulate investors from permanent loss of capital. Companies with pricing power, for example, can offset the negative effects of inflation and devaluations, and companies with high returns on capital do not need to incur debt that can be so damaging in periods of high interest rates. In 2002, when the Argentine peso devalued by 75%, Quilmes, the leading beer company in Argentina, saw its net domestic sales decline from $426 million in calendar year 2001 to $164 million in 2002 largely due to a −59% decline in net realization per liter in dollar terms. However, over the five years that followed, Quilmes was able to impose significant price increases due to its strong brand equity, dominant 65% market share, and higher input costs across the entire industry. By 2006, Quilmes had recovered three-quarters of its lost net realization in dollar terms. Despite suffering an extraordinary macroeconomic shock, Quilmes had restored the value of its business in dollar terms. Similarly, during the Brazilian hyperinflation of the 1980s and 1990s, pricing power helped Nestle grow its Brazilian revenues in Swiss franc terms. Vietnam Dairy Products, known as Vinamilk, the leading dairy products and beverages company in Vietnam, was also able to raise domestic price enough to offset a steady depreciation of the Vietnamese dong from 2006 to 2011. Vinamilk was able to raise prices due to its dominant brands and grow its revenues in U.S. dollar terms at an average yearly rate of 18%, while improving its margins during a difficult period for the Vietnamese economy.

CURRENCY RISK

In assessing international investments, it is important for U.S. investors to make sure all returns are calculated and measured in U.S. dollars. If returns were measured solely in local currency, with inflation running at levels upward of 50% in places like Argentina, Venezuela, and Zimbabwe in the early 2020s, local bonds may appear to offer annual returns as high as 50% in nominal terms, but those returns can disappear when measured in U.S. dollars. Indeed, these high yields reflect an expectation of devaluation. In other words, an analyst must adjust expected returns to reflect the differential in inflation rates between the analyst's base currency (which means the U.S. dollar for U.S. investors) and the local currency. Over long periods, local currencies should theoretically depreciate at this differential. Of course, other variables, such as differentials in real interest rates, changes in terms of trade (the relative prices of exports to imports), and other capital flows, will influence changes in exchange rates, but this simple approximation provides a good baseline.

Foreign exchange risk is something that all international investors need to think about. These risks can be hedged, but as with all forms of insurance, currency hedging involves a cost or premium. These costs or premia are lowest before the storm, when they are most necessary, and most expensive right after the storm, when they are least needed. We are not recommending that investors hedge all their currency exposures, only that all investors be mindful of currency when investing outside their home markets.

It is important to understand the true underlying exposures to currency fluctuations. For example, in 2009 we decided not to hedge our currency exposure in Tata Consultancy Services, an Indian IT services company, because it generated its revenues in U.S. dollars and euros, while most of its costs were in local currency. Thus it benefited from a depreciating Indian rupee. Businesses that benefit from weaker local currencies are particularly valuable in countries that do not have a currency that can be easily hedged, such as Vietnam. We could not hedge our exposure to the Vietnamese dong when we invested in Vietnam Dairy, but we received a measure of protection from the fact that Vinamilk's products competed against imported dairy products from New Zealand, which were priced in U.S. dollars. As the dong depreciated, prices of these imported competitors increased at the rate of depreciation, giving Vinamilk an opportunity to raise prices to fully offset this depreciation.

U.S. investors also need to consider currency risk when investing in developed markets. In the case of the Greek debt crisis of 2012, despite the significant price declines of companies such as the stock exchange (Hellenic Exchanges) and the national lottery (OPAP), there was still additional downside risk if Greece were to leave the euro. As analysts, we estimated our downside exposure in this worst-case scenario. In the case of stocks valued below a company's underlying cash per share, we could bookend our downside and potentially hedge any currency risk on the cash. We generally avoid investing in situations where we were unable to determine an acceptable downside value.

MANAGEMENT COMPETENCE, ALIGNMENT, AND INTEGRITY

Graham and Dodd warn that "future value factors" can affect the realization of the intrinsic value of a security. (Chap. 1) A key future value factor is management competence and reputation. Warren

Buffett astutely noted: "Somebody once said that in looking for people to hire, you look for three qualities: integrity, intelligence, and energy. And if you do not have the first, the other two will kill you. If you hire somebody without integrity, you really want them to be dumb and lazy."[7] While this is important in any market, it is critical when investing abroad. Self-interested or conflicted managements can erode the intrinsic value of a security through unfair treatment of minority shareholders. In many countries, boards of directors in family- or state-controlled companies often do not represent the interests of minority shareholders.

In the United States, when a management is incompetent or conflicted, shareholder activism can often force a change. This means that poor management might present an opportunity for value investors, a low-hanging fruit to be plucked as activists force a change in management. In most international markets, whether developed or developing, this is impossible. Attempts by shareholders to replace managements in Japan, Germany, and France have proven futile, just as they have in developing markets. Quality of management is critical when investing internationally. In most international markets, the management you have when you buy a security is almost always the management you will have to live with.

Many international companies are family-controlled, and the interests of the controlling family may diverge from those of minority shareholders. For example, a family might want a depressed share price for an extended period to minimize estate taxes if the death of a patriarch seems imminent. Or controlling shareholders may engage in unethical but not illegal related-party transactions in order to enhance their personal wealth.

---

[7] Warren Buffett, Lecture to the University of Florida School of Business, Graham-Buffett Concentration, University of Florida, Gainesville, Florida, October 15, 1998, https://www.youtube.com/watch?v=2MHIcabnjrA.

Having internationally accepted auditors and highly regarded local board members may not provide sufficient protection. Satyam Computer Services Limited, often called "India's Enron," was audited by the Indian affiliate of PricewaterhouseCoopers, and its board of directors included a preeminent technologist, an accounting professor from a leading American business school, and highly regarded former government officials. Satyam was regarded as a leading global information technology company. In 2008, it reported revenues of over $2 billion, employed over 53,000 employees, and operated in 66 countries. In 2004, its ADRs were listed on the New York Stock Exchange, and the World Council for Corporate Governance awarded it the "Golden Peacock Award" for excellence in corporate governance. But on January 7, 2009, Satyam's founder and CEO, Ramalinga Raju, shocked the markets when he confessed that Satyam had overstated its cash balances by over $1 billion and understated its liabilities by $252 million. He had siphoned funds out of Satyam to pay for real estate investments made by private companies owned by his family.

Identifying competent and ethical managements is not necessarily difficult. Graham and Dodd's financial analysis must be combined with Phil Fisher's scuttlebutt methods.[8] As in many U.S. small towns, reputations are well-known among locals—another reason why creating a local network is critical. Proof of actual cash flow generation, such as dividends or share buybacks at attractive prices, is also important.

INTERNATIONAL CREDIT INVESTMENTS

Investors need to look beyond the legal formalities associated with their investments. Yes, bonds and loans are legal contracts between debtors and creditors, but they are only valuable if enforceable. Credit investors in international markets must thoroughly understand the

---

[8] Phil A. Fisher, *Common Stocks and Uncommon Profits* (later printing), New York, Harper & Brothers Publishers, 2022.

enforceability of these contracts, the relevant bankruptcy codes, and the enforceability of the foreign judgments before investing in international debt securities. Overlapping jurisdictions and conflicting laws can make enforcement costly, time-consuming, and unpredictable. A judgment regarding bonds subject to New York law that is handed down in a U.S. court may take decades to enforce if the underlying collateral is located in Mexico or Argentina.

WITH ASSETS OF NATIONAL SIGNIFICANCE, CAVEAT EMPTOR

It is sometimes profitable to invest in companies that play an important role in significant industries in a country—they may receive a degree of protection because they are a national champion. There can also be pitfalls in purchasing shares in an asset of national significance controlled directly or indirectly by a foreign government, as in the case of Électricité de France ("EdF"). In November 2005, the French government sold a 12.7% stake in EdF, raising €6.35 billion at €32 per share. However, after an initial run-up to €70 per share within two years of its November 2005 IPO, EdF shares slowly and steadily ground their way down to a July 2022 price of €7.85 per share. Over the years, EdF has continued to sell power below market price, a policy that is popular among ratepayers. EdF also maintained a bloated employee base to keep its unions happy. The offshore minority shareholders of EdF, who do not vote in local elections, have suffered as a result of this mismanagement of EdF by the politicians. EdF has remained a political football: in 2022, as the French president sought a way to show he was seeking to ease rising energy costs caused by the Russia-Ukraine war, he talked about renationalizing EdF, likely at a price far below that of its 2005 IPO.

The case of Coal India Limited mirrors the case of EdF. Coal India went public in October 2010 by selling 10% of its equity to domestic and foreign investors while the government of India retained the remaining 90%. Coal India was pricing its coal at a significant discount to the landed cost of imported coal, as a means of lowering the cost of electricity in India. In October 2012, a U.K. activist sued the board of directors of Coal India for breach of its fiduciary duties and accused the government of India of "abusing its powers as a majority shareholder and for improperly exerting pressure on CIL directors."[9] In the end, the activist failed to get Coal India to increase its prices of coal.

Of course, government ownership alone does not make a business uninvestable; our investment in Vinamilk illustrates this. The state owned 47.6% of Vinamilk, yet it did not interfere with Vinamilk management's decision to raise prices during inflation, allowing the company to continue earning high returns on capital. In this case, the government wanted to promote domestic food production to reduce its need to import food and to increase food security; thus, in this case, minority shareholders were aligned with the Vietnamese government.

Governments can control critical assets of national significance even without significant share ownership, by using regulation and taxation to achieve the same result. Any investment in any asset or company of national significance should be analyzed and undertaken with great caution. It is critical to understand the motives of the controlling shareholders, especially governments, to ensure their interests are aligned with the interests of foreign investors.

ATTRACTIVE ALTERNATIVES TO INVESTING IN INTERNATIONAL SECURITIES

The myriad risks specific to international markets might make U.S. investors wary of investing directly in international securities,

---

[9] Times of India, "The Children's Investment Fund Sues Government, Coal India Directors over Loss," *Times of India*, October 13, 2012, https://timesofindia.indiatimes.com/business/india-business/the-childrens-investment-fund-sues-government-coal-india-directors-over-loss/articleshow/16790705.cms.

particularly those listed in developing countries. However, there is an
alternative that allows investors to capture the superior long-term
growth prospects of international markets without taking all the risks
involved in doing so. Global businesses such as Nestlé, Diageo, Pernod
Ricard, Unilever, Colgate, Ambev, Heineken, Mastercard, and Visa
earn a significant share of their revenues from their operations outside
the United States. The shares of these companies are listed in the
United States or have American or global depository receipts that
trade in New York or London, and these companies adhere to the
highest regulatory, accounting, and governance standards. By
investing in these global businesses, investors benefit from the growth
prospects of international markets. Even more enticing, at times these
businesses trade at a significant discount to their counterparts in the
developing markets, enabling investors to capture all the upside of
global growth, without the risks uniquely inherent in offshore
securities, and with a larger margin of safety.

Company	Headquarters	Market Capitalization 6/30/2009	% off Sales from International Markets	6/30/09 NTM P/E	6/30/09 EV/ EBIT
Diageo	United Kingdom	24,001	65.1%	13.8	11.9
United Spirits	India	93,363	100.0%	27.0	13.7
Heineken	Netherlands	12,922	68.2%	17.0	10.2
SAB Miller	United Kingdom	30,661	99.4%	13.4	15.5
United Breweries	India	29,465	100.0%	45.9	16.9
Nestlé	Switzerland	149,358	67.4%	20.1	14.1
Nestlé India	India	192,986	100.0%	32.5	20.3
Unilever	United Kingdom	46,673	83.6%	11.7	10.1
Hindustan Lever	India	617,593	100.0%	29.8	22.8

CONCLUSION

In summary, the investment approach articulated by Graham and Dodd, although focused on U.S. securities, turns out to be equally useful for investing in international markets. However, there are additional considerations that prudent investors must consider in international markets.

First, determining a business's intrinsic value is more difficult in many international markets than for U.S. businesses because of issues such as currency risks, uncertain regulatory regimes, and volatile local macroeconomic and political forces. In addition, minority investors may face additional risks because of potentially poor corporate governance. These risks, when coupled with limited scope for shareholder activism, not only significantly affect the future value of businesses, but they could also cause a security to trade at a significant discount to its intrinsic value for an indeterminate period. Consequently, investors require a larger margin of safety, via a deeper discount to intrinsic value, in international markets.

Investors investing outside their home markets should also raise the bar in considering management and business quality. In addition to assessing the outlook for the company's markets, investors need to invest the time and effort to thoroughly investigate management competence, motivations, and integrity. In seeking businesses with the potential to grow intrinsic value, the quality of a company may well be as important as its valuation, because quality businesses can preserve and grow their value during periods of macroeconomic volatility, which are more common in these markets. This growth potential provides added protection against an incorrect assessment of intrinsic value or a decrease in intrinsic value due to factors that may be beyond the control of a company's management.

At the Intersection of Public and Private Investing: A Case Study

by David Abrams

The goal of investing is to eat well and sleep well, to generate profits in a way that never threatens your solvency or causes you a restless night. That is the essence of *Security Analysis*. Its prescription for conservative investing has served many generations well, despite—or, in fact, because of—the dramatic changes that have transpired since this book was first published in 1934.

Throughout these pages, Graham and Dodd advise investors to continually seek a margin of safety. Doing so is not a formula into which numbers can be blindly inserted; it is a mindset that helps one minimize the probability of loss and maximize gain. Those who buy stable assets focus mostly on a discounted entry price, which means less risk is incurred and greater potential return is available. Those who purchase companies, either publicly traded stocks or privately held enterprises, must weigh many qualitative considerations, such as the competency of management, the stability of the company and its growth prospects, the degree to which barriers to entry exist, the alignment of interests among the various constituencies (or lack thereof), and the ability of the company to allocate capital intelligently. Graham and Dodd were wary of these intangibles and preferred hard numbers, like entries on a balance sheet or income statement, and discernible facts, such as the terms of a debt instrument. Indeed, they wrote that "the quantitative factors lend themselves far better to thoroughgoing analysis than the qualitative factors." (Chap. 2)

We are all products of our times. As James Grant has noted, the first edition of *Security Analysis* came into the world amid the challenging backdrop of economic depression and the sparks that would soon ignite into World War II, a time when national unemployment in the United States topped 25%, and in the immediate aftermath of a stock market crash that had seen the market plunge 87% between its 1929 peak and 1932 nadir. After this crash and the ensuing Great Depression that had just wiped out an entire generation of investors, Graham and Dodd approached stocks with extreme caution. To help their readers avoid the same devastating losses, the authors recommended they pay less than two-thirds of "net working capital."[1] Buying at such a discount to the value of a company's hard assets makes it difficult to lose money, especially if a portfolio of similarly undervalued securities can be assembled to diversify and mitigate the risk of owing a single enterprise. This approach, however, turns operating companies into asset plays, a strategy that made sense in 1934, but no longer does. When today's stocks trade at a very distressed price, it's typically because the underlying business is facing an existential struggle.

Graham and Dodd distinguished between investing and speculation. "Investment," they wrote, "is grounded in the past whereas speculation looks primarily to the future." (Chap. 4) Yet those who buy ongoing companies (which is what most investors do) have no choice but to contemplate the future and to wrestle with qualitative issues that are at least as important as price.[2] The purpose of demanding a margin of safety is to tip the odds in favor of the

---

[1] Defined as working capital less all liabilities (so-called net nets).

[2] The irony is that, despite his advice to avoid "speculation," Graham's greatest investing triumph was his ownership in Geico, an operating business, which made him more money than all his beloved net-nets.

investor. A high going-in valuation does not guarantee a bad result; it just makes it less likely. Likewise, mediocre management, lousy capital allocation, and misaligned interests do not ensure failure, but they do lower the chances of success. Conversely, excellent leadership, intelligent capital deployment, and aligned interests put the wind at the investor's back. Though Graham and Dodd were reticent to take these intangible and sometimes ephemeral factors into consideration, I believe the conservative principles espoused in *Security Analysis* can and should be applied to them. Doing so is part of creating a margin of safety in today's investment landscape.

While this book's central themes remain critically important, the deployment of those ideas has necessarily changed over time. Markets shift and evolve. Information is rapidly disseminated; dislocations that cause large discrepancies between price and value are rapidly exploited and then quickly disappear. Those who discover a profitable niche usually attempt to exploit it further. This brings additional capital to the asset class, spreads the word of its attractiveness, and hastens the closing of that window of opportunity. I have seen several such opportunities come and go during my own career.

Years before I arrived on Wall Street, people like Gus Levy of Goldman Sachs figured out that once a company had become the subject of a takeover bid, investors would tend to dump the stock without much thought, leaving a "small" amount of money on the table. Levy understood that the dollar of profit gained by buying a company at $20 before it was to be acquired for $21 produced a high annualized return that more than compensated for the losses that occurred when deals fell apart. Such situations lent themselves to analysis that not everyone was equipped to perform. But by the time I got to Wall Street, where my first job was in the merger arbitrage department of a boutique firm, the jig was practically up. Word had gotten out that juicy profits could be had in risk arbitrage, and so firms dedicated to the strategy sprang up. Within a short while, most of the excess returns had been squeezed out and it was time to seek another hunting ground.

In the mid-to-late 1980s, bankrupt and distressed securities were shunned by most investors. Many institutions had adopted internal rules forcing them to sell a company's bonds when it went bankrupt or got downgraded below investment grade. Furthermore, the complexity of Chapter 11 encouraged many to leave the court process and haggling to others. The savings and loan crisis, the recession of 1990–1991, and the bankruptcy of Drexel Burnham Lambert created a flood of bonds in a market with few buyers. Great assets and companies could be bought at bargain prices. Successful investment firms were formed, careers launched, and fortunes made. As with risk arbitrage, talent and capital rushed in, and funds were created with mandates to buy distressed bonds. Today, those easy pickings are long gone, and the world of distressed investing has become fiercely competitive.

As I continued the search for attractive investments, in recent years I have begun actively pursuing private assets. Many investors see public and private investing as separate and distinct worlds, but to me the line between them is blurry at best and often nonexistent. The fundamental principles of each are the same, opportunities within an industry can be found in both, and wisdom gleaned in one can be applied in the other. I have also learned that moving between public and private holdings can help one find investments whose intangible factors are more likely to act as a tailwind than a headwind, and thereby increase the margin of safety. Some of the most successful investors in the world, those such as Warren Buffett, enjoy a flexible mandate. The longtime involvement of my own firm, Abrams Capital—17 years and counting—in auto retailing illustrates this and highlights some of the trade-offs between liquid and illiquid assets.

In 2005, Abrams Capital bought shares in two publicly traded auto retailers because the stocks were trading at bargain multiples and we had a higher opinion of the business than Wall Street did. Dealerships, of course, sell and repair cars. Selling cars is volatile, which makes this part of the business difficult to value, but fixing them is stable, predictable, and lucrative. We believed the market was too focused on the former, not enough on the latter. When researching the industry, we came across David Rosenberg, who has spent his life in the automobile business. His father, Ira, was a legendary auto dealer who operated a well-known chain in New England, and David had worked there as a teenager. When we first met him, he was a manager for Group 1 Automotive, one of the companies we owned. He deepened our understanding of the business, and we struck up a friendship. An entrepreneur at heart, David left Group 1 a year or two later, hoping to find dealerships to purchase and run. He soon reached an agreement to buy 11 franchises and two body shops from the Clair family. Its patriarch, Ernie Clair, had left the stores to his children when he died, but their heart wasn't in it, operations languished, profits shrank, and within a few years they were ready to exit. David needed capital to complete the deal and approached us about providing it.

David believed the franchises were dramatically underperforming and thought he could turn them around. I have heard many pitches over the years, during which the buyer claims she or he can breathe life into a company's operations because prior management had done a poor job. Often, the hoped-for improvements don't materialize, so I was skeptical of David's claims. He took us through his analysis line by line and showed us how $250,000 could be saved here, another $500,000 there. None of the changes seemed difficult. We decided to back him even though the price was high relative to the company's then-current earnings. After closing, the company was renamed Prime Motor Group.

Warren Buffett has reportedly said that you should buy a business any fool could run because eventually one will. But the human element can't be removed from commerce. Customers, employees, and counterparties must all be managed. Furthermore, the world often presents challenges for which there is no textbook answer, and individuals must exercise their judgment to develop custom solutions. Capitalism is competitive, and many businesses find their firms under attack. Fending off threats takes intelligence, creativity, and skill. Leadership matters. Some CEOs—such as David Rosenberg—are more talented than others. The management of companies is not unlike compound interest, where small differentials in rates of return eventually yield vastly disparate outcomes. The gap between what a capable executive team and an incompetent one achieve might be barely discernible in the short term, but in the long run talented managers soar, average ones muddle along, and the worst drive their companies off the cliff. Determining the good from the bad, however, is not easy. Someone who's risen to the top of the corporate ladder surely possesses political and oratorical skills even if she or he isn't a superstar. Aware of what investors want to hear, corporate managers tend to craft their words and presentations to resonate with their audience. Despite sounding polished, the pronouncements from public companies rarely reflect the unvarnished opinions of its executives. This obscures management's true thoughts and makes it hard for outside investors to correctly judge and trust them.

One benefit of owning private companies, such as Prime Motor Group, is that the investor gets to know with a great degree of certainty whether the team is strong. The conversations investors have with board members and with managers (who are typically also significant investors) are almost always honest. Negatives and positives are discussed candidly. Deliberations of difficult issues are frank. Privy to this dialogue, an investor can determine whether the managers are facile with both quantitative and qualitative analyses. In private companies, an investor can rely on both words and actions; in public companies, more weight must be placed on deeds.

Another crucial factor in determining the attractiveness of a company is its ability to allocate capital intelligently. Funds generated from operations can be plowed back into the business, invested in other ventures, or returned to shareholders. Enterprises that deploy cash well create value for owners, while those that do it poorly destroy wealth. With public companies, it can be hard to know if their investments are thoughtful, or whether management is engaged in empire building at the expense of shareholders. An investor who has insights into whether a company is making sound decisions may be able to peer into the future with greater clarity than the market can. Owning private car dealerships opened our eyes to opportunities in the auto-retailing industry that dramatically increased the value of Prime Motor Group. Later, this knowledge gave us the confidence to make commitments to two public companies, Lithia and Asbury.

We learned a lot about the acquisition market for car dealers during the time we owned Prime Motor Group. For example, most transactions in the industry require approval from the manufacturer, so it's necessary to have a successful track record and a good reputation to obtain that consent. This requirement limits the number of buyers. In addition, some sellers transact without an intermediary. Thus personal relationships can yield opportunities to acquire dealerships at attractive prices. Finally, there can be ways to profitably invest in a seemingly mature business. One day David told us that Mercedes-Benz had been embroiled in a dispute with a dealership on Cape Cod that had devolved into litigation, but the parties were now ready to settle. To resolve the situation, Mercedes wanted Prime Motor Group to buy the small Cape Cod franchise, which didn't have much upside and wouldn't have been interesting in and of itself. As part of the deal, however, Prime Motor

Group would be allowed to build a new Mercedes dealership on Boston's south shore. This required the construction of a new facility. Moreover, Prime Motor Group would incur a couple of years of operating losses before the new dealership turned a profit. Together, the cost of the facility and the operating losses meant a significant investment, yet we were confident it would ultimately be profitable. It was.

When we first purchased Prime Motor Group, we focused on improving the existing operations. After we realized how much value could be created through capital allocation, we reinvested all the profits into real estate and acquisitions for 10 years. These investments paid off handsomely. Under our stewardship, Prime became the second-largest dealership group in New England and one of the 50 largest in the country.

While we held Prime Motor Group, we were prohibited from buying shares in public auto dealers due to restrictions imposed by framework agreements.[3] In 2017, shortly after we exited, these restrictions were lifted and we turned our attention back to publicly traded dealers. Lithia Motors had a history of buying underperforming dealerships and improving their performance—the same strategy Prime Motor Group first pursued. This, along with Lithia's track record of growing its earnings and management's ownership of a significant amount of stock, prompted us to make a large investment in that company. Had we not already owned Prime Motor Group, we probably would have been wary of Lithia's aggressive pursuit of acquisitions and doubted that its capital-allocation program made sense.

The biggest difference between liquid and illiquid securities, of course, is that public securities are traded daily. The most challenging part of investing is psychological. Market fluctuations often stimulate

---

[3] Large dealers often enter into framework agreements with manufacturers. These agreements limit the number of stores of a manufacturer (e.g., Toyota) the dealer can own. The purpose is to prevent the retailer from gaining too much power vis-à-vis the manufacturer.

strong feelings of, yes, greed and fear. Money is a fraught topic. Whether you are investing your own savings, overseeing a large endowment, or managing a hedge fund, you must grapple with not only your own state of mind but also that of your family members, other community constituents (e.g., faculty, alumni, boards), and clients. In trying to help investors think intelligently about market movements, Graham and Dodd stressed that stocks are fractional ownership interests in companies and that the market is, in their oft-quoted phrase, a voting machine in the short term but a weighing machine in the long run. Owning private companies reinforces the idea that *all* equities are fractional interests in businesses, not just ticker symbols flashing on a screen.

One paradox of private investing is that there can be a silver lining in *not* being able to sell. Bad things frequently happen to businesses. Our initial investment in Prime Motor Group was made at the end of 2007. I half-jokingly tell people that it closed about five minutes before the recession began. The next year was brutal for the markets and the economy, and no industry was hit harder than the automotive sector. Auto dealers finance their inventory through a structure called floor-plan financing. As is their tendency, the banks freaked out when the markets swooned. One day in the middle of the crisis, our floor-plan lender called and asked for immediate repayment. Had we been forced to pay off the loan, the company would have suffered severe financial distress and might have sought bankruptcy protection. Fortunately, the bank had no right to call the loan, and by the time the debt matured, the crisis had passed, the company was performing well, and the lender was happy to keep extending credit.

We owned Prime Motor Group for more than a decade and made many times our money. If we had had the option to sell during the panic, we might have succumbed to fear and dumped the stock. Owning private companies means you must ride out the inevitable

bumps in the road and not seek a quick exit. This has helped
condition us to take a longer view when the public enterprises in our
portfolio experience turbulence.

At Abrams Capital, our increased patience has had an interesting
effect. I have noticed that our relationships with the top managers at
some of our public companies have become more like the ones we
have with the leaders of our private companies. Several public
companies in which we hold shares now regularly seek our input
before engaging in major transactions, and one CEO asked one of my
partners to join his board even though we had not requested a seat. I
believe what has happened is that we have communicated our long-
term perspective through our actions and words, and managers have
responded positively.

Despite the psychological challenges that come with publicly
traded securities, the price of a stock itself can be an asset. Around the
same time that we purchased Lithia, we also bought another public
auto dealer, Asbury Group, which had two things going for it. First, its
CEO, David Hult, is quite talented; the company's operating metrics
are among the best in the industry. Second, Asbury had pursued a
capital-allocation strategy that created value, although its path was
different than Lithia's. For many years, Asbury took advantage of Mr.
Market's grumpiness (he seems to perpetually frown on the industry)
by repurchasing a significant portion of its shares. Between 2005 and
2020, Asbury increased its earnings per share from $1.84 to $12.89, a
nearly sevenfold jump. Almost half of that growth was due to the
company's share-repurchase program, which slashed the number of
outstanding shares from 33 million to 19 million over those 15 years.

When the incentives of management, the board of directors, and
investors are all aligned, a company's performance tends to be better—
often vastly better—than when they are not. The private-company
investor can insist that managers invest a significant portion of their

savings in the company and structure compensation packages so that the fortunes of managers and investors rise or fall together. In public companies, though, the major constituencies frequently don't march to the beat of the same drum. Some directors are primarily interested in protecting their fees and staying in the good graces of their fellow board members; some managers want the company to grow, regardless of the impact on shareholders, because managing a larger enterprise typically makes their paycheck swell. As a result, shareholders can become disenfranchised. Having witnessed the powerful effect of shared incentives in achieving great outcomes at private companies, I am now willing to pay a premium for public ones whose top managers are clearly cultivating the long-term value of the business.

I have noted the many benefits of investing in private companies, but there are downsides worth mentioning. Not all the individuals with whom we've worked are exceptional as managers. Among the duds was a CEO who defrauded the company (and the U.S. government) and ran it into bankruptcy. If things start to go badly, it takes a very long time to get out; every day is misery until your stake is gone. You come into the office each morning with the position staring you in the face, and you can't help but ask yourself, "What was I thinking? How *could* I have been so dumb?"

In my nearly 40 years of investing, I have experienced many challenges: outright fraud, general incompetence, value-destroying capital allocation, market crashes, terrorist attacks, deep recessions, a pandemic, and more. I have watched masters of the universe go from the top of the hill to bankruptcy—or reach the edge of it—in a matter of weeks. I have seen investors get psychologically broken by a bear market. These events have left deep scars. Investing is harder than it looks. Staying in the game is a prerequisite to success. Seth Klarman once said that the secret to investing is that there is no secret to investing. Instead, hard work, intellectual honesty, and a flexible mind are what fuel success. Investors must modify their tactics as the world changes, but keeping Graham and Dodd's essential concepts in mind, and seeking a margin of safety—whether in public or private securities—will enable them to invest comfortably in the face of a future which is always uncertain.

Endowment Management Principles and Practices

by Seth Alexander

When I started my investment career 27 years ago, I viewed *Security Analysis* as better suited for financial historians than modern-day investors. The book seemed quaint, belonging to a simpler and very much bygone era of finance. What could a modern-day investor learn from reading descriptions of investments in railroad bonds and companies trading for less than the value of the tangible assets on their balance sheet?

Today, I have a very different perspective. By looking at principles and insights as opposed to investment ideas from nearly a century ago, the lessons of Graham and Dodd spring to life. While many people only associate Graham and Dodd with outdated investment examples, it is more accurate to characterize these examples as expressions of their investment philosophy using the opportunity set at that time, not the inevitable output of their thinking. Like the investment manager who told me he used a photograph of Warren Buffett's office to position his desk in the same orientation to the window, I had definitely been missing the point.

I write from the perspective of an endowment investor. I am part of the team that helps invest MIT's financial assets. Like many American universities, MIT has an endowment, a pool of capital built from donations that has been set aside to pay for things such as financial aid, faculty salaries, and building maintenance. Each year, MIT spends around 5% of its endowment to support these and other immediate needs. We invest the remaining capital in hopes of generating sufficient investment returns to maintain the purchasing power of the endowment. Our goal is to support MIT in perpetuity with the same level of resources on an inflation-adjusted basis, allowing future scholars to advance our thinking in the same way past researchers at MIT have made advancements in fighting cancer, alternative energy research, space exploration, and much more. If, over the very long term, inflation averages 3% and we spend 5% per year, we need to earn roughly 8% annualized returns to meet this goal.

A book about investing in stock and bond instruments may not at first appear to offer insights into managing an endowment. Endowments are rarely direct purchasers of securities, because they maintain significant competitive disadvantages in that world. Universities cannot match the compensation commonly paid to the elite ranks of investment managers. Universities lack the internal culture and fast decision-making processes needed to move at the speed of trading in global markets. In most investment arenas, endowments are poorly situated to compete with more specialized local investors. For example, we would struggle to be a leading investor in start-up companies in Bangalore or Lagos from our office in Cambridge, Massachusetts.

While they may not be well-suited to buy assets directly, endowments maintain distinct competitive advantages in establishing partnerships with exceptional external investment managers. Because an endowment is a stable pool of funds, they are a good fit for investment managers looking for a steadfast source of capital through thick and thin. An endowment's time horizon matches the long process of building enduring, valuable, and mutually beneficial relationships with external managers. Amazingly, MIT maintains several active investment manager relationships that date back over 35 years. University endowments can sometimes gain access to capacity-constrained investment strategies by appealing to an investment manager's desire to support our twin missions of educational excellence and cutting-edge research. Large communities of alumni, faculty, parents, and friends provide a built-in network of people who help us find and diligence new investment managers. As a result, most endowments build portfolios of investment managers, rather than buying assets directly. Endowment investment staff appropriately focus their time on the external investment manager selection process and the allocation of capital between these managers to gain desired exposures.

An endowment's competitive advantages naturally lead to portfolios that look very different from your average 401(k) retirement account. With a stable capital base and a long time horizon, endowments are able to invest with fund managers pursuing long-duration, more illiquid investment strategies. Endowments can participate with managers in the redevelopment of real estate assets, the purchase of private businesses, the sustainable harvesting of timberlands, and investment in venture capital start-ups. The main attraction of these arenas is that they lend themselves to active involvement, allowing investment managers to add value above baseline market returns. For example, we might work with a real estate manager who purchases a run-down, half-empty building. If the manager can successfully refurbish and re-lease the building, they may be able to earn compelling returns, even if market rents in the area remain flat. As a result of these opportunities to add value and the ability to tolerate illiquidity, it is not uncommon for endowments to allocate a significant portion of their portfolios to private equity, venture capital, and real estate strategies, rather than investing only in more traditional stock and bond strategies.

Yet even with these differences, endowments can learn a great deal from *Security Analysis*. One of the keys to success in any industry is to understand the natural forces that drive behavior, for good or for bad. In the endowment world, for example, quasi-academic norms of debate and deliberate, collective decision-making help endowments make carefully considered long-term decisions. At the same time, the fact that decisions can almost always be postponed another week without discernable impact often leads to suboptimal outcomes in areas such as building internal data systems and new manager sourcing, where a strong sense of urgency might lead to better results. Endowments that understand their natural tendencies and create processes and cultural norms to lean against them, where appropriate, have a better chance of success.

In the Graham and Dodd world of stock picking and direct asset purchases, and in the endowment world of manager selection, one feature of the investment landscape that leads to suboptimal outcomes is an overabundance of choice. Investors have the opportunity to select from among thousands of different securities across dozens of industries and countries (or in the case of endowments, invest with thousands of different investment managers.) While it would seem beneficial to have a significant number of choices, human nature unfortunately tends to translate this cornucopia of riches into a lack of focus and a resulting inability to develop a competitive advantage over other market participants. Our curiosity, love of novelty, and the dopamine rush of a new piece of information (or new twitter post) push us to look at too many ideas, collect too many unimportant pieces of data, and debate too many unknowable or irrelevant issues. As a result, very few investors develop the well-defined, differentiated expertise that leads to compelling investment outcomes.

The length and depth of *Security Analysis* provides a solution to this excess of choice. In page after page, Graham and Dodd describe and provide examples of the characteristics they are looking for in a compelling investment, what characteristics to avoid, and how to research and collect needed information. This distinct filter leans back against the overabundance of choice by focusing Graham and Dodd on a rare set of companies and a circumscribed set of information to be examined.

When trying to select exceptional investment managers for our endowment, we use this concept of an investment filter as a first step in our process. In our way of thinking, a compelling investment filter has several characteristics. First, the filter must allow a manager to quickly discard the vast majority of potential investments on offer. One can easily imagine Graham and Dodd fairly rapidly dismissing most securities they examined as overly speculative, or engaged in a low-quality business endeavor, or not obviously inexpensive, instead directing their full attention to a manageable set of opportunities.

Second, a good investment filter should lead naturally to a good universe of opportunities. Investment managers whose filters lead them to out-of-favor areas, misunderstood industries, arenas of dynamic change, or assets where significant involvement can add value are more likely to find securities with attractive return prospects. Finally, a good investment filter must match an investor's temperament, resources, and capabilities. An investor may see opportunity in Silicon Valley's latest start-ups, but without the network needed to find the company early, the technical background needed to assess the opportunity, the operating background needed to offer valuable advice to the founders, the prior track record of success that helps convince companies to take capital from one investor over another, and the deep-pocketed capital base needed to support start-up companies to profitability, investors are unlikely to succeed in this arena no matter how compelling the underlying opportunity set.

A few managers in our portfolio use an owner-operator filter. Investment managers with this filter search for publicly listed companies led by an involved founder who owns a meaningful percentage of the company. Because large founder ownership stakes are rare, these investment managers can focus their energy and attention on a manageable number of potential opportunities. Because the long-term benefits of an exceptional owner-operator driving operating and capital allocation decisions do not necessarily show up in the historic or current financial statements of a business, there exist good possibilities of finding mispriced securities. You can imagine that examining the financial records of Warren Buffett's Berkshire Hathaway in 1965 would have provided few clues as to the subsequent record of stock price performance. The skills required to underwrite such a business leader—an ability to develop a deep understanding of management's motivations, decision-making discipline, willingness to chart a different path than others, long-term vision, and other softer factors—are difficult to acquire. The patience needed to hold onto these companies through bouts of volatility and underperformance is rare. Consequently, investment managers with this focus may be able to develop differentiated expertise in owning these types of companies versus other market participants.

Good investment filters are not rules based. There are many examples of founder-led public companies that turn out to be bad investments. Nor are investment managers likely to thrive as one-trick ponies—they will need to develop other insights and other types of expertise. Starting with a clear investment filter, however, allows an investment manager to spend their time well, develop a focused expertise, and thoughtfully expand their investment universe without suffering from the overabundance of choice.

Like other advice gleaned from Graham and Dodd, the benefits of a good investment filter appear obvious, yet in our experience few investment managers actually maintain a disciplined filter. It is far more common to see managers whose target universe changes based on the flavor of the day—they become excited about software companies when technology is booming, Chinese companies when China appears to be on an economic tear, and oil and gas stocks when inflation appears on the horizon. These investors put themselves in the worst position to find investment bargains by filtering for areas with high investor interest and large investor capital flows, and by shifting their focus instead of developing deep expertise. Because we also fall prey to this lack of discipline as hard as we try to avoid it, we think we understand the cause—the quirks of natural human behavior. It is difficult for humans to identify potential moneymaking opportunities but decide not to pursue them in the name of focusing on their areas of competitive advantage. These feelings are harder to control during market upswings, when other people appear to be making significant amounts of money without any discernible focus, discipline, special expertise, or competitive advantage.

Graham and Dodd also teach endowment investors valuable lessons in the area of risk management. Although risk management is of paramount importance to any investor, the budgetary structure of a university makes it particularly vital for us. A university's budget is composed primarily of salaries and benefits. Without other line items to focus on, budget reductions often fall on people, our greatest asset. Given this tendency, the sanctity of tenured positions, the desire to preserve a campus culture of stability and long-term thinking, and the restricted nature of funding resources (endowment funds usually have a specific legally designated purpose and cannot be shifted around to fill budgetary holes elsewhere), budget cuts are particularly painful to a university. As a result, investment policies that produce reasonably stable results, reducing the periodic need for large budget cuts, are of significant benefit to endowment-supported institutions.

An endowment's biggest risk is a large and permanent impairment of capital that hinders its ability to maintain the value of annual spending to the institution it supports, and there are numerous ways endowments can impair capital. Endowments can invest with managers that hold overvalued assets and generate poor returns. Endowments can have an overly volatile portfolio and lock in losses at a market bottom through annual spending. Endowments can maintain an overly illiquid portfolio and be forced to sell good assets at large discounts to fund spending needs. Endowments can hold a portfolio that is not sufficiently diversified to protect against changes in the environment such as inflation, an economic downturn, pandemic, war, or other downside shock.

Many of Graham and Dodd's insights in *Security Analysis* are directly applicable to avoiding these risks. Graham and Dodd caution against overly confident predictions of the future, instead recommending investments that will produce good returns in a wide variety of potential future environments. By buying with a margin of safety, by favoring high quality assets with high quality management teams, by being prudent with financial leverage and illiquidity, stock pickers and endowment investors can avoid downside disaster scenarios.

One complication for endowments is that they typically do not directly control which assets they own—those decisions are up to the external managers with whom they partner. As a result, an endowment's first line of defense against risk is its manager selection process. One important question we ask ourselves when deciding whether to partner with a manager is if we would be happy to go through a crisis with that manager. Partnering with managers who borrow too much money, overconcentrate in their positions, and plan only for upside scenarios will multiply risk. Partnering with managers who adhere to the principles of Graham and Dodd helps mitigate risk in the portfolio instead.

We have learned through painful experience that our manager risk assessments must go well beyond an examination of a manager's underlying investments. One of our scars from the Global Financial

Crisis in 2008–2009 was an investment with a manager that purchased high quality credit instruments senior in the capital structure of a company. Unfortunately, the manager used leverage to boost their returns. As a result, when prices declined in the credit market meltdown of that era, the manager faced margin calls on the lines of credit it used to hold its investments. Although the underlying credit investments ultimately did fine, the manager was forced to sell many of them at the worst possible time, locking in losses that could not be recovered. We have similarly locked in losses by investing with managers who go out of business in bad markets due to large investor redemptions, key employee departures, or other types of business instability. As a result, we explore if potential manager partners are sufficiently capitalized as a business to endure periods of negative returns, sufficiently generous with economics to retain talented staff in a downturn, sufficiently long-term oriented and motivated to work through difficult times, and have a sufficiently high quality investor base to avoid run-on-the-bank scenarios where investors compete to pull money from a dying fund.

We have tried to identify other attributes of managers that help mitigate risk. For example, we prefer managers who love the process and challenge of investing, not simply the financial rewards. These managers are more likely to stay the course and even thrive in difficult markets when investment bargains are rampant but near-term economic rewards are lower. We prefer managers with a willingness to limit their capital base by closing their funds and turning away potential investors. These managers prepare for downside scenarios by maintaining excess demand from investors that can be used to replace possible future redemptions, protecting themselves from business disruptions during market dislocations. We prefer managers with a focus on absolute returns, rather than those who view success as outperforming an index. In our experience, managers with absolute return goals tend to be more aware of potential downside scenarios as they are unlikely to view losing money over the long term as a good outcome, regardless of how the market performs.

You may wonder how venture capital fits into this manager selection risk rubric. Aren't venture capitalists supposed to swing for the fences? Yes, they are—but while prudent venture capitalists may take bets on inexperienced entrepreneurs and unproven business models, they are also aggressive about mitigating every other risk they can. They set aside cash reserves to support companies through inevitable tough times, they help recruit proven operating executives to provide grounding to visionary founders, they advocate for sustainable long-term business practices, and they push companies to raise excess capital in good times. By preparing for downside scenarios, venture capitalists give start-up companies the best shot at surviving difficult times long enough to see if their disruptive idea works, preserving the upside potential for which venture capital is famous.

Portfolio-level risk controls represent an endowment's second line of defense after manager selection. Investment managers may make individually sensible decisions that create unhealthy portfolio-level exposures when aggregated across multiple managers, and an endowment must act to limit these exposures. Thoughtful top-down limits impose diversification on a portfolio, ensuring that negative events, political changes, or macroeconomic headwinds will not similarly impair all parts of the portfolio simultaneously. For example, in 2013, we established a top-down limit on our China exposure. Our investment committee correctly identified potential future downside scenarios that could impair value for a U.S. investor, no matter how well we diversified our exposure within China. A U.S.-based endowment that looked only at bottom-up investment opportunities could easily become overexposed to China before changing geopolitics made such investments less attractive.

A final set of risk defenses are the broader financial policies of an endowed institution. In addition to investment policies that limit risk, institutions can protect against budgetary cuts through thoughtful spending and reserve policies. For example, institutions can leave room for endowment values to drop without leading to spending cuts, by not aggressively increasing endowment payouts to the maximum level each year. Similarly, institutions can build alternate financial reserves to be used to support the budget through difficult economic times.

Investors of all types can learn from Graham and Dodd. Unfortunately, *Security Analysis* suffers from its own fame. The works of Graham and Dodd are so well-known and so well-referenced in investment circles that many people may believe they are already eminently familiar with the lessons contained within before reading any of their books. I certainly believed this when I entered the industry and looked around for books to read. Picking up *Security Analysis*, however, opened a world far beyond the simplistic summaries commonly cited in the financial press. Perhaps what was most surprising was how much of this investment tome remains relevant today, even to an adjacent field such as endowment management. I hope that by reading through these pages, you are enjoying a similar journey to mine.

See the Appendix online at www.mhprofessional.com/SecurityAnalysis7.

About This Edition

It has been an unusual 14 years since the sixth edition of *Security Analysis* was published, shortly before the Great Financial Crisis of 2008–2009. So much has happened over this period that in early 2022 we made the decision to produce a seventh edition. There is much new ground to cover.

The backbone of this edition is the second edition of *Security Analysis*, published in 1940, with only sections we considered obsolete removed. As with the sixth edition, we recruited some of today's leading investors and financial thinkers to comment on the original. By proceeding in this fashion, we hope that readers will gain an appreciation for what has changed since the era of Graham and Dodd and what hasn't, while garnering insight into contemporary practices, innovations, trends, and challenges.

Soon after the sixth edition of Security Analysis was published, a major financial crisis ensued that was triggered by significant excesses in the U.S. housing market. Enormous volumes of residential and commercial mortgages had been sliced and diced into various tranches and then securitized for sale to investors. While credit agencies blessed the newfangled securities with investment grade ratings, these instruments were not created with a rainy day in mind; they had never been stress-tested by a widespread and sustained decline in housing prices nationally, which few imagined could happen. When such a decline occurred, these securities plummeted and bloodied the balance sheets of many major financial institutions, including Bear Stearns, Lehman Brothers, AIG, Fannie Mae, Freddie Mac, and Merrill Lynch.

The damage soon spread to the real economy, spurring a stock market collapse, a widespread sell-off in corporate credit, and a severe economic downturn, resulting in the worst financial crisis in three-quarters of a century. The Federal Reserve immediately cut interest rates to next to nothing, and the U.S. Congress passed a variety of bills to support both enterprises on the brink and individuals who were struggling. Central banks and legislators around the world responded similarly.

As the United States and other global economies began to recover, the financial markets went on an 11-year bender through March of 2020, the longest equity bull market on record, a period during which the S&P 500 rose fivefold. It then doubled again from April 2020 through January 2022. Continued zero interest rate policy, massive buying of Treasury bonds and mortgage securities by the Fed, and a variety of other unprecedented interventions fueled the market exuberance.

As economic activity was normalizing, the March 2020 emergence of the first global pandemic since the influenza of 1918–1919 essentially shut down parts of the United States and global economies, precipitating another series of stimulative measures. By early 2022, the ongoing impact of enormous economic stimulus as well as supply chain difficulties caused by an uneven economic recovery, growing worker shortages, Chinese Covid-related shutdowns, and the Russian invasion of Ukraine contributed to the worst bout of inflation in four decades. This, in turn, triggered a sharp reversal of Fed policy, leading to considerably higher interest rates and a sharp stock market sell-off, especially in the shares of the highest flyers. The previous, unprecedented economic stimulus and accommodative monetary policy measures are only starting to be reversed as we write, leaving investors and markets in a heightened state of uncertainty. An economic downturn seems increasingly likely.

Will the surge of inflation experienced as 2022 unfolded come under control, or will it become ingrained? At the time of this writing, no one knows if the Fed will be able to tame it or if they will come to the rescue once again if markets falter. But the contributors to this edition offer a fresh framework built upon Graham and Dodd's timeless commonsense principles to help readers navigate whatever may come next.

The preface to the seventh edition is an extensive update and expansion of the one I wrote for the sixth edition. In it, I attempt to convey how value investors can and should adhere to Graham's time-tested principles in a world that has changed significantly since the sixth edition and is unimaginably different from Benjamin Graham's time. In addition to this essay:

- Financial historian Jim Grant has significantly updated his exceptional piece that places Benjamin Graham in a historical perspective, shining light on the conditions and circumstances of the era in which he formulated and practiced his investment approach.

- Acclaimed financial writer and historian Roger Lowenstein offers his perspective on the eternal wisdom of Graham's approach in the context of the fads and follies that arose during the lengthy post-financial crisis bull market.

- Investor and author Howard Marks, widely known for his regular missives and books on investing, provides a freshly updated perspective on navigating the fixed-income markets with a steady focus on risk as well as potential return.

- Investor and author Dominique Mielle shares her insights on a specialized subset of the debt markets, investing in distressed credit.

- Todd Combs offers his perspective on his stock-in-trade—equity investing. He discusses the keys to identifying investment opportunity and shares strategies for assessing the value of businesses, delving into his own approach to due diligence and analysis.

- Steve Romick discusses his opportunistic approach to value investment that includes equities, debt, and mortgage-backed securities.

- Ben Stein and Zach Sternberg focus on a narrow subset of the investable universe, investing alongside passionate owner-operators, an approach they hatched in their Wharton School dorm room. They value the alignment of interests that results from such an approach, while accepting significant volatility in performance as a result of a very long-term holding period and an unusually concentrated portfolio.

- Nancy Zimmerman shares her insights on an important subset of special situations—arbitrage investments—recounting the many ways securities can depart from their underlying value and how investors may profitably exploit those mispricings.

- I offer a perspective on the ongoing importance but also the contemporary shortcomings of balance-sheet analysis as an investment tool.

- While Graham and Dodd did not cover international investing, Bill Duhamel, Ashish Pant, and Jason Moment offer a perspective on the challenges and opportunities inherent in non-U.S. markets. Our economic horizons have gone global; companies increasingly do business beyond their countries of origin, and most investors can easily invest internationally. As with all markets, the basic principles of Graham and Dodd fully apply to global investing in both developed and emerging markets. But global investing requires attention to additional considerations, such as currency exchange rates, different laws and regulations in every jurisdiction, varying cultural norms, often much less liquid markets, and the risk of substantial information disadvantages. At my firm, we often joke that in most countries, only a couple of dozen people know what's really going on, and we know that we're not one of them. An investor must figure out how to deal with such challenges and overcome any disadvantages. Of course, such challenges may also cause other investors to shy away from markets where these issues are particularly profound, which, in turn, may lead to prices that more than fully discount such challenges. In such cases, price is truly the great equalizer.

- David Abrams follows with his unique perspective on a multistrategy investment approach, describing the symbiotic effects of investing in both public securities and private equities.

- Given the large and growing amount of capital now held by educational, philanthropic, medical, and other endowments, I asked Seth Alexander, president of MIT Investment Company, to share his framework on the best contemporary strategies for the management of large pools of institutional capital. Seth demonstrates his acumen and invaluable perspective as a steward who doesn't pick individual investments himself but who seeks to determine the best sectors, strategies, and managers to which and whom to allocate capital.

All of the contributors to this seventh edition are well-known to me. They are superb investment thinkers as well as strong writers. Readers stand to learn a great deal from each of them. Together, the original Graham and Dodd text, combined with the essays written by our distinguished roster of contributors, offers up a paradigm through which those who are participants in, or simply observers of, financial markets can gain a sense of how these markets function and how investors can and should successfully engage with them.

This project has brought together 15 contributors in a collaboration that is emblematic of the nature of the value investing community. Many of us are investment rivals, but we are also friends and colleagues. We regularly learn from each other; each of us knows that we don't possess all the answers. We all vividly remember our biggest mistakes as if they happened yesterday. Similarly, we recognize that none of us has perfected the art of value investing; there are always new challenges and considerations, and there is always room to improve. A value investor must constantly be in the process of reinvention, of raising his or her game to navigate the terrain of new eras, novel securities, nascent businesses, emerging industries, shifting standards, and evolving market conditions. By assembling the diverse perspectives of these experienced and able contributors, we hope to make this seventh edition of *Security Analysis* a rich, varied, and highly informed tapestry of investment thinking that will be a worthy and long-lived successor to the six preceding editions.

Seth A. Klarman
Boston, MA
November, 2022

Acknowledgments

I owe a great debt to the many contributors who took time out of their very busy lives to share their insights, experiences, and practices with the readers. I'm profoundly grateful. On behalf of them all, I would also like to acknowledge the enormous accomplishments of Benjamin Graham and David Dodd. Through their writings and legacy, they have touched and inspired each of us in important and lasting ways. I would also like to recognize Warren Buffett, who is the living embodiment of Graham and Dodd's principles of value investing. His example regularly demonstrates how modern-day investors can remain true to value-investing principles while flexibly applying them amid an ever-changing market and business environment.

Judith Newlin at McGraw Hill initiated and captained this project through the usual shoals, and her acumen and editorial hand repeatedly made the writing crisper while retaining each contributors' unique perspective and writing style. Also, our external editors, Harvey Shapiro and Katherine Messenger, worked assiduously and tirelessly over many months to impact these contributions for the better.

I dedicate this edition to Lailah—the future—my joy and inspiration. And to Ashley and Morgan—my team—whose can-do attitude and energetic commitment make so much possible. With gratitude and appreciation.

Seth A. Klarman
Boston, MA
November, 2022

About the Contributors

Seth A. Klarman, CEO and portfolio manager of the Boston-based Baupost Group, LLC, has managed a series of successful investment partnerships using value-investing principles since 1983. In his preface, Klarman discusses the timeless applications of this philosophy, as well as the many profound changes in the business, market, and competitive environment with which value investors must contend. He is also the author of *Margin of Safety*, an investment classic. Klarman served as coeditor of the sixth edition of *Security Analysis* and is the editor of this seventh edition.

James Grant, founder and editor of *Grant's Interest Rate Observer*, has been writing about markets and the people who operate in them for a half-century. Among his nine books are biographies of the financier Bernard Baruch and of the Victorian financial journalist Walter Bagehot. Grant's introduction lends historical context to *Security Analysis* by taking us back to the era in which Graham and Dodd lived and worked. He served as coeditor of the sixth edition of *Security Analysis*.

Roger Lowenstein is one of America's top financial journalists and the author of seven books on economic history and finance. His journalism has appeared in the *Wall Street Journal*, the *New York Times*, the *Financial Times*, the *Washington Post*, *Substack*, and many more. He is the bestselling author of the books *Buffett: The Making of* an American Capitalist and When Genius Failed: The Rise and Fall of Long-Term Capital. His most recent book, Ways and Means, Lincoln and His Cabinet and the Financing of the Civil War, was awarded the 2022 Harold Holzer Book Prize. Mr. Lowenstein is also an outside director of the Sequoia Fund.

Howard S. Marks, CFA is chairman and cofounder of Oaktree Capital Management based in Los Angeles. He was an early investor in high-yield bonds and a devotee of Graham and Dodd. At first glance, those two ideas appear to be antithetical, but Marks says that's not the case. His introduction to Part II, which covers fixed-income investments, explains how the ideas in Security Analysis can be profitably applied to today's corporate bond market.

Dominique Mielle is a former partner and portfolio manager at a major hedge fund primarily focused on distressed investments. She played key roles in complicated bankruptcies, serving on the board of PG&E during its Chapter 11 proceeding and leading creditors' committees for the Commonwealth of Puerto Rico and major U.S. airlines in the wake of the tragic events of September 11, 2001. In 2017, she was named one of the "50 Leading Women in Hedge Funds" by the Hedge Fund Journal and E&Y. She is the author of Damsel in Distressed, the first hedge fund memoir written by a woman, and is also a contributor to Forbes.

Todd A. Combs is chairman, president, and CEO of GEICO, as well as an investment officer at Berkshire Hathaway Inc., a holding company whose subsidiaries engage in a number of diverse business activities, including finance, insurance and reinsurance, utilities and energy, freight rail transportation, manufacturing, retailing and services. Prior to joining Berkshire in 2010, Mr. Combs was CEO and managing member of Castle Point Capital, an investment partnership he founded in 2005 to manage capital for endowments, family foundations, and institutions. Mr. Combs has served as a director of various Berkshire Hathaway subsidiaries and has served as a director of JPMorgan Chase & Co. since 2016.

Steven Romick is managing partner of Los Angeles–based First Pacific Advisors, LP, a role in which he manages funds employing value-oriented investment strategies. The FPA Crescent Fund, comanaged by Mr. Romick, has provided the best risk-adjusted returns of all allocation mutual funds (with assets over $1 billion) that invest in equities and have been managed by the same manager since its inception, according to Morningstar. He was awarded Morningstar's U.S. Allocation Fund Manager of the Year (2013) and was a nominee for Morningstar's Domestic Manager of the Decade (2009) and Morningstar's U.S. Allocation/Alternatives Fund Manager of the Year (2016). In the introduction to Part V, "The Evolution of a Value Investor," Mr. Romick discusses his evolution as a value investor, the importance of continuous learning, and responding to the world as it is and not as what we want it to be.

Zachary S. Sternberg and Benjamin F. Stein are the cofounders of the Spruce House Partnership, a New York–based investment partnership that they started in 2005 when they were both sophomores at the University of Pennsylvania. Spruce House (which was the name of their freshman dormitory) is committed to investing in and partnering with a small group of both public and private owner-operated businesses to support building companies for the long term across a range of industries. In their section, "Investing with Owner Operators," they discuss the benefits and risks of investing alongside owner operator CEOs as they outline their value-investing journey.

Nancy Zimmerman is cofounder and managing partner of Boston-based hedge fund Bracebridge Capital, a pioneer in the field of absolute return investing. In her introduction to Part VII, "The Market Is Still Not Efficient," Zimmerman explores the many ways in which Graham and Dodd's ideas remain relevant in the world of modern finance and brings an arbitrage investor's perspective to the discussion of the ways investors can seek to benefit from discrepancies between price and value.

William F. Duhamel, Jason E. Moment, and Ashish Pant are principals of Route One Investment Company, L.P., which they founded in 2010. Route One is an institutional investment manager that invests globally following a value-investment approach. Prior to Route One, each of them were partners at Farallon Capital Management. In their chapter on international investing, they discuss their application of Graham and Dodd's value-investing methods to finding opportunity in international markets.

David Abrams has been the CEO of Boston-based Abrams Capital Management, a leading hedge fund manager since 1999. In "At the Intersection of Public and Private Investing: A Case Study," which appears as Part IX of the Seventh Edition, Abrams discusses how investors can apply Graham and Dodd's principles to both public and private markets and may find synergies between those disciplines. For the introduction to Part VII of the sixth edition of *Security Analysis*, "The Great Illusion of the Stock Market and the Future of Value Investing," Mr. Abrams describes his early experiences in and lessons from the investment business while making the dry subject of warrants and options come alive.

Seth Alexander is president of the MIT Investment Management Company (MITIMCo), a division of the Massachusetts Institute of Technology. MITIMCo manages the endowment, retirement plan, retiree welfare benefit plan, and other financial assets of MIT. In his essay, Alexander discusses how the principles of Graham and Dodd apply to endowment management.

About the Authors

Benjamin Graham was a seminal figure on Wall Street and is widely acknowledged to be the father of modern security analysis. The founder of the value school of investing and founder and former president of the Graham-Newman corporation investment fund, Graham taught at Columbia University's Graduate School of Business from 1928 through 1957. He popularized the examination of price-to-earnings (P/E) ratios, debt-to-equity ratios, dividend records, book values, and earnings growth, and also wrote the popular investors' guide *The Intelligent Investor*.

David L. Dodd was a colleague of Benjamin Graham's at Columbia University, where he was an assistant professor of finance.

Index